AF443499

NEW TRENDS IN SOFTWARE METHODOLOGIES, TOOLS AND TECHNIQUES

Frontiers in Artificial Intelligence and Applications

FAIA covers all aspects of theoretical and applied artificial intelligence research in the form of monographs, doctoral dissertations, textbooks, handbooks and proceedings volumes. The FAIA series contains several sub-series, including "Information Modelling and Knowledge Bases" and "Knowledge-Based Intelligent Engineering Systems". It also includes the biennial ECAI, the European Conference on Artificial Intelligence, proceedings volumes, and other ECCAI – the European Coordinating Committee on Artificial Intelligence – sponsored publications. An editorial panel of internationally well-known scholars is appointed to provide a high quality selection.

Volume 161

Recently published in this series

Vol. 160. I. Maglogiannis et al. (Eds.), Emerging Artificial Intelligence Applications in Computer Engineering – Real World AI Systems with Applications in eHealth, HCI, Information Retrieval and Pervasive Technologies

Vol. 159. E. Tyugu, Algorithms and Architectures of Artificial Intelligence

Vol. 158. R. Luckin et al. (Eds.), Artificial Intelligence in Education – Building Technology Rich Learning Contexts That Work

Vol. 157. B. Goertzel and P. Wang (Eds.), Advances in Artificial General Intelligence: Concepts, Architectures and Algorithms – Proceedings of the AGI Workshop 2006

Vol. 156. R.M. Colomb, Ontology and the Semantic Web

Vol. 155. O. Vasilecas et al. (Eds.), Databases and Information Systems IV – Selected Papers from the Seventh International Baltic Conference DB&IS'2006

Vol. 154. M. Duží et al. (Eds.), Information Modelling and Knowledge Bases XVIII

Vol. 153. Y. Vogiazou, Design for Emergence – Collaborative Social Play with Online and Location-Based Media

Vol. 152. T.M. van Engers (Ed.), Legal Knowledge and Information Systems – JURIX 2006: The Nineteenth Annual Conference

Vol. 151. R. Mizoguchi et al. (Eds.), Learning by Effective Utilization of Technologies: Facilitating Intercultural Understanding

ISSN 0922-6389

New Trends in Software Methodologies, Tools and Techniques

Edited by

Hamido Fujita

Iwate Prefectural University, Iwate, Japan

and

Domenico Pisanelli

ISTC-CNR, Rome, Italy

IOS
Press

Amsterdam • Berlin • Oxford • Tokyo • Washington, DC

ISBN 978-1-58603-794-9
Library of Congress Control Number: 2007935641

Publisher
IOS Press
Nieuwe Hemweg 6B
1013 BG Amsterdam
Netherlands
fax: +31 20 687 0019
e-mail: order@iospress.nl

Distributor in the UK and Ireland
Gazelle Books Services Ltd.
White Cross Mills
Hightown
Lancaster LA1 4XS
United Kingdom
fax: +44 1524 63232
e-mail: sales@gazellebooks.co.uk

Distributor in the USA and Canada
IOS Press, Inc.
4502 Rachael Manor Drive
Fairfax, VA 22032
USA
fax: +1 703 323 3668
e-mail: iosbooks@iospress.com

New Trends in Software Methodologies, Tools and Techniques
H. Fujita and D. Pisanelli (Eds.)
IOS Press, 2007

v

Preface

Software is the essential enabler for the new economy and science. It creates new markets and new directions for a more reliable, flexible, and robust society. It empowers the exploration of our world in ever more depth. However, software often falls short of our expectations. Current software methodologies, tools, and techniques remain expensive and not yet reliable enough for a highly changeable and evolutionary market. Many approaches have been proven only as case-by-case oriented methods.

This book, as part of SOMET series, contributes on new trends and theories in the direction in which we believe software science and engineering may develop to transform the role of software and science integration in tomorrow's global information society.

This book is an attempt to capture the essence on a new state of art in software science and its supporting technology. The book also aims at identifying the challenges such a technology has to master. It contains highly extensively reviewed papers lectured at the Sixth International Conference on New Trends in Software Methodology Tools, and Techniques, V, (SoMeT_07) held in Rome (CNR), Italy, from 7 to 9 November 2007, (http://www.somet.soft.iwate-pu.ac.jp/somet_07). This conference brought together researchers and practitioners to share their original research results and practical development experiences in software science, and its related new challenging technology.

One of the important issues addressed by this book is software development security tools and techniques. Another example we challenge in this conference is intelligent software design from the human aspect and the technology aspect. This book and the series it continues will also elaborate on such new trends and related academic research studies and development.

A major goal was to gather scholars from the international research community to discuss and share research experiences on new software methodologies, and formal techniques. The book also investigates other comparable theories and practices in software science, including emerging technologies, from their computational foundations in terms of models, methodologies, and tools. These are essential for developing a variety of information systems research projects and to assess the practical impact on real-world software problems.

For an outline of the past series of related events that contributed to this publication, **SoMeT_02** was held on October 3–5, 2002, in Sorbonne, Paris, France.

SoMeT_03 was held in Stockholm, Sweden, **SoMeT_04** in Leipzig, Germany, **SoMeT_05** in Tokyo, Japan, **SoMeT_06** in Quebec, Canada, and most recently **SoMeT_07** held in Rome, Italy. These events also initiate a future event to be organized in October 2008, (http://www.somet.soft.iwate-pu.ac.jp/somet_08/).

This book provides an opportunity for exchanging ideas and experiences in the field of software technology, opening up new avenues for software development, methodologies, tools, and techniques, especially, software security and program coding diagnosis and related software maintenance techniques aspects. Also, we have emphasized human centric software methodologies, end-user development techniques, and human emotional reasoning for best performance harmony between the design tool and the user.

Issues discussed are research practices, techniques and methodologies proposing and reporting solutions needed for global world business. We believe that this book creates an opportunity for us in the software science community to think about where we are today and where we are going.

The book is a collection of **33** carefully reviewed best-selected papers by the reviewing committee.

The areas covered are:

- Software engineering aspects on software security, programs diagnosis and maintenance
- Static and dynamic analysis on Lyee-oriented software performance model
- Software security aspects on Java mobile code, and networking
- Practical artefact on software security, software validation and diagnosis
- Software optimization and formal methods
- Requirement engineering and requirement elicitation
- Software methodologies and Lyee oriented software techniques
- Automatic software generation, reuse, and legacy systems
- Software quality and process assessment
- Intelligent software systems and evolution
- End-user requirement engineering and programming environment
- Ontology and philosophical aspects on software engineering
- Business software models and other kinds of software application models, based on Lyee theory

All papers published in this book have been carefully reviewed and selected by the SOMET international reviewing committee. Each paper has been reviewed by between three and six reviewers and has been revised based on the review reports. The papers were reviewed on the basis of technical soundness, relevance, originality, significance, and clarity.

This book outcome is also a collective effort from many industrial partners and colleagues from around the world. We also gratefully thank Iwate Prefectural University, especially its President Prof. Makoto Taniguchi, CNR Rome, Italy, Catena Co., SANGIKYO Co., ARISES and others for their overwhelming support of this work. We especially are thankful to the reviewing committee and others who participated in the hard effective review of all submitted papers and thanks also for the hot discussions we have had at the review evaluation meetings which selected the contributions in this book.

This outcome is another milestone in mastering new challenges in software and its new promising technology, within SoMeT's consecutive events. It also gives the reader new insights, inspiration and concrete material to elaborate and study this new technology.

Last but not least, we would like to thank and acknowledge the Microsoft Conference Management Tool team for the support it has provided on the use of Microsoft CMT System as a conference-supporting tool during all the phases of the SOMET transactions.

The Editors

SoMeT Organization

Program Chairs

Hamido Fujita, *Iwate Prefectural University, Iwate, Japan*
e-mail: issam@soft.iwate-pu.ac.jp

Domenico Pisanelli, *ISTC-CNR, Rome, Italy*
e-mail: d.pisanelli@istc.cnr.it

Reviewers and Program Committee of SoMeT_07

(http://www.somet.soft.iwate-pu.ac.jp/somet_07)

Anna-Maria Di Sciullo, University de Quebec de Montreal, Canada
Mohamed Mejiri, Laval University, Quebec, Canada
Béchir Ktari, Laval University, Quebec, Canada
Luigi Logrippo, University of Quebec at Hull, Quebec, Canada
Kamel Adi, University of Quebec at Hull, Quebec, Canada
Kone Mamadou Tadiou, Laval University, Quebec, Canada
Mourad Debbabi, Concordia University, Montreal, Canada
Marite Kirikova, Riga Technical University, Latvia
Rimantas Butleris, Kaunas University of Technology, Lithuania
Kasem Saleh, American University of Sharjah, UAE
Remigijus Gustas, Karlstad University, Sweden
Love Ekenberg, Stockholm University, Sweden,
Paul Johannesson, Royal Institute of Technology, KTH, Stockholm, Sweden
Benkt Wangler, University of Skovde, Sweden
Rudolf Keller, Zuehlke Engineering AG, Switzerland
Volker Gruhn, Leipzig University, Germany
Heinrich Herre, Leipzig University, Germany
Clemens Schaefer, Leipzig University, Germany
Sergei Gorlatch, Muenster.University, Germany
Bipin Indurkhya, International Institute of Information Technology, Hyderabad, India
Ernest Edmonds, University of Technology, Sydney, Australia
George Feuerlicht, University of Technology, Sydney, Australia
Colette Rolland, University de Paris_1-Pantheon Sorbonne, Paris, France
Selmin Nurcan, University de Paris_1-Pantheon Sorbonne, Paris, France
Pierre-Jean Charrel, Toulouse_2 University, France
Victor Malyshkin, Russian Academy of Sciences, Russia
Yury Zagorulko, A.P.Ershov Institute of Informatics Systems, Russia
Gregers Koch, Copenhagen University, Denmark
Roberto Poli, Trento University, Italy
Domenico Pisanelli, ISTC-CNR, Rome, Italy
Amedeo Cesta, ISTC-CNR, Rome, Italy

Claudio De Lazzari, IFC-CNR, Rome, Italy
Soundar Kumara, The Pennsylvania State University, USA
Margeret M Burnett, Oregon State University, USA
Michael Oudshoorn, Montana State University, Bozeman, USA
Gregg Rothermel, Nebraska University, Lincoln, USA
Kenneth Baclwaski, Northeastern University, Boston, USA
Hatem Ben Sta, Institute Superior of Informatique, Tunisia
Shaoying Liu, Hosei University, Japan
Tu Bao Ho, JAIST, Japan
Jun Hakura, Iwate Prefectural University, Iwate, Japan
Masaki Kurematsu, Iwate Prefectural University, Iwate, Japan
Yutaka Funyu, Iwate Prefectural University, Iwate, Japan
Jun Sasaki, Iwate Prefectural University, Iwate, Japan
Yasuaki Nishitani, Iwate University, Japan
Debasish Chakraborty, Tohoku University, Japan
Norio Shiratori, Tohoku University, Japan

Organizing Chairs

Angelo Oddi, ISTC-CNR, Rome, Italy
Gabriella Cortellessa, ISTC-CNR, Rome, Italy
Nicola Policella, ISTC-CNR, Rome, Italy

Contents

Preface   v
SoMeT Organization   ix

Chapter 1. Software Engineering Best Practices

On the Challenges of Correctly Using Metamodels in Software Engineering   3
Brian Henderson-Sellers

Software Engineering Practices: An Auditor's Perspective   36
Krzysztof Sacha

Technology Neutral Business Process Design Using URDAD   52
Fritz Solms

Chapter 2. Software Development and Related Methodologies

A Method of Software Structure Designing Based on Graph Planning   73
Mingzhi Mao, Yunfei Jiang and Xiaolong Chai

ASOP: An Agile Service-Oriented Process   83
Asif Qumer and Brian Henderson-Sellers

Approaching OWL and MDA Through Knowledge Management System:
Application to Project Memory   93
Hatem Ben Sta and Khaled Ghedira

Methodology of Building and Using Ontology for Providing Content-Based
Access to Scientific Information Resources   105
Yury Zagorulko and Olesya Borovikova

**Chapter 3. Cognitive Modeling on Software Design and Natural Language
Representation**

The Art of Programming or Programs as Art   119
Ernest Edmonds

A Remark on Natural Language Processing from the Biolinguistic Perspective   126
Anna Maria Di Sciullo

Cognitive Modeling in Software and Relation to Human Emotional Reasoning   145
Hamido Fujita, Jun Hakura and Masaki Kurematu

Establishing Research Criteria for Performed Gestures and Emotional Interaction
in an Interactive Gestural Film Game: To Be or not To Be   166
Roman Danylak, Zafer Bilda and Ernest Edmonds

Chapter 4. Network Software Security

Formal Technique for Discovering Complex Attacks in Computer Systems   185
Lamia Hamza and Kamel Adi

Automatic Enforcement of Security in Computer Networks   200
T. Mechri, M. Langar, M. Mejri, H. Fujita and Y. Funyu

Chapter 5. Software Security and Validation

New Verification of Reactive Requirement for Lyee Method   225
Osamu Arai and Hamido Fujita

Model Checking Communicative Agent-Based Systems   239
Jamal Bentahar and John-Jules Meyer

Chapter 6. Program Conversion and Related Software Validation

Constructing Higher-Level Transformation Languages Based on XML   269
Daniel Foetsch and Elke Pulvermueller

Toward Solving Equations in Kleene Algebras   285
F. Lajeunesse-Robert and B. Ktari

Analyzing Software Engineering Processes on Source Code Level   305
Dirk Wilking and Stefan Kowalewski

Automated Design Improvement by Example   315
Mark O'Keeffe and Mel Ó Cinnéide

Experience of XML-Based Source Code Representation with Parsing Actions   330
Kazuaki Maeda

Chapter 7. Intelligent Software Design and Maintenance

Normative Systems: The Meeting Point Between Jurisprudence and Information Technology? A Position Paper   343
Luigi Logrippo

On Implementability of the Formal Specifications   355
Victor Malyshkin

An Introduction to the Quantitative, Rational and Scientific Process of Software Development (Part 1)   361
Zenya Koono, Hui Chen and Hassan Abolhassani

An Introduction to the Quantitative, Rational and Scientific Process of Software Development (Part 2)   372
Zenya Koono, Hui Chen and Hassan Abolhassani

Measurement Analysis and Fault Proneness Indication in Product Line Applications (PLA)   391
Zeeshan Ahmed

Chapter 8. User Requirement Engineering and Development

Clayworks: Toward User-Oriented Software for Collaborative Modeling and Simulation   403
Sergei Gorlatch, Jens Müller, Martin Alt, Jan Dünnweber, Hamido Fujita and Yutaka Funyu

A Unique Trial of Developing Software for the Actual Application by an Engineer with Non-Software Background   416
Shogo Hayashida, Noriko Taniguchi and Rikio Maruta

Algorithm Library Based on Algorithmic CyberFilms   427
Yutaka Watanobe, Nicolay Mirenkov and Rentaro Yoshioka

A Novel Intuitive GUI Method for User-Friendly Operation   448
Kohei Sugawara and Rikio Maruta

Chapter 9. Service Oriented Systems

Determinants of Service Reusability   467
George Feuerlicht and Amalka Wijayaweera

Development of a Maintenance Environment that Enabling Users to Revise Existing Web Applications   475
Hidaka Yano, Sota Honda, Jun Sasaki, Michiru Tanaka, Keizo Yamada and Yutaka Funyu

ROME: A Reference Ontology in Medicine   485
Domenico M. Pisanelli, Massimo Battaglia and Claudio De Lazzari

A Collaborative Environment for User-Initiated Development of Web Applications   494
Sota Honda, Hidaka Yano, Michiru Tanaka, Keizo Yamada, Jun Sasaki and Yutaka Funyu

Author Index   505

Chapter 1

Software Engineering Best Practices

New Trends in Software Methodologies, Tools and Techniques
H. Fujita and D. Pisanelli (Eds.)
IOS Press, 2007

On the Challenges of Correctly Using Metamodels in Software Engineering

Brian HENDERSON-SELLERS[a,1]
[a]Faculty of Information Technology, University of Technology, Sydney, Australia

Abstract. Metamodels are increasingly being used in software engineering, particularly in standards from both the OMG and ISO. It is therefore critical that these metamodels be used "correctly". In this paper, we investigate some of the pitfalls observed in the use of metamodelling ideas in software engineering and, from these observations, deduce some rules of thumb to help increase the quality of usage of metamodels in software engineering in the future.

Keywords. Metamodelling. Software Engineering.

1. Introduction

The use of metamodelling in software engineering, particularly in the context of object-oriented software engineering, has been increasingly gaining credence and visibility since it was first proposed as a vehicle for facilitating convergence of OO modelling languages [1]. Although frequently described as "a model of a model" e.g. [2-4], this is a mistake [5]; metamodelling is in fact "a model of models" [6, 7] or, equally, "a model of a set of models" [8] or perhaps "a model of a modelling language" [8]. Seidewitz [9] states that "A *metamodel* is a specification model for a class of SUS[2] where each SUS in the class is itself a valid model expressed in a certain modelling language. That is, a metamodel makes statements about what can be expressed in the valid models of a certain modeling language." For example, while a detailed map at a scale of say, 1:60,000, is a model of real terrain, a regional-scale map, say at 1:500,000, is a model of the (terrain-resolving) map and a continental-scale map (e.g. 1:5,000,000) is a model of the regional-scale map, none of these can lay claim to be a metamodel since the SUS (system under study) is identical in each case – the hallmark of a series of models at different granularity/abstraction levels. For a true metamodel, the domain of discourse (SUS) changes as do the metalevels. For example, a UML model of the banking domain represents entities within a bank; a UML metamodel, on the other hand, represents concepts such as *class* or *association* that are totally independent of the

---

[1] Corresponding Author: Brian Henderson-Sellers, Faculty of Information Technology, University of Technology, Sydney, P.O. Box 123, Broadway, NSW 2007, Australia; E-mail: brian@it.uts.edu.au
[2] SUS = system under study

banking (or indeed any other) domain (Figure 1) and instead represent *types* of entities in the SUS.

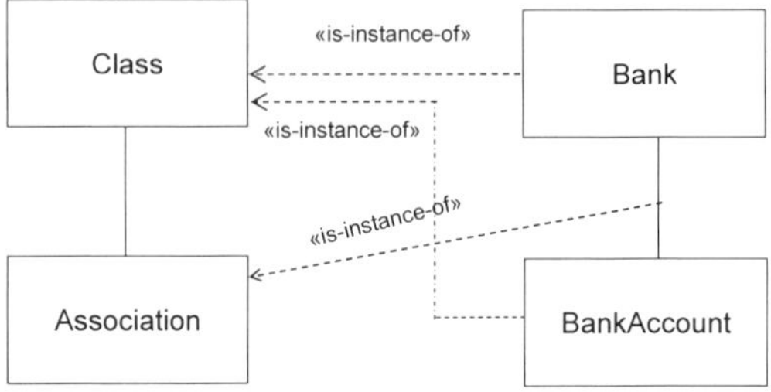

Figure 1 Elements in the banking domain (OMG level M1) and their metamodel counterparts (OMG level M2).

While this would appear to be relatively straightforward, the whole area of modelling at multiple abstraction levels turns out to be cognitively challenging for most humans. Consequently, many published (so-called) metamodels in software engineering contain flaws, such as mixed metalevels; (incorrect) use of metamodelling semantics when modelling semantics are all that is needed; incorrect appellation of a model (of a real-world domain) as a metamodel; incorrect or inappropriate use and neglect of a definition of domain-specific stereotypes; etc. In this paper, we analyze these and similar errors in an attempt to lay clear guidelines for improved use of metamodelling within software engineering.

In Section 2, we discuss two of the most popular multi-level "architectures" – one based on instantiation semantics and one aligned to a perception of how various roles within software engineering require information at different so-called metalevels. In Section 3, we reiterate issues identified in the literature – largely those arising from the former and longer established (i.e. instantiation-based) architecture, and see how the insistence on "strict metamodelling" [10-12] within this context has led to numerous apparent inconsistencies, especially when the process and product aspects of software are integrated, as discussed in [13]. This leads to consideration, in Section 4, of some larger scale inaccuracies in the literature: in particular, misuse of the metamodel appellation, the mixing of metalevels in a number of recent papers and the confounding that can occur when powertype patterns [14, 15] are misapplied. In Section 4, we also analyze some detailed metamodels for method chunks, method fragments and process elements wherein it can be argued that the solutions published violate some of the well-established OO *modelling* rules – after all, a contemporary metamodel is just a model, often expressed using UML, and so the quality of its design can be evaluated in *exactly* the same way as that of a domain model such as the model for a banking information system.

2. Creating a metalevel hierarchy

It is often said that metamodelling naturally leads to the need for several "layers of abstraction". However, this is not a precise description since abstraction simply means removal of detail and hence a type-supertype relationship in OO programming fulfils such a role; yet, traditionally, no-one would try to link an inheritance hierarchy in an OO program with the multiple layers in a metamodel hierarchy such as that of the OMG (Figure 2). In this diagram, four layers are shown such that there is a classification relationship between any consecutive pair of layers. In fact, it is more common to show the inverse of this in the diagram i.e. the "instance-of" relationship between layers. Thus one can say that every entity in the layer Mx is an instance of a single entity in the layer Mx+1 i.e. it is a many to one relationship. The "higher level" entity *classifies* those appropriate entities in the lower level. Flastcher [7] describes this in terms of the higher level entity as defining the intension for models at the lower level, the latter being the extension. Although these layers are therefore "artificially defined", they are related, as shown in Figure 2 and in the context of the UML, to

M0: data elements

M1: elements that comprise the model of the data

M2: elements that comprise UML itself i.e. "metamodel"

M3 MOF – the OMG's so-called meta-object facility (incorrectly called a metametamodel originally and now [16, p16] recognized as being another metamodel – see also [17]).

The layering can thus be said to have been accomplished from a linguistic viewpoint (see later discussion) because it is based on the concepts of object modelling and not on any specific user domain.

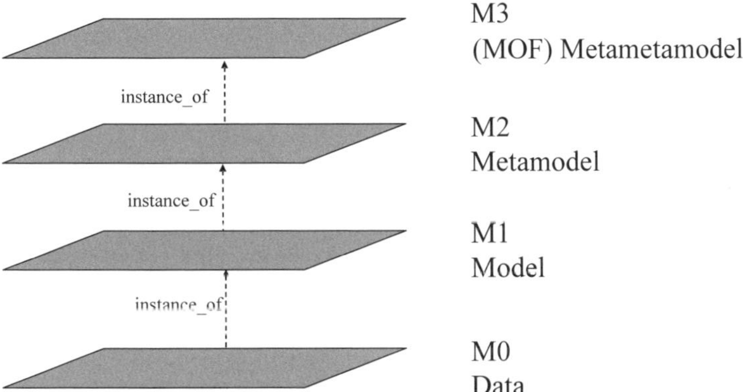

Figure 2 The four layer hierarchy of the OMG, itself based on [18] (after [19]) © Pearson Education Limited

In some little contrast is the architecture adopted in AS4651 and ISO/IEC24744 (Figure 3). Rather than starting with the layer discrimination mechanism (instantiation/classification in the previous example), this newer approach identifies first what kinds of things can be observed in real life. Thus identified are actual people working on actual projects in real time. Secondly, they use a set of tools, guidelines, methodologies etc. Thirdly, the developers trust that these tools have been well defined. This is done, by methodologists and/or tool vendors and/or standards bodies, in the topmost layer. The three layers are thus defined around the communities that create and use them, and are named Endeavour domain, Method domain and Metamodel domain.

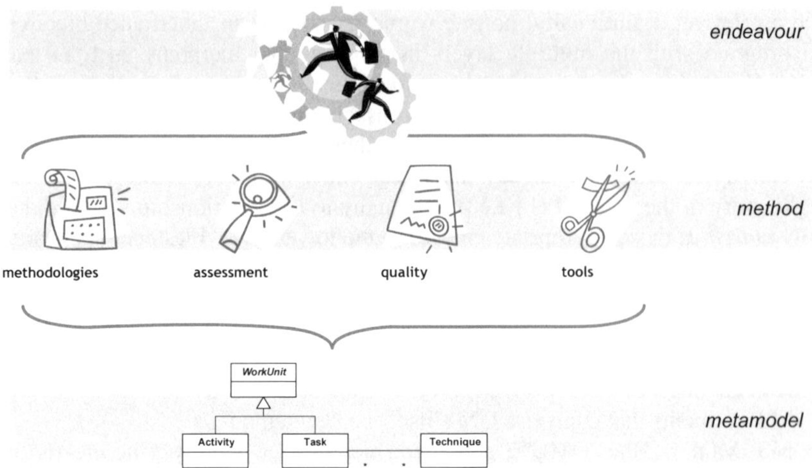

Figure 3 Three layer architecture of recent standards (after [20])

The use of these two multi-level/domain architectures will be demonstrated throughout the following sections.

3. Inherent problems requiring resolution

Problems occurring in metamodelling of work products, particularly those described by UML, have been documented in many places, primarily in the proceedings from the UML, now MODELS, conference series. An immediate consequence of the ANSI/OMG architecture is that instantiation produces an object from its class i.e. an object is an instance of a class. But in the OMG architecture, instantiation is used three times. For example, if Class is a M2 entity and it is instantiated, then the result must be an object. Yet this "object" is the entity that modellers draw in their UML class diagram e.g. a box labelled Book. This is meant to represent a set of individual people's books i.e. it is intended to be a classification mechanism or a type. Clearly this is a contradiction within the strict metamodelling OMG architecture. As pointed out in [21], what is happening is a sleight of hand by which the modeller introduces the necessary mapping between the object instantiated from the M2 class Class and the M1 class (say Book) that he/she needs in their design (Figure 4).

This paradox has led some authors e.g. [22] to propose a pattern to underpin this "leap of faith". Named by them the Type-Object pattern, it is said to "Decouple instances from their classes so that those classes can be implemented as instances of a class." Interestingly, two earlier but parallel developments led to similar results but differently named. Pirotte *et al.* [23], in the context of database design, introduced a relationship named "materialization" while, at about the same time, Odell [24] introduced the notion of "powertype" based on a loose interpretation of power sets in mathematics. This latter idea was also taken up by [15, 25] who used the powertype pattern [14] to underpin a revision to the way we understand metamodelling and, particularly, "layering" within this context (an example is shown in Figure 5).

Intertwined with these challenges has been an ongoing debate between so-called ontological (or logical) and linguistic (or physical) metamodelling (e.g. [2] in which two different styles of metamodelling are evaluated). Atkinson and Kühne argue that some modelling pertains to the domain (SUS) and can be called ontological. In contrast, linguistic models are those that define the abstract syntax of languages and hence feature concepts such as class, entity and relationship. Problems are said to occur when these two axes of modelling are not carefully discriminated. Atkinson and Kühne [26] investigate several non-linear descriptions that allow the two to apparently co-exist. One such proposal is shown in Figure 6, called by them the "Orthogonal Classification Architecture" [27].

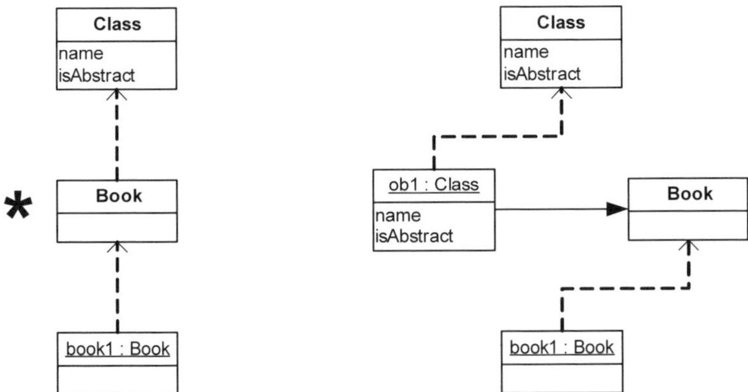

Figure 4 On the left-hand side, Book is shown as a class that is also an instance of Class, which is impossible within the conventional object-oriented paradigm; the asterisk signals this diagram as illegal. On the right-hand side, Book is shown as a class that is specified by the object ob1 through a forward-looking isotypical interpretive mapping (depicted as a solid arrow) (after [21][3]).

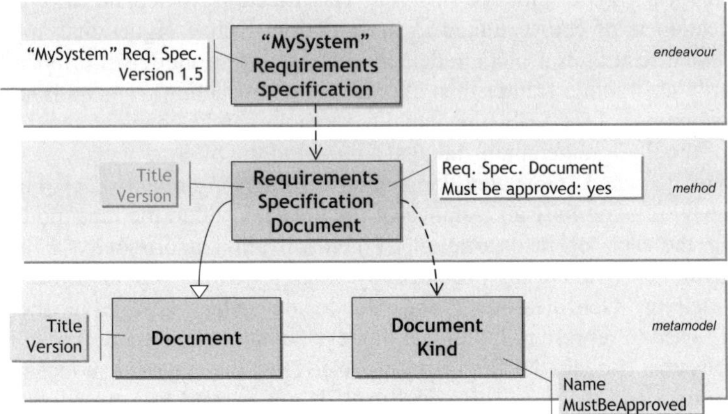

Figure 5 Application of the powertype pattern for Document/Kind in the context of the three levels of Figure 3 (after [20])

---

3 Reprinted from Journal of Systems and Software, 80, Gonzalez-Perez, C. and Henderson-Sellers, B., Modelling software development methodologies: a conceptual foundation, doi:10.1016/j.jss.2007.02.048, Copyright Elsevier (2007)

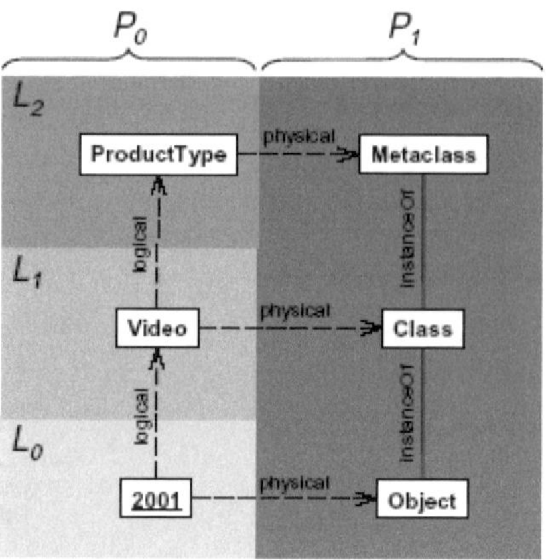

Figure 6 Proposed two-dimensional framework options from [26]. L = logical (ontological), P = physical (linguistic). © 2002 ACM, Inc. Reprinted by permission.

Seidewitz [9] and, later, Gonzalez-Perez and Henderson-Sellers [15] link some of these problems to the insistence on the "instance-of" relationship between metalayers, as dictated by the adoption and strict adherence to the notions of strict metamodelling [11]. Seidewitz prefers a more generic interpretative mapping while Gonzalez-Perez and Henderson-Sellers use the term "represents". This issue of the utility of strict metamodelling is important when one considers metalevel architectures that utilize powertypes since these combine instantiation semantics with generalization semantics "across layers". It is indeed perhaps the lack of generalization semantics "between layers" in strict metamodelling especially within the OMG/UML community that has led to the kind of restrictions discussed above [21].

There are also parallels with the proposals of Kühne [3, 4] of type models and token models. Type models rely on classification to create a type hierarchy. Classification is of course linked to instantiation. Kühne argues that applying a type model twice results in a metamodel. In contrast, token models are those that rely on granularity abstraction (rather than classification abstraction). Thus a fine grained map is a token model of the SUS (the actual topography) and a coarse grained map is both a model of the fine-grained map and also a model of the SUS.

Favre [8] and Gonzalez-Perez and Henderson-Sellers [21] both note the inadequacy of using *only* an instance-of relationship within the metamodelling sphere, decrying the lack of incorporation of generalization additionally. This leads to a solution to this conundrum provided by linking powertypes to these two types of metamodelling. Gonzalez-Perez and Henderson-Sellers [21] have shown that the language used to represent the logical model (the ontological model) is in fact identical to the physical model (the linguistic model). Thus the physical model represents the logical model and the physical model itself is represented by some defining language (Language1 in Figure 7).

If we apply this idea (that the physical model is the language used to represent the logical model) together with the powertype pattern to the apparent paradox as exemplified in Figure 6, then we derive two domains: the model domain (previously the ontological model) and the metamodel domain (previously the linguistic model) –

as shown in Figure 8. ProductType and Video are clabjects[4] because they have a powertype instantiation relationship to elements in the metamodelling and modelling domains respectively. Consequently, as demonstrated theoretically in Figure 7, we are using the physical model (on the right hand side of Figure 8) to represent the logical model (of Videos etc. on the left hand side of Figure 8).

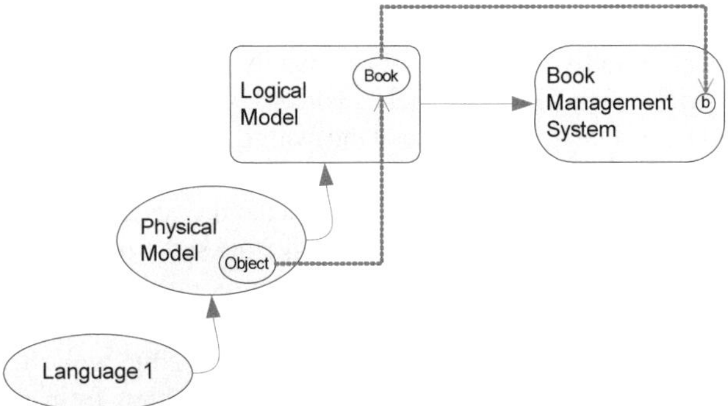

Figure 7 Physical Model is the language used to represent the Logical Model. Language 1 is the language used to represent the Physical Model (after [21][5]).

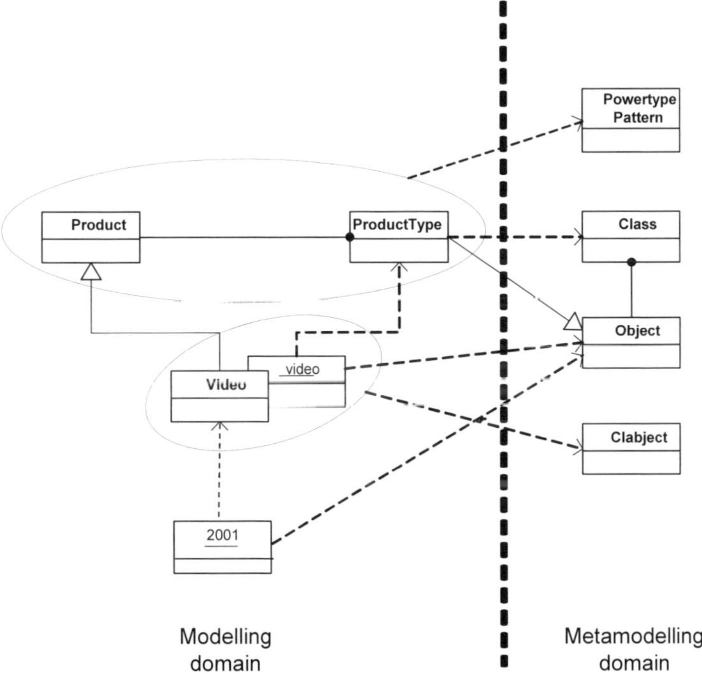

Figure 8 Revision of Figure 6 by the application of powertypes.

---

[4] clabject = cla(ss) + (o)bject [11]

[5] Reprinted from Journal of Systems and Software, 80, Gonzalez-Perez, C. and Henderson-Sellers, B., Modelling software development methodologies: a conceptual foundation, doi:10.1016/j.jss.2007.02.048, Copyright Elsevier (2007)

Subsequent to these UML-focussed and work-product-focussed studies, process-focussed metamodels were investigated; for example, within the OMG in their creation of the Software Process Engineering Metamodel or SPEM [28]. One of their unsolved problems was how to define an attribute of a process element in the definition layer (M2) and refrain from having to allocate it a value until level M0. The problem is that under the rules of strict metamodelling and instantiation semantics, any definition at level Mx *must* be given a value at the next lower level, Mx-1. It is not possible to defer that value allocation until Mx-2. Yet this is exactly what is needed. For example, let us suppose (not strictly true in metamodels such as ISO/IEC 24744) that all tasks need to have a duration associated with them. One would then suppose to define, at M2, an attribute of class Task, called *duration* of type Time. But if we allocate this a value at the next lower level, M1, then we will have dictated that *all* tasks of a particular kind (such as the task "write the use case model") take the same time (the value of which we have just allocated at the M1 level). Instead, what is needed is a "flag" to say that all tasks: "write the use case model" will need a duration but the duration allowed will be allocated at the individual level i.e. M0. This is not possible with the UML and SPEM architecture. This and other metamodelling issues resulting from trying to solve this conundrum are well documented in a series of papers [12, 29, 30, 13, 2, 27] and summarized here.

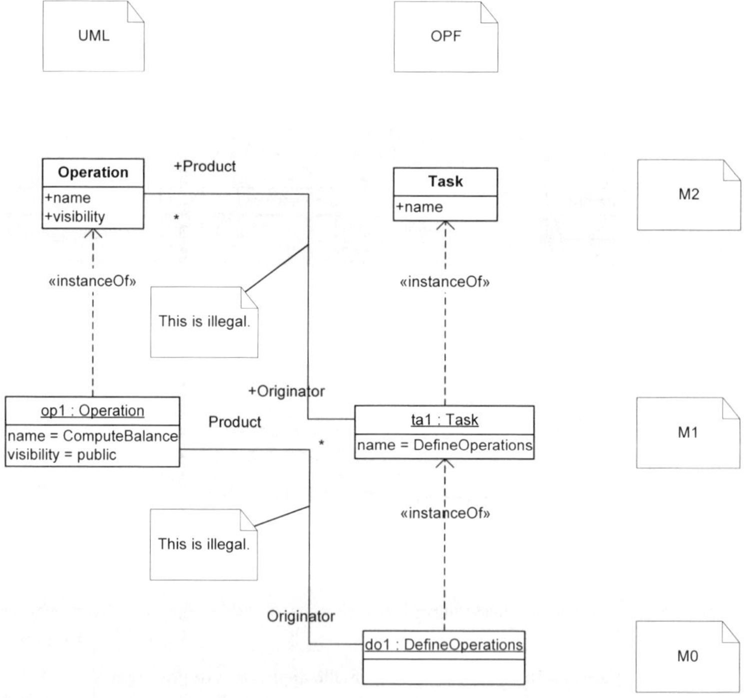

Figure 9 Problems arise when metamodels for process and work product are linked (after [15, figure 3]) © Springer-Verlag, 2006. With kind permission of Springer Science and Business Media.

When amalgamating process and product aspects of a method, the most straightforward modelling hierarchies (M0-M3) result in a transgression of strict metamodelling rules by virtue of an association linking M1 diagrams to the M0 task of drawing those diagrams (Figure 9) – equality, as shown in Figure 10, is in fact gained either by pulling standardized meta-elements into the M1 layer or displacing such conceptual definitions upwards to M3 – with the added disadvantage of placing all derived method/process fragments into the "standardized" M2 layer (Figures 9-11).

Figure 9 shows the linkages necessarily introduced when juxtaposing a work product three layer model (such as used in UML) with a process model description language (such as used in OPF or SPEM). Since M2 is the definitional (standards) layer, it is clear that Operation and Task[6] belong there i.e. it is appropriate that standards are defined for these two concepts. But the links between product and process cross the metalevel boundaries. For instance, a person working on a project is executing the (M0) task of defining an operation (on a class). That operation from a work product viewpoint (e.g. in a UML diagram) exists at the M1 level. The association is the only relationship that is appropriate to link these two and thus crosses the boundary – illegal in the strict metamodelling world.

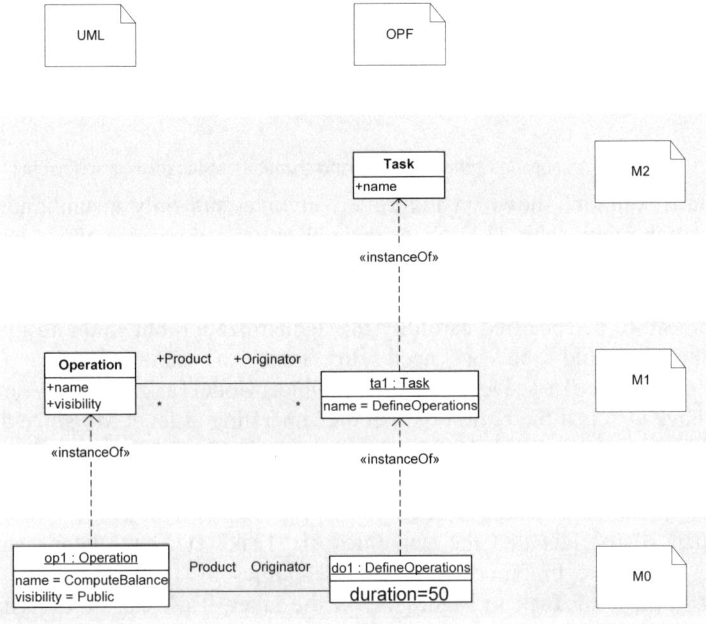

Figure 10 Vertical realignment offers some solution but introduces new problems (after [15, figure 4]) © Springer-Verlag, 2006. With kind permission of Springer Science and Business Media.

An obvious "solution" is shown in Figure 10 wherein the right hand side of Figure 9 is moved up (or equivalently the left hand side is moved down). Now the associations are (correctly) within layers. If we equate level M2 with standards committees and M1 with users' applications (as assumed in the OMG suite of standards), then it can be seen that there is a problem resulting from the fact that Operation is now at level M1 i.e. the user level. This takes it away from the realm (and responsibility) of the standards committees, thus somewhat negating the idea of having a standardized modelling language if the users can effectively create their own standard (but see

---

[6] We shall discuss later the inappropriateness of the name "Task" and its implied semantics (see, e.g. Figure 12)

discussion on the standardization of M1 libraries in the method engineering literature e.g. [31-33] and in [27]).

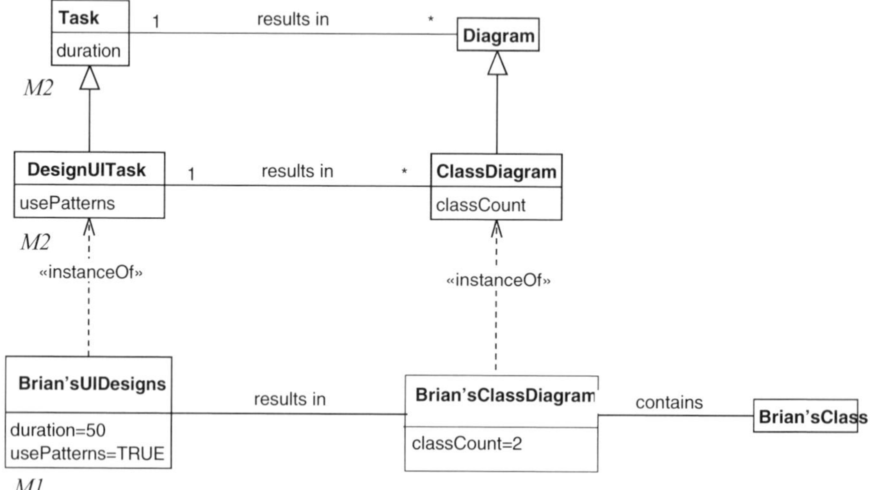

Figure 11 An apparent solution using generalization – using ideas described in [13]

A third solution, shown in Figure 11, involves not only instantiation but also a generalization relationship [13]. Since generalization can occur *within* a layer, this also compounds the architecture into only two layers. However, we now have four elements within the M2 (standards) layer, which means that not only do concepts like Task and Diagram need to be specified carefully for standardization but so do all their subtypes. Thus there would be a need to issue a standard for CodingTask, DesignUserInterfaceTask, DevelopBusinessObjectModelTask etc. etc. – an open-ended set. We have also lost the notion of "people" operating at level M0 since they are now necessarily part of level M1. [Of course, this can be fixed by dropping everything by one level – but at the expense of leaving nothing in the M2 level!]

Finally, what is in danger of being lost in these diagrams is the awareness (by the user/reader) of the fact that the semantics of "Task" etc. have been changed whilst retaining the name. In other words, the semantics of Task in Figure 10 are very different to those of Task in Figure 11. In the latter, Task can be described by a set containing many different actual tasks (Figure 12, left hand side) while the former is described by a different set with a much smaller number of elements (right hand side Figure 12).

This name and semantics change occurs when/if instantiation semantics are substituted by generalization semantics (or vice versa). Atkinson and Kühne [13] characterize this in their discussion about whether specific elements, such as Task, should be regarded as a class (generalization semantics) or a metaclass (instantiation semantics).

An important issue is whether all elements of the modelling language in fact need to belong to the M2 level – this is certainly the implicit assumption made by the OMG – that the UML standard, for instance, is at the M2 level and is the only level to contain pre-defined elements, all user-defined elements residing in M1 [12]. Loosening this rule permits a wide range of other options, notably that of creating a standard that has some elements pre-defined at level M2 and others pre-defined at level M1 [12]. This has been called the "Unified Modeling Library" by Atkinson and Kühne [27] and has strong similarities to the notion of method fragment in a methodbase [33, 31] in the area of situational method engineering. The Unified Modeling Library concept allows both generalization relationships (to superclasses in the M1 layer) as well as instantiation relationships (to classes in the M2 layer) – Figure 13.

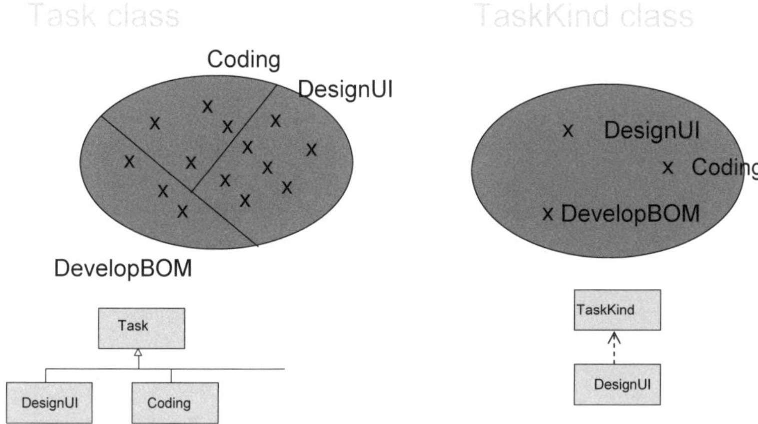

Figure 12 Semantic differences between Activity in Figures 10 and 11.

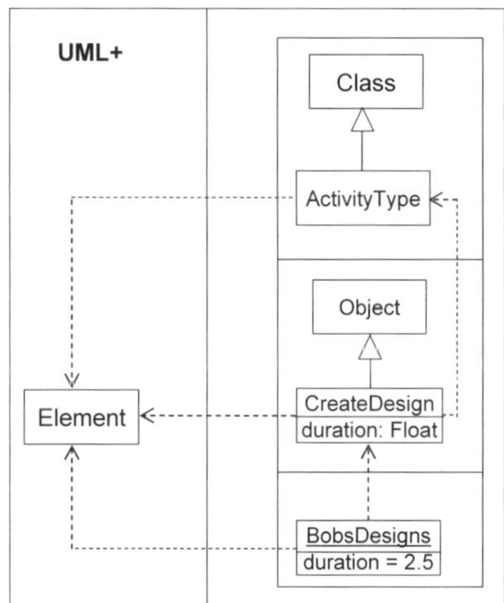

Figure 13 Library metaphor (after [27, figure 12b]) © Springer-Verlag, 2005. With kind permission of Springer Science and Business Media.

In resolution, these authors [26] invent what might be called an "attribute field" named potency (Figure 14), which they attach to each attribute – a solution applied to both modelling and also, more recently, to programming [34]. The value of the potency determines how many levels the attribute must be transferred down the instantiation chain before it is given a value. However, the existing UML architecture clearly requires an extension in order to support "potencies" e.g. [30]. Figure 14 also shows an alternative solution to this puzzle: the use of powertypes [24] as employed in standards such as AS461 [35] and ISO/IEC 24744 [36]. Here, a more natural mechanism is used to project values over two depths – although it must be stressed that this solution is incompatible with the OMG four layer architecture of Figure 2 if strictly applied (although potentially compatible with the modifications proposed by [27] as shown in Figure 13) but requires the newer architecture of Figure 3 in order for it to be successfully applied if one prefers to keep the whole of the powertype pattern [14] (here Task and TaskKind) within a single layer.

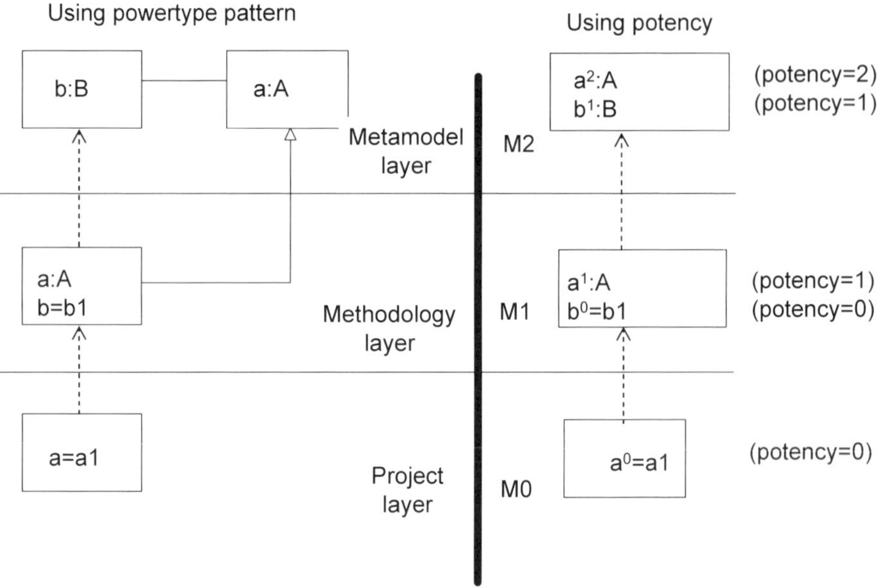

Figure 14 Comparison of powertype patterns and potency in terms of transmission of attribute values over several layers (adapted from [15, figure 20]). With kind permission of Springer Science and Business Media.

4. Explicit problems found in literature

While there are many papers that utilize these ideas of metamodelling appropriately e.g. [7, 37-42], there are as many (unfortunately perhaps even more) that do not follow such a quality metamodelling approach. In this section, we highlight, by example only, some of the pitfalls that we have seen ensnare the unwary modeller.

4.1. Modelling a model as "metamodel" (while acknowledging that the term is relative)

It is generally agreed that a metamodel is useful for defining the "abstract syntax" of a (modelling) language. In the UML context, a M2 level class diagram is used to describe "the concepts from which models are created" [2, table 1]. This M2 class diagram is thus equivalent to the abstract syntax i.e. the notions of abstract syntax and metamodel are here synonyms. Thus, when Dubé and Vangheluwe [43] discuss the abstract syntax of a modelling language for use in interface design, it is appropriate to evaluate it as if it were a (linguistic) metamodel. The metamodel of these authors shows syntactic elements, e.g. Watch, Button, Time, Alarm, which are all in fact concepts in the domain (SUS) and do not belong to the linguistic domain of the abstract syntax of a modelling language. In other words, their "metamodel" can be most appropriately interpreted as a (M1) model and not at the (OMG) M2 level. An alternative description of this model would be as an ontological model i.e. one that uses domain concepts and not linguistic concepts. It would thus fit into the left-hand column of Figure 8, using the modelling language depicted in the right-hand column for its descriptor. Such an alternative use of the term "metamodel" (an ontological metamodel) relies on uses clabject-instantiation relationships between elements in consecutive layers. The use of metamodelling solely in an ontological sense would, in fact, appear to be at the root of many of the uses of UML stereotypes that have been identified in [44] as "incorrect" when viewed against the basically linguistic rules of UML (see further discussion in Section 4.3).

In the process domain, one would anticipate seeing a class called, say, Task in the metamodel and a class called IdentifyUseCases in the model. However, in the formal analysis of OO methods by Hong *et al.* [45], their proposed meta-process model contains elements such as "Find responsibilities in requirements specification" and "Assign responsibilities to classes". Furthermore, it is said to "describe the analysis and design steps advocated by the methodology" – clearly at the M1 level.

4.2 Mixing of layers

A serious challenge in metamodelling, in whatever hierarchical framework is selected, is the allocation of a concept to an appropriate metalevel (a.k.a. domain in some metamodelling frameworks) and the *communication* of that to the reader. This is especially true in a strict metalevel framework such as that of the OMG since it is commonly understood in OO (and UML) modelling that a class is understood as standing as a surrogate for its instances. This immediately introduces a potential ambiguity when talking of, say, a class (M1) which is an instance of an M2 level class Class. [The UML documents try to use a lower case initial letter for instances and upper case for their types (i.e. one metalevel higher)]. Thus the very definite strict metamodelling "rule" [11] blurs rapidly – this is a natural consequence of the necessary discretization of a continuum. Notwithstanding, it is necessary to be as precise as possible to which metalevel one is referring, especially in diagrams using UML or similar notation which, as a notation, is meta-level agnostic. In the OMG documents, for instance, a UML class diagram is used to document the M2 metamodel of UML itself, the M3 MOF model (and its current variants) as well as regular design models at the (OMG) M1 level. This is not unreasonable since at any abstraction level, what is being depicted is simply "a model". The "meta-"ness is a useful label to indicate the displacement (up or down) by one artificially-induced metalevel (= abstraction level)[7].

With the above caveats, it is reasonable to examine the literature in the context of evaluation as to whether published diagrams contain elements that really do belong to the metalevels as stated. For instance, if the diagram is offered as being at a level commensurate with the OMG level M2, then are all its elements at a concomitant level of abstraction appropriate to such a level in the stated metamodelling hierarchy?

Van de Weerd *et al.* [46] propose a mutant UML diagram that they name a "process-data" diagram (Figure 15). The question is how we are to interpret this. The

---

[7] It should be noted that associating OMG metalevels with abstraction levels is not one-to-one since there is obviously need for abstraction techniques *within* each of the Mx levels of the OMG architecture.

text states "The process-data diagram we use consists of two integrated meta-models". On the left hand side is a "meta-process model based on a UML activity diagram". Both these statements suggest a metalevel (=OMG level M2). However, rather than notating this using UML's class diagram notation as is typically used for M2-level models, an activity diagram style is utilized. At first glance, this activity diagram appears to be an instance level (M1) diagram with generic names for the activities and subactivities, in which case its appropriate metalevel specification would be (adapted from the UML Activity diagram metamodel) something akin to that depicted in Figure 16.

Turning our attention to the second part of this process-data diagram. At first glance, this could be seen as depicting M2 concepts e.g. OPENCONCEPT – yet this (and SIMPLECONCEPT) appears many times. One conclusion is that an identifier (e.g. a numerical suffix as in the left hand side) has been omitted. Adding this then leads to a similar discussion to that for the "meta-process" component of the process-data diagram, with a consequent "true" metalevel diagram as given in Figure 17[8].

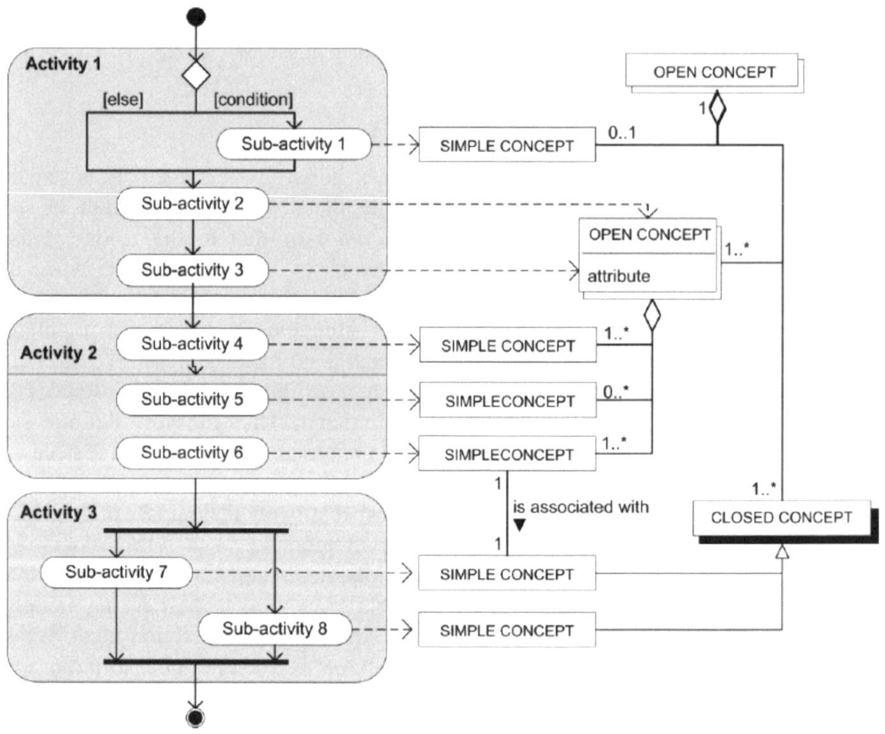

Figure 15 Example process-data diagram (after [46]) © John Wiley and Sons Limited. Reproduced with permission.

---

[8] This figure also contains a common notational "error" by representing several binary relationships (e.g. associations, aggregations) by a single notational arc i.e. a "yoke".

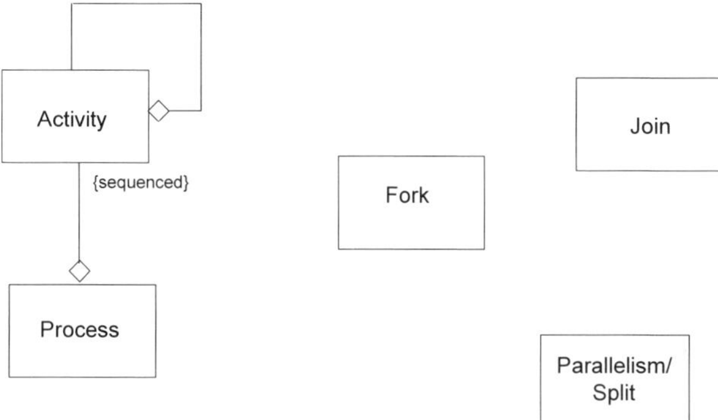

Figure 16 Inferred metamodel fragment for the process part of Figure 15. [Note that in this and following diagrams, the white UML "aggregation" diamond is given the semantics of (all) whole-part relationships.]

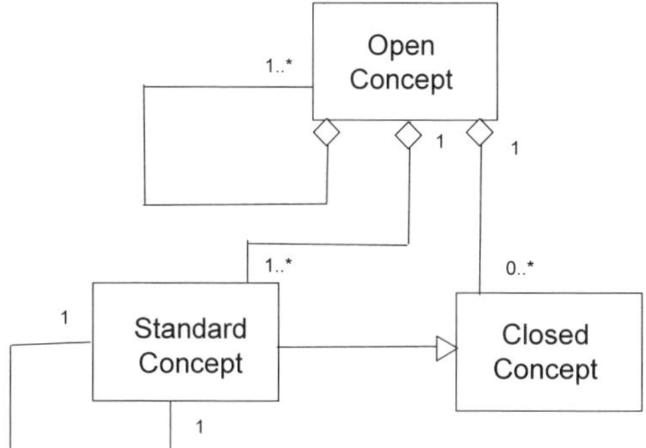

Figure 17 Inferred metamodel fragment for the data part of Figure 15

Linking these diagrams, both at the M1 (instance) level, introduces a relationship (the dashed arrow in Figure 15) that must be defined in addition to the concatenation of the two (M2) metamodels (that we have deduced here) into a single metamodel for this process-data diagram (Figure 18).

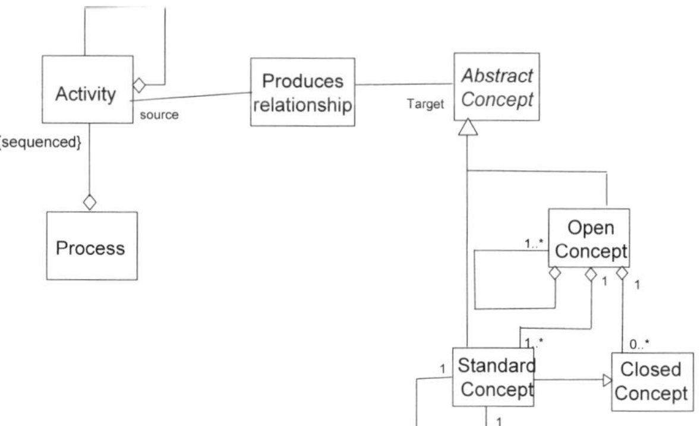

Figure 18 Combination of the metamodel fragments of Figures 16 and 17 together with a class for the linking relationship (produces)

It is clear from most of the figures later in the Van de Weerd *et al.* paper [46] that the above interpretation is appropriate. Figure 19 shows one such example in which the generic names of Figure 15 are replaced by actual names. Clearly, based on the names alone in Figure 19, this is at the regular modelling level. However, this is not substantiated by their figures 2 and 3 (Figure 20 here) where the right hand side readily matches the metamodel (M2) fragment of the UML specification [47] – shown here as Figure 21.

Finally, *in the context of model and metamodel precision*, there are some unanswered questions:

- Why is a SimpleConcept a subtype of ClosedConcept (their figure 1)?
- Why is ClosedConcept defined as a collection of (sub)concepts? (which itself contradicts the content of the first bulleted point)?
- In the definitions of Open and Closed Concept, what is the definition of "unexpanded"?
- In [46], a class diagram is contradictorily said to be a good example of both an OpenConcept and a ClosedConcept – which is it?

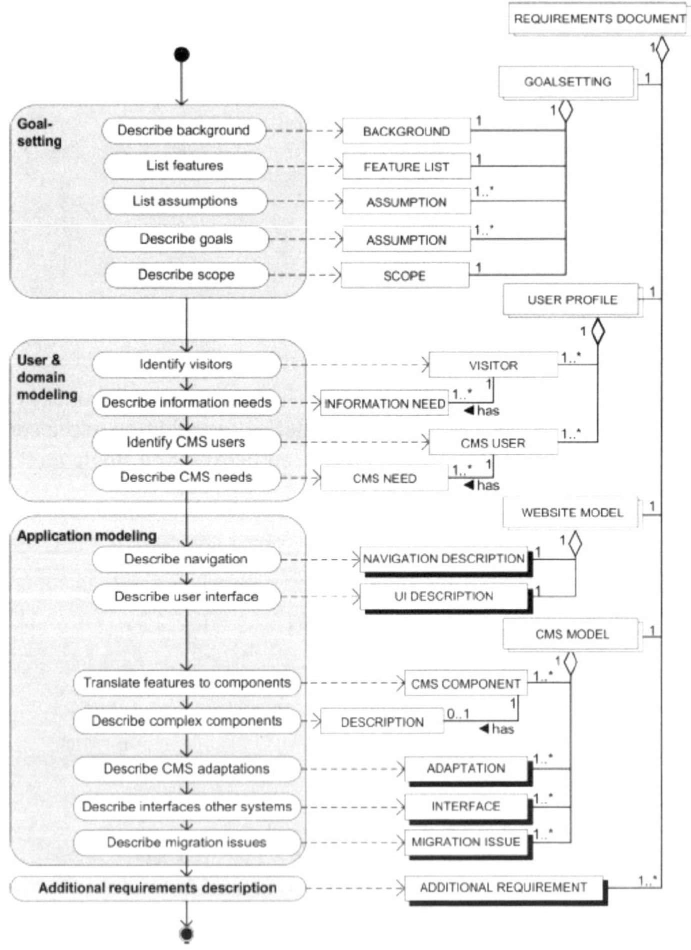

Figure 19 Process-data diagram of the standard Definition phase (after [46]) © John Wiley and Sons Limited. Reproduced with permission.

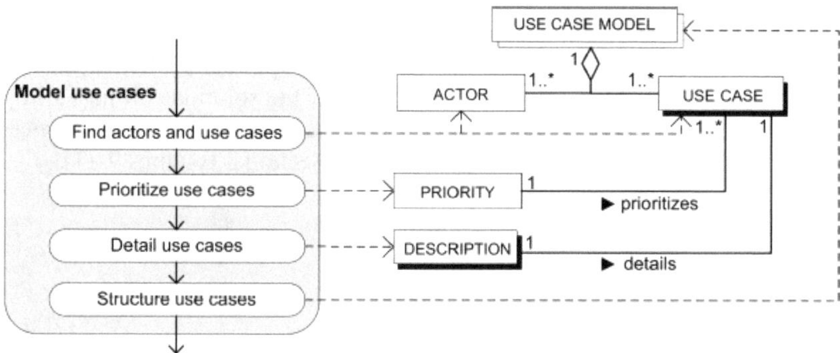

Figure 20 Implementation situation characteristics (after [46]) © John Wiley and Sons Limited. Reproduced with permission.

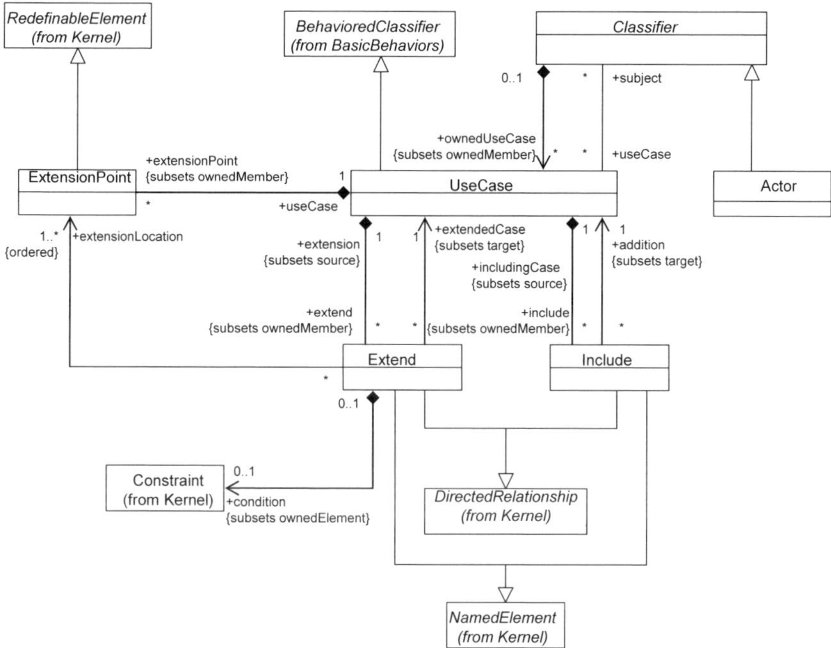

Figure 21 Use case/Actor fragment from UML 2. Reprinted with permission. Object Management Group, Inc. © OMG. 2005 [47]

Similar issues can be identified in another, slightly earlier, paper [48]. Although that study is focused on metrics, an attempt is also made to address the challenge of linking the process and product aspects of a method engineering approach. In Figure 22, the product (artifact) part is linked to the activity or process part. The right hand side describes steps in a real development process (clearly at the method level or M1 equivalent). Yet the left hand side is clearly aligned with similar diagrams in the UML metamodel. At first glance, this seems to be a contravention of strict metamodelling rules since M1 entities (right hand side) are linked to M2 entities (left hand side) with a relationship other than is-instance-of. Furthermore, these non-instantiation relationships are said to "stand for the artifacts that are produced by an activity". This may be confusing to the reader since the concept of a relationship and the concept of an entity are generally regarded as being orthogonal[9].

However, Saeki [48] also documents this approach using MEL [50], the Method Engineering Language (Figure 23). With this form of expression, all elements appear to be on the same level. This is, in fact, akin to one of the solutions proposed in [13] in their attempt to resolve the well-known problem that when amalgamating process and product aspects of a method, as discussed above, in Section 3 (Figures 9-11).

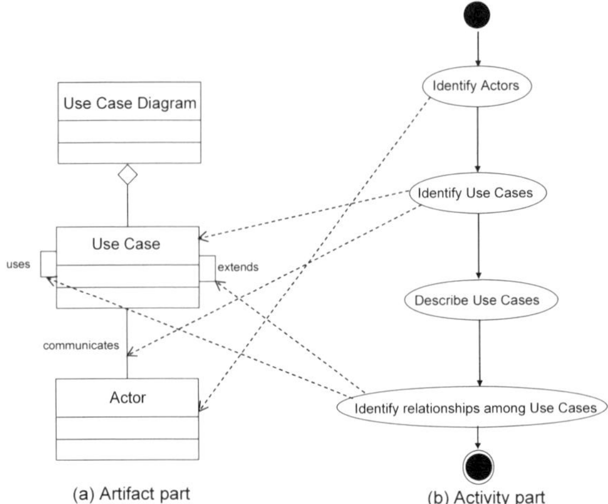

Figure 22 Proposed metamodel example from [48, figure 1] © Springer-Verlag, 2003. With kind permission of Springer Science and Business Media.

PRODUCT Use Case Model;
  ID Use Case Model;
  IS_A Diagram, Structured Text;
  LAYER Diagram;
  PART OF Analysis Model;
  NAME TEXT;

PRODUCT Use Case:
  LAYER Concept;
  PART OF Use Case Model;
  SYMBOL Oval;
  NAME Text;
  ASSOCIATED WITH {(uses,), (extends,), (hasUseCase,), (communicates,)}.

ASSOCIATION has UseCase:
  ASSOCIATES (Use Case Diagram, Use Case);
  CARDINALITY (1..n; 1..1).

(a) Product fragment

PROCESS Construct a Use Case Diagram:
  LAYER Diagram;
  TYPE Creation;
  PART OF Create an Analysis Model;
  REQUIRED {Interview results};
  REQUIRED OPTIONAL
    Current information system;
  (- Identify Actors ;
  - Identify Use Cases ;
  - Describe Use Cases ;
  - Identify Relationships among Use Cases ;
)
  DELIVERABLES {Use Case Diagram}.

(b) Process fragment

Figure 23 An example of a MEL description (after [48, figure 2]) © Springer-Verlag, 2003. With kind permission of Springer Science and Business Media.

---

[9] Association classes in UML would appear to be a counter-example but they introduce a paradox as identified in [49]

Interestingly, in a very recent paper, van de Weerd and colleagues [51] formalize their process data diagram approach. The metamodel they propose is shown in Figure 24 and is clearly aligned with the class diagram style of the UML M2-level metamodel – yet interestingly labelled by them as a "meta-meta model". Contrasting its contents with those deduced here in Figure 18 based on their earlier papers, one should note that Figure 24 does not explicitly support the difference between open and closed concepts and appears to rename Process as Method. It also introduces a differentiation between ProcessFragment and DeliverableFragment, which is in line with many authors' interpretation of situational method engineering [31].

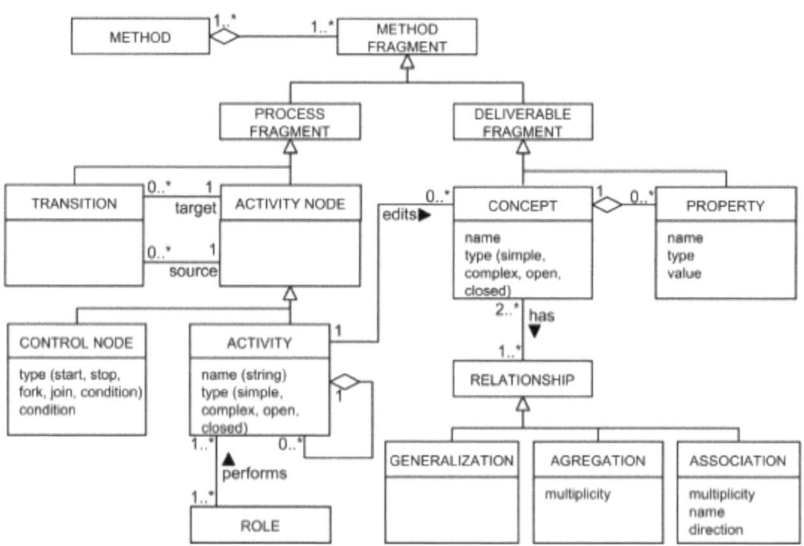

Figure 24 Metamodel of process-data diagram (after [51, figure 3]) © Springer-Verlag, 2007. With kind permission of Springer Science and Business Media.

4.3 Modelling issues at the "meta" level

Although metamodelling is often discussed independently of modelling, for the most part the mindset required to undertake a good quality metamodel is exactly those for good modelling. The concepts to be modelled are of course more abstract but the notion of a "class", the various kinds of "relationships" between these classes and so forth are identical. The use of generalization, for instance, to link two classes in a parent-child relationship, or an "aggregation" to represent whole-part or an association to indicate a peer to peer linkage are the same and the same rules for good modelling that apply in domain level modelling also apply to metamodelling. With this in mind, we can evaluate whether models correctly positioned at the higher abstraction level and appropriately labelled as "metamodels" are of an appropriate quality, based on standard modelling rules and guidelines.

A commonly misunderstood area of metamodelling is the use of UML stereotypes e.g. [44, 52]; the associated notion of profiles being widely recognized as being of poor quality [53]. Although stereotypes were reformulated in UML2, there are still identifiable concerns [27]. In addition to the concerns raised in [52], a further explanation of the statement there that stereotypes only appear to be able to be attached to classes is needed. Figure 25 shows the fragment of the UML2 metamodel that supports this statement. Extension is associated with Class (and notably Class not Classifier) thus suggesting that instances of Extension can only be attached to instances of Class. However, this diagram is not as straightforward as it seems. The rolename "/metaclass" would appear to be an attempt to say that the M2 Class should be regarded as if it were the M3 Class (from MOF). Since MOF::Class is able to have instantiated from it all the UML::Classifier types, then if this interpretation is correct, the Stereotype (via the Extension class) can be applied to many instances in an M2 model. This is borne out by the statement [16, page 178] that "Stereotype is the only kind of metaclass that cannot be extended by stereotypes". However, this introduces a violation of strict metamodelling (i.e. a contradiction) as follows. On the one hand it states that extensions apply to metaclasses but on the other hand it states that extensions apply to user classes (since we must remember that the class Class in UML (M2) stands for classes in user models (M1). In fact, the "/metaclass" rolename appears to be a disguise for an association that crosses the M2/M3 boundary (Figure 26) since the M2 class Class plus the rolename suggests in fact that what is meant is the M3 class Class.

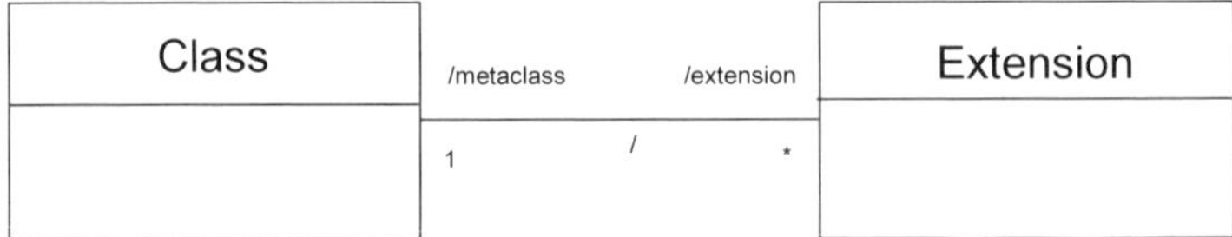

Figure 25 Fragment of UML 2.0 metamodel for the stereotype mechanism – the link between Class and Extension

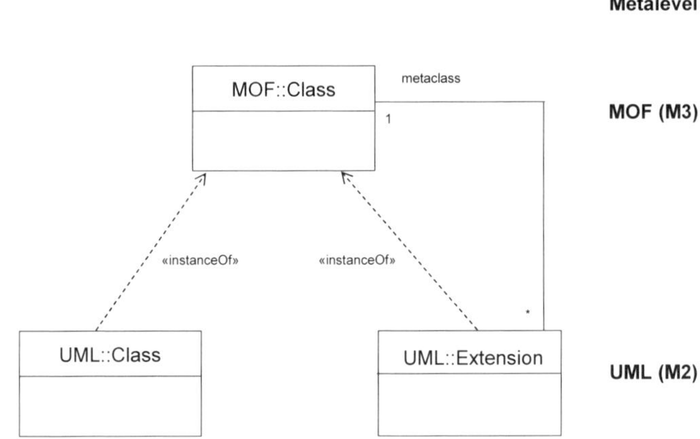

Figure 26 Reformulation of Figure 25 to make the link to MOF::Class explicit

Furthermore, the formal OMG documentation that describes the UML standard e.g. [54, 47] stresses the need to *define* any stereotype before use – they proffer two alternatives for doing such a definition. Secondly, the stereotype must conceptualize a notion at the metalevel i.e. commensurate with all the other elements in the UML modelling language (i.e. the "M2" metamodel). In other words, the concept represented by a stereotype must, by definition, be at the metamodelling level and not the modelling level. Notwithstanding, as noted by e.g. [44], there are very many occurrences in the literature where the names of the stereotypes clearly pertain to concepts in the real world and the model that represents that real world e.g.

"ShoppingTrolley", "VideoRental" (akin to an ontological model). In other words, metamodelling has been used (in the case of UML with instantiation semantics) when a more correct approach would be to use a regular modelling approach such that all classes represents "things" in the real/business world. Typically, misused stereotypes would be replaced by regular generalization relationships between a pair of classes.

Unfortunately, such errors, whilst pointed out repeatedly over the last several years, persist. Now, not only the object-oriented community but more recently the agent-oriented modelling community has begun to use both metamodels and, particularly in the current context, UML stereotypes. Fuentes-Fernandez *et al.* [55] include a large number of stereotypical annotations (a name in guillemets) without any definitions of these stereotypes. Figure 27 (their figure 1) contains ten apparent stereotypes. But all the stereotype names are identical to the class names! Secondly, as discussed above, the stereotype names are clearly names of things in the model domain not the metamodel domain. For example, a DivisionOfLabout stereotype on a class would indicate the presupposition of the virtual existence of a subtype of Class in the UML M2 metamodel which was a DivisionOfLaboutClass. This makes absolutely no sense. (Later diagrams such as their figure 3 add other inappropriate stereotypes such as Task, Agent and Goal).

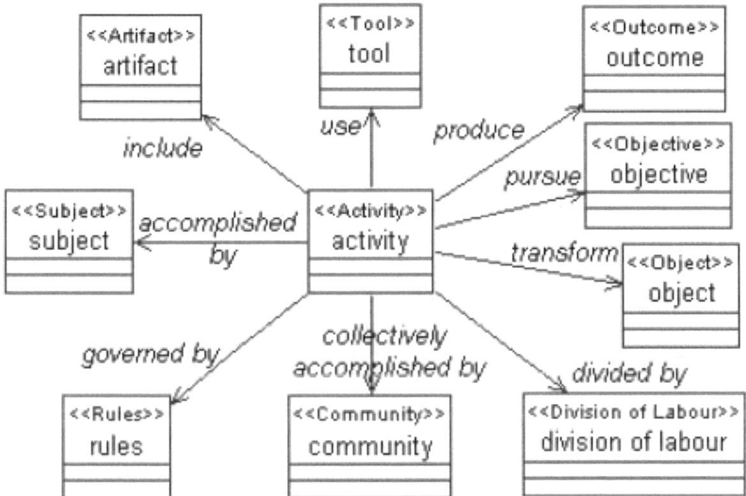

Figure 27 Example of incorrect use of stereotypes in agent-oriented methodology (after [55])

A different error of usage of stereotypes is seen in figure 2 of [56], also in the AOSE context. They propose a class in their MAS fragment metamodel called FragmentsDependency that is stereotyped as «Guideline». This suggests a subtype at a higher metalevel called Guideline. While this is not impossible, there are two issues: Guideline is defined in the same diagram and is therefore at the same level as FragmentsDependency and/or an "M3" level class called Guideline is needed. This is not possible using UML since MOF does not define a stereotype mechanism, which is a necessary precondition to the existence of a stereotype within a (M2) metamodel such as the one presented by these authors.

Stereotypes are sometimes understood as allowing the addition of elements accidentally omitted from the metamodel itself. An alternative is of course to actually add these elements to the metamodel. For instance, in the OPF metamodel, figure G.5

of [57] describes very many subtypes of Work Product (Figure 28). In contrast, figure G.10 of [32] models the various kinds of role as method fragments rather than as actual subtypes in the metamodel (Figure 29). Yet, there appears no conceptual difference between a link such as "Plan is a subtype of WorkProduct" (Figure 28) and "SoftwareArchitect is an instance of Role" (Figure 29). This means that the metamodel, as described in Appendix G, does not have the integrity it could and should have. This is due to the lack of the powertype mechanism, which resulted in indecision as to the "level" for many of the classes described. Kühne [4] captures this in his litmus test for a metamodel. He proposes that if the instances of their models are *not* instances of them holds true, then it is a true metamodel. For example, the freeway F1 is an instance of motorway which is an instance of ConnectorType but it is untrue to say that the freeway F1 is an instance of ConnectorType.

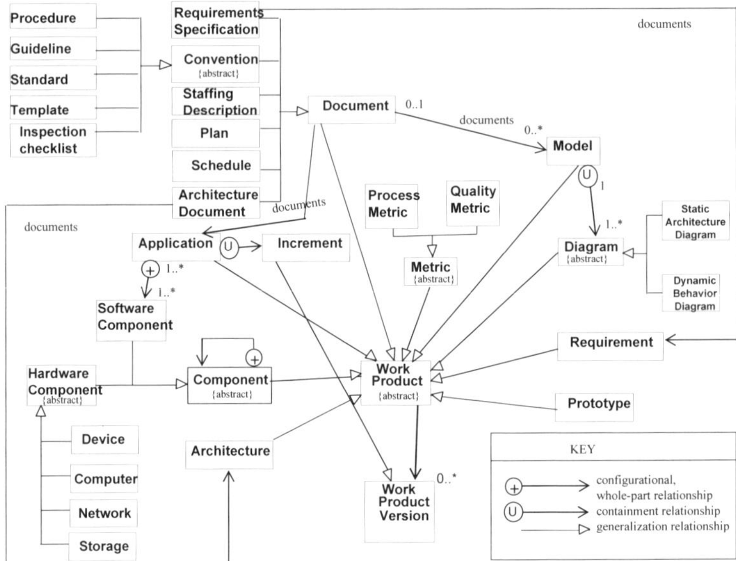

Figure 28 Predefined classes of Work Products (after [32]) © Pearson Education Limited

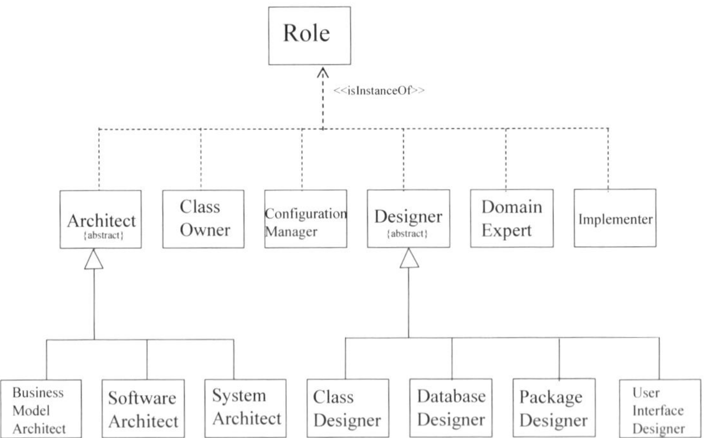

Figure 29 A selection of the predefined classes of Roles (after [32]) © Pearson Education Limited

Misleading and erroneous statements abound, for example, Lin and Ding [56] state that there are three subtypes of activity: generalization, aggregation and classification[10]. Furthermore, Activity is said to be "a central concept which composes a process". If this statement is to be understood as implying some kind of whole-part relationship between an activity and a process, then it is contradicted in Definition 2 of these authors: "An activity can be considered as a simple process".

SPEM 1.1 allows itself to move away from technology independence. For example, in its need to be viewed as a UML Profile, various claims are made such as "an Activity is an Operation" [28, figure 7-1], meaning an operation on some (unspecified) class in an architectural model (we presume). Classes in the SPEM (process) metamodel should really belong to a different domain from the metaclasses (product) in the UML yet in the SPEM's very definition these two areas are confounded.

Finally, and less importantly, scoping can be a problem in metamodels. For instance, the original OMG MOF specification was proposed as a metametamodel. Such a model should contain around 4-6 classes, as exemplified by the CDIF work [7, 57]; yet despite all review comments, the MOF scope, when published, was observed to be almost equivalent to that of UML and in UML 2, the MOF metamodel is regarded as a subset of the UML metamodel, perhaps even a UML profile [58]. Other examples of scope problems in metamodels can be found in some of the published papers on method chunks, such as those of [59, 60], the classes included in their "fragment/chunk metamodel" delving into areas well outside the declared scope [21].

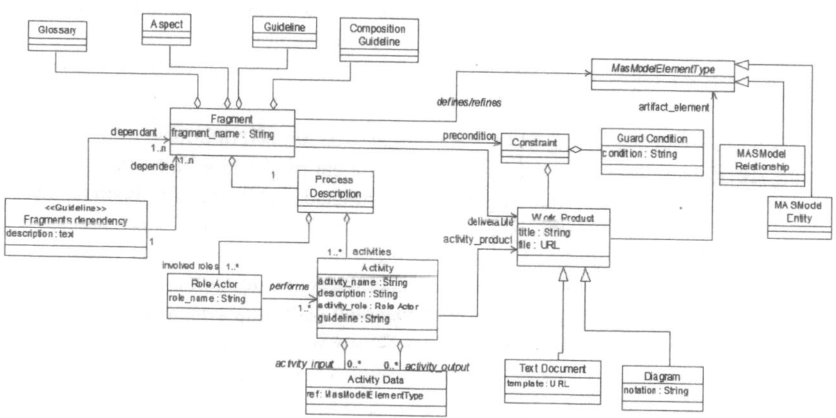

Figure 30 The FIPA method fragment metamodel (after [59])

For instance, although the FIPA study that resulted in Figure 30 is in the domain of agents, its fragment metamodel is, in fact, technology-independent. The first obvious comment is that there are many classes in this diagram that *do not* contribute to the definition (i.e. metamodel) of the concept of "fragment". A fragment includes[11] a glossary and a list of terms that facilitate the understanding of fragment concepts when applied to a context different from the one from which it was extracted. The aspect is useful to detect the field of fragment application, for instance a tool to be used to aid in

---

[10] Although later in the paper they are defined more correctly as "semantic relationships between activities".

[11] Note we are interpreting the white diamond, undefined in UML 2, very loosely here.

the performance of an activity. An aspect has the form of a textual description. A method fragment has two kinds of guidance to indicate its own purpose; *guideline* relates to the fragment as a portion of a process i.e. a set of rules providing a detailed description on how to perform an activity, a *composition guideline* describes the context from which it is extracted, indicating the reuse possibility for the fragment. However, this might seem to imply the use of multiple fragments and is therefore, again, out of scope (for the definition of "fragment").

The fragment dependency, in the third area, is the only element belonging to the methodbase; it is composed of a list of dependee and dependant fragments useful for composing different fragments. However, this means that these relationships involve more than one fragment and must necessarily be out of scope for the definition of "fragment".

It is also possibly worth showing the pre- and post-conditions for a fragment although these should probably not be an intrinsic part of the *definition* of a method fragment.

The other classes in Figure 30 can all be challenged as being out of scope. A fragment only has a process description if it is a process-focussed method fragment! However, it turns out [61] that this metamodel is for a *chunk* (with a process part and a product part) not for a generic fragment. This means that the aggregation relationship (white diamond) to ProcessDescription should be balanced by a similar relationship to WorkProduct. Furthermore, the generalization relationships to WorkProduct are clearly out of scope and should be omitted as should the coarse granular classes in Figure 30 of GuardCondition and Constraint. The link to MetaModelElement Type is arcane and, in any case, its subtypes are unnecessarily technology-specific (to agent technology). In Figure 30, ProcessDescription is shown as an aggregation of RoleActor and Activity. While the semantics of these classes may need tightening[12], this does illustrate nicely the concept of granularity since, at a coarse granularity, one would only need ProcessDescription – the other two aggregated classes showing more detail revealed if a finer granularity is required. The resultant metamodel (two possible levels of metamodel granularity) is more tightly focused and is shown in Figure 31.

A second chunk model is presented in Figure 32, which shows the metamodel published in e.g. [60] to define their notion of a method chunk. (As discussed above, this is a combination of a product part and a process part). Similarly to our observation of the FIPA metamodel (Figure 30), this metamodel defines not only the chunk but a significant number of methodology elements outside of the scope of a definition of what a chunk itself is.

A chunk consists of a process portion plus a product portion. A Chunk has a ProductPart because it inherits the association to Guideline. The complement, ProcessPart, does not appear under this name. Instead, the ProcessPart appears under its synonym of Guideline [63]. What is immediately problematical is that if Guideline is the process part of the chunk, then this is contradicted by the Generalization between Chunk and Guideline, which states that a Chunk _is_ (only) a Process Part.

This part of the chunk metamodel (Figure 33) obfuscates the definition as described textually (as above). The many-to-many relationship (undirected yet labelled "is based on") between Guideline and ProductPart is also contradictory to the textual

---

[12] For example, the association between RoleActor and Activity is two way as a result of the attribute activity_role on Activity (Figure 26) although such a two-way relationship introduces problems of semantic integrity [62]

definition. There is also overlapping subsetting (without a discriminator) between Guideline subtyped as Chunk or non-Chunk and Guideline subtyped as either StrategicGuideline, TacticalGuideline or SimpleGuideline (Figure 33). The latter subtyping relates to the *process* of creating a "map" whereas the former aims to represent the entities that may appear in that map. We therefore respectfully suggest

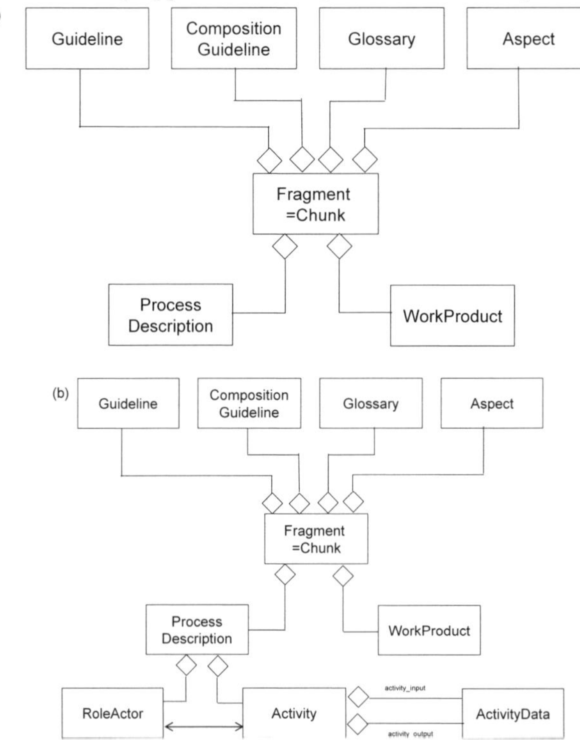

Figure 31 Revised FIPA fragment metamodel (=Figure 30 with extraneous classes removed) at (a) coarse granularity and (b) fine granularity

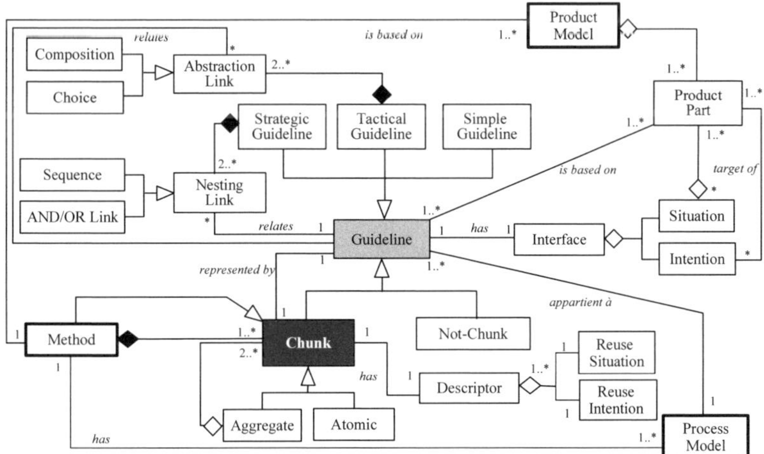

Figure 32 The chunk metamodel of Ralyté and Rolland [60, figure 3] © Springer-Verlag, 2001. With kind permission of Springer Science and Business Media.

that Figure 33 is an inappropriate metamodel to describe the clear intentions of chunk modelling as represented textually or in diagrams like Figure 34. It is speculation that perhaps the method *construction* idea encapsulated in earlier publications as a "map" [64], which relies on Strategic, Tactical and Simple Guidelines, have been concatenated with the static architectural demands of a chunk metamodel. At the very best, this is multiple partitioning (with no discriminator) going on here.

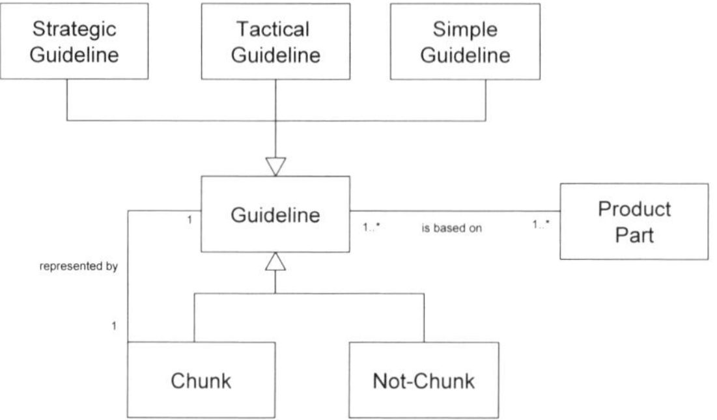

Figure 33 The core of the chunk metamodel of e.g. [60]

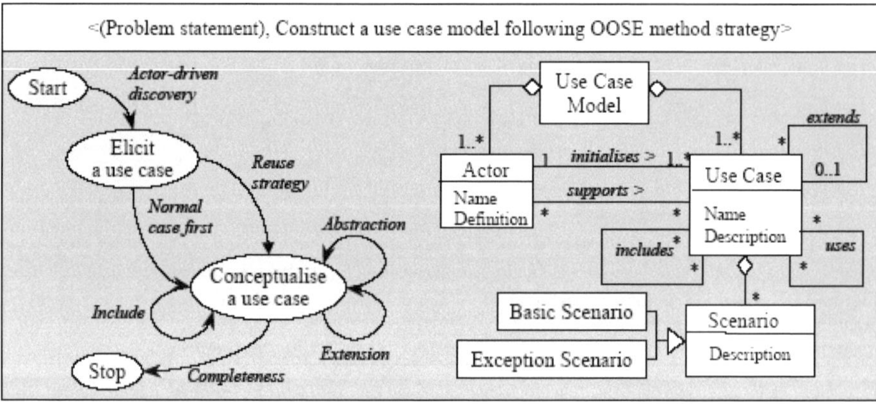

Figure 34 An example of a method chunk, consisting of a single process fragment and a single product fragment (after [65])

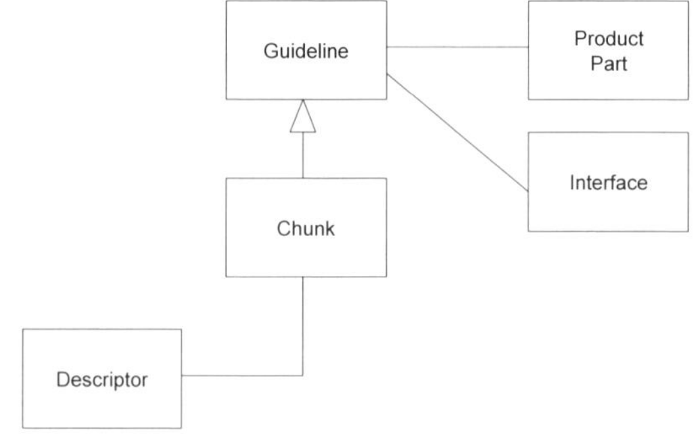

Figure 35 More tightly focused definition of method chunk derived from Figure 32.

Other classes can be readily eliminated. Although stating that a method can be viewed as a combination of chunks or a single chunk is relevant to method engineering in general, it is not relevant for a chunk definition. Similarly out of scope for defining a Chunk is a class called Non-Chunk. More problematic are the classes focused around a) Interface and b) Descriptor.

The resultant metamodel for method fragment, after mere pruning of irrelevant classes, is shown in Figure 35 and in Figure 36 is shown a more radical revision, which eliminates Guideline as a superclass of Chunk.

While Interface can be misinterpreted as implying a visibility constraint, it in fact only refers to knowledge stored about the context of the use of the method chunk [66]. Thus it consists of two parts, one relating to the situation (the pre-condition for usage) and one to the intention (the post-condition of the use of this chunk).

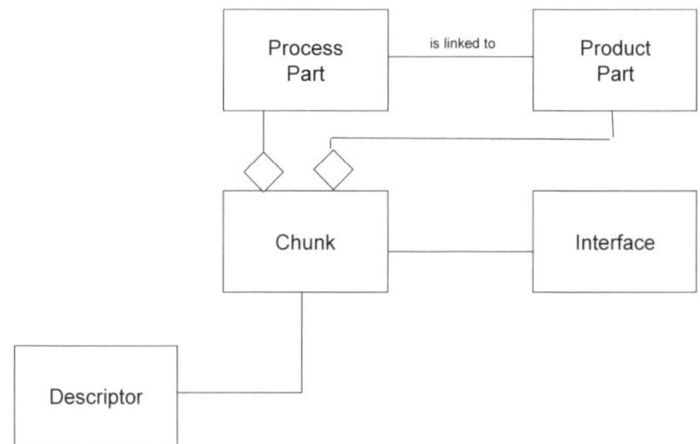

Figure 36 A more radical revision of Figure 32 in which are added whole-part relationships to represent the exemplar of Figure 34.

The descriptor is used to add information relevant to chunk retrieval, formalized and extended by [67. 68] as shown in Figure 37. As well as a name, id, type (i.e. atomic or aggregate) and objective (a narrative description) for the chunk, the descriptor also has a *Reuse Context* and *Reuse Intention*, only hinted at in [65]. Mirbel and Ralyté [67] suggest that the reuse intention, which describes the objective of the chunk and has the same structure as the intention of the chunk, can be formally stated as verb + target + parameters [69]. For example, the informal intention "Construct a use case model following the OOSE approach" can be reformatted as Construct$_{verb}$ (as use case model)$_{target}$ (following the OOSE approach)$_{parameter=manner}$. However, it should be noted that such an example underlines the one-to-one nature of chunks (process to product part). Thus, the process focussed nature of this approach prevents it from being of use in situations where, for example, one processes is linked with (creates, modifies or deletes) more than one work product.

Descriptors, as seen in Figure 37, also have connections to other elements, also potentially useful for consolidating the interface. These are (i) the origin of the chunk (i.e. from which method was it derived/abstracted), (ii) incompatible chunks, (iii) alternative chunks, (iv) experience gained from previous usage and (v) an example. Descriptors give information on which method the chunk has been extracted from in terms of the Method class in Figure 37. However, this contradicts the Method class in Figure 32 where there it represents the constructed method itself. Since Figure 37 is in fact an amplified portion of Figure 32 there is a serious name clash. We respectfully recommend renaming of Method in Figure 37 as SourceMethod.

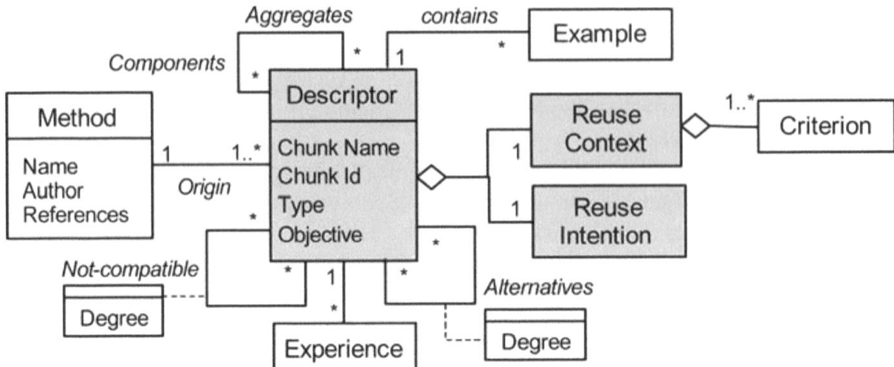

Figure 37 Metamodel for the Descriptor (after [67, figure 8]) © Springer-Verlag, 2006. With kind permission of Springer Science and Business Media.

Finally, since chunks can be at any granularity (see also [70]), it is argued e.g. [65] that the full method itself can also be regarded as a chunk. This is similar to the model adopted more recently in SPEM Version 1 [28] in which a Process is modelled as a special kind of ProcessComponent. However, while this could work for fragments, since, by definition, a chunk is ONE process-focussed fragment plus ONE product-focussed fragment, then there is no meaningful way to model a full SEP as a combination of one process-focussed fragment plus one product-focussed fragment.

A comparison and contrast between chunks and fragments is undertaken in [66, 71]. While there are many similarities, there are also many differences. It could be conjectured that fragments and chunks could be united in a metamodel such as that shown in Figure 38. However, it should be noted that there are implicit problems here. In particular, it should be noted that since a single method chunk consists of one process fragment plus one product fragment, the statement that one process fragment can be associated with several product fragments provides an internal inconsistency i.e. a contradiction within the tenets of chunk modelling.

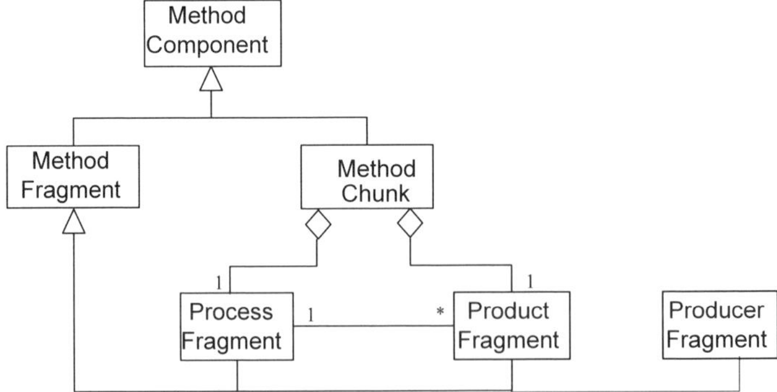

Figure 38 Part of a metamodel linking Method Components, Chunks and Fragments, including the three kinds of fragments

5. Solutions and Guidelines

The best architecture of a multi-layer framework for metamodelling is still uncertain. The ANSI/OMG four-layer approach, shown in Figure 2, has been used for the longest period of time but has led to the discovery of very many anomalies in its use, particularly when product and process modelling are integrated. The Orthogonal Classification Architecture has also been proposed [2], perhaps together with the notion of standardizing a language over a combination of two layers (Figure 13) [27]. As an alternative, the practice-based architecture of Figure 3 is newer but supports the use of powertypes more successfully within a single "metamodel" layer.

The integration of process and product aspects of a methodology has led to many apparent paradoxes, resolved either by potency or powertypes (Figure 14) but deeper analysis leads to the identification of more and more anomalies. For instance, when one instantiates a class (in OO terms) one gets an object – which is itself non-instantiable. Consequently, since the UML metamodel (OMG level M2) consists of classes (sometimes labelled as metaclasses but with no stated differentiating semantics), one would anticipate that the instantiated M1 level entities should be objects, yet they are normally understood to be classes (e.g. in a user-drawn UML class diagram). Indeed, the whole OMG architecture is based on the notion that the instance of a M3 class is a M2 class and the instance of an M2 class is a M1 class. Only the instantiation of an M1 class results in an object. There is a missing metatypical mapping, as identified in [21], as demonstrated in Figure 4. This needs to be made visible.

A second issue is the realization that there are in fact two distinct kinds of metamodelling: so-called linguistic (or logical) and ontological (or physical). One normally thinks of metamodelling in terms of the UML/MOF hierarchy which is focussed primarily on linguistic modelling. In this case, the guideline is that the SUS and the modelling language used to describe the SUS are different e.g. bank account as opposed to UML Classifier. When ontological modelling is accidentally interspersed, this is ready identifiable by the fact that apparent metaclasses are in the same domain and use the same modelling language and terminology e.g. breed as a metaclass for dog.

A common problem observed (as outlined in Section 4.2) is the intermixing of meta-layers in the one diagram. Based on traditional OO modelling, one would expect only one example of, say, Class in the metalevel diagram with several example instances of that class in the layer below. This ties in strongly with the notion that the Type/Object relationship is representable by set theory or category theory is a useful basis for object orientation e.g. [72]. A test therefore is whether there are linguistic classes like Classifier or Operation in the same diagram as multiple classes all with the same domain-specific name (as in Figure 15). A subsidiary test for ontological modelling is whether a generalization could alternatively be used; for instance, many stereotyped classes can be more appropriately modelled as a class and its superclass.

A second common problem, often linked, is that of scoping. Many fragment metamodels, as used in method engineering, state that they define a "fragment" but in fact have a much broader scope, bearing on domains at very different granularities or purpose. Another example is the number of classes in MOF 1.0 which far exceed the minimum set envisaged by e.g. [9] or CDIF [57]. Guidelines here require simply common sense and a tighter constraint on what is and isn't in scope.

A final rule of thumb is provided by [44] who suggests that, when evaluating if a particular stereotype named 'S' is appropriate, we should ask the following question:

"Do I under any circumstance want instances of the stereotyped element to be understood as "S"- instances?"

If the answer is yes, then the stereotype name is wrong. These authors offer, as an example, the case in which an OnlineGame instance ought to be regarded as an "applet" instance then "Applet" is a good candidate for an Applet superclass name, but not for the stereotype. Atkinson *et al.* note that a good guideline is to remember that, just as a class name dictates what its own instances (i.e., objects) are (e.g., applets), then any good stereotype name should similarly spell out what its instances (i.e., types) are (e.g., AppletType).

These insights, rules of thumb and guidelines, appropriately applied by all metamodellers, should increase the quality of all metamodels as needed for an increasing number of aspects of modern-day software engineering.

Acknowledgements

I wish to thank Dr Cesar Gonzalez-Perez for useful comments on an earlier draft of this manuscript, especially for Figure 8 and for the example shown in Figures 25 and 26. Also thanks to Professors Thomas Kühne and Colin Atkinson for permission to use diagrams and for providing feedback regarding the cited Atkinson/Kühne papers. This is contribution number 07/25 of the Centre for Object Technology Applications and Research of the University of Technology, Sydney.

References

[1]   Monarchi, D., Booch, G., Henderson-Sellers, B., Jacobson, I., Mellor, S., Rumbaugh, J. and Wirfs-Brock, R., 1994, Methodology standards: help or hindrance?, *Procs. Ninth Annual OOPSLA Conference, ACM SIGPLAN,* 29(10), 223-228

[2]   Atkinson, C. and Kühne, T., 2003, Model-driven development: a metamodelling foundation, *IEEE Software,* 20(5), 36-41

[3]   Kühne, T., 2004, What is a model? *Procs. Dagstuhl Seminar 04101 "Language Engineering for Model-Driven Software Development"* (eds. J. Bézivin and R. Heckel) http://drops.dagstuhl.de/portals/index.php/semnr=04101

[4]   Kühne, T., 2006, Matters of (meta-) modelling, *Software and Systems Modeling,* 5(4), 369-385

[5]   Favre, J.-M., 2004, Foundations of model (driven) (reverse) engineering: models. Episode I: Stories of The Fidus Papyrus and of The Solarus, *Procs. Dagstuhl Seminar 04101 "Language Engineering for Model-Driven Software Development"* (eds. J. Bézivin and R. Heckel) http://drops.dagstuhl.de/portals/index.php/semnr=04101

[6]   OMG, 2003, *MDA Guide Version 1.0.1,* OMG document omg/03-06-01

[7]   Flatscher, R.G., 2002, Metamodeling in EIA/CDIF – meta-metamodel and metamodels, *ACM Trans. Modeling and Computer Simulation,* 12(4), 322-342

[8]   Favre, J.-M., 2004, Foundations of meta-pyramids: languages vs. metamodels. Episode II. Story of Thotus the Baboon, *Procs. Dagstuhl Seminar 04101 "Language Engineering for Model-Driven Software Development"* (eds. J. Bézivin and R. Heckel) http://drops.dagstuhl.de/portals/index.php/semnr=04101

[9]   Seidewitz, E., 2003, What models mean,. *IEEE Software* 20(5), 26–31

[10]   Atkinson, C., 1997, Metamodelling for distributed object environments, *First International Enterprise Distributed Object Computing Workshop (EDOC'97).* Brisbane, Australia, 1997

[11]   Atkinson, C. 1998, Supporting and applying the UML conceptual framework. *The Unified Modeling Language. «UML» 1998: Beyond the Notation* (eds. J. Bézivin and P.-A. Muller), LNCS 1618, Springer-Verlag, Berlin, 21-36.

[12]   Atkinson, C. and Kühne, T., 2000, Strict profiles: why and how, *Procs. Third Intl. Conf. on the Unified Modeling Language,* LNCS1939, Springer-Verlag, 309-322

[13] Atkinson, C. and Kühne, T., 2001, Processes and products in a multi-level metamodelling architecture, *Int. J. Software Eng. and Knowledge Eng.*, 11(6), 761-783

[14] Henderson-Sellers, B. and Gonzalez-Perez, C., 2005, Connecting powertypes and stereotypes, *J. Object Technol.*, 4(7), 83-96

[15] Gonzalez-Perez, C. and Henderson-Sellers, B., 2006, A powertype-based metamodelling framework, *Software and Systems Modeling*, 5(1), 72-90

[16] OMG, 2006, Unified Modeling Language: Infrastrcture. Version 2.0. formal/05-07-05, 218pp

[17] Seidewitz, E., 2001, Organizing the UML 2.0 Infrastructure, OMG document ad/01-09-15. Available from http://www.omg.org

[18] ANSI, 1989, *Information Resource Dictionary System (IRDS)*, American National Standards Institute, New York

[19] Henderson-Sellers, B. and Unhelkar, B., 2000, *OPEN Modeling with UML*, Addison-Wesley, 245pp

[20] Henderson-Sellers, B., 2006, Method engineering: theory and practice, *Information Systems Technology and its Applications. 5th International Conference ISTA 2006. May 30-31, 2006. Klagenfurt, Austria* (eds. D. Karagiannis and H.C. Mayr), Lecture Notes in Informatics (LNI) – Proceedings, Volume P-84, Gesellschaft für Informatik, Bonn, 13-23

[21] Gonzalez-Perez, C. and Henderson-Sellers, B., 2007, Modelling software development methodologies: a conceptual foundation, *J. Systems Software* doi:10.1016/j.jss.2007.02.048 (in press)

[22] Johnson, R. and Woolf, B., 1997, The type object pattern. Pattern Languages of Program Design 3, Addison-Wesley, Boston, 47-65

[23] Pirotte, A., Zimányi, E., Massart, D., Yakusheva, T., 1994, Materialization: a powerful and ubiquitous abstraction pattern. In: Bocca, J., Jarke, M., Zaniolo, C. (eds.) Procs. 20th Int. Conf. Very Large Data Bases (VLDB '94) pp. 630–641

[24] Odell, J.J., 1994, Power types, *Journal of Object-Oriented Programming*, 7(2), 8–12

[25] Henderson-Sellers, B. and Gonzalez-Perez, C., 2005, The rationale of powertype-based metamodelling to underpin software development methodologies, Conferences in Research and Practice in Information Technology, 43 (eds. S. Hartmann and M. Stumptner), Australian Computer Society, 7-16

[26] Atkinson, C. and Kühne, T., 2002, Rearchitecting the UML infrastructure, ACM Trans. Modeling and Computer Simulation 12(4), 290–321. http://doi.acm.org/10.1145/643120.643123

[27] Atkinson, C. and Kühne, T., 2005, Concepts for comparing modeling tool architectures, *Model Driven Engineering Languages and Systems*, LNCS 3713. Springer-Verlag: Berlin, 398-413

[28] OMG, 2002, *Software Process Engineering Metamodel Specification*, OMG document formal/02-11-14

[29] Atkinson, C. and Kühne, T., 2000, Meta-level independent modelling. *International Workshop on Model Engineering at the 14th European Conference on Object-Oriented Programming 2002*. Sophia Antipolis and Cannes, France

[30] Atkinson, C. and Kühne, T., 2001, The essence of multilevel metamodelling.In: Gogolla,M., Kobryn, C. (eds.) «UML»2001 – The Unified Modeling Language. Modeling Languages, Concepts and Tools LNCS 2185, pp. 19–33. Springer-Verlag, Berlin

[31] Brinkkemper, S., 1996, Method engineering: engineering of information systems development methods and tools. *Inf. Software Technol.*, 38(4), 275-280

[32] Firesmith, D.G. and Henderson-Sellers, B., 2002, The OPEN Process Framework. An Introduction, Addison-Wesley, 330pp

[33] Saeki, M., Iguchi, K., Wen-yin, K. and Shinohara, M., 1993, A meta-model for representing software specification & design methods, *Procs. IFIP WG8.1 Conf on Information Systems Development Process*, Come, 149-166

[34] Kühne, T. and Schreiber, D., 2007, Can programming be liberated from the two level style? Multi-level programming with DeepJava, *Procs. OOPSLA*, ACM Press (in press)

[35] Standards Australia, 2004, *Standard Metamodel for Software Development Methodologies.*

[36] International Organization for Standardization / International Electrotechnical Commission (2007). ISO/IEC 24744. *Software Engineering - Metamodel for Development Methodologies.*

[37] Demeyer, S., Tichelaar, S. and Steyaert, P., 1999, FAMIX 2.0, http://www.iam.unibe.ch/~famoos/FAMIX/Famix20/Html/ famix20.html (accessed 13 June 2007)

[38] Dominguez, E. and Zapata, M.A., 2000, Mappings and interoperability: a meta-modelling approach, *ADVIS 2000* (ed. T. Takhno), LNCS 1909, Springer, Berlin, 352-362

[39] Vrandečić, D., Völker, P.H., Duc, T.T. and Cimiano, P., 2006, A metamodel for annotations of ontology elements in OWL DL, in *Meta-Modelling and Ontologies. Proceedings of the 2nd Workshop on Meta-Modelling, WoMM 2006*, LNI Volume P-96, 109-123

[40] Bertoa, M.F., Vallecillo, A. and Garcia, F., 2006, An ontology for software measurement, Chapter 6 in *Ontologies for Software Engineering and Software Technology* (eds. C. Calero, F. Ruiz and M. Piattini), Springer, Heidelberg, 175-196

[41] Zaiez, S., Huget, M.-P. and Oquendo, F., 2007, Approach for multiagent metamodelling, *Multiagent and Grid Systems* (in press)

[42] Lin, Y. and Sølvberg, A., 2007, Goal annotation of process models for semantic enrichment of process knowledge, *CAiSE 2007* (eds. J. Krogstie, A.L. Opdahl and G. Sindre), LNCS 4495, 355-369

[43] Dubé, D. and Vangheluwe, H., 2006, Multi-paradigm modelling and synthesis of user interface, *Procs. Workshop W5: Model Driven Development of Advanced User Interfaces (MDDAUI 2006)* (eds. A. Pleuss, J. Van den Bergh, H. Hussmann, S. Sauer and A. Boedcher), MODELS conference, Genova, 2 October 2006, 4pp. http://sunsite.informatik.rwth-aachen.de/Publications/CEUR-WS//Vol-214/ (accessed 7 August 2007)

[44] Atkinson, C., Kühne, T. and Henderson-Sellers, B., 2003, Systematic stereotype usage, *Software and System Modelling,* 2(3), 153-163

[45] Hong, S., van den Goor, G. and Brinkkemper, S., 1993, A formal approach to the comparison of object-oriented analysis and design methodologies, *Procs. 26th HICSS,* 689-698

[46] van de Weerd, I., Brinkkemper, S., Souer, J. and Versendaal, J., 2006, Situational implementation method for web-based content management system-applications: method engineering and validation in practice, *Software Process: Improvement and Practice,* 11(5), 521-538

[47] OMG, 2005, Unified Modeling Language: Superstructure, version 2.0, formal/05-07-04, 709pp

[48] Saeki, M., 2003, Embedding metrics into information systems development methods: an application of method engineering technique, *CAiSE2003* (eds. J. Eder and M. Missikoff), LNCS 2681, Springer-Verlag, Berlin, 374-389

[49] Stevens, P. with Pooley, R., 2000, *Using UML Software Engineering with Objects and Components,* updated edition Addison-Wesley, Harlow, England, 256pp

[50] Brinkkemper, S., Saeki, M. and Harmsen, F., 2001, A method engineering language for the description of systems development methods (extended abstract), *Procs CAiSE 2001),* LNCS 2068, Springer-Verlag, Berlin, 473-476

[51] van de Weerd, I., Brinkkemper, S. and Versendaal, J., 2007, Concepts for incremental method evolution: empirical exploration and validation in requirements management, *CAiSE 2007* (eds. J. Krogstie, A.L. Opdahl and G. Sindre), LNCS 4495, 469-484

[52] Henderson-Sellers, B. and Gonzalez-Perez, C., 2006, Uses and abuses of the stereotype mechanism in UML1.4 and 2.0, *Model Driven Engineering Languages and Systems, 9th International Conference, MoDELS 2006, Genoa, Italy, October 2006* (eds. O. Nierstrasz, J. Whittle, D. Harel and G. Reggio), LNCS 4199, Springer-Verlag, Berlin, 16-26.

[53] Englebert, V. and Heymans, P., 2007, Towards more extensible metaCASE tools, *CAiSE 2007* (eds. J. Krogstie, A.L. Opdahl and G. Sindre), LNCS 4495, 454-468

[54] OMG, 2000, *OMG Unified Modeling Language Specification, Version 1.3.* June 1999. OMG Document formal/00-03-01,

[55] Fuentes-Fernandez, R., Gomez-Sanz, J.J. and Pavon, J., 2007, Integration in agent-oriented development, *Int. J. Agent-Oriented Software Eng.,* 1(1), 2-27

[56] Lin, Y. and Ding, H., 2005, Ontology-based semantic annotation for semantic interoperability of process models, *Procs. 2005 Int. Conf. on Computational Intelligence for Modelling, Control and Automation, and Int. Conf. on Intelligent Agents, Web Technologies and Internet Commerce (CIMCA-IAWTIC'05)*

[57] ISO/IEC, 1998, ISO/IEC 15474. *CDIF Framework.*

[58] Seidewitz, E., 2003, What do models mean? OMG document ad/03-03-31. Available from http://www.omg.org

[59] Cossentino, M., Gaglio, S., Garro, A. and Seidita, V., 2007, Method fragments for agent design methodologies: from standardization to research, *Int. J. Agent-Oriented Software Eng.,* 1(1), 91-121

[60] Ralyté, J. and Rolland, C., 2001, An approach for method engineering, *Procs. 20th Int. Conf on Conceptual Modelling (ER2001),* LNCS 2224, Springer-Verlag, Berlin, 471-484

[61] Cossentino, M., 2006, personal communication

[62] Graham, I.M., Bischof, J. and Henderson-Sellers, B., 1997, Associations considered a bad thing, *J. Obj.-Oriented Programming,* **9(9),** 41-48

[63] Ralyté, J., 2006, personal communication

[64] Rolland, C., Prakash, N. and Benjamen, A., 1999, A multi-model view of process modelling, *Requirements Eng. J.,* 4(4), 169-187

[65] Ralyté, J., 2004, Towards situational methods for information systems development: engineering reusable method chunks, *Procs. 13th Int. Conf. on Information Systems Development. Advances in Theory, Practice and Education* (eds. O. Vasilecas, A. Caplinskas, W. Wojtkowski, W.G. Wojtkowski, J. Zupancic and S. Wrycza), Vilnius Gediminas Technical University, Vilnius, Lithuania, 271-282

[66] Henderson-Sellers, B., Gonzalez-Perez, C. and Ralyté, J., 2008, Evaluating the efficacy of method chunks versus method fragments for situational method engineering, submitted to APCCM 2008, Wollongong.

[67] Mirbel, I. and Ralyté, J., 2006, Situational method engineering: combining assembly-based and roadmap-driven approaches, *Requirements Engineering*, 11, 58-78

[68] Mirbel, I., 2006, Method chunk federation, *CAiSE'06. 18th Conference on Advanced Information Systems Engineering – Trusted Information Systems. Luxembourg 5-9 June, 2006. Proceedings of the Workshops and Doctoral Consortium* (eds. T. Latour and M. Petit), Namur University Press, Belgium, 407-418

[69] Prat, N., 1997, Goal formalisation and classification for requirements engineering, *Procs. 3rd Int. Workshop on Requirements Engineering: Foundations of Software Quality REFSQ'97*, Barcelona, 145-156

[70] Rolland, C. and Prakash, N., 1996. A proposal for context-specific method engineering. in Method Engineering. Principles of Method Construction and Too Support. Procs. IFIP TC8, WG8.1/8.2 Working Conference on Method Engineering, 26-28 August 1996, Atlanta, USA (eds. S. Brinkkemper, K. Lyytinen and R.J. Welke), Chapman & Hall, London, 191-208.

[71] Henderson-Sellers, B., Gonzalez-Perez, C. and Ralyté, J., 2007, Situational method engineering: chunks or fragments? *Procs. CAiSE Forum* (eds. J. Eder, S.L. Tomassen, A.L. Opdahl and G. Sindre), 89-92

[72] Whitmire, S., 1997, Object-Oriented Software Design Measurement, Wiley, 494pp.

New Trends in Software Methodologies, Tools and Techniques
H. Fujita and D. Pisanelli (Eds.)
IOS Press, 2007

Software Engineering Practices:
An Auditor's Perspective

Krzysztof SACHA[1]
Warsaw University of Technology, Poland

Abstract. This report details part of the results of five software audits that were done to evaluate various aspects of the quality in five very big software projects. One result of our work was a method for software quality evaluation, which is described in detail elsewhere. Another result was a review of the software engineering practices and methods that were used throughout those projects by the development companies. The paper presents a survey of these practices and tries to answer the question which software development paradigms, processes and methods are used in the software industry and which of them can contribute to the final success of the project more than the others.

Keywords. Software quality, quality evaluation, software engineering, software development

Introduction

Software systems are used in many application areas in which a malfunction of the system can be a source of serious losses or disturbances to the functioning of the society. Examples of such application areas are not only command and control systems, but also public administration, social insurance or post delivery services. The quality of services offered in these areas depends heavily on the quality and dependability of software systems that support the functioning of the appropriate public or private organizations (service providers).

Software development processes consist of a selection of methods and tools that vary from project to project. It is interesting to know which of the methods described in the literature are used in everyday practice and how do they work. The question is vital, as research shows that the success ratio of the software projects is low, when comparing to other branches of engineering. According to The Chaos study [1, 2] of the Standish Group, in 1994 only 16% of projects were completed on-time and on budget, 53% were challenged, i.e. completed but over-budget and over time estimates and 31% of projects were cancelled. Ten years later The Chaos study reported 29% of successful projects, 53% challenged, and 18% cancelled. Despite a significant improvement (Table 1), the success ratio of the software projects is still far from satisfaction. Similar data can also be found in American Programmer [3].

---

[1] Krzysztof Sacha: Warsaw University of Technology, Nowowiejska 15/19, 00-665 Warszawa, Poland; E-mail: k.sacha@ia.pw.edu.pl

Table 1. Project resolution (source: The Chaos Study, The Standish Group)

Year of research[*]	Successful	Challenged	Cancelled
1994	16%	53%	31%
2000	28%	49%	23%
2002	34%	51%	15%
2004	29%	53%	18%

[*] The data were published one year later

The methodology of The Chaos studies was based on questionnaires and interviews responded to by IT executive managers of over 50,000 IT projects (during 12 years of research), with the most important part aimed at discovering the key factors of a project success or failure. The list of the most important factors that cause projects to succeed changed over the years, and in 2004 was the following [2]: User involvement, executive management support, clear business objectives, minimized scope, agile process, experienced project manager, formal methodology, and standard tools and infrastructure. Those results reflected a managerial point of view. More technically-oriented aspects of the software processes and the development methods were outside the scope of these surveys.

This paper relies on a different methodology. The results presented in this report are based on the observations that I did during a series of audits and quality evaluations of five big software development projects ($300 million the biggest) that were conducted for public administration in Poland in the last five years. During those evaluations, the evaluating team was positioned just between the customer and the development company, and dealt with the deliverables of the projects. Therefore, the research came closer to the technical level and was aimed at identification and evaluation of processes and methods that were used by software developers in their work.

The goal of this paper is to summarize our observations pertaining to the software processes and the development methods that are used by big development companies. Because the contract awards for building the systems considered in the paper were made through a competitive bid process with a participation of huge global companies, we believe that the results of our observations are representative to the contemporary IT market. According to our contracts we are not allowed to describe the details of particular systems and the development of these systems. Therefore the paper does not present a case study, but is a survey of practices that are used.

The main body of the paper is divided into five parts, the first of which provides the reader with an overview of the characteristics and the context of projects and systems that were subject to our evaluation. The results of projects considered in this paper are described, and related to major success/failure factors of The Chaos study in Section 2. Development processes and methods used throughout these projects are described in Section 3, and the evaluation of several process and product metrics is given in Section 4. Section 5 refers to a specific aspect of the development that is best visible to the customer of an IT contract, i.e. acceptance testing. Final remarks and statistics are gathered in Conclusions.

1. Evaluated Projects

The projects under evaluation were typical on the IT market: The developed systems were going to deliver common services, the development contracts were awarded through a competitive bid process and the development companies applied well known, yet different, development methods and tools.

All the development companies were big and had strong market position. One was a branch of a huge global company headquartered in US, while the other four were big national companies ($500 million annual revenue the biggest) with strong international cooperation. Therefore the observations described in this paper can be considered representative of the global software development market.

The systems covered in this paper are the following:

- Integrated Information System for Social Insurance Institution that supports individual accounts of all employees and all employers in the country.
- Integrated Administration and Control System (IACS) that supports direct payments within the European Union common agriculture policy.
- Common Agriculture Policy System (CAPS) that supports intervention purchase, storage and sale within the European Union common agriculture policy.
- Computerized Postal System that controls the process of transferring and tracking of registered shipments across the country.
- District Level Elections Support System.

All of those systems cover the area of the entire country and influence the living conditions of millions of people. Therefore, they fall into the category of big or very big systems. A set of attributes to characterize the size of the information systems considered in this paper is given in Table 2.

Table 2. Size attributes of the information systems considered in the paper

Number of	Social Insurance	IACS	CAPS	Postal System	Elections
Accounts	17 000 000	2 300 000	800 000		
Documents per year	300 000 000	12 000 000	1 000 000	540 000 000[*]	
Users	23 000	8 500	500	2 500	6 000
Sites	300	330	17	17	5 500

[*] 1 500 000 registered shipments per day

The attributes given above are not quite comparable. Nevertheless, we believe that they characterize the size of an information system much better than traditional measures of lines-of-code or function points. In the first three cases the number of documents per year means the number of real documents that are sent by the customers and that must be scanned and processed by the system. In case of the postal system this number refers to the bulk of registered shipments that must be handled. The number of sites equals to the number of local branches of the organization, each of which has usually multiple users. However, in case of Election System those sites contained in most cases a single user only.

In the final result, two of five systems considered in this paper were built within the budget and schedule, in two cases the schedules were not met but the core elements of the systems were deployed with an acceptable delay. One project failed completely and did not provide the required services at the deadline. These statistics (40% of success, 40% of challenged and 20% of failed projects) look a bit better than the data of the Chaos study shown in the last two rows of Table 1.

The processes of building systems listed in Table 2 were subject to a number of evaluations made on behalf of the customers or of the state institutions of control. One of the evaluators was the Software Engineering Group at Warsaw University of Technology. The evaluation took place in the years of 2002-2004 and was based on an in depth analysis of the deliverables of the particular development activities. The primary goal of our evaluation was the assessment of the expected quality of software under development in one case, and the evaluation of the quality of phases of the software process in three cases; in one case we tried to find the reasons of a catastrophe.

The typical audit methodology, focused on the quality evaluation of the development process [4, 5], could offer only a limited set of means for the quality evaluation of the software product. Software quality evaluation methods described in the literature [6-10] represented the software development organization point of view. Neither of those methods fitted well into the environment of a software quality evaluation, which was done on behalf of external authorities by people from the outside of the development company. One difference was such that we had only limited access to the project data, and the quality evaluation had to be based on an evaluation of the deliverables of the software process that had been enumerated in the contract. Another difference was such that we had no historical data of the manufacturer related to a set of similar projects. Therefore we had to develop a new method, which was based on a modification to the GQM measurement model [6]. A detailed description of the methodology that was developed by us for the purpose of evaluation can be found in [11, 12].

2. Project Success/Failure Factors

It is not easy to isolate and evaluate the influence of the key success factors, identified in The Chaos [1] and cited in the Introduction, on the final result of a project. An attempt of such an evaluation is given below.

(1) User involvement and (2) executive management support were high in all but one project considered in this paper. The customer organizations that contracted the systems created special departments to help the development companies and to supervise the project. In one case user feedback was missing; this project failed.

(3) Business objectives were clear in four of five cases: Because of a change in legal regulations, the customer organizations could not function without a new support system any more. These four systems were built and put into operation. In one case the system was not indispensable for the customer organization; this project failed.

(4) Minimized scope means a decomposition of one huge project into a series of smaller projects, each of which can be completed within a shorter period of time and smaller budget. Such a type of project planning was applied in two cases, however, in a different way. In one case a huge centralized system was functionally decomposed into

a set of independent subsystems and modules coupled through a common database. The development of the system was then divided into a series of projects, each of which was restricted in scope to a subset of modules. This project has been delayed, but went ahead despite significant evolution of the requirements.

In the second case a project of an inherently distributed system was decomposed into two completely separate projects. One of them covered full functionality of a single business site, while the second project, started after full completion of the first one, covered the cooperation between the business sites. Both of these subprojects were finished within time and budget.

(5) Agile process. There is confusion in understanding agility in The Chaos study. None of the projects considered in this paper used an agile method, e.g. Scrum or XP [13]. Public systems are contracted through a competitive bid process, which requires a complete requirements specification available at the very beginning. Also the deadline, the price and the number of iterations are always written into the contract. None of these data is available at the beginning of an agile project. Therefore, I can hardly imagine the use of an agile method to contracting and building a public system.

However, if one identifies agility with iterativeness of the development process, then two of five projects were conducted this way. Both of these projects were finished within time and budget.

(6) Experienced project manager. In one case a system was built by a consortium of a few independent companies, with no hierarchical dependencies defined between them. The stakeholders discussed and agreed upon the schedule and the scope of tasks performed by the development teams. This way a sort of collaboration management was implemented, with no single project manager on top of the project structure. This project failed. In the other cases project management responsibilities were clearly defined and the results of those projects were much better.

(7) Strict methodology, though not very formal, was used in four of the projects. All of them were ultimately completed. In one case no strict methodology was used. This project failed.

(8) Standard software tools and infrastructure can resolve many technological problems and allow the development team to concentrate on business aspects of the application. In all but one project described in this paper, standard middleware was used as the main integrating keystone of the application. In one case a proprietary middleware package was used. This project failed, and an improper functioning, or improper usage, of this tool contributed to the defeat of the project.

There is one key factor missing in the list of 2004, which was present at the earlier editions of the Chaos study. This is the clearness and stability of the requirements specification. In two projects considered in this paper the requirements were stable; these projects were finished successfully. In two other cases the requirements varied. Both of those projects were delayed and over budget.

A detailed description of the final results of five projects considered in this paper (Table 2) can be summarized as follows.

Integrated Information System for Social Insurance Institution has not been completed within the schedule and budget. In fact, it is still being built, with the time overrun over 100%. However, the delay cannot be attributed to the methods that were applied during the project, but rather to the changes in the external environment of the project. It was clear from the very beginning that a powerful, quite new information system was indispensable to support the implementation of a very general reform of the rules of social insurance system in the country. The starting day of the reform was fixed by the government. A feasibility study of the system had been done, and the date at which the development had to start (in order to have the system ready at the date of reform) was known. However, the legislation process was late and when the development-start-date arrived, the necessary legal acts had still not been passed by the parliament. At that point in time the decision either to start the development or not, created the following risks:

- If they waited for the legislation, the time remaining for development would shorten dramatically and the deadline could not be met.
- If they started the development process immediately, the risk appeared of implementing requirements that differed from those ultimately present in the legislation act.

There was no good answer to resolve this dilemma. In our case the project was started on the basis of a draft version of the appropriate acts. Unfortunately, a parliamentary election arrived and the new government changed the acts and the requirements of the information system significantly. An annex to the contract was signed nearly one year after the development had been started and three years before the expected release of the system.

The final result of the project was not catastrophic, however. The core elements of the system were deployed and started working five months after the deadline. Due to the one year clearance of the social insurance payments, the delay appeared not essential to the success of the entire insurance reform. The legislation pertaining to social insurance is still evolving and the remaining modules of the system are still being built. The development used an Oracle-based structured method [14] and tools.

The story of IACS system was a bit similar. The system had to be built because of the accession of Poland to the European Union (EU). The date of the accession was agreed upon, but very detailed negotiations related to the Polish benefits of the common agriculture policy of EU lasted nearly to that date. As result, the development of IACS started on the basis of a draft version of the agreement. When the final agreement appeared different, an annex that changed the requirements was signed two and a half year after signing the original contract. The core elements of the modified system were released about half a year later, just in time to enable farmers to benefit from the common agriculture policy. However, a few auxiliary elements of the system were built much later. The system was built using RUP-based object-oriented methods [15].

Two systems: CAPS and Post Delivery Support System were developed in time and within the budget. Both of the two had well established requirements specifications that did not change during the development process. The development processes relied on Oracle-based methods and tools, however, use case specification was also created in one of these two projects.

The District Level Elections Support System crashed at the date of election. Investigation showed the lack of proper project management, the lack of sound methodology, and significant technological problems.

The lesson, which I learned from the above stories, is such that the key factors of success are user feedback, competent project management and a stable requirements specification. If the requirements evolve, then restricting the scope of the project and adding a dose of agility to the development process can create a good base to cope with the problem. The development methods are less important, provided that a certain level of technology competence is preserved. Such a conclusion matches quite well the conclusions of the Chaos studies [1] cited in the Introduction.

3. Software Processes and Development Methods

There are two major approaches to software development and two groups of methods that are currently used by the development companies on the IT market: Structured approach and object-oriented approach. The methods of both groups can be used within the framework of various software processes. Two of these processes that dominate nowadays in the industrial practice are waterfall model [14], and incremental and iterative RUP software process [15].

Software systems that are considered in this paper were created using various combinations of a software process and a development method. We identified both of these two constituents of the development process using the following metrics [12]:

- A list of methods declared in the contract and in the analytical specification.
- A mapping from the steps of the software process into the set of methods.
- A list of artifacts and a mapping from the set of artifacts to the set of methods.
- Qualitative evaluation of the deliverables of the particular steps of the process.

The results of the evaluation are shown in Table 3. Two projects were conducted using structured methods and tools, one project relied on an object-oriented methodology and in one case a mixture of methods was used. This data is in quite a good correlation with data of The Chaos study, which reported that 70% of projects developed from scratch in 2000 used structured methods and languages, while the other 30% was based on object-oriented methods and models.

Table 3. Processes and methods used in the development of software

	Structured methods	Object-oriented methods	*ad hoc*
Waterfall process	2.5[*]	0.5[*]	
RUP process		1	
ad hoc			1

[*] One project started with an object-oriented use case model, but was continued using structured methods.

The use of the waterfall model did not necessarily mean that the entire system was developed, implemented and deployed within a single sequence of consecutive steps. On the contrary, the system under development was usually decomposed into a set of functionally independent subsystems that were built independently of others. The system could then be integrated by the manufacturer and deployed at the customer's site in one step (as an entity). However, it could also be constructed incrementally, with particular subsystems created and deployed within separate runs of the waterfall process.

The initial requirements statement, which began the development of systems considered in this paper, consisted mainly of legal acts passed by the national parliament or by the European Union, accompanied by several business demands and constraints. In all cases the requirements analysis began by doing the context analysis, which led to a definition of the context schema that documented the external systems, organizations and users, and the required inflows and outflows of the developed system. The expected size and frequency of those inflows and outflows were estimated. The values of those estimates corresponded to the number of 'documents per year' in Table 2.

The kind of methods that were used to perform the analytical activities, or steps, varied from project to project. We identified and evaluated those methods using a set of metrics, which can be exemplified by the following samples [12]:

- A list of methods declared for the project.
- A mapping from the steps of the software process into the set of methods.
- A mapping from the set of user documents and reports identified in the acts to the set of inflows and outflows.
- An evaluation of the analytical products.

The analysis of the required behaviour of systems under development was done in two of five cases using object-oriented use case method, while in another two cases a hierarchy of functions was built. Data structures were modelled at this stage of development using entity-relationship diagram notation (ERD) or class diagrams created from the conceptual perspective. In one case the requirements analysis was performed intuitively, without being specified in any formal document.

Detailed analysis and design relied in three cases on a principle of structured functional decomposition. The initial requirements statement was subject to a critical requirements analysis, which led to a multi-level hierarchy of functions. The flows of data between the functions at each level of the hierarchy were defined and documented by means of data flow diagrams. The structure of data that was stored and passed within the system was modelled using entity-relationship diagrams. The processing assigned to each particular function was documented by means of flowcharts and textual specifications, accompanied by paper-based prototypes of the user interface (screenshots). Program structure and data base structure were derived from the above models using Oracle-based methods and tools [14].

Object-oriented analysis and design was based on the RUP methodology. First, the use case method was applied within a two-step process. In the first step business actors and procedures were identified, and the scenarios together with the pre- and post-conditions of those procedures were defined and documented. In the second step the definitions of actors were refined, and the user functions that were to be implemented by the system were derived and specified. The specification of a user function included a set of alternative scenarios, a definition of exceptions and exceptional actions, and the conditions to start and stop each particular function. The structure of data that was identified within the application domain was modelled using class diagram notation, and the behaviour of the most important classes was described by means of state transition diagrams.

Then, the logical structure of the application was designed using patterns [16] and documenting the results by means of class and interaction diagrams. Finally, physical components were defined and implemented. According to our observations the dominating implementation languages were SQL, Java and C++.

4. Evaluation of Methods

It was a superficial similarity between the final results of the analysis done by means of structured and object-oriented methods. In both cases a set of functions was defined, accompanied by a set of ERD or class diagrams. There was, however, one big difference between the two.

Hierarchy of functions and data flow diagrams resulted from a functional decomposition of the required processing. The top level functions within the hierarchy were nearly independent, as they referred to different business processes at the customer organization. The second-level functions had also very limited interplay, as they referred to different aspects and procedures within a given business process. The hierarchy of functions was then converted into the hierarchy of subsystems and modules, in which the top-level functions became subsystems that were developed independently, and the second level functions became modules of those subsystems. An advantage of such a development process was a good traceability of the design to the analysis. A disadvantage was such that the functions did not correspond directly to the business procedures at the customer organization and were not very useful in defining the acceptance testing scenarios.

The set of user functions, identified by means of the use case method, did not create any hierarchical structure. Such a flat and huge set of functions (about five hundreds in IACS) was nearly useless for the design purposes. Instead, a class model was developed with several thousands of classes. The classes were packed into packages that had very little to do with the initial user functions. As result, traceability from the design to the analysis was poor, and we found the verification of the design with respect to the analysis very difficult.

The advantages of using the use case method were: Completeness of the functional requirements and direct support of the acceptance testing process. The analytical artefacts that were created consisted of:

- Use case specifications and preliminary data model.
- A working prototype of the user interface.
- Preliminary test plan, closely related to the use case scenarios.

In this package the use case scenarios defined precisely the desired behaviour of the software, the prototype enabled the user to play with the (non-existing yet) software, and the test scenarios defined the verification method of the requirements. Usually, test scenarios corresponded directly to the respective use case scenarios. Preliminary data model (class diagrams) created a bridge towards future design activities.

Our evaluation of the quality of **functional** requirements specification in structured as well as object-oriented version was, in general, positive. Unfortunately, this positive evaluation did not spread out on the area of **non-functional** requirements. Performance requirements were, in general, not stated clearly during the analysis. Sometimes, an estimation of the number and the volume of input documents were given. Quantitative metrics, like response time or throughput measured in transactions per time unit [17], appeared in the specification of one system only. Instead, arbitrary (usually high) requirements for the performance of hardware were sometimes formulated.

Security requirements were described in an extensive, but qualitative and untestable way. A typical requirement was such that the system should use "*the most effective and up to date tools in order to guarantee perfect protection of data and other resources*". The position and length of the security requirements showed, however, that the customers were aware of the threat and were willing to spend money on the protection mechanisms.

The only kind of non-functional requirements that was stated in a clear and testable way was availability. The following metrics were used to define the required reliability and availability of the developed software systems:

- The percentage of time during a year that the system services must be available.
- The maximum time for recovery after a crash.
- The minimum period of time, within which a local server must provide the required functionality after a break to the communication links to a central server.
- The ability of process migration in case of hardware break down.
- The ability of re-running all the transactions that were lost as result of hardware break down.

The first three metrics were written into a service contract between the customer and the manufacturer of software. Test cases to verify the last two metrics were built into the test plans of the acceptance testing phase.

Comparing the quality of the four systems and their development processes, we did not observe definite superiority of one approach over the other. However, any kind of methodology worked better than *ad hoc* development that did not adhere to any method or standard and eventually led the project to a total collapse.

A surprising observation was instability of the development progress exposed by the RUP process. The development was driven by a use case model, which was created in the elaboration phase, and then used to plan the incremental development of the software in the construction phase. The construction phase started with the core requirements (a set of core use cases), and proceeded in such a way that the consecutive increments added functionality to the previously developed part of the software. It was said [15, 18] that this should lead to a stable architecture and modules.

In order to measure the stability of the development progress we counted the files of the source code that had been issued in the consecutive iterations, and compared the size of files that had the same name. If names and sizes of two files were the same, we assumed that the code in those files had not been changed. If the names were the same, but the sizes were different, we assumed that the code was retained with modification. Then, we calculated the following metrics:

- The percentage of files that were retained without modification in the next consecutive iteration.
- The percentage of files that were retained without modification in the final product.
- The percentage of files that were retained, but modified, in the final product.

The values of metrics, calculated for two components (subsystems) of the IACS system are shown in Figures 1 through 3. One of these components was responsible for collecting submissions and handling direct payments within the European Union common agriculture policy. The other component was responsible for the identification and registration of bovine animals. (There were also other components in IACS, such as: geographical information subsystem, accounting component, farm and animals data bases.) The characteristics of code of the two components are given in Table 4.

Table 4. Characteristics of the sample components of IACS

Characteristic	Payments	Animals
Number of classes	1 879	2 370
Number of lines of code	277 948	288 873
Number of lines of comment	82 343	60 410
A relation of comments to code	29.63%	20.91%
Percentage of classes with the relation of comments to code less than 10%	4.00%	33.50%
Percentage of classes with no comments	0.11%	12.57%
Percentage of classes with cyclomatic complexity [19] of a method ≥ 10	6.44%	6.82%
Percentage of classes with cyclomatic complexity [19] of a method ≥ 20	1.54%	1.54%

The stability metrics showed that the integration of code after a subsequent iteration required usually deep modification to that part of software that had been constructed and released earlier. The scope of changes to the code, which we measured between two consecutive increments, exceeded in average 40% of the total size of the existing code (Figure 1). Percentage of code that was retained without modification in the final product increased from iteration to iteration, but was well below 50% in the first half of the development process.

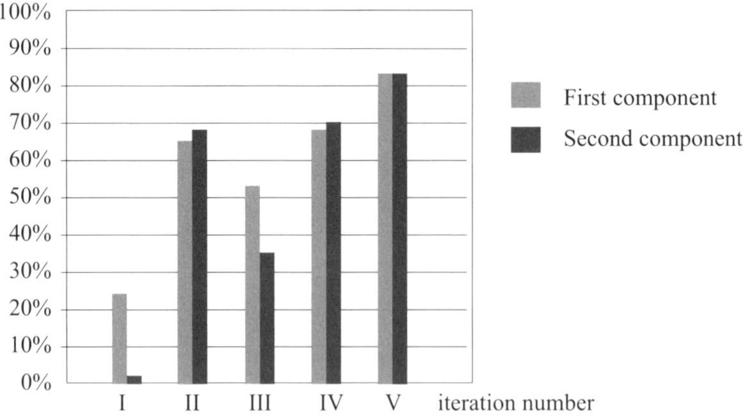

Figure 1. Percentage of code retained without modification in the next iteration

One explanation of this phenomenon is such that the method was not clearly understood by the developers and was misused. The other one is such that the partitioning of the developed software system driven by the use cases violated the rules of modularization: A particular increment of software did not constitute an internally consistent module with relatively weak interfaces to its environment. Instead, just the opposite was true, and the subsequent increments that were added within the loop of the construction phase, were strongly interrelated to the previously constructed part of software. The integration of such strongly related components imposed huge refactoring of the existing code.

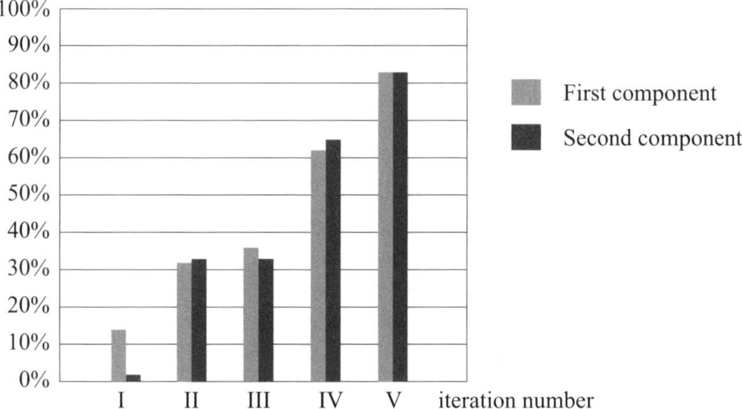

Figure 2. Percentage of code (issued in an iteration) retained in the final product

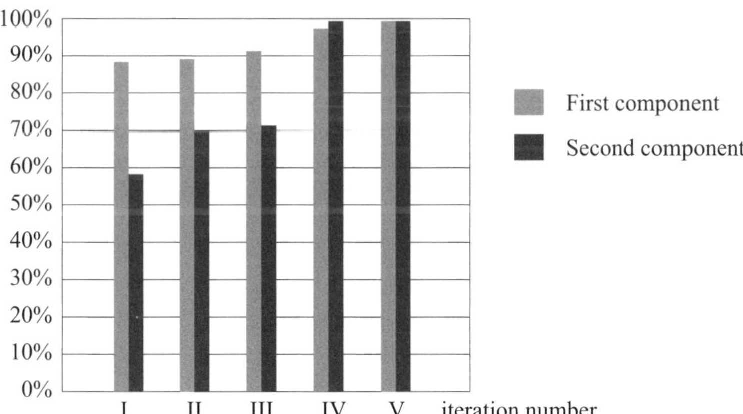

Figure 3. Percentage of files retained with modification in the final product

A major problem, which we observed in relation to such a development practice, pertained to the acceptance testing that was done after each iteration. The modifications to the code that had been released earlier made the development process unstable in that some errors that had appeared and had been fixed in an earlier version of the software, re-appeared again in a subsequent release of the same software component. Such a phenomenon was particularly disappointing for the customer, who wanted to use the existing part of the system that had been released in the latest iteration.

A minor problem was the scope of verification that was needed after each iteration of the software construction process. Because the modifications affected all kinds of development artefacts: Analytical, design and code, the same artefact, e.g. a sequence diagram, had several versions that had to be evaluated many times in a sequence.

5. Acceptance Testing

All the weak and strong points of the requirements specification, described in Section 4, were reflected in the artifacts prepared for acceptance testing. The well defined functional requirements were converted into well defined test scenarios, composed of test cases defined in terms of input data, output data and evaluation criteria. The set of test scenarios created a test plan with defined schedule and allocated resources (a testbed and a test team). Similarly, the lack of well defined non-functional requirements resulted in poor quality of non-functional testing.

A unit of acceptance testing was an "application", i.e. a functional module of a system. The scope of the application was defined by a set of functions (system use cases) that was subject to testing. We assessed the test plan of an application and the actual testing process using the metrics similar to the following:

- The coverage of functions by test cases.
- The coverage of functions by the sets of test data.
- The coverage of non-functional requirements by test scenarios.
- Qualitative evaluation of the actual test procedure.

The range of values of the first two metrics that we measured for a set of applications of a system is given in Table 5. The values below 1 were definitely too low and warned about those cases, in which only the main runs of functions were tested. The values above 1 could be confronted with the number of runs of the tested functions.

Planning of acceptance testing was the step of the development process in which the application of use case method appeared particularly beneficial. Use case scenarios could nearly directly be converted into test scenarios, and the coverage of the main and alternative use case scenarios by test scenarios was one of the best understood metrics that could characterize the quality of the testing process.

Table 5. Measured values of test coverage metrics

Metric	Range	Average value
Number of: Test cases / Functions	0.70 ... 7.00	2.34
Number of: Data sets / Functions	0.67 ... 15.00	3.80

The most important shortcomings that we found in test plans of the acceptance testing were the following:

- Low coverage of functional requirements by test scenarios – the set of tests offered by the development company covered sometimes the main scenarios of the use cases only, while neglected at least part of the alternative scenarios and exceptions (Table 5).
- Incomplete definition of the actual system state at the start of the testing process – this included the lack of component version numbers, lack of a specification of the initial contents of the data base and of a specification of deviations from the target hardware architecture.
- Imprecise definition of the expected test results – in some cases the expected results were defined by a statement *"Correct results of the computation."*

The first of the above listed shortcomings (low coverage of tests) decreased the credibility of the acceptance testing process. The second one affected reproducibility of the test results and made the analysis of the current project status difficult when a total disaster happened. The last drawback disorganized the testing process and provoked discussions about whether or not the results that had been obtained were correct, which was not always obvious.

Despite the shortcomings described above, the evaluation of the quality of the functional part of the test plans was positive. The evaluation of non-functional part looked, however, much worse. The lack or precise definition of performance and other non-functional requirements led to the lack of systematic tests within the test plan. The evaluation criteria offered by the development company could not be traced back to the requirements, but rather reflected the "achievements" of the actual design and implementation. If the data was questioned by the customer, a negotiation process was started at the level of the Steering Committee of the project. In one case the performance tests had to be developed by our team.

The way in which the acceptance tests were executed showed that the customers made a significant effort in order to make this process credible. In all but one case the testing process was planned in the project schedule, the test procedure was defined and the necessary resources were allocated.

The mechanics of testing was not uniform. In one case the testing process was centralized and all tests were executed in sequence on a single workstation with the results being displayed on a screen by a computer projector, and evaluated by the commission. In other cases the tests were performed by testers sitting on a set of individual workstations. All the events that occurred during the testing process were formally recorded in a log and the errors revealed were classified according to their importance, and submitted for fixing according to a predefined procedure.

6. Conclusions

The observations related to software development that are presented in this paper are based on the analysis of project documentation and evaluation of metrics exemplified in the previous sections of the paper. Not all of those metrics are quantitative, i.e.

evaluate to a numerical value [10]. However, many of them are formal, i.e. take the form of a mapping between the sets of artefacts or documents.

The results of our work confirmed the results of the survey [1]. Even though the number of projects in our research was small, we could observe a good correlation between the key success factors identified in [1] and the results of the projects evaluated within the scope of our research.

Another result of our study was an observation of a gap between the scope of university courses in software engineering and the reality of the software industry. The majority of software engineering courses are concentrated on object-oriented methods, while structured methods are usually considered obsolete. The reality is different, and structured methods still occupy at least half of the software development market.

Some numerical data that were collected during our study in order to characterize the current practices in software engineering are shown in Table 6.

Table 6. The observed characteristics of the software projects

Characteristic	Values	
Software process	waterfall	– 3
	iterative	– 1
Development methodology	structured	– 2.5[*]
	object-oriented	– 1.5[*]
Use of CASE tools	upper case	– 4
	lower case	– 5
Data base architecture	centralized	– 5
Quality of functional testing	adequate	– 3
	low coverage	– 1
	lack of tests	– 1
Quality of non-functional testing	adequate	– 1
	low coverage	– 3
	lack of tests	– 1

[*] One project started with an object-oriented use case model, but was continued using structured methods.

References

[1]   The Chaos Report, Standish Group International, Inc, West Yarmouth, MA (1995, 2001, 2003) www.standishgroup.com.

[2]   Hartmann, D.: Interview: Jim Johnson of the Standish Group, http://www.infoq.com/articles/Interview-Johnson-Standish-CHAOS

[3]   American Programmer, 5 (1996).

[4]   CISA Review Manual. Information Systems Audit and Control Association, (2002).

[5]   ISO 9001: Quality management systems – Requirements. ISO (2001).

[6]   Basili, V.R., Caldiera, G., Rombach, H.D.: The Goal Question Metric Approach. In: Encyclopedia of Software Engineering, Wiley-Interscience, New York (1994).

[7]   Erikkson, I., McFadden, F.: Quality Function Deployment: A Tool to Improve Software Quality. In: Information & Software Technology, 9 (1993), 491-498.

[8]   Haag, S., Raja, M.K., Schkade, L.L.: Quality Function Deployment Usage in Software Development. In: Communications of the ACM, 1 (1996), 41-49.

[9]   Fenton, N: Software Metrics: A Rigorous Approach, Chapman and Hall (1993)

[10] Lethbridge, T.C., Sim, S.E., Singer, J.: Studying Software Engineers: Data Collection Techniques for Software Field Studies, Empirical Software Engineering, 10 (2005), 311-341.

[11] Sacha, K.: Evaluation of Software Quality. In: K. Zielinski, T. Szmuc (eds.) Software Engineering: Evolution and Emerging Technologies, IOS Press, Amsterdam (2005), 381-388.

[12] Sacha, K., Evaluation of Expected Software Quality: A Customer's Viewpoint, in. L. Baresi, R. Heckel (eds) Fundamental Approaches to Software Engineering, LNCS 3922, Springer-Verlag, Berlin Heidelberg (2006), 170-183.

[13] Beck, K., Andres, C.: Extreme Programming Explained: Embrace Change, Addison-Wesley (2000).

[14] Rodgers, U.: Oracle: A Database Developer's Guide, Prentice-Hall (1998).

[15] Kruchten, P.: Rational Unified Process: An Introduction, Addison-Wesley Longman (2003).

[16] Gamma, E., Helm, R., Johnson, R., Vlissides J.: Design Patterns: Elements of Reusable Object-Oriented Software, Addison-Wesley (1995).

[17] ISO/IEC TR 9126-2: Software engineering – Product quality – Part 2: External metrics. ISO/IEC (2001).

[18] Fowler, M., Scott, K.: UML Distilled, Addison-Wesley Professional (1997).

[19] McCabe, T.J., A Complexity Measure, IEEE Trans. on Software Engineering, SE-2, 4 (1976), 308-320.

New Trends in Software Methodologies, Tools and Techniques
H. Fujita and D. Pisanelli (Eds.)
IOS Press, 2007

Technology Neutral Business Process Design using URDAD

Fritz SOLMS

*Solms Training and Consulting CC, PostNet Suite 237, Private Bag X9, Melville, 2109,
Johannesburg, South Africa; E-mail: fritz@solms.co.za.*

Abstract. This paper presents the Use Case, Responsibility Driven Analysis and Design methodology, URDAD. URDAD aims to provide a simple algorithmic design methodology which generates a technology neutral business process design in the context of model driven development. The design methodology has been formulated in such a way that it includes core drivers for widely accepted requirements for good design.

Keywords. URDAD, design methodology, model driven development, design principles, analysis, design, technology neutral, MDA, business process design

1. Introduction

The aim of this paper is to present an implementable algorithmic analysis and design methodology which generates a technology neutral design model satisfying accepted requirements for a "good design". The resultant model is meant to represent the Platform Independent Model (PIM) of the *Model Driven Architecture* (MDA) published by the Object Management Group (OMG), [17,9].

1.1. Model driven development

OMG's MDA forms the bases for most model driven development (MDD) processes[16, 15]. A high level view of a model driven approach is shown in figure 1.

The input for the technology neutral business process design are the functional or use-case requirements. The output of the design phase is the Platform Independent Model (PIM) which can be mapped onto one's choice of implementation architecture and technologies resulting in a Platform Specific Model (PSM). Both, the PIM and the PSM are UML models. The Platform specific model is then taken through an implementation mapping which includes the generation of all deployable artifacts including the code, the database structures, the deployment scripts, the user documentation. MDA effectively separates design from architecture.

URDAD targets

- the analysis phase resulting in a use case contract, as well as
- the design phase resulting in a technology neutral business process design.

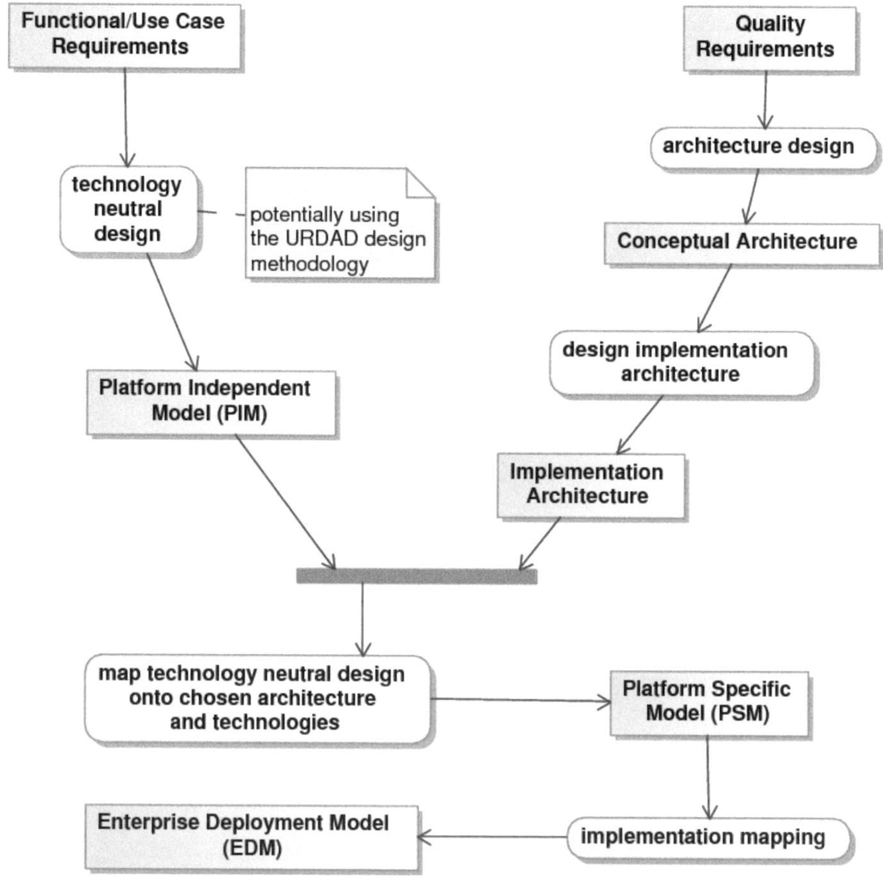

Figure 1. High level view of a model driven approach.

The use case contract contains both, functional and non-functional requirements around a use case. The functional requirements drive the design process while the non-functional and in particular the quality requirements like scaleability, reliability, integrability, ... requirements drive the architectural process. The output of the architectural process is an infrastructure into which the business processes are to be deployed. This may span, both, organizational and systems architecture as business processes will often be realized across manual and automated processes [1].

URDAD is usually embedded within an iterative realization or development process. A typical model driven development process is shown in figure 2. Note that the technology neutral business process design is performed by business analysis. The technical team comprising both, architecture and implementation (development), is responsible for the realization of the business process within the chosen architecture and technologies.

---

[1] The implementation mapping around manual business process steps would typically involve training of workers.

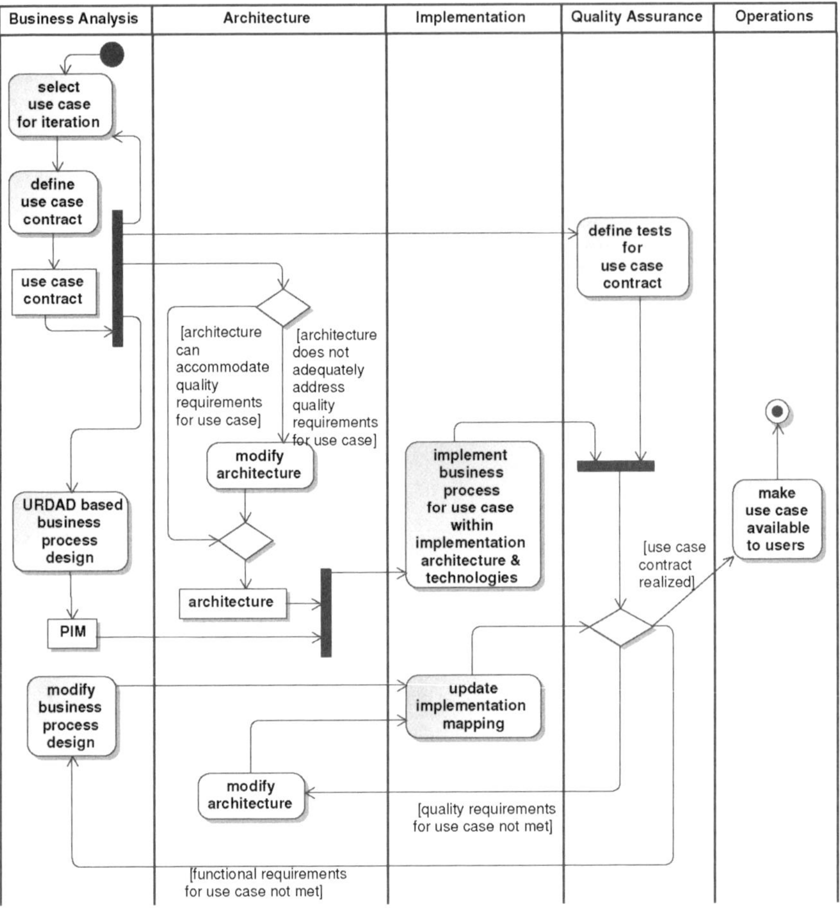

Figure 2. Outline of a model driven development process.

After passing quality assurance and actual deployment, operations takes over the management of the business process execution.

1.2. Requirements for the design methodology

A good process design needs to fulfill the functional requirements of all the various stake holders. The quality requirements (the non-functional requirements) are generally addressed via architecture. For example, in order to achieve a specific level of scalability and reliability one may decide on a clustered architecture supporting load balancing and session replication. Any business process deployed in such an architecture would acquire these qualities through the architecture – these requirements need not be realized through process design.

Our aim was to formulate a design methodology which satisfies Berard's requirements for a methodology [4]. In particular, the methodology should represent an engineering process which

- can be used repeatedly, each time achieving similar results,
- can be taught to others within a reasonable time frame,
- can be applied by others with a reasonable level of success,
- is applicable to a relatively large percentage of cases, and
- is able, on average, to achieve better results than either other techniques, or an ad hoc approach.

In order to generate "good results", one requires an understanding of the required attributes of a "good design". One can then attempt to identify design activities which ensure that the design will have these desired attributes.

Robert C. Martin has compiled a widely quoted list of accepted design principles [12]. Many of these design principles including the interface segregation, dependency injection and the Liskov substitution principles are realized by following a strict contracts based approach. One of the most important principles is the single responsibility principle which requires that at any level of granularity, each contract or class should address only a single responsibility. All the services should be narrowly aligned with the this responsibility focus. The reuse/release equivalence principle can be addressed by enforcing that one only reuses components which are released with realizing a published contract. If one would like to enforce the open-closed principle, one would do so separately from a design methodology.

In addition to the design principles listed by Robert C. Martin, the generated design should also satisfy the simplicity principle, [19], realize a high level of reusability [11], exhibit clean layers of granularity, [12,2] be testable across the levels of granularity [18], and facilitate bidirectional traceability across layers of granularity [7,1].

Figure 3 shows the final list of attributes we would want to realize within a design generated by the design methodology.

2. Other design methodologies

URDAD has grown out of Responsibility Driven Design (RDD) methodology pioneered by Rebecca Wirfs-Brock and Brian Wilkerson (see [21], and [20] [19]). Like RDD, UR-DAD focuses during the early stages of the design on identifying and assigning responsibilities. Also, like RDD, URDAD puts a lot of emphasis on client-server contracts. UR-DAD adds a step-for-step algorithm which generates different layers of granularity, enforces decoupling within each level of granularity via work flow controllers and enforces, through the methodology, a number of widely accepted design principles.

The *ICONIX* process from Doug Rosenberg discussed in [13] provide a structured process for evolving the static model from the collaboration requirements, but are not really responsibility driven, nor do they project out clean layers of granularity.

Methodologies like the Rational Unified Process [10] and Extreme Programming are incorporate aspects of a design methodology, but are, in many respects more software development than design methodologies.

3. Design activities realizing desired design attributes

Figure 3 also shows the design activities which have been inserted into the design methodology in order to realize the desired design attributes as well as the dependency

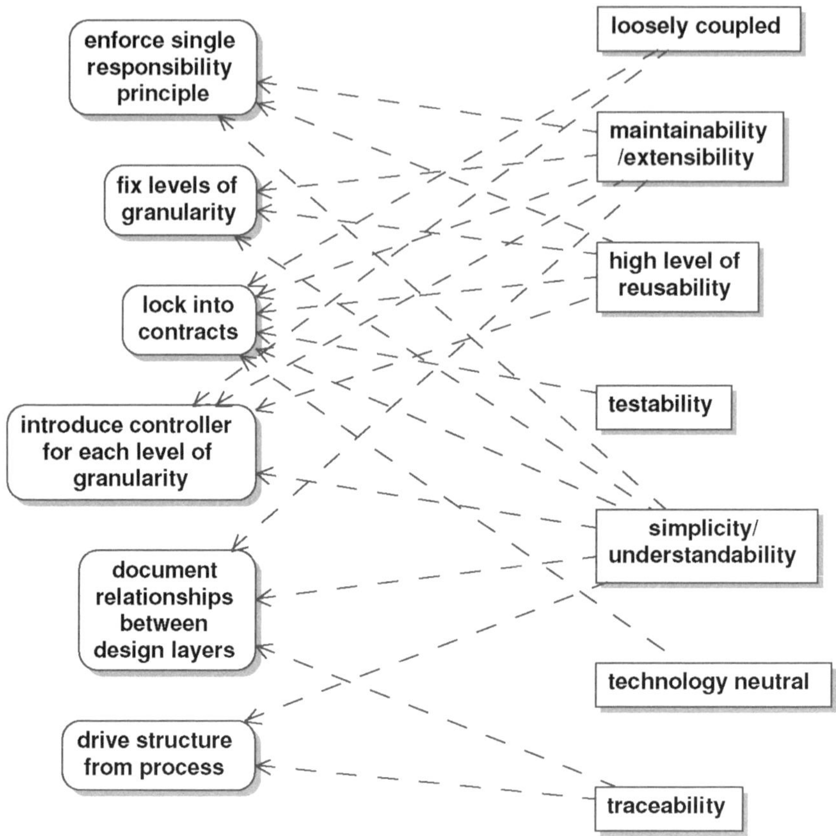

Figure 3. Design attributes and their dependencies on design activities.

of design attributes on various design activities. Each of these design activities has been directly built into the URDAD methodology:

3.1. Enforce the single responsibility principle

The single responsibility principle is enforced by grouping functional requirements into responsibility domains and assigning each responsibility domain to a separate services contract. Any system or organizational component as well as any external service provider realizing the full contract would be pluggable. Enforcing the single responsibility principle directly drives pluggability and reusability.

In addition, it makes each object more understandable through being able to understand the contract(s) it realizes without having to understand the way in which the services specified in the contract are implemented.

Finally, enforcing the single responsibility principle also facilitates simpler maintainability as

- maintenance is often required around a particular responsibility (enforcing the single responsibility principle leads to localized maintenance).
- One can verify whether, after maintenance work, the contractual obligations are still met.

3.2. Fix the levels of granularity

In the context of a work break down structure, one is automatically led to define different levels of granularity [6]. In order to generate clean layers of granularity, URDAD starts by identifying the first level responsibilities and assigns them to contracts. The business process and ultimately the service provider contracts are specified for this level of granularity before going, in a structured way, to the next lower level of granularity.

This improves the maintainability of the design as changes to a business process often only need to be applied to the controller of a particular level of granularity.

Fixing the levels of granularity also improves the understandability and usability. It facilitates incremental understanding of a design, enabling one to look at a high level business process before specifying how each of the individual high level work flow steps are realized through lower level business processes. Furthermore, a particular role player often only needs to work at a specific level of granularity without there being a need to understand either the higher or lower levels of granularity.

3.3. Lock into contracts

For each responsibility domain one assigns a separate services contract. The business process is designed to be realized across abstract service providers realizing these contracts. Design by contract rules are enforced ensuring the pluggability of service providers realizing the contract as well as the pluggability of specializations. This results in a loosely coupled design.

Enforcing that service providers realize services contracts increases the reusability of such service providers as the client can compare the services requirements with what is guaranteed through the contract.

Furthermore, enforcing contracts facilitates testability. It is difficult to write a sensible test if one does not know what the contractual obligations are which need to be tested.

A contracts based approach improves maintainability and extensibility through enhanced pluggability and testability.

If all participants in a business process lock into contracts, the individual contracts can be realized within different technologies. A contract driven approach can be used to generate a technology neutral design.

3.4. Define for each level of granularity and each responsibility domain a controller

Introducing for each level of granularity and each responsibility domain a controller localizes the business process information within the controller and decouples the service providers from that level of granularity. Taking any business process decisions out of individual service providers and localizing it within a controller results in simpler business process management and maintenance[2] Furthermore, the increased decoupling leads to a higher level of reusability.

The introduction of a controller for each level of granularity also simplifies the design and improves understandability as one only needs to look at the controller logic to understand the business process for the current level of granularity.

3.5. Derive structure from process

Going from a use case directly to defining structure is difficult and often leads to complexity which may not be required. A simpler approach which leeds to reduced complexity is that of defining first the process through which the use case is realized at a particular level of granularity. One can then project out the minimal structure required to support the process.

Furthermore, driving structure from process facilitates the traceability of any structural element to the process it supports and across the layers of granularity to the use cases for which it is required. Similarly, one can trace from a use case to the structural elements required across the levels of granularity to realize the use case.

3.6. Document relationships between layers of granularity

Finally, documenting the relationships between the layers of granularity is required to support full bidirectional traceability across the layers of granularity.

4. The URDAD methodology

Having identified a use case or service one would like to realize, URDAD attempts to provide an algorithmic analysis and design methodology which incorporates the above design activities in order to ensure that the resultant technology neutral business process design has the desired design attributes. The methodology starts with an initial analysis phase followed by a design phase which incrementally generates a design across different levels of granularity. The steps of the algorithm are shown in 4.

This paper uses the example of processing an insurance claim to illustrate the algorithm. This example is taken through two levels of granularity in order to illustrate the incremental refinement of the technology neutral business process design.

4.1. The analysis phase

The analysis phase aims to elicit, verify and document the stake holder requirements. As one takes the business process design through lower levels of granularity, one may require further input from the stake holders regarding the detailed requirements around the lower level use cases.

---

[2]This strategy is also directly used within Services Oriented Architectures.

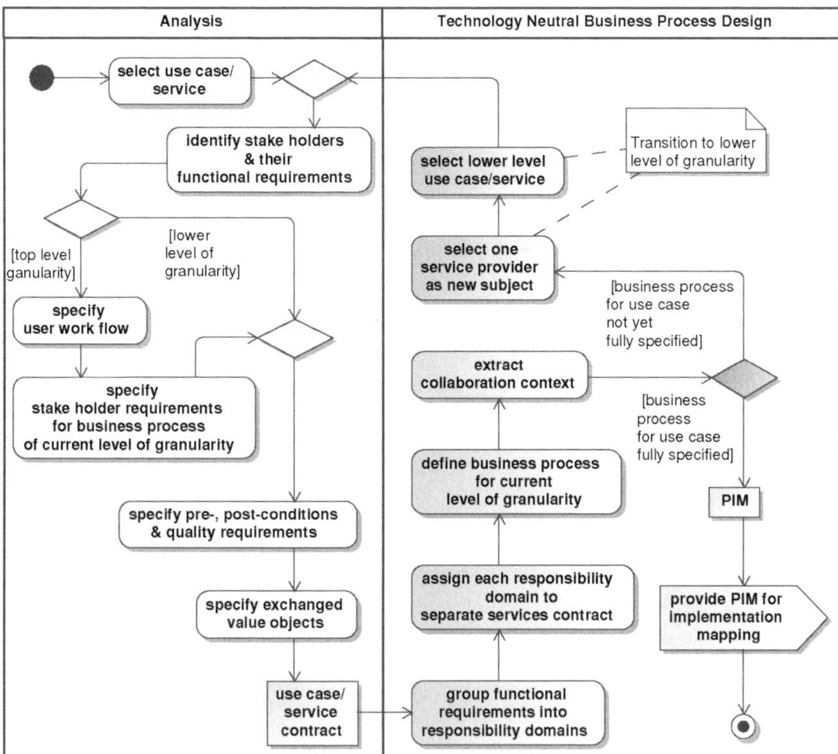

Figure 4. Outline of the URDAD methodology.

4.1.1. Functional requirements

During the analysis phase one first identifies all those stake holders who have an interest in the use case. Each stake holder is prompted for their mandatory and conditional functional requirements around a use case. Maintaining the linkage of any functional requirement to the stake holder who requires it facilitates full traceability of any business or system activity back to the stake holder requirements they realize and ultimately to the stake holder itself.

For example, figure 5 shows the high level functional requirements for a process claim use case. One can up-front elicit the requirements across levels of granularity or one can do that incrementally in the context of designing the business process across layers of granularity. In the case where full functional requirements across levels of granularity are elicited up-front, the functional requirements would be decomposed into lower level functional requirements.

For example, the functional requirement of determining to what extend a policy covers a claim may include lower level functional requirements like that of determining to what extend the contract covers the claim, assessing any further constraints placed by public legislation and ultimately generating a claim coverage report.

Often the detailed requirements around the different domains of responsibility are obtained from different role players; i.e. while certain domains of business may be able to provide information around the higher level business process, the details concerning

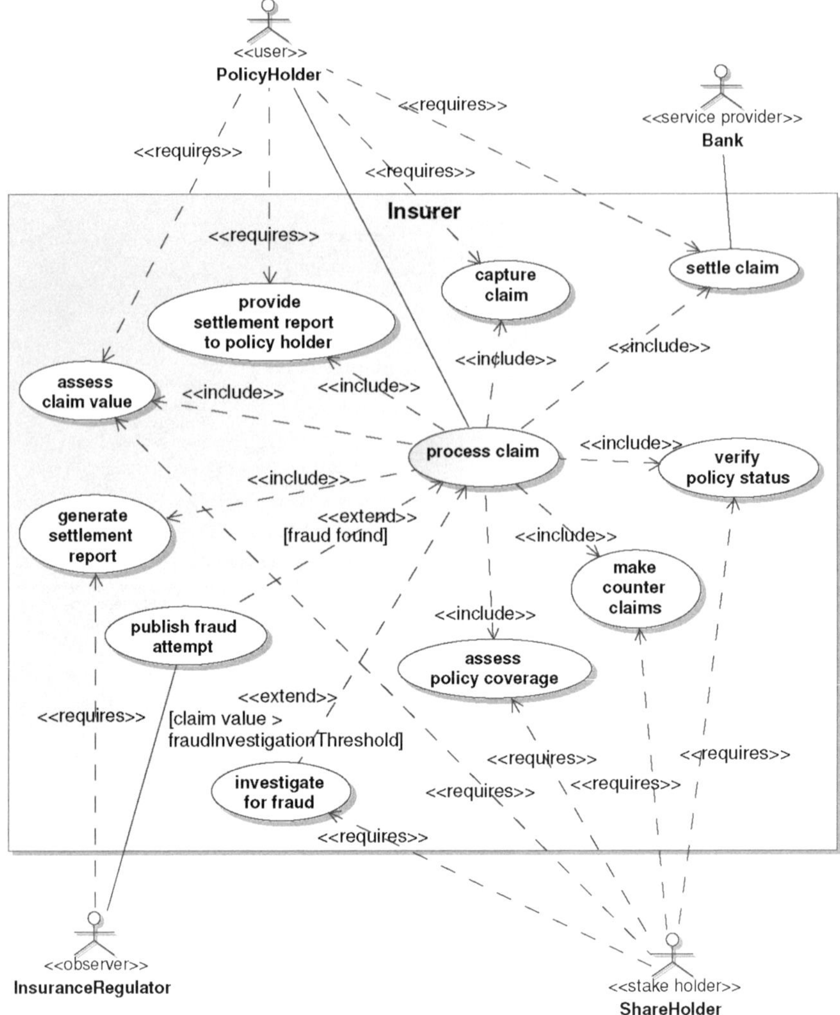

Figure 5. Functional requirements for the process claim use case.

lower level responsibilities are often determined from domain experts in the appropriate domains of responsibility. This can be done in the context of designing the lower levels of granularity of the business process.

4.1.2. User work flow

The required user work flow is documented via interaction diagrams showing the messages exchanged between the subject responsible for realizing the use case and the actors.

For example, figure 6, shows the interactions of the subject with the actors for a particular scenario and specifies the value objects exchanged between them.

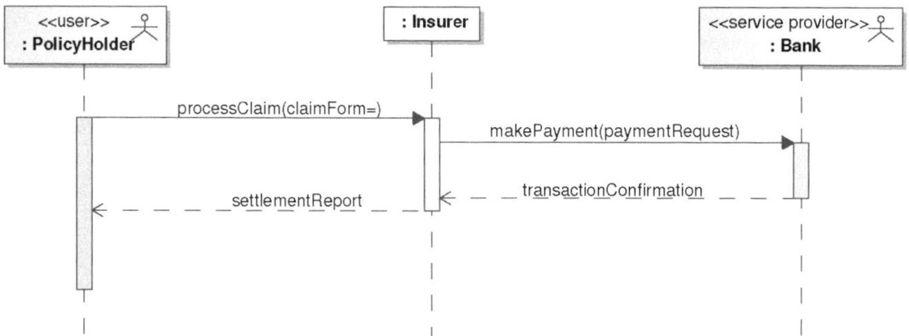

Figure 6. The user work flow for a success scenario of the use case.

4.1.3. Business process requirements

The business process as required by stake holders is specified using a high level activity diagram. It shows partitions for the actors participating in the use case as well as a partition for the subject which is responsible for realizing the use case. Note that this diagrams shows the required activities without specifying how they are realized within the subject.

Figure 7 shows example business process requirements for the process claim use case.

4.1.4. Exchanged value objects

Part of the analysis phase is the specification of the exchanged value object. For example, the policy holder receives a settlement report. There will be a class diagram specifying the information which should be contained in the settlement report.

In a similar way one specifies the information which must be provided with a claim, a payment request and a payment confirmation. As we go through lower levels of granularity we may need to add further structure to some of the value objects, particularly those which are provided by actors (e.g. the claim).

4.1.5. Adding pre- and post-conditions and quality requirements

In order to be able to tale a full services contract view for the use case we need to assign pre- and post-conditions as well as quality requirements to the use case. The pre-conditions are those conditions under which the service may be refused without breaking the contract.

The post-conditions are those conditions which must hold once the service has been provided. They apply to the success scenarios of the use case.

Finally, there may be quality requirements which are specific to this use case. Quality requirements are non-functional requirements referring to the realizable quality of service [3]. They refer to aspects like scaleability, reliability, performance, integrability, ... and are the core drivers behind architecture and infrastructure. While the pre- and post-conditions are part of the functional requirements which are realized through design, the quality requirements are used to assess whether the target architecture for the use case can indeed host the use case or whether architectural adjustments need to be made in order to realize the required quality requirements.

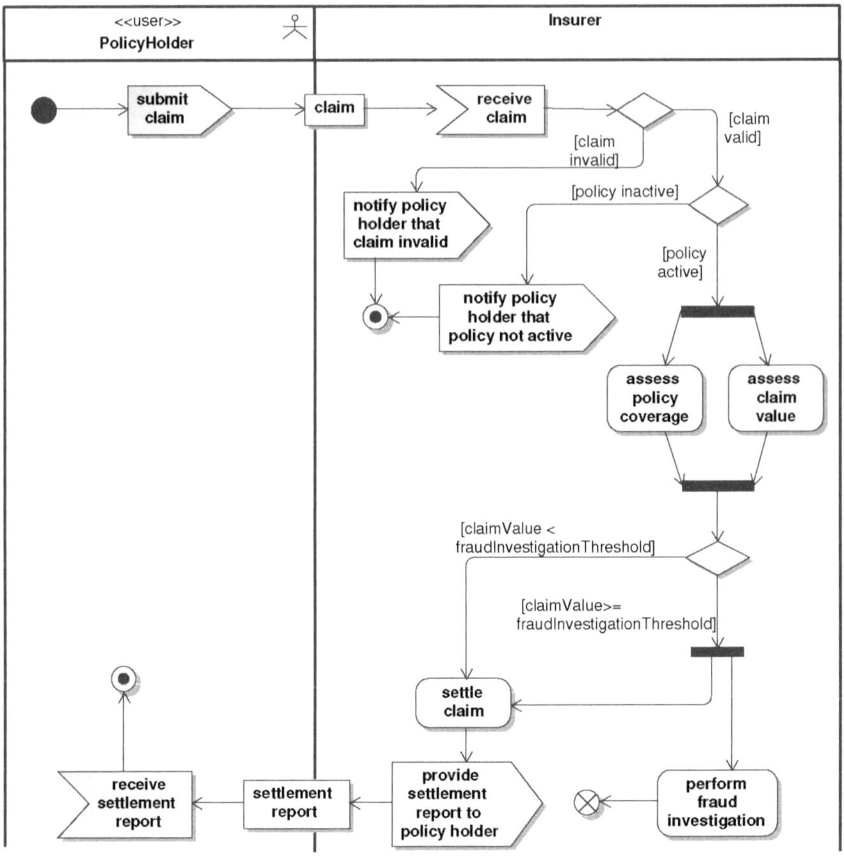

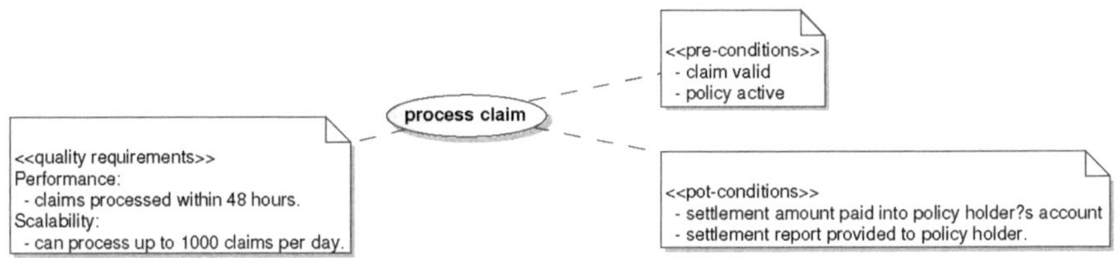

Figure 7. The general business process as required by the stake holders.

Figure 8. Pre- and post conditions as well as quality requirements for the process claim use case.

Figure 8 shows an example of pre- and post-conditions as well as quality requirements assigned to the "buy product" use case.

4.2. The design phase

During an URDAD design phase one identifies the responsibilities for the current level of granularity, assigns them to services contracts and specifies the business process the role

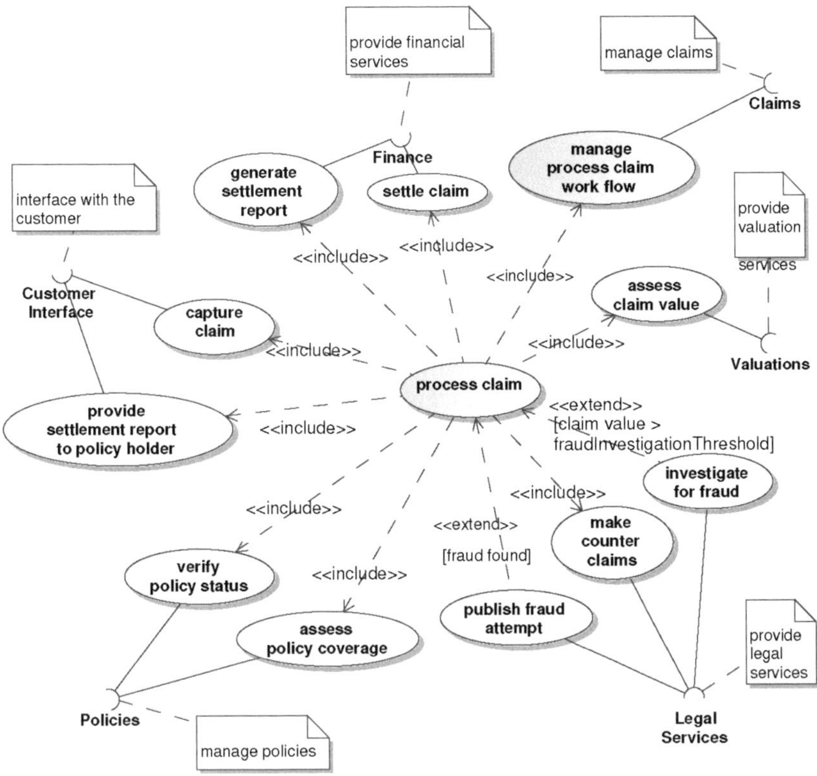

Figure 9. Responsibility identification and allocation for the process claim use case.

players realizing the contract need to execute. One then projects out the collaboration context, i.e. the static structure supporting the collaboration which realizes the use case.

The output of the design phase is the technology neutral business process design for that level of granularity.

4.2.1. Responsibility identification and allocation

During the first step of an URDAD design phase one groups functional requirements into responsibility domains and assigns each responsibility domain to a separate services contract. Note that the technology neutral design specifies contracts for service providers required within a business process. In the context of a model driven development process, the choice of a concrete service provider or the technology within which a service provider is o be realized is made during the implementation mapping phase. A services contrac can be realized by a system, an organizational component (e.g. a business unit) or an external service providers to whom the organization has outsourced certain responsibilities.

URDAD requires that one adds the responsibility for managing the work flow and assigns the responsibility to a separate services contract. This decouples the service providers from one another, localizes the business process information for the current level of granularity and removes any business process information from the service providers themselves. They are simply there to provide reusable services around a responsibility domain without knowledge of the business processes for which these services are required.

Figure 9 shows the responsibility identification and allocation for the process claim use case.

4.2.2. Business process specification

The services contracts are first introduced abstractly without specifying the services which service providers realizing the services contract need to provide. Instead one next designs the business process for the current level of granularity, showing how these abstract service providers need to collaborate in order to realize the use case. The business process design feeds the services required for the business process into the services contracts for the service providers required for the business process.

An interaction diagram like a sequence diagram is used to show how the role players from the current level of granularity collaborate to realize the use case. It shows the messages value objects exchanged between these role players in a technology neutral way. one can show multiple scenarios in a single diagram or use a separate sequence diagram for any scenario which has significantly different interactions.

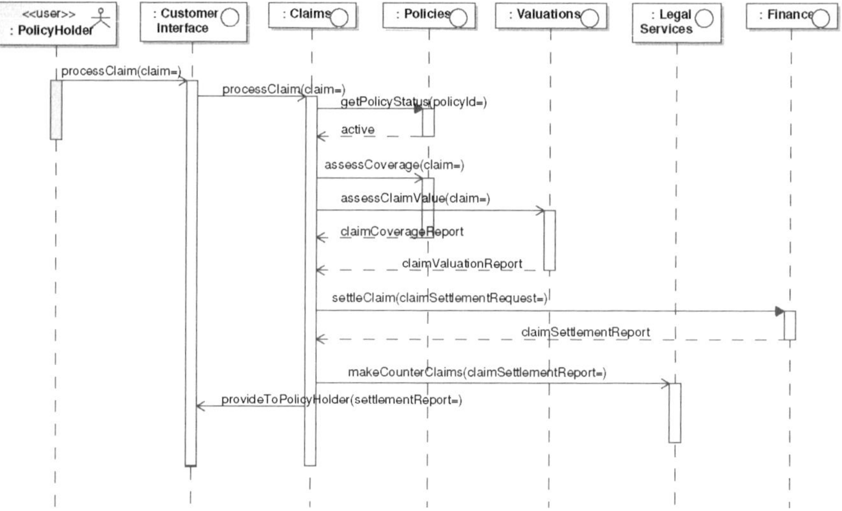

Figure 10. Role players collaborating to realize a success scenario of the process claim use case.

Note that in figure 10 the lowest level granularity messages are those between the controller and the service providers. Any further messages exchanged in the context of these service providers realizing these service requests is deferred to lower levels of granularity.

The full business process (seee 11 is then specified using an activity diagram with swim lanes for each of the service providers participating in the current level of granularity.

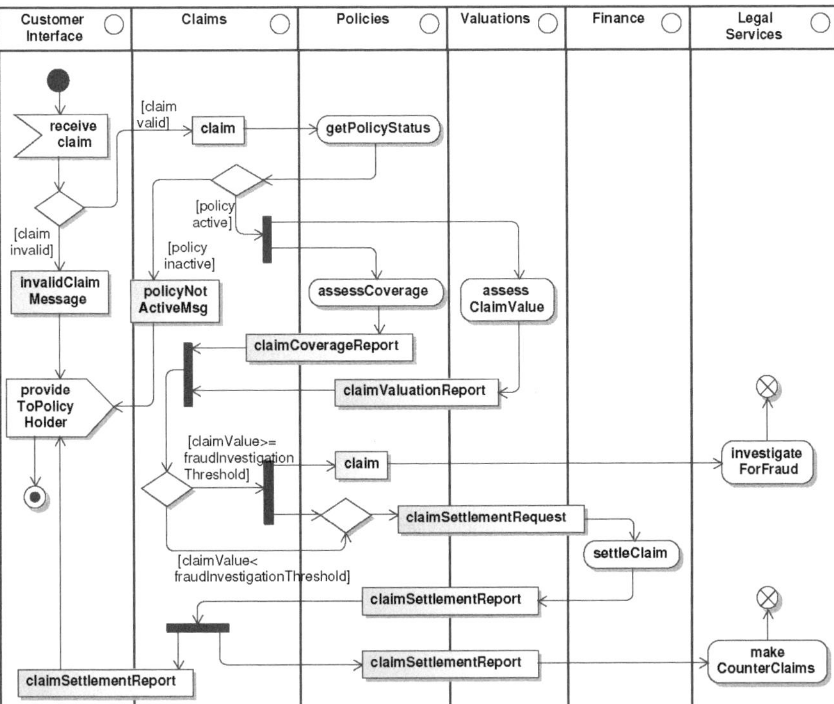

Figure 11. The business process for the process claim use case (at the current level of granularity).

4.2.3. Projecting out the collaboration context

The collaboration context shows the service providers required, at a specific level of granularity, to realize the use case, the services they need to provide for this use case and the message paths we require in order for the service providers to be able to collaborate to realize the use case.

Figure 12 shows the collaboration context for the process claim use case. Note that the dynamics (i.e. the business process specification) will already have fed in the services required for the business process into the contracts for the individual service providers.

4.3. Transition to next level of granularity

Having completed one analysis/design cycle, one needs to ask oneself whether the business process for the use case has been fully specified or not. If not, one may need to go to lower levels of granularity for some or all of the service providers from the current level of granularity.[3] This is done by selecting one of the service providers as the new context. The services from the current level of granularity become the lower level use cases. After all, a use case is defined as a service of value[14]. One then selects a particular service or use case and repeats the lower level analysis and design process.

---

[3] Often the lower level granularity design is done by different business analysts who understand that domain of responsibility (e.g. from a different department of the organization) or by the business analysts of other organizations to whom the realization of the services contract is outsourced.

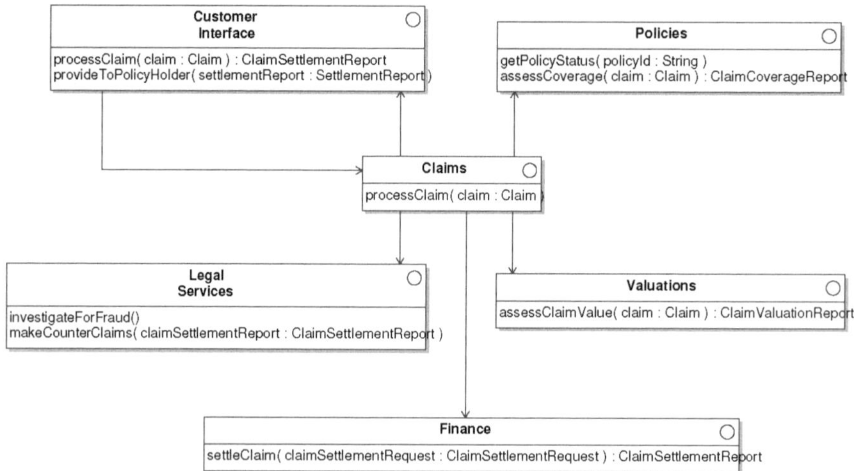

Figure 12. The collaboration context for the process claim use case.

Some of the information required we have already from the higher level granularity design phase. This includes the user work flow, the stake holder requirements for the business process and the specification of the value objects. However, one typically will need to do the identification of the lower level functional requirements and specification of the formal contract parameters (the pre- and post-conditions and quality requirements).

Figure 13 shows an example of stake holders around the lower level use case of assessing the policy coverage together with their functional requirements around that use case.

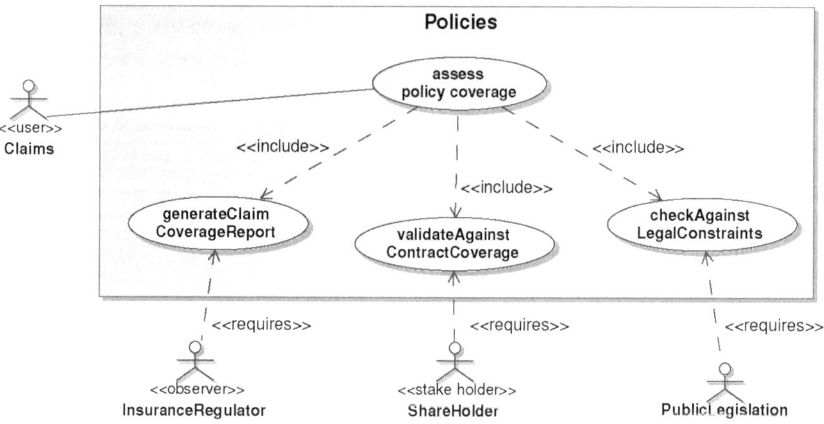

Figure 13. Functional requirements for the assess coverage service.

The lower level design phase is executed in the same way as one was done for the higher level of granularity. It start with the grouping of functional requirements into responsibility domains and the allocation of each responsibility domain to a separate services contract. Figure 14 shows an example of identifying and allocating the lower level responsibilities around assessing the policy coverage.

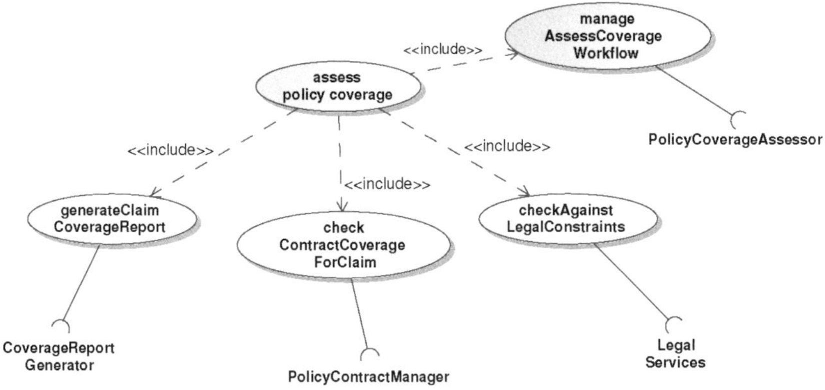

Figure 14. Responsibility allocation for the assess coverage service.

4.3.1. Facilitating navigation across levels of granularity

In URDAD a service from one level of granularity is mapped onto a use case at the next lower level of granularity. In order to be able to conveniently navigate across levels of granularity, one needs to maintain the link between the the service and its corresponding use case. This can be done in various UML tools by adding a link with an appropriate stereotype.

5. How are the design activities realizing the desired design attributes embedded in URDAD?

The single responsibility principle is directly enforced by grouping functional requirements into responsibility domains and requiring the each responsibility domain is assigned to a separate contract.

The levels of granularity are fixed by including only those contracts to which the responsibilities for a particular level of granularity have been assigned. Furthermore, the level of granularity is further fixed be requiring that the lowest level service requests at a particular level of granularity are those which come from the controller for that level of granularity.

The locking into services contracts is enforced by directly assigning responsibility domains to contracts and specifying the work flow across these contracts. The URDAD design process then generates the contract details and requires the specification of pre- and post-conditions as well as quality requirements.

URDAD directly enforces the introduction of a work flow controller for each responsibility domain and each level of granularity, resulting in the localization of the business process information and decoupling of the service providers used in the business process.

The relationship between the layers of granularity are documented through an explicit transition across the layers of granularity, facilitating bidirectional traceability.

Finally, the minimal conceptual (technology neutral) structure supporting the collaboration is projected out from the dynamics of the business process realizing the use case.

6. Evaluating an URDAD based design

In order to assess an URDAD based design one will

- validate that each functional requirement is indeed adressed by the business process,
- assess the grouping of functional requirements into responsibility domains in order to verify that there are no overlaps between responsibility domains and that each responsibility domain does indeed comprise a single responsibility,
- verify that the process at any level of granularity is intuitive and simple,
- verify that the service providers are represented by services contracts (UML interfaces) and not by implementation or technology specific classes,
- verify that each services contract has been fully specified including the functional and non-functional requirements,
- verify that the structure of all exchanged value objects is defined using class diagrams.

7. Implementation mappings

The implementation mappings would be quite technology specific. Thus, while the technology neutral business process design is usually done by business analysts, the implementation mappings are usually done by the technical team.

Often a business process is realized across manual work flow steps, services provided by external service providers and automated processing steps executed within systems. The services contracts coming out of the technology neutral business process design can be used as a basis for the service provider contracts which are either realized by external service providers or by business units hosted within the organization. The implementation mapping of such work flow steps may require training certain staff members to execute them.

Often, however, the technology mapping may result in mapping the technology neutral design onto a realization using current systems with perhaps some additional development, buying technology components and customizing them or developing an entire system hosting the various services. MDA tools aim to automate this process.

7.1. Notes on mapping onto a service oriented architecture (SOA)

In a services oriented architecture (SOA) [8] the work flow controllers for the various levels of granularity would map onto service specifications with higher level services being assembled from lower level services. The exchanged value objects would typically be mapped onto XML data structures usually specified using an XML schema. Some lower level services would be realized not as composite services defined on a bus, but as atomic services which have been published on the bus, but which are hosted in external systems.

7.2. *Notes on mapping onto a Java EE based architecture*

As a second example of a technology mapping, consider a typical Java EE architecture [5]. The work flow controllers at the various levels of granularity would be typically mapped onto either session or message driven beans. The value objects would map onto Java data objects or onto entity beans.

8. Conclusions

The set of accepted design principles which are seen as required characteristics of a good design can be supported by a set of design activities through which these design principles are realized. URDAD defines an algorithmic design process which incorporates these design activities. It generates a technology neutral business process design in the form of services contracts for each level of granularity together with the business process for that level of granularity. URDAD can be embedded within a model driven development process where the technology neutral business process design is ultimately mapped onto one's choice of implementation architecture and technologies.

9. Acknowledgments

I would like to thank my college, Dawid Loubser, as well as our clients and students. The many discussion we had helped to solidify the vision and practical implementation of the URDAD methodology.

References

[1]   N. Aizenbud-Reshef, J. R. Brian T. Nolan, and Y. Shaham-Garifi. Model traceability. *IBM Systems Journal*, 45(3):515–526, 2006.

[2]   D. J. Artus. Soa realization: Service design principles. Technical report, IBM, February 2006.

[3]   L. Bass, P. Clements, and R. Kazman. *Software Architecture in Practice, Second Edition*. Addison-Wesley Professional, April 2003.

[4]   E. V. Berard. What is a methodology? White paper, The Object Agency, 1995.

[5]   S. Corporation. Java ee at a glance. http://java.sun.com/javaee/.

[6]   T. DeMarco. *Structured Analysis and System Specification*. Yourdon Press, 1979.

[7]   J. Dick. Design traceability. *IEEE Software*, 22(6):14–16, November 2005.

[8]   T. Erl. *Service-Oriented Architecture (SOA): Concepts, Technology, and Design*. Prentice Hall PTRs, August 2005.

[9]   D. S. Frankel. *Model Driven Architecture: Applying MDA to enterprise computing*. John Wiley & Sons, New York, 2003.

[10] P. Kruchten. *The Rational Unified Process*. Addison Wesley, 2000.

[11] M. Lenz, H. A. Schmid, and P. F. Wolf. Software reuse through building-blocks. *IEEE Software*, 4(4):32–42, 1987.

[12] R. C. Martin. *Agile Software Development, Principles, Patterns, and Practices*. Prentice-Hall, 2002.

[13] D. Rosenberg and K. Scott. *Use Case Driven Object Modeling with UML: A Practical Approach.* Addison-Wesley Professional, New York, 1999.

[14] J. Runbaugh, I. Jacobson, and G. Booch. *Unified Modeling Language Reference Manual, 2nd Edition.* Addison-Wesley Professional, July 2004.

[15] D. C. Schmidt. Model driven engineering. *IEEE Computer*, 39(2):25–31, February 2006.

[16] B. Selic. The pragmatics of model driven development. *IEEE Software*, 20(5):19–25, September/October 2003.

[17] J. Siegel. Developing in omg's model-driven architecture. White paper, Object Management Group, November 2001.

[18] J. M. Voas and K. W. Miller. Software testability: The new verification. *IEEE Software*, 12(3):17–28, MAY 1995.

[19] R. J. Wirfs-Brock. Toward design simplicity. *IEEE Software*, 24(2):9–11, March/April 2007.

[20] R. J. Wirfs-Brock and A. McKean. *Object Design: Roles, Responsibilities and Collaboration.* Addison-Wesley Professional, New York, 2002.

[21] R. J. Wirfs-Brock and B. Wilkerson. Object-oriented design: A responsibility-driven approach. In *OOPSLA '89 Proceedings*, pages 71–75. TeX Users Group, October 1989.

Chapter 2

Software Development and Related Methodologies

A Method of Software Structure Designing

Based on Graph Planning

Mingzhi Mao[1,2] , Yunfei Jiang [1], Xiaolong Chai[1]

Software Research Institute, Sun Yat-sen University, Guangzhou 510275, China

Department of Computer Science, Sun Yat-sen University, Guangzhou 510275, China

Abstract: With the rapid growth in the development of sophisticated modern software, the complexity of the software has increased enormously, posing an urgent need for the automation of the more time-consuming structure designing. In this paper, we proposed SDGP which is an automatic generating method of software structure designing based on the graph planning technique. The method has properties of self-adaptation, finite terminating and complete.

Key Words: Software Structure Designing, AI Planning, Planning Graph, Automated Method

1. Introduction

Since the modern software is being more and more sophisticated, it is not only necessary to understand the contents of the software designing structure. But it is also required to clarify the structure of the system and the mutual influence among all of the subsystem in the software designing since the designing structure of different software part are influenced each other, and sometimes even conflict with each other since the system is so large nowadays. Automated software engineering is a new field in the software engineering [1].

A variety of automated structure designing tools currently exist but most of these tools cannot ensure that the generated structure data will take the system to the desired state. AI planning techniques seem to be quite promising in this field because of their emphasis on goals[1], i.e., the structure can be generated step by step by sequences of actions, thus the designing structure of software generated specifically to fulfill some purpose such as the function requirements. Some of the classical AI planning techniques, including STRIPS, SAT, CSP, PSP, Graph planning [2], plan-space planning [3], HTN planning [4, 5], and temporal logic planning [6, 7, 8], can be potential planning techniques for automated structure generating process.

Among such planning techniques, Blum and Furst's Graphplan algorithm [2] seems to be a promising development. Graphplan is a simple, elegant algorithm based on a technique called Planning Graph Analysis that yields an extremely speedy planner that, in many cases, is orders of magnitude faster than the total-order planner Prodigy [9] and the partial-order planner UCPOP [3].

In this paper, we propose SDGP (Structure Designing Graph Planning) which is a method of software structure designing based on graph planning which gives a algorithm for generating the automation function framework from the requirement analysis by applying AI planning techniques for software systems and using a comprehensive example to describe how the algorithm automatically generates the designing structure of the software system.

2. Related AI Planning Techniques

A planning problem is a triple $P = (O, s_0, g)$, where O is a collection of operators, s_0 is an initial state, and g is a set of goal formulas. A plan is a sequence of actions $<a_1, a_2, ..., a_n>$ such that each a_i is an instance of an operator in O. State s_i is obtained by executing a_i in state s_{i-1}.

The *Graphplan* algorithm has two phases, namely, graph expansion and solution extraction. In the graph expansion phase, the planning graph is extended forward to a fixed level or until the extended graph has achieved a necessary (but perhaps insufficient) level for plan existence. The solution extraction phase then performs a backward chaining search on the graph, looking for a valid plan from the goal states which must be meet back to the initial state. If no plan is found then the cycle repeats by further expanding the planning graph with more levels.

The planning graph generated is a directed, leveled graph with two kinds of nodes, i.e., proposition nodes and action nodes. Level 0 of the planning graph consists of proposition nodes representing the initial conditions. The levels contain proposition nodes (i.e., ground literals) and the levels contain action nodes (i.e., action instances) whose preconditions are present at the previous proposition level are alternated appeared, as shown in Figure 1.

Edges connect proposition nodes to the action nodes (at the next level) whose preconditions include those propositions, and additional edges connect action nodes to subsequent propositions made true by the actions' effects as shown in Figure 1. Actions that do nothing to a proposition are called maintenance actions that encode persistence.

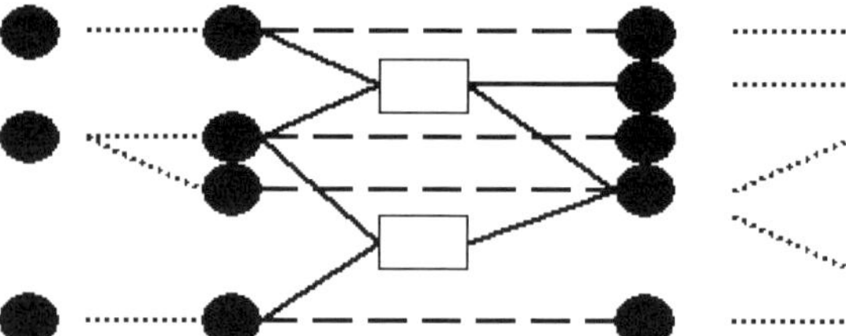

Figure 1.   The levels contain proposition nodes and action nodes

Figure 1: The Planning graph with action nodes represented by squares, proposition nodes represented by solid-rounds, dashed horizontal gray lines between proposition nodes representing the maintenance actions that encode persistence, and solid lines from proposition nodes to action nodes representing the preconditions of the action, solid lines from action nodes to proposition nodes representing the effects of the action.

The planning graph constructed during the extended process makes the mutual exclusion relation among nodes at the same level explicitly available. Also, a valid plan found during the solution extraction phase is a planning-graph where actions at the same level are not mutual exclusion, each action's preconditions are made true by the plan, and all the goals are satisfied.

If the solution cannot be extracted out when the last two adjacent proposition levels of the forward planning-graph are identical, i.e., they contain the same set of propositions and have the same exclusivity relations, then the planning-graph has leveled off and the algorithm terminates without a solution.

The algorithm of Graphplan planning is finite terminate, sound and complete. The Graphplan algorithm seems to be an appropriate planner for generating the designing structure based on the requirement analysis automated since the planning graph constructed during the planning process makes useful constraints, such as interactions and conflicts among subsystems, explicitly available that might provide a better understanding of the properties of the subsystems.

3. SDGP

3.1 Several Concepts

In order to apply AI planning techniques for testing software systems, the conceptual ingredients of a software system should include a model of the possible states, a model of effects of actions which denotes how the system can be changed, and a specification of the global constraints in the system.

Definition 1 (Designing state) $S = \{s_1, s_2, ..., s_m\}$ is a set of designing states. Each designing state is depicted by some propositions.

Definition 2 $\Sigma = \{S, A, R\}$ is a state transition system, where

$S = \{s_1, s_2, ..., s_m\}$ is a set of states.

$A = \{a_1, a_2, ..., a_n\}$ is a set of actions.

$R :$ is a state transition relation from the states to the others via actions in A.

Definition 3 (*Planning Domain*) A planning domain D is a triple $<\Sigma, s_0, G>$, where Σ is a state transition system, s_0 is the initial state, and G is the goal states.

Definition 4 (Designing Precondition)

Precond(a) is a proposition set that only after all propositions in Precond(a) are satisfied, the action a could be exccuted.

Definition 5 (Designing Effect)

Effect(a) is a proposition set which includes all new propositions that would be generated by action a.

Definition 6 (Mutual Exclusion)

We say that proposition p_1 and p_2 are mutual exclusion if p_1 and p_2 cannot be true in the same state. We say that action a_1 and a_2 are mutual exclusion if $precond(a_1) \cup precond(a_2)$ include two propositions which are mutual exclusion. Or $Effect(a_1) \cup Effect(a_2)$ include two propositions, which are mutual exclusion.

3.2 Framework of SDGP

In the requirement analysis, there are many constraints and relations between the contents. Requirement analysis structure is the input data, after being dealt with SDGP, output the designing structure, as shown in Figure 2.

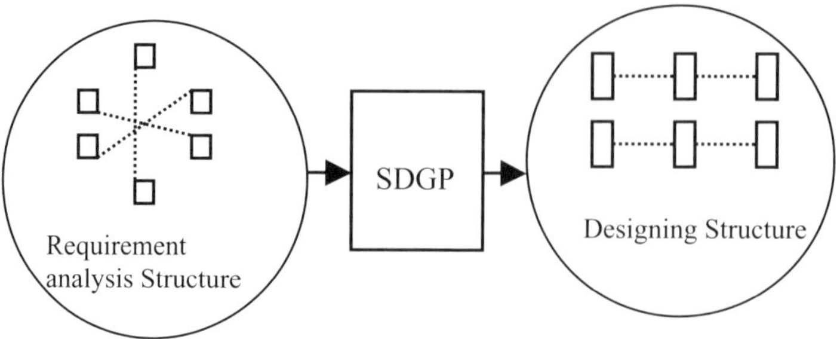

Figure 2.　The framework of the system

3.3 Designing Algorithms of SDGP

Algorithm 1. Put Requirement Analysis set R' into the Unit Valid Requirement R

Input: Requirement Analysis set R'

Output: the Unit Valid Requirement R

Begin Algorithm1

$R = \phi$

Loop

　　Break if $R' = \phi$

　　$R \leftarrow R - \{r\}$; $\forall r \in R$

　　$T \leftarrow Modularization\ of\ r$

　　$R \leftarrow R \cup T$

End Loop

End Algorithm1

Algorithm 2. Get the mapping relation C between the Unit Valid Requirement Set R and the designing Action Set A.

Input: Constraints, Relations and Structure characteristic among the Unit Valid Requirement R

Output: the Designing Action set A and the mapping relation C in which: $\forall a \in A$, $\{< precond, a, precond(a) >\} \in C$, $\{< Effect, a, Effect(a) >\} \in C$

Begin Algorithm2

Build the Designing Action set A according to R, such that:

$\forall r \in R$, $\exists a \in A$, $r \in Execute(a)$

$B \leftarrow A$, $C \leftarrow \phi$

Loop

　　　Break if $B = \phi$

　　　select $\forall a \in B$

$$B \leftarrow B - \{a\}$$

Build the precondition set of a $precond(a)$ according to R

$$C \leftarrow C \cup \{< precond, a, precond(a) >\}$$
$$C \leftarrow C \cup \{< Effect, a, Effect(a) >\}$$

End Loop

End Algorithm2

Algorithm 3. Extend the next layer in the Graph G.

Input: R_{i-1}, which is Level $i-1$ of the Graph G, the Unit Valid Requirement R, the Designing Action set A, and the mapping relation C.

Output: R_i, which is Level i of the Graph G.

ExpandNextLevel(R_{i-1}, R, A, C)

Begin

$$R_{i-1} \leftarrow \{r \mid \forall r \in Level(i-1)\}$$

$$A_i \leftarrow \{a \in A \mid precond(a) \subseteq R_{i-1}\}$$

$$R_i \leftarrow \{r \mid \exists a \in A_i , r \in Effect(a) \}$$

for each $a \in A_i$ do:

    Link a with precondition arcs to precond(a) in R_{i-1}

    Return R_i

End

Algorithm 4. Extend the Graph G from ϕ to any level k.

Input: the planning problem $p =< s_0, R, A, C >$, in which: s_0 is the initial designing state, R is the Unit Valid Requirement set, A is the Designing Action Set, C is the mapping relation between R and A. The level number is k.

Output: the Graph G, which includes k levels.

Expand(s_0, R, A, C, G, k)

Begin

    $R_0 \leftarrow s_0$, $i \leftarrow 0$

    Loop:

        Break if $i = k$

        $i \leftarrow i + 1$

        $R_i \leftarrow ExpandNextLevel\,(R_{i-1}, R, A, C)$

    End Loop

    $G \leftarrow < R_0, R_1, ..., R_k >$

End

Algorithm 5. Extract a solution from the Graph G.

Input: the extended Graph G, the planning problem P.

Output: the Designing Action Sequence Π.

Extract(G, P, k)

Begin

    $k \leftarrow$ *the last level number of G*

    Break if *the goal designing propositions* in $R \not\subset R_K$ and return *failure*

    $i \leftarrow k$

    Loop:

        Break if Π is a solution

        Break if all ways had been tried without a solution and return *failure*

        Select $B_i \subseteq A_i$, such that: (1). $\forall a, b \in B_i$, a and b are not mutex.

$$(2). \bigcup \{ \mathit{Effect}(b) \big| \forall b \in B_i \} \subseteq R_i$$

$$(3). \bigcup \{ \Pr econd(b) \big| \forall b \in B_i \} \subseteq R_{i-1}$$

        $\Pi \leftarrow \;<< B_i >, \Pi >$

        $i \leftarrow i - 1$

    End loop

    Return Π

  End

Algorithm 6. SDGP

Step1: Put Requirement Analysis set R' into the Unit Valid Requirement R. By Algorithm 1.

Step2: Get the mapping relation C between the Unit Valid Requirement Set R and the designing Action Set A. such that:

    $\forall a \in A$, $\{< precond, a, precond(a) >\} \in C$, $\{< \mathit{Effect}, a, \mathit{Effect}(a) >\} \in C$

By Algorithm 2:

Step3: Rewrite the designing problem according to the requirement into a planning problem $P = < s_0 , R , A , C >$

Step4: Generate the Designing Action Sequence Π as follows:

    $m \leftarrow |A| \cdot |R|$, where m is the most deep level that would be extended in Graph.

    $k \leftarrow 0$

    Loop:

        Break if $k > m$ and return *failure*

Set a level number k that the Graph would be extended to, where $k \leq m$

$\Pi \leftarrow$ Expand(s_0, R, A, C, G, k)

Break if Π is a solution and return Π

$k \leftarrow k+1$

   End Loop

Step5: Translate the planning solution Π into the designing description.

End of Algorithm 6.

3.4 The Characteristic of SDGP

Theorem 1. The algorithm of SDGP is sound.

Proof: Suppose SDGP returns the sequence $\Pi =< \pi_1, \pi_2, ..., \pi_n, >$, where π_i is a set of actions in A. Because $precond(\pi_1) \subseteq R_0$, and $precond(\pi_1)$ is not a mutex. So, in state s_0, π_1 is executable. After the execution of π_1, the current state is changed to state s_1. Thus $Effect(\pi_1)$ is not a mutex, and $precond(\pi_2) \subseteq Effect(\pi_1)$, so π_2 is executable in state s_1, ... In the same way, it can be induced that π_n is executable in state s_{n-1}, and after the execution of π_n, all the requirements are meet, thus the solution of SDGP is sound.

3.5 An Example of SDGP

There is a Requirement Analysis set $R' = \{r_1'\}$, we can deal with R' by algorithm 1 into the Unit Valid Requirement $R = \{r_1, r_2\}$ for an instance. r_1 and r_2 are depicted by proposition p_a and p_b respectively. The initial designing state is depicted as the propositions: $\{p_1, p_2\}$. To realize p_a and p_b, we have the designing action set $A = \{a_1, a_2, a_3, a_4, a_5\}$. The precondition and the effect proposition set is $\{p_1, p_2, ..., p_7, p_a, p_b\}$.

The constraints of mapping relation C is :

Table 1. The mapping relation C.

Action	Precondition	Effect
a_1	p_1, p_2	p_3, p_4
a_2	p_2	p_5
a_3	p_3, p_4	p_6, p_a
a_4	p_4	p_b
a_5	p_5	p_b, p_7

The mutual exclusion pairs are: $< p_3, p_5 >, < p_4, p_5 >, < p_a, p_7 >$ By SDGP, the Graph is extended as Figure 3 shows: The extraction process was shown by the wide black line. And a solution of the planning problem is: $< \{a_1\}, \{a_3, a_4\} >$.

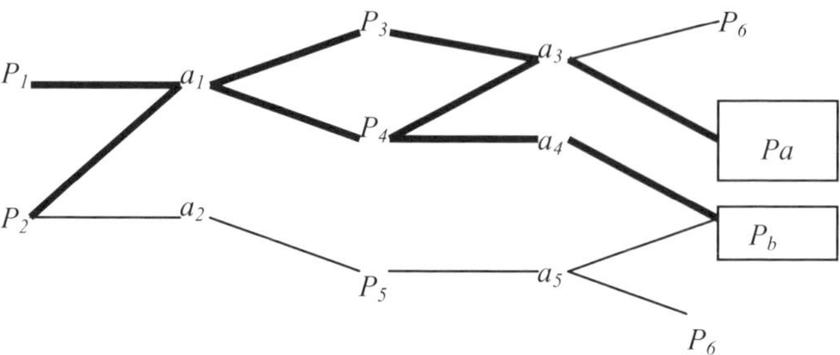

Figure 3.　Extended Graph

4. Conclusions and Some Directions of the Further Work

In this paper, we proposed an algorithm SDGP which is a method of software structure designing based on graph planning technique and it gives a realization for generating the automation function framework from the requirement analysis by applying AI planning techniques for software systems. The algorithm SDGP is sound. The algorithm SDGP is used to get a designing structure in the form of action sequence which is designed mainly based on the general technique Graphplan. When the scale is large, the efficiency of SDGP is not pleased. So the algorithm of SDGP should be better extended or improved along different directions. Here are two of them.

4.1 Use the Technique of Heuristic Search

Heuristic search technique can be added in the SDGP. For example, in state s_i, action a_1 and a_2 are both executable, and a goal proposition p is both included in $Effect(a_1)$ and $Effect(a_2)$. In SDGP, it will use a_1 or a_2 freely. Yet there are some differences between $Effect(a_1)$ and $Effect(a_2)$, the different infection for the even latter stage between a_1 or a_2 hasn't been shown in state s_i and state s_{i+1}, but the difference is something in the even latter states. We can take a heuristic function $h^*(x)$ which means the cost of the action x. The least of $h^*(x)$ is, the better of action x is chosen from the similar actions.

4.2 Use AND/OR relations

In SDGP, it is supposed that all propositions in $precond(a)$ should be meet. But in fact, the real situation is more complex, and different propositions often have the relations of AND, OR, etc. there is an example showed in Figure 4:

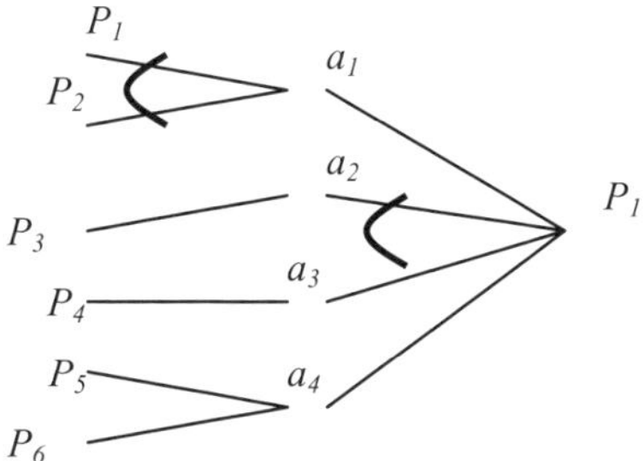

Figure 4.　SDGP with AND/OR Relations

In this example, we have:

(1), p_1 and p_2 are both in $precond(a_1)$.

(2),action a_2 and a_3 must both be executed in one stage.

(3), p_5 and p_6 are both preconditions of action a_4. Yet the relation between p_5 and p_6 is OR, which means, only one of p_5 and p_6 is needed to execute a_4.

Our work can also be extended in several other directions. There are some different techniques to improve the planning efficiency with the rapid development of planning technique in about recent 10 years. After all, our work is a new method in the field of structure designing of software engineering.

References

[1] M. Gupta, F. Bastani, L. Khan, and I. L. Yen, "Automated test data generation using MEA-Graph Planning", In Proc. of the 16th IEEE International Conference on Tools with Artificial Intelligence (ICTAI'04), Boca Raton, Florida (USA), 2004, pp. 174-182.

[2] A. Blum and M. Furst, "Fast planning through planning graph analysis", Artificial Intelligence, 1997, 90: 281-300,

[3] J. S. Penberthy and D. Weld, " UCPOP: A sound, complete, partial order planner for ADL", In Proc. 3rd Intl. Conf. Principles of Knowledge Representation and Reasoning, 1992, pp. 103-114

[4] D. Nau, Y. Cao, A. Lotem, and H. Muñoz-Avila, "SHOP: Simple hierarchical ordered planner", IJCAI-99, 1999, pp. 968-973

[5] K. Erol, J. Hendler, and D. S. Nau, "UMCP: A sound and complete procedure for hierarchical task-network planning", In Proc. of the International Conference on AI Planning Systems (AIPS), 1994, pp. 249-254

[6] F. Bacchus and M. Ady, "Planning with resources and concurrency: A forward chaining approach", International Joint Conference on Artificial Intelligence (IJCAI-2001), 2001, pp. 417-424

[7] F. Bacchus and F. Kabanza, "Using temporal logic to express search control knowledge for planning", Artificial Intelligence, vol 116, 2000.

[8] F. Bacchus and F. Kabanza, "Using temporal logic to control search in a forward chaining planner", New Directions in Planning, M. Ghallab and A. Milani (Eds.) IOS Press, 1996, pp. 141-153,

[9] M. M. Veloso, J. Carbonell, M. A. Perez, Daniel Borrajo, Eugene Fink, and Jim Blythe, "Integrating planning and learning: The prodigy architecture", Journal of Experimental and Theoretical Artificial Intelligence, 1995, 7(1): 81-120

Correspond author: Mingzhi Mao(1966-),
Associate Professor at Sun Yat-sen University ,P.R.China. He is the secretary-general of the Computing Mathematics Federation of Guangdong Province of China, and Senior Member of China Computer Federation. His main research interesting: Graph Plan; Software Engineering; Software MatMeric.
Corresponding Address: Department of Computer Science
School of Information Science and Technology
Sun Yat-sen University
No.135, Road Xingang West, Guangzhou, 510275, China.
Post Code: 510275

New Trends in Software Methodologies, Tools and Techniques
H. Fujita and D. Pisanelli (Eds.)
IOS Press, 2007

ASOP: An Agile Service-Oriented Process

Asif QUMER, Brian HENDERSON-SELLERS
Faculty of Information Technology, University of Technology, Australia

Abstract. The increasing prevalence of service-oriented architecture (SOA) has introduced another layer of abstraction (service-oriented) on top of already well-known object-oriented and component-oriented layers of abstractions. However, it has been found that the current traditional phase-based approach towards the development of SOA-based applications, contrarily, lacks agility, which mitigates against the needed ability to quickly respond to changes in business processes. Therefore, here, we suggest an agile approach to implement a flexible SOA. This paper, based on our industrial experience and case studies, presents the agile service-oriented process (ASOP) that had been constructed by using the agile software solution framework (ASSF), agile toolkit (ATK), situational method engineering (SME) and agile adoption and improvement model (AAIM) for the development of one of our industry (case study) service-oriented e-health project.

Keywords. Agile Methods, Service-Oriented Architecture, Method Engineering

Introduction

The dynamic and complex nature of business processes and large scale enterprise applications such as embedded systems, e-health, e-government and e-business has led to the creation of an emerging service-oriented computing architecture (SOA) [1-2], currently being adopted by many software development organizations worldwide. SOA is considered suitable for capturing the veiled complexity of the loosely coupled reusable distributed services of such large scale applications and for their full development [3]. However, the problem is that the current traditional approach for the development of service-oriented applications is not sufficiently capable of quickly matching changing business needs by quick releases of a working software application. On the other hand, we believe that the agile approach is capable of providing quick software releases, resulting in a decrease in the overheads often imposed by a traditional SOA development approach that lacks agility [4]. This paper presents an agile service-oriented process (ASOP) in order to find an appropriate agile mechanism for the implementation of SOA by testing our hypothesis that "the core practice of agile such as customer interaction and short releases shall be helpful in the implementation of service-oriented architectures in comparison with traditional SOA implementation approaches".

We have developed a comprehensive method-independent framework, the ASSF [5], that includes an agile toolkit and an agile adoption and improvement model that can be used together with situational method engineering [6] for the construction of situation-specific and abstraction-specific (object-oriented, agent-oriented, service-oriented) agile software processes. This paper presents the agile service-oriented process (ASOP), based, in part, on an earlier industrial case study [7], for the demonstration of the applicability of an agile approach for the development of service-oriented applications. The ASOP had been constructed for a specific organizational development environment and a specific e-health project and consequently cannot necessarily be generalised for every situation. The paper is organized as follows: Section 1 discusses SOA and method engineering. Section 2 outlines agile competence, the ASSF, method construction, the agile tool kit (ATK) and the agile adoption and improvement model (AAIM). Section 3 presents the ASOP followed by conclusions in Section 4.

1. Background

The purpose of this section is to give an overview of service-oriented architecture and the method engineering approach and its application in the context of the situational engineering of the service-oriented application development method.

1.1 Service-Oriented Architecture

A software service is a logical view or an abstraction of a business process such as a program or database for carrying out business-level operations [8-9]. A service is a contractually defined behaviour that is developed and provided by a service provider and is used by other services or service consumers in compliance with a service contract. According to Arsanjani [10], a service is a software resource (discoverable) with an externalized service description. This service description is available for searching, binding and invocation by a service consumer. A service-oriented architecture (SOA) is a system with a collection of services, interactions and inter-connecting patterns [11]. A service-oriented software system is a platform-independent system that is designed to follow a standard interface and flexible collaboration contract, and can communicate in any mode at any time [12]. We have identified the key elements of service-oriented analysis and design that have been distilled from existing service-oriented analysis and design architectures [10], [12-13], [14-17]. The main identified elements of SOA are: domain decomposition, goal-service modelling, existing system analysis, service specification, service flow specification, message and event specification, component specification, component flow specification, service allocation to components and component layer. The concepts of service-oriented analysis and design together with the concepts of agile practices have been considered reasonable and used for the construction of agile service-oriented process fragments or practices.

1.2 Method Engineering and Application

The method engineering approach uses standard method fragments (based on an underpinning metamodel) and guidelines, stored in a methodbase for the construction of the project-specific method [6], [18-20]. According to [21], a metamodel should be used to describe and specify a family of methodologies in terms of concepts, rules and relationships. Here, we demonstrate the application of method engineering along with our newly developed agile framework (ASSF) [5] for the construction of an agile service-oriented process (ASOP). ASSF assists method engineers and managers in selecting the most appropriate method fragments or practices (stored in the method repository) with the appropriate degree of agility for the construction of a situation-specific agile processes. Here, the method engineering approach offers three benefits: first, facilitating the construction of a problem-specific or project-specific process; second, facilitating the self-organizing and empowered agile teams to tune or adjust the engineered process to handle day-to-day issues on the course of development; third, building trust in the agile team's ability to make use of their own process ownership.

2. The Agile Case

This section points out the agile competence together with the description of the important components of the agile software solution framework (ASSF).

2.1 Agile Competence

An agile software process is more flexible, responsive and people-focused in comparison with traditional software methodologies (process-focused), and has the ability to quickly produce and deliver quality software products in small executable-increments by using an iterative feedback mechanism. The duration of each increment or working-code delivery (release) may span from 2 to 8 weeks, thus giving visibility into the progressive state of both the development process and solution product. The working-code, minimal documentation, test-first, iterative and incremental planning and development, continuous testing and integration, and self-organizing teams are the highlighted features of agile processes and methods [22]. An ideal agile organization should have all the ingredients to execute agile processes in a smooth fashion. There are six elements (ingredients) of an agile methodology or method that has been identified [23] including agile teams (people), agile processes, agile workspace (tools and development environment) that encompass the attributes of agility (flexibility, leanness, responsiveness etc.) to support a specific abstraction-mechanism (object, agent, service etc.) and combined by using a recipe (mental-model) to produce software products.

2.2 Agile Software Solution Framework (ASSF)

The extant fixed agile processes cannot be used off-the-shelf for any specific software project. Although agile methods offer many powerful agile practices, this profusion can often confuse software organizations as to which practices to choose for a particular situation. Therefore, we have developed a method-independent framework that provides a shared vision, guiding vision or mental-model to guide the software development organization choosing the best suite of agile practices for their local development and business environment. The main components of ASSF [5] are: agile method, agile knowledge, agile governance, business value and agile (business-agile alignment bridge) and business. Agile method represents the different but related core aspects of an agile method/ methodology: agility, abstraction, people, process, product and tools (agile workspace); which can be combined by using a method engineering approach for the construction of agile situation-specific methods to achieve desired business value.

2.3 Agile Toolkit and Method Construction and Adoption

The embedded java-based agile toolkit (ATK) in ASSF [24] is used to create, tailor and customize agile agent-oriented or agile service-oriented process fragments (an agile process fragment represents an individual agile practice) and to create multiple abstraction paradigm-based (called here "m-abstraction") agile software development processes by using a method engineering approach. The seven main components of ATK are: agile knowledge-base, providing the basic components for the construction of agile process fragments and an agile process; agile process fragment and agile process composer, services for the composition of agile process fragments and agile processes by using the process meta-model; publisher, to transform the composed process fragments and process into an XML format and then export that to the registry; registry, containing agile process fragments; agility calculator, knowledge-transformer, performing the transformation of process fragments in different formats; and a visualizer, an interactive toolkit client interface. The ATK engineered process fragments are then put into production by using the AAIM [25] - vision guiding model. The following section describes AAIM.

2.4 Agile Adoption and Improvement Model

The construction, adoption and then improvement of agile practices is a continuous and evolutionary process and takes time, depending upon various factors. AAIM [25] is a standard guiding vision model developed to facilitate the adoption and then assessment or improvement of the engineered agile method in practice in a software development organization. The notion and structure of AAIM can be characterized in terms of three agile blocks (an agile-prompt, an agile-crux and an agile-apex) and six agile stages or levels embedded in these blocks, whereas, in each block, there are specified agile practices to follow in order to achieve the particular AAIM level (AAIML). The AAIM levels are: AAIML 1: agile infancy; AAIML 2: agile initial; AAIML 3: agile realization; AAIML 4: agile value; AAIML 5: agile smart and the AAIML 6: agile progress. AAIM provides a road map to successfully establish agile practices in the development environment of an organization to achieve the desired aims through agile transition over the period of time. We have applied AAIM on our pilot projects [7] in industry for the purpose of agile-transition.

3. Agile Service-Oriented Process (ASOP)

Existing traditional service-oriented application development processes lack the ability to embrace the flexible and dynamic nature of modern business processes. The challenge is to construct a methodology that can deliver and be flexible enough to cater for a number of e-health service-oriented applications. Therefore, based on our industrial experience and case studies, we propose and have engineered an agile service-oriented process (Figure 1) for the e-health application by using the ASSF and a method engineering approach.

In one of our case studies, focussing on e-health software applications, we have constructed an agile service-oriented process (ASOP) for the e-health consultancy services (EHCS) project of one specific (anonymous) software development company. The EHCS provides a remote clinical interface and services to both patients and consultants and enables them to interact with each other. The main identified services in the domain of EHCS are: patient service, quality service (security and reliability service), consultant service, treatment service, administrative service, clinical service and report service including business operations. The EHCS also provides a patient-consultant forum service, messaging service and query service. A service is a logical view or an abstraction of a business process such as a program or database for carrying out business-level operations.

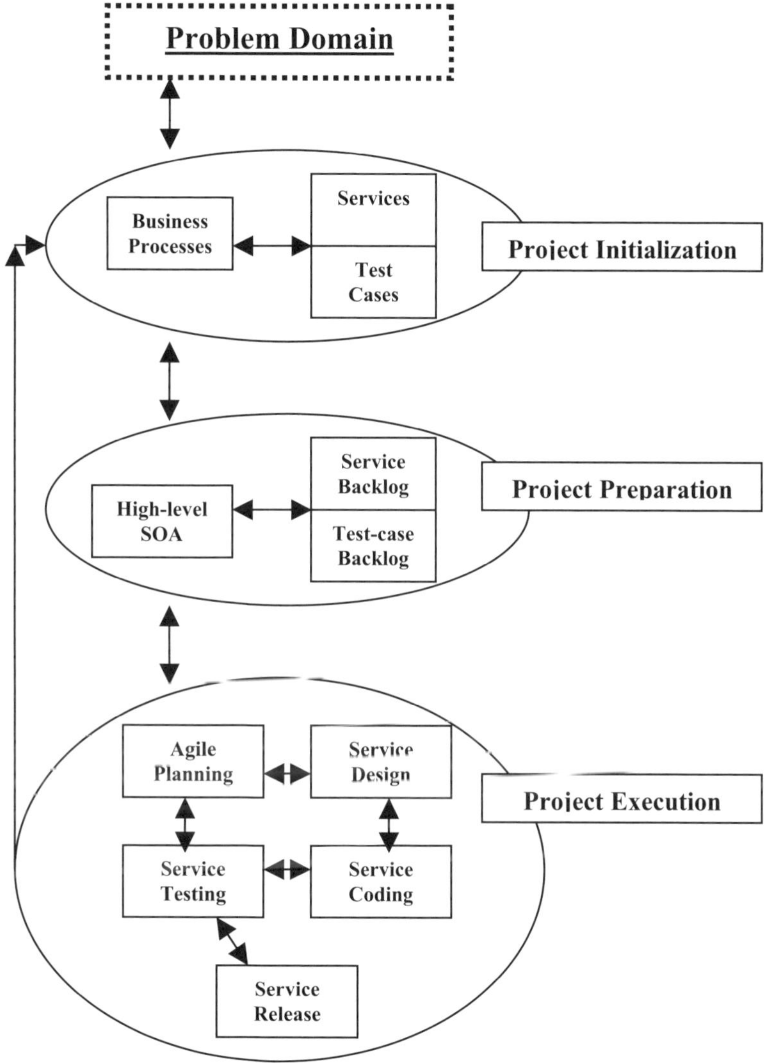

Figure 1. Agile service-oriented process

The existing service-oriented analysis and design process was a traditional phased approach and lacked the attributes of agility; it therefore took months or years to show real business value in terms of executable working software services. In contrast, agile development provides a value-driven and results-oriented approach that attempts to increase the business value throughput through the rapid release of working software in small iterations of 2-3 weeks. Therefore, an agile process (ASOP) has been engineered (by focusing on AAIM level 1 agile practices) to iteratively carry out a systematic test-driven development for the EHCS project. Prior to the construction of a full-scale agile process (ASOP), an experimental scenario had been envisaged and only three agile practices had been engineered for the e-health application followed by the engineering of a full scale agile process on the basis of the obtained results of the application of these practices. The results of this case study highlighted that the adoption of agile approach is not possible without its challenges and a step-by-step approach may be considered reasonable and less risky for a gradual and successful adoption of agile process, rather than all at once. It has been observed that agile is highly appropriate and suitable for the development of service-oriented e-health applications. The mapping of business processes is very easy in terms of independent (loosely coupled) services and then, therefore, easier to assign their development to individual developers to incrementally develop the software services in short iterations.

The ASOP has three main phases: project initialization, project preparation, project execution (Figure 1); and includes ten main practices: identification of the business processes and service-mapping, service backlog, test-cases backlog, high-level service-oriented architecture, release planning, iteration planning, software services-components mapping and design, enhanced pair programming, pair review and user acceptance testing, and service release and final documentation. In the project initialization phase, the problem domain is explored and perceived in terms of business processes, and then the identified business processes are visualized in terms of software services along with their test cases. Quick and effective feedback from the client or its representative (business analyst) is the key for the identification of business processes, services and test cases. The next phase in ASOP is project preparation, where the service and test-case are formally put in their respective backlogs, and then are iteratively used to define the high-level architecture of the service-oriented software systems. Finally, in the third phase of a project execution, agile planning is done for the design, coding, testing and release of each service. Taken as a whole in ASOP, this back-and-forth mechanism is used to iteratively move within the phase (intra-phase loop) and among the phases (and inter-phase loop). The following sections describe the practices of ASOP in detail.

3.1 Identification of the Business Processes and Service-Mapping

A business process is a sequence of activities or operations with specific business goals in the given problem domain or client requirements. The client requirements or business domain is iteratively analysed, defined and specified in terms of currently known and utilized business processes. It is often impossible to get the complete requirements list at the start of a project from customers; therefore an iterative approach is recommended. The currently known business processes are then further iteratively identified and conceptualized in terms of services, called service-mapping. A service is a logical view or an abstraction of a business process such as a program or database for carrying out business-level operations. Face-to-face communication with a client is preferred here in this phase of ASOP; however, other means of communications (email, fax, teleconferencing, video conferencing, telephone etc.) may be used, if appropriate.

3.2 Service Backlog

The service backlog is a repository for formally documenting and prioritising the currently known and identified services, and is updated as the new services iteratively emerge during the course of an agile development. The intensity of the details of the documentation varies from project to project and problem to problem. There are various factors that can be considered contextually for deciding upon the documentation details such as the ability of the business analyst or a customer to convey requirements, availability of the tools and the skill of the developers.

3.3 Test-Case Backlog

Test-driven approach is a key and a fundamental aspect of an agile development and considered critical towards the development of a quality system. The associated test-cases, with currently known services, are also identified and specified by the interaction of a developer and client. The developers directly communicate with a client or client representative (business analyst) to develop, prioritise (from a criticality point of view) the service test-cases and put into the test-case backlog.

3.4 High-Level Service-Oriented Architecture

The service-oriented architecture includes two types of architectures: enterprise service-oriented system architecture and service-oriented application architecture. The enterprise service-oriented system architecture (J2EE, .NET etc.) specifies hardware and a software infrastructure or environment that is required to support the execution of the service-oriented application and may involve application transactions, service distribution and clustering, messaging, security and session management. Whereas the application architecture is a domain-specific, service-oriented software application (such as E-Health Consultancy Services Application) architecture that is built on top of the enterprise system architecture. Instead of a detailed up-front design of architecture, a high-level service-oriented architecture is developed, which is updated after each iteration as the development progresses. The focus and preference should be given to the development of an executable high-level architecture and should be used as a feedback tool from a client, rather than simply detailed documentation, although necessary documentation cannot be avoided and is likely to depend upon the project.

3.5 Agile Planning: Release and Iteration

A detailed plan is not possible at the start of the project, since a wrongly estimated plan may lead toward the wrong decision. Therefore agile planning is done at two levels: release and iteration planning. At a high level, release planning is done by the agile manager to estimate (at a high level) the number of iterations, service functionality, cost and duration with agile burndown charts being used for project tracking and monitoring. As agile development focuses on the frequent delivery of executables, the release duration should be between 2-3 months. At a low level, the developers are responsible for providing the estimate (low-level) for the current iteration in hand. The duration of each iteration may span from 3-4 weeks but, ideally, the preferred duration of any iteration should be 1-2 weeks.

3.6 Software Services-Components Mapping and Design

The enabling of interactive and quick feedback mechanism (as advised by agilists) eliminates the production waste generation activity (unnecessary documentation) and its overheads and, therefore, focuses more on production by using direct and less-burdened communication means. Client feedback and a developed high-level architecture is used for the iterative mapping and adaptive design of the currently known services (modelling services) in terms of the configurations of software components and objects (a further low level abstraction) before implementation. Any desired and agreed changes in these artefacts are quickly adjusted to satisfy the customer needs.

3.7 Service Implementation: Enhanced-Pair Programming

The services that are ready (according to the priority order of the service-backlog) for implementation are fetched from the service backlog together their test-cases from the test-case backlog, and are implemented iteratively by using an enhanced pair programming (EPP [24]) approach (J2EE or .NET specific implementation for the services). In enhanced pair programming, two or more developers may work together and are responsible for the service that is allocated them for development. One of the developers should be senior and the other developer(s) may be junior. The benefits of such a pairing are not only to develop the quality service by using economical means but also to provide the hands-on training to the junior developer. It has been observed that a junior developer's per/hour rate is less than a senior developer and, when both work in a cooperative manner on individual machines on the different parts of the same service or component, produce better results then working together on a single machine. However, it is the responsibility of the developers (collective-ownership) to make sure that the developed service should work according to the specified test-cases. If there are any changes that are required in the service-backlog or test case-backlog, these must be reported and realised in the affected artefacts, accordingly. In future, more quantitative research and metrics are required to measure the productivity of the newly developed enhanced-pair programming approach.

3.8 Pair Review and User Acceptance Testing

Pair review includes the individual testing and exchange testing techniques before the integration testing is undertaken in each iteration. The developed services are tested individually by the developers concerned and then developers use exchange testing by testing the services of each other. There are two benefits and purposes of an exchange testing: first, to test the quality of the service; second, to communicate and share the developed work using executable artefacts. Any further testing is done in pairs (pair-reviews). Finally, after internal testing of the developed service, user acceptance testing is done with the collaboration of the client and developer in each iteration and before each release.

3.9 Service Release and Final Documentation

The release of a software service may include several iterations of small duration (for example 2 week iterations). The immediate executable or usable quality service that has passed the user acceptance testing is prepared for release with the necessary user documentation and is shipped to the client. This agile practice makes it possible to quickly deliver the results to clients while shipping the software services in short releases to test their utility in the real production environment on the client site. The earlier possible deployment of the software services in the client production environment gives factual feedback on the operability and quality of the service.

4. Conclusions

In this paper, we have demonstrated the applicability of method engineering together with ASSF for the construction of a project-specific, agile, service-oriented process (ASOP), created for an e-health project within industry. We found in our qualitative industrial case study that agile practices are appropriate for the construction of service-oriented architecture based applications. It has been observed that the ability to define, solve and refine improved with the application of test-driven agile practices. The quick feedback mechanism and short iterations helped to get the meaningful appropriate response on the development of the services (work done or in progress). Agile planning at two levels, pair reviews and user acceptance testing (release and iteration level) gave a rigorous insight on the development state of the software services. However, the constructed agile process, ASOP, is specific to the problem domain of e-health service-oriented although we propose to experiment further with agile practices for the development of other service-based software domains and applications.

Acknowledgements: We wish to acknowledge financial support from the Australian Research Council. This is contribution number 07/29 of the Centre for Object Technology Applications and Research.

References

[1] Endrei, M., Ang, J., Arsanjani, A., Chua, S., Comte, P., Krogdahl, P., Luo, M. and Newling, T.: *Patterns: Service-Oriented Architecture and Web Services*. IBM Redbooks, 2004.

[2] Omar, W. M. and Taleb-Bendiab, A.: Service Oriented Architecture for E-Health Support service Based on Grid Computing Overlay. *IEEE International Conference on Services Computing*, IEEE Computer Society, 2006

[3] Kodali, R. R. : What is service-oriented architecture: An introduction to SOA. www.javaworld.com, 2005.

[4] Stiehm, T., Foster, R., and Hulen, R. : SOA, Meet Agile: Adopting SOA with Agile Teams. Digital Focus – a Command Information Company, 2006.

[5] Qumer, A., and Henderson-Sellers, B.:: Method engineering tools for agile teams in practice. *IEEE Software* (submitted), 2007.

[6] Kumar, K. and Welke R.J.: Methodology Engineering: a Proposal for Situation-Specific Methodology Construction. *Challenges and Strategies for Research in Systems Development*, John Wiley & Sons: Chichester, UK, pp. 257-269, 1992.

[7] Qumer, A. and Henderson-Sellers, B. : Construction of an Agile Software Product-Enhancement Process by Using an Agile Software Solution Framework (ASSF) and Situational Method Engineering. *Proceedings of the 31st IEEE International Computer Software and Application Conference (COMPSAC 2007)*, Beijing, China, 2007.

[8] Krogdahl, P., Luef, G. and Steindl, C.: Service-oriented agility: Methods for successful Service-Oriented Architecture (SOA) development, Part 1. IBM. http://www-128.ibm.com/, 2005.

[9] Feuerlicht, G.: System Development Life-Cycle Support for Service-Oriented Applications. *In New Trend in Software Methodologies, Tools and Techniques (SoMeT2006)*, IOS Press, Quebec, Canada, 2006.

[10] Arsanjani, A.: Service-oriented modeling and architecture. http://www-128.ibm.com/

[11] Nickull, D. 2005. Service-Oriented Architecture. Adobe Systems, Inc., San Jose, CA, 2004.

[12] Tsai, W.T., Malek, M., Chen, Y. and Bastani, F.: Perspectives on Service-Oriented Computing and Service-Oriented System Engineering. *In Proceedings of the Second IEEE International Symposium on Service-Oriented System Engineering (SOSE'06) IEEE*, 2006.

[13] Erl, T.: *Service-Oriented Architecture: Concepts, Technology, and Design.* Pearson Education Inc., Upper Saddle River, 2005.

[14] Zimmermann , O., Krogdahl, P., and Gee, C.: Elements of Service-Oriented Analysis and Design. IBM, 2004.

[15] Kruger, I. H., Gupta,D., Mathew, R., and Praveen, M.: Towards a Process and Tool-Chain for Service-Oriented Automotive Software Engineering. *ICSE 2004 Workshop on Software Engineering for Automotive Systems*, Edinburgh, 2004.

[16] Zhong, J.: Step into the J2EE architecture and process. www.JavaWorld.com, 2001.

[17] Castro, V. d., Marcos E., and Cáceres, P.: A User Service Oriented Method to Model Web Information Systems. *WISE 2004 : Web information systems*, Brisbane, Australia, Springer, Berlin, 2004.

[18] Cockburn, A.: Selecting a project's methodology. *IEEE Software*, 17(4), pp. 64-71, 2000.

[19] Glass, R.L.: Matching methodology to problem domain. *Comm. ACM*, 47(5), pp.19-21, 2004.

[20 Henderson-Sellers, B. : Process Metamodelling and Process Construction: Examples Using the OPEN Process Framework. *Annals of Software Engineering*, 14, pp. 341-362, 2002.

[21] Henderson-Sellers, B., and Gonzalez-Perez, C.: A comparison of four metamodels and the creation of a new generic standard. *Information and Software Technology*, 47, pp. 49-65, 2004.

[22] AgileManifesto.: Manifesto for Agile Software Development.http://www.agilemanifesto.org/, 2001.

[23] Qumer, A. and Henderson-Sellers, B.: Six aspects of an agile software development methodology. *Proceedings of European and Mediterranean Conference on Information Systems*, Valencia, 2007.

[24] Qumer, A. and Henderson-Sellers, B.: Agile Toolkit to Support Agent-Oriented and Service-Oriented computing Mechanisms. *Procs. PROFES 2007*, Springer, LNCS, 2007.

[25] Qumer, A. and Henderson-Sellers, B.: Agile adoption and improvement model. *Proceedings of European and Mediterranean Conference on Information Systems*, Valencia, 2007.

Approaching OWL and MDA through Knowledge Management System: Application to project Memory

Hatem BEN STA[1], Khaled GHEDIRA
Ecole Nationale des Sciences de l'Informatique

Université la Manouba, Campus Universitaire de la Manouba,. Tunisia

Abstract: The knowledge preservation of design project is an important issue for high technological industry. A general framework for managing knowledge pertaining to design projects is proposed. The objective is to allow preserving relevant information to be used later, thanks to a product design project memory. We introduce a generic platform-independent model that fits requirements of project memory management; this platform is based on UML generic models. We describe the original implementation over object-relational technology in a multi-tier architecture; model transformation based on Model Driven Architecture (MDA) is developed. We present some ontology concepts, three mechanisms for exportation database under Oracle to platform dedicated for representation and exploitation Knowledge, Protégé platform. Finally, we discuss the benefits of ontology engineering for Project Memory management.

Keywords: Project Memory, Object-Relational, Knowledge Management, Ontology.

Introduction

In design projects characterized by a high level of technological and organizational complexity, an important question is to know how a company or partners consortium can maintain competencies generated during an engineering project until their next use, and how the technical choices validated or invalidated within a previous projects can be reused.

In the framework of high technology products, designers use their experience to make choices. The justification of these choices is sometimes stored in documents, which are exploitable with difficulty or at the very worst remains in the implicit domain, and is never formalized. These choices depend on the context: economic constraints for example can change during the time; new technologies can appear, as well as new requirements concerning comfort or security. If a team has to design a new product version some time later, it is interesting to retrieve the different considered solutions and the reason why they were rejected. The cost of a particular component

---

[1] Correspondence: LI3 – Laboratoire de l'Ingénierie Intelligente des Informations; la Manouba 2010, E-mail: Hatem.Bensta@ensi.rnu.tn ; Khaled.ghedira@isg.rnu.tn

was perhaps prohibitive, but it is now acceptable, and so a previously abandoned solution becomes possible.

So, the traceability of reasoning process can ensure going faster in the design of future products, by reusing. Furthermore, it is often necessary to know who by, when and why, the decision was made, to determine the responsibilities when a problem occurs. Another problematic is to preserve information about a product configuration. An aircraft for example is often a particular case, and to be able to ensure the airplane's maintenance, a company has sometimes to call actors who have left the firm, because these persons are the only ones to have the appropriate knowledge. This situation is unacceptable.

So, the question is: how to store design choices, their justifications, working hypotheses, context and authors of these choices. The proposed answer is to implement a method of expert's knowledge management using a software tool: a product design project memory [1]. This software must be considered as a means serving a learning organization, including human aspects. In this paper only technical aspects are considered.

1. A model for project memory

1.1. Definitions of Project Memory

A project memory can be defined as a memory of both knowledge and information acquired during the realization of projects [2]. [3] distinguishes the memory of the projects characteristics (concerning the context, the organization, the result) from the memory of the design reasoning (relating to the decisions and the resolution of problem). In the field of the engineering and knowledge management, some traditional methods can be quoted, like REX [4] (individual memory of experiment), MKSM [5] and CommonKADS [5] (memory of activities). Several approaches are proposed more specifically for the design memory. For example, "Design Rationale Capture Design" [7] based on a representation language (language DRCS) is adapted to concurrent engineering. Other approaches like IBIS [8] or QOC [9] are interested in the decision-making process in design.

Other non-technical aspects must be taken into account. In [10], the author shows that it is necessary to develop a new culture to transform an organization by project into a learning organization. In [11], the author has shows the interest to capitalize on the failures and missed opportunities. Many aspects require nevertheless to be improved, in particular the problem of the traceability of the design choices is still of topicality.

We can find other related definitions about project memory in [12].

1.2. General Architecture of the Information System dedicated Project Memory

Our approach consists in proposing a generic model allowing the implementation of project memories. In reference to model levels proposed by [13], we suggest a three level architecture (Figure 1).

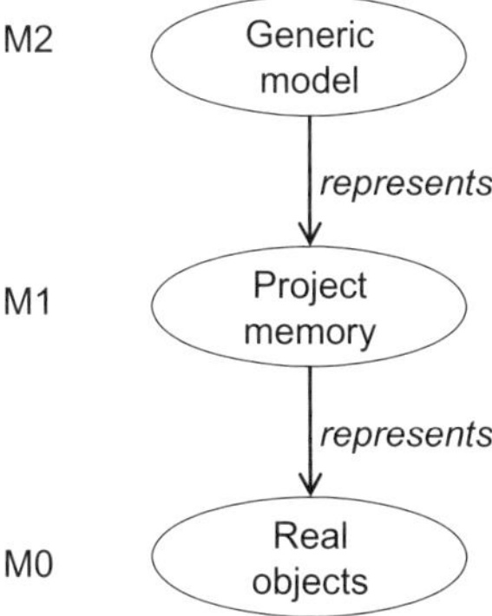

Figure 1. The three levels architecture

Level M0 is relative to real world "objects", such as product, human or material resources, calculation resources, CAD models, documentation, etc. Level M1 corresponds to the models of the previous real objects, and constitutes a project memory; it structures the pertinent information without redundancies, but indicating where to find this information. Lastly, level M2 is the more abstract one; it describes the model allowing project memories instantiation. This level is generic and ensures the possibility to memorize all projects' information. For example, it is possible to add dynamically attributes to a class, to associate it to one or several viewpoints. It also allows linking to the actor who is responsible of its values' validity and to elements from which it is issued (documentation, calculation resource, etc.). By instantiation of the model, the software's developer of a particular project memory for an enterprise has to define the appropriate information to store, depending on its next use. For example, if the concern is tracking the responsibilities in case of default, the software will store the tasks, the actors, the organization and the date of each action.

1.3 A Generic Data Model

In the framework of product design project, real objects can often be represented by tree structures. The search of a generic concept leads to representation of such models by the use of a pattern (design scheme) **[1]** adapted from those proposed in **[14]**. A pattern is in a sense a motif duplicable and adaptable according to necessities. This pattern contains a class Root-Element intended to represent the root of the structure, because it was noticed that this one is stable. Indeed, if one represents the WBS of a project for example, the root is at once the name of the project and remains unchanged.

On the other hand, for Gamma, leaves have to remain leaves, without possibility of continuing the breakdown. This limit does not correspond to what was noticed in real design cases. The users often have to break down elements that were previously leaves. As a result, the pattern we propose contains a class called Element representing a node of the breakdown. This class contains a reflexive association (a node can consist of nodes).

The association between Root-Element and Element as well as the reflexive association represented on **[1]** are of composition type; a node belongs only to a father node, and the suppression of this father leads to suppression of all children nodes. But the pattern can be adapted according to necessities, and one or some of these compositions can become aggregations; in this case, a node can be shared between several fathers, and the lifecycles of a node and its father can be different.

We may also notice that such a pattern can be enriched by constraints described with a language such as **[15]** to specify for example the impossibility to create a circular breakdown structure (if Element_1 consists of Element_2, then Element_2 can not consist of Element_1). These constraints are specified once. The pattern described allows only keeping the last version of the arborescence, administering neither its history nor any other constraint such as exclusivity between children nodes, etc. These aspects are managed by the means of relations which are defined between entities in the package Core **[1]**. In **[1]**, the author has given :

- The global view of the information system models structure in packages.
- The passage from the generic model to the practical case.
- Case of study for how to implement the project memory in study office specialized in civil engineering and design.

2. Prototype architecture of the project memory

The models proposed were implemented by using multi-tier J2EE architecture **[1]**.
- The first tier is the database tier supported by an Oracle database management system in version 9iR2 and is in charge of:

- The definition of the database type hierarchy using the object/relational feature of the server (type inheritance, nested tables, type references…)
- data storage in one object relational table named "entity_tab"
- data filtering with object views associated to database triggers "instead of…"

- The second tier consists of a business application server hosting one entity EJB per object view and one session EJB implementing the classical façade pattern. This pattern provides a unified interface to a set of interfaces in a subsystem. Façade defines a higher-level interface that makes the subsystem easier to user **[14]**.
- The third tier is the presentation tier composed of JSP and html pages.
- The last tier is the client tier. The client uses the application trough a simple web browser.

For the implementation of the project memory, one of the main interesting features of this database management system is to provide the developer with the object relational technology. The object-relational model is based on the extension of the relational model by the essential concepts of the object. The system main part thus remains relational, but all the key concepts of the object are added there in a form particularly designed to facilitate the integration of the two models. In addition to built-in data types, the developer can define new object types that make it possible to model complex structures such as type hierarchy, object references, etc.

In general, the object-type model is similar to the class mechanism found in C++ and Java. Like classes, objects make it easier to model complex, real-world business entities and logic, and the reusability of objects makes it possible to develop database applications faster and more efficiently. By natively supporting object types in the database, Oracle enables application developers to directly access the data structures used by used by their applications. Object abstraction and the encapsulation of object behaviours also make applications easier to understand and maintain **[16]**. In **[1]**, the author has given a transformation and implementation guide for different models dedicated Project Memory.

3. Ontologies for Project Memory

3.1. Cartographies of Ontologies Concepts

Over the past decade, knowledge representation research has focused on ontology, which are, as [17] defines them, formal specifications of conceptualizations. In [18], the author has presented the state of the art of ontologies and synthesizes it. He made a synthesis of definitions, languages, ontology classifications, ontological engineering, ontological platforms and application fields of ontology. He presented a new vision of the ontological concepts through the proposition of a number of cartographies related to these concepts.

Ontology typically consists in a set of formally defined concepts and properties. By applying inference rules defined by ontology, a software agent can compute inferred knowledge from a given ontology asserted knowledge. Several general inference tasks are referenced by ontology engineering, the main one being the subsumption problem, which consists in finding all the classes a given object, belongs to. Ontologies usually rely on a subset of first order predicate logic known as Description Logics [19]. Depending on the constructs an ontology is built upon, a given ontology can be proven decidable, in the sense of subsumption, and therefore ensure tractability of applications using it. SHOIN (D) is one of the most popular Description Logics, since a well-known implementation of it is OWL-DL, the Description Logic compliant subset of the Web Ontology Language (OWL) [20]. The World Wide Web Consortium (W3C) has recently issued a recommendation for OWL as a core technology of the Semantic Web, but only with its DL restriction can one ensure an EXPTIME decidability regarding the subsumption problem.

Unlike expert systems that aim at building the most extensive knowledge base or ontology pertaining to a specific domain and to compute it, Semantic Web ontologies tend to focus on knowledge interchange and interoperability. The Semantic Web can be regarded as a http-based network of XML-serialized ontologies, such that any resource is identified by an URI (Uniform Resource Identifier, of which URL are a subset). On the Semantic Web, a resource can assert a relation involving some instances of a concept defined by another ontology, simply by referencing the URI of that concept. Therefore, using applications that are aware of a limited set of primitives, a machine can compute knowledge formalized in distinct ontologies, and have access to the meaning of a description rather than to plain text strings.

3.2. From Models to Ontologies

Many related works concerning the projection between models based MDA (Model Driven Architecture) technology and ontologies based on OWL (Web Ontology language) technology like [21], [22], [23] and others. The link between the two worlds can be considered acceptable [24]: the ontology elements and the link between those elements are a sub-set of the elements in MOF [13].

A model is a basic element of a process conceptualization, it represent a conception of application; the ontologies represent a Knowledge domain. It's important to define a projection mechanism from a model application conception to domain Knowledge and inversely. In [21], the author has defined a projection mechanism from ontologies to models. A set of steps has been created that compose the process of transformation. He describes the transformation of ontology to a model by selling the integration of ontologies in the MDE (Model Driven Engineering) [25] process. In the next paragraph, we present the opposite projection. It means from the conception of models to an ontology implementation: application to Project Memory.

3.3. From Data-Model Oriented Object-Relational Technology to OWL-DL Technology

All the models of Project memory were designed by using the Objecteering case [26]. A guide of models transformation was defined in [26], this guide show the crossing from UML diagram to an implementation of type Objet-Relational type under the system Oracle database 9iR2. Although Object-Relational databases offer a very powerful environment for knowledge management, several insufficiencies remain under this paradigm that an ontology-based approach might help to solve.

The main difference between Object-Oriented modelling, and frame-based systems (built upon Description Logics) come from the way classes (or types, concepts...) are defined. When creating a new object type in an Oracle application, one can assert that the new type extends any previously defined type, but there is no other way to create a subtype than to explicitly state what type it extends. Under the Description Logics paradigm, a concept is defined by asserting a set of necessary conditions, under which any instance in the knowledge base will be classified as an instance of the considered concepts, whenever those conditions are met. Thus, a knowledge base (KB) has to be classified, and depending on the complexity of the concepts necessary or necessary and sufficient conditions, a software agent, known as a reasoner, will achieve classification of the KB in a tractable time. Therefore, from a set of asserted concepts and roles definitions, a DL-based KB will compute an inferred ontology, including concept taxonomy. For these reasons, ontology-based modelling can be regarded as much more extensible than UML-based models, since whenever a new concept has to be defined, there is no need for a complete redesign of the model.

Under the Semantic Web, one will also benefit from another kind of flexibility due to ontology-based modelling: since concepts can be formally identified by an URI, there is no need to maintain an exhaustive database of any concept one might have to refer to inside the system. By using external URIs, and thanks to Web Services, one can model projects involving externalized resources. Let's suppose a product is completely designed and the model makes use of external references through the URI mechanism. Whenever someone will need a new functionality for which no form was intended (e.g. to check that all the parts of a product, including subcontracted ones, are free of certain particles), the ability to scale a query up to the semantic web will be a powerful advantage.

3.4 Implementation details

Among the advantages of using Oracle 9iR2, that it include XML technology and the Fusion cash technology. Protégé 3.11 has been the editor of choice of ontology. This editor can build a domain for ontology, define forms to input and output data like an instances of this ontology. It is also be possible to reason on the ontologies by using an inference engine like JESS [27] or other inference engine basic on logic description like RACER. The both tools can be integrated easily to protégé platform.

Many others ontology editor can be found in [18]. The main reasons of using protégé are:

¶   free software
¶   Protégé integrates almost of ontology languages: RDF, RDFS, OWL, CLIPS, XML, UML, etc ;
¶   It allows the conversion of ontology from a format to another by using different plug-in.
¶   It has a convivial interface and easy for managing the instances.

3.4.1. An XDK Approach

XDK tool was adopted a first approach for extracting instances from the database on XML format, because the Protégé editor can accept to built ontologies with importing XML files. For using this tool we have to prepare configurations:
-decompress: *xdk_nt_10_1_0_2_0_production.zip* in c*:\temp\;*
- configure file:
c:\temp\xdk_nt_10_1_0_2_0_production\bin\env.bat by defining the installation folder and the variables *ORACLE_HOME* and *JAVA_HOME;*
- be sure that the variable CLASSPATH contains the access way to the file ZIP (or JAR) for JDBC.
After the configuration we can test the XDK tool. The test has concerned a part of the database. We have concerted only the view concerning the element Product of the Project memory in order to extract the instances of the element Product by typing the command:

```
Java OracleXML getXML
-user   "projects_memory_v2/projects"   #user   name   and
password
-conn "jdbc:oracle:thin:@oracle.Li3.tn:1521:li32"
"Select * from PRODUCT_VIEW" > produit.xml
```
Considering:
- thin is the driver JDBC;
- @oracle.li3.tn:1521:li32 is the access way to the database. After extracting instances in the file produit.xml, we import it by using our ontology editor and when we open it we choice a project type using .XML files as shown in the figure 2.

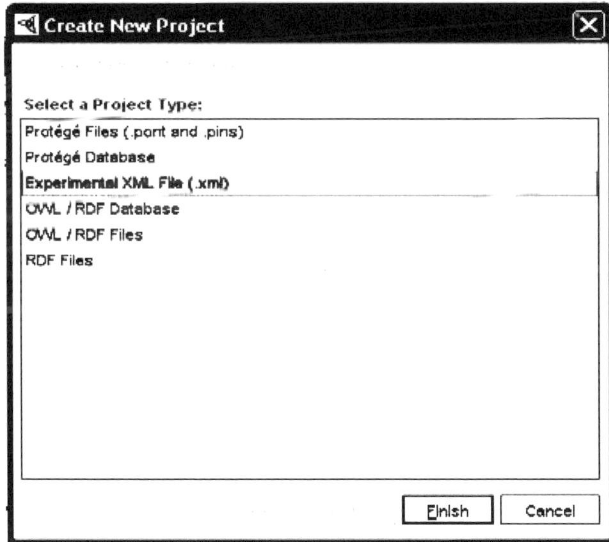

Figure 2: Choice project type

After, using XML option of the protégé editor we import the file generated by XDK. After the import of this file containing the instances, we can get all the instances of the Products elements that exist in the database as shown in the figure 3.

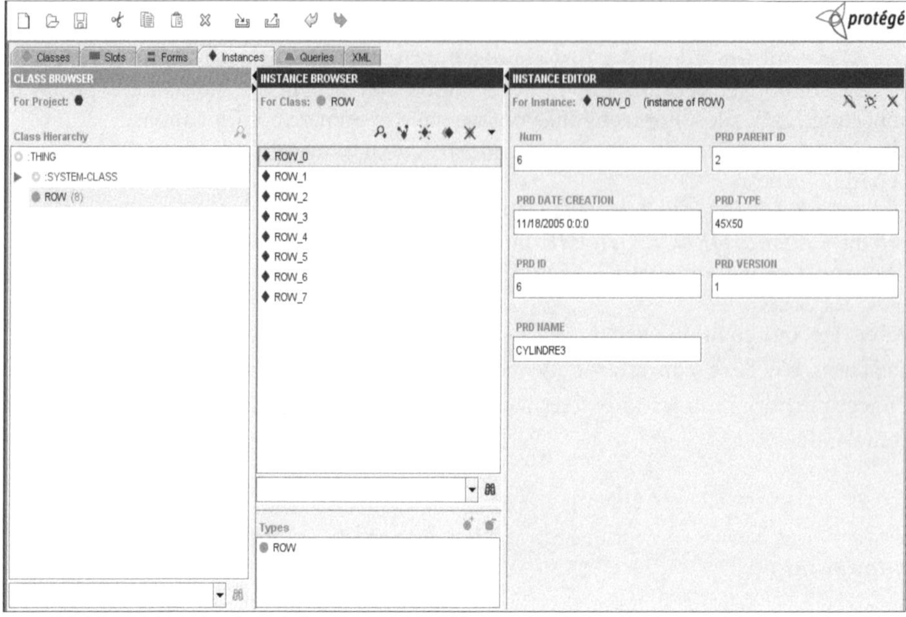

Figure 3: Instances of Product elements

Using XDK tool we imported instances from the database but we met some problems: we should repeat the same task for every table and every view of the database. There is no an automatically way allowing the import of all the instances of the database and the hierarchy of the instances. Our database dedicated to project memory contains many views and the goal is to obtain a complete ontology with getting the relations between the instances. This method was quickly given up. It was evident that we must find another solution that allows us to get acceptable results. We have opted for the DataGenie plugin.

3.4.2. An DataGenie Approach

A DataGenie is a plugin; it can read the data from a database trough protégé **[28]**. It can also use the ODBC/JDBC driver to establish the connection to a specific database. It allows the user to import a part or all databases. Each table is transformed to a class and attributes to slots [29]. The figure 4 shows the configuration procedure of DataGenie plugin.

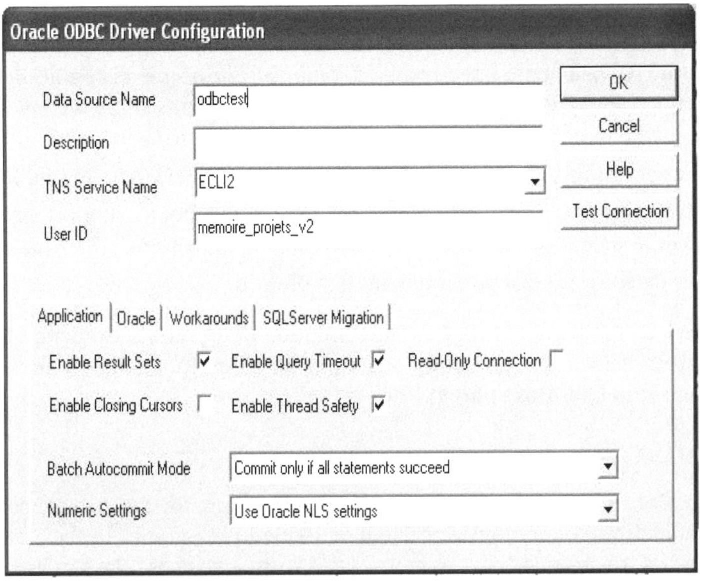

Figure 4: DataGenie Configuration

After typing the name and password of the user and after the configuration of the ODBC driver, we can access to the database containing all the information about the project memory. The DataGenie plugin has examined all the databases on oracle server. It does not give us the possibility to choice witch table/view/instance that we need to export. Also by using DataGenie plugin, it takes so much time for exporting. In fact, the use of DataGenie plugin, allow us to consult the data of our project memory and we can display all the entities and the instances from the head view ENTITY_VIEW as shown in the next figure:

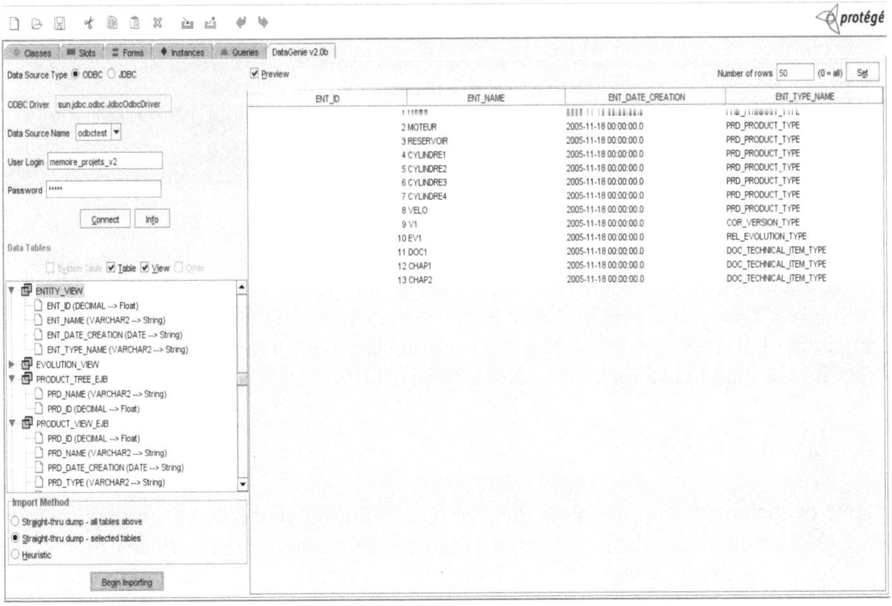

Figure 5: DataGenie Configuration

So now we can display all the class attributes and the instances. The ontology is ready for exploitation; we can update instances, add other instances, and class with the Protégé editor. A DataGenie have resolved a part of our needs: access to the database, export structures and data for building ontology but it presents some inconvenient:

- It can't give choice to the user for each table, view, or instance would like to export.

- User must wait the check of the entire database by DataGenie plug-in. It takes very

- Long time (in our case it was around One hour) before import process start.

It can't export instances or class after updating; it means the opposite way (from ontology to database) is not possible with this plug-in.

It's necessary to think and to find another solution that permits exchange data on the both way: from database to ontology and from ontology to database. In this context, we had recourse to OntoBase plugin.

3.4.3. An OntoBase Approach

The plug-in OntoBase use the interface of Protégé editor for the representation of the relational database like ontology and the data like a hyper-graph. In fact, each table of the database is represented by a meta-class with instances class representing the attributes and the constraints. The instances are created during the navigation in the hyper-graph **[30]**.

OntoBase can be downloaded; it's an OntoBase.zip file that we must decompress it in the root folder of Protégé editor. We introduce the Oracle server address, database name, user name and password and the driver JDBC as shown in the next figure:

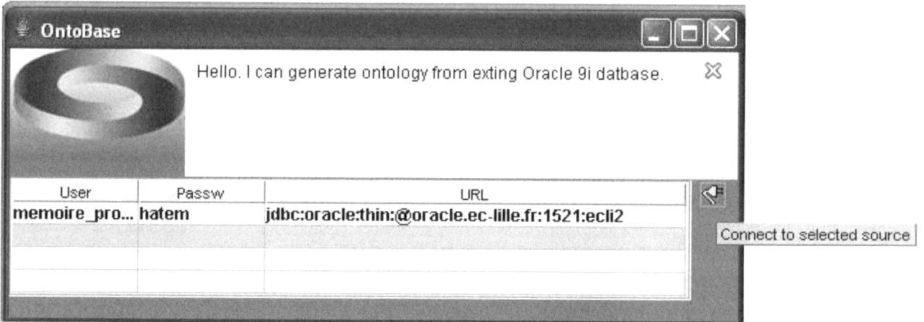

Figure 6: *Plugin OntoBase*

The principal problem that we have got by using OntoBase plugin is the long time for waiting the export of the database. We can see at the figure 6, in the OntoBase window a message: « I can generate Ontology from exting Oracle 9i database ». It's mean if we change the Oracle 9i by Oracle 10g we can't do the exportation because the Ontobase plugin is designed to use only with Oracle 9i platform.

4. Benefits of ontologies

In spite of the entire test, it's clear that the built ontology dedicated to project memory allow us to exploit the data. We have very easy and convivial interfaces of Protégé, opposite to database where it's necessary to develop the interfaces. It's the same advantages for updating and retrieving data.

We don't need any development; all the interfaces come with the Protégé platform. We can access to the ontology without any constraints. The ontology can be saved in different formats (HTML, OWL, XML, RDF, etc.) and exploited by other platform or software. Another advantages, consists of checking the syntax, reasoning using for example Racer Pro software.

5. Conclusion and future work

We have designed a generic framework suited for project memory management. We present its platform independent model, and explain its implementation over object-relational technology, in compliance with the model-driven application (MDA) paradigm. We discuss an extension of our work to support ontologies for project memory, and present its benefits. After the implementation, we present some ways for how to export the database dedicated Project Memory (structure and data) to another environment under Protégé platform, so our database become an ontology that we can exploit. In the near future, we aim at extending our work using another solution for export and to validate our work in an industrial context.

Acknowledgements

This study has been completed within the IS3C group on "Design System Engineering and Product Life Cycle" and supported by the GDR-MACS from the CNRS (http://www.univ-valenciennes.fr/GDR-MACS/).
The authors would thank their colleagues from the Industrial Engineering Department of the Ecole Centrale Paris, the Research team on Industrial Engineering from the Ecole Centrale Lille for their helpful comments during the whole process of this study.

References

[1] Ben Sta Hatem Contribution de la modélisation Conceptuelle a l'Ingénierie du Knowledge Management : Application dans le cadre de la mémoire de Projet, Thèse de Doctorat, Ecole Centrale de Lille, Lille, 2006.

[2] R. Dieng, O. Corby, A. Giboin and M. Ribière, "Methods and Tools for Corporate Knowledge Management", International Journal of Human-Computer Studies, 51:567-598, Academic Press, 1999.

[3] N. Matta, O. Corby and M.Ribière, "Méthodes de capitalisation de mémoire de projet", INRIA, Rapport de recherche n°3819, 1999.

[4] P.Malvache and P. Prieur, "Mastering Corporate Experience with the REX Method", Management of Industrial and Corporate Memory, ISMICK'03, Compiègne (France), pp.33-41, 1993.

[5] J.L. Ermine, M. Chaillot, P. Bigeon, B. Charenton and D. Malavielle, "MKSM a method for knowledge management", Knowledge management: organization, competence and methodology, ISMICK'96, Schreimenmakers ed., Rotterdam (Neederlands), pp.288-302, 1996.

[6] G. Schreiber, H. Akkermans, A. Anjewierden, R. De Hoog, N. Shadbolt, W. Van de Velde, B. Wielinga, "Knowledge engineering and management: The CommonKADS Methodology", The MIT Press ed., ISBN 0-262-19300-0, 1999.

[7] M. Klein, "Capturing Design Rationale in Concurrent Engineering Teams", IEEE, Computer Support for Concurrent Engineering, January, 1993.

[8] Conklin, 1998 J.E. Conklin and M.L. Begeman, "gIBIS: A Hypertext Tool for exploratory Policy Discussion", ACM Transactions on Office Informations Systems, 6:303-331, 1998.

[9] Buckingham Shum, 1997, "Negotiating the construction and reconstruction of organizational memories", Journal of Universal Computer Science, 3(8):899-928, 1997.

[10] J.J. Kasvi, M. Vartiainen and M. Hailikari, "Managing knowledge and knowledge competences in projects and project organizations", International Journal of Project Management, Pergamon ed., 2003.

[11] M. Jarke, Experience-based knowledge management: a cooperative information systems perspective, Control Engineering Practice Vol 10 (2002) 561 – 569.

[12] Ben Sta Hatem, Michel Bigand; Ghédira Khaled; Jean-Pierre Bourey: An approach of the project memory development using a diagram of conception; CCCT'05 (International Conference on Computing, Communications and Control Technologies); July 2005.

[13] OMG-Meta Object Facility Specification v1.4, July 2005.

[14] Gamma E., R. Helm, R. Johnson, and J. Vlissides, "Design Patterns: Elements of Reusable Object-Oriented Software", Reading, Addison-Wesley, 1995.

[15] Object Constraint Language Specification. OMG Unified Modeling Language specification version 1.5, http://www.OMG.org/uml, 2005.

[16] "Oracle Application Developer's Guide- Object-Relational Features", Release 2 (9.2), Part No. A96594-01, March 2006.

[17] T. R. Gruber, "A translation approach to portable ontologies", Knowledge Acquisition, 5(2):199-220, 1993.

[18] Ben Sta Hatem; Ben Said Lamjed; Ghedira Khaled; Michel Bigand, Jean Pierre Bourey Cartographies of ontology concepts; International Conference on Enterprise Information Systems(ICEIS); 2005.

[19] Baader, F., D. Calvanese, D. McGuiness, D. Nardi, 2003 "The Description Logics Handbook", *Theory Implementations and Applications*, Cambridge, 2003.

[20] D. McGuiness, F. VanHermalen, "OWL Web Ontology Language Overview", http://www.w3.org/TR/2004/REC-owl-features-20040210/, W3C recommendation, 2004.

[21] MDA_Ontology_ biblio, 2005, MDA et Ontologie : une bibliographie, Une Bibliographie, Pierre Parrend, 2005.

[22] Bezivin, J, Devedzic, V, Djuric, D, Favreau, J, Gasevic, D, and Jouault, F: An M3-Neutral infrastructure for bridging model engineering and ontology engineering, Springer, INTEROP ESA 2005.

[23] Gašević, D., Djurić, D., Devedžić, V., Damjanović, V., "Approaching OWL and MDA through Technological Spaces," In Prceedings of the 3rd Workshop in Software Model Engineering - WiSME2004 at 7th International Conference on the Unified Modeling Language: Modeling Languages and Applications, Lisbon, Portugal, 2004.

[24] Atkinson, Colin, 2004 Unifying MDA and Knowledge Representation Technologies Colin Atkinson, University of Mannheim, edoc 2004.

[25] www.omg.org/news/meetings/workshops/RT_2006_Workshop_CD/04-3-Tambe.pdf

[26] Objecteering, 2005, http://www.objecteering.com/, 2005

[27] JESS, 2004, www.ida.liu.se/~her/protege-reasoning-ws04/Wang.pdf (JESS)

[28] DataGenie, faculty.washington.edu/gennari/Protégé-plugins/DataGenie/Index.html, 2006.

[29] Protégé, 2006, protege.cim3.net/cgi-bin/wiki.pl?ProtegePluginsLibraryByType, 2006

[30] www.ontospace.net/pages/3/index.htm, 2006

New Trends in Software Methodologies, Tools and Techniques
H. Fujita and D. Pisanelli (Eds.)
IOS Press, 2007

Methodology of Building and Using Ontology for Providing Content-Based Access to Scientific Information Resources[1]

Yury Zagorulko[2], Olesya Borovikova[3]
AI Laboratory
A.P. Ershov Institute of Informatics Systems
Russian Academy of Science

Abstract. The paper is devoted to the discussion on the problem of provision of the content-based access to scientific information resources. We suggest solving this problem by means of creation of specialized topic-oriented Internet portals. The information basis of such portals is an ontology that supports integration of information resources relevant to the subject domain of a portal into a uniform information space and provides formulation of user queries in terms of the subject domain and knowledge-driven navigation through the information space of the portal.

Keywords. Scientific Information Resources, Content-based Access, Ontology, Knowledge Portal

Introduction

Recently, a great amount of scientific knowledge and information resources relating to various areas of knowledge has been accumulated in the Internet. However, the access to and the use of this knowledge and resources is rather complicated as they are disembodied and ill-structured, or distributed over various Internet sites, electronic libraries and archives.

At the same time, researchers need an efficient access to scientific papers and other information resources containing descriptions of methods and approaches developed in the framework of the branch of science interesting to them.

For example, increasing needs for natural language interfaces and facilities for automatic processing of documents necessitate content-based access to scientific papers and reports relating to this topic – various dictionaries, program components and algorithms implementing one or another task or stage of text or speech processing. (Here by the content-based access we mean the advanced semantic search and knowledge-driven navigation through information resources relating to a certain topic.)

---

[1] The authors are grateful to the Russian Foundation for the Humanities (grant 07-04-12149) for financial support of this work.
[2] 630090, Novosibirsk, RUSSIA, zagor@iis.nsk.su
[3] 630090, Novosibirsk, RUSSIA, olesya@iis.nsk.su

Traditional search engines are not able to provide such access to information resources. They usually return to user a flood of useless information. The reason for this is that the modern search engines use primarily keyword search mechanisms, which are insensitive to the query semantics, and index Web resources with virtually no tools for analysis of the information presented in them. Besides, as a rule, search engines do not provide convenient navigation through information resources that have been found.

In recent years, there have been attempts to provide semantic access to information allocated in Internet by means of using ontologies for describing the Web resource semantics. There are many examples of tools currently being developed for semantic annotation of Web-pages or documents, when each document is linked to its semantic content. Using such annotations, the intelligent search agents provide more relevant responses to a user query as compared to existing engines. For example, the SHOE system [1] supplies HTML documents with a set of special tags for knowledge presentation, and the Semantic Web initiative [2] presumes supplying documents with annotations in the RDF language [3]. There has been certain progress in this direction, however that does not improve the situation in general, since Web-pages annotated in such a manner are an infinitesimal drop in the sea of the Web.

Now, to solve the problem of content-based access to knowledge and data related to certain topic, the so-called Semantic Web Portals using ontologies and other components of Semantic Web technologies are developed.

For example, the Esperonto Portal [4] can serve as a source of information on state of the art of ontology research. For the Esperonto portal five different domain ontologies (Project, Documentation, Person, Organization and Meeting) were developed. Though these ontologies are connected through several relations, only direct attributes within a single ontology are considered for search.

The OntoWeb Portal [5] is a community portal for both academic and industrial partners who share an interest in the Semantic Web. The OntoWeb portal is structured according to an ontology which serves as a shared basis for supporting communication. OntoWeb community members can publish annotated information on the web, which is then crawled by a syndicator and stored in the portal knowledge base.

We should note that these two portals are aimed to description of projects and/or establishing communication between their participants and not oriented to presentation of scientific knowledge and resources.

It is worth mentioning one more portal that uses ontology-based approach. This is the semantic portal "MuseumFinland" that is intended for publishing collections of Finnish museums on the web [6]. The portal allows to perform navigation through and semantic search of cultural artifacts in these collections basing on seven domain ontologies. This is an excellent portal, but it, just as the above two portals, is not intended for providing effective access to scientific information resources.

To provide content-based access to information resources related to certain area of scientific knowledge we have suggested a conception and architecture of specialized Internet portals – knowledge portals [7] that must support:

1. A sufficiently complete and consistent representation of some branch of science, its components and various aspects of research activity (persons, organizations, events, methods, objects and results of researches etc.)
2. Integration of knowledge and information resources relating to a given branch of science into a uniform information space.

3.   Semantic search and effective content-based navigation through the integrated knowledge and information resources.

The users of the portal can be researchers, lecturers and students that teach or study one or another branch of science, as well as specialists, whose professional activity is concerned with this science.

To play such an important role, the portal must have not only flexible means for presentation of heterogeneous information, but also it must be adjustable to any area of knowledge as well as provide operative management of information content.

We could achieve the objectives and satisfy the requirements described above due to using ontology as a conceptual basis and information model of knowledge portal.

In this paper we would like to define cognitive, structural and functional requirements to ontology of knowledge portal as well as to discuss problems that arise in the process of its building and application.

1. General requirements to portal ontology

Before describing the requirements to (the) portal ontology we have to clarify what we mean by ontology.

We use the concept of "ontology" in such sense as it is used in computer science and artificial intelligence [8, 9]. We consider that one of the goals of ontology is to describe and to investigate entities that are assumed to exist in real world and/or in the human mind. For AI systems and, in particular, knowledge portals there exists only what is already represented or can be represented in them. Therefore we will follow the definition given in the paper [9]. According to it, the ontology is an explicit specification of conceptualization. Where conceptualization is an abstract, simplified view of the world serving a certain purpose. Conceptualization includes objects, concepts, and other entities that are assumed to exist in some area of interest, as well as the relationships between them.

It is worth stressing that paper [10] emphasizes that the ontology is a specification of conceptualization in its only part, which depends on some area of interest.

In paper [11] the ontology is considered as an agreement on the area of interests for achievement certain purposes.

Basing on the definitions presented above we can say that the ontology is an explicit specification (model) of some part of the world as applied to a specific area of interests. Later on we will follow this interpretation of ontology.

From the informal point of view the portal ontology serves for representing concepts that are required for the description of both research activity and scientific knowledge in whole and specific area of knowledge in particular.

Formally, the portal ontology is a group of six:

$<C, A, T, D, R, F>$, where

C – set of classes describing concepts of some subject or problem domain;

A – set of attributes describing simple properties of concepts;

T – set of standard types attribute values ("string", "integer", "real", "date");

D – set of "domains" (set of values of standard type "string");

R – set of relations defined on classes (concepts);

F – set of constraints defined on attribute values.

In context of this work, the ontology has to not only provide formal description of subject domain of the portal, but also support all necessary functionality, i.e. to serve as the basis for implementation of effective representation of diverse information relating to the portal topic and convenient content-based access to it.

To support an effective representation of subject domain knowledge the ontology must provide a description of concepts that have a complex structure, and diverse semantic relations between them. An important requirement to the portal ontology is the possibility of ordering subject domain concepts in a "generic-specific" hierarchy and supporting inheritance of properties through this hierarchy.

When describing concepts it must be taken into account that there exist such properties of concepts that can get concrete instance of other concepts as their values. Such properties are convenient to present in form of binary relations. Thus, from informal point of view, properties of concepts are both attributes and relations. Therefore to keep logical integrity of knowledge system both attributes of concepts-parents and relations defined on them must be inherited in concepts-descendants.

Since the ontology has to provide content-based declarative adjustment of the portal on given area of knowledge and support its whole functionality, it must be designed in such a way that it could be used for automatic generation of portal data base scheme, forms for filling data base, forms of query to DB as well as scheme of navigation through portal information space.

2. Ontology structuring

To meet the portal objectives, the ontology must be well-structured. Therefore the portal ontology is divided into domain-independent ontologies and subject domain ontology.

2.1. Base ontologies

Base ontologies are the ontology of research activity and the ontology of scientific knowledge (see Figure 1) that are independent from the subject domain of the portal.

The ontology of research activity is based on the ontology that was suggested in [12]. Practically, it is a top-level ontology and includes base classes of concepts related to the organization of research activities such as *Person (Scientist), Organization, Event, Activity, Publication.* These classes are used for describing participants of research activity, scientific events, research programs and projects, various types of publications and the materials represented in printed or electronic format (such as monographs, articles, reports, proceedings of conferences, periodicals, photo and video data, etc.). This ontology includes class Information resource that serves for describing information resources presented in the Internet.

The ontology of scientific knowledge is virtually meta-ontology. It states main structures that are used for building of subject domain ontologies describing specific areas of knowledge or branches of science. In particular, this ontology contains the meta-concepts specifying structures for the description of concepts of specific subject domain such as *Subdivision of science, Research method, Object of research, Scientific result.* Using these meta-concepts we can describe divisions and subdivisions that are significant for given science, determine classification of methods and objects of research, and describe results of research activity.

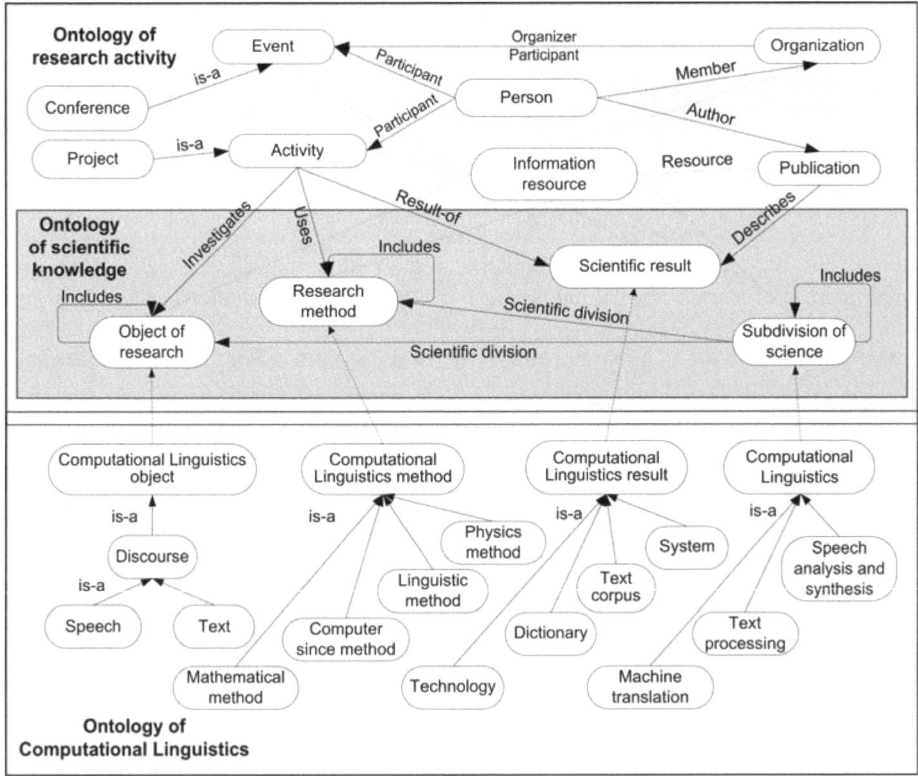

Figure 1. Fragment of ontology of computational linguistics

The concepts of ontology of scientific knowledge are interconnected with each other and well as with the concepts of ontology of research activity by associative relations, main of which are the following:

- "Scientific division" – links events, publications, organizations, persons or information resources with subdivisions of science;
- "Describes" – links publication with a scientific result, method or object of research;
- "Uses" – links research method with activity, person or organization;
- "Investigates" – attaches some activity to the object of research;
- "Result of" – serves for linking scientific results with the activity;
- "Resource" – links information resources with any concept of ontology.

2.2. Subject domain ontology

Subject domain ontology describes some branch of science. It is built for organization of effective access to information resources related to certain research area and also meets the requirements described in section 1.

The concepts of subject domain ontology, describing some branch of science, are at the same time realizations of meta-concepts of ontology of scientific knowledge and can be ordered in the "generic-specific" hierarchy.

For example, the ontology of computational linguistics (see Figure 1), which is under development now, includes four base hierarchies: Subdivision of science hierarchy, Research method hierarchy, Object of research hierarchy, Scientific results hierarchy.

Subdivision of science hierarchy based on classification of main theoretical directions of computational linguistics determines significant divisions and subdivisions of computational linguistics. Divisions of computational linguistics are *Machine translation, Text processing, Speech analysis and synthesis* etc. These general divisions are divided into more specific subdivisions. For example, *Machine translation* includes *Automatic* and *Automatized machine translation*.

Research method hierarchy serves for systematized description of various methods that are applied in computational linguistics. Here such groups of methods as *Linguistic methods, Computer Science methods, Mathematical methods* are distinguished.

Object of research hierarchy determines classification of objects of research. A discourse as base object of research is considered as form of existence and use of natural language. In particular, phonetic, syntactic and other linguistic phenomena are taken into consideration as well as such forms of discourse as *Text* and *Speech*.

Scientific results hierarchy serves for structuring and description of results of research activity. It includes such kinds of results as *Technologies, Systems, Dictionaries* and *Text Corpuses*.

All hierarchies of computational linguistics are connected by means of associative relations. One part of these relations is inherited from base ontologies, the other part of them is specific relations of given subject domain.

When building subject domain ontology, in particular, when choosing concepts and relations between them as well as defining the above mentioned hierarchies of concepts, it is necessary to take into account not only preciseness and completeness of the ontology description of the subject domain and related information resources, but also convenience of navigation through portal information space and content-based search.

3. Adjustment of the portal on given area of scientific knowledge

Adjustment of the portal to some area of scientific knowledge is performed with the help of ontology editor that allows one to create, modify and delete any elements of the portal ontology (classes, relations, domains, constraints) as well as define a mode of knowledge and data visualization.

When class is created, its parent can be selected from a set of already created classes. Thereby this class inherits from parent class not only all its attributes, but also its relations; whereas the parent class gets linked to a new class by "class-subclass" ("is-a") relation.

Classes of ontology can be linked by directed binary relations. The peculiarity of these relations is their (relations') ability to have own attributes that specify nature of link between arguments of relation. The relation has the following form:

R (Arg1, Arg2, Matr), where

R – name of relation, *Arg1, Arg2* – arguments of relation (classes of ontology), *Matr* – set of attributes describing additional properties of relation.

To make representation of information more convenient for user, possibility of adjustment of knowledge and data visualization is provided. For this purpose, templates of visualization of objects for each class of ontology and templates of visualization of reference to such objects are created.

A template of visualization of class objects contains all its attributes and all relations associated with it. By default, attributes of class and its relations are depicted in the same order as defined in the ontology; but the user can change this order.

A template of visualization of reference to class object can include both attributes of this class and attributes of classes that are linked with it by relations and attributes of these relations. Values of attributes included in this template are used for building text presentation of hyperlink to class object.

4. Management of information content of a knowledge portal

Introducing formal description of concepts of subject domain in the form of classes of objects and relations between them, portal ontology defines structures for presentation of real data and relations between them. The portal data themselves are presented as a set of linked information objects.

An information object (IO) is a structured aggregate of data presenting a description of a certain object of subject domain. Each IO corresponds to certain class of ontology (is the instance of this class) and has a structure defined by this class. There can exist connections between information objects. Semantics of these connections are defined by relations between corresponding classes of ontology.

Description of information resources is an important component of the information content of a portal. According to the definition of base ontologies from section 2.1, each resource corresponds to such concept of ontology as *Information resource*, and its description includes an instance of this concept (an information object) and a set of instances of relations that link this IO with other IOs and concepts of ontology.

The set of attributes and relations of *Information resource* is based on Dublin Core standard [13] and includes the following units: Title of the resource, Address in the Internet (URL), Subject of the resource, Resource type, Language, etc. Each resource can be linked by relations with persons, organizations, events, results of researches etc.

Thus, the information content of a knowledge portal includes both general knowledge (presented in ontology) and knowledge on concrete objects of subject domain (presented by information objects and relations between them).

Extension of information content of a knowledge portal can be performed in two ways that both use the ontology actively.

The first way assumes that extension of information content is performed by the expert with the help of data editor that allows one to create, modify and delete information object and relations between them.

Operation of data editor is based on portal ontology. Therefore when a new information object is created, first of all, the expert selects the corresponding class of ontology. Then based on description of this class a form for data input is automatically generated.

Simultaneously with the object creation, the expert can specify its connection with other objects already existing in the internal data base. These connections and their attributes are defined by the corresponding relations of ontology; and a form for their input is automatically generated on the base of description of these relations.

An important feature of conception of knowledge portal being proposed is its ability to not only provide the access to its own information resources, but also to support an effective navigation through relevant Internet resources. Information on these resources is accumulated by a special programme module – the ontology information collector working in automatic mode.

The ontology information collector performs the function of extracting knowledge and data from the Internet. It comprises two basic modules: the Internet document collection module and the semantic indexing and classification module.

The former provides the search of text resources or documents by keywords (that describe knowledge area of the portal) at Internet sites and pages, whose Internet links are stored in a special data base. This data base can be filled with new links both manually (by the expert) or automatically (with links found in downloaded documents). The module supports management of data base of downloaded documents.

The semantic indexing and classification module, using ontology and thesaurus, analyzes each downloaded document and builds its semantic index (semantic annotation) and defines to what subdivision of science it refers.

Semantic index of document (resource) contains a set of objects and relations that present its content in terms of portal ontology. For each document an information object – instance of class *Information resource* is built and linked with all objects included in its semantic index. All these objects and their relations are inserted in internal data base and become accessible for searching and navigation engine. In this manner, the information content of the portal can be automatically updated.

5. Providing content-based access to portal content

Content-based access to portal content provides advanced facilities for searching and navigation. Their operation is based on ontology.

5.1. Navigation

Navigation through portal information space is realized in accordance with the content of its ontology. Navigation engine provides transition from the concepts of ontology to their instances (information objects) and then transition along the ontological links (relations) from one information objects to others.

List of objects corresponding to the selected class of ontology is presented in a form of HTML-page containing a set of hyperlinks to these objects. For big lists a compound page including list of pages and facilities of navigation through this list is formed.

All the information on each concrete object and its connections is presented in the form of HTML-page. The format and content of this page depend on the class of the object and the template of visualization defined for this class. At the same time, the objects linked with a given object are presented at its page by their hyperlinks (a form and content of these hyperlinks are defined by the expert during the adjustment of visualization). Using these hyperlinks the user can proceed to their detailed description.

For example when we look through information on concrete publication we can see values of its attributes and its connections with other objects. Using presented connections as elements of navigation we can proceed to detailed information by both direct connections (on authors, on described object of research) and inverse connections (on information resource presented this publication).

When we move along a certain link of any information object we can get a rather big list of objects (for example, list of printed works of well-known scientist). To solve this problem, the procedure of filtration of lists was implemented.

The filter is a set of conditions that define admissible values of attributes of information object and requirements to existence of connections with other IOs. This method allows one to filter a set of publications by date (condition on attribute), by scientific result described in this publication or by object of research (conditions on object connected with given object).

5.2. Search

Due to the search being based on ontology, the user can formulate his query in terms of a portal subject domain. Basic elements of such query are concepts and relations of ontology as well as constraints on the data under the search.

Constraints on attribute depend on type of its values. For example, for attribute that has numeric type (type "integer") and date (type "date") an exact value or an interval of admissible values can be defined.

To define constraints on objects connected by associative relations with the sought object, the user has a possibility to define conditions on values of any attributes of connected objects. Thereby the user can define conditions on values of attributes of corresponding relations.

For example, the query "Find printed works on Text processing for period from 1970 to 1992 writing by Eduard Popov" will be presented as follows:

```
Class "Publication":
   Attribute "Date of publication": (>= 1970) & (<=1992)
   Relation "Author":
      Class "Scientist"
         Attribute "Family name" =  "Popov"
         Attribute "First name"  =  "Eduard"
   Relation "Scientific division":
      Class "Subdivision of Science"
         Attribute "Name of subdivision" = "Text processing".
```

Retrieval queries are formed by means of special graphic interface driven by portal ontology. When user selects a class of the sought information objects, retrieval form is generated where the user can define constraints on values of attributes of the sought object and objects connected with the sought object by associative relations.

So, the query presented above will be built as follows. At the beginning, the user will select a class of the sought object ("Publication") and define constraints on the attribute "Date of publication". Then the user will specify connections of the sought object: first, he will define that the sought object must be linked by relation "Author" with some object of class "Scientist" having the value of attribute "Family name" equal to "Popov" and the value of attribute "First name" equal to "Eduard"; next, the user will "link" the sought object by relation "Scientific division" with "Subdivision of Science" that is named as "Text processing".

6. Implementation

At present, the core of a portal (see Figure 2) including user interface, the search engine, the ontology and data editors, the ontology information collector has been implemented. The base ontologies also have been developed.

The user interface along with the search engine provides the users with ergonomic ontology-based representation of search queries and results, and with ontology-driven navigation through information space of the portal.

The ontology editor and data editor are implemented as Web-applications. Using these editors the expert can perform remote adjustment of the portal to required area of knowledge and form/manage its information content.

The ontology information collector performs extension of information content of the portal in automatic mode.

Internal database stores all local data, including information objects and their links with other objects, the indices of documents and the descriptions of information resources. To hold and manipulate data and knowledge, the database and Internet technologies and services are used.

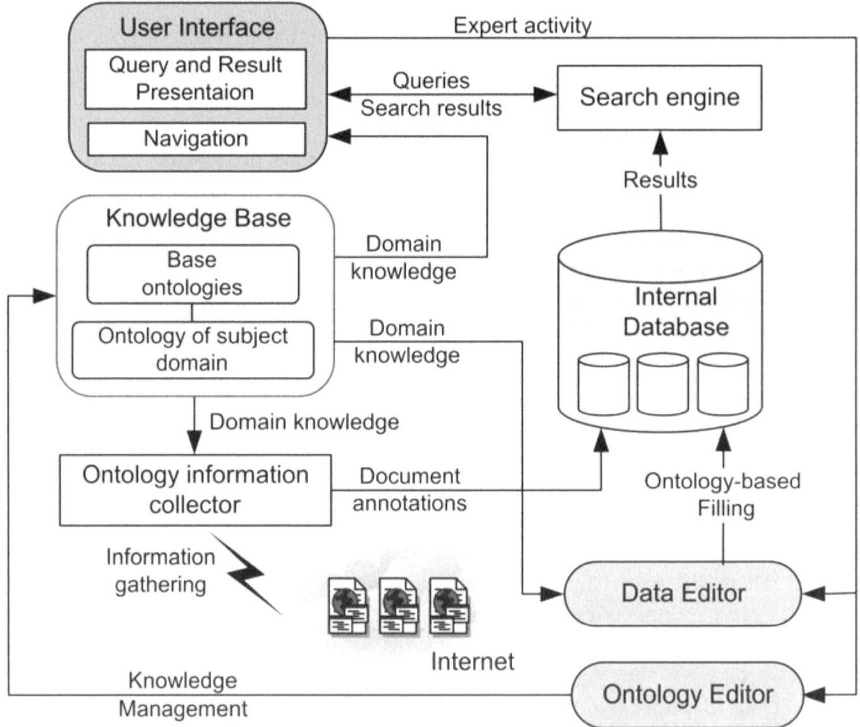

Figure 2. Architecture of the knowledge portal

Conclusions

The paper presents an approach to providing content-based access to scientific information resources on the base of ontology. Ontology ensures facilities for effective representation of diverse information on given subject, supports systematization and integration of relevant information resources and semantic access to them.

Ontology is used for automatic generation of a scheme of internal data base of the portal, forms for filling internal data base, forms for formulating query in terms of concepts and relations of ontology as well as a scheme of navigation through portal information space.

The structuring of portal ontology to domain-independent and subject domain ontology, makes the knowledge portal easily adjustable to any area of knowledge.

Due to using ontology as information model of a knowledge portal, it not only provides access to one more catalogue of information resources, also but supports semantic search in and convenient navigation through network of knowledge and data.

Based on the core of the portal, a specialized Internet portal providing semantic access to systematized knowledge and information resources relating to archeology has been successfully developed (Russian version of this portal is available at http://www.sati.archaeology.nsc.ru/classarch2/). This development demonstrates the soundness and productivity of the proposed approach. At present this approach is used for building a knowledge portal on computational linguistics.

References

[1] Heflin J., Hendler J. Searching the Web with SHOE // Artificial Intelligence for Web Search. — Menlo Park: AAAI Press, 2000, 35–40.

[2] Berners-Lee T., Hendler J., Lassila O. The Semantic Web // Scientific American. — 2001. — Vol. 284, N 5, 34–43.

[3] Brickley D., Guha R. RDF Vocabulary Description Language 1.0: RDF Schema W3C Recommendation 10 February 2004. — http://www.w3.org/TR/2004/REC-rdf-schema-20040210/

[4] Corcho O., Gómez-Pérez A., López-Cima A., López-García V., MC. Suárez-Figueroa. ODESeW. Automatic Generation of Knowledge Portals for Intranets and Extranets. LNCS 2870. The Semantic Web - ISWC 2003. Springer-Verlag, October 2003, 802-817.

[5] Spyns P., Oberle D., Volz R., Zheng J., Jarrar M., Sure Y., Studer R., Meersman R.. OntoWeb a Semantic Web Community Portal. In Proc. Fourth Int. Conf. on Practical Aspects of Knowledge Management (PAKM), December 2002, Vienna, Austria, LNAI 2569, Springer Verlag, 189-200.

[6] Hyvönen E., Salminen M., Kettula S., Junnila M. A Content Creation Process for the Semantic Web. Proceedings of OntoLex2004: Ontologies and Lexical Resources in Distributed Environments, May 29, 2004, Lisbon, Portugal.

[7] Zagorulko Yu., Borovikova O., Bulgakov S., Sidorova E. Ontology-based approach to development of adjustable knowledge internet portal for support of research activity // Bull. of NCC. Ser.: Comput. Sci. – 2005. – Is. 23.

[8] Guariano N., Giaretta P. Ontologies and Knowledge Bases. Towards a Terminological Clarification // Towards Very Large Knowledge Bases: Knowledge Building and Knowledge Sharing. – Amsterdam, IOS Press, 1995, 25–32.

[9] Thomas R. Gruber. Towards Principles for the Design of Ontologies Used for Knowledge Sharing // International Workshop on Formal Ontology, March, Padova, Italy, 1993.

[10] Mike Ushold, Michael Gruninger. Ontologies: Principles, Methods and Applications // Knowledge Engineering Review, Volume 11, Number 2, 1996.

[11] Takeda H., Takaai M., and T. Nishida. Collaborative development and Use of Ontologies for Design // Proc. of Tenth Inter. IFIP WG 5.2/5.3 Conference PROLAMAT 98, September, Trento, Italy, 1998.

[12] Benjamins V. R., Fensel D., et. all, 1998, "Community is Knowledge! in KA2", Proceedings of the KAW'98, Banff, Canada, 1998.

[13] Using Dublin Core. http://dublincore.org/documents/usageguide/

Chapter 3

Cognitive Modeling on Software Design and Natural Language Representation

New Trends in Software Methodologies, Tools and Techniques
H. Fujita and D. Pisanelli (Eds.)
IOS Press, 2007

The Art of Programming or Programs as Art

Ernest Edmonds
Creativity and Cognition Studios
Faculty of Information Technology
University of Technology, Sydney
Australia

Abstract The paper reviews developments in the implications of software programming in art practice whilst pointing to a recognition of the art in programming. The concerns in software-based art are significantly more conceptual than was often the case before. Following the Russian constructivist artists, the software artist is more concerned with the plan for making the work than for conventional rules of composition. The paper reviews a history of the author's use of various software representations in his art practice and proposes that art is all the richer for embracing software but, in so doing, the challenge to the artist is to be at least as deeply involved in software as in any other aspect of their practice.

1. The art of and in programming

The computer provides a significant enhancement to artists' ability work with the underlying structures of art works and art systems. New concepts and constructs have become available to us in ways that enable new forms in art. One significant such concept is generative art [1]. Here, the artist specifies their intentions and a computer program builds the artwork from that specification. Many new possibilities arise from this development and a number of challenges also present themselves. One such challenge is to find appropriate methods and notations in which to represent the specification of the artwork. These specifications amount to programs providing that they completely describe the generative processes involved.

Donald Knuth famously promoted programming as an art. In fact, he called his much read compendium "The Art of Computer Programming" [2]. This goes beyond a concern for just how the code looks, as in for example the Unix 'cb' command (C program beautifier). Software coding is itself an art. This art is mostly executed by software engineers who are deeply concerned with the technical aspect of their work. However, the design process that that they use has strong aesthetic values. If the resulting code control structure is like spaghetti, for example, it is not highly rated even if it performs its functions perfectly. In many ways the aesthetics of software design are derived from the aesthetics of formal mathematics, where brevity, elegance and clarity are much admired.

Hence, programming is well known as an art, but generative artists are turning computer programs *into* art.

However, as Cramer puts it:-

"While software, i.e. algorithmic programming code, is inevitably at work in all art that is digitally produced and reproduced, it has a long history of being overlooked as a conceptual and aesthetic factor" [3].

This paper attempts to address this overlooked issue.

2. Software and interaction design

Today, the majority of software is probably interactive. Hence, integral with the design of the algorithms embodied in the software is the design of the interactions that the 'user' will have with the system. This fact does not change the core nature of the art of programming, but it does extend the range of the issues of concern. Our desire for elegance (for example) in the algorithms and their expression in the code is extended to an additional desire for elegance in the interaction design and *its* expression in the code.

As before, concerns for the aesthetics of interaction design in computer programs go beyond user interface presentation design. The issues are to do with the abstract representation of interaction processes and the realization of those representations in software architectures and code. This area has been widely discussed in the field of human-computer interaction. A review of much of the foundation work is contained in the author's book 'The Seperable User Interface' [4].

Interaction design is, of-course, important for many artists working in this field. Hence, the following discussion of programs as art is directly concerned with the most complex and elusive topic of interactive programs as art.

3. Art theory and the implications of software

Jack Burnham was an extremely important early theorist in the area of software as art. As Shanken describes his concept:-

"He conceived of 'software' as parallel to the aesthetic principles, concepts, or programs that underlie the formal embodiment of the actual art objects, which in turn parallel 'hardware'" [5].

Shanken also quotes Kosuth explaining a key implication for art practice:-

"here meaning and value are not embodied in objects, institutions, or individuals so much as they are abstracted in the production, manipulation and distribution of signs and information." [5].

Burnham saw very significant implications for art in the developments of information technology. In particular, he saw art as being redefined, with a central concern moving to systems rather than objects.

"Information processing technology influences our notions about creativity, perception and the limits of art ... It is probably not the province of computers and other telecommunications devices to produce works of art as we know it, but they will, in fact, be instrumental in redefining the entire area of esthetic awareness" [6: p11].

"The central thesis of my book ... is that we are moving from an art centred upon objects to one focused on systems" [7]

In a later interview he drew a specific parallel between the concerns of the programmer with those of the artist:-

"all this business about recursion ... and I thought to myself, you know, this is the way artists think, you know" [8].

To return to a computer science viewpoint discussed above, von Neumann, discussing mathematical theorems, said:-

"... One also expects 'elegance' in its 'architectural' and structural makeup. These criteria are clearly those of any creative art ..." [9]

4. Conceptual art and software

In many visual art forms, for example painting, the artist works directly with the materials that form the final work. In traditional western music, on the other hand, the composer will normally work with a score, which is an abstract representation of their intentions. The adequacy of such representations largely depends upon the composer's ability to mentally map the notation to sound. Such mappings are difficult and sometimes very complex but, nevertheless, are direct and one-to-one. They are specified in a presentation notation, the process being an implicit linear progress in time. The one-to-one nature of the notation used makes it relatively easy to move between abstract and concrete representations of the music. However, this exact mapping between representations does not apply to generative art.

Perhaps the most obvious starting point for generative art was in the discussions of the General Working Group of Objective Analysis in 1921 in Moscow [10]. This was the beginning of the art movement generally known as Constructivism. The group drew a distinction between composition and construction in making their art. Briefly, composition was seen to be about arranging forms according to relationship rules and construction was about making a work according to a plan for its production. The discussions of the group were complex and they did not all take the same position. It is probably best understood through Gough's careful analysis of the composition/construction drawing pairs that the group made [11]. For our concerns, however, the key point was the introduction of the notion of making a visual art work according to a plan rather than by the application of rules of composition. In 1921, of-course, the plans were executed by the artists themselves, but in generative art they are executed by computers.

The art theorist, Goodman, drew an important distinction between what he called notional and non-notional works of art. In a novel, for example, he argued that any sequence of letters that corresponds with the original text is a genuine instance of the work. One might say that the essence of the novel is not the book object at all. It is in the 'notional object' that we access through the book [12]. He drew a distinction between execution, e.g. the writing of a novel and its implementation as a book [13].

Sol Lewitt made clear contributions to the practical realisation of conceptual art that made full use of the execution/implementation distinction without using software.

"In conceptual art the idea of concepts is the most important aspect of the work ... (t)he idea becomes a machine that make the art" [14].

Burnham, again, emphasises the importance of the 'invisible':-

"But since the early 1960s Hans Haacke has depended upon the invisible components of systems. In a systems context, invisibility, or even invisible parts, share equal importance with things seen" [15].

Of one artist he said:-

"I suggested ... that his pages of computer data ... were more intriguing than the resulting sculpture" [16].

The boundaries of art are changed by the advent of software. In practice, the software itself becomes a key component of the art (if not its core) and the art object becomes the implementation of the work in Goodman's meaning. In this sense, art becomes more conceptual than before.

"The traditional notion of consecrated art objects and settings will gradually give way to the conclusion that art is conceptual focus, and that the boundary conditions of form as process and system transcend the more literal notions of geometrically defined form" [16].

The art in software is increasingly recognized [17]. Software in art has been underrated, however. The artist's challenge is software, not because it is difficult but because it is the conceptual representation of the new art.

5. Representations: a personal history

5.1. Generative composition

In generative art, such as my video constructs [18], the composition is notated as a set of rules, constraints or logical structures, together with a computer program that automatically generates the artwork using them. There is an important distinction between the structures that define the work's progress in time and the mappings [19] from those structures to specific images and sounds. Whereas the former are not necessarily perceivable in the art object, the mappings directly result in the artwork as seen and/or heard. The terms process notation and presentation notation can be used to distinguish between the two distinct representations that correspond to defining the progress in time and the mappings respectively.

In generative artworks, the representations that artists create specify the rules that must be used in the process of realizing the work. These rules may be of many forms, such as constraints or contingencies, but in all cases they cannot be mapped by a simple one-to-one relationship onto the concrete artwork. Instead, they must be used together with some well-defined process, normally a computer program, in order to make the work. For example, the specification of a piece of music might be as a set of rules that govern the evolution of a given 'life' game [20]. It is specified in a process notation. This can give us the structure of the work, but then a one-to-one mapping must also be defined so as to select which sounds and sound features relate to the various aspects of the structures. For this reason, two forms of representation are required for generative works, both a presentation and a process notation. One notation relates abstract entities, which could be for example letters or numbers, to colours, shapes, sounds or other physical attributes of an artwork. The other notation specifies the rules by which the generation process should proceed. This second type of notation could, for example, be an algorithm that leads to a drawing or a process that produces an infinite piece of music. Whereas the implications of the first can be inspected and reviewed by placing the notation next to the physical elements, a list of numbered colours for example, the second has a more distant relationship to the final work. In generative art the artist may truly not know how the work will look or sound in detail until the generative process is performed.

5.2. Procedural representations

From 1968 and in the early 1970s, I used the procedural programming language, Fortran [21], in which to implement problem-solving algorithms used in art practice. From this experience, it became apparent by 1980, that the steps in the operation of a program, know as its 'trace', could be used to define a sequence of events. The process of the program running could be the centre of interest rather than the result that the program came up with. Thus, a computer program could be used to define a generative process for a time-based work. A significant issue was to find appropriate ways in which to specify work of this kind.

At around this time the Atari 400 and 800 computers appeared on the market [22]. They had, for the time, significant computer graphics capability built into their firmware. This could be accessed from the languages that were available for the machine. The key programming language available was Basic. In some respects, of-course, this was not unlike Fortran. However, there were also significant differences.

One difference was that Basic was an interpreted language rather than a compiled one. Interpreted representations seemed then, as they have since proved, to be extremely important in supporting creative system development. Just as the composer often sits at the piano and switches frequently between writing a score and listening to the equivalent sounds, so this flexibility of an interpreted language allows the artist to switch at will between composition and execution. All of the representations used subsequently have this property.

Another difference that applied to the Atari version was the integration of computer graphics functions. These were very significant for the production of generative visual work because it was possible to specify an algorithm that produced or modified graphical objects on the screen, as it was executed, instruction-by-instruction. Almost certainly, the main intention of the developers of this version of Basic was to enable programmers to construct static images and graphical user interfaces. However, because the changes to the images were made after each graphical instruction was executed, it was a system in which a time-based generative work could be specified in terms of the execution of a program.

In the Atari Basic representation, the presentation notation was direct and intuitive. The process notation, however, was that of a procedural programming language and, hence, was weak in expressing the rules that define the generative artwork. In any case, the Atari was limiting and it was necessary to move to other machines. I settled on the significant new machine of the time, the Apple Macintosh [23].

5.3. Logic

The next step was to recognize that logic programming could be used as a method for handling structures in time and as a more appropriate process notation. It can be used to make generative work in which the rules specified in logic control the form and order of a sequence of images. The sequence can potentially go on forever without loops, depending on the rules.

A further development has been the integration of audio and visual elements in the generative pieces. Whilst, at first, the Prolog-based notation was used together with more-or-less conventional scores for the music, recent work with sound artist, Mark Fell, has integrated the audio-visual production into a single generative process [24]. This work has raised new issues in the choice of notation, because of the added complexity, and a new approach has been developed based on Max/MSP [25]. The simple presentation notations used previously no longer seemed adequate. This was because of the need to specify both audio and visual elements and, in addition, to specify the sound processing that was to be used so as to but the specification into real-time effect.

5.4. Graphical representations

The Max/MSP system is a graphical object-based notation using familiar sound art constructs, such as patching, in its language. It is natural in this notation to provide sound, shape and colour pallets, whilst composing the code to determine exactly how those elements are employed on the screen and through the sound system. In this way, the presentation notation itself is divided into two parts: the pallets and the realization methods.

Max/MSP, on the other hand, does not include any logic programming constructs. However, it has not proved difficult to add appropriate elements to the system so that the equivalent to the earlier logic programming process notation can be incorporated into the Max/MSP environment.

6. Conclusion

It is very instructive that computer scientists consider programming an art. They see aesthetic issues as significant ones for their work. It is not altogether surprising from that point of view that programs can be seen as art. The important point, however, is that software art is a radical and relatively new step forward for art. Notwithstanding much said above, software art does not remove the importance of art objects anymore than an understanding of the 'executed object' that is the novel reduces the importance of the book. Rather, software art adds a conceptual dimension to art that changes the focus from a largely object oriented one to a broader and perhaps deeper systems oriented one. Art is all the richer for embracing software but, in so doing, the challenge to the artist is to be at least as deeply involved in software as in any other aspect of their practice.

7. Acknowledgements

This paper extends a discussion published in [18], which benefited from valuable comments by Linda Candy. Valuable comments were also made on a draft version of this publication by Hamido Fujita.

8. References

[1] Brown, P. (ed) "Special Issue on Generative Art". *Digital Creativity*, 14(1) (2003).

[2] Knuth, D. E, *The Art of Computer Programming*. Addison Wesley, Reading, MA. 1973-1998.

[3] Cramer, F. "Software Art and Writing". American Book Reviews, 18th August 2001.

[4] Edmonds, E.A (editor) *The Separable User Interface*. Academic Press, London, 1992.

[5] Shanken, E. A. "Art in the Information Age: Technology and Conceptual Art". *Leonardo*. 35(4). (2002) 433-438.

[6] Burnham, J. "Notes on Art and Information Processing" *Software Information Technology: Its New Meaning for Art. Burnham*, J. B. (ed) The Jewish Museum, New York, NY. 1971.

[7] Burnham, J. "Letter: Art's End". *New York Review of Books*. 20th November 1969.

[8]Dammbeck, L. "Excerpts from an Interview with Jack Burnham" 2001. *http://www.volweb.cz/horovitz/burnham/lutz-interview.html*. Last accessed 1.7.2007.

[9] Von Neumann, J "The Mathematician". *The World of Mathematics*. Newmann, J, R, (ed). Simon and Schuster, New York, NY. (1956) 2053-2063.

[10] Lodder, C. *Russian Constructivism*. Yale University Press. London. 1983.

[11] Gough, M. *The Artist as Producer: Russian Constructivism in Revolution*. University of Calafornia Press, Berkeley, CA. 2005.

[12] Goodman, N. *Ways of Worldmaking*. Hackett Publishing, Indianapolis, IN.1978.

[13] Goodman, N. "Implementation of the Arts". *Journal of Aesthetics and arts Criticism*. 40. (1982) 281 283.

[14] Lewitt, S. "Paragraphs on Conceptual Art". *Theories and Documents of Contemporary Art*. Stiles, K. and Selz, P. (eds). University of California Press, Berkeley, CA. (1996) 822-825.

[15] Burnham, J. "Systems Esthetics". *Artforum* 7(1). (1968) 30-35.

[16] Burnham, J. *On the Future of Art*. Viking, New York, NY. 1970.

[17] Fishwick, P. A. (ed). *Aesthetic Computing*. MIT Press, Cambridge, MA. 2006.

[18] Edmonds, E. A. *On New Constructs in Art*. Artists Bookworks, Forest Row, East Sussex. 2005.

[19] Doornbusch, P. "Composers Views on Mappings in Algorithmic Composition". *Organised Sound* 7(2) (2002) 145-156.

[20] Gardner, M. The fantastic combinations of John Conway's New Solitaire Game of 'Life'. *Scientific American* 223(4) (1970) 120-123.

[21] Katzan,H. *Fortran 77*, Van Nostrand Reinhold Co, 1978.

[22] *http://oldcomputers.net/atari400.html*. Last accessed 1.7.2007.

[23] *http://www.apple.com*. Last accessed 1.7.2007.

[24] Edmonds, E. A. and Fell, M. "Broadway One". *Electronic Art and Animation Catalogue, SIGGRAPH2004*. ACM Press, New York. (2004) 30.

[25] *http://www.cycling74.com*. Last accessed 1.7.2007.

New Trends in Software Methodologies, Tools and Techniques
H. Fujita and D. Pisanelli (Eds.)
IOS Press, 2007

A Remark on Natural Language Processing from the Biolinguistic Perspective

Anna Maria DI SCIULLO
Université du Québec à Montréal

Abstract. In this paper, I discuss basic elements of the biolinguistic approach to language and language processing. First, I provide evidence that linguistic expressions have hierarchical structure where asymmetric relations hold. Second, I relate biolinguistics to language processing, and I discuss central aspects of natural language processing based on the properties of natural languages. Third, I identify some connections between biology, language, and information processing.

Keywords. Biolinguistics, natural languages, natural language processing, hierarchical functional structure, pronominal anaphora resolution

1. Language

1.1. Recursion and Hierarchy

Recent works on the language faculty [1], [2], suggest that the narrow syntactic component of the language faculty (FLN) satisfies conditions of highly efficient computation, and could be close to an optimal solution to the problem of linking the sensori-motor (SM) and the conceptual-intentional (CI) systems.[1] In other words, the language system would provide a near optimal solution that satisfies the interface conditions of interpretability.

According to [1], recursivity is the central property of FLN and is part of the genetic endowment that makes humans capable of developing a grammar on the basis of experience. The recursive operation Merge, (1), applies to pairs of elements and generates linguistic expressions which take the form of hierarchical structures, (2). Merge sub-divides into external and internal Merge. External Merge applies to two syntactic objects and forms a new object; internal Merge displaces an already merged syntactic object. In (2), the material in < > is the silent copy of a displaced syntactic constituent. In this configuration, Subject is abbreviated to Sub, Object to Obj, Verb to

---

[1] The FLN corresponds to overt syntax, and differs from the language faculty in a broad sense (FLB), which includes the external systems, CI and SM.

V, and Tense to T, where VP stands for Verb Phrase and TP stands for Tense Phrase. The hierarchical structure generated by Merge is interpreted by the semantic rule of Functional Application, (3).

(1) *Merge*:   Target two syntactic objects α and β, form a new object Γ $\{\alpha,\beta\}$, the label LB of $\Gamma(LB(\Gamma)) = LB(\alpha)$ or $LB(\beta)$. [3]

(2) [$_{TP}$ Sub   T   [$_{vP}$ <del>Sub</del> > v [$_{VP}$ V   Obj]]]

(3) *Functional Application:*   If α is a branching node and $\{\beta,\gamma\}$ the set of its daughters, then, for any assignment g, $\|\alpha\|^g = \|\beta\|^g(\|\gamma\|^g)$. [4]

The computational efficiency of FLN should be part of an efficient natural language processing system. I illustrate this on the basis of the processing of expressions found in medical texts, [5], [6], [7], [8].

1.2. Functional Structure

Sentence processing systems should rely on the rich properties of the hierarchical structure derived by Merge. In languages such as English, a sequence of substantive words cannot be interpreted without being part of a hierarchical structure headed by functional categories, such as prepositions and determiners.[2] Consider the following examples, where PP stands for prepositional phrase and VauxP stands for auxiliary phrase.

(4)   a.   Ticlopidine is a potent inhibitor for CYP2C19.

      b.   [$_{TP}$ [$_{DP}$Ticlopidine] [[$_{T}$ is [$_{vauxP}$ <del><is></del> [<[$_{DP}$ <del>Ticlopidine</del>]> [$_{DP}$ a potent inhibitor]]]] [$_{PP}$ for [$_{DP}$ CYP2C19]]]]

(5)   a.   Ticlopidine potent inhibitor CYP2C19

      b.   [Ticlopidine] [potent] [inhibitor] [CYP2C19]

The syntactic expression in (4a) is straightforwardly interpretable, whereas the expression in (5a) is not. Namely, the expression in (4a) is interpreted by the application of Functional Application to the constituents of the syntactic structure in (4b). In contrast, the interpretation of the expression in (5a), consisting of a set of words unrelated to one another, is undetermined. Given that its functional structure is lacking, it cannot be interpreted as a proposition, i.e., it cannot be assigned a value, true or false, with respect to a domain of interpretation D.

Functional structure is a necessary ingredient in natural language processing by humans. Without functional hierarchical structure, it would be impossible for humans to identify the abstract relations between the parts of a linguistic expression, and to

---

[2] The set of functional categories includes all the grammatical categories, but not nouns and verbs. In information processing systems, such as Information Retrieval systems, the functional categories are considered to be stop words, and are eliminated from processing.

compute the interpretation of a linguistic expression on the basis of the semantics of its parts.

1.3. Asymmetric Relations

Asymmetric relations, such as the asymmetric c-command relation, play a central role in the representations generated by the grammar.[3] The following paragraphs illustrate the role of asymmetry in selection, displacement, and interface conditions.

1.3.1. Selection

Selectional relations, such as the relation between a verb and its complement, map onto hierarchical structure, where asymmetric relations hold.

The selection relation is a local relation holding between a head H and its complement C. H asymmetrically selects the head Z of C. Such a relation does not hold between a head H and the head W of a constituent superior to H. For example, in (6a), the auxiliary verb *is* selects for the complex DP including the DP [a potent inhibitor] and does not select for the complement of the preposition *for*, i.e., the DP [CYP2C19] which is generated higher in the structure and thus is not asymmetrically c-commanded by the auxiliary verb. If this were the case, the PP [$_{PP}$ for [$_{DP}$ CYP2C19]] would wrongly (*) be predicted to be a complement of the auxiliary verb, as in the structure (6b).

(6)   a.   [$_{TP}$ [$_{DP}$ Ticlopidine] [[$_T$ is [$_{vauxP}$ <is> [< [$_{DP}$ ~~Ticlopidine~~]> [$_{DP}$ a potent inhibitor]]] [$_{PP}$ for [$_{DP}$ CYP2C19]]]]]

      b.   *[$_{TP}$ [$_{DP}$Ticlopidine] [$_T$ is   [$_{vauxP}$ <is> [< [$_{DP}$ ~~Ticlopidine~~]> [$_{PP}$ for [$_{DP}$ CYP2C19]]]]]

1.3.2. Displacement

Displacement of constituents is observed in natural languages. For example, in question formation and in passive formation, a constituent originating in the post-verbal position is displaced in the left periphery of the sentence. Displacement is subject to the asymmetrical c-command relation between the displaced constituent and its copy, which is the initial position of the displaced constituent. Whereas a selected constituent is externally merged as a sister to another constituent, a displaced constituent can only be internally merged to a position higher than the position to which it was externally merged. For example, in (7)-(9), the displaced constituent asymmetrically c-commands its copy; whereas it does not in * (10).

---

[3] In syntactic representations, the precedence, dominance, and asymmetric c-command relations are the more common asymmetric relations. The definition of C(onstituent)-command, and asymmetric c-command are the following:

C-command: X c-commands Y iff X and Y are categories and X excludes Y, and every category that dominates X dominates Y. [9]

Asymmetric c-command: X asymmetrically c-commands Y, if X c-commands Y and Y does not c-command X. [9]

(7) a.   [_TP_ [_DP_ Ticlopidine] [[_T_ is [_vauxP_ <is> [<[_DP_ ~~Ticlopidine~~]> [_DP_ a potent inhibitor]]]
      [_PP_ for [_DP_ CYP2C19]]]]]

      ←

   b.   [_TP_ [_DP_ A potent inhibitor for CYP2C19] [_T_ is [_vauxP_ <is> [[_DP_ Ticlopidine]
      <[_DP_ ~~A potent inhibitor for CYP2C19~~] >]]]]

      ←

(8)   [_TP_ They discovered [[_DP_ genes] of [<[_DP_ ~~genes~~] > [_DP_ this type]]]]

      ←

(9)   [_TP_ They discovered [[_DP_ this type] of [[_DP_ genes] < [_DP_ ~~this type~~] >]]]

      ←

(10) *[_TP_ <[_DP_ ~~Ticlopidine~~]> [_T_ is [_vauxP_ <is> [<[_DP_ Ticlopidine]> [_DP_ a potent

   inhibitor]]]]   →

The examples above illustrate the fact that the operations of the grammar of natural language derive the hierarchical functional structure underlying the linguistic expressions, where asymmetric relations hold.

1.3.3. Interface Conditions

The operations of the grammar derive interface representations interpretable by the external systems, CI and SM. Given the central role of asymmetry in the derivations, one of the interface conditions takes the following form in Asymmetry Theory [10].

(11)   *Interface Interpretability Condition*: Elements in asymmetric relations are optimally interpretable by the performance systems.

Since asymmetry is part of the expressions derived by the grammar, it does not come as a surprise that asymmetric relations are part of the interfaces between the expressions derived by the grammar and the external systems.[4] According to Asymmetry Theory, FLN is the best solution to the interface interpretability conditions because the asymmetry of linguistic expressions matches with the asymmetry of the external systems.

Asymmetry Theory has implications for natural language technologies, including Information Retrieval, and Question Answering. The expressions of natural languages cannot be thought of in terms of ad-hoc sets of words, as it is often the case in natural language processing technologies. The processing of the asymmetric properties of linguistic expressions enables any area where human users can benefit by communicating with their computers in a natural way.[5]

---

[4] According to [2], [11], efficient computation is a factor external to the core properties of the language faculty that contributes to the efficiency of the language design. The interface conditions and the local economy conditions contribute to eliminate complexity, such as choice points, in the course of the derivation and at the interfaces.

[5] Computational implementations of asymmetric relations are available. For example, the asymmetric c-command relation is part of Marcus's parser [12], as well as Government and Binding computational implementations [13], [14], [15], [16], and the recent works on asymmetry and minimalism [17], [18], [19],

2. Language Processing

Experimental evidence reported in [21] shows that cotton-top tamarins have the parsing abilities of Finite State Grammars (FSG), but not Phrase Structure Grammars (PSG). Thus, according to [21], contrary to human primates, cotton-top tamarins cannot process abstract constituent structures and long distance dependencies.

(12) Finite state grammar

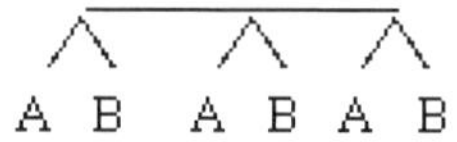

(13) Phrase structure grammar

Chomsky argues that portions of English cannot be described by FSG. FSG may describe local relations, such as local agreement in English, (14), but it cannot describe long distance dependencies, (15).

(14) a. At 373 K, [the mesophilic protein unfolds] rapidly.
      b. [Biophysics proteins unfold] in steps.

(15) a. [The FOX12 gene] did not reveal [itself] sufficient to account for the emergence of language.
      b. The FOX12 gene, much discussed in the recent literature, did not reveal itself sufficient to account for the emergence of language.
      c. The FOX12 gene, which was discovered recently, did not reveal itself sufficient to account for the emergence of language.

There are at least two descriptive advantages of PSG. First, they apply to categories that are not physically manifested in linguistic expressions, and thus they introduce structure. Second, they can relate elements that are distant from one another, such as pronominal anaphors and their nominal antecedents, as in (15a). In several cases, natural language processing technologies process language with FSG. This is the case for stemmers based on Porter's algorithm, as well as finite state part-of-speech taggers, and sentence analyzers. The technologies are not optimal, since there are sorts of linguistic expressions that they cannot analyze, in particular the expressions that include non-local relations between constituents. Given Chomsky's hierarchy of formal grammars, the descriptive power of PSG properly includes the power of FSG, and the descriptive power of Generative Transformational Grammar (GTG) properly includes the descriptive power of PSG. The incorporation of a grammar that has at least the power of FSG contributes to the optimization of natural language processing technologies.

---

[20]). A computational model based on the recovery of asymmetric relations leads to a new paradigm in natural language processing.

2.2. Word Processing

In a biolinguistic approach to natural language processing, systems that process complex lexical terms, find equivalences between words, and relate generic and common names, for entities such as genes, for example, must include recursive rules that generate the abstract hierarchical structures. The morphological hierarchical structure expresses the restrictions on precedence and scope between affixes, for example, the fact that the sequential affix *re-* scopes over the directional affix *en-* in a verb such as *reencode*. Moreover, new compounds including recursive constituent modification, such as *non-human offspring primate*, cannot be generated by a grammar that has less generative power than a FSG. Efficient processing of complex words requires the recovery of the underlying hierarchical structure that supports the semantic interpretation, as discussed in [22], [23]. A morphological parser recovering the hierarchical structure as well as the semantic relations between parts of words is described in [24].

2.2. Sentence Processing

Given the biolinguistic approach to language processing, the analysis of sentences requires recursive operations that generate abstract hierarchical structures, where asymmetric relations between the parts of the linguistic expressions are taken into consideration.

In languages such as English, the linear order of the syntactic constituents plays a role in the syntactic well-formedness as well as in the semantic interpretation of a linguistic expression. Consider the examples in (16).

(16) a. Ticlopidine is a potent inhibitor for CYP2C19.
      b. CYP2C19 is a potent inhibitor for Ticlopidine.

The difference between (16a) and (16b) reduces to a difference in the linear order of two nominal constituents *Ticlopidine* and *CYP2C19*. Yet the semantic interpretation of these expressions differs dramatically: the expressions in (16) cannot be both true in the same world of interpretation D. If the proposition in (16a) is true in D, then the proposition in (16b) is false. Thus efficient computation that meets the interface interpretability condition requires that the linear order of the constituents of linguistic expressions be taken into consideration, the precedence relation being an asymmetric relation. Furthermore, the processing of functional words, such as *a*, *for*, and *of*, is crucial in languages such as English. Such languages lack the rich morphological case system of other languages such as Modern Arabic and the Slavic languages. In languages such as English, prepositions and determiners induce case/semantic relations and generic/specific reference. For example, the presence of the preposition *for* in (16a) prevents the DP [CYP2C19] to be interpreted as part of the constituent in the subject position, i.e., the DP [Ticlopidine]. The semantic inclusion relation between these constituents could be conveyed if the preposition immediately dominating CYP2C19 in (16a) were the preposition *in* instead of the preposition *for*. Likewise, the indefinite determiner *a* c-commanding the constituent *potent inhibitor* in (16a) does not convey a restricted interpretation for the constituent of which it is part, as should be the case with the definite determiner *the*. Thus linear order, hierarchical constituent structure, and the properties of the specific functional elements must be analyzed in efficient language processing that meets the interface interpretability condition.

Functional hierarchical structure is also necessary in efficient natural language parsing and understanding. The underlying functional structure of propositions is recovered by the LAD parser, [18], as can be see with the trace in (17) is executed by the LAD.

(17)

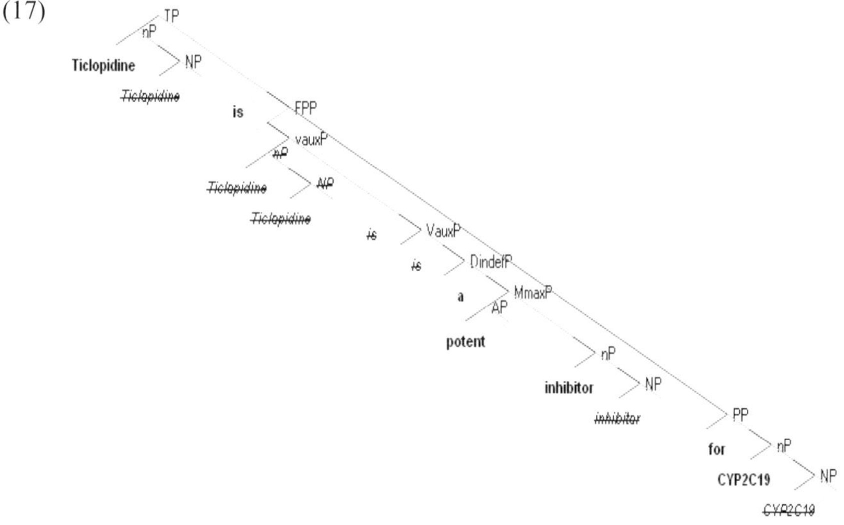

The LAD parser ensures the recovery of the asymmetric relations that are part of the hierarchical structure of linguistic expressions by performing a top-down left-to-right analysis of sentences.

2.3. Pronominal Anaphora Resolution

The ability to process long distance relations between pronouns and their antecedents is part of the near-optimal solution of the language design that meets the interface interpretability conditions.

Efficient computation of pronominal anaphora resolution also requires the processing of the underlying hierarchical structure between the parts of linguistic expressions, as discussed in [25]. For example, in (18b), the antecedent of the possessive pronoun *its* is the DP [CYP2C19's potent inhibitor] that asymmetrically c-commands that pronoun, and not a part of that DP, which does not asymmetrically c-commands the pronoun, i.e., the DP [potent inhibitor], see (19), a trace of (18b) of the LAD parser.

(18) a. Ticlopidine is a potent inhibitor for CYP2C19.

   b. [$_{DP}$CYP2C19's [$_{DP}$potent inhibitor]] manifests its effects.

(19)

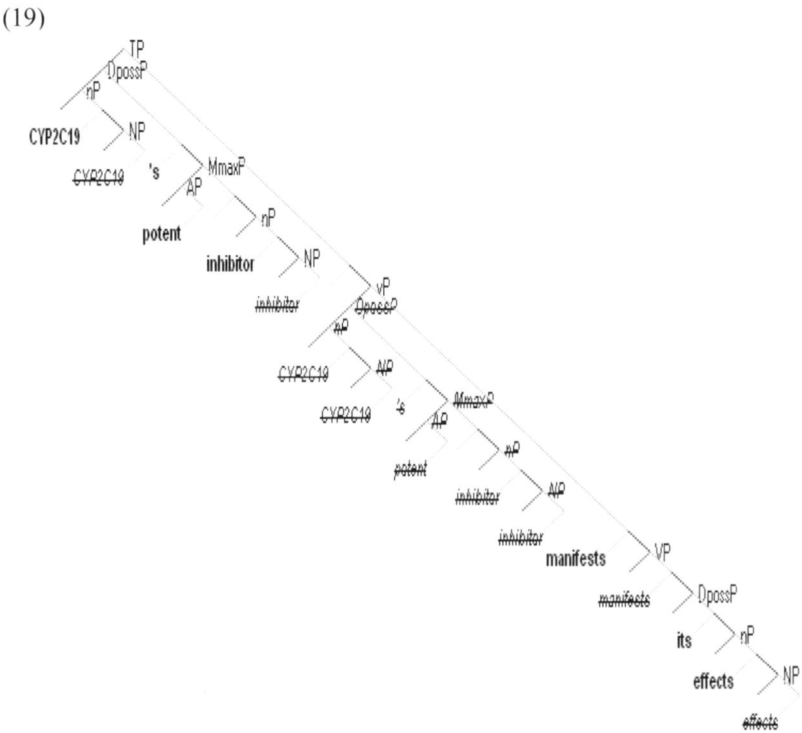

The recovery of the asymmetric relations underlying linguistic expressions must be part of efficient natural language processing systems that meet the interface legibility condition. These systems cannot mainly be based on string-linear proximity relations, but require fine-grained representations provided by parsers such as the LAD parser.

3. Linguistics, Biology, and Language Processing

The biolinguistic approach to language and language processing brings about convergences between linguistics, biology, and information processing. Given that the characteristic property of the FLN is recursivity, and that language processing by humans is based on the processing of abstract hierarchical structures, efficient information technologies process human languages on the basis of recursive operations and properties of hierarchical structures.

3.1. A Misleading Connection

The connection between linguistics, biology, and information processing is, more often than not, based on current practice in information technologies rather than on the properties of FLN.

For example in [26], an analogy is drawn between feature selection in language and feature selection in biology. The analogy is based on the assumption that substantive words (such as *ball, glove, bat, basket*) differ fundamentally from functional words (such as *a, to, the*). Some substantive words (e.g., *ball*) identify the relatedness of documents, while other substantive words (e.g., *glove, bat, basket*) identify their differences. Functional words (e.g., *a, to, the*) are irrelevant for distinguishing the documents from each other and from unrelated ones.

According to [26], word equivalents used in protein sequence language are short stretches of amino acids. Only some amino acid positions are useful in distinguishing different subtypes of a protein-coupled receptor, while the helices (center) are common to all protein-coupled receptors. Other areas cannot be distinguished from any other protein. See (20).

(20)

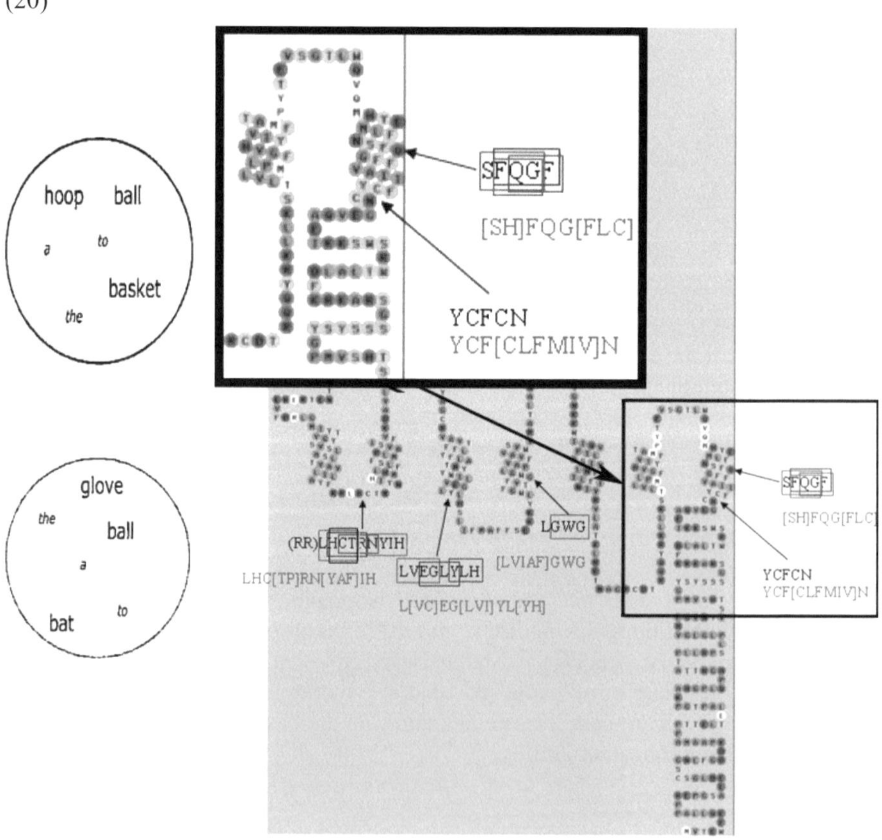

Almost all existing Information Retrieval systems simply represent documents and queries as 'bag-of-words'. Several problems are tied to the simple 'bag-of-words' representation of documents, including the problems related to natural language understanding, e.g., word-sense identification, sentences and texts interpretation processing. The bag-of-words approach to information processing does not take into account the asymmetry of linguistic relations. Consequently the relations between the substantive words and other substantive words mediated by the functional elements are lost, and with them the semantic content conveyed by the expressions of which they are part.

3.2. Promising Convergences

Contrastingly, promising convergences between linguistics, biology, and information technologies take into consideration the properties of the FLN, including the processing of hierarchical asymmetric relations. The recovery of asymmetric relations constitutes a near optimal solution to the semantic interface conditions.

I will point out some promising convergences between linguistics, biology, and information processing in the following paragraphs, taking into consideration Asymmetry Theory, evolutionary developmental biology (evo-devo), and information technologies.

3.2.1. Modularity

The fully parallel model of the language faculty defined in [9] is the expression of the modularity of living organisms. According to Asymmetry Theory, morphological derivations are parallel to syntactic derivations. Morphological and the syntactic operations share the generic properties of the language faculty, while they differ with respect to the instantiations of these properties. Thus, the generic Merge operation, enabling the infinitude of language, is customized to apply in different modules (computational spaces). When it applies in the morphological module, it applies to elements that already have asymmetric properties, affixes and roots. When it applies in the syntactic module, the morphological structure is no longer available for syntactic computation.[6]

A modular architecture is observed in biological systems according to evolutionary developmental biology. One of the elemental ideas of evolutionary developmental biology is that plants and animal bodies are organized into developmentally and anatomically distinct parts. Often these parts are repeated, such as fingers, ribs, and body segments. Evo-devo seeks to understand the genetic and evolutionary basis for the division of the embryo into distinct modules, and for the partly independent development of such modules.

The human brain is also organized in different modules, each module with specialized functions, as illustrated below. From a biolinguistic perspective, the language faculty is biologically grounded, and thus its architecture is modular. This

---

[6] However, a fully modular architecture of the language faculty, where morphology and syntax are distinct modules (with restricted interactions between the derivations) is not assumed in other theories. This is not the case, for example, for Distributed Morphology [27], according to which morphological and syntactic derivations coincide.

view is opposed to non-modular views, such as the ones developed in connectionist models [28], [29], [30].

(21)

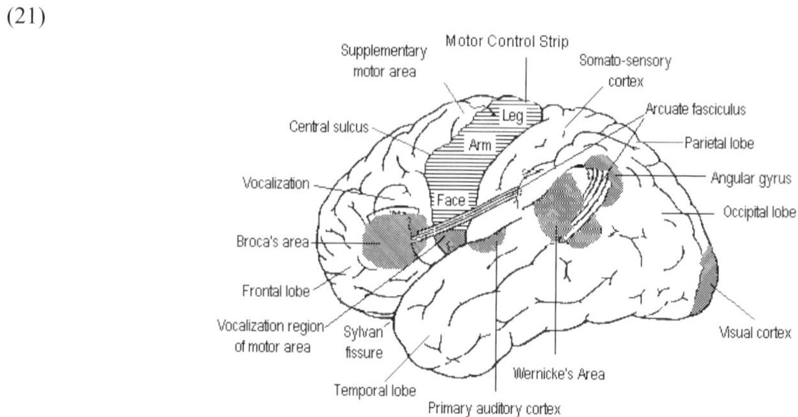

Modularity is also part of the architecture of most information processing systems, including Information Retrieval (e.g. Google) and Question Answering (ex. Start system). The question that arises is the level of granularity of the modular architecture. Generally, the architecture of natural language processing systems is based on coarse modularity. For example, the architecture of Information Retrieval systems includes simple modules for stemming, part-of-speech tagging, and in some cases super-tagging. However, these modules do not perform fine-grained analyses of linguistic expressions. This is also the case for Discourse Anaphora Resolution Systems, such as MARS [31], which includes different modules, but performs shallow parsing only.

From a biolinguistic perspective, the incorporation of the fine-grained modular architecture of the broad language faculty (FLB), including the narrow faculty of language (FLN) and the external systems, the conceptual-intentional (CI) system and the semsori-motor system (SM) (22), leads to the optimalization of natural language processing systems.

(22)

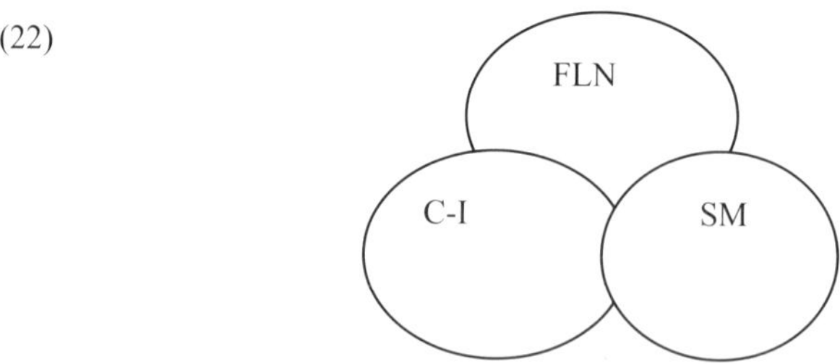

According to [25], the modules of a Discourse Pronominal Anaphora Interpreter (DPAI) include a Sentence Delimiter (SD) that sequentially identifies each sentence of a discourse, preserving the asymmetric precedence relation between the propositions, see (23). The DAI analyses each proposition from left to right with the following modules. The Constituent Boundary Identifier (CBI) and the Relation Recoverer (RR) identify the formal and semantic feature structure of the DPs and the DPros (strong and weak), and the asymmetric c-command relations between them. The Argument Structure Delimiter (ASD) identifies the domains of argument structure asymmetries.

The Discourse Linker (DL) implements the operations of Asymmetry Theory. The output yields an annotated discourse with pronominal anaphora resolution.

(23)   Architecture of Discourse Pronominal Anaphora Interpreter (DPAI)

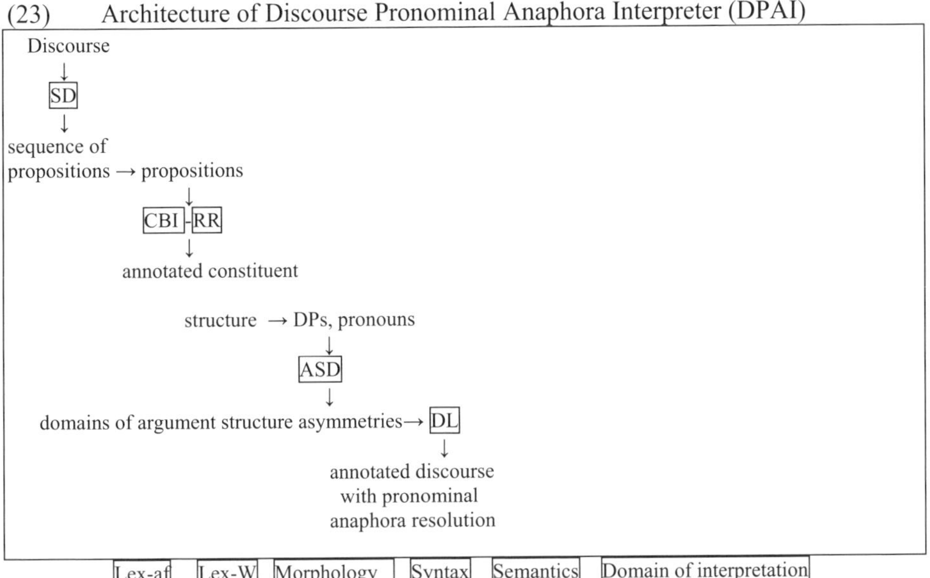

This fine-grained modular architecture contrasts with discourse anaphora resolution systems, such as [31], which do not include fine-grained syntactic modules identifying the local domains of argument structure asymmetries. Most discourse anaphora resolution systems operate on shallow parsing and do not go beyond the analysis of nominal constituents.

The DPAI relies on morphological-syntactic-semantic properties and asymmetric relations. It identifies necessary and possible antecedents for pronouns in linguistically determined domains of argument structure asymmetries. For example, in (24), the DAI will assign no antecedent to the expletive pronoun [it] occurring in the second sentence, whereas it will identify the DP [the company] in the first sentence as a possible antecedent for the pronoun [it] occurring in the third sentence.

(24) [The company] was making progress. [It] seemed as if the market was not ready
      for a breakthrough. However, [it] sold the new X-software very well.

The DPAI contrasts with so-called "knowledge-poor" pronominal anaphora resolution, such as [31], [32]. It develops the view that pronominal anaphora resolution is basically determined by linguistic knowledge, and its architecture is highly modular.[7]

3.2.2. Asymmetry

Asymmetrical relations (hierarchies, structure dependencies) are hard-wired in the grammar and are part of the derivation of words and propositions. They are also part of the genetic system (structure of genes),and widespread in the human biological system (Sylvian fissure in the human brain), as well as more generally in nature (Fibonacci numbers: 1,1,2,3,5,8,13,21,34,56 in the sunflower) .

In genetics for example, the basic structure of amino acids that makes up the proteins is asymmetric. In (25), "R" represents one of the 20 combinations of elements found in different amino acid types. All the amino acids in proteins have the basic structure in (25) and differ only in the structure of the R-group.

(25)

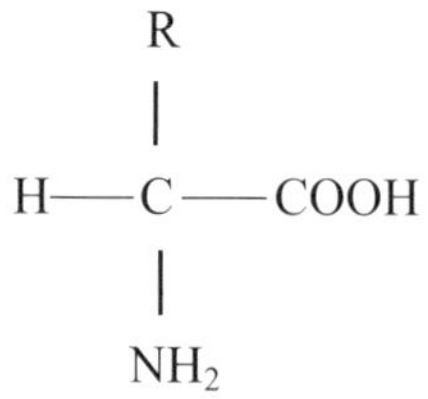

$$R$$
$$|$$
$$H\!-\!C\!-\!COOH$$
$$|$$
$$NH_2$$

Likewise, the nucleic acids in the DNA share a basic structure and exhibit structural asymmetries, (26).

(26)

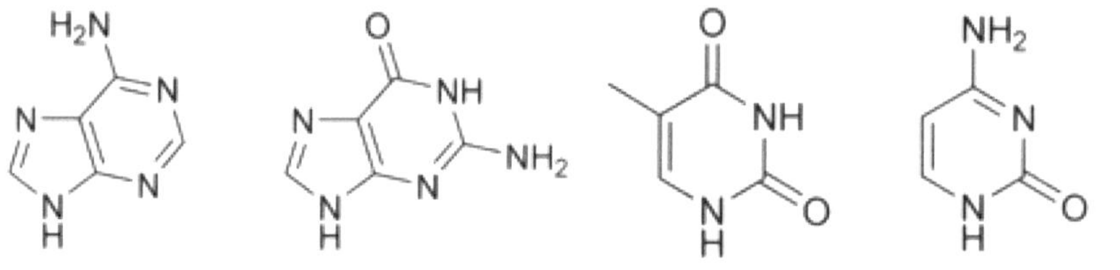

Adenine	Guanine	Thymine	Cytosine

According to [35], the origin of some of the (a)symmetries in syntax would be akin to the physical evolution of molecular chirality. Molecular chirality is an example of asymmetry, since chiral objects, like human hands, are not superposable on their mirror image. Enzymes are constructed from a group of about 20 small molecules called amino acids. All amino acids except one are chiral, thus the enzymes they make are chiral as well.

---

[7] For richer syntax-semantic approaches to discourse pronominal anaphora resolution see also [33], and [34].

Another manifestation of asymmetry in the human biology is the Sylvian fissure (or *lateral sulcus*). It is the deepest and most prominent of the cortical fissures, and it separates the frontal lobes and temporal lobes, see (28). It is in both hemispheres of the brain but longer in the left hemisphere. The areas specialized in language are located close to this fissure.

(27)

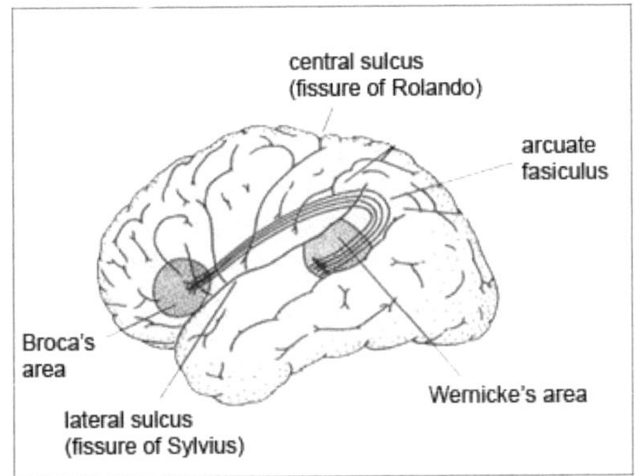

Asymmetry is part of the building blocks of natural systems as it is part of the building blocks of the grammar. In [9], I argued that morphological derivations are strikingly distinct from syntactic derivations. The fact that the parts of a morphological expression cannot be inversed, e.g., *bio-logi-cal, *bio-al-logic, *al-bio-logic, *logic-bio-al, *logic-al-bio, *al-logic-bio*, provides evidence that morphological relations are asymmetrical only. While points of symmetry may arise in syntactic derivations [35], as the examples above in (6)-(9) illustrate with copular and inverse copular expressions, they are never created in morphological derivations. If asymmetry breaks the symmetry of the natural laws and brings about stability to an instable system by creating dominance relations, [36], the absence of points of symmetry in morphological derivations suggests that morphological derivations apply to elements having inherent asymmetric, stable, properties which, according to our view, are preserved through the derivation, [10].

3.2.3.   *Asymmetry-Based Parsing*

Asymmetry is central to both theoretical and computational linguistics. Strong hypotheses on the asymmetry of linguistic relations have been formulated within generative grammar. Computational implementations of asymmetric relations are available. The questions raised by this paper are the following: How does the parser efficiently interpret the grammar? How does it efficiently parse linguistic expressions? A plausible answer to the first question requires a means to restrict the actions of the parser. A plausible answer to the second question requires a means to reduce the search space of the parser.

Asymmetry-based parsing [17] presents direct convergence between linguistics, biology, and information processing. In this model, the grammar derives asymmetric relations, and the parser recovers them.

LAD parser, [18], is an LL(1) parser, which is a computational implementation of the Asymmetry Theory, [10]. The architecture of the parser is such that it limits the search space while it incrementally recovers the asymmetric structure of the input from left to right. We focus on the parsing of simple affirmatives, passives, and questions in order to show that the parser recovers their underlying asymmetric structures, including their argument structure, and relates the elements in the functional domains CP (Complementizer Phrase) and DP to their copies within the VP and NP domains.

The parser computes asymmetric relations and assembles phrase structure, respecting the left-to-right nature of parsing. The incremental parser processes the input of a word at a time, producing one or potentially more partial parses at each step. Each time a word is introduced, it efficiently extends the analyses produced until then, without backtracking or unnecessary search of the derivational history.

The parser interprets the operations of the grammar as applying groups of rules in local domains. The rules of the domains (CP, DP) define the maximal realizations of syntactic projections; the rules of the groups (Grp CP, Grp DP, Grp PP (Prepositional Phrases), etc.) exhaustively enumerate the potential realizations of domains, as in the following sample:

(28) Dom CP

Proj CmaxP

   Spec [getw(word, 'cat') == 'WHadj']

      : shift, link(FPP.Spec);

   H   [word.get_cat() == 'Vaux']

      : shift, link(FauxP.h);

Cmpl shift;#TP …

   Grp DP

(PName <DdefP h> | Dpron <DpronP.h> …

The most inclusive domain is the CP domain, which is open by default at the beginning of the parse. Conditions apply before an action is taken by the parser. After the first word has been matched with a category of the grammar, the next word's category is recovered from the numeration and is matched against the next available positions in the group. If no match is found, no parse is generated. The above procedure is repeated until a word is found that does not belong to the current group. The group is then closed and, together with it, any domain it may have triggered. Following the projection path, the last domain to close is the first opened, i.e., the maximal CP domain.

Thus, a common noun is recognized as a head and is first shifted with a determiner to form a DP, before this DP is shifted in the specifier of the TP. Subsequent links of this DP to positions in the more inclusive domains, including the VP and the NP domains, derive the effects of movement from left to right. The parser makes an optimal use of the operations of the grammar, while it reduces the search space. The parses in (30) for an interrogative, (29a), a declarative, (29b), and a passive, (29c), illustrate the output of the parser, which recovers the underlying asymmetric relations of linguistic expressions.

(29) a. Who discovered FOX12?

  b.   Scientists discovered FOX 12.

  c. FOX12 was discovered by scientists.

(30)   LAD traces

  a. Who discovered FOX12?

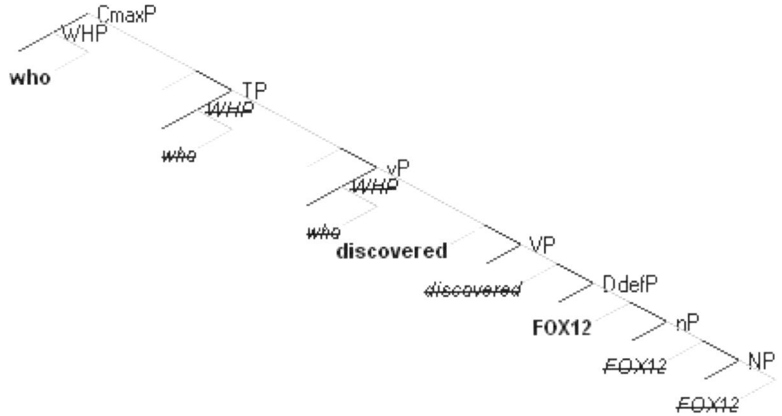

b.   Scientists discovered FOX 12.

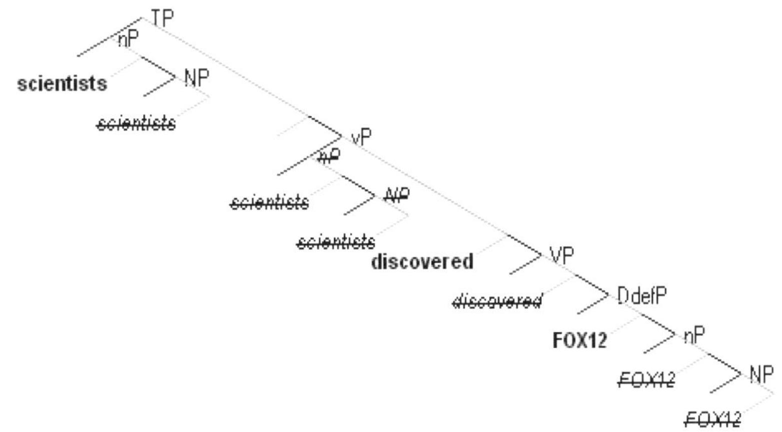

c.   FOX12 was discovered by scientists.

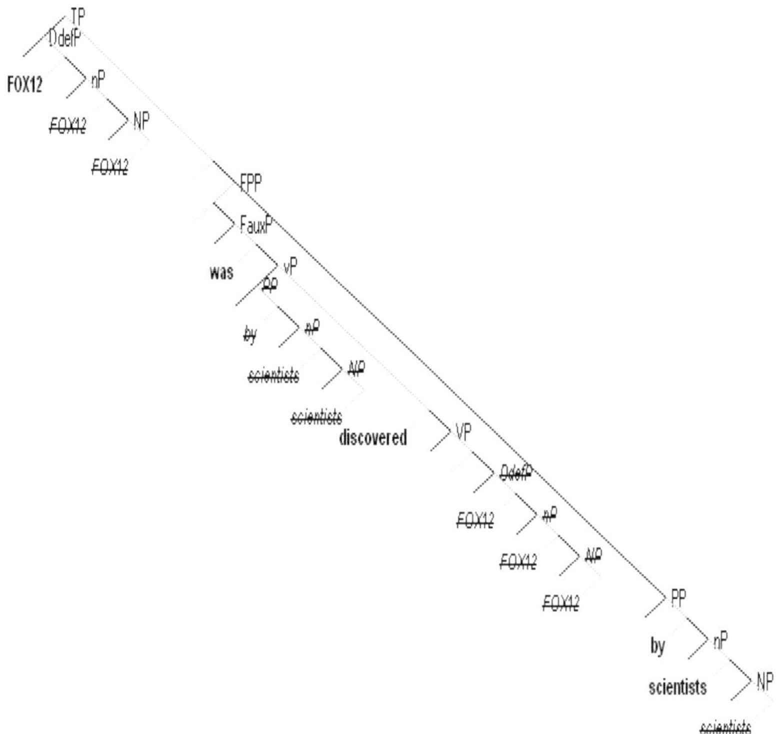

The recovery of asymmetrical relations provides the configurational bases for semantic interpretation. The recovery of fine-grained asymmetric relations, including the DP internal relations, is crucial in efficient information processing.

Given the generic properties of the grammar it implements, the LAD can easily handle cross-linguistic variation. The LAD recovers the asymmetric relations between the elements of linguistic expressions, which makes it closer to human processing. Experimental results reported in [36], [37], provide psycholinguistic evidence that human processing of linguistic expressions is based on the recovery of the asymmetric relations. The processing of these relations in parsing can only improve their efficiency by bringing natural language processing systems closer to human performance.

4. Conclusion

We conclude that, from a biolinguistic perspective, natural language processing cannot be reduced to the bag-of-words technique, to the tagging of the words in documents, to processing of string-linear proximity relations, or to the sole identification of shallow syntactic relations, such as subject and object. The fine-grained asymmetric relations must be recovered in order to identify the semantics of linguistic expressions.

Although the discussion has necessarily been limited, it is easy to see that natural language processing based on the recovery of asymmetric relations is naturally part of a model of the mapping between the expressions generated by the grammar and the external systems.

Further studies on fine-grained connections between language and biology/genetics are needed to develop the biolinguistic program. In particular, the connection between constituent-internal asymmetries and molecular biology should be investigated in detail. Further studies on the connection between biolinguistics and natural language processing are also needed. Natural language processing systems oriented by the recovery of asymmetric relations contributes to the development of efficient software that will analyze, understand, and generate languages, by recovering a central property of relations, asymmetry, which is rooted in human biology.

5. Acknowledgements

This work is supported in part by funding from the SSHRC of Canada to the MCRI on Interface Asymmetries 214-2003-1003, www.interfaceasymmetry.uqam.ca, and by a grant from the FQRSC to the Dynamic Interface research to Professor Anna Maria Di Sciullo at the Université du Québec à Montréal.

6. References

[1] Hauser, M. D., Chomsky, N. and Fitch, W. T. The Faculty of language: What is it, who has it, and how did it evolve? *Science* 298, 2002, 1569-1579.

[2] Chomsky, N. Three factors in language design. *Linguistic Inquiry* 36(1), 2004, 1-22.

[3] Chomsky, N. *The Minimalist Program*. The MIT Press, Cambridge, MA. 1995.

[4] Hein, I. and Kratzer, A. *Semantics in Generative Grammar*. Blakwell, Malden, 1998.

[5] Karamanis, N., Lewin, I., Sealy, R., Drysdaley R., and Briscoe, E. Integrating natural language processing with flybase curation. In *Pacific Symposium on Biocomputing* 12, 2007, 245-256.

[6] Ahler, C. B., Fiszman, M., Demner-Fushman, D., Francois-Lang, M., Rindflesch, T. C. Extracting semantic predications from medline citations for pharmacogenomics. In *Pacific Symposium on Biocomputing* 12, 2007, 209-220.

[7] Neveol, A., Shooshan, S. E., Humphrey, S. M., Rindflesh, T.C., and Aronson, A. R. Multiple approaches to fine-grained indexing of the biomedical literature. In *Pacific Symposium on Biocomputing* 12, 2007, 292-303.

[8] Yu, H. and Kaufman, K. A cognitive evaluation of four online search engines for answering definitional questions posed by physicians. In *Pacific Symposium on Biocomputing* 12, 2007, 328-339.

[9] Kayne, R. *The Antisymmetry of Syntax*. The MIT Press, Cambridge, MA, 1994.

[10] Di Sciullo, A. M. *Asymmetry in Morphology*. The MIT Press, Cambridge, MA, 2005.

[11] Di Sciullo, A. M. and Fong, S. Morpho-syntax parsing. In A. M. Di Sciullo, ed., *UG and External Systems. Language, Brain and Computation*. John Benjamins, Amsterdam-Philadelphia, 2005, 247-268.

[12] Marcus, M. *A Theory of Syntactic Recognition for Natural Language*. The MIT Press, Cambridge, MA, 1980.

[13] Berwick, R. and Weinberg, A. *The Grammatical Basis of Linguistic Performance*. The MIT Press, Cambridge, MA, 1984.

[14] Berwick, R. *The Acquisition of Syntactic Knowledge*. The MIT Press, Cambridge, MA, 1985.

[15] Berwick, R., Abney, S. and Tenny, C., eds., Principle-based parsing: computation and psycholinguistics. *Studies in Linguistics and Philosophy*. Kluwer, Dordrecht, 1991, 301-346.

[16] Fong, S. *Computational Properties of Principle-Based Grammatical Theories*. Ph.D. Thesis, Artificial Intelligence Laboratory, MIT, 1991.

[17] Di Sciullo, A. M., Parsing asymmetries. In *Natural Language Processing*. Computer Science Press, Springler, 2000, 24-39.

[18] Di Sciullo, A. M., Gabrini, P., Batori, C., and Somesfalean, S. Asymmetry, the grammar, and the parser. In *SLI* 2007.

[19] Fong, S. Computation with probes and goals. In A. M. Di Sciullo, ed., *UG and External Systems. Language, Brain and Computation*. John Benjamins, Amsterdam-Philadelphia, 2005, 311-334.

[20] Harkema, H. Minimalist languages and the correct prefix property. In A. M. Di Sciullo, ed., *UG and External Systems. Language, Brain and Computation*. John Benjamins, Amsterdam-Philadelphia, 2005, 289-310.

[21] Fitch, W.T. and Hauser, M. Computational constraints on syntactic processing in a nonhuman primate. *Science*, vol. 303, 2004, 377-380.

[22] Di Sciullo, A. M. Morphological phases. In James Yoon, ed., *Generative grammar in a broader perspective. The 4th GLOW in Asia 2003*. The Korean Generative Grammar Circle & Cognitive Science, Seoul National University, 2004, 113-137

[23] Di Sciullo, A. M. Affixes at the edge. *Canadian Journal of Linguistics* 50 (1/2/3/4), 2005, 83-117.

[24] Di Sciullo, A. M. An integrated competence-performance model, a prototype for morpho-conceptual parsing, and consequences for information processing. *Proceedings of VEXTAL*. Università Ca'Foscari, Venezia, 1999, 369-379.

[25] Di Sciullo, A. M. Domains of argument structure asymmetries. In *Proceedings of WMSCI-The 9th World Multi-Conference on Systemics, Cybernetics and Informatics*, 2005, 316-320.

[26] Cheng, B. Y. M., Carbonell, J. and Seetharaman, J.K. *Biolinguistics: The Use of Analogies for Interdisciplinary Research*, 2004.

[27] Halle, M. and Marantz, A. Distributed morphology and the pieces of inflection. In K. Hale and S. J. Keyser, eds., *The View from Building 20*. The MIT Press, Cambridge, MA, 1993, 111-176.

[28] Rumelhart, D. E., Hinton, G. E., and Williams, R. J. Learning internal representations by error propagation. In D. E. Rumelhart, J. L. McClelland, and the PDP Research Group, eds., *Paralled Distributed Processing. Explorations in the Microstructure of Cognition. Volume 1: Foundations*. The MIT Press, Cambridge, MA, 1986, 318-362.

[29] Smolensky, P. The constituent structure of connectionist mental states: a reply to Fodor and Pylyshyn. *The Southern Journal of Philosophy, XXVI, Supplement*:137-161, 1987.

[30] Fodor, J. A. and Pylyshyn. Z. W. Connectionism and cognitive architecture: a critical analysis. *Cognition*, 28:3-71, 1988.

[31] Mitkov, M. *Anaphora Resolution*. Pearson Education, Edinburgh, London, 2002.

[32] Kennedy, C. and Boguraev, B. Anaphora for everyone: Pronominal anaphora resolution without a parser. In *Proceedings of the 16th International Conference on Computational Linguistics (COLING'96)*. Copenhagen, Denmark, 1996, 113-118.

[33] Carter, D. *Interpreting Anaphora in Natural Language Text*. Ellis Horwood ,Chichester, 1987.

[34] Lappin, S. and Leass, H. An algorithm for pronominal anaphora resolution. *Computational Linguistics*, vol. 4, 1994, 535-561.

[35] Moro, A. *Dynamic Antisymmetry*. The MIT Press, Cambridge, MA, 2000.

[36] Jenkins, L. 2000. *Biolinguistics*. Cambridge University Press.

[38] Tsapkini, K., Jarema, G. and Di Sciullo, A. M. The role of configurational asymmetry in the lexical access of prefixed verbs: Evidence from French. *Brain and Language* 90, 2004, 143-150.

[37] Di Sciullo, A. M. and Tomioka, N. Processing the object/adjunct asymmetry in Japanese compounds, LAD-UQAM, 2007.

New Trends in Software Methodologies, Tools and Techniques
H. Fujita and D. Pisanelli (Eds.)
IOS Press, 2007

Cognitive Modeling in Software and Relation to Human Emotional Reasoning[1]

Hamido Fujita[2], Jun Hakura, Masaki Kurematu
Intelligent Software Systems Laboratory
Iwate Prefectural University

Abstract. The paper reports on our experience to in adapting emotional experiences of the software engineers in evolutionary design of software systems. The works here reported present development progress report in relation to the state-of art that need to create the multidisciplinary technologies, needed to establish best harmony engagement between human user the software application, based on human cognitive analysis. We approach the user best engagement from facial and voice analysis. And through it, we can measure (collectivized and quantified), and observe the user behavior, and accordingly enhance the engagement by generative interactive scenario.   The approach has been experimented using famous literature person (Keni Miyazawa).

Keywords. Intelligent software, cognitive modeling, Human computer Interaction, software development, facial analysis, sound analysis.

1. Introduction

The software designer needs to extend certain cognitive view on the user emotional behaviour in the design process. Having the user mental behaviour be reflected into the system can enhance creativity process on such understanding. Software design is a creative process that needs to stimulate thinking from spatial design prospective, which cooperatively and intellectually participates to establish an engaging harmony to best design practices based on distributed cognition. Computer can stimulate such engagement and create multilayer situated enact for best practices in creative design process. A possible elaboration on the work presented in this paper for software design, is to bring a close look on the adaptability of such innovation on software spatial deployment, that should integrate cognitive process and user usability be integrated, by examining the nonverbal communication skills between the designer and the systems. For example in visual art, of all cultures mental work is done to bring separation together into a whole. Designer should integrate or reflect this aspect into the design principles.

Awareness of their framing within for example, software interface, as well as the knowledge of the separate narratives captured within them, links our visual experience to a known genre, event, or tradition creating a congruence of understanding. This

---

[1] This research is supported by Iwate Prefectural University Research Grants on "Kenji project"..

[2] Correspondence: 020-0193, Iwate, JAPAN, issam@iwate-pu.ac.jp: http://www.fujita.soft.iwate-pu.ac.jp/

mental work of making fragments whole or of shaping clues and cues into a pattern is often thought if as an individual responses. Connections between perceptual and conceptual or linguistics representations emerge in socially interactive situations that punctuate underline and enlarge individual understanding. Verbal language has minimal units of meaning whereas visual and (generally) gestural units would not. It offers the opportunity to lift actions and intentions out of the moment into multiple versions of something else. Metaphors apply to forms to give meaning. Form is therefore a vehicle for inference, and the content of the inference depends on the metaphor.

Mental model of the designer engaged with the tool depends on the role and level of engagement. The minute usage of each component in the tool and also on the system capability to enhance and empower the designer enacts to prompt his/her emotional collective intuition for best practices. Digital virtual worlds as mentioned by Mitchell [13] in not only more pervasive and efficient than ever, it is also generating new cultural complexities. Words not as literature but as signs within the context of space, to confirm and enliven our urban setting in our information age. Urban spaces and places provide setting for communication and at how they conduct complex flows of information through new architectural design. It is the essential interaction between digital media and the built environment. We think our project reported here contributes to such bridge.

People interact with digital technologies through touch manipulation and gesture interaction is increasingly being embodied. People move through environments embedded with digital artefacts, and interact with and through technologies in new ways.   This act as collaboration in design, and specify the design concept as collaborative cognitive process. This participate in generative and evolutionary techniques in architecture[10].   There are digital spaces that participate in architectural design in such digital world that involve people to interact through its space [20], [2].

We think that the practices reported in this work contribute to integrate (corporate) the cognitive intention of the designer with the knowledge of the system. The system designer can use these design practices to inhale the emotional practices into the design using such experiment. [24], [26] described a possible architecture for organizing agents into a flexible, human-like Society of Mind. Rather than seeking a best way to organize agents, their architecture supports multiple 'ways to think', each a different architectural configuration of collaborative agents. [8] identified three different kinds of distribution of cognitive process' across people, across representation, and across cultures. Socially distributed cognition focuses on the role that a group of people have in thinking and knowing and on the phenomena that emerge as a result of these social interactions. Cognitive process makes use of external as well internal representations. These external representations are things such as notes, scripts, and other information artifacts. It is a metaphoric representation, collected from different dimensional representation, (i.e., disciplines), collectively to enact for example Miyazawa Kenji and revive him through such conceptual cognitive representation. Psychology, linguistics, computer science, and philosophy, collectively can lead to cognitive science disciplines. Cognitive Psychology [14], contributes to understand human thought from an individual perspective.

We project the general conceptual framework above through the parts of Miyazawa Kenji project (Fig.1). We present the main four parts of the project. We show our technology on the interaction between human and virtual system representing the cognitive mental model (Self) of other human.

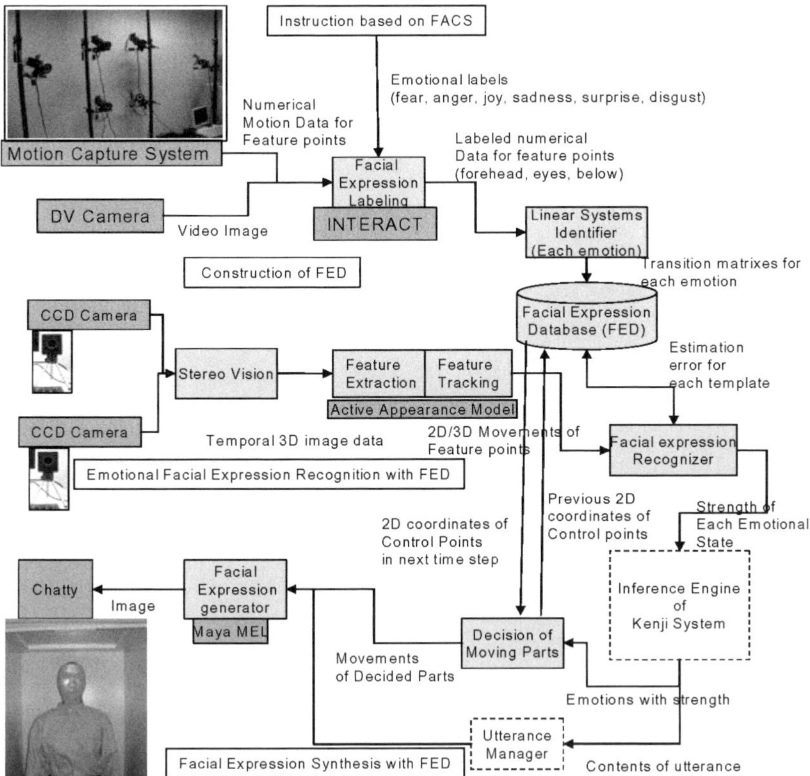

Figure 1. Outline of Virtual Kenji System

Computer program reflecting some concept does have a self, this reflected by the conceptual design, of certain personality, so the self is defined by the personality, of that person reflected in the program. The face and voice emotional representation belong to human mind, or mental representation. They are part of human emotional states representation, reflecting mind transition in different representation reflected as modes. It is part of the language context that be integrated into our vocabulary and language representations.

In this paper, we are using this case study to bridge these issues and move to the direction of intelligent human centric computing that can mimic a specific human cognitive behavior and based on this cognitive modal we can reason on real human interactive behavior for spatial design. The rest of this paper is organized, to show the major part in this case study. In Section 2, we will discuss the example of presenting certain human cognitive model. We have used Miyazawa Kenji cognitive mode. In Sec. 3 we present part 1 of the system, that will create the emotional feature of Kenji system as virtual world. In Sec. 4 we present part 2 of the system, that collect human user cognitive interaction and mental behavior based on Kenji Style reasoning and other knowledge related to common sense reasoning. In Sec. 5 we preset part 3 of the system, that related to voice emotional recognition. In Sec. 6 we deal with Part 4, that initiate the scenarios and responses to the user in role act style to the cognitive behavior of the user state. In Sec. 7 we present conclusions.

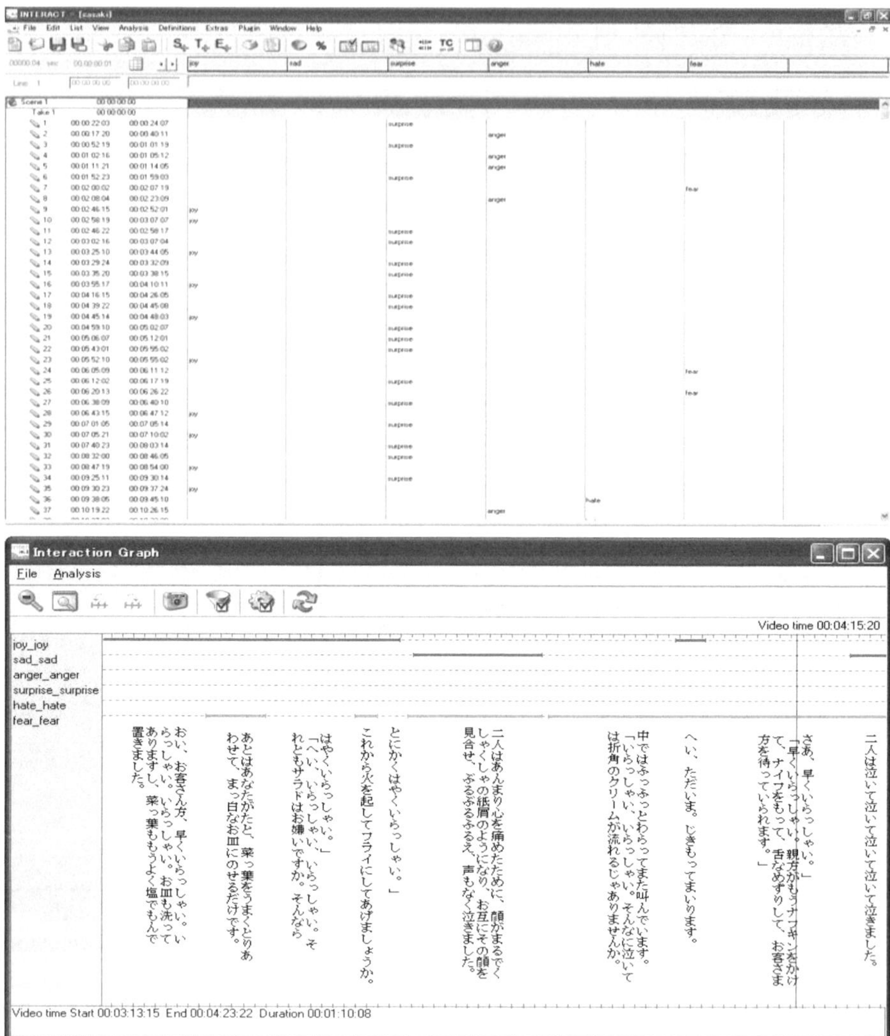

Figure 2. Cognitive analysis of Kenji Scripts using INTERACT software

2. Cognitive style of human cognition: Kenji Style case study

As mentioned in the introduction that we have selected Kenji Miyazawa(MK) to be the virtual model of our experiment on intelligent human interaction cognitive based conceptual model. http://www.kenji-world.net/english/who/who.html; this link give an overview about who is Kenji. Such cognitive behavior reasoning system interacts with human user based on cognizing-based reasoning, and factorized through, based on MK cognitive studies.

Our system thinks on which action it may take to appropriately interact with the user. The outline of the system is shown in Fig.1. This decision making process is based on MK thinking style. The way in which we use our mind becomes the way in which we use our body and the attitudes of mind so that to create its own manifestation in the function of the muscles that implements deliberately the concessions behavior behind it.

Previous or old thoughts (from Aristotle to Darwin) saw facial expressions as the result of internal emotional states. Facial expressions were seen as pre-warning of emotional responses on others. However, why do humans need such non-verbal communication and complex facial muscles when we have language? Darwin tried to extend his theories on evolutions of structures to behavior. He felt that behavior also evolves, and concluded from the universality of many facial expressions (sadness, happiness, etc.) that such behaviors also evolved from lower life forms. Facial expressions are "serviceable habits" that helped the organism react to sensations and internal states. In [26] has introduced the "self," as mechanism to logic related to how to define or represent and put in structures the self to reason cognitively on it. Kenji style is the emotional voice and facial animation that virtual MK is able to speak through in role act to the user. These are the extracted cognitive feature reasoned templates. As stated in the introduction, we need to construct creatively and physiologically Kenji style featured by his personality implicitly hidden within his scripts and from scholars who have acquaintance on his personality reflected through his published artwork. This style is constructed from collected data from testing actual person act and has some knowledge on Kenji scripts, and from general person who can read and cognitively understand Japanese scripts.

The analysis data have been classified according to six emotional modes of EKMAN[4]. We use such style of reasoning to label and understand on how to use the gesture. We have selected scripts from Kenji artwork.

The analysis is based on cognitive feature extraction referenced on reading of above-mentioned Kenji scripts (1) by specialist in Kenji literature and his art pieces. Also, the same has been done by: (2) reading observation analysis on non-expert people, (i.e., general Japanese people).

These extracted patterns based on experimental analysis and reasoning of Kenji scripts projected through (life style, physiological view, philosophical, linguistics reasoning referencing analysis (onomatopoeia and mimesis) and other analytical observations as shown in Fig.2, that shows the emotional analysis using INTERACT tool[9]. As shown in Figure 3, that among 10 observed users we have collected 3 users with 90% match related to the Action units and six Ekman emotional modes [4]. These collected templates have been used to reflect Kenji Style. We used these templates to establish part 1 of the system. For more details on these templates, please refer to [6], [9].

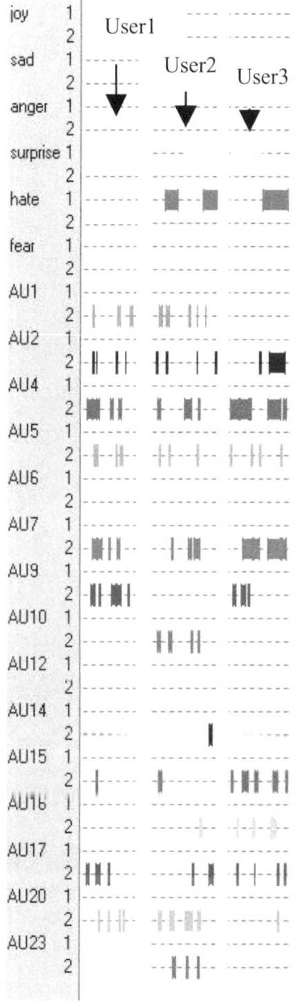

Figure 3.
[INTERACT] software usage in video analysis of human behavior

3.   Emotion Estimation from Facial Expressions of Users

Part 1 of Kenji System presents the hologram, it is as shown in Fig. 5. The total image of Kenji Hologram is on Fig. 5, image_4. The other photos(1-3) snapshots are taken while Kenji is talking through the emotional templates that are created in real time by the Emotion processor (We called it *KANJO* processor, *KANJO* means emotion in Japanese language).   KANJO processor (Figure 4-1) is synchronizing the MAYA images generating in real-time animated facial images, and synchronized through KServer (Figure 4-2), and the emotional sound file extracted Kenji text (refer to: Fig.8), all this is synchronized through KNAJO processor. All this is referenced as Part_1 in our system. The details of the software development (Part_1) here are omitted for space and technological securities issues related reasons.

Figure 4-1. KANJO processor

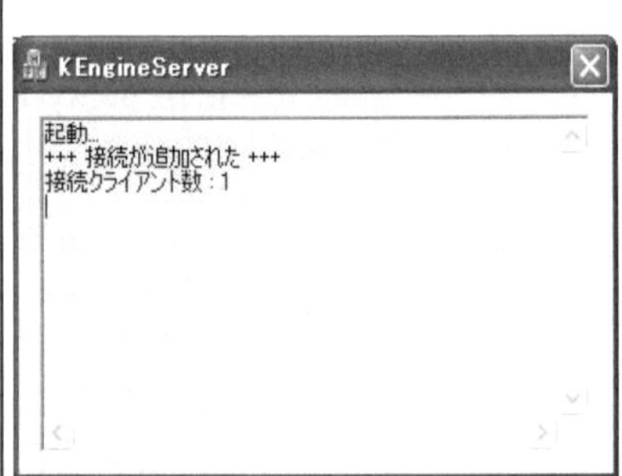

Figure 4-2. KENJI-Engine Server

Figure 4. Virtual Engine component

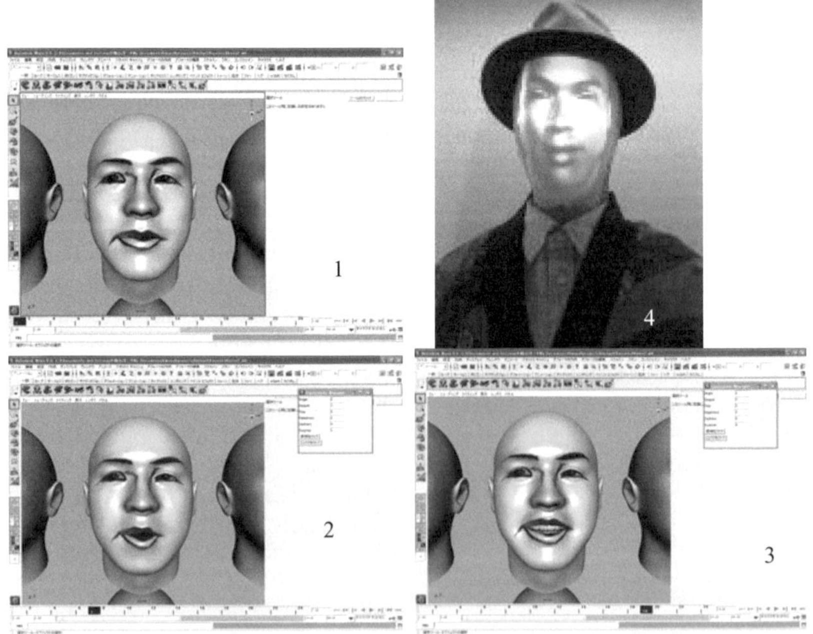

Figure 5. Shows part 1 of the hologram

You can reference to demos on this application by reference to [9] or the link (http://www.fujita.soft.iwate-pu.ac.jp/prof_dir/issam/others/ KenjiOnly.wmv). Please notice that all is done in real time. This section will be reference again in Sec.5, related to creating facial images in harmony with the contents of the spoken text.

4. Emotion Estimation from Facial Expressions of Users

In this section, we preset part 2 of Virtual Kenji system, that to make the interaction between Kenji and human user, to achieve the conceptual cognition engagement with a user, the system is required to react to emotional states of the user. Emotional states of the user can be perceived through emotional signs exhibited in several modalities, such as words, vocal features, and gestures, and recognized collectively through situated reasoning. Gestures are known as one of the essential modalities to perceive the emotional states of the user. Among the gestures, facial expressions afford a great deal of emotional information in human natural communications. In proportion to the importance, there have been a lot of studies concerning facial expressions are conducted not only in psychology and philosophy, but also in computer science. One of the most popular approaches to automatic facial expression analysis is relying on the Facial Action Coding System (FACS), (for FACS, Ekman and Friesen, 1975[4]; for a survey of the literature see, [19]. The FACS uses the combinations of movements of facial parts, named Action Units (AUs). Namely, detecting the AUs is the main subject of the approaches relying on the FACS. The AUs' are defined as typical results of movements of facial parts in facial expressions, such as "left eyebrow up" and so on. Thus, they are apt to focus on the static images of the facial expressions, and require the completion of the expressions. Namely, they do not fully utilize the dynamic aspects of the facial expressions. This would result in the misleading at on the reasoning about the situation: "What triggers the facial expression?"

To know the emotional states of the user together with the exact timing of their appearance is one of the important requirements to the conceptual cognition. For this aim, we have introduced a linear system identification approach to the facial expression analysis [7]. The approach is able to fully utilize the dynamic aspects of facial expressions.

The approach assumes that the movements of the facial feature points are the consequence of the facial muscles modeled as linear systems with several modes. The modes of the system correspond to the represented emotions, and each identified mode of the system can estimate the movements of the facial feature points in expressing the emotion. As shown in Fig. 6, the differences of the estimated movements and actual movements are used to detect the emotional expressions. While we are planning to merge the approach with the FACS approach, yet at the current stage, this section concentrates on the system identification approach. The rest of the section is assigned to the following four topics: Face and feature points' detection's method; Facial expression database realizing system identification approach; Emotion estimation with facial expression database, and an experimental results showing that the proposed method can detect the six basic emotional expressions, i.e., happiness, surprise, sadness, fear, anger, and disgust, with their exact starting points.

4.1. A Face and facial feature points detection method

In contrast to our previous results on this project (e.g.,[6], [7]) that require a motion capture system to detect face and facial feature points, we have adopted Active Appearance Model (AAM) [3] to raise the availability of our system. While there is a defect in the accuracy, there are several advantages in this change such as free from markers (used in motion capture systems), and availabilities of the device and needed real time processing. The AAM is a statistical model/method to detect deformable objects in images. It makes a statistical model of the shapes and appearances from training images with manually added feature points. When applied to the novel image, it finds parameters to adapt the model to the novel image by means of an optimization method. Today's computational advances enable the method to be processed in real time so that it can be applied to object tracking tasks. The points on the facial images in Figure 4 are automatically detected by the implemented AAM system.

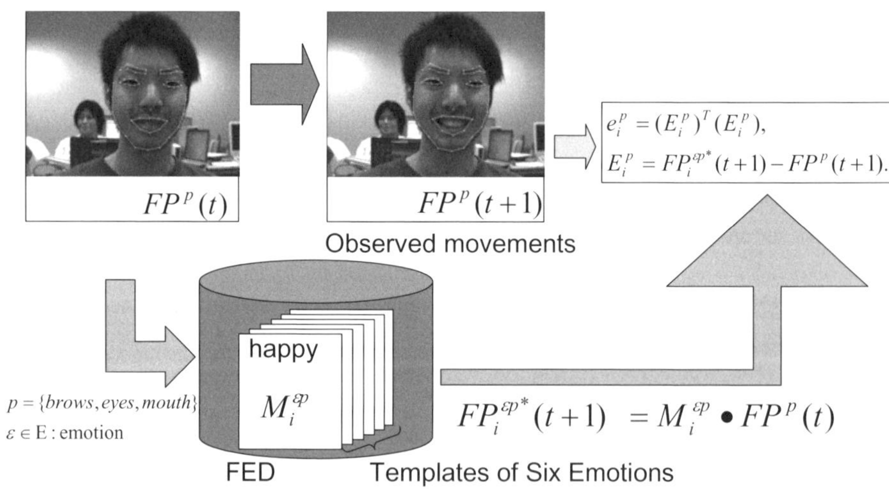

Figure 6. System Identification Approach to Facial Expression Analysis.

4.2. Facial Expression Database (FED)

Facial expressions in this study are considered as the results of movements of facial feature points. Facial feature points are the points that are needed to estimate the target emotional expressions by observing the movements of these points. The movements of the feature points are assumed to be caused by a set of systems as in the

Facial Score [15]. The system identification method, i.e., LSM: Least-Square Method is adopted to identify the systems. A face is divided into roughly three parts: eye brows, eyes, and mouth. Each part is assumed to contain its own emotional signals. The results of the identification for each part would be the six transition matrixes; each of those can estimate the movements of the facial feature points for particular emotional facial expressions. The acquired knowledge is collected as a database, called Facial Expression Database (FED).

To extract typical movements of the facial feature points that express the particular emotion, we should collect facial expressions that represent the particular emotion. For this aim, subjects who have trained to express the six emotions act on each emotion for several times, and the movements at that time are labeled as an emotion. As mentioned above, the movements are represented as result of the system's output. The system has some modes; initially, the duration is assumed to be a mode. A merging algorithm of the modes reduces the number of the modes. The similar movements are considered as results of the system in the same mode. Namely, each mode expresses an emotional category. The detail of the algorithm is described in [6]. As the results of applying the algorithm, each mode corresponds to the most typical movements of these points to express an emotion. For example, when there exists N durations labeled as "fear", the modes that representing fear are described as follows:

$$\mathbf{M^{fear}} = \{\mathbf{M^{brows}}, \mathbf{M^{eyes}}, \mathbf{M^{mouth}}\},$$

$$\mathrm{M}^p = \{M_i^p \mid 1 \le i \le m, i \in I, 1 \le m \le N\}. \tag{1}$$

where, $p = \{brows, eyes, mouth\}$, I denotes a set of positive integers. M^p is obtained for each of the six emotions.

The modes are represented as the transition matrixes. Namely, every facial feature point can be estimated by using the matrixes. Let eye brows require six feature points (three points for each brow) at time t denoted as $FP^p(t) = (px_1, py_1, px_2, py_2, \cdots, px_6, py_6)^T$, where px_i and py_i are the x and y coordinate of i-th feature point respectively. Then, the points at the next time step can be estimated by the following equation:

$$FP_i^{p^*}(t+1) = M_i^p \bullet FP^p(t) \tag{2}$$

where, p* means that it is the estimated value. Note that M_i^p is a 12 x 12 matrix in this example. Note also that every estimation value is calculated by the actual value of the facial points. The estimation process compares the error between actual and estimated values of the facial points for every mode, part, and emotion. The next section describes our method to make estimation with the modes setting.

4.3. Emotion estimation with facial expression database

As mentioned in the previous section, FED provides system identifiers of the systems that control the facial feature points. Therefore, emotional estimation from the facial expression with FED uses these identifiers to know to what emotional categories the presented facial expression belongs. The presented facial expressions can be detected as the movements of the facial feature points with a vision system and the AAM, so that $FP^p(t)$ in Equation (2) are available at every time step. Every identifier estimates $FP_i^{p^*}(t+1)$ at the next time step through Equation (2). These estimated points are compared with the actually observed points at t+1, and then we can calculate the error e_i^p :

$$e_i^p = (E_i^p)^T (E_i^p),$$
$$E_i^p = FP_i^{p^*}(t+1) - FP^p(t+1).$$

$$(3)$$

Note that e_i^p is a scalar value, and E_i^p is a vector. Then, according to Equation (1), we have $|M^p|(=m)$ errors for each facial part with respect to each emotional category. To determine which emotion is observed, we have to cumulate the error values of each part. We simply employ the minimum value for the aim, because the identifier with the minimum error itself implies that the emotion is detected:

$$e^p = \min_i \{e_i^p\}$$

$$(4)$$

Namely, we have now error vectors Δ_e consist of three elements, i.e., on eye brows, eyes, and mouth, for each emotion:

$$\Delta_e = (e^{brows}, e^{eyes}, e^{mouth}),$$
$$e \in \{joy, sadness, anger, disgust, fear, surprise\}$$

$$(5)$$

While the error vector can be used as differently, for now, we simply add the errors. Then, the error is used to estimate the expressed emotions: Here we simply set an empirically obtained threshold to each error. Namely, the emotion with the estimation error below the threshold is considered as the expressed emotions.

4.4. An Experiment on detecting emotions

We have implemented the AAM by means of the aam-api (Stegmann et. al., 2003) coupled with OpenCV library (Open Computer Vision Library). The frame rate of the camera is approximately 20 frames per second.

An experiment to check basic detective abilities of the proposed approach is conducted. For this aim, only a subject who acts on six emotions according to the FACS is assumed to be the target person. Thus, the training data for AAM and the FED is prepared only for the subject. After construction of the AAM and the FED, another sequence of the actions is observed. In the observation phase, emotion estimation process works in real time, and the results are sent to the conceptual cognition engine in response to the facial expressions of the subject. To confirm the above-mentioned abilities of the approach, the subject acts on the six emotions in the following order: happy, surprise, anger, disgust, sadness, and fear. The frames corresponding to the facial expressions are listed in Table 1.

The result of the experiment is depicted in Figure 7. Figure 7(a) shows the transitions of sums of the difference between estimated movements of the feature points and the actual movements of the points, i.e., estimation error, observed in each frame. Namely, the estimations by means of the modes (matrices) corresponds to the six emotions are compared with the actual movements of the feature points. Therefore, the lower error value means that the corresponding emotional facial expression is observed. Comparing Figure 7 with Table 1 reveals interesting facts.

TABLE 1.   Frames and Acted Emotional Facial Expression.

Acted Emotional Facial Expression	Frames
Happy	51 to 105
Surprise	131 to 170
Anger	222 to 268
Disgust	310 to 346
Sadness	394 to 430
Fear	535 to 569

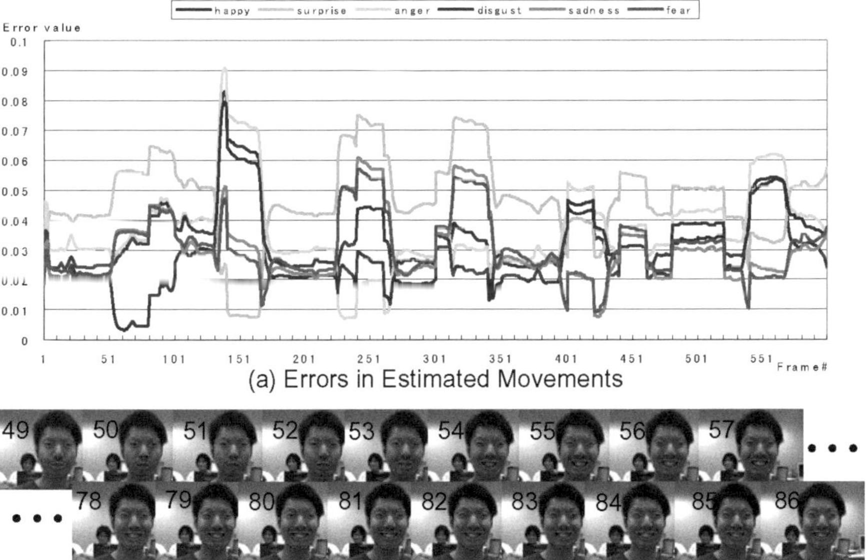

Figure 7. Result for Estimating Acted Emotions.

The error values rapidly decrease at the beginning of each act, and in most cases, continues decreasing until the facial expression becomes the typical one that can be recognized with FACS. Figure 7(b) is the actual sequence of the facial expression expressing "Happy" from beginning to the end. It means that the proposed method is able to detect the very beginning of the facial expressions. It is very important for our aim, i.e., construction of conceptual cognition system, because the system should know what makes the user having that emotion. Although some emotions, disgust and happy, and fear and sadness, seem hard to distinguished by the proposed method, the other emotions are detectable with the method. The undistinguished emotional expressions are sometimes very hard to identify even by the human when forced to identify it only from the facial expression. We are planning to merge and/or analyze the information from the other modalities, i.e., voice (as explained in the following Section), situation, and so on, to overcome this issue.

5. Emotional Voice recognition

This Section resembles what we call as part_3 of Virtual Kenji System. In our system reference to Figure 5 (emotionally generated facial images), the corresponding text with emotional features (represented as templates) generated by the system and spoken by Kenji system as shown in Figure 8, are been synchronized to create the total cognitive real image interface for talking person with cognitive personality specialized as Kenji. The facial movement of the lips has been (real time) synchronized by interface (LipSync mentioned on the reference [11]), which is API (application program interface) with MAYA application.
However, the templates generated on in Figure 8 used conventional rules that we revised as in the following.

Researchers use discriminant rules to estimate emotion in human speech in general [17]. They make these rules as the following steps. First, researchers record human utterance that participants speak certain phrases emotionally in role act, like actor or actress. Second, researchers extract sound features, for example power and fundamental frequency using frequency analysis and get mean and maximum value of these features. Finally, they make discriminant rules from these features using machine-learning methods, for example decision tree and artificial neural network. These rules depend on recorded data. The set of such rules are not the same among different systems. Therefore, the correctness rate is not high.. We think it is necessary to improve such method or invent new one for our system. For the voice emotional recognition system, we propose three methodological steps to improve the referenced method.

First method is that we use variance, skewness and kurtosis from the results of frequency analysis to make discriminant rules in addition to mean and maximum. Variance, skewness and kurtosis express distribution of frequency spectrum in plain. Mean and maximum show frequency spectrum as one value. There are a data set has same mean and different variance. We can see new and recover viewpoints using variance, skewness and kurtosis.

Second method is that we make a regression tree corresponding to emotion. The regression tree is constructed to distinguish the different emotions. We think that people could have several generated emotions simultaneously. For this purpose, we construct a regression tree for each emotion. Each regression tree shows that; whether human speech includes an emotion or not. We use the prediction value gotten by each regression tree to estimate emotion type. If the prediction value gotten by a regression tree, which shows the emotion, is bigger than other prediction values by other trees, then we can estimate the emotion in speech. If there is not; the prediction value shows one emotion, and we have no emotion change in speech.

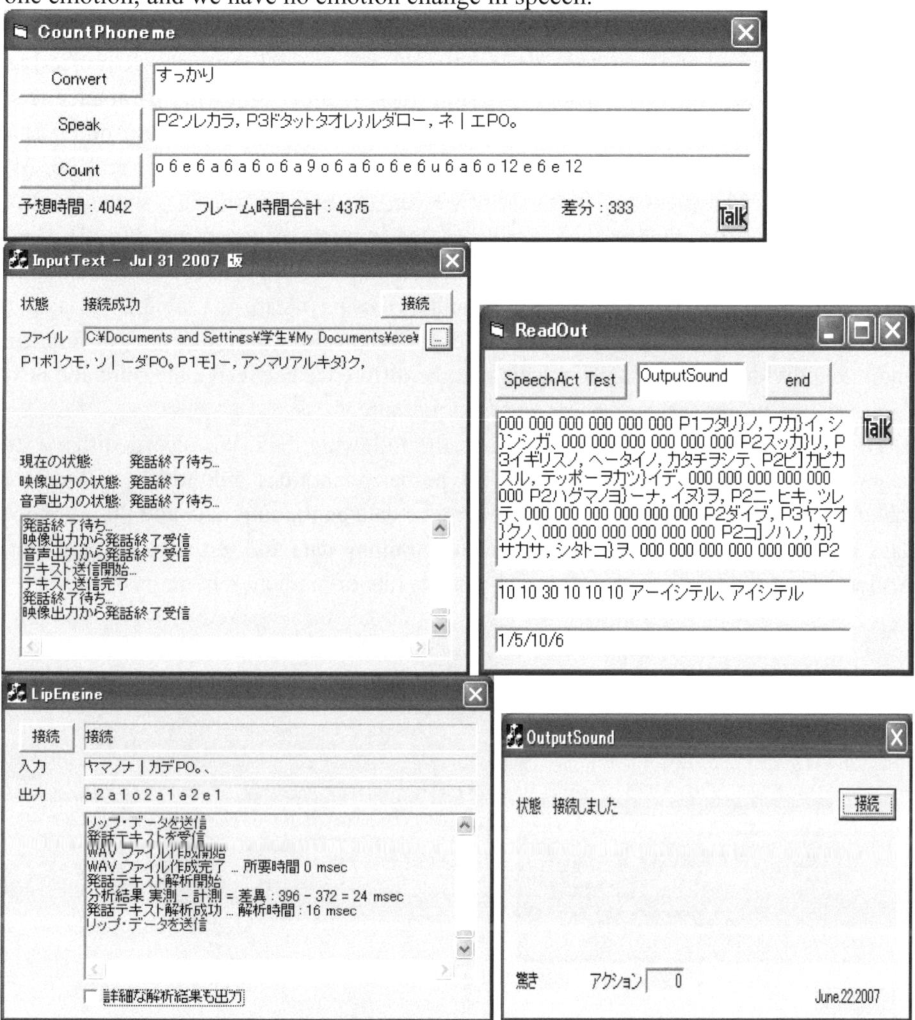

Figure 8. Shows the screens of the Input text window, and readout window

Third method is that we make discriminant rules from speech synthesize. We focus on human speech data. It is difficult for people to express emotion in speech intentionally. Human speech data may include noise, too. So we use speech synthesize to make discriminant rules as following. First, we make speech synthesize data together with variance voice parameters, for example pitch, volume, speed, and intonation. Next, participants would answer emotionally in speech synthesizes data. Finally, we try to get the relation between sound parameters of speech synthesize and emotion extracted by participants. In other word, descriminant rules made by this method depend on human evaluation about speech synthesize.

5.1. Experiments

In order to evaluate proposal methods, we did some experiments. We make descriminant rules by regression trees. The reason is that making regression trees is well-known method and easy to understand rules. We use R Language; [R-project] to make these trees.   First, we make regression trees with the following parameter sets, (1) using mean and maximum of power, (2) using mean and maximum of F0 (F0 means fundamental frequency), (3) using mean and maximum of power and F0, (4) using variance, skewness and kurtosis of power, (5) using variance , skewness and kurtosis of F0, (6) using variance, skewness and kurtosis of power and F0, (7) using mean, maximum, variance, skewness and kurtosis of power, (8) using mean, maximum, variance , skewness and kurtosis of F0 and (9) using mean, maximum, variance , skewness and kurtosis of power and F0. We get these values from measure, difference, and rate individually. Difference means that the difference between a measure and next measure, rate means that a measure and next measure.

To make these regression trees, we used the following data. We recorded that a 20 years aged man spoke 20 phrases with 6 type basic emotions individually. When we make regression tree, we used 90 type utterance data as training data and 30 utterance data as test data. We make 4 data sets whose training data and test data are different. And we compare the average of the each correct rate of prediction by regression trees.

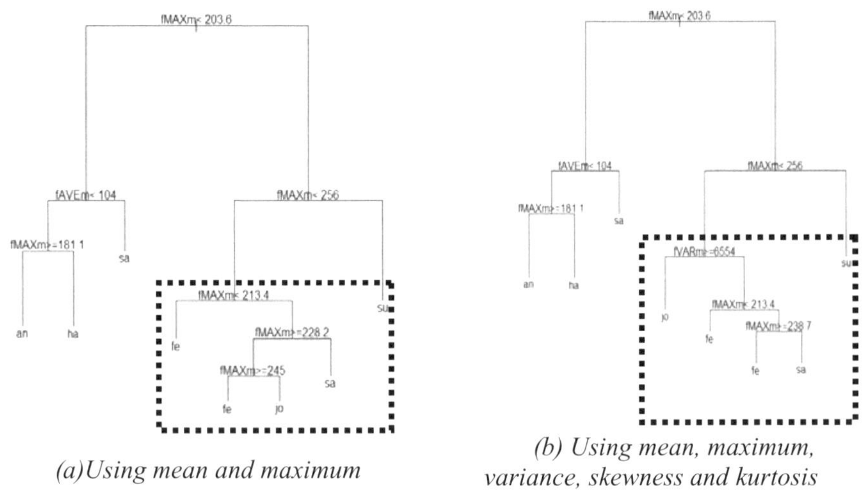

(a)Using mean and maximum   (b) Using mean, maximum, variance, skewness and kurtosis

Figure 9. Example of regression tree

Figure.8 shows the example of regression trees. Fig.9(a) shows the regression tree with mean and maximum of F0 and Fig.9(b) shows the regression tree with mean, maximum, variance, skewness and kurtosis with F0.

These trees made from same data set, but are different. "fVAR" in figure.1(b) means that this tree focus on variance of F0 to discriminate emotion. the correct rate of Fig.9(a) is same as one of Fig.9(b).

TABLE 2. The experimental result of prediction using variance, skewness and kurtosis of voice features (Top 10)

Criteria	Value	Power		F0		Average	Correct rate						
		Mean	Variance	Mean	Variance		Surprise	Anger	Fear	Dislike	Happy	Sadness	total
Gini	Measure					12.75	0.25	0.4	0.35	.6	0.35	0.6	0.43
Gini	Measure					12.75	0.25	0.4	0.35	.6	0.35	0.6	0.43
Gini	Difference					12.75	0.25	0.4	0.35	.6	0.35	0.6	0.43
Gini	Difference					12.75	0.25	0.4	0.35	.6	0.35	0.6	0.43
Deviance	Measure					12.25	0.45	0.3	0.4	.4	0.4	0.5	0.41
Deviance	Difference					11.75	0.45	0.3	0.45	.35	0.3	0.5	0.39
Gini	Measure					11.25	0.3	0.35	0.25	.45	0.4	0.5	0.38
Gini	Difference					11.25	0.3	0.35	0.25	.45	0.4	0.5	0.38
Deviance	Measure					10.75	0.4	0.25	0.3	.4	0.3	0.5	0.36
Deviance	Difference					10.75	0.3	0.4	0.25	.35	0.35	0.5	0.36
Average						8.09	0.25	0.25	0.22	.28	0.30	0.33	0.27

TABLE 3. the experimental result of prediction each data set (Top 10)

Criteria	Value	Power		F0		Average	Correct rate							Data set
		Mean	Variance	Mean	Variance		Surprise	Anger	Fear	Dislike	Happy	Sadness	Total	
Deviance	Ratio	O	O			18	0.6	0.2	0.6	0.8	0.6	0.8	0.6	1
Gini	Ratio	O		O		15	0.4	0.6	0.4	0.8	0.4	0.4	0.5	1
Gini	Measure	O		O		15	0.4	0.6	0.4	0.8	0.4	0.4	0.5	2
Gini	Measure	O		O		15	0.4	0.8	0.4	0.8	0.2	0.4	0.5	2
Gini	Ratio		O		O	15	0.4	0.8	0.4	0.8	0.2	0.4	0.5	4
Gini	Ratio	O		O		15	0.4	0.8	0.4	0.8	0.2	0.4	0.5	4
Gini	Measure		O		O	15	0.4	0.8	0.4	0.8	0.2	0.4	0.5	1
Deviance	Measure		O	O	O	15	0.4	0.6	0.6	0.8	0.2	0.4	0.5	2
Deviance	Ratio		O			15	0.6	0.2	0.4	0.8	0.2	0.8	0.5	2
Deviance	Measure					15	0.6	0.2	0.6	0.6	0.2	0.8	0.5	2

TABLE 4. The experimental result of prediction with multi regression trees (Top 10)

Criteria	Value	Power		F0		Average	Correct rate						
		mean	Variance	Mean	Variance		Surprise	Anger	Fear	Dislike	Happy	Sadness	Total
Gini	Difference		O			2.5	0.55	0.25	0.4	0.3	0.45	0.55	0.42
Gini	Measure		O	O		2.5	0.4	0.3	0.5	0.4	0.4	0.5	0.42
Gini	Difference		O	O		2.5	0.4	0.3	0.5	0.4	0.4	0.5	0.42
Gini	Measure	O				2.5	0.3	0.45	0.3	0.4	0.6	0.45	0.42
Gini	Measure		O			2.25	0.5	0.3	0.3	0.5	0.35	0.5	0.41
Gini	difference	O				1.5	0.25	0.4	0.25	0.4	0.6	0.4	0.38
Deviance	Difference			O	O	1.25	0.3	0.35	0.5	0.35	0.35	0.4	0.38
Deviance	Measure	O				1.25	0.25	0.35	0.4	0.4	0.4	0.4	0.38
Deviance	Measure			O	O	1.25	0.25	0.35	0.45	0.4	0.4		
Deviance	Difference	O				1.25	0.25	0.35	0.4	0.4	0.4	0.45	0.38
Average						7.93	0.24	0.24	0.23	0.27	0.30	0.29	0.26

Table1 shows the part of experimental results. It shows parameter sets that has high correct rate of prediction. Table3 shows parameter sets that has high correct rate of prediction in each data set. To evaluate second method, we make each regression trees for each emotion from same data as first expression and predict by using them.

TABLE 5. The relation between emotions and features of speech synthesize

Emotion	Criteria	Volume	Speed	Pitch	Intonation
Anger	Deviance	Normal, Small	Fast	Low	
Anger	Deviance	Big	Fast	High	
Anger	Gini		Fast	Low	
Anger	Gini	Big	Fast	Normal, high	
Dislike	Deviance	Big		Low	
Dislike	Gini	Big		Low	
Happy	Deviance				Big
Happy	Gini				Big
Sadness	Deviance	Small	Normal. slow		
Sadness	Deviance	Normal, small	Normal. Slow		Small
Sadness	Gini	Small	Normal. Slow	Normal	
Sadness	Gini	Normal, small	Normal. Slow		small
Surprise	Gini	Big	fast	High	

Table 4 shows the part of this experiment. To evaluate third method, we did pre experiment. In pre-experiment, we synthesize two voice patterns for a phrase. Second voice pattern is different from first voice about sound features, for example speed, volume, intonation, and pitch. After hearing two voice patterns, participants evaluate which kind of emotion second voice stress rather than first voice.

Table 5 shows the relation between sound parameters and emotion gotten by this experiment. We use SMARTTALK[23] to do speech synthesize.

5.2. Analysis

5.2.1. Using variance, skewness and kurtosis

Experimental result didn't say that variance; skewness and kurtosis contribute to estimate emotion. Table.2 shows that estimate prediction rate by using mean of F0 is high. Estimate prediction rate by using mean and variances is high, but estimate prediction rate is not high. Estimate prediction rate using mean is 8.76. But estimate prediction rate using variance is 6.84. Estimate prediction rate using mean and variance is 8.94. This value is best of 3 patterns. The experimental result says that variance, skewness and kurtosis support mean and maximum to estimate emotion.

5.2.2 Using multi regression trees

Comparison table.3 with table.2, estimate prediction rate of table.4 is lower than the rate of table.1. The average of estimate prediction rate becomes from 8.08 to 7.94 and the variance becomes from 5.30 to 6.04. Estimate prediction rate got down in 28 data sets and got up in 22 data sets. These results say that using multi regression trees is not good to estimate emotion. One of reasons is that using multi regression trees doesn't match to estimation. So we should rethink how to use multi regression trees.

5.2.3. Using speech synthesis

Table.5 shows that there are parameter sets to feel same emotion. For example, participants feel anger from voice with big volume or voice with normal volume and high pitch. This result let us change some speech features. We have not yet analyzed speech synthesis data. We believe to get useful information from the frequency analysis result about speech synthesis using same method, which we use to analyze human speech. And we should change the experiment style.

We could get some knowledge about emotion estimation from these experimental results. However, it yet has not brought precision improvement in the selection quality. The analysis of the experimental result needs further investigation. It is yet not easy to predicate emotion in speech. However, we have to analyze these experimental results and reflected analysis outcome on our method. We need to new knowledge, like for example psychology-of-music findings, to enhance emotion estimation method.

6. Cognitive Scenario generation according to human cognitive state

We explain here part 4 of the system. How to make a system can act with the user according to a situation, what type of possible scenario or knowledge that the system can provide to the user? These issues should be reflected on memory structure and situated computing.

The User cognitive states been examined and analyzed using Part 2 of the system. The user engagement with Kenji system is computed using Sec.4 that analyze the facial expression of the user to examine the degree of user engagement with Virtual system mode. The system would conclude if the user is interesting in the current created scenario or not interesting. Actively engaged or disconnected. There are four states that the system concludes to reach; according to the conclusion, it takes through the facial analysis of users. Also, this is the same for voice emotional recognition as well. So, we have a view on facial analysis state (using Sec. 4), and view on voice analysis state (using Sec. 5). These two views are integrated to create the cognitive state of user engagement with Virtual Kenji system. We have created several scenarios that prepared according to the expertise in Kenji cognitive style views. Also other views have been prepared according to several situations, that been classified according what is called as 1st imprecision [21]. We use a tool named as digital physiognomy from www.uniphiz.com to test user physiological emotional states before they engaged with KENJI so that to create emotional 1st impression model. According to the type of the user face, we created a scenario that Kenji virtual model can interact. These systematic guidelines are to simplify the best engagement between the human user the virtual system.

Though the experiment is to have the system, be Kenji and the user is general user who has certain knowledge and interest on such famous writer. We think the system can be useful for HCI design to complex creative artwork or eliciting a complex requirement, where the user nonverbal communication work in hand with to stimulate the designer thinking for best harmony with system and user cognitive thinking mutually, with emotional integration of the design.

The templates mentioned in Sec.4 and Sec.5 should include a mechanism to include situations, and user mental background ontological views (vast views: culture views, and mental view and spontaneous views). We human; our intellectual communication is not bounded by fixed templates. Though we use them in learning and adapting our self through them, but we modify them for best performance. For example, we learn templates on driving skills by theory and practices. But on road, we modify these templates to match it to our behavior and cognitive mental performance. Such adaptability is related to the best adjustment that our body system and condition can fit into to create the best harmony that we think such driving performance is best. For the same human, driving style (templates) in downtown Cairo is not as driving style in downtown Tokyo. Looking into the contents of cognitive actions, we notice different patterns, between the proposed virtual system and human user in terms of perceiving a certain space. The spatial space relationship cognitive integration between human and virtual system is essential to best harmony in communication. These issues can be reflected into the Architecture design, when the integration of spatial space in design is essential to evaluate the whole layout of the architecture, where designers compete to new ideas based on their perception of the current state of the integrated spatial design in total be interfered by the cognitive user (mind).

We think the development of new interactive environment (like virtual Kenji system) can employ user interface with spatial cognition integration. This can contribute to reduce the load of mental visual reasoning.

We have in addition this, we added other sub-space, we called tonal sub-space that created a short of musical tone on the generated synthesized voice. Reference to rules of compositions by Marc-Antoine Charpentier (1692), we could notice the perpetual aspect between music and text. Pitch (Melody and harmony), rhythm (tempo and meter), and sonic qualities, (timbre, articulation dynamics, and texture) are the three parts defining the music structure. Such patterns construction, as combination of natural stimuli in well-specified generative forms reflects the source of our voice synthesis to produce sounds with such constructed nature. From this table (below) we have cognitive six Ekman modes be classified into tonal sub-space. The style of wording pronunciation is based on the compositional synthesis summarized in the below table. This sub-space would be integrated with the voice emotional recognition (Sec.5), sub-space. These two sub-spaces constitute the voice emotional synthesis and recognition part.

Sad	C_{Minor}, B_{Minor}, F_{Minor}
Happy	D_{Major}, G_{Major}, A_{Major}
Fear	$B_{FlatMinor}$, E_{Minor}
Surprise	$B_{FlatMajor}$, G_{Minor}, G_{Major}
Anger	F_{Major}, E_{Major}
Disgust	F_{Minor}, M_{Major}

We still are adding issue in regard to the colors and emotional states of the systems. From that prospective, we will have facial recognition space (Sec.4) and color sub-space to be integrated as part of the emotional space (facial, and voice), representation, all together to construct the distributed spatial recognition for best engagement between man and, machine. The color sub-space has not explained yet in this paper. This will be referenced in another to submit paper.

7. Conclusion:

We think that the two sub spatial cognitive spaces model would participate collectively to establish a cognitive interface between human and machine. The voice synthesis explained in Sec.5, integrated with tonal presentation outline in Sec. 6, these two subspaces contributes to create the voice synthesis space of machine recognition. Facial sub space explained in Sec. 4 and the color subspace(mentioned in Sec.6), contribute in establishing the perceptional view of the cognitive interaction (the perceptional synthesis and recognition of human emotional reasoning). This research project contributes to establish the best harmony and engagement between human user and the system based on defining and constructing the "self" in computing style, based on voice and facial construction definition of the self. The self defined in the system interacts with the human user based on the reasoning and recognition of the collected user voice and facial informational features and reasoned according to the self. This experiment would contribute to create new generation of cognitive user interface between man and machine.

Acknowledgement

We would like to thank Iwate Prefectural University for the financial support provided fro this project. Also, gratitude goes to (www.bitage.co.jp), Bitage limited for the hard work development on KANJO processor. Thanks also to Mangold International (www.mangold-international.com/), Mr. Pascal T. Mangold(CEO), for the support on INTERACT software tool, also thanks go to Dr. Kevin Erler of Automatic Sync Technologies (www.automaticsync.com), for technical advises on LipSync. Also, many thanks go to MIYAZAWA KENJI Museum (Mr. Ushizaki), Prof.T. Sasaki (Kenji's Scripts analysis), and Prof. Mochituki.

1. References

[1] ADELMANN, P. K. and ZAJONC, R. B. 1989. *"Facial efference and the experience of emotion."* Annual Review of Psychology, 40: pp249-280.

[2] BILDA Z., 2006. The role of mental imagery in conceptual designing, Doctor Thesis, *Key Centre of Design Computing and Cognition, Faculty of Architecture, University of Sydney, Australia*

[3] COOTES, T., EDWARDS, G. J., Taylor, C. J., Burkhardt, H., Neuman, B., 1998. Active Appearance Models, *Proc. Eur. Conf. Computer Vision*, 2, 484-498.

[4] EKMAN, P. and FRIESEN, W. V., 1975. Unmasking the Face, *Prentice Hall*, NY.

[5] EVANS, W.A., 1994. Approaches to intelligent information retrieval. *Information processing and management,* 7 (2), 147-168.

[6] FUJITA, H., HAKURA J., KUREMATSU, M., 2006. Virtual Cognitive Model for Miyazawa Kenji Based on Speech and Facial Images Recognition, *WSEAS Transactions on Circuits and Systems,* 10(5), 1536-1543.

[7] HAKURA, J., KUREMATSU, M., FUJITA, H., 2007. Facial Expression Recognition and Synthesis for Virtual Miyazawa Kenji System, *WSEAS Transactions on Circuits and Systems,*3(6), 288-295.

[8] HOLLAN, J., et al. 2000. *Distrubuted Cogntion:Toward a New Foundation for Human-Computer Interaction Research.* ACM Trans. On Computer-Human Interaction 7, No.2: 174-196.

[9] INTERACT, 2007. http://www.mangold-international.com/   News: *Japanese Scientist Revive Famous Writer, April 2007. Mangold International*

[10] JANSSEN, P., 2006. A Generative Evolutionary Design Method, *Digital Creativity*, Vol. 17, Issue 1, 2006, pp. 49–63.

[11] LIPSYNC, Automatic Sync Technologies, http://www.automaticsync.com ProductionSync and InstantSync.

[12] MERCER, P.A. AND SMITH, G., 1993. *Private view data in the UK.* 2nd ed. London: Longman.

[13] MITCHELL, W. J., 2005: *Placing Words: Symbols, Space, and the City*, MIT press, ISBN: 10-0-262-63322-1, Sept., 2005

[14] NEISSER, U. 1967. *Cogntive Psychology*, Englewood Cliffs, NJ' Prentice-Hall.

[15] NISHIYAMA, M., KAWASHIMA, H., HIRAYAMA, T., MATSUYAMA, T. 2005, Facial Expression Representation Based on Timing Structures in Faces, *IEEE International Workshop on Analysis and Modeling of Faces and Gestures*, 140-154.

[16] R-Project *http://www.r-project.org/*

[17] OUDEYER Pierre-Yves, 2003. The production and recognition of emotions in speech: features and algorithms, *International Journal of Human Computer Interaction*, Vol.59(1-2) pp.157-183.

[18] OPEN COMPUTER VISION LIBRARY, http://sourceforge.net/projects/opencvlibrary/

[19] PANTIC, M. and ROTHKRANTZ, L J. M., 2000. Automatic Analysis of Facial Expressions: The State of the Art. *IEEE Transactions on Pattern Analysis and Machine Intelligence*, 22(12), 1424-1445.

[20] PENG, W and GERO, J.S., 2007: *"Computer-aided design tools that adapt"*, *CAADFutures2007* (to appear)

[21] TICKLE N.R., 2003. *You can read a face like a book*, Daniels Publishing, 2003.

[22] SILVER, K., 1991. Electronic mail: the new way to communicate. *In:* D.I. RAITT, ed. *9th international online information meeting, 3-5 December 1990 London.* Oxford: Learned Information, 323-330.

[23] SMARTTALK *http://www.oki.com/jp/Cng/ Softnew/JIS/sm.html*

[24] SINGH, P. , and MINSKY M., 2004. *An Architecture for Cognitive Diversity*, In: D. DAVIS , ed. Visions of Mind.

[25] STEHMANN, M. B., ERSBOLL, B. K., LARSEN, R., 2003. *FAME – a flexible appearance modeling environment*, IEEE Transactions on Medical Imaging, 22(10), 1319-1331.

[26] MINSKY M., 2006. *The Emotion Machine,* Simon & Schuster publisher,

New Trends in Software Methodologies, Tools and Techniques
H. Fujita and D. Pisanelli (Eds.)
IOS Press, 2007

Establishing research criteria for performed gestures and emotional interaction in an gestural film game: *To be or not to be*

Roman DANYLAK[a], Zafer BILDA[a b], Ernest EDMONDS[a]
[a]Creativity and Cognition Studios, University of Technology, Sydney
[b]Australasian CRC for Interaction Design, Australia

Abstract. This paper describes practice-based research using an interactive gestural film game *To be or not to be,* to study the relationship between performed gestures and emotional response. The work is the result of a collaboration between an intermedia artist (first author), and a programmer / designer. The content of the interactive film game is based on lines from Act 3 scene i from Shakespeare's play *Hamlet.* Attention is given first to the original design method based on gestural expression in theatre using the key techniques of *text, rehearsal and performance.* A primary design goal was to construct an interface where coherent and continuous gestural and emotional interaction occurred. This is followed by observation and evaluation of audience / user interaction with the work (collaboration with second author) establishing research criteria to evaluate performed gestures and emotional responses of the audience.

Keywords. Theatre, performed gesture, emotion, human-computer interaction, game.

1. Introduction
The problem: the emotional content of gesture in human-computer interaction

1.1 A technological perspective

A persistent problem in human-computer gestural interface design has been the *interpretation of gestural content.* This may be characterised as an attempt to establish gestural meaning where it can be clearly stated that 'he moved *this way* and it meant *this...*'.

Achieving this end has been difficult because gestures are often ambiguous as they may differ in their function [1, 2]; gestures in common usage may sometimes be consciously expressive, or serve a functional need, or may merely be an incidental

---

[a] Correspondence author: rdanylak@it.uts.edu.au, ernest@ernestedmonds.com

movement as Martinec[3] points out. For this reason, it is difficult to pinpoint precise expressed content from observed gestures.

Queck, McNeill et al[4] who have published prodigious research in human-computer gestural interaction have stated that new paradigms are required to exploit gestural multimodal interaction, suitable, effective use having not yet been demonstrated. Kadous[5] furthermore, describes the state of research in this area as not lacking in hardware techniques for gathering information regarding body positioning, but that '....getting the data is only the first step. The second step, that of recognising the sign or gesture once it has been captured is much more challenging, *especially* in a continuous stream'. As such, the research problem to which this artwork responds to is the recognition of emotional content in gestures.

1.2 An artistic perspective

Attempts at creating gestural interfaces using artistic expression would seem to alleviate the problem significantly in that artistic gestures are *performed gestures*. Gestures used in traditional, stage- based gestural art forms mostly have a clear expressive function making emotional content apparent[6]. However, artists working in collaborative technological environments with gesture have also met with significant obstacles. Electronic artists Chadabe[7] and Rovan[8] have stated that differentiating expressed gestures as perceptible in interactive artworks is difficult due to the extreme temporal accuracy of gestural programs. For example, programs such as Max/MSP, commonly used in such artworks, are capable of defining commands to the millisecond, defining processes where humanly perceptible actions disappear and with it, perceived meaning of the gesture. As such, a clear attachment of the gesture to emotional content has also been difficult to achieve in artistic, expressive contexts of human-computer interaction.

As such, creating an interactive artwork where coherent and continuous expressed gestural and emotional interaction occurred was a primary design goal, responding to the persistent problem of emotional content and gesture.

2. Method: Practice-based research and Practice-led research

There are two critical distinctions in the adopted research approach that evolves the design, construction and evaluation of the interactive gestural film game *To be or not to be* [9], (short title *To be*; see reference for video site).

The first distinction is to recognise the research method of art and technology collaboration in practice-based research as defined by Candy and Edmonds[10] a specialist approach within human factors design in human-computer interaction[11]. Practice-based research is research that focuses upon practice where an artefact may be generated to respond to research questions with the goal of making an original contribution to an existing body of knowledge[12].

The second distinction is that of practice-led research; this is design research where a practitioner evolves new techniques in design process through reflective practice[13]. Outcomes of the research are often the evolution of new processes or techniques within the design discipline. What follows in the first part of this paper is practice-led research in that it describes a novel approach in design process; the second part, the evaluation, is practice-based, responding to the broader problem of emotion and gesture in the field of human-computer interaction.

3. Practice-led research: evolving the design of *To be*

3.1 Approach: making art

The overarching concept for the work was to *create* the emotions attached to a gesture experience, not unlike choreographing a dance with certain expressive moves or to be more precise, choosing how an actor moves on stage expressing a character's inner emotional state. The process uses the foundations of gesture making in theatre - a linear process - and then rearranges the elements so as to function as an interactive gestural film game in segmented cycles of interaction.

3.2 Gesture manufacture based on theatrical practice

Gestures made in professional theatre have a precise, focused, expressive goal as opposed to casually observed and experienced gestures of day to day interaction. Audiences watch a performance they receive a specific, directed emotional message as communicated through the gestural and speech patterns of the actors. Watching the same performance on another day and experiencing more or less the same message, indicates a process is present by which the expression of the gestures are constructed and regulated. Without such conscious structures, the repetition of the art form would not be possible.

The theatrical process adopted here is the creation of dramatic performance from literary scripts, which has been practiced in Western culture from the time of Ancient Greek theatre to the modern day performance [14]. The process by which such traditional mainstream theatre is developed can be defined in three stages. This process will be described as *text, rehearsal and performance* (see Figure 1); this is the process by which a director, who envisages the details of the performance from a script, works with actors, constructing the work with its emotional content and expressive gestures. These key elements are described as follows:

3.2.1 Text

This first stage, involves the reading of the script by the actors and director; it is at this point that the director decides on the *intent* of the work, developing the message that will be conveyed in the performed play. This is an act of interpretive reading, a process by which directors in theatre construct an intended message into the work not unlike designing a message in prose or conveying feeling through a painting or film [15]. A script of textual dialogue may be interpreted in a number ways, this interpretation altering the delivered emotional message of the work. One director might see a work as tragic and serious; another may see the message of the same script as humorous, and as such, construct scenes to convey that message. This is a primary consideration when generating emotions in developed gestural artforms and is the content design phase of a work. The text, as such, contains the main blueprint of emotional content from which gestural action is evolved by actors and directors.

3.2.2 Rehearsal

Secondly, rehearsal occurs where development of the physical gestures and speech occurs. The goal is to discard the text, actors and director then developing the *spatial reality* of the characters. At this point script and gestures are memorised, reinforced by constant repetition.

The specific rehearsal process to establish stage movement is called blocking [16]. Blocking is the process by which actors and directors decide where an actor should be on stage when delivering lines as they appear in the written script of the play. Where one stands and how one moves upon the stage is critical as this forms the character's behaviour communicating the intended emotion to an audience. As such, a key requirement for all actors is to be in the right place at the right time, so as that all perform the sequences of speech and gesture eventually in synchronisation. The characters, through actor rehearsal, emerge from the two-dimensional text into the three dimensions of the stage.

3.2.3 Performance

Finally, there is the performance; actor gestures and speech communicate the work in a fixed pattern to a passive audience from memory. The actors of the written page now exist mimetically, a simulation of the textual world on stage. This performance has the capacity to be repeated because the spatial coordinates of gestures and delivered speech exist in the constructed space of the stage. To achieve this end, text, rehearsal and performance follow one another as separate processes.

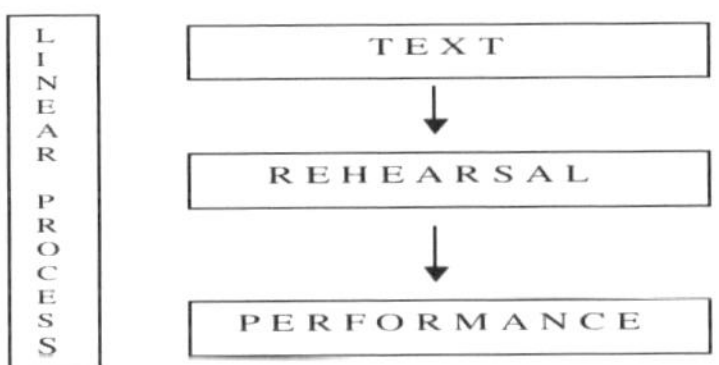

Figure 1. Process used in theatre to create expressive gestures in a narrative context

3.3 A new model: interactive gestural film game

3.3.1 Recurring cycles of theatrical media forms in To be

The interactive gestural film game *To be* utilises the foundations of the theatrical process. *Text, rehearsal* and *performance* are altered and function in recurring cycles in an interactive game format, to which is added also the medium of film. Gestures made by the audience / user in the game control the playing of the film. The steps of this process can be described as: *text phrase; rehearsal and performance; virtual theatre: film;* and *game.* Their configuration is represented in Figure 2 and are described as follows:

3.3.2 Text phrase

Text phrase is the segmentation of the text into syllabic units. The process of continuous narrative text is divided into rhythmic pulses, presented as either single syllables or groups of syllables written in large font on the screen. These pulses form the basis on which the floor pad pattern is executed. The audience / user then dances the text, assembling the narrative text as they proceed.

3.3.3 Rehearsal and performance

The audience / user walks to solve the gestural floor puzzle with the goal of creating a fixed pattern as defined by the program. This is similar to the process of blocking, where an actor adopts a fixed time and place to deliver lines. When the fixed pattern is achieved, this is considered performance.

3.3.4 Virtual theatre: film

As each word gesture puzzle is solved, sections of a pre-shot film based on the *Hamlet* narrative text, is played back to the audience / user. The virtual quality of film creates the illusion of theatrical space adding performers to the interactive experience.

3.3.5 Game

The work is a game in that the gestures are puzzle-patterns to be achieved. The aim of the game is to solve all twenty-three gesture puzzles triggering target squares in the pre-programmed patterns. Once this occurs, the entire film is played back. The experience is that the gestural exertion of the audience / user has assembled the film as a single narrative unit. *Text phrase, rehearsal and performance, virtual theatre / film* are part of interlocking cycles by which a final game goal can be achieved progressively. Table 1 shows these three elements as a modified sample storyboard of the game.

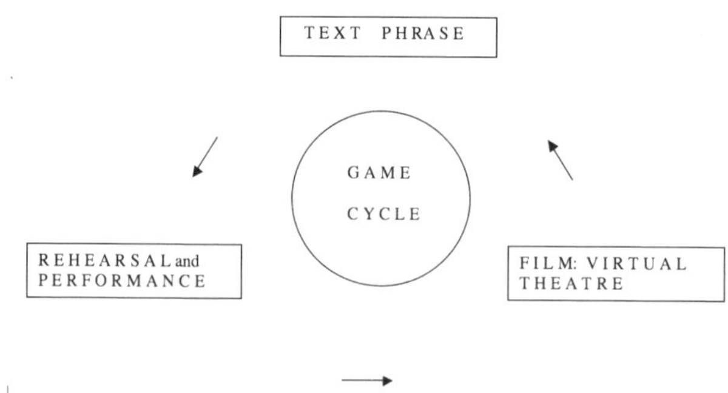

Figure 2. Arrangement of key elements in interactive gestural film game *To be*

Table 1. Modified sample storyboard showing screen shots and floor plan of first five word / gesture puzzles in *To be*. Note gesture position map in left hand corner of screen. There are twenty-three puzzle sequences in total. Entire film plays back once all puzzles are solved as game goal.

G A M E				
C Y C L E	**syllabic units**	**STEP 1** **TEXT PHRASE**	**STEP 2** **REHEARSAL to PERFORMANCE**	**STEP 3** **VIRTUAL THEATRE: FILM**
F U N C T I O N		Gesture/word puzzle based on syllabic units as indicated by flashing left hand square codes on screen. Proceed to Step 2 (solving all twenty-three puzzles, entire assembled film plays back)	User/audience performs gestures on floorpads with the goal of achieving pre-programmed pattern. If achieved, triggers playing of *virtual theatre; film.* Proceed to Step 3	Segmented /film sequence of short Hamlet film. Film generates emotional response. Playing of next text phrase. Return to Step 1
1	to be	To be	1 2	
2	or	or	3	
3	not to be	not to be ?	4 5 6	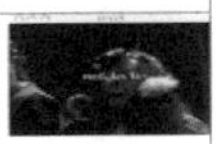
4	that	That	7	
5	is	is	8	

4. The user experience: a description

4.1 Generating gestures

Users walk upon an array of a thirty-six square interactive floorpad measuring 3m x 3m connected to a Mac G5 computer which also controls an adjacent 2m x 3m back projected multimedia screen with sound which the user faces when interacting with the floor pad.

When audience / users enter the room the work is in a steady default state displaying a title and brief description. As the audience / user walks onto the floorpad this triggers the game cycle. The second screen gives a brief description of the game rules and the function of the gesture map: green squares show a user where they are actively walking; blue squares are an indication of where users should walk to; red squares indicate that the user has hit a target, being in the right place at the right time. The goal of the game – to solve all twenty-three gesture / word puzzles– is also stated and that the film will play back in full with all sequences once all puzzles are solved.

Figure 3. a, b. Audience / user in two different gesture positions, engaging Step 1 *text phrase,* the reading of syllabic units and Step 2 *rehearsal and performance,* generating gestures according to game map (upper left hand corner).

Table 2. Map codes

Blue	**Green**	**Red**
target squares established in program to be extinguished; flashing in set sequences	show active walking position of user to aid navigation to find the blue square position	the target has been achieved; user has extinguished a blue square, being in the right place at the right time. Move to next target or film proceeds.

The audience / user is presented with large on-screen text, where sections of Hamlet's monologue appear (Figure 3 a, b) A small map in the upper left-hand corner shows the player's active position on the floorpads, represented by interactive green squares allowing navigation. Blue squares flash simultaneously in a pre-programmed pattern; these are target squares where the user must stand to engage the game. When the user has performed the correct gesture by standing on the blue square position at the right time, the square turns red on the map until each square of the syllabic sequence is extinguished. This causes as section of film to play. The next word / gesture puzzle to be solved will then appear. A progressive text-map of all sequences completed appear in the right hand corner. The codes of the map are summarised in Table 2.

4.2 The game goal

The audience / user ideally solves twenty-three word / gesture sequences each sequence delivering a film segment. Once all twenty-three word / gesture sequences are performed followed by twenty-three pieces of narrative film, the entire film plays back as one narrative. What is observed by the user is the achievement of the gestural exertions in assembling the twenty-three sequences into one continuous film. In this way, the gestures of the audience control the playing of the film.

4.3 Generating emotions
Directorial intent and emotional response in 'To be or not to be'

The emotional material in *To be* is present in the film which forms an integral part of the game. The short film is based on lines from Shakespeares' play *Hamlet* Act 3 sc. 1 lines 56-61 [17], a well known scene where the prince, Hamlet, is suffering from conflicting emotions about his father's murder and his desire for revenge and reflects deeply upon the meaning of life. The film is based on the *Hamlet* text as a script. Actors workshopped this material with the artist, the film storyboarded as a narrative film, then shot, edited and loaded into the game.

The interpretation adopted is tragi-comic, meaning it communicates a sad and also a humorous message. The film has three groups of characters played by the same three actors alternatively. The three groups are office workers, pirates and spirits. The life of office workers is shown to be colourless and uninteresting; the pirates are fun-loving, playful but temperamental; whilst the spirits watch and react to these two other worlds. The material is designed for teenage audiences.

These three character dimensions form the basis of the directorial intent and establish the emotional range of the film as: negative, that is sad emotions; positive, that is happy emotions; and neutral or other, as represented by the spirits. The characters associated with theses emotions are shown in Figure 4 a, b, c.

Sprits (neutral)   *Pirates (happy)*   *Office workers (sad)*

Figure 4. a, b, c. Scenes from play back sequences in *To be or not be*, activated when the audience / user solves a word /gesture sequence (multimedia text removed).

5. Method of Evaluation

This section now discusses our approach to audience experience evaluation, where we focus on the gestural and emotional responses of the audience. We start with describing what the criteria could be for evaluating the audience experience of *To be*. The goal is to establish the validity of criteria through data collection, analysis and preliminary measurements.

5.1 Criteria

The evaluation was designed firstly to respond to two factors: performed gestures and emotional response. We do not aim to describe the relationship between these two, but only aim to establish our criteria to understand how they change over the timeline of each experience.

5.1.2 Defining gestural response

A performed gestural response was any execution of the pre-programmed floorpad moves required to solve the word/gesture sequence. This comprised of standing on the blue target floorpad at the correct place and time according to VR testing requirements[18]. According to the game rules, a change from a blue square to a red square registered in the program as a performed standing gesture

5.1.3 Defining emotional response

Three main categories were established for recording emotional responses to the film based on the notion that audiences emotionally respond to film[19]. These emotions were *happy, sad* and *neutral* based on the three character types of the tragic, the comic and the spiritual respectively as stated in the directorial intention of the artist. The participants were tested using thirteen words in three groups. These groups were:

- (sad)   A/ bored; disappointed; troubled; frustrated.
- (happy)   B/ funny; playful; colourful; foolish; jovial.
- (neutral) C/ angel-like; watchful; sensitive.

A 'pass' criteria (no response) was also possible. A control emotional criteria was established through a statement of directorial intent.

5.2 Data collection

5.2.1 Participant selection

Nine teenage subjects were tested for whom ethical approval was obtained. The subjects were visiting the *Beta_space* exhibition and evaluation facility at Sydney's Powerhouse Museum – a technology museum - as part of a schools program. Selection was based on teachers asking for interested volunteers from the class to participate. Participants P1 to P5 were from a co-educational school and were aged between fifteen and sixteen years of age; students P5-P9 were from an all boys school aged between thirteen and fourteen years of age. Parental consent had been established in writing prior to the visit.

5.2.2 Performed gestures

To obtain data on performed gestures participants were instructed to use the interface for as long as they wished. Responses were obtained through tabulating the rate at which users completed the target sequences as recorded in the Beta_space computer program that regulated the game process through the floorpads. Electronic log records of floorpad interactions were retained in the hard drive of the computer.

5.2.3 Emotional responses

Immediately after the subject user had completed the interface user test, each participant was interviewed in a separate room by a researcher. Twenty-three of word / gesture puzzle short films were shown plus two concluding scenes. The participant was also shown the interview form on which the emotion criteria of thirteen words appeared in three groups of happy, sad and neutral and asked to select one of the words as a response to each film scene they were being shown. These responses were recorded on a sheet by the interviewer (appendix 1). This process was based on verbal protocol analysis where playback of significant user experiences are commented on by the user after the using the interface[20]. The process was limited to what users had viewed in their experience only.

5.3 Data analysis

5.3.1 Performed gestures

To capture the levels of performed gestures, the interactions of participants on the floorpad as recorded in Beta_space computer program was analysed. This data was transferred by data clip from the Beta_space computer and analysed on a laptop computer. Gestures performed per syllabic unit could be established from these records and are represented in Figure 5. Figure 6 shows total comparisons of all nine participants and the number of walking gestures recorded on the floorpad before converting blue squares to red following the word / gesture puzzle. This is marked by the syllabic units present in the game marked on the x axis. A trend line is included.

5.3.2 Emotional response

The criteria of 'happy', 'sad' or 'other', recorded on the questionnaire sheet in the post experience interview were then represented as responses to the twenty-five film images played after each word / gesture puzzle had been solved. In Table 3 each of the three emotional states are represented by a pattern code (see key) occurring one after the other. This has been tabulated in one chart for all nine participants. A control category of directorial intent, that is the intended emotional response created by the film director / artist, is also present.

6. Results

Figure 5 shows the change in number of hits to the floor pads, as participants perform gestures as part of playing the interactive game. The high peaks in the chart occur when the user is not able to solve the puzzle, although s/he is making several attempts to hit the blue square to turn it into red. The more unsuccessful attempts are made to hit the blue square, the more the number of gestures performed during the experience, indicated by peaks. Troughs indicate that the user has hit the target with a low number

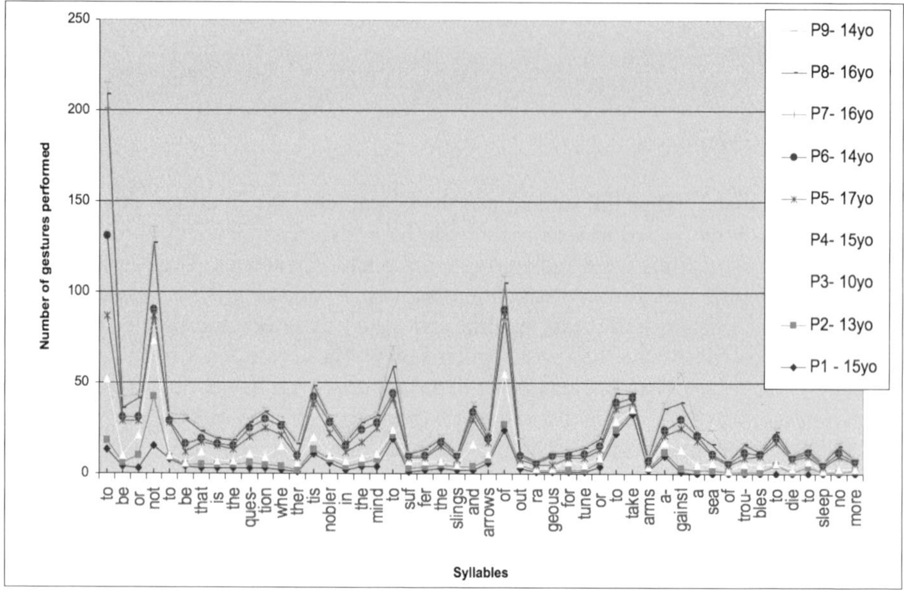

Figure 5. Performed gestures per syllable, nine subjects

of gestural attempts. The x-axis of the graph shows the twenty-three text phrase syllable units. The experience timeline starts from the left hand side of the graph and progresses through to right hand side of the graph. The right end of the graph indicates that the game was completed having solved all twenty-three episodes and that the participant achieved the game goal of playing back the entire film, an assembly of all the episodes.

In summary, Figure 5 shows the number of gestural actions of all nine participants as a response to each syllable game unit activating the floor pads while the puzzle was being solved. Here, there are significant features. For example P7 (participant 7) showed a very high rate of gesture performance being unable to hit the target square but the rate dropped down quite quickly and subsequent gestures as per the average. This was also the case for P2, this participant not completing the game abandoning the process at the word 'arrows'. P3 showed a very high peak in the middle of the game at the syllable 'to', experiencing a delay. P8 had a minimum number of peaks indicating a low gesture rate succeeding to perform the gestures with a minimum number of moves. Eight of the nine participants completed the game.

Figure 6 shows the total trend of all gestures performed (Total) and the average fitted trendline with a minus slope. The minus slope of the average trendline means that the number of gestures performed decreased along the timeline of the interactive game experience. In other words, the participants showed an increased ability to perform fewer gestures, suggesting that familiarity of the interactive process grew as they used the system. The peaks and troughs however indicate that difficulty and ease of the gesture puzzle sequence varied.

Table 3 demonstrates the emotional responses in the three criteria of 'happy', 'sad' and 'neutral' as occurring in response to the film play back sequence. A pass

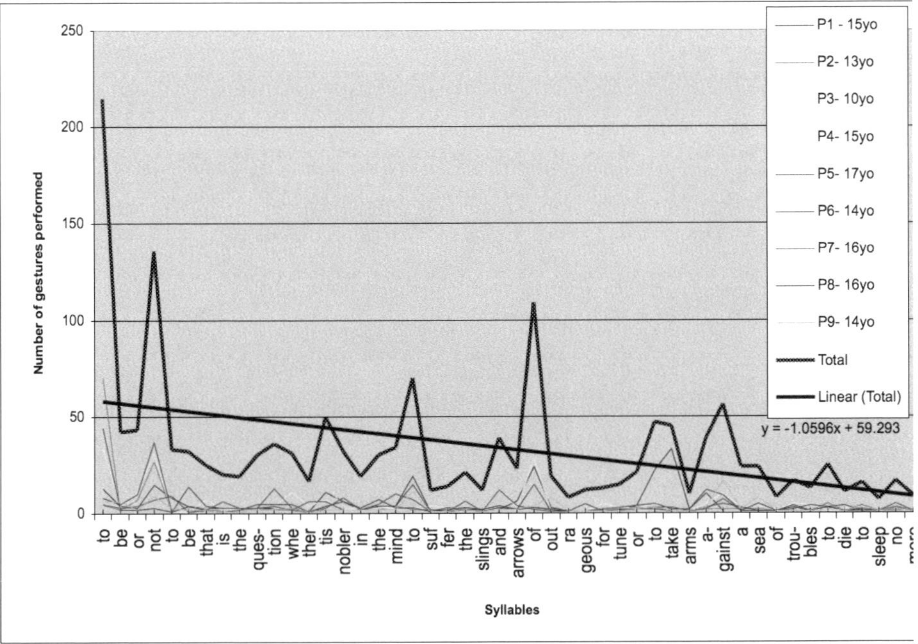

Figure 6. Total number of performed gestures of individual participants, and trendline

category of 'no response' was also present during testing. Each participant has chosen one of the three emotion categories as a response to the film. The column 'control' is the directorial intent determined by the artist who designed the film, constructing scenes with the emotional intention of 'happy', 'sad' or 'neutral' scenes. P5 showed the greatest percentage of aberration from the anticipated pattern at 14% whilst P9 showed the highest level of concurrence at 68%. P2 who did not complete the game was tested only for the relevant gestural responses. The average number of scenes responses meeting the directorial intent was 13.3 out of the 25 total scenes – almost half, standing at 52%. The general pattern shows that the 'happy' message of the first half and its 'sad' second half was communicated to the audience.

7. Discussion

7.1 Methodology

The collaborative relationship between the Creativity and Cognition Studios, UTS and The Powerhouse Museum was very effective in that the museum being a public exhibition space, generates significant user interest in exhibited artefacts. The research team utilised the museum's school program to randomly recruit a variety of subjects, gaining parental permission in support of the methodology ethics.

The face to face interview held with the participants was digitally recorded; at times, noise levels from accompanying exhibitions interfered with the conversation during the interview process with questions requiring repetition. Identification of pre-

Table 3. Tested emotional responses: nine test participants versus control (director intent)

syllabic units	scene	control	P1	P2	P3	P4	P5	P6	P7	P8	P9	P versus control	average
to be	1											8	
or	2											1	
not to be	3											8	
that	4											3	
is	5											4	
the	6											9	
ques	7											0	
tion	8											0	
whether	9											1	
'tis nobler	10											0	
in	11											8	
the	12											9	
mind	13											8	
to suffer	14											5	
the slings	15											5	
and arrows	16											8	
of..fortune	17											7	
or	18											1	
to take arms	19											5	
a... troubles	20											6	
to die	21											0	
to sleep	22											1	
no more	23											0	
mask scene	24											7	
violin scene	25											9	
no. of emotions correct per participant		25	12	16	11	14	7	14	15	14	17		13.3
% correct		100	48	64	44	56	14	56	60	56	68		52

KEY	
sad	
happy	
neutral	
pass / na	

defined emotion types to replayed video was an effective technique to collect teenagers' emotional responses; the purpose and procedure were easy to communicate to the participants.

7.2 Results

The design of the interactive gestural film game based on the theatrical model was effective in generating performed gestures and emotion. Users had little difficulty in understanding the operations of the interface as a gestural game and showed above average levels of emotional response to the narrative material. The high levels of game completion showed that this arrangement was coherent and engaging.

Measuring levels of emotional response could be achieved by choosing a simpler narrative; *Hamlet* is a complex play with complex emotions; sometimes the design of characters were necessarily ambiguous in nature, for example, the pirates were designed to be humorous but sometimes also showed negative emotions such as greed or jealousy, as typical of their ironic nature. A simpler script would allow for more direct emotional analysis.

This however, may have an adverse effect on completion rates as an interesting narrative aids completion: an aim is to balance between the two. An advantage of

Hamlet is that its strong expressive material makes the strong polarity of tragi-comic interpretation possible; it is also well known, gaining user attention readily.

8. Conclusions

The anticipated outcome was to establish research criteria for performed gestures and emotional response occurring in the interactive gestural film game *To be*. The preliminary findings have indicated that the interactive gestural film game format generates a coherent, continuous and varied expression of performed audience / user gestures with a range of emotions that can be measured.

Future activity further evolving the design could incorporate a variety of sensor devices, altering the nature of the gestural interaction, for example, also incorporating hand movements. Further, the film design could be evolved to create an even greater variation in emotional response using different arrangements of media input and output. Designing the narrative message of the film specifically to different categories of age, gender and culture is also worth considering. Other perspectives, such as group game playing could also be explored as well as research into the experience of spectator gaming, that is, the experience of watching another engage in the game.

Acknowledgements

Thanks to Dr Linda Candy for invaluable guidance in the evaluation process; Professors Margaret Boden, Tom Hewitt, Nigel Cross, Ted Selker, and Hamido Fujita for their inputs; also Glen Pead, Pas Accuri, Johanna de Ruyter, Lucinda Gleeson, UTS Faculty of Humanities, Toula Anastos, Alex Turenko and Viveka Wiley who assisted in making and presenting the artwork; Deborah Turnbull and to Matthew Connell, curators; and to the parents, teachers and children who gave their time to support the research. This research / work was partly funded by the Australasian CRC for Interaction Design, which is established and supported under the Australian Government's Cooperative Research Centres Program. Special thanks to Alastair Weakley whose collaborative work and patience enabled the technical plan of the interface.

References

[1]   Abercrombie, D., *Paralanguage*, in *Communication in Face to Face Interaction*, J. Laver and S. Hutcheson, Editors. 1972, first published 1968.

[2]   Barre, W.L., *The Cultural Basis of Emotions and Gestures*, in *Communication in Face to Face Interaction*, J. Laver and S. Hutcheson, Editors. 1972, first print 1947, Penguin: England. p. 207.

[3]   Martinec, R., *Interpersonal resources in action.* Semiotica, 2001. 1(4): p. 117-145.

[4]   Quek, F., McNeill, D., Bryll, R., Duncan, S., Ma, X.F., Kirbas, C., McCullogh, K.E., and Ansari, R., *Multimodal Human Discourse: Gesture and Speech in ACM Transactions on Computer-Human Interaction.* 2002. 9(3): p. 172-176.

[5]   Kadous, W., *Machine Gesture and Sign Language Recognition.* 2007, School of Computing Science and Engineering, Autonomous Systems and Sensing Technologies, University of New South Wales, Sydney, Australia http://www.cse.unsw.edu.au/~waleed/gsl-rec/.

[6]   Vaganova, A., *Basic Principles of Classical Ballet: Russian Ballet Technique.* 1969, New York.

[7]   Chadabe, J. *The Limitations of Mapping as a Structural Descriptive in Electronic Instruments* in *Conference on New Instruments for Musical Expression*. 2002. Dublin, Ireland p 1-5.

[8]   Rovan, J.B., Wechsler, R., and Weiss, F., *Seine hohle Form: Artistic Collaboration in an Interactive Dance and Music Performance Environment*. Crossings: eJournal of Art and Technology, 2001. 1(2).

[9]   Danylak, R. and Weakley, A., *To be or not to be*. 2006, http://www.youtube.com/watch?v=jKNvSpXG0Z0.

[10]   Edmonds, E. and Candy, L., *Explorations in Art and Technology*. 2002, London: Springer-Verlag.

[11]   Preece, J., *Human-Computer Interaction*, ed. p.vii. 1994, Harlow, England: Pearson.

[12]   Candy, L., *Practice-Based Research: A Guide*. 2006, Creativity and Cognition Studios, University of Technology, Sydney http://www.creativityandcognition.com/resources/PBR%20Guide-1.1-2006.pdf.

[13]   Schon, D., *The Reflective Practitioner*. 1983: Basic Books.

[14]   Nagler, A.N., *A Source Book in Theatrical History*. 1952, Dover: New York.

[15]   Monaco, J., *How to Read a Film: The Art, Technology, Language, History and Theory of Film and Media p.1-20*. 1977: Oxford University Press.

[16]   Brockett, O.G., *Theatre: An Introduction*. 1964, New York: Holt, Rhinehart and Winston. 541-2.

[17]   Shakespeare, W., *Hamlet: a tragedy in five acts, by William Shakespeare, as arranged for the stage by Henry Irving, London: Printed at the Chiswick Press, 1879* in *Horace Howard Furness Memorial (Shakespeare) Library*. First Folio 1623 http://dewey.library.upenn.edu/sceti/printedbooks.

[18]   Patel, H., Cruz, M.D., Cobb, S., and Wilson, J., *Initial Report on Existing Evaluation Methodologies; VR and Human factors best practices*. 2004, Information Society Technologies (IST) Programme http://www.intuition-eunetwork.net/documents/deliverables.p. 10-15.

[19]   Smith, G.M., *Film Structure and the Emotion System*. The Velvet Light Trap, University ofTexas, 2004. 54: p. 76-79.

[20]   Russo, J.E., Johnson, E.J., and Stephens, D.L., *The Validity of Verbal Protocols*. Memory & Cognition, 1989. 17(6): p. 759-769.

Appendix 1

PHASE 2
WRITTEN RESULTS   **SUBJECT NAME:**
TEST
WATCH SCREEN SHOTS   **RUN BY:**

DATE:

As we show the sections of the movie in the appearing order on a computer screen, we
ask the participant to assign an emotion / mood or feeling to each scene.

Scene	Emotion/ mood / feeling	Choose one word from List 1 List 2 or List 3 using the alphabet code
1 to be		List 1
2 or		
3 not to be		(A) SAD
4 that		(B) BORED
5 is		(C) DISSAPOINTED
6 the		(D) TROUBLED
7 ques		(E) FRUSTRATED
8 tion		
9 whether		List 2
10 tis nobler		
11 in		(S) FUNNY
12the		(T) PLAYFUL
13 mind		(U) COLOURFUL
14 to suffer		(V) FOOLISH
15 the slings		(W) JOVIAL
16 and arrows		
17of ...fortune		List 3
18 or		
19 to ..arms		(H) ANGEL-LIKE
20 aga....troubles		(I) WATCHFUL
21 to die		(J) SENSITIVE
22 to sleep		
23 no more		
24 mask scene		
25 violin scene		

Chapter 4

Network Software Security

New Trends in Software Methodologies, Tools and Techniques
H. Fujita and D. Pisanelli (Eds.)
IOS Press, 2007

Formal Technique for Discovering Complex Attacks in Computer Systems [1]

Lamia Hamza [a] Kamel Adi [b,c]

Computer Security Research Laboratory

[a] *Computer Science Department*
Université de Béjaia
hamzalamia@gmail.com

[b] *Computer Science and Engineering Department*
Université du Québec en Outaouais
Gatineau, Québec, Canada
Kamel.Adi@uqo.ca
[c] *Advanced Research Institute on SoftwarE Strategies (ARISES)*
Morioka, Japan

Abstract. Computer systems security management can be largely improved by the installation of mechanisms for automatic discovery of complex attacks due to system vulnerabilities and middleware misconfigurations. The aim of this paper is to propose a new formal technique for modeling computer system vulnerabilities and automatic generation of attack scenarios exploiting these vulnerabilities.

Keywords. Computer security, Intrusion detection, Modelling, Attacks scenarios, Formal technique

1. Introduction

With the growing need for computer systems opened to the Internet, computer security became a major concern. The current approach for securing computer systems consists in setting up firewalls and intrusion detection systems in addition to panoply of other ad-hoc solutions. Each one of these mechanisms, used independently or in conjunction, have not proved to be a fool-proof strategy to protect the network assets. This can be attributed to the fact that these systems are put in place without preliminary and meticulous network vulnerability analysis and the possibilities of exploitation of these vulnerabilities by the intruder for network attacks. In this context, automatic generation of attack scenarios is of crucial importance for the analysis and the configuration of computer systems security. Our work contributes in this field by proposing a new formal technique for system modelling and analysis in order to generate automatically attack scenarios of the system.

---

[1] This research is supported by NSERC (the Natural Sciences and Engineering Research Council of Canada)

The remainder of this paper is organized as follows: Section 2 presents the related work. Section 3 details our approach. Section 4 presents example showing how our technique can be used to generate the attack scenarios. Section 5 concludes this paper.

2. Related Work

Nowadays, the generation of attacks scenarios is the intense research object and several works [1,2,3,5,6,7,9,10,11,12,13,14,15,17,18] was published on this subject. This work basically follows one of these three approaches:

First approach, based on the definition of logical rules that relate events through pre-conditions and post conditions, a second based on the representation of the relationships among events as a graph and a third describes how attack graphs can be used to group the large numbers of alerts that are produced by Intrusion Detection Systems (IDS). The description of an attack scenario requires a multi-events language for signature recognition. Templeton and Levitt [17] propose a language for describing attacks, JIGSAW, centred on the expression of attack pre-conditions and their effects with respect to the attacker. Note that JIGSAW is intended to describe attacks; and not to describe attack scenarios.

Cuppens and Ortalo [2] define a language, called Lambda, for the specification of attack scenarios. In the approach of Cuppens [2,3], the work of the experts is confined to the description, in Lambda, of the attacks with their pre- and post-conditions. The possible scenarios are built automatically, starting from a description of a base attack, by the mapping of the pre and post-conditions.

Mé and Michel [9] propose a description language for attack scenarios called ADeLe. An attack in ADeLe is described with its pre and post conditions. The authors of ADeLe did not push the details up to the level reached in the language Lambda where each useful information for the attack is codified in a form similar to the Prolog facts.

The languages discussed above imply that we know, a priori, all the scenarios we want to detect, but without any guaranty that we will be able to generate those scenarios. In order to overcome the limits of the language based attack correlation approach, the authors of [1,5,7,11,12,13,14,15,18] propose an approach based on attacks graph. An attack graph is a collection of attack scenarios showing how a malicious user can compromise the integrity of a target system.

The authors of [13,14,15] envisage the automatic generation of an attack graph by resorting to model checking, which is known to suffer from the combinatorial explosion problem. To analyse exploits in large networks, Ammann and Al [1] propose a « *scalable»* network vulnerability analysis method based on the assumption of monotonicity [2], which decreases the analysis complexity from exponential to polynomial. Jajodia and Al [5], use this approach to develop a tool for Topological Vulnerability Analysis (TVA), TVA

---

[2]This means the attacker never loses her abilities to further the attack in network due to any action taken in her attack.

is one of the most comprehensive tools developed to now for the approach of building and analysing attack graphs, the author of [7,11,12,18] extend these approach by the further details that explain how network hardening recommendations are made in the TVA system and they describes various approaches to collapse parts of attack graphs generated by the TVA system to make visual understanding easier. TVA tool generates a graph of dependencies among exploits that represents all possible attack paths but it does not explicitly specify the security policy to enforce and it cannot provide information as to whether a potential attack sequence is really harmful.

In [4], Dacier introduces the concept of a « *privilege graph*»İn this graph, a privilege is defined as being a set of rights that a subject can have on an object. The nodes of the graph are sets of privileges that each user has on a set of objects. The existence of an edge from a set of privileges to another one indicates that ownership of the first set makes it possible to acquire the second, by applying one or more access control rules. This approach analyzes only a single host and uses graph-building tools and measures that may not scale to large networks.

In order to detect complex attacks and to increase the level of granularity of alerts, the authors of [10] propose a technique of alerts correlation based on type graph to reason about attacks possibly missed by the IDSs. This is accomplished by first building attack graphs for a computer network that is being protected by the IDS. If IDS alerts can be associated with actions in the attack graph, then alerts that arrive in a sequence that is predicted when proceeding along a single attack graph path may indicate that an attacker is successfully performing the steps in that path. Constructing a type graph does not have the scalability problem but it is one of alert correlation method which depends on the underlying IDSs to provide alerts and no practical application has yet been constructed.

A common observation in the related research literature is that the existing approaches for the generation of the attack scenarios turn out to be not very reliable. Although research has made significant progress in the past few years, a computation for most approaches suffer from the problem of « *scalability*» they are impracticable for networks with a hundred computers. Current approaches also are limited because many of the existing attack graph tools adopt an ad-hoc way to represent input information and output graph data structures, many assume that host-to-host reachability information between all hosts is already available, many produce an attack graph but do not automatically generate recommendations from that graph, many does not explicitly specify the security policy to enforce, and the resulting attack graphs are often hard to comprehend and use by a human. These have made those attack graph tools difficult to use in practice.

3. Our Approach

In this article, we propose a new formal approach based on the use privileges of graph and a security policy to produce attacks graph. The proposed approach consists in building attack scenarios using a formal proof. The choice of the formal proof is justified by the fact that it has the capacity to treat systems with an infinite number of states since it is capable to infer conclusions directly starting from an abstract description of the

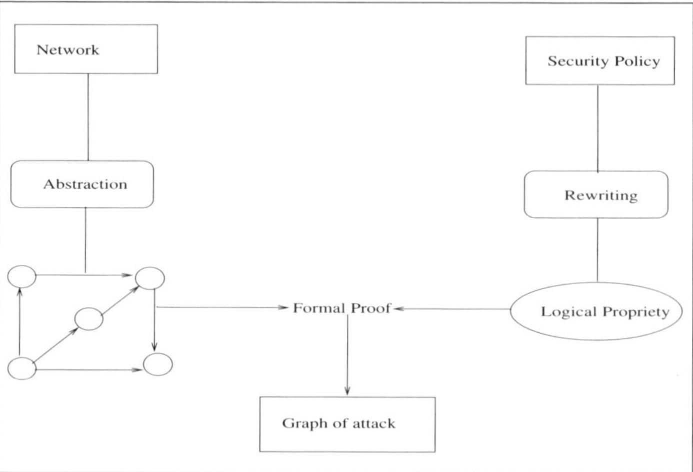

Figure 1. Proposed approach.

system and a security policy; In our representation, a node in the graph is a privilege acquired by exploitation of a vulnerability. This privilege does not encode the entire state of the network, but only some aspect of it. The edges in the graph specify the causality relations between these privileges. Our contribution is to formally represent such dependency relations and generate attack graphs through automatic logic deduction. Moreover, our approach specifies explicitly the security policy to enforce using the power of temporal logic. The main steps of this approach are summarized in Figure 1.

The proposed approach uses a privilege graph. Thus, we define an attack as being the acquisition of a privilege by exploiting vulnerability, and an attack scenario as being the acquisition of a set of privileges whose last privilege is an intrusions objective. Note that, an attack scenario ends as soon as intrusion objective is reached. Thus, principal steps of our approach are:

- Define a network attack model;
- Rewriting the security properties;
- Build an attack graph.

3.1. Network Attack Model

The model of attack is represented as a finite state machine. The choice of this model is justified by the fact that it includes all the families of the models policy security, each one is characterized by the way of defining a state, the transition function or the unit from the states which violate security. The model suggested described the system by the following components:

H: the set of computers connected to the network;
C: the connectivity relation;
A: the set of the individual actions that an intruder can apply to carry out the attacks scenario;
O: the whole of the intrusions objectives.

Hosts.   The principal interest of modeling host is to capture the maximum of information on these vulnerable components. According to Sheyner [15], a computer $h \in H$ is described by the tuple $(id, svcs, sw, vuls)$, where:

- id is the single identifier of the computer (machine name, network addresses);
- $svcs$ is the list of service (service name, listen port);
- sw is the list of the actifs software (in operation);
- $vuls$ is the list of the vulnerable components.

Connectivity Relation.   Connectivity are expressed by the relation $C \subseteq H \times H \times P$ where P is the set of the port numbers. The relation $C(h_1, h_2, p)$ means that the computer h_2 is accessible from h_1 on the port p, note that the connectivity relation incorporates the filtering of the firewalls rules which restrict the activity of a computer on another.

Intruder Actions.   Intruder actions are based on the exploitation of an existing vulnerability of an element in the set H. Thus, we will need to model attacks associated with each vulnerability.

3.2. Network Security Policy

The networks security management is made very difficult by their heterogeneity and their complexity. The abstraction of these constraints recommends the specification of security policies in high level terms. Let $action$ be the set of events which can be authorized or prohibited by a security policy. Within the framework of this article, these events represent the access of a malevolent user to a resource. Inspiring from [16], we give the following definitions of a security policy:

Definition 3.1. *A security policy defined on a set of action sequences is a property indicating for sequence of actions if it is authorized or not.*

Definition 3.2. *A computer system is in conformity with a security policy if no action (or sequence of actions) can violate that policy.*

From an attacker view point, the intrusion objective is the motivation which justifies its actions. From the detection view point, the intrusion objective is all violation of the security policy. In our approach, the intrusion objective is the intruder motivation. From the definition 3.1, we consider an attack scenario as the set of the malevolent actions authorized by the security policy whose last action is a prohibited action.

Definition 3.3. *An attack scenario is a set of privileges acquired by the exploitation of vulnerabilities whose last privilege is an intrusions objective.*

The intruder seeks to violate the security policy and his strategy is to exploit the system vulnerabilities in order to acquire more and more privileges while it did not reach his objective intrusion.

Before creating an attacks graph for a computer system, we must define in a formal language the system security policies. So, we have to choose an adequate logic in order to

Table 1. syntax

$$\Phi, \Psi \; ::= \; p \mid \neg\Phi \mid \Phi \vee \Psi \mid \Phi.\Psi \mid \Phi \cup \Psi$$

---

generate attacks scenarios. Definition 3.3 expresses that a particular situation will occur and thus corresponds to a property of equity or way (property having to be checked on any way of the privileges graph). The property, therefore, can be expressed by means of a Linear Temporal Logic (LTL) [18].

3.2.1. Specification of Security Policies

As we mentioned in the introduction, we work on an attack scenario which is a sequence of privileges acquired by exploiting system vulnerabilities. Before we define our security policy specification language, we give in the following some auxiliary definitions.

Scenario.   A scenario $\tau \; =< priv_0.priv_1 \; \ldots \; priv_n >$ is a sequence of privileges. The ith privilege is noted by τ_i, the prefix of a trace τ until the ith action is noted $\tau_i^<$ and the suffix of the trace starting by event i is noted $\tau_i^{>=}$. Let τ be a trace, we denote by τ^+ the set of actions composing the trace. More formally:
$$a.\tau^+ = \{a\} \cup \tau^+$$
$$\epsilon^+ = \emptyset$$

Attack.   An event in a scenario τ is an exploitation of a vulnerability which we define as the acquisition of a privilege.

Intrusion objective.   It is a prohibited action defined by the security policy.

In the sequel we define a simple logic for specifying security policies. The later is used to build complex attack scenarios of the system. The syntax of this logic is illustrated in Table 1 and its semantics is given in Table 2.

Syntax.   In Table 1, p indicates an atomic proposition used to check the exploitation of a vulnerability, we denote this atomic proposition by $priv(v_x(h))$ this indicates an acquisition of privilege on the host h by the exploitation of the vulnerability x. This privilege could include the discovery of network information, acquisition of confidence relations with other hosts, as well as other effects. Before exploitation of vulnerability, some conditions must be met, we denote this condition by the set $Cond()$ these conditions may include the existence of the vulnerability on the host and the connectivity between the two hosts. A logical formula is built on a set of atomic propositions, logical operators $\neg$, $\vee$, $\cup$ and the sequence concatenation operator « . ».

Semantics.   We denote by $\tau \models \Phi$ a trace τ satisfying the logical formula Φ. This satisfaction relation between execution traces and formulas is defined in the Table 2.

The first three clauses of Table 2 coincide with the semantics of propositional logic, a trace satisfies $p.\Phi$ if its first action satisfies the predicate p and if its remainder satisfies Φ. The formula $\Phi \cup \Psi$ is satisfied by a trace τ if there is a suffix of τ, say τ_i^+, which satisfies Ψ and that all the preceding suffixes (without exception) satisfy Φ.

Table 2. Semantics.

$$\tau \models priv(v_x(h)) \quad \text{iff} \quad \tau_0 = priv(v_x(h))$$
$$\tau \models \neg\Phi \quad \text{iff} \quad \neg(\tau \models \Phi)$$
$$\tau \models \Phi \vee \Psi \quad \text{iff} \quad (\tau \models \Phi) \vee (\tau \models \Psi)$$
$$\tau \models p.\Phi \quad \text{iff} \quad \tau_0 = p, \tau_i^+ \models \Phi$$
$$\tau \models \Phi \cup \Psi \quad \text{iff} \quad \exists i > 0, \tau_i^{>=} \models \Psi \text{ and } (\forall (0 < k < i), \tau_k^< \models \Phi)$$

Table 3. Intruder rule

$$\frac{\Box}{priv_I = priv_{Int}}$$

$$\frac{priv_I^+ \supseteq cond(v_x(h)) \wedge priv_I.priv(v_x(h)) \models \Phi}{priv_I = priv_I.priv(v_x(h))}$$

$priv_I$: the sequence of intruder privileges

$priv_{Int}$: the sequence of the initial intruder privileges

Φ : the intruder strategy

3.3. Attacks Graphs

The execution of the intruder strategy organized in an intrusion scenario allows changing the state of the system from an initial safe state, where the security policy is respected, to a final state where the intrusion objective is achieved and the policy security violated. In the initial state we suppose that the conditions of exploitation of a first vulnerability are satisfied, in other words the intruder should have one or more initial privileges. The question now is to check if it is possible to reach an intrusion objective indirectly by following a complex attack scenario. The construction of privileges graph is based on the fact that an attack cannot be realized until all of its required conditions have been satisfied, whereas a condition can be satisfied by any one of the realized attacks, thus the construction of graph is done gradually by the application of an intruder deduction rule given in table 3. In this rule condition-vulnerability dependency relation $cond(v_x(h))$ indicates that a set of conditions is required for exploiting the vulnerability v_x on the destination host h. The intruder-strategy rule means that the intruder can across from one node to the other and increase his set of privileges $priv_I^+$ if only if the acquired privilege satisfies Φ.

3.4. Building the Attacks Graph

Synthesizing the attacker's start point, host information and network topology information, the based-graph description represents the threat to security of information system, and it is called attack graph. To analyze the network security, based on the analysis of network security incidents and attacker's actions, we make assumptions as follows:

1. The intruder does not have knowledge, a priori, of the complete graph. He only sees the attacks that he can immediately conduct.

2. The intruder is endowed with a memory that remembers the set of accumulated privileges.
3. The intruder is endowed with reason, he does not implement an attack which would bring back privileges he already has.

To build the attack scenarios seeking to exploit the network vulnerabilities, we present the attack model with an attack graph AG. The construction of this graph is based on the fact that the process of attack changes state when a new privilege was acquired by application of the intruder rule described in Table 3, the graph nodes can be labelled by the attacks associated with the acquired privilege. When the process of attack passes from a state to another, total set of privileges which it holds after the transition is always a superset of that which it had with the folding screen. We formally characterize attack graphs in this definition.

Definition 3.4. *Given the sequence of intruder privileges $priv_I$ and a set of edges $R \subseteq priv_I \times priv_I$ which corresponds to the intruder rules, an attack graph AG is the directed graph AG($priv_I$, R).*

4. Case Study

In this section we present two examples. The first illustrates the use of firewalls to restrict internal user activity by disallowing most outgoing connections whereas the second illustrates a user without restrictions.

4.1. First Example

Figure 2 shows the network configuration for our first example. This network contains a firewall which separates the internal sub-network from the external world. The internal network contains two computers; computer A under NT4 is running IIS (Microsoft's Internet Information Server), the computer B under UNIX, is running send mail, SSH (Secure Shell) and WUFTPD (Washington University FTP Daemon) services. In this example, a restrictive firewall protects the machines that support public web and email services, this example shows how vulnerable services on a network can be exploited even when direct access to services is blocked. The firewall implements the following policy to restrict connectivity from the attack machine:

1. Incoming ssh traffic is permitted to both A and B, although only B is running the service;
2. Incoming web traffic is permitted only to A, which is running (IIS);
3. Incoming email is permitted to B, which is running the send mail server;
4. Incoming File Transfer Protocol (FTP) traffic is blocked because B is running the wuftpd server;
5. All outgoing traffic is permitted.

We specify the state of the network to include services running on each host, existing vulnerabilities, and connectivity between hosts. There are four Boolean variables for

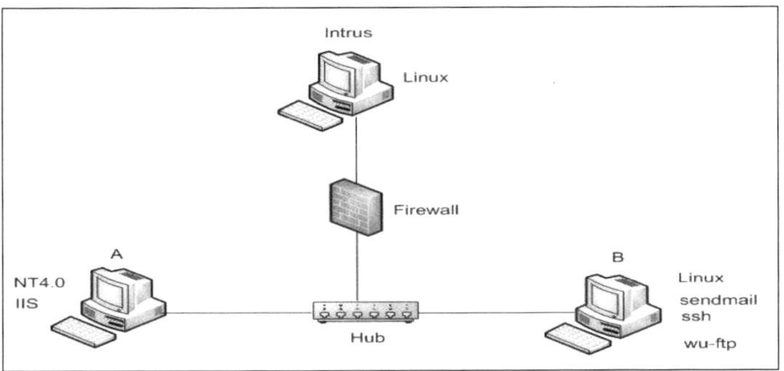

Figure 2. Example of network.

each host, specifying whether any of the two services are running and whether either of two other vulnerabilities is present on that host. The following table shows the services and the vulnerabilities of the network describes on Figure 2.

Variable	Meaning
ssh_h	The computer h runs the ssh service
rpc_h	The computer h runs the rpc service
$v_{IIS}(h)$	The exploitation of the vulnerability IIS enables the attacker to execute programs on h at super user privilege level
$v_{ftp}(h)$	The exploitation of this vulnerability gives root Shell in the target

The intruder launches his attack starting from a single computer, which lies on the outside network. To be concrete, let us assume that his eventual goal is to disrupt the functioning on B. To achieve this goal, the intruder needs root access on host Linux(B). The four actions at his disposal are:

- IIRDS(att_0) IIS Remote Data Services: This attack exploits one of many vulnerability associated with IIS this exploit enables the attacker to execute programs on A.
- RCPDOWNLOAD(att_1): The RCP (Remote Control Program) program is included in the default Windows NT installation, on which the IIS web server runs. This attacks Binds rsh access to the ability to transfer programs (e.g., rootkits[3]) from victim machine using the rcp program.
- PORTFORWARD (att_2): One of few exploits that implements "middleman" machine to direct exploits against victim machine. This attack enables attacker to work around firewall when foothold obtained on an internal machine. Program port forwarding opens a port in a router or firewall in order to allow outside traffic to reach a particular client or server in the private network.
- WUFTPD (att_3): The wuftpd server has a history of vulnerabilities; thus, this attack yields super user on many UNIX platforms that run the wuftpd.

---

[3]A "rootkit" is a hacker term that refers to tools an attacker often transfers to a compromised machine for the purpose of expanding access or escalating privileges.

The model of the target network includes connectivity information among the three hosts. The initial value of the connectivity relation R is shown the following table. An entry in the table corresponds to a pair of hosts (h_1, h_2). IIS listens on port 80 and the ftp listens on port 21, and the connectivity relation specifies which of these services can be reached remotely from other hosts. Each entry consists of three Boolean values. The first value is 'y' if h_1 and h_2 are connected by a physical link, the second value is 'y' if h_1 can connect to h_2 on port 80, and the third value is 'y' if h_1 can connect to h_2 on port 21.

The connectivity relation is presented in the following table:

R	I	A	B
I	y,n,n	y,y,n	y,n,n
A	y,y,n	y,y,n	y,y,y
B	y,n,n	y,y,y	y,n,y

We use the connectivity relation to reflect the settings of the firewall as well as the existence of physical links. In the example, the intruder machine initially can reach only the Web server on port 80 due to a strict security policy on the firewall. The intrusion objective is to obtain super user (root) access on B. This is not directly possible because. The firewall blocks access to the vulnerable wuftpd service from the attack machine. The question now is whether the intrusion objective can be realized indirectly, through attack scenarios, and which are the attacks scenarios making it possible to achieve this objective. The formula Φ in the intruder rule limits the transitions in order to produce only the scenarios of attacks which violate the security policy. Thus, the transitions from the intruder of machine A to the machine B can be obtained by observing the intruder's rule. In this example the intruder strategy is to gain all the privileges on A until reaching an access on the target B, to write this formula in LTL we define three atomic propositions.

$priv(v_x(A))$: The privilege on the host A
$priv(v_x(B))$: The privilege on the host B
$root(B)$: The privilege root on the host B

The firewall blocks access to the vulnerable wuftpd service from the attack machine. Thus, the objective of intruder can be expressed by the following formula LTL:

$$\Phi ::= priv(v_x(A)) \cup priv(v_x(B)) \cup root(B)$$

This LTL formula makes it possible to describe the strategy of the intruder who is closely related to network configuration, thus in the networks the access to the machine B is blocked by the firewalls, in this case the intruder will exploit all the vulnerabilities of the machine A when he will have an access on the machine B he changes strategy and the traces which does not satisfy the formula will be pruned by the intruder.

To build the attack scenarios exploiting the vulnerabilities of the network, we specify the attack model described above using an attack graph. The application of the intruder rule on this attack model gives the attack routes.

At the beginning, the set of the initial intruder privileges is $priv_{Int} = \{v_{IIS}(A), v_{ftp}(B)\}$. Since, the firewall blocks access to the vulnerable ftp service from the attack machine, the intruder begins its scenario with the exploitation of IIS vulnerabilities. Given the access provided by the IISRDS exploit, the remote copy (rcp) program on A is executed to download a rootkit from the attack machine, a port-forwarding program from the root kit is then executed to set up access from the attack machine through A to the ftp service on B.

The attack IIRDS(att_0) can be obtained by applying the rule R_0

$$R_0 \frac{priv_I^+ \supseteq Cond(v_{IIS}(A)) \ \wedge \ priv_I.priv(v_{IIS}(A)) \models \Phi}{priv_I' = priv_I \cdot priv(v_{IIS}(A))}$$

Given the access provided by the IISRDS exploit, a port-forwarding program is executed to set up access from the attack machine through A.

$$R_1 \frac{priv_I'^+ \supseteq Cond(v_{ssh}(A)) \ \wedge \ priv_I'.priv(v_{ssh}(A)) \models \Phi}{priv_I'' = priv_I' \cdot priv(v_{ssh}(A))}$$

The ftp exploit is executed through the forwarded connection against B to obtain root access there.

$$R_2 \frac{priv_I''^+ \supseteq Cond(v_{ftp}(B)) \ \wedge \ priv_I''.priv(v_{ftp}(B)) \models \Phi}{priv_I''' = priv_I'' \cdot priv(v_{ftp}(B))}$$

In Figure 3, we represent the computed attack scenarios of the example network. The attack graph shows that the initial exploitation of the IIS vulnerability on A ultimately leads to the compromise of B. Once the intruder succeeded in having the access on B, it will not carry out other attacks on A and this arc will be pruned. The trace $priv(v_{IIS}(A)).priv(v_{ssh}(B)).priv(v_{rpc}(A))$ which corresponds to the rule R3 of figure 3 does not satisfied the formula $\Phi ::= priv(v_x(A)) \cup priv(v_x(B)) \cup root(B)$ because it allow the acquisition of privileges on A after the privileges acquisition on B.

4.2. Second Example

This network contains a firewall which separates the internal sub-network from the external world and an intrusion detection system (IDS) which sees the traffic network between the internal network and the external world. The internal network contains two computers under UNIX; computer A is running ftp and sshd services, the computer B is running ftp and database services. The intruder launches his attack starting with only one computer which is in the external network. To be more concrete, we assume that the intruder goal is to disturb the normal database functioning in computer B. To achieve this goal, the intruder needs a root access to the database of B. The states of the model include running services on each computer, the connectivity relation between computers, and the existing vulnerabilities.

The following table shows the services and the vulnerabilities of the network described in Figure 4.

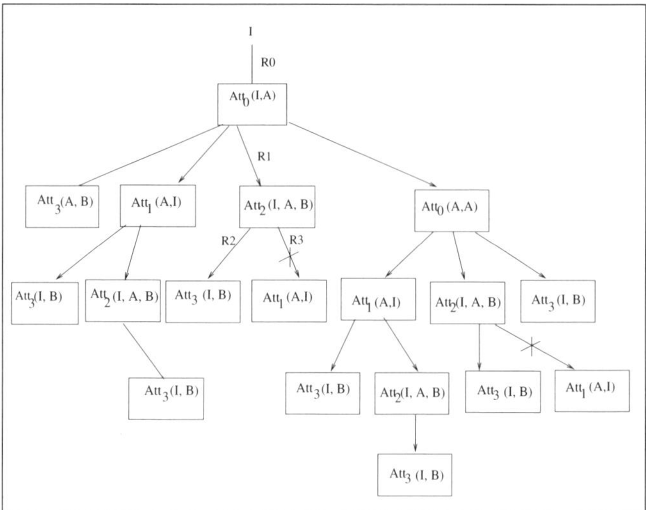

Figure 3. Graph of the attack scenarios.

Variable	Meaning
$sshd_h$	The computer h runs the sshd service
ftp_h	The computer h runs the ftp service
$vul_{sshd}(h)$	The exploitation of the vulnerability sshd gives root Shell in the target machine
$vul_{ftp}(h)$	The exploitation of vulnerability ftp creates a trustworthy relation (r-trust) between the machine h and the target machine.
$vul_{at}(h)$	At is a binary file vulnerable to overflow memory on the host h

The connectivity relation is presented in the following table:

R	I	A	B
I	y,n,n	y,y,y	y,y,n
A	y,n,n	y,y,y	y,y,n
B	y,n,n	y,y,y	y,y,n

Each entry of this table corresponds to a pair of computer (h_1, h_2), and consists of a triplet of Boolean values. The first value is "y" if there is a physical connection between nodes. The second value is "y" if the first node is connected to the second node on the ftp port. The third value is "y" if the first node is connected to the second node on the sshd port.

I corresponds to the intruder computer and A, B is the internal network computers. The intruder actions can be:

- sshd buffer overflow (attack0): This attack exploits the vulnerability sshd which immediately gives "root shell" in the target machine.

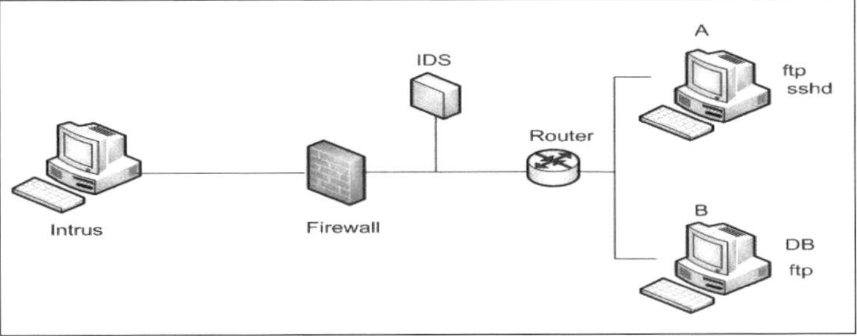

Figure 4. Example of network.

- ftp.rhost(attack1): This attack uses the ftp vulnerability; the intruder creates a "rhost" file in the ftp home directory; this creates a confidence relation between his machine and the target machine.
- remote login (attack 2): The intruder uses the relation of confidence between two machines and reaches a terminal user of the target machine without password.
- local buffer overflow (attack 3): Once the intruder has access to user shell on the target machine, the next step is the exploitation of the "buffer overflow" vulnerability on the file "setuid root" to get root access.

The intrusion objective is represented in the network description as a root access to the database of B, the intruder can exploit all the vulnerabilities of A and B in order to achieve his goals, to write this formula in LTL we define three atomic propositions.

$priv(v_x(A))$: The privilege on the host A
$priv(v_x(B))$: The privilege on the host B
$root(B)$: The privilege root on the host B

Thus, the objective of intruder can be expressed by the following formula LTL:

$$\Phi ::= [priv(v_x(A)) \lor priv(v_x(B))] \cup root(B)$$

To build the attack scenarios exploiting the network vulnerabilities, we specify the attack model described above using an attack graph. The application of the intruder rule on the attack model gives the attack scenarios graph.

The set of the initial intruder privileges is $priv_{Int} = \{v_{ftp}(A), v_{ftp}(B), v_{ssh}(A)\}$, thus the intruder can make three privileges :

$$R_0 \frac{priv_I^+ \supseteq Cond(v_{sshd}(A)) \land priv_I.priv(v_{sshd}(A)) \models \Phi}{priv_I' = priv_I.priv(v_{sshd}(A))}$$

$$R_1 \frac{priv_I^+ \supseteq Cond(v_{ftp}(A)) \land priv_I.priv(v_{ftp}(A)) \models \Phi}{priv_I'' = priv_I.priv(v_{ftp}(A))}$$

$$R_2 \frac{priv_I^+ \supseteq Cond(v_{ftp}(B)) \land priv_I.priv(v_{ftp}(B)) \models \Phi}{priv_I''' = priv_I.priv(priv(v_{ftp}(B)))}$$

These three rules correspond to the three roots graph. If the intruder continues with $priv_I'$, one of the rules which can applied is R3.

$$R_3 \frac{priv_I'^+ \supseteq Cond(v_{ftp}(B)) \land priv_I'.priv(v_{ftp}(B)) \models \Phi}{priv_I'''' = priv_I'.priv_I(v_{ftp}(B))}$$

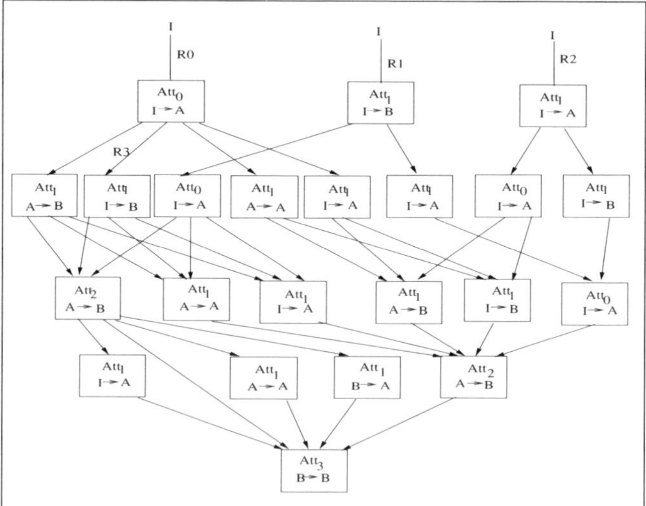

Figure 5. Graph of the attack scenarios.

The intruder has a memory; certain scenarios differ only by the order of the attacks. This is translated in the graph by the fact that certain states can be reached from several others. Moreover, since the intruder remembers the acquired privileges, each transition can lead to only one state, in which he will acquire a superset of privileges comparatively to the one he detains in the present state. Therefore, No cycles can exist in the graph.

In Figure 5, we represent the computed attack scenarios of the example network. In this example the intruder exploits all the vulnerabilities, thus the graph of this figure represents all the possible ways without pruning of arc because the configuration of this network makes it possible to the intruder to achieve his goal with any way.

5. Conclusion

In this paper, we have proposed a new technique that models vulnerabilities and analyses a system in order to automatically build attack scenarios that exploit those vulnerabilities. This technique is based on deduction rules that model intruder capabilities. The attack graph generated by this approach can be used to enrich IDS. Indeed, it is possible to identify on the graph the state in which the potential intruder is. The level of severity of alert can be adjusted according to the distance which still separates it from the intrusion objectives. Our representation avoids the exponential explosion problem and specifies explicitly the security policy to enforce, thereby making our approach a candidate for realistic networks with tens or hundreds of hosts, thus allowing our approach to be candidate in the security configuration of the wide-area networks. Our future work will aim on the one hand obtaining better data sources, and on the other hand, the production of better recommendations; the ultimate objective being to improve the network security configuration.

References

[1]   P.Ammann, D. Wijesekera, S. Kaushik, Scalable, Graph-Based Network Vulnerability Analysis in Proceedings of 9th ACM Conference on Computer and Communications Security (CCS), Washington, DC, November 2002.

[2]   F.Cuppens, R. Ortalo, LAMBDA: A Language to Model a Database for Detection of Attacks, Proceedings of the Third International Workshop on the Recent Advances in Intrusion Detection (RAID'2000), LNCS 1907,October 2000, pp. 197-216.

[3]   F. Cuppens, A. Miège., Alert correlation in a cooperative intrusion detection framework in Proceedings of the IEEE Symposium on Research in Security and Privacy, Oakland, CA, May 2002.

[4]   M. Dacier. Vers une évaluation quantitative de la sécurité informatique. Thèse de doctorat, Université Catholoque de Louvain, December 1994.

[5]   S. Jajodia, S. Noel, B. O'Berry, Topological Analysis of Network Attack Vulnerability in Managing Cyber Threats:Issues, Approaches and Challenges, V. Kumar, J. Srivastava, A. Lazarevic (eds.), Kluwer Academic Publisher, 2004.

[6]   L. Hamza, K. Adi, K. El Guemhioui, Automatic generation of attack scenarios for intrusion detection systems, Intl. Conf. on Internet and Web Applications and Services (ICIW 2006), Gosier, Guadeloupe, Feb. 21-25, 2006.

[7]   K. Ingols, R. Lippmann, K . Piwowarski, Practical Attack Graph Generation for Network Defense , In: Proceedings of Computer Security Applications Conference, ACSAC '06, Miami Beach, FL, USA, pp.1-12. December, 2006.

[8]   J.P. Katoen, Principles of Model Checking, Lecture Notes System validation, 2003.

[9]   C. Michel, L. Mé, ADeLe: an Attack Description Language for Knowledge based Intrusion Detection, Proceedings of the 16th International Conference on Information Security(IFIP/SEC2001), Paris, France, June 2001, Kluwer, pp. 353-365.

[10]   P. Ning, D. Xu, C. Healey, R. St. Amant, Building Attack Scenarios through Integration of Complementary Alert Correlation Methods, in Proceedings of the 11th Annual Network and Distributed System Security Symposium, February, 2004.

[11]   S. Noel, S. Jajodia, B. O'Berry, and M. Jacobs, Efficient Minimum-Cost Network Hardening Via Exploit Dependency Graphs, Proceedings of the 19th Annual Computer Security Applications Conference, Las Vegas, Nevada, 2003.

[12]   S. Noel and S. Jajodia, Managing Attack Graph Complexity Through Visual Hierarchical Aggregation, Proceedings of the 2004 ACM Workshop on Visualization and Data Mining for Computer Security, New York: ACM Press, 2004.

[13]   R. Ritchey, P. Ammann, Using Model Checking to Analyze Network Vulnerabilities, In Proceedings of the IEEE Symposium on Security and Privacy, Oakland, California, 2000. pp. 156-165.

[14]   O.M. Sheyner, Scenario Graphs and Attack Graphs, Thesis, School of Computer Science Computer Science Department Carnegie Mellon University, Pittsburgh, April, 2004

[15]   O. Sheyner, J. Haines, S. Jha, R. Lippmann, J. Wing, Automated Generation and Analysis of Attack Graphs, In: Proceedings of the IEEE Symposium on Security and Privacy, Oakland, California, 2002. pp.1-12.

[16]   F.B. Schneider. Enforceable security policies, ACM Transactions on Information and System Security (TISSEC), 2000.

[17]   S. Templeton, K. Levitt, A requires/provides model for computer attacks, in proceedings of the 2000 New Security Paradigmes Workshop (NSPW'00).

[18]   L.Wang, S. Noel, S.Jajodia, Minimum-cost network hardening using attack graphs, Computer Communications, Volume 29, Issue 18 , 28 November 2006, Pages 3812-3824.

New Trends in Software Methodologies, Tools and Techniques
H. Fujita and D. Pisanelli (Eds.)
IOS Press, 2007

Automatic Enforcement of Security in Computer Networks [1]

T. Mechri [a], M. Langar [a], M. Mejri [a], H. Fujita [b], and Y. Funyu [b]
[a] *Laval University, Quebec, Qc, Canada.*
[b] *Iwate Prefectural University, Japan.*

Abstract.

The main issue of this paper is to propose a formal technique allowing to automatically configure a given network so that it will respect a given security policy. In other words, given a computer network N and a security policy Φ, we introduce a formal technique that automatically produce another network N' such that $N' \models \Phi$ and N and N' behaves in an "equivalent" (with respect to a given de finition of equivalence) way. To that end, we define a new process algebra allowing to better specify and analyze monitored network. We also define an operator $\otimes$ that produce from an initial network N and a security policy Φ another version of the network, denoted by $N \otimes \Phi$, configured in such a way that the security policy is always respected.

Keywords. Network security, Process Algebra, Logic, Monitoring.

1. Introduction

It is a well known fact that purchasing the best and the most powerful security tools and equipments is far from being sufficient to reduce the risks of intrusions. In fact, the weakest link in the computer security chain is often the human interventions which is sometimes necessary to install and configure these tools. Therefore, reducing this human interventions will decrease, without any doubt, both the security risks together with the costs involved by the security solution. It is important, for example, to develop formal methods making it possible to automatically configure a computer network so that its behavior is in conformity with a given security policy.

What we propose in this paper is a technique which could be considered as a first step toward a formal and automatic configuration of computer networks so that they respect their security policies. The analyzed computer network is specified as a term in a new process algebra called **CMN** (Calculus for Monitored Networks) and designed to easily capture the behaviors of network components and specially those behaving as monitors (firewalls, etc.). Security policy, in the other hand, is specified, in this paper, using a simple propositional logic called L_M. After that, we define an enforcement operator, denoted by $\otimes$, that aims to automatically configure the network so that it respects it security policy.

[1]This research is supported by NSERC (the Natural Sciences and Engineering Research Council of Canada), FQRNT (Fonds Québécois de la Recherche sur la Nature et les Technologies) and the project ARISES.

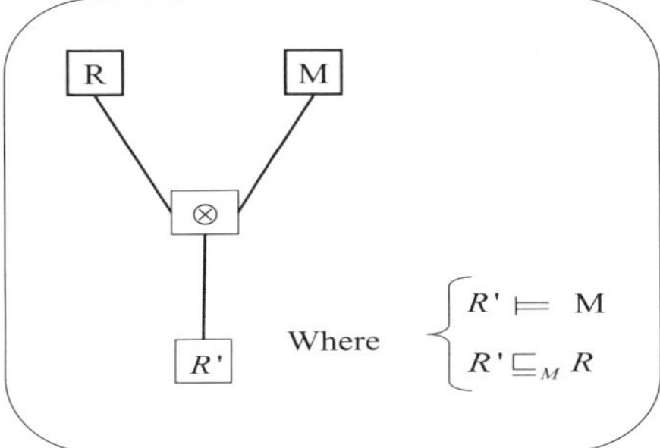

Figure 1. Enforcement operator $\otimes$.

More precisely, as shown by Figure 1, given a network R (specified in **CMN**) and a security policy M (specified in L_M), we automatically produce a new network R' such that the two following properties hold:

- $R' \models M$, i.e: R' satisfies the security policy M.

- $R' \sqsubseteq_M R$, i.e: The configured version, R', of the network behaves like R except that it does not perform actions (e.g. sending a message) that violate the security policy. A more precise definition of $\sqsubseteq_M$ will be given later in this paper.

Another interesting technique given by this paper is what we call the selective monitoring. The idea is that given a security policy and a network together with a set of selected nodes or components (firewalls, etc.) from this network, then we generate, when it is possible, a new configured version of this network that respects the security policy and where monitors are placed only on the selected nodes.

The remainder of this paper is organized as follows: Section 2 presents the syntax and the operational semantics of the **CMN** which is the language used to specify networks. Section 3 defines the logic L_M. Section 4 defines our enforcement operator $\otimes$ and proves that it has the requested properties. Section 5 defines an extension of $\otimes$, denoted by $\otimes_S$, allowing a selective monitoring. Section 6 illustrates our method by a complete example. Finally, some concluding remarks and perspectives are given by Section 7.

2. Network specification

This section gives the syntax and the semantics of the formal language that we use to specify computer networks [4,7,8,9]. Mainly, it is a modified version of CCS (Calculus of Communicating Systems) which is developed by Robin Milner [7]. Denoted by **CMN** (Calculus for Monitored Networks), this new algebra has the particularity of explicitly handling the monitoring concept through its operator "$[-]_-^-$". For instance, the process $[P]_M^C$ can send and receive only messages respecting the security policy M.

2.1. Syntax

We suppose that we have a set of channel names $\mathcal{C}$, a set of messages $\mathcal{M}$ and a language L_M to write monitors (the exact definition of this language will be given in

Section 3). The syntax of **CMN** is as shown by the BNF grammar given in Table 1, where $a \in \mathcal{C}$, $C \subseteq \mathcal{C}$, $m \in \mathcal{M}$, $M \in L_M$ and x is variable that ranges over $\mathcal{M}$. Basically, a process is a combination, according to some rules, of atomic actions and other processes using some operators. Also, we introduce the concept of a **Net** (network) which contains composition of processes having some specific forms.

Actions $\alpha :=$		$a(m)$		Sending a message.
	$\mid$	$\overline{a}(x)$		Waiting for a message.
	$\mid$	$\vec{\widetilde{a}}\,(m)$		Floating message.
	$\mid$	τ		Silent action.
Process $P :=$		0		Empty Process.
	$\mid$	$\alpha.P$	$\alpha \neq \vec{\widetilde{a}}$	Prefix.
	$\mid$	$X \stackrel{def}{=} P$		Definition.
	$\mid$	$\displaystyle\sum_{i \in I} P_i$		Choice (I is an indexing set).
	$\mid$	$\vec{\widetilde{a}}\,(m)\|Q$		Parallel 1.
	$\mid$	$P\|Q$		Parallel 2.
	$\mid$	$P[f]$		Relabeling.
	$\mid$	$P\backslash L$		Restriction.
Net $N :=$	$\mid$	$[P]_M^C \mid \vec{\widetilde{a}}\,(m)\|N \mid N\|N$		Monitored Network.

Table 1. Syntax of CMN.

An atomic action can be one of the following:

- $a(m)$: used to specify the act of sending a message $m \in \mathcal{M}$ over a channel a.

- $\overline{a}(x)$: used to represent the act of waiting for a message coming from a channel a.

- $\vec{\widetilde{a}}\,(m)$: used to specify a floating message, i.e., a message $m \in \mathcal{M}$ was sent over a channel a but it has not reached its destination yet.

- τ: used to specify a silent or an hidden action.

A process in **CMN** can have only one of the following forms:

- 0: a process that cannot perform any action.

- $\alpha.P$: a process that executes the action α and then behaves as P.

- $X \stackrel{def}{=} P$: a definition of X as P. In particular, it is useful for specifying processes having infinite behaviors.

- $P_1 + P_2$: a process that behaves as P_1 or P_2.

- $\vec{\widetilde{a}}\,(m)\|Q$: specifies that Q sees a floating message $\vec{\widetilde{a}}\,(m)$. The process Q can then receive m if it is waiting for a message coming from the channel a.

- $P_1 \| P_2$: specifies that P_1 is running in parallel (interleaving meaning of parallel) with P_2.

- $P[f]$: specifies a process P where its action are renamed by f which is a mapping that respects the following conditions: $f(\overline{a}) = \overline{f(a)}$ and $f(\tau) = \tau$.

- $P \backslash L$: a process that behaves as P except that it cannot communicate with its environment using channels in L.

A **Net** has one of the following forms:

- $[P]_M^C$: is a node or component that behaves as P except that it can communicate with its environment using only channels in C and where its external actions are controlled (monitored) by M.

- $\vec{a}(m) \| N$: is a network N where a message m coming from a channel a is floating (sent but has not reached its destination yet).

- $N \| N$: the composition of two networks.

The set of processes, will be denoted in the sequel by $\mathcal{P}$ and the set of networks by $\mathcal{N}$. Finally, note that contrarily to the restriction operator which do not allow a process to send or receive from a list of channels L , the monitoring operator does not block the process, but it intercepts the sent messages.

2.2. Semantics of a process

Intuitively, the meaning of a process P is a labeled transition system $(P, \mathcal{P}_P, \mathcal{A}, \longrightarrow)$ showing its different behaviors, where:

- P is the initial state.

- $\mathcal{P}_P$ is a subset of $\mathcal{P}$ containing the different states in which the process can be.

- $\mathcal{A} = \{\tau,\ a(m),\ c(a(m))\}$ is the set of labels, where $c(a(m))$ represents a synchronization (communication) over the channel a using the message m. We assume that we extend the definition of f so that $f(c(a(m))) = c(f(a(m)))$.

- $\longrightarrow\ \subseteq\ \mathcal{P}_P \times \mathcal{A} \times \mathcal{P}_P$ is a transition relation defined by Table 3, where $\equiv$ is a simplification relation used to reduce the number of rules and defined as the smallest relation satisfying the axioms given in Table 2.

$$
\begin{array}{rcll}
P + Q & \equiv & Q + P & (A_1) \\
P + 0 & \equiv & P & (A_2) \\
P \| Q & \equiv & Q \| P & (A_3) \\
P \| 0 & \equiv & P & (A_4)
\end{array}
$$

Table 2. Axioms of $\equiv$.

It is important to highlight the following facts related to this semantics:

$$(R_\equiv) \quad \frac{P \equiv P' \quad P' \xrightarrow{\alpha} Q \quad Q \equiv Q'}{P \xrightarrow{\alpha} Q'} \qquad \text{(Equivalence)}$$

$$(R_.) \quad \frac{\Box}{a(m).P \xrightarrow{a(m)} \widetilde{a}\,(m) \parallel P} \qquad \text{(Prefix)}$$

$$(R_=) \quad \frac{P \xrightarrow{\alpha} P' \quad Q \overset{def}{=} P}{Q \xrightarrow{\alpha} P'} \qquad \text{(Definition)}$$

$$(R_+) \quad \frac{P_i \xrightarrow{\alpha} P'}{\sum_{i \in I} P_i \xrightarrow{\alpha} P'} \qquad \text{(Choice)}$$

$$(R_{\parallel}) \quad \frac{P \xrightarrow{\alpha} P'}{P \parallel Q \xrightarrow{\alpha} P' \parallel Q} \qquad \text{(Interleaving)}$$

$$(R_|) \quad \frac{\Box}{\widetilde{a}\,(m) \parallel \overline{a}(x).P \xrightarrow{c(a(m))} P\{m/x\}} \qquad \text{(Communication)}$$

$$(R_\backslash) \quad \frac{P \xrightarrow{a} P'}{P \backslash L \xrightarrow{a} P' \backslash L} \; Si \quad a \notin L \cup \overline{L} \qquad \text{(Restriction)}$$

$$(R_f) \quad \frac{P \xrightarrow{a} P'}{P[f] \xrightarrow{f(a)} P'[f]} \qquad \text{(Relabeling)}$$

Table 3. Operational semantics of CMN's basic operators.

- When a process is ready to send, it do that in asynchronous way (it doesn't need to find a process waiting for the message that it wants to send). The result of a sending action is a floating message, meaning that the message was send but it has not reached its destination yet.

- $\overline{a}(x).P$ means that the process is waiting for a message coming from the channel a. Furthermore, this process cannot move forward until it finds a floating message coming from the channel a.

2.2.1. Semantics of "net"

The operational semantics of **Net** is given in Table 4. It is an extension of the relation "$\longrightarrow$" where we assume that the relation $\equiv$ is also extended by the following axiom:

$$N_1 \| N_2 \equiv N_2 \| N_1 \; (A5)$$

In the following we gives the intuitive meaning of each monitoring rule:

- $R_{[\rightleftharpoons]}$, $R_{[\tau]}$ and $R_{[\rightarrow]}$: these rules state the fact that a monitor does not control the internal communications of a process.

$$(R_{[]}^{\equiv}) \quad \frac{N_1 \equiv N_1' \quad N_1' \xrightarrow{\alpha} N_2 \quad N_2 \equiv N_2''}{N_1 \xrightarrow{\alpha} N_2'} \qquad \text{(Equivalence)}$$

$$R_{[]}^{\parallel} \quad \frac{N_1 \xrightarrow{\alpha} N_1'}{N_1 \| N_2 \xrightarrow{\alpha} N_1' \| N_2} \qquad \text{(Parallel)}$$

$$R_{[\rightleftharpoons]} \quad \frac{P \xrightarrow{c(a(m))} P'}{[P]_M^C \xrightarrow{c(a(m))} [P']_M^C} \qquad \text{(Communication)}$$

$$R_{[\tau]} \quad \frac{P \xrightarrow{\tau} P'}{[P]_M^C \xrightarrow{\tau} [P']_M^C} \qquad \text{(Silent action)}$$

$$R_{[\rightarrow]} \quad \frac{P \xrightarrow{a(m)} \vec{\tilde{a}}\,(m) \| P'}{[P]_M^C \xrightarrow{a(m)} [\vec{\tilde{a}}\,(m) \| P']_M^C} \qquad \text{(Send)}$$

$$R_{[\vdash} \quad \frac{\square}{[\vec{\tilde{a}}\,(m) \| P]_M^C \xrightarrow{\tau} \vec{\tilde{a}}\,(m) \| [P]_M^C} \quad a \in O(C), a(m) \models M \qquad \text{(External output)}$$

$$R_{[\nvdash} \quad \frac{\square}{[\vec{\tilde{a}}\,(m) \| P]_M^C \xrightarrow{\tau} [P]_M^C} \quad a \in O(C), a(m) \not\models M \qquad \text{(Blocked external output)}$$

$$R_{[\dashv} \quad \frac{\square}{\vec{\tilde{a}}\,(m) \| [P]_M^C \xrightarrow{\tau} [\vec{\tilde{a}}\,(m) \| P]_M^C} \quad a \in I(C), a(m) \models M \qquad \text{(External input)}$$

$$R_{[\,]\nvdash} \quad \frac{\square}{\vec{\tilde{a}}\,(m) \| [P]_M^C \xrightarrow{\tau} [P]_M^C} \quad a \in I(C), a(m) \not\models M \qquad \text{(Blocked external input)}$$

Table 4. Semantics of the monitoring operator [ ].

- $R_{[\vdash}$ and $R_{[\dashv}$: these rules state that a floating message $\vec{\tilde{a}}\,(m)$ can cross a zone controlled by the monitor M ($[-]_M^C$) only if it is coming from a channel in C and it satisfies the security policy of M ($a(m) \models M$). Note that, the formal meaning of $a(m) \models M$ is given in Section 3. In addition, in the process $[P]_M^C$, C means the set of channels that can be used by this process to communicate with the outside. More precisely, $C = I(C) \cup O(C)$, where $I(C)$ is the set of channels that can be used by $[P]_M^C$ to receive messages from outside and $O(C)$ is the set of channels that can be used by $[P]_M^C$ to send messages to outside.

- $R_{[\nvdash}$ and $R_{[\,]\nvdash}$: these rules state that any message trying to cross a zone controlled by a monitor M will be blocked if it doesn't satisfy the security policy specified by M.

2.3. Example

This section gives a simple example showing how to specify a network using **CMN**. Suppose that we have the network containing four hosts H_1, H_2, H_3, H_4 connected as shown by Figure 2. Suppose also that we haven't any further detail about the programs

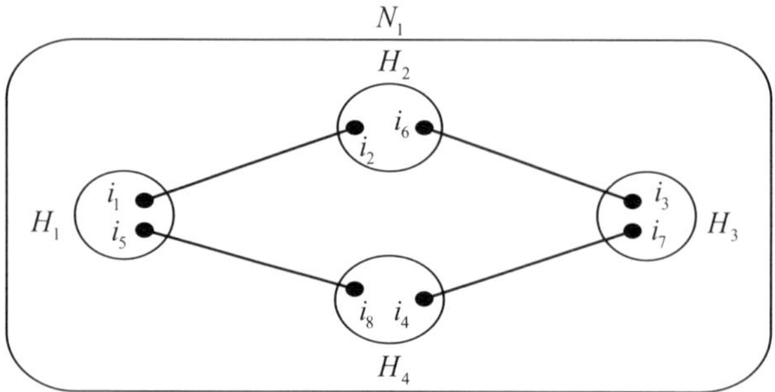

Figure 2. Network's architecture.

that are running inside these computers. The specification for this network is given by the following process:

$$N_1 \overset{def}{=} [H_1]_{M_1}^{C_1} \| [H_2]_{M_2}^{C_2} \| [H_3]_{M_3}^{C_3} \| [H_4]_{M_4}^{C_4}$$

where :

$$H_1 \overset{def}{=} (\sum_{m \in \mathcal{M}} i_1(m).H_1) + \overline{i_2}(x).H_1 + (\sum_{m \in \mathcal{M}} i_5(m).H_1) + \overline{i_8}(y).H_1$$

$$H_2 \overset{def}{=} (\sum_{m \in \mathcal{M}} i_2(m).H_2) + \overline{i_1}(x).H_2 + (\sum_{m \in \mathcal{M}} i_6(m).H_2) + \overline{i_3}(y).H_2$$

$$H_3 \overset{def}{=} (\sum_{m \in \mathcal{M}} i_3(m).H_3) + \overline{i_6}(x).H_3 + (\sum_{m \in \mathcal{M}} i_7(m).H_3) + \overline{i_4}(y).H_3$$

$$H_4 \overset{def}{=} (\sum_{m \in \mathcal{M}} i_4(m).H_4) + \overline{i_7}(x).H_4 + (\sum_{m \in \mathcal{M}} i_8(m).H_4) + \overline{i_5}(y).H_4$$

and

$$I(C_1) = \{\overline{i_2}, \overline{i_8}\} \qquad O(C_1) = \{i_1, i_5\}$$
$$I(C_2) = \{\overline{i_1}, \overline{i_3}\} \qquad O(C_2) = \{i_2, i_6\}$$
$$I(C_3) = \{\overline{i_4}, \overline{i_6}\} \qquad O(C_3) = \{i_3, i_7\}$$
$$I(H_4) = \{\overline{i_5}, \overline{i_7}\} \qquad O(C_4) = \{i_4, i_8\}$$

We can read H_1 for example as following: It is a process that can send any value over channels i_1 and i_5 and then behaves like H_1 (recursively). Also, it can receives any message coming from channels i_2 and i_8 and behaves like H_1.

Note that from a network specified as a graph, we extract its specification in **CMN** using the following convention: Each line in the graph is considered as two bidirectional channels, where one is used to send and the other is used to receive. For example, the network given by Figure 3(a) will be considered as shown in Figure 3(b). Using this convention, it is possible to find the graph of a network from its **CMN** specification.

Also, we suppose in this example that we haven't inserted any monitor yet, i.e : each monitor in $\{M_1,\ M_2,\ M_3,\ M_4\}$ acceptes all the crossing messages. To simplify the presentation, we use in the rest of this paper the following shortcuts:

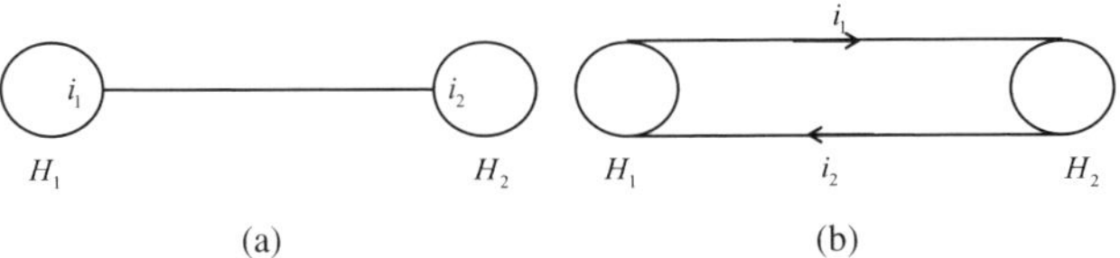

Figure 3. Two connected nodes.

- $a.P$ to mean $\sum_{m \in \mathcal{M}} a(m).P$. In other words, $a.P$ is a process that can send any value over a channel a.

- $\overline{a}.P$ to mean $\overline{a}(x).P$ where the name of the variable x isn't important.

- $[P]^C$ to mean $[P]_M^C$ where M is a monitor that acceptes any message, i.e., the security policy can be captured by the formula "true".

Using these shortcuts, the specification of the network given by Figure 2 becomes as following:

$$N_1 \stackrel{def}{=} [H_1]^{C_1} \| [H_2]^{C_2} \| [H_3]^{C_3} \| [H_4]^{C_4}$$

where :

$$H_1 \stackrel{def}{=} i_1.H_1 + \overline{i_2}.H_1 + i_5.H_1 + \overline{i_8}.H_1$$
$$H_2 \stackrel{def}{=} i_2.H_2 + \overline{i_1}.H_2 + i_6.H_2 + \overline{i_3}.H_2$$
$$H_3 \stackrel{def}{=} i_3.H_3 + \overline{i_6}.H_3 + i_7.H_3 + \overline{i_4}.H_3$$
$$H_4 \stackrel{def}{=} i_4.H_4 + \overline{i_7}.H_4 + i_8.H_4 + \overline{i_5}.H_4$$

3. Security policy specification

In this section, we present a simple propositional logic [1,5], denoted by L_M, that we use to specify security policies. A monitor M is a formula in L_M.

3.1. Syntax

The syntax of the logic L_M is given by the BNF grammar shown in Table 5. The possible values of $Field$, $Operator$ and $Value$ are given just as examples and the language L_M can be easily enriched by other possibilities. In addition, the symbol $*$ is used to indicate an unspecified value. The intuitive meaning of the proposition of L_M is as given in the following:

- $\top$: it is used to mean "true".

- p: is a proposition which represents a condition having the form: $\langle$ Field Operator Value $\rangle$. For example, the proposition $ip\_src = 132.203.114.23$ can be used to indicate that the source address of messages must be $132.203.114.23$.

Moniteur	M	$::=$	$\top \mid p \mid a(p) \mid \overline{a}(p) \mid \neg M \mid M_1 \wedge M_2$
	p	$::=$	$Field\ Operator\ Value$
	$Champ$	$::=$	$ip\_src \mid ip\_dst \mid port\_src \mid port\_dst \mid prot$
	$Operateur$	$::=$	$= \mid < \mid \in$
	$Valeur$	$::=$	$Num \mid \text{TCP} \mid \text{UDP} \mid \text{ICMP} \mid Num.Num.Num.Num \mid *$
	a	$::=$	name of a channel

Table 5. Syntax of L_M.

- $a(p)$ (respectively $\overline{a}(p)$): is a formula used to mean that all messages sent over (respectively coming from) the channel a must satisfy p. For example, the formula $\neg(i_1(ip\_dst >= 132.203.114.23) \wedge i_1(port\_dst = 25))$ specifies that the channel i_1 cannot send messages having the destination address 132.203.114.23 and the destination port 25.

In addition to syntactic construction of L_M, we use others shortcuts such that:

- $\bot = \neg\top$

- $M_1 \vee M_2 = \neg(\neg M_1 \wedge \neg M_2)$

- $a(p_1 \wedge p_2) = a(p_1) \wedge a(p_2)$

3.2. Semantics

$a(m) \models \top$ $\quad \overline{a}(m) \models \top$		$\tau \models M$
$a(m) \models Field\ Operator\ Value$	if	$m.Field\ Operator\ Value = true$
$\overline{a}(m) \models Field\ Operator\ Value$	if	$m.Field\ Operator\ Value = true$
$a(m) \models i(p)$	if	$a = i$ and $m.Field\ Operator\ Value = true$
$\overline{a}(m) \models \overline{i}(p)$	if	$a = i$ and $m.Field\ Operator\ Value = true$
$a(m) \models \neg M$	if	$a(m) \not\models M$
$\overline{a}(m) \models \neg M$	if	$\overline{a}(m) \not\models M$
$a(m) \models M_1 \wedge M_2$	if	$a(m) \models M_1$ and $a(m) \models M_2$
$\overline{a}(m) \models M_1 \wedge M_2$	if	$\overline{a}(m) \models M_1$ and $a(m) \models M_2$
$c(a(m)) \models M$	if	$a(m) \models M$ and $\overline{a}(m) \models M$

Table 6. Semantics of L_M.

The semantics of L_M is as shown by Table 6, where a and i are names of channels. We write $a(m) \models M$ to say that a message m send over the channel a satisfies M. Also, $\overline{a}(m) \models M$ to say that the message m coming from the channel a satisfies M.

Hereafter, we present some examples of properties specified in L_M.

- "$\neg(ip\_dst = 132.203.114.*)$" : This monitor intercepts any packet sent to the sub-network 132.203.114.*.

- "$\neg i(port\_src = 80)$" : This monitor intercepts any packet send over the channel i and the value of $port\_src$ field is equal to 80.

Finally, we say that a process P respects the security policy M, denoted by $P \models M$ if for any action α: $P \xrightarrow{\alpha} P'$ then $\alpha \models M$ and $P' \models M$.

4. Enforcement operator $\otimes$

Recall that our goal is to define an operator $\otimes$ allowing to generate from a network N and a security policy M a configured version $N \otimes M$ such that:

(i) $N \otimes M \models M$
(ii) $N \otimes M \sqsubseteq_M N$

We have already formalized the definition of "$\models$" and now it is time to formalize the definition of "$\sqsubseteq_M$".

Definition 4.1. *Let P and Q be two processes in $\mathcal{P}$ and M a monitor. We say that P is smaller then Q modulo M, denoted by $P \sqsubseteq_M Q$, if all the following conditions are satisfied:*

- $P \xrightarrow{a} P'$ *then* $Q \xrightarrow{a} Q'$ *and* $P' \sqsubseteq_M Q'$.
- $Q \xrightarrow{a} Q'$ *and* $a \neq c(a)$ *or* $Q \xrightarrow{c(a)} Q'$ *and* $(a \models M \wedge \bar{a} \models M)$ *then* $P \xrightarrow{a} P'$ *and* $P' \sqsubseteq_M Q'$.
- $Q \xrightarrow{c(a)} Q'$ *and* $(a \not\models M \vee \bar{a} \not\models M)$ *then* $P \xrightarrow{c(a)} P'$

The problem that we are trying to solve has in general many solutions [6]. In other words, it is possible to find many enforcement operators having the desired properties (i) and (ii). In fact, an obvious solution of the problem is to place the monitor M on every component of the network M. This means that the following enforcement operator $\otimes$ has the desired properties:

$$[P]^{C}_{M_0} \otimes M = [P]^{C}_{M_0 \wedge M}$$

$$([P_1]^{C_1}_{M_1} \| \ldots \| [P_1]^{C_n}_{M_n}) \otimes M = [P_1]^{C_1}_{M_1 \wedge M} \| \ldots \| [P_1]^{C_n}_{M_n \wedge M}$$

$$(\vec{\tilde{a_1}} \| \ldots \| \vec{\tilde{a_m}} \| [P_1]^{C_1}_{M_1} \| \ldots \| [P_1]^{C_n}_{M_n}) \otimes M = \vec{\tilde{a_1}} \| \ldots \| \vec{\tilde{a_m}} \| [P_1]^{C_1}_{M_1 \wedge M} \| \ldots \| [P_1]^{C_n}_{M_n \wedge M}$$

where:

$$\vec{R} = \vec{\tilde{a}}_1(m_1) \| \ldots \| \vec{\tilde{a}}_n(m_n)$$

4.1. Example

Let's consider again the example given by Figure 3. We have said that this network can be specified in **CMN** by the following process:

$$N_1 \overset{def}{=} [H_1]^{C_1} \| [H_2]^{C_2} \| [H_3]^{C_3} \| [H_4]^{C_4}$$

Suppose now that we have the following security policy:

- H_1 cannot send message to H_2 using the channel i_1 and the port 25.

- H_2 cannot receive from H_3 on channel i_6.

- H_3 cannot send messages using the port 80.

This security policy, denoted by M, can be specified in L_M as following:

- $M = M_1 \wedge M_2 \wedge M_3$:

  where:

  - $M_1 = \neg i_1(ip\_src = ip\_src(H_1) \wedge ip\_dst = ip\_dst(H_2) \wedge port\_src = 25)$.
  - $M_2 = \neg i_6(ip\_src = ip\_src(H_3) \wedge ip\_dst = ip\_dst(H_2))$.
  - $M_3 = \neg(ip\_src = ip\_src(H_3) \wedge port\_src = 80)$.

Now, if we apply the enforcement operator, we obtain the following result:

$$N \otimes M = [H_1]_M^{C_1} \| [H_2]_M^{C_2} \| [H_3]_M^{C_3} \| [H_4]_M^{C_4}$$

As we can see, the solution provided by the enforcement operator $\otimes$ is not optimal (the monitors placed at different components of the network could be simplified). For example, the component $[H_1]_M^{C_1} \| [H_2]_M^{C_2}$ "behaves" like $[H_1]_M^{C_1} \| [H_2]_{M_1 \wedge M_3}^{C_2}$. In the sequel, we define the notion of network behaviors and we show how it could be used to better simplify the solution given by the enforcement operator $\otimes$.

4.2. Optimization

In our case, the optimization is a sequence of modifications where each one of them consists in substituting a component of the network by another equivalent one. For example $N = N_1 \| [P]_M^C$ can be replaced by $N = N_1 \| [P]_{M'}^C$ if M and M' do the same job. To prove the correctness of this transformations, we need the following ingredients:

- An equivalence relation $\sim$: this will be used to say for example that $[P]_M^C \sim [P]_{M'}^C$ under some conditions.

- The equivalence relation $\sim$ needs to be a congruence at least with respect to the "$\|$" operator: Such a property allows us to say that if $[P]_M^C \sim [P]_{M'}^C$ then $N = N_1 \| [P]_M^C \sim N = N_1 \| [P]_{M'}^C$.

- The required properties of $\otimes$ must be preserved by $\sim$, i.e: this allows us to say that if

  if $N' \sim N$ and $N \models M$ then $N' \models M$.

  if $N' \sim N$ and $N \sqsubseteq_M N''$ then $N' \sqsubseteq_M N''$.

Definition of $\sim$:   Before giving the definition of $\sim$, we need to introduce the notion of week besimulation:

Definition 4.2 (Weak bisimulation). *A binary relation $S \subseteq \mathcal{N} \times \mathcal{N}$ is a weak bisimulation if for any couple $(P, Q) \in S$, and for any action α we have:*

1- $P \xrightarrow{\alpha} P'$ then there exists Q' in $\mathcal{P}$ such that $Q \stackrel{\hat{\alpha}}{\Longrightarrow} Q'$ and $(P', Q') \in S$.

2- $Q \xrightarrow{\alpha} Q'$ then there exists P' in $\mathcal{P}$ such that $P \stackrel{\hat{\alpha}}{\Longrightarrow} P'$ and $(P', Q') \in S$.

where $"\stackrel{\hat{\alpha}}{\Longrightarrow}"$ is an abbreviation of $"(\xrightarrow{\tau})^* \xrightarrow{\alpha} (\xrightarrow{\tau})^*"$ and $\hat{\alpha} = \alpha$ if $\alpha \neq \tau$ and $\hat{\tau} = \varepsilon$.

Now we denote the largest week bisimulation by $\approx$, i.e:

Definition 4.3 (Week bisimulation $\approx$). *Two networks N_1 and N_2 are weakly bisimilar, denoted by $N_1 \approx N_2$, if it exists a weak bisimulation S containing the couple (N_1, N_2), i.e:*

$$\approx = \bigcup \{S : S \text{ is a weak bisimulation}\}$$

Unlike CCS, a week bisimulation doesn't allow us to see the different possible behaviors of a network in **CMN**. This is because the reception is asynchronous. For instance, the process $P_1 = \overline{a}(x).b(m).0$ cannot exhibit any behavior (there isn't any transition rule in the semantics of **CMN** allowing this process to evolve) without the presence of an explicit environment. The same case for the process $P_2 = \overline{b}(x).a(m).0$ and it is therefore meaningless to compare these two processes using the week bisimulation. However, if we consider the process $P_3 = a(m).0$ (an environment) we run $P_1 \| P_3$ and $P_2 \| P_3$, then we will get different behaviors, i.e., $P_1 \approx P_2$ but $P_1 \| P_3 \not\approx P_2 \| P_3$.

Within **CMN** the only way that a process or a network has to interact with its environment is via floating messages (what we have denoted by $\tilde{a}(m)$). Therefore it is suffisent to put a process or a network within different kind of floating messages to see its complete behavior. This idea is captured by the equivalence relation $"\sim"$ that is defined as following.

Definition 4.4 (Testing equivalence $\sim$). *We say that two process (or networks) P and Q in $\mathcal{P}$ (or in $\mathcal{N}$) are testing equivalent, or simply $P \sim Q$ if:*

$$\forall \vec{R} \in \mathcal{R} : \vec{R} \| P \approx \vec{R} \| Q$$

where:

$$\mathcal{R} = \{\tilde{a}_1(m_1) \| \tilde{a}_2(m_2) \| \dots \| \tilde{a}_n(m_n) \mid n \geq 1, m_i \in \mathcal{M}, a_i \in \mathcal{C}, 1 \leq i \leq n\}$$

Some important properties of $\sim$: The following theorem shows that testing equivalence has the required properties allowing us to easily doing some optimization on a monitored version of a network generated by $\oplus$.

Theorem 4.5 (Congruence). *Let $N1$, N_2 and N_3 bet three networks in* **CMN** *and M a monitor in L_M. The equivalence relation $\sim$ is congruent with respect to "$\|$", $\models$ and $\sqsubseteq_M$, i.e:*

- *if $N_1 \sim N_2$ then $N_1\|N_3 \sim N_2\|N_3$*
- *if $N_1 \sim N_2$ and $N_1 \models M$ then $N_2 \models M$*
- *if $N_1 \sim N_2$ and $N_1 \sqsubseteq_M N_3$ then $N_2 \sqsubseteq_M N_3$*
- *if $N_1 \sim N_2$ and $N_3 \sqsubseteq_M N_1$ then $N_3 \sqsubseteq_M N_2$*

Proof. The proofs of this kind of properties are classic and they will not be given in this paper. $\qquad\square$

Optimization function $\mathcal{O}$: Before optimizing a network, let us first give some rewriting rules allowing to simplify a monitor.

Definition 4.6 (Simplification operator). *Given a monitor M and a set of channel C, the simplified version of M with respect to C, denoted by $M_{\downarrow_C}$, is the normal form of M modulo AC (Commutativity and Associativity) using the following rewriting rules.*

$$
\begin{aligned}
\neg\top &\longrightarrow_C \bot \\
\top \wedge M &\longrightarrow_C M \\
\bot \wedge M &\longrightarrow_C \bot \\
M \wedge \neg M &\longrightarrow_C \bot \\
a(m) &\longrightarrow_C \top \quad \text{if } a \notin C \\
\overline{a}(m) &\longrightarrow_C \top \quad \text{if } \overline{a} \notin C
\end{aligned}
$$

Notes that the previous rewriting rules are classical and it is not difficult to prove that such a normal form exists. Having this definition and the result of the previous theorem, it is not complicated to see that the following function $\mathcal{O}$ has the requested properties to be used as an optimization function.

$$
\mathcal{O}([P]_M^C) = [P]_{M_{\downarrow_C}}^C
$$

$$
\mathcal{O}([P]_M^C\|N) = \mathcal{O}([P]_M^C)\|\mathcal{O}(N)
$$

Example We have seen within the example given in section 4.1 that when we apply the enforcement operator $\otimes$ we get the following result:

$$
N \otimes M = [\, [H_1]_M^{C_1}\|[H_2]_M^{C_2}\|[H_3]_M^{C_3}\|[H_4]_M^{C_4}]^C
$$

where the security policy M is equal to $M_1 \wedge M_2 \wedge M_3$ and

- $M_1 = \neg i_1(ip\_src = ip\_src(H_1) \wedge ip\_dst = ip\_dst(H_2) \wedge port\_src = 25)$.

- $M_2 = \neg i_6(ip\_src = ip\_src(H_3) \wedge ip\_dst = ip\_dst(H_2))$.

- $M_3 = \neg(ip\_src = ip\_src(H_3) \wedge port\_src = 80)$.

Now, if we apply the optimization function to $N \otimes M$, we obtain the following result:

$$\mathcal{O}(N \otimes M) = [[H_1]_{M_1 \wedge M_3}^{C_1} \| [H_2]_M^{C_2} \| [H_3]_{M_2 \wedge M_3}^{C_3} \| [H_4]_{M_3}^{C_4}]^C$$

since:

$$\mathcal{O}([H_1]_M^{C_1}) = [H_1]_{M_1 \wedge M_3}^{C_1} \qquad \mathcal{O}([H_2]_M^{C_2}) = [H_2]_M^{C_2}$$

$$\mathcal{O}([H_3]_M^{C_3}) = [H_3]_{M_2 \wedge M_3}^{C_3} \qquad \mathcal{O}([H_4]_M^{C_4}) = [H_4]_{M_3}^{C_4}$$

4.3. Discussion

As we have already said, the problem that we want to solve has in general many solutions. The simplest one is given by the the operator $\otimes$ that we have previously defined. An ameliorated version of this solution can be obtained after applying the optimization function $\mathcal{O}$. The solution given by $\otimes$ consists in placing the monitor at each node of the analyzed network. In real life, this solution is not interesting in all the situations. To surmount this drawback, one can try to find all the possible solutions of the problem. However, even if it is interesting as a problem, it is obviously more complicated. Also, giving all the solutions to the end-user it is not necessarily a good direction since he can be confused to choose the best one. For that reason, we find interesting the fact of giving the end-user the possibility to provide more information about the solution that he wants to get. An example of these informations could be the nodes on which he wants to place his monitors (the names of the firewalls in the network, etc.). This kind of information could give more interesting and practical solutions. The next section formalize and resolve this problem.

5. Selective monitoring

As shown by Figure 4, the problem of selective monitoring consists in finding new operator $\otimes_S$ that can, like $\otimes$, configure a network according to a security policy where the monitors are placed only at nodes in S. To simplify, the presentation of this section, we suppose that the analyzed network N doesn't initially contain any monitor, i.e, the monitors of all the node in the initial version of the network behave like $\top$. Assuming that, the formalization of the problem can be given as follows:

Problem 5.1 (Selective Monitoring). *Given a network N, a monitor M, a set of selected components S, we want to define an operator $\otimes_S$ that is able to produce, when it is possible, a configured version $N \otimes_S M$ that respects the following conditions:*

(i) $N \otimes_S M \models M$
(ii) $N \otimes_S M \sqsubseteq_M N$
(ii) *If* $N \otimes_S M = [P]_{M'}^C \| N''$ *and* $[P]^C \notin S$ *then* $M' = \top$

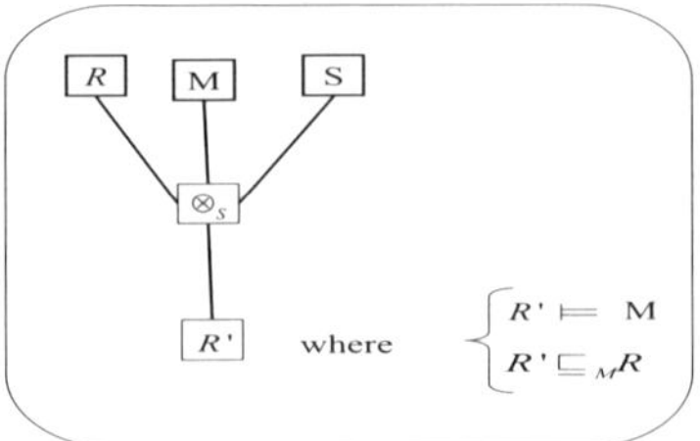

Figure 4. Selective enforcement operator $\otimes_S$.

5.1. Approach

To find a configured network that respectes the desired properties, we proceed as following:

- First we start by defining an operator $\otimes$ that respects the conditions (i) and (ii) of the problem. This has already been done in the previous sections.

- Using $\otimes$, we define some rewriting rules allowing us to move a monitor form one node to another so that we complete the messing property. As pictured by Figure 5, the task of this rewriting rules is denoted by $\otimes_1$ and $N \otimes_S M = (N \otimes M) \otimes_1 S$

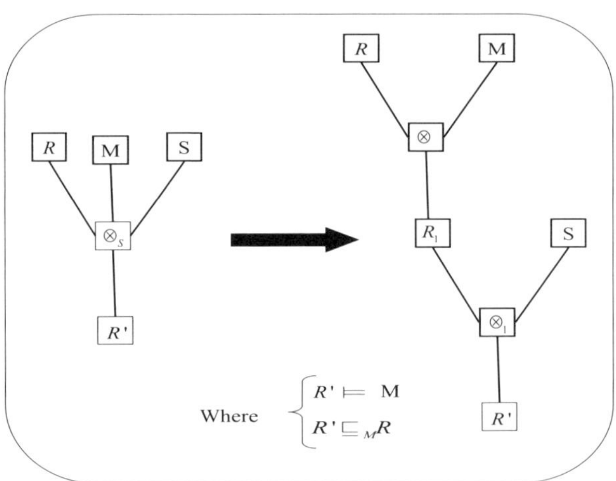

Figure 5. Selective enforcement operator $\otimes_1$.

It is implicit, that the idea of the approach works only if the operator $\otimes_1$ preserves the properties of (i) and (ii) of $\otimes_S$. We know, however that the testing equivalence $\sim$ preserves these properties. Therefore to show that $\otimes_1$ respects the conditions (i) and (ii) of the problem, it will be enough to prove that

$$\forall N, \forall S : \; N \otimes_1 S \sim N$$

Before defining $\otimes_1$ and proving that it respects the required conditions, we need the definitions given in the following.

5.2. Notations and definitions

For the sake of simplicity, the word node is used to mean a network component having the form of $[P]_M^C$. In addition, if $N = [P_1]_{M_1}^{C_1} || \ldots || [P_r]_{M_r}^{C_r}$, then we denote by $\overline{N}$ the set of the nodes in N, i.e, $\overline{N} = \{[P_1]_{M_1}^{C_1}, \ldots, [P_r]_{M_r}^{C_r}\}$.

We introduce, hereafter, the concept of a disc having a radius d and a center η in a network $\mathcal{N}$ as the set of all the reachable nodes from η using a path with a length less or equal to d (the length of a path is the number of its arcs).

Definition 5.2 (Disc). *Let N be a network and η a node in $\overline{N}$. A disc of center η and radius d, in $\overline{N}$, denoted by $D_N^d(\eta)$, is defined as follows:*

$$D_N^0(\eta) = \{\eta\}$$
$$D_N^{d+1}(\eta) = D_N^d(\eta) \cup$$
$$\{\eta' \in N \mid \exists \eta'' \in D_N^d(\eta) \wedge (O((\eta'')) \cap I(\eta') \neq \emptyset \vee O(\eta') \cap I(\eta'') \neq \emptyset)\}$$

In addition, we introduce the concept of a disc limited by a set of nodes S as follows:

Definition 5.3 (Disc limited by S). *Let N be a network, η a node in $\overline{N}$ and S a set of nodes in $\overline{N}$. A disc, in $\overline{N}$, with a center η, a radius d and limited by S, denoted by $D_{calN}^d(eta >, s)$, is defined in the following way:*

$$D_N 0(\eta, S) = \{\eta\}$$
$$D_N^{d+1}(\eta) = D_N^d(\eta, S) \cup$$
$$\{\eta' \in N \mid \exists \eta'' \in (D_N^d(\eta, S) - S)$$
$$\wedge (O((\eta'')) \cap I(\eta') \neq \emptyset \vee O(\eta') \cap I(\eta'') \neq \emptyset)\}$$

From the definition of a disc, we can find the notion of the neighbors of a node as following:

Definition 5.4 (Neighbors of a node). *Let N be a network and η a node in $\overline{N}$. The neighbors of η of level i in N, denoted by $V_N^i(\eta)$, are defined as follows:*

$$V_N^0(\eta) = \emptyset$$
$$V_N^{i+1}(\eta) = D_N^{i+1}(\eta) - D_N^i(\eta)$$

Also, we can define the neighbors limited by S as follows:

Definition 5.5 (Neighbors limited S). *Let N be a network and η a node in $\overline{N}$. The neighbors of η in N limited by S and having the level i, denoted by $V_N^i(\eta, S)$, are defined as follows:*

$$V_N^0(\eta, S) = \emptyset$$
$$V_N^{i+1}(\eta, S) = D_N^{i+1}(\eta, S) - (D_N^i(\eta, S) - S)$$

The trafic controlled by a monitor M is defined hereafter.

Definition 5.6 (Trafic monitored by M). *Let N be a network, M a monitor, and η_1 and η_2 two nodes in $\overline{N}$. We say that the trafic between η_1 and η_2 is monitored by M, denoted by $\eta_1 \triangleright_M \eta_2$ if one of the following conditions holds:*

- *There exists $m \in \mathcal{M}$ and $i \in O(\eta_1)$ such that $\overline{i} \in I(\eta_2)$ and $(i(m) \not\models M$ or $\overline{i}(m) \not\models M)$.*
- *There exists $m \in \mathcal{M}$ such that $(m.ip_{src} \in O(\eta_1) \wedge m.ip_{dst} \in I(\eta_2)$ and $m \not\models M$*

We use also the following notations:

- *$\eta_1 \triangleleft\triangleright_M \eta_2$ to say that $\eta_1 \triangleright_M \eta_2$ or $\eta_2 \triangleright_M \eta_1$.*
- *$S_1 \triangleleft\triangleright_M S_2$ to say that there exist $\eta_1 \in S_1$ and $\eta_2 \in S_2$ where $\eta_1 \triangleleft\triangleright_M \eta_2$, and S_1 and S_2 are two sets of nodes.*

We conclude our definitions with the following one.

Definition 5.7. $[S_1[S_2 \dagger M]]$ *Let S_1 and S_2 be two sets of nodes, and M a monitor. We denote by $S_1[S_2 \dagger M]$ the set defined as following:*

$$(\emptyset)[S_2 \dagger M] = \emptyset$$
$$(\{[P]^C_{M_0}\} \cup S_1)[S_2 \dagger M] = \{[P]^C_{M_0}\} \cup (S_1[S_2 \dagger M]) \quad si \ [P]^C_{M_0} \notin S_2$$
$$(\{[P]^C_{M_0}\} \cup S_1)[S_2 \dagger M] = \{[P]^C_{M_0 \wedge M}\} \cup (S_1[S_2 \dagger M]) \ si \ [P]^C_{M_0} \in S_2$$

5.3. Definition of $\otimes_1$

The definition of $\otimes_1$ is based on the two rules given by Table 7 and it is:

$$\otimes_1 = (R_1^*.R_2)^*$$

The notation $(R_1^*.R_2)^*$ means that we apply the rule R_1 recursively until we reach a fixed point (the rule is no longer applicable), then we apply the rule R_2 and we repeat these two operations until a global fixed point is reached. Notice that $\otimes_1$ can fail to place the monitor on the selected node. However, in this case, solution does'nt exist.

$$\mathbf{R_1} \qquad \frac{< \overline{N} \cup \{[P]^C_M\}, \ S >}{< \overline{N} \cup \{[P]^C_{M\downarrow_C}\}, \ S >}$$

$$\mathbf{R_2} \qquad \frac{< \overline{N} \cup \{[P]^C_M\}, \ S >}{< \overline{N}[V^i(\eta, S) \dagger M] \cup \{[P]^C\}, \ S >} \qquad [P]^C_M \notin S \ \text{and} \ C$$

$$C = ((\exists i > 0 \mid V^i(\eta, S) \subseteq S) \ \wedge \ (\neg((D^{i-1}(\eta, S) - S) \triangleleft\triangleright_M (D^{i-1}(\eta, S) - S)))$$

Table 7. Selective monitoring algorithm's rules

The rules R_1 and R_2 have the following intuitive meaning:

- R_1 allows to simplify the monitors attached with the nodes of the analyzed network as much as possible.

- R_2 allows to move a monitor attached to a given node to it's neighbors in S located at $V^i(\eta, S)$ (neighbors at level i limited by S) only if the monitor doesn't control the trafic between the nodes in $\neg((D^{i-1}(\eta, S) - S))$. This idea is pictured by figure 6. This figure aims to show that a monitor is moved from a black node in the center to the nodes in the border, if all of them are in S and no trafic coming from the outside can reach the node in the center without crossing a node in a border. For that reason, moving the monitor in these conditions is safe if it doesn't control the trafic between nodes inside the border limited by the continuous line. Note that a complete example showing when and how these rules are applied is given later in this paper as a case study.

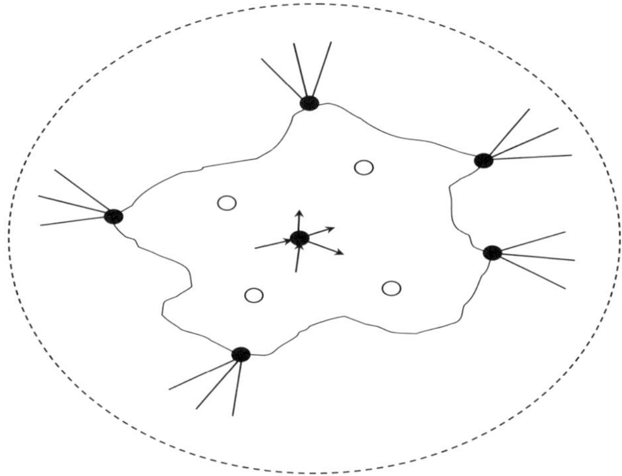

Figure 6. Moving monitors.

5.4. Correction of $\otimes_S$

Proposition 5.8. *Let N be a network in* **CMN** *and S a set of selected components. We have :*

$$N \otimes_1 S \sim N$$

Proof. Since $\otimes_1 = (R_1^*.R_2)^*$, then it is enough to prove that R_1 and R_2 preserve the equivalence with respect to $\sim$.

- It is clear that $\sim$ is preserved by R_1. In fact R_1 is same as the optimization function defined in 4.2.
- The testing equivalence $\sim$ is also preserved by R_2. This proof will not be detailed in this paper. However the intuition behind this proof is what is captured by Figure 6.

$\square$

Theorem 5.9. *Let N be a network in* **CMN**, *M a monitor in L_M and S a set of selected components. If the problem 5.1 has a solution then $(N \otimes M) \otimes_1 S$ is a solution, i.e:*

    (i) $(N \otimes M) \otimes_1 S \models M$
    (ii) $(N \otimes M) \otimes_1 S \sqsubseteq_M N$
    (ii) $(N \otimes M) \otimes_1 SM = [P]^C_{M'} \| N''$ *and if* $[P]^C \notin S$ *then* $M' = \top$

Proof. Hereafter the proof each property:

    (i) We know, from Section 4, that $N \otimes M \models M$. By proposition 5.8, it follows that $(N \otimes M) \otimes_1 S \sim N \otimes M$. We conclude, from theorem 4.5, that $(N \otimes M) \otimes_1 S \models M$ meaning that $N \otimes_S M \models M$.

    (ii) We know, from Section 4, that $N \otimes M \sqsubseteq_M M$. By proposition 5.8, it follows that $(N \otimes M) \otimes_1 S \sim N \otimes M$. By theorem 4.5, we conclude that $(N \otimes M) \otimes_1 S \sqsubseteq_M M$, i.e., $N \otimes_S M \sqsubseteq_M M$.

    (iii) The proof of this property follows directly from the definition of the rule R_2. Indeed, if the algorithm terminates and this property is not satisfied, we conclude that the problem hasn't a solution.

$\square$

6. Case study

The network that we want to secure in this section is the one given by Figure 7.

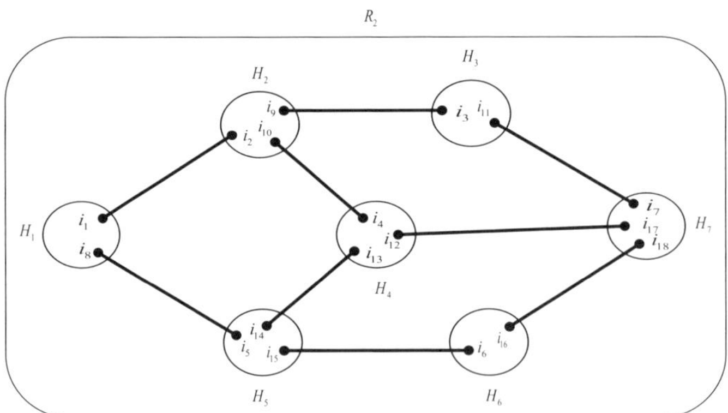

Figure 7. A network specified by CMN.

The security policy that we want to enforce is the following:

    $\bullet$ H_1 cannot send any packets to H_7 using the protocol $icmp$.
    $\bullet$ H_4 cannot send any packets to H_5 using the port 21.
    $\bullet$ H_6 cannot receive from H_5 on port 25 via the channel i_{15}.

Our selected components in which we want to put the monitor are H_2, H_4 and H_6. To reach our goal we apply in the sequel all the steps of the approach.

Specification of the network   Following the same ideas and abbreviations used in the first example of this paper, the network of Figure 7 is specified in CMN as following:

$$H_1 \stackrel{def}{=} i_1.H_1 + \overline{i_2}.H_1 + i_8.H_1 + \overline{i_5}.H_1$$
$$H_2 \stackrel{def}{=} i_2.H_2 + \overline{i_1}.H_2 + i_9.H_2 + \overline{i_3}.H_2 + i_{10}.H_2 + \overline{i_4}.H_2$$
$$H_3 \stackrel{def}{=} i_3.H_3 + \overline{i_9}.H_3 + i_{11}.H_3 + \overline{i_7}.H_3$$
$$H_4 \stackrel{def}{=} i_4.H_4 + \overline{i_{10}}.H_4 + i_{12}.H_4 + \overline{i_{17}}.H_4 + i_{13}.H_4 + \overline{i_{14}}.H_4$$
$$H_5 \stackrel{def}{=} i_5.H_5 + \overline{i_8}.H_5 + i_{14}.H_5 + \overline{i_{13}}.H_5 + i_{15}.H_5 + \overline{i_6}.H_5$$
$$H_6 \stackrel{def}{=} i_6.H_6 + \overline{i_{15}}.H_6 + i_{16}.H_6 + \overline{i_{18}}.H_6$$
$$H_7 \stackrel{def}{=} i_7.H_7 + \overline{i_{11}}.H_7 + i_{17}.H_7 + \overline{i_{12}}.H_7 + i_{18}.H_7 + \overline{i_{16}}.H_7$$
$$N \stackrel{def}{=} [H_1]^{C_1} \| [H_2]^{C_2} \| [H_3]^{C_3} \| [H_4]^{C_4} \| [H_5]^{C_5} \| [H_6]^{C_6} \| [H_7]^{C_7}$$

where:

$$I(C_1) = \{\overline{i_2}, \overline{i_5}\} \qquad O(C_1) = \{i_1, i_8\}$$
$$I(C_2) = \{\overline{i_1}, \overline{i_3}, \overline{i_4}\} \qquad O(C_2) = \{i_2, i_9, i_{10}\}$$
$$I(C_3) = \{\overline{i_7}, \overline{i_9}\} \qquad O(C_3) = \{i_3, i_{11}\}$$
$$I(C_4) = \{\overline{i_{10}}, \overline{i_{14}}, \overline{i_{17}}\} \qquad O(C_4) = \{i_4, i_{12}, i_{13}\}$$
$$I(C_5) = \{\overline{i_6}, \overline{i_8}, \overline{i_{13}}\} \qquad O(C_5) = \{i_5, i_{14}, i_{15}\}$$
$$I(C_6) = \{\overline{i_{15}}, \overline{i_{18}}\} \qquad O(C_6) = \{i_6, i_{16}\}$$
$$I(C_7) = \{\overline{i_{11}}, \overline{i_{12}}, \overline{i_{16}}\} \qquad O(C_7) = \{i_7, i_{17}, i_{18}\}$$

Specification of the security policy   The security policy can be specified in the langage L_M by the monitor M defined as following :

$$M = M_1 \wedge M_2 \wedge M_3$$

where

- $M_1 = \neg(ip\_src = ip\_src(H_1) \wedge ip\_dst = ip\_dst(H_1) \wedge prot = icmp)$.
- $M_2 = \neg(ip\_src = ip\_src(H_4) \wedge ip\_dst = ip\_dst(H_5) \wedge port\_src = 21)$.
- $M_3 = \neg i_{15}(ip\_src = ip\_src(H_5) \wedge ip\_dst = ip\_dst(H_6) \wedge port\_src = 25)$.

Compute $N_1 = N \otimes M$

$$N_1 = N \otimes M = [H_1]^{C_1}_M \| [H_2]^{C_2}_M \| [H_3]^{C_3}_M \| [H_4]^{C_4}_M \| [H_5]^{C_5}_M \| [H_6]^{C_6}_M \| [H_7]^{C_7}_M$$

For the sake of simplicity, we use the following notation in the sequel:

$$N_1 = 1_M \| 2_M \| 3_M \| 4_M \| 5_M \| 6_M \| 7_M$$

where $1 = [H_1]^{C_1}$, $2 = [H_2]^{C_2}$, ... and $7 = [H_7]^{C_7}$

Compute $N \otimes_S M = (N \otimes M) \otimes_1 S = N_1 \otimes_1 S$ For this, we need to apply the rule R_1 and R_2 following the order given by $(R_1^* . R_2)^*$ and using the configuration $< \overline{N_1}, S >$. As shown hereafter, the details of the computation of $\otimes_1$ will be given for only one step and the details related to the other steps could be obtained in a similar way.

$$\begin{cases} S = \{2,4,6\} \\ \overline{N_1} = \{1_M, 2_M, 3_M, 4_M, 5_M, 6_M, 7_M\} \end{cases}$$

$$\Longrightarrow \{\text{We apply } R_1 \text{ on each node}\}$$

$$\begin{cases} S = \{2,4,6\} \\ \overline{N_1} = \{1_{M_1 \wedge M_2}, 2_{M_1 \wedge M_2}, 3_{M_1 \wedge M_2}, 4_{M_1 \wedge M_2}, 5_M, 6_M, 7_{M_1 \wedge M_2}\} \end{cases}$$

$$\Longrightarrow \{ \text{We apply } R_2 \text{ on the node } 1\}$$

First, we need to fin an integer i satisfying the following condition:

$$V_{\mathcal{N}_\infty}^{i+1}(1_{M_1 \wedge M_2}, S) = D_{\mathcal{N}_\infty}^{i+1}(1_{M_1 \wedge M_2}, S) - D_{\mathcal{N}_\infty}^i(1_{M_1 \wedge M_2}, S)$$

This can be done recursively from $i = 1$ to, at worst, the diameter (maximal distance between nodes) of the network.

$$\begin{aligned} \text{Case } i = 1 : \quad V_{\mathcal{N}_\infty}^1(1_{M_1 \wedge M_2}, S) &= D_{\mathcal{N}_\infty}^1(1_{M_1 \wedge M_2}, S) - D_{\mathcal{N}_\infty}^0(1_{M_1 \wedge M_2}, S) \\ &= \{1,2,5\} - \{1\} = \{2,5\} \not\subseteq S \end{aligned}$$

$$\begin{aligned} \text{Case } i = 2 : \quad V_{\mathcal{N}_\infty}^2(1_{M_1 \wedge M_2}, S) &= D_{\mathcal{N}_\infty}^2(1_{M_1 \wedge M_2}, S) - D_{\mathcal{N}_\infty}^1(1_{M_1 \wedge M_2}, S) \\ &= \{1,2,4,5,6\} - \{1,5\} = \{2,4,6\} \subseteq S \end{aligned}$$

So, we found that $i = 2$. Now we need to verify the second condition required by R_2:

$$\neg((D_{\mathcal{N}_\infty}^{i-1}(\eta, S) - S) \triangleleft \triangleright_M (D_{\mathcal{N}_\infty}^{i-1}(\eta, S) - S))$$

$$\begin{aligned} D_{\mathcal{N}_\infty}^1(1_{M_1 \wedge M_2}, S) - S &= \{1,2,5\} - \{2\} \\ &= \{1,5\} \end{aligned}$$

The above condition is satisfied because $M_1 \wedge M_2$ doesn't monitor communication between hosts H_1 and H_5.

Since the two conditions of R_2 are satisfied, we can move the monitor from node 1 to it's neighbors at level 2 an we obtain:

$$\{1, 2_{M_1 \wedge M_2 \wedge M_1 \wedge M_2}, 3_{M_1 \wedge M_2}, 4_{M_1 \wedge M_2 \wedge M_1 \wedge M_2}, 5_M, 6_{M \wedge M_1 \wedge M_2}, 7_{M_1 \wedge M_2}\}$$

$$\begin{cases} S = \{2,4,6\} \\ \overline{N_1} = \{1, 2_{M_1 \wedge M_2 \wedge M_1 \wedge M_2}, 3_{M_1 \wedge M_2}, 4_{M_1 \wedge M_2 \wedge M_1 \wedge M_2}, 5_M, 6_{M \wedge M_1 \wedge M_2}, 7_{M_1 \wedge M_2}\} \end{cases}$$

$$\Longrightarrow \{R_1^*\}$$

$$\begin{cases} S = \{2,4,6\} \\ \overline{N_1} = \{1, 2_{M_1 \wedge M_2}, 3_{M_1 \wedge M_2}, 4_{M_1 \wedge M_2}, 5_M, 6_M, 7_{M_1 \wedge M_2}\} \end{cases}$$

$\Longrightarrow \{$ We apply R_2 to the node 3 $\}$

$$\begin{cases} S = \{2,4,6\} \\ \overline{N_1} = \{1, 2_{M_1 \wedge M_2 \wedge M_1 \wedge M_2}, 3, 4_{M_1 \wedge M_2 \wedge M_1 \wedge M_2}, 5_M, 6_{M \wedge M_1 \wedge M_2}, 7_{M_1 \wedge M_2}\} \end{cases}$$

$\Longrightarrow \{R_1^*\}$

$$\begin{cases} S = \{2,4,6\} \\ \overline{N_1} = \overline{N} = \{1, 2_{M_1 \wedge M_2}, 3, 4_{M_1 \wedge M_2}, 5_M, 6_M, 7_{M_1 \wedge M_2}\} \end{cases}$$

$\Longrightarrow \{$ We apply R_2 to the node 5 $\}$

$$\begin{cases} S = \{2,4,6\} \\ \overline{N_1} = \{1, 2_{M_1 \wedge M_2 \wedge M}, 3, 4_{M_1 \wedge M_2 \wedge M}, 5, 6_{M \wedge M}, 7_{M_1 \wedge M_2}\} \end{cases}$$

$\Longrightarrow \{R_1^*\}$

$$\begin{cases} S = \{2,4,6\} \\ \overline{N_1} = \{1, 2_{M_1 \wedge M_2}, 3, 4_{M_1 \wedge M_2}, 5, 6_M, 7_{M_1 \wedge M_2}\} \end{cases}$$

$\Longrightarrow \{$ We apply R_2 to the node 7 $\}$

$$\begin{cases} S = \{2,4,6\} \\ \overline{N_1} = \{1, 2_{M_1 \wedge M_2 \wedge M_1 \wedge M_2}, 3, 4_{M_1 \wedge M_2 \wedge M_1 \wedge M_2}, 5, 6_{M \wedge M_1 \wedge M_2}, 7\} \end{cases}$$

$\Longrightarrow \{R_1^*\}$

$$\begin{cases} S = \{2,4,6\} \\ \overline{N_1} = \{1, 2_{M_1 \wedge M_2}, 3, 4_{M_1 \wedge M_2}, 5, 6_M, 7\} \end{cases}$$

We conclude that the solution is:

$$N \otimes_S M = [H_1]^{C_1} \| [H_2]^{C_2}_{M_1 \wedge M_2} \| [H_3]^{C_3} \| [H_4]^{C_4}_{M_1 \wedge M_2} \| [H_5]^{C_5} \| [H_6]^{C_6}_M \| [H_7]^{C_7}$$

7. Conclusion and future work

In this paper, we have introduced a formal technique allowing to automatically configure, according to a given security policy, a network so that we have a secure version. The network is specified in a new process algebra called **CMN** and the security policy is specified in a propositionnal language called L_M. After that, we have defined an enforcement operator $\otimes$ allowing to generate a secured configuration of the analyzed network. Finally, we have extended this enforcement operator to $\otimes_S$ to be able to give to the end-user the possibility of specifying where he wants to place his security policy.

As a future fork, we want to consider the LTL logic instead of L_M to be able to enforce more interesting properties. We want also to develop a tool that implements our approach.

References

[1]   E. Allen Emerson, *Temporal and modal logic*, Handbook of theoretical computer science (vol. B): formal models and semantics, 995–1072, 1990.

[2]   Angelos D. Keromytis and Jason L. Wright, *Transparent network security policy enforcement*, In proceedings of the Annual Technical Conference, 47–59, San Diego, California, USA, 2000.

[3]   Tomás E. Uribe and Steven Cheung, *Automatic Analysis of Firewall and Network Intrusion Detection System Configurations*, In proceedings of the ACM Workshop on Formal Methods in Security Engineering, 66–74, Washington, D.C., USA, 2004.

[4]   C. Hoare, *Communication Sequential Processes (CSP).*, Prentice Hall International, 1985.

[5]   Fred Kröger, *Temporal logic of programs*, Springer-Verlag New York, USA, 1987.

[6]   A. Lacasse, M. Mejri and B. Ktari, *Formal Implementation of Network Security Policies*, In proceedings of the confernce on privacy, security and trust, 161–166, New Brunswick, Canda, 2004.

[7]   R. Milner, *Communication and concurrency*, Prentice Hall International, Hertfordshire,UK, 1995.

[8]   R. Milner, *Lectures on a calculus for communicating systems*, In proceedings of the NATO Advanced Study Institute on Control flow and data flow: concepts of distributed programming, 205–228, Marktoberdorf, Germany, 1986.

[9]   J. L. M. Vrancken, *The algebra of communicating processes with empty process*, Theoretical Computer Science, vol. 177, no. 2, pp. 287–328, Essex, UK, 1997.

[10] S. Wolthusen, *Layered multipoint network defense and security policy enforcement*, In proceedings of the Second Annual IEEE SMC Information Assurance Workshop, 100–108, United States Military Academy, West Point, NY, USA, 2001.

Chapter 5

Software Security and Validation

New Trends in Software Methodologies, Tools and Techniques
H. Fujita and D. Pisanelli (Eds.)
IOS Press, 2007

New Verification of Reactive Requirement for Lyee Method

Osamu ARAI [1] and Hamido FUJITA
ARISES, Iwate Prefectural University, Japan

Abstract. Software development in general lacks richness in expressing appropriately the requirement, as well related supportive tools. Despite the advances in this field, the solutions have still not overcome and the proposed way of thinking is far from resolving the problems on software development and maintenance. Recently, a new promising methodology, called Lyee, has been proposed. It aims to generate programs automatically from user requirement. Program structure in terms of Lyee was formalized. However, when requirement and operation are not correct, Lyee program may not perform correctly. Especially, when requirements are reactive type, the validation mechanism have not proposed yet to show correctness or appropriateness of the running requirement. For this purpose, in this paper, the structure of Lyee program with multi SF is linked to process model. The properties that requirement and operation should have are described as a proposition in terms of temporal logic and are verified by such logic. Fairness property of excursion of program is used. New verification of reactive requirement for Lyee Method puts together as a design rule.

Keyword. Lyee, temporal logic, verification, reactive program, user requirement.

1. Introduction

From research practices in industry, a new promising methodology, called Lyee, has been proposed. It aims to generate programs automatically from user requirement. Program structure in terms of Lyee was formalized in the paper [2,3,4,5,6]. The Lyee program generation principle [1] is applicable to Lyee requirement specification. This means that the program is either providing the user with the correct computation results, or indication to the user that the specification is incorrect. In Lyee methodology, requirement specification is described using word and process root diagram that is automatically expanded to routing vector (a kind of word). The correctness of Lyee in the fixed-point setting [2], extension of this for parallel and distributed computing [3] is already discussed. Also, in the case of Lyee methodology, Structure of Lyee and Lyee requirement was formalized [4].

However, we think that almost all of Lyee style program behaves as reactive system program. In the case with multi screen and database management system or external equipments, the behavior of system depends on the external employment such as human or external equipment reaction. If requirement is well defined and appropriately expressed, software methodologies can realize them correctly for system

---

[1] Correspondence: 020-0193, Iwate, JAPAN, arai@fujita.soft.iwate-pu.ac.jp, <Hamido Fujita>: issam@soft.iwate-pu.ac.jp

built up. But, in order to evaluate the program run correctly beforehand, we should be able to clarify that requirement and operation should have a certain property for evaluation purposes.

Therefore, it is necessary that we apply another style of verification for such reactive requirement. As an example, Lyee requirements representing Light Control System are discussed. In the case of Process Control System such as Light Control System of buildings, the users' intension (requirement) is to save energy. Such intension (requirement) cannot verify without using process model.

In a previous paper [7], we considered the whole system including not only the structure of its program but also its external requirement and operation of human to behave as *reactive system*. We formalize whole system by process model, which consist of processes, states and shared variables as a bulletin board type communication tool. For this purpose, a *language* called L is defined by shared variables declaration and process definition been embedded in its syntax. The semantics is represented by the *labeled transition system* extracted from the program. By constructing the *Temporal Frame* (TF) that is the semantics in terms of temporal logic extracted from the calculation sequence of that system, the linkage of semantics of temporal logic and that of L, is presented. Based on such provision, the property, (i.e., users' intension) which the requirement specification should have, is described as a proposition in temporal logic using fairness property.

In this paper, we introduce that process model to the structure of Lyee program. Such reactive system is verified by the theorem of temporal logic, and its derivation rule. The remainder of this paper is organized as follows. In Section 2, we introduce Lyee Methodology and we describe the intension (property) of program of reactive system in temporal logics. In Section 3, we show the way to verify those properties in terms of reactive program. In Section 4, we verify an example. In Section 5, we discuss classification of condition and fairness, and transition of state and transition of SF in PRD in Lyee method. As summary of discussion, the design rule is shown. Finally, Section 6 provides concluding remarks on this work, and related future work.

2. Lyee Methodology and Lyee requirement

In the Lyee methodology, requirement specification is described using specific component which is called Word, that is part of language, and PRD which is connecting every Scenario Function (SF), and others. SF is a unit in which inputs, process computations and outputs are reached in fixed-point representation. If SF is an object for screen, then the output is displayed waiting for input. With pushing the enter button after a value of variable input, it is restarted and processing is performed. Using transition of screen or database management system (DBMS), at least two SF are required. One SF is assigned to every single button of screen, and to every single table of database management system. Accordingly, Process Route Diagram (PRD) is constructed. PRD expresses transition among screens, the correlation of screens and DBMSs, etc. as transition between SFs. A routing vector is defined for this purpose. Transition among two or more SFs is defined as PRD. For more details on Lyee refer to [1] and http://www.lyee-project.soft.iwate-pu.ac.jp.

In the case of dialogue between human and computer system by screen and keyboard, Lyee requirement of such system have reactive property in itself or whole system including environment such as human operation.

2.1. Reactive System

In recent years, not only Lyee requirement the computing system has developed into online system style computation. Such systems are called reactive system. Functional modeling cannot capture reactive system feature. Therefore, it is necessary to investigate all states during calculation. Since the sequence of these states continues in-deterministically, a program does not have deterministic output value at the time of program end, so the formulization by input/output relation is not simple. A program continues reacting over input from outside.

To confirm whether the reactive system runs correctly as intended, even if such system itself does not have concurrent property, the whole system which consists of system and its exteriors have concurrent property.

2.2. Composition of reactive system

A reactive system consists of the following.

- Process

The subject that calculates by running a program is called a process. Reactive system consists of two or more calculation subjects called process, and each process runs in parallel, communicating with other processes.

- State

The global running status of a process that is named as *state* is used to grasp internal state of the system. The state includes not only allocation of value to variable but also working situation of process.

- Inter-process communication

Communication is done by shared variables or channels [2] that is representing message exchange among processes. We use a bulletin board type communication that uses the shared variable as communication means.

2.3. Reactive System on Lyee Specification

In [7], we have defined a program L for reactive system and give its syntax and semantics for formal representation. L program consists of declaration of shared variables and definition of processes. Process definition has two attributes such as state and action. In declaration of a shared variable, this L-program declares to use the variable shared between each process. The other part of L-program defines the action of a process. A process changes its state, by updating shared variables. An action of a certain process is defined as in the following: when a process is in state α, if the value of a shared variable fulfills conditions B, performing substitution A of an assigned value to a shared variable then such process transfers itself to state β. The below formula shows such representation:

$$\alpha \overset{t}{\underset{B \Rightarrow A}{\rightarrow}} \beta$$

where t is the name of an action. Hereafter, we call this representation *process model*. The conditional expression B about the value of a shared variable is called the execution conditions of action t. The substitution of the value to a shared variable is called the command A of action t.

In Lyee Method structure, Scenario Function (SF) which has pallets W04-W02-W03 [1] and is shown in Fig.1 can be expressed by process model as shown in Fig. 2. Pallet W02 has two processes, one is a computer (C) and the other is an external event such as human operation (H). If processes have more than two outputs, to describe which

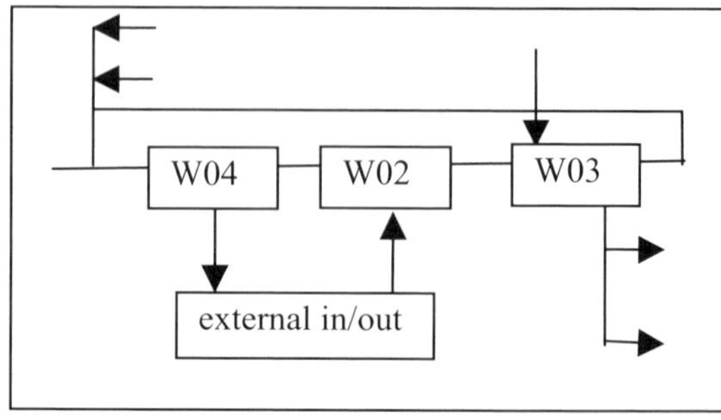

Figure 1. SF of Lyee Program

output should be selected, Process Route Diagram (PRD) is needed. Generally, output is selected by human operation or executed result of W03. The left part (a) of Fig.2 can be summarized to right part (b). This is because the variable domain for routing is limited inside SF; W04-W02-W03. The requirement of reactive type system could be described as a transition of SF shown in (b) of Fig.2. In Fig 2, state of process is surrounded by circle; $\bigcirc$ and action name, condition and command are omitted.

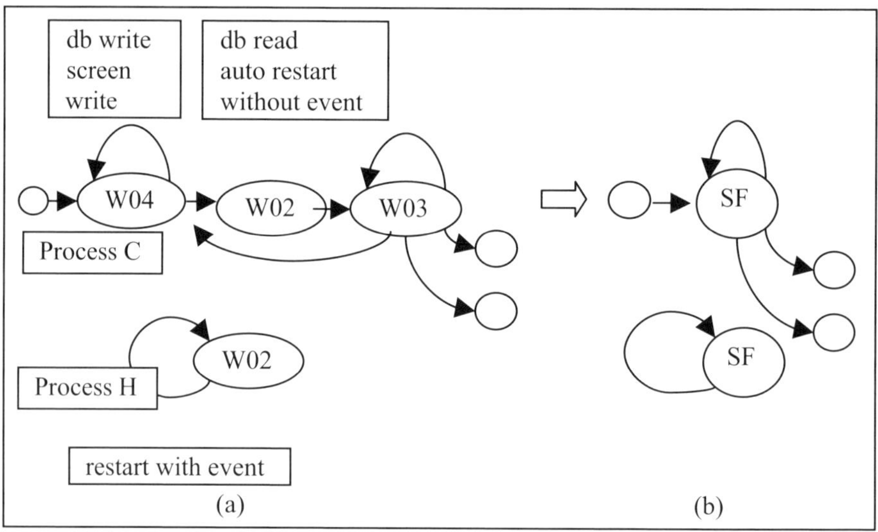

Figure 2. Process Model Representation of Lyee Program

A sample program of reactive system type is shown as Fig. 3, where two variables *start* and *finish* (includes initial value) are defined by {*start*:=undefined, *finish*:=false }.Two processes named H (Human) and C (Computer) react with each other using shared variables *start* and *finish*. At state *SF*, when shared variable *start* is false, process H transfer its state from *SF* to *itself* changing *start* variable. Then Process C can transfer its state from *SF* to *Child SF* without changing any variables. At state *Child SF*, Process C can transfer its state from *Child SF* to *itself* changing the value of variable *finish* from false to true after memory reading is complete. In the case to transfer another SF, variable start have value another. We call SF as Parent SF in the case to distinguish from Child SF.

$\{start := \text{undefined}, finish := \text{false }\}$

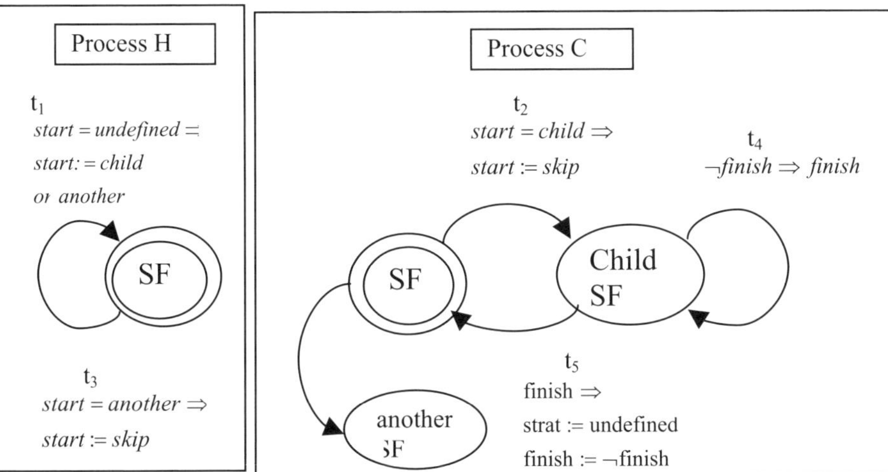

Figure 3. Process model of Reactive System

3. Verification Lyee Reactive Requirement by Temporal Logic

Using process model, we can represent the structure of Lyee reactive style program. To treat such representation more formally, we introduce a formal language L on process model. At first, we define the syntax of L-program. The semantics of L-program is defined as a set of calculation sequence represented by LTS extracted from the program. We introduced temporal logic to verify requirement described as a proposition of temporal logic. At the definition of semantics of temporal logic, we introduced temporal frame as a structure. Building a temporal frame from the calculation sequence of a program performs mediation with the semantics of L and the semantics of temporal logic. We describe the property of inner state which is changing according to the program execution of reactive system as the proposition of temporal logic, and then verify it with a rule of temporal logic such as live rule. For more detail, please refer the paper [7].

Generally, the fairness of processes execution should be maintained to some extent by scheduling. In Process route diagram of Lyee structure, at the connection of SF, such fairness of execution is needed. If the execution of routing is not fair, user's intension such as termination of program and saving energy result of process execution cannot be achieved. For the verification of requirement, two types of fairness (week and strong) are introduced. To verify the statement [a property Q will be satisfied at a certain time] on execution, liveness property is used as fairness property.

Our design provision is as follows;
1. Describe a state transition diagram based on L-language.
2. Verify Property which design intension (requirement) wants.
3. Repeat 1) and 2) until the state transition diagram is fixed.

Based on such provision as shown above, the intension that specification should have is described as a proposition of temporal logic, and is verified by the axiom of temporal logic, and related reduction rules.

For the use of proofing, we introduce some definitions and theorems. In the temporal logic, we use time modality connector $\Box, \Diamond, \bigcirc$ are shown

$$P := p \qquad\qquad (\textit{The notation showing a proposition})$$
$$|(\neg P)|(P \to Q) \quad (\textit{not } P)\,(\textit{if } P \textit{ then } Q)$$
$$|(P \wedge Q)|(P \vee Q) \quad (P \textit{ and } Q)\,(P \textit{ or } Q)$$
$$|(\Box P) \qquad\qquad (P \textit{ is true } \textit{allways})$$
$$|(\Diamond P) \qquad\qquad (P \textit{ is true } \textit{some time})$$
$$|(\bigcirc P) \qquad\qquad (P \textit{ is true } \textit{at the next time})$$

The symbol string p showing a proposition is defined as below.

$$p ::= B \mid at\ P_i.\,\alpha \mid enabled_\tau \mid executed_\tau$$

where, P_i is a process name, τ is transition name. B is a Boolean formula in the syntax of L. [$at\ P_i.\alpha$] expresses that the present state of Process P_i is α . [$enabled_\tau$] expresses that transition τ is under execute permission. [$executed_\tau$] expresses the transition that just pre-performed is τ .The semantics of L-program $\|C\|_{T,F}$, that is the calculation sequence, defined as follows. When the calculation

sequence $\sigma = s_0 \xrightarrow{\tau_0} s_1 \xrightarrow{\tau_1} \cdots \xrightarrow{\tau_{n-1}} s_n \xrightarrow{\tau_n} \cdots$ belongs to $[\![C]\!]_{T,F}$, a temporal frame $M_{C,\sigma}$ is built from σ as follows, where $s_i = \langle \rho, \alpha_1, \cdots, \alpha_m \rangle$.

$$M_{C,\sigma}(i)(B) \overset{def}{=} \begin{cases} true & if\ [\![B]\!]\rho = true \\ false & otherwise \end{cases}$$

$$M_{C,\sigma}(i)(at\ P_j.\alpha) \overset{def}{=} \begin{cases} true & if\ \alpha = \alpha_j \\ false & otherwise \end{cases}$$

$$M_{C,\sigma}(i)(enabled_\tau) \overset{def}{=} \begin{cases} true & when\ s_i, \tau\ is\ enabled \\ false & otherwise \end{cases}$$

$$M_{C,\sigma}(i)(executed_\tau) \overset{def}{=} \begin{cases} true & \tau_{i-1}\ is\ exist\ and\ \tau = \tau_{i-1} \\ false & otherwise \end{cases}$$

To verify that a program C written by L-program satisfies a property P that is described in temporal logical, we have to verify that P is universally valid in C. In this case, we argue about the property *"to be universally valid in the temporal frame made from the calculation sequence of LTS extracted from C"*; although it is not universally valid in any other temporal frame. For this purpose, the following theorems are provided.

(Theorem 3.1) Suppose that $P_i, ..., P_n \models_{IM} P$ is true in a set IM of temporal frame and logical expressions $P_1, \cdots, P_n$ and P . Then, $Q_1, \cdots, Q_m \models_{IM} Q$ is true if Q can be extracted from $Q_1, \cdots, Q_m$ by adding $P_1, \cdots, P_n \vdash P$ as reduction rule.

IM is the set of a temporal frame. Moreover, the following general theorems are used for our use.

(Theorem 3.2) Let P, Q be logical formula. $P \rightarrow \bigcirc Q$ is universally valid formula on C, when the statement [*If P is realized before the execution of τ and then τ is performed, and Q will be true after execution of τ.*] is realized to arbitrary transition τ in terms of LTS that is extracted from Program C.

Liveness property is used to prove the statement [a property Q will be satisfied at a certain time], therefore the rules below are used. If P is satisfied then P or Q will be satisfied at a certain time. If P continues to be satisfied then τ can be done at a certain time. If P is satisfied before execution of τ then Q is satisfied after execution. Therefore, it will be warranted that if P is satisfied then Q will be satisfied at a certain time. What formulized above as reduction rule of liveness shown below. This is used to verify the property of specification that is written as a proposition in temporal logic.

(Theorem 3.3) (rule of liveness) The following are satisfied when the set $\left\{ \tau \right\}$ which consists of transition τ of the LTS extracted from Program C are a weak fairness set or a strong fairness set on C.

$$P \rightarrow \bigcirc (P \vee Q),$$
$$P \rightarrow (Q \vee enabled_\tau),$$
$$P \rightarrow \bigcirc (executed_\tau \rightarrow Q)$$
$$\models \left\{ M_{C,\sigma} \mid \sigma \in [\![C]\!]_{J,F} \right\} P \rightarrow \diamondsuit Q$$

$\Box$

$\models \left\{ M_{C,\sigma} \mid \sigma \in [\![C]\!]_{J,F} \right\}$ means that to the temporal frame $M_{C,\sigma}$, $P \rightarrow \diamondsuit Q$ is universally valid in terms of $C_{J,F}$ under strong and weak fairness where σ is a calculation sequence belonging to $[\![C]\!]_{J,F}$.

(Theorem 3.4) (rule of chain) The following is satisfied on arbitrary natural number i.

$$P_0 \rightarrow \diamondsuit Q$$
$$P_1 \rightarrow \diamondsuit (P_0 \vee Q)$$
$$\vdots$$
$$P_i \rightarrow \diamondsuit (P_0 \vee P_1 \vee \cdots \vee P_{i-1} \vee Q)$$
$$\models (P_0 \vee P_1 \vee \cdots \vee P_i) \rightarrow \diamondsuit Q$$

$\Box$

These two Theorems 3.3 and 3.4 are proven by deduction. According to Theorem 3.1, we can use the formula, which used $\vdash$ instead of $\models$.

4. Example of verification

As an example, Lyee requirement specification which represents Light Control Case Study [8] is discussed. Its intension is to save energy. The property of Lyee requirement (intension) specification is described as proposition of temporal logic.

4.1. Representation of example system

Our example is a program specification, which represents the Light Control Case Study [8]. This case study is about saving energy and security control of a building. If

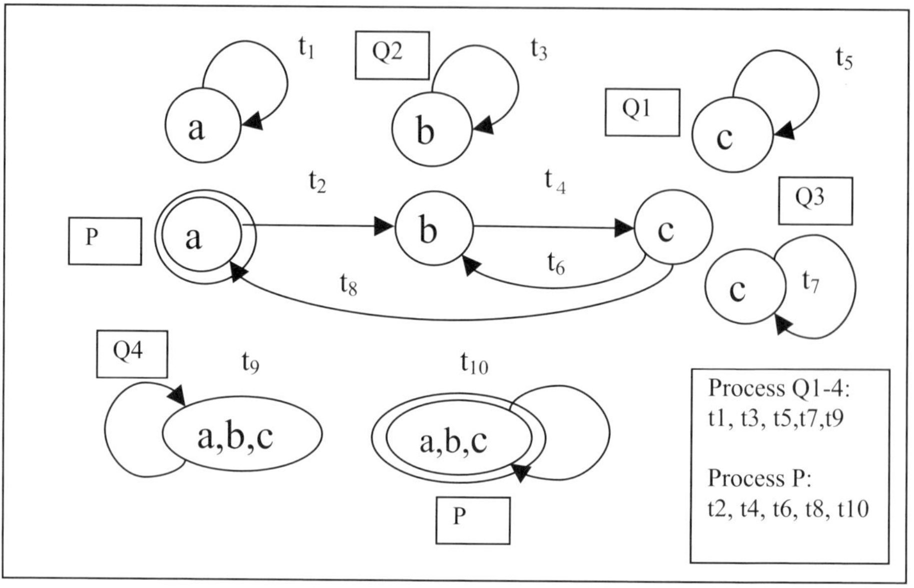

Figure 4. Example of program Light Control Case Study

nobody is in the room, light is turned off in fixed time. The program is shown in Fig 4. Related processes and its states are shown in Table 4.1.

Table 4.1   Process and state of example

name	description
Process Q1	human detector on
Process Q2	human detector off
Process Q3	deemed-timer time up
Process Q4	light sensor scanning timer time up (repeat)
Process P	computer whose role is governor
State a	nobody in one room
State b	somebody in the room
State c	deemed-timer running
State a,b,c	deemed somebody in the room

Shred variables shared by processes control state transition and common variables that are used plural states commonly is defined. Declaration of shared variables and common variables is shown in Table 4.2. An unstated item is Boolean.

Table 4.2   Declaration of shared and common variables

Declaration of shared and common variables	Description
shared variable $s = \{0,1\}$	0: nobody in, 1: somebody in
shared variable $t = \{0,1\}$	0: deemed-timer stopped, 1: running
shared variable $x = \{0,1\}$	0: light sensor scan off, 1: scan on
common variable $z = \{0,1\}$	0: not deemed, 1: deemed

Process definition is shown in Table 4.3. Since the variable which controls transition is expressed as a shared variable, then this variable is specified in command A. The shared variable is cleared by transition before turning into its initial state. s, t, z, x = 0, 0, 0, 0.

States (SFs) c have two outgoing transitions (routes). In state c, transition t6 and t8 are selectable. In this case, fair selection is needed. In order to save energy, program selects transition from state c to state a in a certain time.

Table 4.3 Process definition

Process	τ	α	β	B	A
Q1	t_1	a	a	s, t = 0, 0	s, t, z = 1, 0, 0: some one detected
P	t_2	a	b	s, t = 1, 0	s, t, z = 1, 0, 1: deemed
Q2	t_3	b	b	s, t = 1, 0	s, t, z = 0, 0, 1: no one detected,
P	t_4	b	c	s, t = 0, 0	s, t, z = 0, 1, 1: deemed-timer start
Q1	t_5	c	c	s, t = 0, 1	s, t, z = 1, 1, 1: some one detected
P	t_6	c	b	s, t = 1, 1	s, t, z = 1, 0, 1: deemed-timer reset
Q3	t_7	c	c	s, t = 0, 1	s, t, z = 0, 0, 1: deemed-timer time up
P	t_8	c	a	s, t = 0, 0	s, t, z = 0, 0, 0: not deemed
Q4	t_9	a,b,c	a,b,c	x = 0	x = 1: light-sensor-scan on
P	t_{10}	a,b,c	a,b,c	x = 1	x = 0: light-sensor-scan off control room light on z

4.2. Verification of example

Our aim is to verify "*Whole system including operation surely saves energy*". In such verification, we should clarify the conditions of fairness, which requirement and operation should have. Liveness property of "*save energy*" is influenced by fairness property. Verification of Liveness is the proof of logical formula deploying fairness sets defined in section 2.

The property which specification should have is described as a proposition in terms of temporal logic, and is verified by the axiom of temporal logic and its reduction rule. The requirement that represents Light Control Case Study is defined as an example.

If people go out of the room, a timer will surely be finished after a while and the light will be put out. That is, fairness is required between the frequency of incomings and outgoings of people, and interval setting of a timer. As the proposition of temporal logic, [*save energy*] is expressed as at P. c $\rightarrow \diamondsuit$ at P. a .

At this time, Processes P and Q are located in state c, and uses shared variables t (initial value of which is $\{t := 0\}$). For this reason, hereafter, [$at\ P. c \rightarrow \diamondsuit at\ P. a$] is verified; where [$at\ P_i. \alpha$] expresses that the present state of Process P_i is α .

Hereafter, logical formula [$at\ P. c \rightarrow \diamondsuit at\ P. a$] is verified. Using the state c of process P and the value of variable t, $at\ P. c$ is *classified* as in the following two cases:

(1) $at\ P.\,c = (at\ P.\,c \wedge t = 0)$

(2) $at\ P.\,c = (at\ P.\,c \wedge t = 1)$

Since $t = \{0, 1\}$, this classification is comprehensively inclusive and exclusively not overlapped internally in this case. Since the value of t is 0 in the case of (1), Process P can approach into a immediately. On the other hand, (2) is far from reaching the end.

In order to return to a, as timer is over, input 0 for t is required in Process Q.

(Apply Chain rule)

The name P_0, P_1 is given to each term according to the order near the goal ($at\ P.a$) for (1) to (2).

$P_0 \equiv at\ P.\,c \wedge t = 0$

$P_1 \equiv at\ P.\,c \wedge t = 1$

The following reduction will be obtained when the chain rule of Theorem 3.4 is applied to such logical formula.

$P_0 \rightarrow \Diamond at\ P.\,a\,,$

$P_1 \rightarrow \Diamond (P_0 \vee at\ P.\,a),$

$\vdash\ (P_0 \vee P_1) \rightarrow \Diamond at\ P.\,a$

Liveness property is verifiable when the premise of rule from (1) to (2) is derived because $(P_0 \vee P_1)$ is $at\ P.\,c$.

(Apply Live rule)

Logical expressions P_0, P_1 named above are derived using the temporal logic shown below.

1) Derivation of (1)

Since P_0 is $at\ P.\,c \wedge t = 0$, when this is true, $\langle P, t_8 \rangle$ is performed at a certain time and the state of P should be set to a. That is, fair execution is required for t_8 as mentioned above. Therefore, in applying the live rule (Theorem 3.3) to $P_0 \rightarrow \Diamond at\ P.\,a$ and $\langle P, t_8 \rangle$, the following derivation can be obtained:

$$P_0 \rightarrow \bigcirc (P_0 \vee at\ P.\,a)\,, \qquad (a)$$

$$P_0 \rightarrow (at\ P.\,a \vee enabled_{\langle P, t_8 \rangle})\,, \qquad (b)$$

$$P_0 \rightarrow \bigcirc (executed_{\langle P, t_8 \rangle} \rightarrow at\ P.\,a) \qquad (c)$$

$$\vDash_{\{M_{C,\sigma} | \sigma \in [[C]]_{T,F}\}} P_0 \rightarrow at\ P.\,a$$

The logical expressions $(a),(b),(c)$, are the premise of this derivation and verified as below.

(Verification of (a)) $\qquad\qquad P_0 \rightarrow \bigcirc (P_0 \vee at\ P.\,a) \qquad\qquad (a)$

In P_0, since states of process P and Q are both $c = 0$ and $t = 0$, possible transition is restricted to $\langle P, t_8 \rangle$; (case 1) and the idling transition τ_I ;(case 2).

(case 1) When $\langle P, t_8 \rangle$ is performed, since variable $at\ P.\,c$ is true, the formula (a) is verified using Theorem 3.2.

(case 2) When τ_I is performed, since P_0 is true, the formula (a) is true by theorem 3.2.

Therefore, formula (a) is verified.

(Verification of (b)) $\qquad\qquad P_0 \rightarrow (at\ P.\ e \vee enabled_{\langle P, t_8 \rangle}),$ (b)

When P_0 is true, Process P is at c and $t = 0$ is true. So, execution of $\langle P, t_8 \rangle$ is permitted.

Therefore, since $enabled_{\langle P, t_8 \rangle}$ is true, (b) is verified.

(Verification of (c)) $\qquad\qquad P_0 \rightarrow \bigcirc(executed_{\langle P, t_8 \rangle} \rightarrow at\ P.\ a)$ (c)

When P_0 is true, if $\langle P, t_8 \rangle$ is performed, the state of process P is set to a. So, (c) is verified by Theorem 3.2.

Therefore, it is verified that formula (1), (i.e., $P_0 \rightarrow \Diamond at\ P.\ a$) turns into a universally valid formula of L-program.

2) Derivation of (2)

Since P_1 is $at\ P.\ c \wedge t = 1$, $\langle Q_3, t_7 \rangle$ is performed at a certain time and t should be set to 0.

Therefore, the live rule is applied to $P_1 \rightarrow \Diamond(P_0 \vee at\ P.\ a)$ and $\langle Q, t_7 \rangle$, the following derivation can be obtained.

$$P_1 \rightarrow \bigcirc(P_1 \vee (P_0 \vee at\ P.\ a)), \qquad (a)$$
$$P_1 \rightarrow ((P_0 \vee at\ P.\ a) \vee enabled_{\langle Q, t_7 \rangle}), \qquad (b)$$
$$P_1 \rightarrow \bigcirc(executed_{\langle Q, t_7 \rangle} \rightarrow (P_0 \vee at\ P.\ a)) \quad (c)$$
$$\models_{\{M_{C,\sigma}|\sigma \in [[C]]_{T,F}\}} P_1 \rightarrow (P_0 \vee at\ P.\ a)$$

The logical expressions denoted above as $(a), (b), (c)$, are the premise of this derivation, and verified as below.

(Verification of (a)) $\qquad\qquad P_1 \rightarrow \bigcirc(P_1 \vee (P_0 \vee at\ P.\ a))$ (a)

In P_1, since state of processes P and Q are both $c = 1$ and $t = 1$, transition is restricted to $\langle Q_3, t_7 \rangle$ (case 1) ; $\langle Q_1, t_5 \rangle$ and the idling transition τ_I ; (case 2).

(case 1) When $\langle Q_3, t_7 \rangle$ is performed, since $at\ P.\ a$ is true, $t = 0$ is true. By assuring that $t = 0$ will be true at a certain time by fair execution, P_0 is true. Therefore, formula (a) is verified using Theorem 3.2.

(case 2) When $\langle Q_1, t_5 \rangle$ or τ_I is performed, since P_1 is true, the formula (a) is true. Therefore, the formula (a) is verified by Theorem 3.2.

(Verification of (b)) $\qquad\qquad P_1 \rightarrow ((P_0 \vee at\ P.\ a) \vee enabled_{\langle Q, t_7 \rangle})$ (b)

When P_1 is true, $t = 1$ is true. So, execution of $\langle Q, t_7 \rangle$ is permitted.

Therefore, since $enabled_{\langle Q, t_7 \rangle}$ is true, (b) is verified.

(Verification of (c)) $\qquad\qquad P_1 \rightarrow \bigcirc(executed_{\langle Q, t_7 \rangle} \rightarrow (P_0 \vee at\ P.\ a))$ (c)

When P_1 is true, if $\langle Q_3,\ t_7 \rangle$ is performed, the state of process P and variable is set to *at P. a*, *sf* = Start or *sf* = End . By assuring that *sf* = End will be true at a certain time by fair execution, P_0 is true. Therefore, formula (c) is verified using Theorem 3.2.

Therefore, when fair execution (*sf* = End is performed at a certain time) is performed in the execution of $\langle Q_3,\ t_7 \rangle$, it is verified that formula (2), (i.e., $P_1 \to \bigcirc (P_0 \vee at\ P.\ a)$), turn into a universally valid formula of L-program.

Since it is verified that (1) and (2) are universally valid formulas, the liveness property *at P. c* $\to \diamondsuit at\ P.\ a$ which is our objective, is verified.

$\square$

Consequently, the property that energy is saved correctly is verified under the fair execution when satisfying the following.

1) Using the combination of shared variables; a special classification is necessary to carry out such execution. In this classification, condition must be comprehensively inclusive and exclusively defined. This means that the conditions of transition of SF is defined only once over the domain of a vector.

2) It is demanded that fair execution (i.e., Timer time up should surely be occurred some time) need to be done.

5. Discussion

The program in terms of Lyee structure is correctly performed only after a definition and operation of requirement of Lyee are executed correctly. Calculation conditions of words and the conditions of transition of SF are the reference of requirement correctness.

5.1. Transition of states in process model and transition of SFs in PRD

From the state transition diagram (STR), extract SF pattern of STR according to event. Unify asynchronously simultaneous events (SF pattern of STR) to one SF. This is the SF division rule. One Parent SF is a group of events that may happen there. A screen (SF) has some buttons, i.e. events, in human interface with screen and keyboard, machine (sensor, actuator) interface event. If these events happen asynchronously, it needs to be received from one parent SF. That is, a group of events in which one of these events happens and the other event does not happen, compose one parent SF. Event transfers process from one state to another state (event driven). Therefore, more than one state exists in one parent SF.

In Process Control Application, there are many events such that communication that include Internet, timer, human interface with screen and keyboard, machine (sensor, actuator) interface event. If these events happen asynchronously, it needs to be received from one Parent SF. That is, a group of events in which one of these events happens and the other event does not happen, compose one Parent SF. Event transfers process from one state to another state (i.e., event driven). Therefore, more than one state exists in one SF. The variable in one SF that is used commonly by plural states is called common variable.

5.2. Classification of condition and Fairness

In classification of transition condition, using the combination of shared variables needs fair classify. All conditions must be comprehensively inclusive and exclusively defined. This means that the conditions of transition of SF is defined only once over the domain of variable. Fair execution should be done. In example, Timer should surely time-up some time.

5.3. Expression as a Design Rule

PRD of Lyee specification is expressed in L-program by considering SF as a state using the process model. Since a state is an atomic action, SF cannot be partitioned into at least one atomic action. If SFs are unified and enlarged, an excessive calculation will be carried out and its execution speed may become slow. It is important to extract the boundary of SF appropriately. For this reason, it is effective to apply the process model proposed here for safety checking .

In order to apply the above discussion result from now on, it puts together as a design rule.
1.　Describe a state transition diagram based on L-language.
2.　Verify Property which design intension (requirement) wants.
3.　Repeat 1) and 2) until fix the state transition.
4.　Divide system to program (PRD).
5.　Divide program (PRD) to SF based on the SF division rule above.
6.　Draw PRD (transition between SF) based on state transition diagram.
7.　Realize state as a set of common variable in SF by Lyee method such as memory table, action vector, and word.

Terms from 1 to 3 are about process model, term from 4 to 7 is about Lyee Methodology.

6. Conclusion

To verify the reactive property of requirement that multi screen, database management and process control system have, we should apply to reactive style of verification. For this purpose, we introduced new verification way of reactive requirement for Lyee Method. As an example, the requirement that represents Light Control System is defined to verify that this program calculates correctly (saves energy of buildings). Consequently, we clarify the conditions of fairness in which the execution conditions of requirement and operation should have.

In classification presented at the proof of the example, conditions must be comprehensively inclusive and exclusively defined. Moreover, operation should be executed fairly. These requirements are common in PRD of Lyee methodology.

Especially, in Process control such as Light Control Case Study, the trace of logic is difficult, and so maintainability is poor, the concept of state of process model is effective as an approach on visualizing and catching the program structure. When using a structured program such as Lyee for reactive application with many state transitions, this model is effective.

In Lyee Methodology, requirement specification is not verified in itself. To use this methodology for actual system development, system design intension is desired to be verified beforehand. Using the process model, we can verify other reactive property of intension (requirement) such as safety, partial correctness, avoidance of dead lock, mutual exclusion of critical resource, total correctness, in the future.

References

[1] F.Negoro. "Principle of Lyee Software", Proceedings of 2000 International Conference on Information Society in the 21st Century (IS2000), Aizu, Japan, November 5-8, 2000, pp441-446.

[2] S.Gorlatch. The Lyee programming model: Analysis correctness in a fixed point setting. In H.Fujita and P.Johannesson, editors, New Trends in Software Methodologies, Tools and Techniques, pages 214-224. IOS Press, 2003.

[3] S.Gorlatch. Declarative Programming with Lyee for Distributed Systems In H.Fujita and V. Gruhn, editors, New Trends in Software Methodologies, Tools and Techniques, pages 129-137. IOS Press, 2004.

[4] H.Fujita, M.Mejri and B.Ktari. A process algebra to formalize the Lyee methodology, pages 263-282. Knowledge-Based Systems, Volume 17, issues 7-8, December 2004, ISSN 0950-7051

[5] O.Arai and H.Fujita, Mathematical structure model for Word-Based Program, pages399-411, Knowledge-Based Systems, Volume 16, issues 7-8, November 2003, ISSN 0950-7051

[6] O.Arai and H.Fujita. Declarative and Procedural Representation of Lyee Software, In Hamid Fujita and Volker.Gruhn, editors, New Trends in Software Methodologies, Tools and Techniques, pages 138-152. IOS Press, September 2004, Proceedings of the 3rd SoMeT_W04, Germany.

[7] O.Arai and H.Fujita Verification of the Lyee Requirement, In Hamid Fujita and Mohamed Mejri, editors, New Trends in Software Methodologies, Tools and Techniques, pages 340-361. IOS Press, September 2006, Proceedings of the 5th SoMeT_06, Qubec.

[8] S.Queins and Others "Requirement Engineering: The Light Control Case Study", Journal of Universal Computer Science, Volume6 Issue7, 2000.

New Trends in Software Methodologies, Tools and Techniques
H. Fujita and D. Pisanelli (Eds.)
IOS Press, 2007

Model Checking Communicative Agent-Based Systems

Jamal Bentahar[1] and John-Jules Meyer[2]
[1] *Concordia University, Concordia Institute for Information Systems Engineering,*
Montreal, QC, Canada
[2] *Utrecht University, Department of Information & Computer Science, The Netherlands*

Abstract. Model checking is a formal technique used to verify communication protocols against given properties. In this paper, we address the problem of verifying systems designed as a set of autonomous interacting agents using such a technique. These software agents are equipped with knowledge and beliefs and interact with each other according to protocols governed by a set of logical rules. We present a tableau-based model checking algorithm for these systems and provide the termination and complexity results.

Keywords. Multi-agent systems, model checking, temporal logic

Introduction

Although formal verification methods are not yet widely used to check large and complex systems, they are useful for the verification of some properties in relatively small systems involving concurrency and communication protocols. *Deadlock* (two or more processes are each waiting for another to release a resource), *safety* (same bad situation may never occur), and *reachability* (some particular situation can be reached) are examples of such properties. Formal methods offer a potential to obtain an early integration of verification in the design process, and to reduce the verification time. However, they are only applicable for finite state systems and they generally operate on system models and not on the actual system.

We distinguish two main formal verification approaches: proof-based approaches and model-based approaches. In the proof-based approaches, the system description is a set of logical formulae Γ and the specification is another formula ϕ. The verification method consists of trying to find a proof that $\Gamma \vdash \phi$. This typically requires guidance and expertise from the user in order to identify suitable lemmas and auxiliary assertions. In the model-based approaches, also called *model checking*, the system (the protocol) is represented by a finite model M modeled as a *Kripke structure* using an appropriate logic. The specification is again represented by a formula ϕ expressed in the same logic, and the verification method consists of computing whether the model M satisfies ϕ or not ($M \vDash \phi$). This is an algorithmic-based technique and usually done automatically.

Recently, model checking has been used to verify agent-based systems [1,2,3,4]. Verifying these systems is becoming more and more necessary because they are increasingly used in several critical application domains, such as e-commerce, simulation, distributed collaborative systems, etc [5,6,7]. In these systems, agents are equipped with reasoning and communicative abilities. This is generally expressed using epistemic logics (logics about beliefs, knowledge, goals, etc.) and logic-based protocols [8]. Such protocols are modeled as a set of rules describing the allowed communicative acts in different situations. How an agent selects the communicative act to perform at a given moment is decided by his reasoning. In order to allow agents to flexibly and autonomously communicate within multi-agent systems, these protocols are specified as a set of policies, called dialogue games, about which agents can reason [9,10,11,12]. Dialogue games are interaction games in which each agent plays a move in turn by performing utterances according to a predefined set of logical rules. Dialogue game protocols are a combination of different dialogue games.

In this paper, we present an efficient *model checking algorithm* to verify interacting agent-based systems, in which agents have knowledge and beliefs and communicate by combining and reasoning about dialogue games. This algorithm is based on a tableau-based technique we developed in [13]. In this paper, we focus on the algorithmic description of this technique and on its termination and complexity. We specify a dialogue game protocol as a transition system in which transitions are labeled with communicative acts. Such acts are modeled as actions performed by agents *on Propositional Commitments* (*PC*), for example, creating, accepting, or challenging a propositional commitment [10]. Propositional commitments are used to capture the *public utterances* in the sense that each utterance is viewed as a propositional commitment.

To use model checking, we specify dialogue game protocols and the properties to be verified in a new logic extending CTL* by adding formulae representing propositional commitments. The verification method is based on the translation of formulae into a variant of alternating tree automata called *Alternating Büchi Tableau Automata* (*ABTA*) [14]. Unlike the model checking algorithms proposed in the literature, our on-the-fly efficient algorithm uses only one depth-first search instead of two. This is due to the fact that our algorithm explores directly the product graph of the dialogue game protocol and the ABTA representing the property to be verified using the sign of the nodes.

Paper Overview. The rest of the paper is organized as follows. In Section 1, we summarize and discuss related work. In Section 2, we develop a logic for communicating agents that we use to specify the properties to be checked. Section 3 presents the tableau rules associated to this logic. Section 4 presents the specification of dialogue game protocols agents use to communicate and gives some examples of the properties to be checked. In Section 5, we discuss the model checking technique of these protocols using tableau rules. In Section 6, we prove the termination property of the technique and we discuss its complexity. Section 7 concludes the paper.

1. Related Work

Bernholtz, Vardi, and Wolper [15] argued that *alternating tree automata* are the key to a comprehensive and satisfactory automata-theoretic framework for branching temporal logics. Alternating tree automata on infinite trees generalize the standard notion of non-deterministic tree automata by allowing several successor states to go down along the same branch of the tree. Tree automata generalize sequential automata in the following way: on a given binary tree, the automaton starts its computation at the root in an initial state and then simultaneously works down the paths of the tree level by level. The transition relation specifies the two states that are the two sons of a node. The tree automaton accepts the tree if there is a run built up in this fashion which is *successful*. A run is successful if all its paths are successful in a sense given by an acceptance condition for sequential automata.

The model checking approach we use in this paper is based on an alternative view of model checking proposed by Bhat and Cleaveland [16] and Bhat et al. [14]. This view relies on translating formulae into intermediate structures, *Alternating Büchi Tableau Automata* (ABTA). Unlike the other model checking techniques, this technique allows us to verify not only temporal formulae, but also action formulae. Because our logic for communicating agents is based on an action theory, this technique is more suitable. This approach is called *tableau-based model checking* [13].

Recently, the verification of agent-based systems has become an attractive field of research and several proposals have been put forward. Some of these proposals use existing model checkers (for example SPIN and JPF2) by translating some agent specification languages (for example MABLE and AgentSpeak) to the languages used by these model checkers [1,2,17]. Other proposals adapt some model checking techniques (for example bounded and unbounded model checking) and propose new algorithms for verifying temporal and epistemic properties [4,5,6]. Giordano and her colleagues [3] addressed the problem of specifying and verifying systems of communicating agents in a Dynamic Linear Time Temporal Logic (DLTL).

Except the work done in [3], all the other proposals on model checking of agent-based systems are based only on temporal and epistemic logics. In this paper, we propose a model checking-based verification of dialogue game protocols using a temporal and dynamic logic. In contrast to [3], the dynamic aspect of our logic is represented by action formulae and not by strengthening the *until* operator by indexing it with the regular programs of dynamic logic. Our protocols are specified as actions that agents apply to propositional commitments. In addition, the model checking procedure that we propose allows us to verify not only that the dialogue game protocol (the theoretical model) satisfies a given property, but also that the tableau semantics of the communicative acts is respected. The idea is to integrate this semantics in the specification of the protocol, and then to propose a parsing method to verify that the protocol specification respects the semantic definition. Consequently, if agents respect these protocols, then they also respect the semantics of the communicative acts. We have here a mechanism for checking the agents' compliance with the semantics without accessing the agents' internal programs. Indeed, we have only one procedure to verify: 1) the correctness of the protocols relative to the properties that the protocols should satisfy; and 2) the conformance of agents to the semantics of the communicative acts. The purpose of this technique is to verify the temporal properties of the protocol and to ensure that the structures of the communicative acts are the same in both the protocol and the specification.

To our knowledge, until now there is no work that addressed the verification problem of agent-based systems communicating by dialogue game protocols. The contribution of this paper is an efficient algorithm for model checking software interacting agent-based systems and its termination and soundness proofs.

2. A Logic for Communicating Agents

2.1. Syntax

In this section, we present CTL^{*CA} an extended logic from CTL^* for Communicative Agents. This logic extends CTL^* by adding propositional commitments and action formulae. In what follows we use p, p_1, p_2... to range over the set of atomic propositions Φ_p. The syntax of this logic is as follows:

$$\mathcal{S} ::= p \mid \neg\mathcal{S} \mid \mathcal{S} \wedge \mathcal{S} \mid \mathcal{S} \vee \mathcal{S} \mid A\mathcal{P} \mid E\mathcal{P}$$

$$\mathcal{P} ::= \mathcal{S} \mid \mathcal{P} \wedge \mathcal{P} \mid \mathcal{P} \vee \mathcal{P} \mid X^+\mathcal{P} \mid X^-\mathcal{P} \mid \mathcal{P}\, U^+\, \mathcal{P} \mid \mathcal{P}\, U^-\, \mathcal{P} \mid \mathcal{P} \therefore \mathcal{P}$$

$$\mid C(Ag_1, PC(Ag_1, Ag_2, t, \mathcal{P}))$$

$$\mid Act(Ag_i, PC(Ag_1, Ag_2, t, \mathcal{P}))$$

The formulae generated by $\mathcal{S}$ are called state formulae, while those generated by $\mathcal{P}$ are called path formulae. We use $\psi, \psi_1, \psi_2,...$ to range over state formulae and $\phi, \phi_1, \phi_2,...$ to range over path formulae. The meaning of most of the constructs is straightforward (from CTL^* with next (X^+), previous (X^-), until (U^+), and since (U^-) operators). The formula $\phi_1 \therefore \phi_2$ means that ϕ_1 is an argument for ϕ_2. We can read this formula: ϕ_1, so ϕ_2. This operator introduces argumentation as a logical relation between path formulae.

The formula $C(Ag_1, PC(Ag_1, Ag_2, t, \mathcal{P}))$ means that agent Ag_1 commits at the moment t towards agent Ag_2 that the path formula $\mathcal{P}$ is true. The formula $Act(Ag_i, PC(Ag_1, Ag_2, t, \mathcal{P}))$ means that agent Ag_i ($i \in \{1, 2\}$) performs an action on the propositional commitment made by Ag_1 towards Ag_2. The set of actions performed on propositional commitments are *Withdraw, Satisfy, Violate, Reactivate, Challenge, Accept, Refuse, Justify, Attack, Defend* (see [9] for more details).

2.2. Semantics

The formal model M associated to this logic corresponds to the dialogue game protocol agents use to communicate. Formally, this model is defined as follows: $M = \langle S_m, Lab_m, Act_m, \xrightarrow{Act_m}, Agt, R_{PC}, S_{m_0} \rangle$ where: S_m is a set of states; $Lab_m : S_m \to 2^{\Phi_p}$ is the labeling state function; Act_m is the set of actions performed on Propositional commitments; $\xrightarrow{Act_m} \subseteq S_m \times Act_m \times S_m$ is the transition relation; Agt is a set of agents; $R_{PC} : S_m \times Agt \times Agt \to 2^\sigma$ with σ is the set of all paths in M is an accessibility modal relation that associates to a state s_m the set of paths representing the propositional commitment along which an agent can commit towards another agent; s_{m_0} is the start state. The paths that path formulae are interpreted over have the form

$$x^i = s_{m_i} \xrightarrow{\alpha_{i+1}} s_{m_{i+1}} \xrightarrow{\alpha_{i+2}} s_{m_{i+2}} ... \quad \text{where} \quad x^i \in \sigma \ , \quad s_{m_i}, s_{m_{i+1}},... \quad \text{are states and}$$

$\alpha_{i+1}, \alpha_{i+2},...$ are actions.

The semantics of CTL*^{CA} state formulae is as usual (semantics of CTL*). A path satisfies a state formula if the initial state in the path does. Along a path x^i, $\phi_1 \therefore \phi_2$ holds if ϕ_1 is true and at next time if ϕ_1 is true then ϕ_2 is true. Formally:

$$x^i \vDash_M \phi_1 \therefore \phi_2 \; iff \; x^i \vDash_M \phi_1 \; \& \; x^{i+1} \vDash_M \phi_1 \Rightarrow \phi_2$$

A path x^i satisfies $C(Ag_1, PC(Ag_1, Ag_2, t, \phi))$ if C is in the label of the first transition on this path and if every accessible path to Ag_1 towards Ag_2 from the first state of the path using R_{PC} satisfies ϕ. Formally:

$$x^i \vDash_M C(Ag_1, PC(Ag_1, Ag_2, t, \phi)) \; iff$$
$$\alpha_{i+1} = C \; \& \; \forall x^i \in \sigma, \; x^i \in R_{PC}(s_{m_i}, Ag_1, Ag_2) \Rightarrow x^i \vDash_M \phi$$

A path x^i satisfies $Act(Ag_i, PC(Ag_1, Ag_2, t, \phi))$ if Act is in the label of the first transition on this path and if in the past (P) Ag_1 has already created the social commitment. Formally:

$$x^i \vDash_M Act(Ag_1, PC(Ag_1, Ag_2, t, \phi)) \; iff \; \alpha_{i+1} = Act \; \& \; P(C(Ag_1, PC(Ag_1, Ag_2, t, \phi)))$$

We notice that the past (P) and future (F) operators are abbreviations from until operator (U) in the usual way of CTL* logic.

3. Tableau Rules for CTL*^{CA}

Tableau-based algorithms for model checking are based on the use of assertions and tableau rules which are *proof rules*. Assertions are typically of the form $s \vdash_M \phi$ and mean that state s in model M satisfies the formula ϕ. Using a set of tableau rules we aim to prove the truth or falsity of assertions. But unlike traditional proof systems which are bottom-up approaches, tableau-based algorithms work in a *top-down* or *goal-oriented* fashion. Tableau rules are used in order to prove a certain formula by inferring when a state in a Kripke structure satisfies such a formula. According to this approach, we start from a goal, and we apply a proof rule and determine the sub-goals to be proven. The proof rules are designed so that the goal is true if all the sub-goals are true. The advantage of this method is that the state space is explored in a need-driven fashion. The algorithm searches only the part of the state space that needs to be explored to prove or disprove a certain formula.

The tableau rules of CTL*^{CA} are given in Figures 1, 2, 3 and 4. We introduce a syntactical operator "?" to express the tableau rule of the challenge action. Semantically, "?ψ" means that, a given agent does not know whether ψ is true or not.

Tableau rules enable us to define top-down proof systems. The idea is: given a formula, we apply a tableau rule and determine the sub-formulae to be proven. Tableau rules are inference rules used in order to prove a formula by proving all the sub-formulae. The labels of these rules are the labels of states in the automata constructed from a given formula. For example, rule $R1$ of Figure 1 labeled by "∧" indicates that ψ_1 and ψ_2 are the two sub-formulae of $\psi_1 \wedge \psi_2$. This means that, in order to prove that a state labeled by "$\wedge$" satisfies the formula $\psi_1 \wedge \psi_2$, we have to prove that the two children of this state satisfy ψ_1 and ψ_2 respectively. According to rule $R2$, in order to prove that a state labeled by "$\vee$" satisfies the formula $\psi_1 \vee \psi_2$, we have to prove that one of the two children of this state satisfies ψ_1 or ψ_2. Rule $R3$ labeled by "$\vee$" indicates that ψ is the sub-formula to be proved in order to prove that a state satisfies E(ψ). According to rule $R4$ (resp. $R5$), the formula $\neg\psi$ (resp. $?\psi$) is satisfied in a state labeled by "$\neg$" (resp. ?), if this state has a successor representing ψ. Rule $R6$ is defined in the usual way where Φ is a set of path formulae.

$$R1 \quad \wedge : \frac{\psi_1 \wedge \psi_2}{\psi_1 \; \psi_2} \qquad R2 \quad \vee : \frac{\psi_1 \vee \psi_2}{\psi_1 \; \psi_2} \qquad R3 \quad \vee : \frac{E(\psi)}{\psi}$$

$$R4 \quad \neg : \frac{\neg\psi}{\psi} \qquad R5 \quad ? : \frac{?\psi}{\psi} \qquad R6 \quad \neg : \frac{A(\Phi)}{E(\neg\Phi)}$$

Figure 1. Tableau rules for propositional and universal formulas

The label "$<C>$" (rule $R7$) is the label associated with the creation action of a propositional commitment PC. According to this rule, in order to prove that a state satisfies $C(Ag_1, PC(Ag_1, Ag_2, t, \phi))$, we have to prove that an accessible state via a transition labeled by the creation action satisfies the sub-formula $PC(Ag_1, Ag_2, t, \phi)$. The rules $R8$ to $R17$ are defined in the same way.

Rule $R18$ of Figure 3 indicates that $E(\phi)$ is the sub-formula of the formula $E(PC(Ag_1, Ag_2, t, \phi))$. Thus, in order to prove that a state satisfies $E(PC(Ag_1, Ag_2, t, \phi))$, we have to prove that the accessible state via a transition labeled by "$[PC_{Ag_1}]$" satisfies $E(\phi)$.

Finally, the rules $R19$ to $R27$ of Figure 4 are defined in the usual way. For example, according to rule $R24$, in order to prove that a state satisfies $E(X^+\varphi)$, we have to prove that the next state via the transition labeled by "X^+" satisfies the sub-formula $E(\varphi)$.

4. Protocol for Communicating Agents

4.1. Protocol Specification

In this section, we define the theoretical model of our model checking procedure. This model specifies the dialogue game protocols. These protocols are specified as a set of rules describing the entry condition, the dynamics and the exit condition of the protocol [10]. These rules can be specified in the logic for communicating agents as action formulae (actions on propositional commitments). We define these protocols as transition systems. The purpose of these transition systems is to describe not only the sequence of the allowed actions (classical transition systems), but also the structure of these actions. The states of these transition systems are sub-transition systems (called *structure transition systems*) describing the structure of the actions labeling the entry transitions. Defining transition systems in such a way allows for the verification of: 1) the correctness of the protocol (if the model of the protocol satisfies the properties that the protocol should specify); 2) the compliance to the structure of the communicative actions (if the specification of the protocol respects the structure).

$$R7 <C>: \frac{E(\Phi, C(Ag_1, PC(Ag_1, Ag_2, t, \phi)))}{E(\Phi, PC(Ag_1, Ag_2, t, \phi))}$$

$$R8 <W>: \frac{E(\Phi, Withdraw(Ag_1, PC(Ag_1, Ag_2, t, \phi)))}{E(\Phi, \neg PC(Ag_1, Ag_2, t, \phi))}$$

$$R9 <S_{PC}^{Ag1}>: \frac{E(\Phi, Satisfy(Ag_1, PC(Ag_1, Ag_2, t, \phi)))}{E(\Phi, \phi)}$$

$$R10 <V_{PC}^{Ag1}>: \frac{E(\Phi, Violate(Ag_1, PC(Ag_1, Ag_2, t, \phi)))}{E(\Phi, \neg\phi)}$$

$$R11 <Rea>: \frac{E(\Phi, Reactivate(Ag_1, PC(Ag_1, Ag_2, t, \phi)))}{E(\Phi, PC(Ag_1, Ag_2, t, \phi))}$$

$$R12 <Ch>: \frac{E(\Phi, Challenge(Ag_2, PC(Ag_1, Ag_2, t, \phi)))}{E(\Phi, PC(Ag_2, Ag_1, t', ?\phi))}$$

$$R13 <Acc>: \frac{E(\Phi, Accept(Ag_2, PC(Ag_1, Ag_2, t, \phi)))}{E(\Phi, PC(Ag_2, Ag_1, t', \phi))}$$

$$R14 <Ref>: \frac{E(\Phi, Refuse(Ag_2, PC(Ag_1, Ag_2, t, \phi)))}{E(\Phi, PC(Ag_2, Ag_1, t', \neg\phi))}$$

$$R15 <Jus>: \frac{E(\Phi, Justify(Ag_1, PC(Ag_1, Ag_2, t, \phi' \therefore \phi)))}{E(\Phi, PC(Ag_1, Ag_2, t', \phi' \therefore \phi))}$$

$$R16 <Att>: \frac{E(\Phi, Attack(Ag_2, PC(Ag_1, Ag_2, t, \phi' \therefore \neg\phi)))}{E(\Phi, PC(Ag_2, Ag_1, t', \phi' \therefore \neg\phi))}$$

$$R17 <Def>: \frac{E(\Psi, Defend(Ag_1, PC(Ag_1, Ag_2, t, \phi' \therefore \phi)))}{E(\Phi, PC(Ag_1, Ag_2, t', \phi' \therefore \phi))}$$

Figure 2. Tableau rules for action formulas

$$R18 [PC_{Ag_1}]: \frac{E(\Phi, PC(Ag_1, Ag_2, t, \phi))}{E(\Phi, \phi)}$$

Figure 3. Tableau rule for propositional commitment formula

$$R19 \ <\equiv>: \frac{E(\Phi, l)}{l, \ E(\Phi)} \qquad R20 \ \wedge: \frac{E(\Phi, \phi_1 \wedge \phi_2)}{E(\Phi, \phi_1, \phi_2)} \qquad R21 \ \vee: \frac{E(\Phi, \phi_1 \vee \phi_2)}{E(\Phi, \phi_1) \ E(\Phi, \phi_2)}$$

$$R22 \ ?: \frac{E(\Phi, ?\psi)}{E(\Phi, \psi)}$$

$$R23 \ X^-: \frac{E(\Phi, X^-\phi_1, ..., X^-\phi_n)}{E(\Phi, \phi_1, ..., \phi_n)} \qquad\qquad R24 \ X^+: \frac{E(\Phi, X^+\phi_1, ..., X^+\phi_n)}{E(\Phi, \phi_1, ..., \phi_n)}$$

$$R25 \ \wedge: \frac{E(\Phi, \phi_1 \therefore \phi_2)}{E(\Phi, \phi_1, X^+(\neg\phi_1 \vee \phi_2))}$$

$$R26 \ \vee: \frac{E(\Phi, \phi_1 U^-\phi_2)}{E(\Phi, \phi_2) \ E(\Phi, \phi_1, X^-(\phi_1 U^-\phi_2))} \qquad R27 \ \vee: \frac{E(\Phi, \phi_1 U^+\phi_2)}{E(\Phi, \phi_2) \ E(\Phi, \phi_1, X^+(\phi_1 U^+\phi_2))}$$

Figure 4. Tableau rules for state formulas

The definition of the transition system of dialogue game protocols is given by the following definitions:

Definition 1 *A structure transition system T' describing the structure of an action formula is a 6-tuple $<S', Lab', F, Ls', R, \rightarrow, s'_0>$ where:*
- *S' is a set of states,*
- *$Lab' : S' \rightarrow 2^{\Phi p}$ is the labeling state function, where Φ_p is the set of atomic propositions,*
- *F is a sub-set of $CTL*^{CA}$ formulae (F does not include the action formulae i.e. Satisfy, Accept, etc.),*
- *$Ls' : S' \rightarrow F$ is a function associating to each state a formula,*
- *$R \in \{ \wedge, \vee, \neg, ?, <\equiv>, X^+, X^-, PC_{Ag} \}$ is the set of tableau rule labels (without the rules for action formulae),*
- *$\rightarrow \subseteq S' \times R \times S'$ is the transition relation,*
- *s'_0 is the start state.*

Intuitively, states s' contain the sub-formulae of the action formulae, and the transitions are labeled by operators associated with the formula of the starting state. Semantic transition systems enable us to describe the semantics of formulae by sub-formulae connected by logical operators. Thus, there is a transition between states s'_i and s'_j iff $L'(s'_j)$ is a sub-formula or an semantically equivalent formula of $L'(s'_i)$. Following traditional usage we write $s \rightarrow^r s'$ instead of $<s, r, s'> \in \rightarrow$ where $s, s' \in S'$ and $r \in R$.

Definition 2 *A transition system T for a dialogue game protocol is a 6-tuple $<S, Lab, \wp, L, Act, \rightarrow, s_0>$ where:*
- *S is a set of states,*
- *$Lab : S \rightarrow 2^{\Phi p}$ is the labeling state function,*
- *$\wp$ is a set of structure transition systems with $\varepsilon \in \wp$ is the empty semantic transition system,*

- $L : S \rightarrow \wp$ *is the function associating to a state $s \in S$ a semantic transition system $T' \in \wp$ describing the semantics of the action labeling the entry transition,*
- *$Act \in \{C, Withdraw, Satisfy, Accept, Refuse, Challenge, Justify, Defend, Attack\}$ is the set of actions,*
- $\rightarrow \subseteq S \times Act \times S$ *is the transition relation,*
- *s_0 is the start state with $L(s_0) = \varepsilon$ (i.e. there is no structure transition system in s_0).*

The transitions are labeled by the actions applied to propositional commitments. We write $s \rightarrow s'$ instead of $<s, \bullet, s'> \in \rightarrow$ where $s, s' \in S$ and $\bullet \in Act$. Figure 5 illustrates a part of a transition system for a dialogue game protocol.

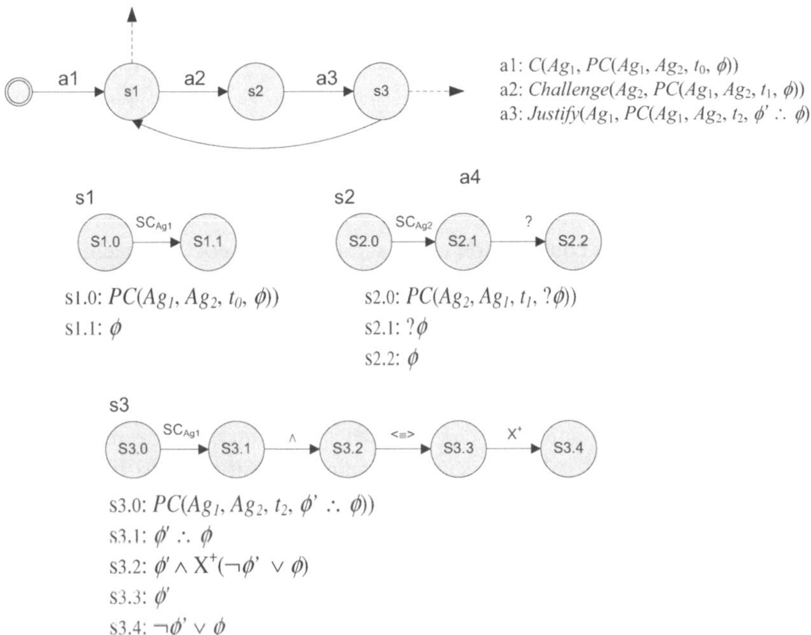

4.2. Examples of Protocol Properties

The properties to be verified in the dialogue game protocols specified in CTL^{*CA} are action and temporal properties. For example, we can verify if a model of dialogue game protocol satisfies the following property:

$$AG^+(Challenge(Ag_2, PC(Ag_1, Ag_2, t, \phi)) \Rightarrow F^+Justify(Ag_1, PC(Ag_1, Ag_2, t, \phi' \therefore \phi)))$$

This property says that in all paths (A), globally (G^+), if an agent Ag_2 challenges the content ϕ of an Ag_1's propositional commitment (PC), then in the future (F^+) Ag_1 will justify this content by an argument $\phi' \therefore \phi$.

Another interesting property to be checked in dialogue games is related to the communicative acts an agent is allowed to perform at a given moment. For example, it is prohibited to attack a commitment content if the addressee did not commit about this content. This property is specified using the past operator F^- as follows:

$$AG^+(Attack(Ag_2, PC(Ag_1, Ag_2, t, \phi)) \Rightarrow F^- C(Ag_1, PC(Ag_1, Ag_2, t, \phi)))$$

A third property capturing the deontic notion of propositional commitments is given by the following formula:

$$AG^+(Attack(Ag_2, PC(Ag_1, Ag_2, t, \phi' \therefore \neg \phi)) \Rightarrow$$
$$(F^+Defend(Ag_1, PC(Ag_1, Ag_2, t, \phi'' \therefore \phi))$$
$$\vee F^+Attack(Ag_1, PC(Ag_2, Ag_1, t', \phi'' \therefore \neg \phi'))$$
$$\vee F^+Accept(Ag_1, PC(Ag_2, Ag_1, t', \phi'))))$$

Using this property, we can verify if a model of a dialogue game protocol satisfies the fact that if an agent Ag_2 attacks the content of an agent Ag_1's propositional commitment PC, then Ag_1 will defend its propositional commitment content, attack the Ag_2's argument or accept it.

5. Model Checking Technique

In this section, we use a combination of an automata-theoretic approach and a tableau-based approach to model-checking communicating agent-based systems.

5.1. Alternating Büchi Tableau Automata for CTL*^{CA}

As a kind of Büchi automata, ABTAs [14] are used in order to prove properties of *infinite* behavior. These automata can be used as an intermediate representation for system properties. Let Φ_p be the set of atomic propositions and let $\Re$ be a set of tableau rule labels defined as follows:

$\Re = \{\wedge, \vee, \neg, ?\} \cup \Re_{Act} \cup \Re_{\neg Act} \cup \Re_{SC} \cup \Re_{Set}$ where $\Re_{Act}$, $\Re_{SC}$ and $\Re_{Set}$ are defined as follows:

$\Re_{Act} = \{<C>, <W>, <S_{PC}^{Ag}>, <V_{PC}^{Ag}>, <Rea>, <Ch>, <Acc>, <Ref>, <Jus>, <Att>, <Def>\}$.

$\Re_{SC} = \{[PC_{Ag}]\}$.

$\Re_{Set} = \{<\equiv>, X^+, X^-\}$.

The associated tableau rules are given in Figures 1, 2, 3 and 4.

Formally, we define ABTAs for CTL*^{CA} logic as follows:

Definition 3 *An ABTA for CTL*^{CA} is a 5-tuple $<Q, l, \rightarrow, q_0, F>$, where:*

- *Q is a finite set of states,*
- *$l: Q \rightarrow \Phi_p \cup \Re$ is the state labeling,*
- *$\rightarrow \subseteq Q \times Q$ is the transition relation,*
- *q_0 is the start state,*
- *$F \subseteq 2^Q$ is the acceptance condition.*

ABTAs allow us to encode *"top-down proofs"* for temporal formulae. Indeed, an ABTA encodes a proof schema in order to prove, in a goal-directed manner, that a transition system satisfies a temporal formula.

Example

Let us consider the following example. We would like to prove that a state s in a transition system satisfies a temporal formula of the form F1 $\wedge$ F2, where F1 and F2 are two formulae. Regardless of the structure of the system, there would be two sub-goals if we want to prove this in a top-down, goal-directed manner. The first would be to prove that s satisfies F1, and the second would be to prove that s satisfies F2. Intuitively, an ABTA for F1 $\wedge$ F2 would encode this "proof structure" using states for the formulae F1 $\wedge$ F2, F1, and F2. A transition from F1 $\wedge$ F2 to each of F1 and F2 should be added to the ABTA and the labeling of the state for F1 $\wedge$ F2 being "$\wedge$" which is the label of a certain rule. Indeed, in an ABTA, we can consider that: 1) states correspond to "formulae", 2) the labeling of a state is the "logical operator" used to construct the formula, and 3) the transition relation represents a "sub-goal" relationship.

In order to decide about the satisfaction of formulae, we use the notion of the *accepting runs* of an ABTA on a transition system. These runs are not considered to be finite, but rather infinite, while cycling infinitely many times through acceptance states. In order to define this notion of the ABTA's run, we need to introduce three types of nodes: *positive*, *negative* and *neutral* (neither positive nor negative). Intuitively, nodes classified positive are nodes that correspond to a formula without negation (for example $C(Ag_1, PC(Ag_1, Ag_2, t, \phi))$), and negative nodes are nodes that correspond to a formula with negation (for example $\neg Justify(Ag_1, PC(Ag_1, Ag_2, t, \phi' \therefore \phi))$). Neutral nodes are used in order to verify the semantics of an action formula ($act \in Act$) written in the formula to be verified under the form $\neg act$. From the semantic point of view, $\neg act$ means that the action act is not performed. For example, if in the formula to be verified appears the sub-formula: $\neg Justify(Ag_1, PC(Ag_1, Ag_2, t, \phi' \therefore \phi))$, we use in the ABTA neutral nodes in order to verify the semantics of: $Justify(Ag_1, PC(Ag_1, Ag_2, t, \phi' \therefore \phi))$. The reason is that in transition systems, and consequently in the sub-transition systems, we have only action formulae without negation, whereas in the formula to be verified, we can have action formulae with negation. We note that we can not use here negative nodes because we do not interested in the formula in itself (i.e. in the example $\neg Justify(Ag_1, PC(Ag_1, Ag_2, t, \phi' \therefore \phi))$) but in the semantics of the underlying action (i.e. $Justify(Ag_1, PC(Ag_1, Ag_2, t, \phi' \therefore \phi))$). In other words, we are not interested in the semantics of the negation action, but in the semantics of the action itself. We note here that in order to verify that an action formula $\neg act$ is satisfied, we have to verify that from a given state there is no transition in the transition system labeled by act. Definition 4 gives the definition of this notion of run. In this definition, elements of the set S of states are denoted s_i or t_i. The explanation of the different clauses is given after the definition.

Definition 4 *A run of an ABTA $B = <Q, l, \rightarrow, q_o, F>$ on a transition system $T = <S, Lab, \wp, L, Act, \rightarrow, s_0>$ is a graph in which the nodes are classified as positive, negative or neutral and are labeled by elements of $Q \times S$ as follows:*

1. *The root of the graph is a positive node and is labeled by $<q_0, s_0>$.*
2. *If φ is a positive node with label $<q, s_i>$ such that $l(q) = \neg$ and $q \rightarrow q'$, then φ has one negative successor labeled $<q', s_i>$ and vice versa.*

- *Otherwise, for a positive node φ labeled by $<q, s_i>$:*

    3. *If $l(q) \in \Phi_p$ then φ is a leaf.*

    4. *If $l(q) \in \{\wedge, <\Leftrightarrow>\}$ and $\{q' \mid q \rightarrow q'\} = \{q_1, ..., q_m\}$, then φ has positive successors $\varphi_1, ..., \varphi_m$ with φ_j labeled by $<q_j, s_i>$ $(1 \le j \le m)$.*

    5. *If $l(q) = \vee$ then φ has one positive successor φ' labeled by $<q', s_i>$ for some $q' \in \{q' \mid q \rightarrow q'\}$.*

    6. *If $l(q) = X^+$ and $q \rightarrow q'$ and $\{s' \mid s_i \rightarrow^{\bullet} s'\} = \{t_1, ..., t_m\}$ where $\bullet \in Act$, then φ has positive successors $\varphi_1, ..., \varphi_m$ with φ_j labeled by $<q', t_j>$ $(1 \le j \le m)$.*

    7. *If $l(q) = X^-$ and $q \rightarrow q'$ and $\{s' \mid s' \rightarrow^{\bullet} s_i\} = \{t_1, ..., t_m\}$ where $\bullet \in Act$, then φ has positive successors $\varphi_1, ..., \varphi_m$ with φ_j labeled by $<q', t_j>$ $(1 \le j \le m)$.*

    8. *If $l(q) = <\bullet>$ where $\bullet \in Act$ and $q \rightarrow q'$, and $s_i \rightarrow^{\bullet} s_{i+1}$ then φ has one positive successor φ' labeled by $<q', s_{i+1,0}>$ where $s_{i+1,0}$ is the initial state of the semantic transition system of s_{i+1}.*

    9. *If $l(q) = <\bullet>$ where $\bullet \in \neg Act$ and $q \rightarrow q'$, and $s_i \rightarrow^{\neg \bullet} s_{i+1}$ then φ has one neutral successor φ' labeled by $<q', s_{i+1,0}>$ where $s_{i+1,0}$ is the initial state of the semantic transition system of s_{i+1}.*

    10. *If $l(q) = <\bullet>$ where $\bullet \in \neg Act$ and $q \rightarrow q'$, and $s_i \rightarrow^{\bullet'} s_{i+1}$ where $\bullet \neq \neg \bullet'$ and $\bullet' \in Act$, then φ has one positive successor φ' labeled by $<q', s_{i+1}>$.*

- *Otherwise, for a negative node φ labeled by $<q, s_i>$:*

    11. *If $l(q) \in \Phi_p$ then φ is a leaf.*

    12. *If $l(q) \in \{\vee, <\Leftrightarrow>\}$ and $\{q' \mid q \rightarrow q'\} = \{q_1, ..., q_m\}$, then φ has negative successors $\varphi_1, ..., \varphi_m$ with φ_j labeled by $<q_j, s_i>$ $(1 \le j \le m)$.*

    13. *If $l(q) = \wedge$ then φ has one negative successor φ' labeled by $<q', s_i>$ for some $q' \in \{q' \mid q \rightarrow q'\}$.*

    14. *If $l(q) = X^+$ and $q \rightarrow q'$ and $\{s' \mid s_i \rightarrow^{\bullet} s'\} = \{t_1, ..., t_m\}$ where $\bullet \in Act$, then φ has negative successors $\varphi_1, ..., \varphi_m$ with φ_j labeled by $<q', t_j>$ $(1 \le j \le m)$.*

    15. *If $l(q) = X^-$ and $q \rightarrow q'$ and $\{s' \mid s' \rightarrow^{\bullet} s_i\} = \{t_1, ..., t_m\}$ where $\bullet \in Act$, then φ has negative successors $\varphi_1, ..., \varphi_m$ with φ_j labeled by $<q', t_j>$ $(1 \le j \le m)$.*

    16. *If $l(q) = <\bullet>$ where $\bullet \in Act$ and $q \rightarrow q'$, and $s_i \rightarrow^{\bullet} s_{i+1}$ then φ has one negative successor φ' labeled by $<q', s_{i+1,0}>$ where $s_{i+1,0}$ is the initial state of the semantic transition system of s_{i+1}.*

    17. *If $l(q) = <\bullet>$ where $\bullet \in \neg Act$ and $q \rightarrow q'$, and $s_i \rightarrow^{\neg \bullet} s_{i+1}$ then φ has one neutral successor φ' labeled by $<q', s_{i+1,0}>$ where $s_{i+1,0}$ is the initial state of the semantic transition system of s_{i+1}.*

    18. *If $l(q) = <\bullet>$ where $\bullet \in \neg Act$ and $q \rightarrow q'$, and $s_i \rightarrow^{\bullet'} s_{i+1}$ where $\bullet \neq \neg \bullet'$ and $\bullet' \in Act$, then φ has one negative successor φ' labeled by $<q', s_{i+1}>$.*

- *Otherwise, for a neutral node φ labeled by $<q, s_{i,j}>$:*

19. *If $l(q) = <\equiv>$ and $\{q' \mid q \rightarrow q'\} = \{q_1, q_2\}$ such that q_1 is a leaf, and $s_{i,j}$ has a successor $s_{i,j+1}$, then φ has one positive leaf successor φ' labeled by $<q_1, s_{i,j}>$ and one neutral successor φ'' labeled by $<q_2, s_{i,j+1}>$.*
20. *If $l(q) = <\equiv>$ and $\{q' \mid q \rightarrow q'\} = \{q_1, q_2\}$ such that q_1 is a leaf, and $s_{i,j}$ has no successor, then φ has one positive leaf successor labeled by $<q_1, s_{i,j}>$.*

- *Otherwise, for a positive (negative) node φ labeled by $<q, s_{i,j}>$:*
21. *If $l(q) = <\equiv>$ and $\{q' \mid q \rightarrow q'\} = \{q_1, q_2\}$ such that q_1 is a leaf, and $s_{i,j}$ has a successor $s_{i,j+1}$, then φ has one positive leaf successor φ' labeled by $<q_1, s_{i,j}>$ and one positive (negative) successor φ'' labeled by $<q_2, s_{i,j+1}>$.*
22. *If $l(q) = <\equiv>$ and $\{q' \mid q \rightarrow q'\} = \{q_1, q_2\}$ such that q_1 is a leaf, and $s_{i,j}$ has no successor, then φ has one positive leaf successor φ' labeled by $<q_1, s_{i,j}>$ and one positive (negative) successor φ'' labeled by $<q_2, s_i>$.*

- *Otherwise, for a positive (negative, neutral) node φ labeled by $<q, s_{i,j}>$:*
23. *If $l(q) \in \{\wedge, \vee, ?, X^+, X^-, [PC_{Ag}]\}$ and $\{q' \mid q \rightarrow q'\} = \{q_1\}$, and $s_{i,j} \rightarrow^r s_{i,j+1}$ such that $r = l(q)$, then φ has one positive (negative, neutral) successor φ' labeled by $<q_1, s_{i,j+1}>$.*

The notion of run of an ABTA on a transition system is a non-synchronized product graph of the ABTA and the transition system. This run uses the label of nodes in the ABTA ($l(q)$), the transitions in the ABTA ($q \rightarrow q'$), and the transitions in the transition system ($s_i \rightarrow s_j$). The product is not synchronized in the sense that it is possible to use transitions in the ABTA while staying in the same state in the transition system (this is the case for example of the clauses 2, 4, and 5).

The second clause in the definition says that if we have a positive node φ in the product graph such that the corresponding state in the ABTA is labelled with $\neg$ and we have a transition $q \rightarrow q'$ in this ABTA, then φ has one negative successor labelled with $<q', s_i>$. In this case we use a transition from the ABTA and we stay in the same state of the transition system. In the case of a positive node and if the current state of the ABTA is labelled with $\wedge$, all the transitions of this current state of the ABTA are used (clause 4). However, if the current state of the ABTA is labelled with $\vee$, only one arbitrary transition from the ABTA is used (clause 5). The intuitive idea is that in the case of $\wedge$, all the sub-formulae must be true in order to decide about the formula of the current node of the ABTA, and in the case of $\vee$ only one sub-formula must be true.

The cases in which a transition of the transition system is used are:

1. The current node of the ABTA is labelled with X^+ (which means a next state in the transition system) or X^- (which means a previous state in the transition system). This is the case of the clauses 6, 7, 14, and 15. In this case we use all the transitions from the current state s_i to next or previous states of the transition system.

2. The current state of the ABTA and a transition from the current state of the transition system are labelled with the same action. This is the case of the clauses 8 and 16. In this case, the current transition of the ABTA and the transition from the current state s_i of the transition system to a state $s_{i+1, 0}$ of the associated semantic transition system are used. The idea is to start the parsing of the formula coded in the semantic transition system.

3. The current state of the ABTA and a transition from the current state of the transition system are labelled with the same action which is preceded by $\neg$ in the ABTA. This is the case of the clauses 9 and 17. In this case, the current transition of the ABTA and the transition from the current state s_i of the transition system to a state $s_{i+1,\,0}$ of the associated semantic transition system are used. The successor node is classified neutral. This allows us to verify the structure of the formula coded in the transition system.

4. The current state of the ABTA and a transition from the current state of the transition system are labelled with different actions where the state of the ABTA is labelled with a negative formula. This is the case of the clauses 10 and 18. In this case, the formula is satisfied, but its structure cannot be verified. Consequently, the current transition of the ABTA and the transition from the current state s_i of the transition system to a next state s_{i+1} are used. This means that, we do not visit the associated semantic transition system.

Finally, the clauses 19, 20, 21, 22, and 23 deal with the case of verifying the structure of the commitment formulae in the sub-transition systems. In these clauses, transitions $s_{i,\,j} \rightarrow s_{i,\,j+1}$ are used. We note here that when $s_{i,j}$ has no successor, the formula contained in this state is an atomic formula or a boolean formula whose all the sub-formulae are atomic (for example $p \wedge q$ where p and q are atomic).

We also need to define the notion of *success* of a run for the correctness of the model checking. To define this notion, we first introduce *positive* and *negative paths*. In an ABTA, every infinite path has a suffix that contains either positive or negative nodes, but not both. Such a path is referred to as *positive* in the former case and *negative* in the latter.

Let $p \in \Phi p$ and let s_i be a state in a transition system T. Then $s_i \models_T p$ iff $p \in Lab(s_i)$ and $s_i \models_T \neg p$ iff $p \notin Lab(s_i)$.

Let $s_{i,\,j}$ be a state in a semantic transition system of a transition system T. Then $s_{i,j} \models_T p$ iff $p \in Lab'(s_{i,j})$ and $s_{i,j} \models_T \neg p$ iff $p \notin Lab'(s_{i,j})$.

Definition 5 *Let r be a run of ABTA $B = <Q, l, \rightarrow, q_0, F>$ on a transition system $T = <S, Lab, \wp, L, Act, \rightarrow, s_0>$. The run r is successful iff every leaf and every infinite path in r is successful. A successful leaf is defined as follows:*

1- A positive leaf labeled by $<q, s_i>$ is successful iff $s_i \models_T l(q)$ or $l(q) = <\bullet>$ where $\bullet \in Act$ and there is no s_j such that $s_i \rightarrow^\bullet s_j$.

2- A positive leaf labeled by $<q, s_{i,\,j}>$ is successful iff $s_{i,j} \models_T l(q)$

3- A negative leaf labeled by $<q, s_i>$ is successful iff $s_i \models_T \neg l(q)$ or $l(q) = <\bullet>$ where $\bullet \in Act$ and there is no s_j such that $s_i \rightarrow^\bullet s_j$.

4- A negative leaf labeled by $<q, s_{i,\,j}>$ is successful iff $s_{i,j} \models_T \neg l(q)$

5- All neutral leaves are not successful.

A successful infinite path is defined as follows:

1- A positive path is successful iff $\forall f \in F, \exists q \in f$ such that q occurs infinitely often in the path. This condition is called the Büchi condition.

2- A negative path is successful iff $\exists f \in F, \forall q \in f$, q does not occur infinitely often in the path. This condition is called the co-Büchi condition.

We note here that a positive or negative leaf labeled by $<q, s>$ such that $l(q) = <\bullet>$ where $\bullet \in Act$ and there is no s' such that $s \rightarrow^\bullet s'$ is considered a successful leaf because we can not consider it unsuccessful. The reason is that it is possible to find a transition labeled by $\bullet$ and starting from another state s'' in the transition system. This is the case of the leaf labeled by $(<Ch>, s_0)$ in the *Case Study* we will discuss in Section 5.3 (see Figure 11). If we consider such a leaf unsuccessful, then even if we find a successful infinite path, the run will be considered unsuccessful. However this is false.

We also note that an ABTA B accepts a transition system T iff there exists a successful run of B on T.

5.2. Translation Procedure

The procedure for translating a CTL^{*CA} formula $p = E\phi$ to an ABTA B uses goal-directed rules in order to build a tableau from this formula. Indeed, these proof rules are conducted in a top-down fashion in order to determine whether states satisfy properties or not. The tableau is constructed by exhaustively applying the rules contained in Figures 1, 2, 3 and 4 to p. Then, B can be extracted from this tableau as follows. First, we generate the states and the transitions. Intuitively, states will correspond to state formulae, with the start state being p. To generate new states from an existing state for a formula p', we determine which rule is applicable to p', starting with $R1$, by comparing the form of p' to the formula appearing in the "goal position" of each rule. Let $rule(q)$ denote the rule applied at node q. The labeling function l of states is defined as follows. If q does not have any successor, then $l(q) \in \Phi_p$. Otherwise, the successors of q are given by $rule(q)$. The label of the rule becomes the label of the state q, and the sub-goals of the rule are then added as states related to q by transitions.

A tableau for a CTL^{*CA} formula p is a maximal proof tree having p as its root and constructed using rules $R1$-$R27$. If p' results from the application of a rule to p, then we say that p' is a child of p in the tableau. The height of a tableau is defined as the length of the longest sequence $<p_0, p_1, ...>$, where p_{i+1} is the child of p_i [18]. Finally, in order to compute the successful run of the generating ABTA, we should compute the acceptance states F. For this purpose we use the following definition.

Definition 6 *Let q be a state in an ABTA B and Q the set of all states. Suppose $\phi = \phi_1 \, U^+ \, \phi_2 \in q^l$. We define the set F_ϕ as follows:*
$F_\phi = \{q' \in Q \mid (\phi \notin q' \text{ and } X^+ \phi \notin q') \text{ or } \phi_2 \in q'\}.$
The acceptance set F is defined as follows:
$F = \{F_\phi \mid \phi = \phi_1 \, U^+ \, \phi_2 \text{ and } \exists q \in B, \, \phi \in q\}.$

According to this definition, a state that contains the formula ϕ or the formula $X^l \phi$ is not an acceptance state. The reason is that according to Definition 4, there is a transition from a state containing ϕ to a state containing $X^+ \phi$ and vice versa. Therefore, according to Definition 5, there is a successful run in the ABTA B. However, we can not decide about the satisfaction of a formula using this run. The reason is that in an infinite cycle including a state containing ϕ and a state containing $X^+ \phi$, we can not be sure that a state containing ϕ_2 is reachable. However, according to the semantics of U^+, the satisfaction of ϕ needs that a state containing ϕ_2 is reachable while passing by states containing ϕ_1.

Case Study

Let us show a practical case on how a CTL^{*CA} formula is translated to an ABTA. We consider the following propositional formula: $E(G^+ F^+ p)$. In the context of dialogue

---

[1] Here we consider "until" formula because is the formula that allows paths to be infinite.

game-based agents, this formula says that along some transitions, globally in the future a commitment content holds. The first step is to build the tableau for this formula using tableau rules. The first rule we can apply is $R27$ labeled by "$\vee$" for the until formula (G^+ is an abbreviation defined from U^+). The second rule is also $R27$ for F^+p (F^+ is also an abbreviation defined from U^+). Thereafter rules $R19$ and $R24$ can be applied. We obtain the tableau illustrated in Figure 6 where the rule labels are indicated.

The ABTA obtained from this tableau is illustrated in Figure 7. In this ABTA, states (1), (3), (5) and (6) are the acceptance states according to Definition 6. The formula ϕ we consider is the following: $\phi = True\ U^+\ p \equiv F^+p$. Notice that ϕ and $X^+\phi$ do not appear in these states. State (5) is the acceptance state in the finite case. On the other hand, ϕ appears in states (2) and (7), and $X^+\phi$ appears in state (4). Therefore, these states are not in F_ϕ. The path $\Pi = (1, (2, 4, 7)^*)$ is not a valid proof of $E(G^+F^+p)$. However, a path that visits infinitely often the states (1), (3) and (6) is a valid (infinite) proof. The reason is that in such a path there is always a chance to meet the proposition p (state (3)). Therefore, this path satisfies the Büchi condition. The Büchi condition is not satisfied in the path Π since there is no chance to visit infinitely often a state containing p.

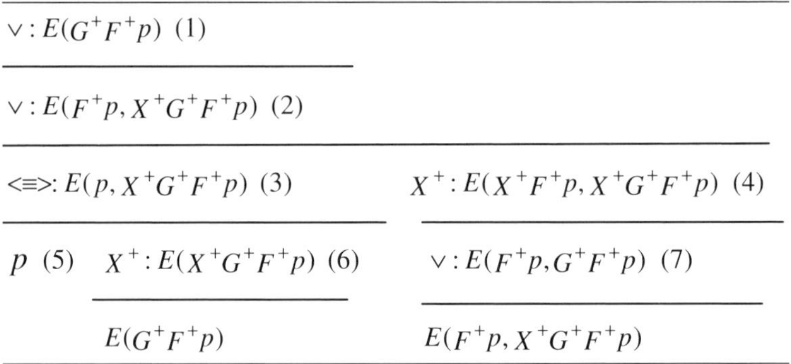

Figure 6. The tableau for $E(G^+F^+p)$

5.3. Model Checking Algorithm

The idea behind our model checking algorithm is to explore the product graph of an ABTA for CLT*^{CA} and a transition system for a dialogue game. This algorithm is *on-the-fly* (or *local*) algorithm consisting of checking if a transition system is accepted by an ABTA. This model checking is reduced to the emptiness of the Büchi automata [19].

Let $T = \langle S, Lab, \wp, L, Act, \rightarrow, s_0 \rangle$ be a transition system for a dialogue game and let $B = \langle Q, l, \rightarrow, q_0, F \rangle$ be an ABTA for CTL*^{CA}. The procedure consists of building the ABTA product $B_\otimes$ of T and B while checking if there is a successful run in $B_\otimes$. The existence of such a run means that the language of $B_\otimes$ is non-empty. The automaton $B_\otimes$ is defined as follows: $B_\otimes = \langle Q \times S, \rightarrow_{B\otimes}, q_{0B\otimes}, F_{B\otimes} \rangle$. There is a transition between two nodes $\langle q, s \rangle$ and $\langle q', s' \rangle$ iff there is a transition between these two nodes in some run of B on T. Intuitively, $B_\otimes$ simulates all the runs of the ABTA. The set of accepting states $F_{B\otimes}$ is defined as follows: $q_{0B\otimes} \in F_{B\otimes}$ iff $q \in F$.

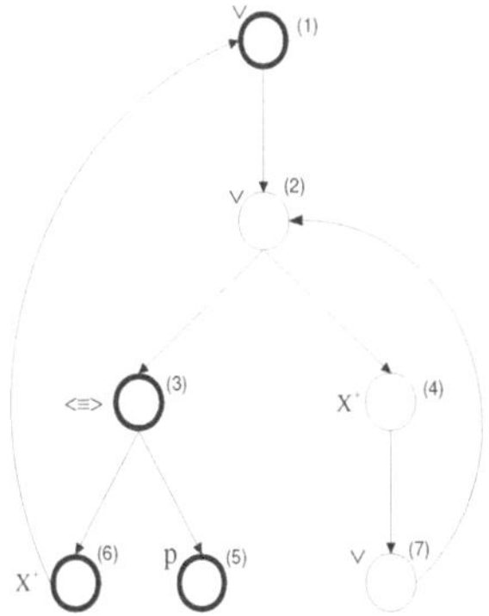

Figure 7. The ABTA of the formula $E(G^+F^+p)$

Unlike the algorithms proposed in [14, 16, 20], our algorithm uses only one depth-first search (DFS) instead of two. This is due to the fact that our algorithm explores directly the product graph using the sign of the nodes (positive, negative or neutral). In addition, unlike the algorithm proposed in [14], our algorithm does not distinguish between recursive and non-recursive nodes. Therefore, we do not take into account the strongly-connected components in the ABTA, but we use a marking algorithm that works on the product graph.

The pseudo-code of this algorithm is given in Figure 8. The idea is to construct the product graph while exploring it. However, in order to make it easy to understand, we omit the instructions relative to the addition of nodes in the product graph. The construction procedure is directly obtained from Definition 4. The algorithm uses the label of nodes in the ABTA, and the transitions in the product graph obtained from the transition system and the ABTA as explained in Definition 4.

In order to decide if the ABTA contains an infinite successful run, all the explored nodes are marked "visited". Thus, when the algorithm explores a visited node, it returns false if the infinite path is not successful. If the node is not already visited, the algorithm tests if it is a leaf. In this case, it returns false if the node is a non-successful leaf. If the explored node is not a leaf, the algorithm calls recursively the function DFS in order to explore the successors of this node. If this node is labeled by "∧", and signed neutrally or positively, then DFS returns false if one of the successors is false. However, if the node is signed negatively, DFS returns false if all the successors are false. A dual treatment is applied when the node is labeled by "∨". We note that if the DFS does not explore a false node (i.e. it does not return false), then it returns true.

Theorem 1 (Correctness) *Let B an ABTA and T a transition system. DFS(q_0, s_0) returns true if and only if T is accepted by B.*

The proof of this theorem is developed in [9][2].

---

[2] The proof is developed in Chapter 8 and could be checked online:
http://users.encs.concordia.ca/~bentahar/Thesis/BNJ-Thesis1.pdf

DFS(v = (q, s)): boolean {
 if v marked visited {
  if (sign(v) = "+" and not accepting(v)) or (sign(v) = "-" and accepting(v))
   return false
 } // end of if v marked visited
 else {
  mark v visited
  switch(l(q)) {
   case (p $\in \Phi$p):
    switch(sign(v)) {
     case("+"): if s is a sub-state and l(q) $\notin$ L'(s) return false
     case("-"): if s is a sub-state and $\neg$l(q)) $\notin$ L'(s) return false
     case("neutral"): return false
    } // end of switch(sign(v))
   case($\wedge$):
    if s is a leaf return false
    else
     switch(sign(v)) {
      case(neutral): for all v'' $\in$ {v' / v $\rightarrow_{B\otimes}$ v'}
          if not DFS(v'') return false
      case("+"): for all v'' $\in$ {v' / v $\rightarrow_{B\otimes}$ v'}
         if not DFS(v'') return false
      case("-"): for all v'' $\in$ {v' / v $\rightarrow_{B\otimes}$ v'}
         if DFS(v'') return true else return false
     } // end of switch(sign (v))
   case($\vee$):
    if s is a leaf return false
    else
     switch(sign(v)) {
      case(neutral): for all v'' $\in$ {v' / v $\rightarrow_{B\otimes}$ v'}
          if DFS(v'') return true else return false
      case("+"): for all v'' $\in$ {v' / v $\rightarrow_{B\otimes}$ v'}
         if DFS(v'') return true else return false
      case("-"): for all v'' $\in$ {v' / v $\rightarrow_{B\otimes}$ v'}
         if not DFS(v'') return false
     } // end of switch(sign (v))
   case(<•>):
    if s is a leaf return true
    else for the v'' $\in$ {v' / v $\rightarrow_{B\otimes}$ v'} if not DFS(v'') return false
   case(X^+, PC_{Ag}, AC_{Ag}, <⇒>, ?):
    if s is a leaf return false
    else for the v'' $\in$ {v' / v $\rightarrow_{B\otimes}$ v'} if not DFS(v'') return false
  } // end of switch(l(q))
 } // end of else
 return true }

Figure 8. Model checking algorithm

Case Study

To show how the model checking technique works, let us consider the following case study. The idea is to check if the dialogue game protocol specified in Section 4.1 and illustrated by Figure 5 satisfied the following property explained in Section 4.2:

$$AG^+(Challenge(Ag_2, PC(Ag_1, Ag_2, t, \phi)) \Rightarrow$$
$$F^+Justify(Ag_1, PC(Ag_1, Ag_2, t, \phi' \therefore \phi)))$$

In order to simplify this formula, we use *Ch* for *Challenge* and *Jus* for *Justify*. The tableau of this formula is illustrated by Figure 9. The associated ABTA of this formula is given by Figure 10. This formula is equivalent to:

$$AG^+(\neg Ch(Ag_2, PC(Ag_1, Ag_2, t, \phi)) \vee F^+Jus(Ag_1, PC(Ag_1, Ag_2, t, \phi' \therefore \phi)))$$

The first rule we can apply is *R6* labeled by "¬". We obtain then the formula (2) of Figure 9. From this formula we obtain the formula Φ that we consider in order to compute the acceptance states:

$$\Phi = F^+(Ch(Ag_2, PC(Ag_1, Ag_2, t, \phi)) \wedge G^+(\neg Jus(Ag_1, PC(Ag_1, Ag_2, t, \phi' \therefore \phi))))$$

In the ABTA of Figure 10 state (1) and states from (3) to (18) are the acceptance states according to Definition 6. States (2) and (4) are not acceptance states. Because only the first state is labeled by ¬, all finite and infinite paths are negative paths. Consequently, the only infinite path that is a valid proof of the formula Φ is (1, (2, 4)*). In this path there is no acceptance state that occurs infinitely often. Therefore, this path satisfies the Büchi condition. The path visiting the state (3) and infinitely often the state (9) does not satisfy the formula because there is a challenge action (state (3)), and globally no justification action of the content of the challenged propositional commitment (state (9)).

Figure 11 illustrates the automaton $B_\otimes$ resulting from the product of the transition system of Figure 5 (noted TS[5]) and the ABTA of Figure 10 (noted ABTA[10]). In order to check if the language of this automaton is empty, we check if there is a successful run. The idea is to verify if $B_\otimes$ contains an infinite path visiting the state (3) and infinitely often the state (9) of ABTA[10]. If such a path exists, then we conclude that the formula is not satisfied by TS[5]. Indeed, the only infinite path of $B_\otimes$ is successful because it does not touch any accepted state and all leaves are also successful. For instance, the leaf labeled by ($<Ch>,s_0$) is successful since there is no state s_i such that $s_0 \rightarrow^{Ch} s_i$. The leaf labeled by ($\neg\phi' \vee \phi$, $s_{3,4}$) is successful because it is a positive leaf and $s_{3,4} \models \neg\phi' \vee \phi$. Therefore, TS[5] is accepted by ABTA[10]. Consequently, TS[5] satisfies the formula and respects the structure of challenge and justification actions.

$$\neg : AG^+(\neg Ch(Ag_2, PC(Ag_1, Ag_2, t, \phi)) \vee F^+ Jus(Ag_1, PC(Ag_1, Ag_2, t, \phi' \therefore \phi))) \quad (1)$$

$$\vee : EF^+(Ch(Ag_2, PC(Ag_1, Ag_2, t, \phi)) \wedge G^+(\neg Jus(Ag_1, PC(Ag_1, Ag_2, t, \phi' \therefore \phi')))) \quad (2)$$

$$<Ch>: E(Ch(Ag_2, PC(Ag_1, Ag_2, t, \phi)) \wedge G^+(\neg Jus(Ag_1, PC(Ag_1, Ag_2, t, \phi' \therefore \phi)))) \quad (3)$$

$$<X^+>: EX^+(F^+(Ch(Ag_2, PC(Ag_1, Ag_2, t, \phi)) \wedge G^+(\neg Jus(Ag_1, PC(Ag_1, Ag_2, t, \phi' \therefore \phi))))) \quad (4)$$

$$[PC_{Ag2}]: E(PC(Ag_2, Ag_1, t, ?\phi) \wedge G^+(\neg Jus(Ag_1, PC(Ag_1, Ag_2, t, \phi' \therefore \phi')))) \quad (5)$$

$$EF^+(Ch(Ag_2, PC(Ag_1, Ag_2, t, \phi)) \wedge G^+(\neg Jus(Ag_1, PC(Ag_1, Ag_2, t, \phi' \therefore \phi)))) \quad (2)$$

$$? : E((?\phi) \wedge G^+(\neg Jus(Ag_1, PC(Ag_1, Ag_2, t, \phi' \therefore \phi)))) \quad (6)$$

$$<\Leftrightarrow>: E(\phi \wedge G^+(\neg Jus(Ag_1, PC(Ag_1, Ag_2, t, \phi' \therefore \phi)))) \quad (7)$$

$$\varphi \ (8) \quad \vee : E(G^+(\neg Jus(Ag_1, PC(Ag_1, Ag_2, t, \phi' \therefore \phi)))) \quad (9)$$

$$<\neg Jus>: E(\neg Jus(Ag_1, PC(Ag_1, Ag_2, t, \phi' \therefore \phi)), X^+ G^+(\neg Jus(Ag_1, PC(Ag_1, Ag_2, t, \phi' \therefore \phi)))) \quad (10)$$

$$[PC_{Ag1}]: E(PC(Ag_1, Ag_2, t, \phi' \therefore \phi), X^+ G^+(\neg Jus(Ag_1, PC(Ag_1, Ag_2, t, \phi' \therefore \phi)))) \quad (11)$$

$$\wedge : E(\phi' \therefore \phi, X^+ G^+(\neg Jus(Ag_1, PC(Ag_1, Ag_2, t, \phi' \therefore \phi)))) \quad (12)$$

$$<\Leftrightarrow>: E(\phi', X^+(\neg \phi' \vee \phi), X^+ G^+(\neg Jus(Ag_1, PC(Ag_1, Ag_2, t, \phi' \therefore \phi)))) \quad (13)$$

$$\phi' \ (14) \quad X^+ : E(X^+(\neg \phi' \vee \phi), X^+ G^+(\neg Jus(Ag_1, PC(Ag_1, Ag_2, t, \phi' \therefore \phi)))) \quad (15)$$

$$<\Leftrightarrow>: E((\neg \phi' \vee \phi), X^+ G^+(\neg Jus(Ag_1, PC(Ag_1, Ag_2, t, \phi' \therefore \phi)))) \quad (16)$$

$$\neg \varphi' \vee \varphi \ (17) \quad X^+ : E(X^+ G^+(\neg Jus(Ag_1, PC(Ag_1, Ag_2, t, \phi' \therefore \phi)))) \quad (18)$$

$$E(G^+(\neg Jus(Ag_1, PC(Ag_1, Ag_2, t, \phi' \therefore \phi)))) \quad (9)$$

Figure 9. The tableau for
$$AG^+(Ch(Ag_2, PC(Ag_1, Ag_2, t, \phi)) \Rightarrow F^+ Jus(Ag_1, PC(Ag_1, Ag_2, t, \phi' \therefore \phi)))$$

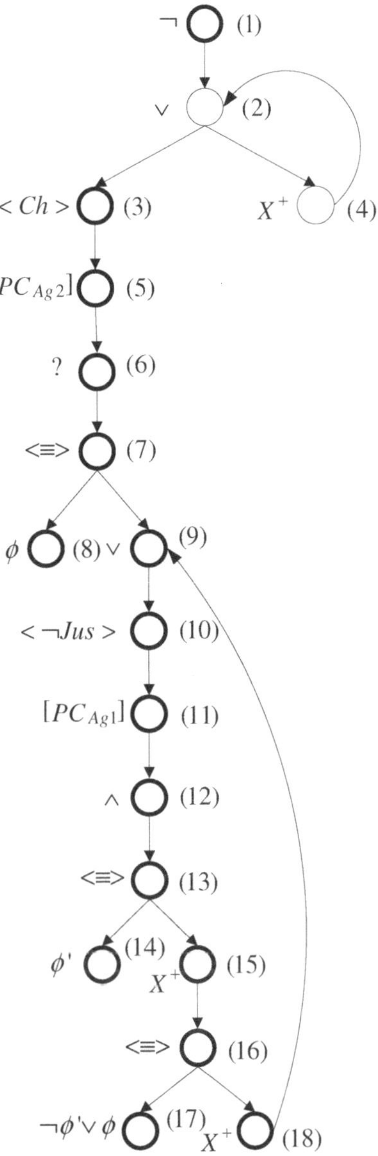

Figure 10. The ABTA for The formula
$AG^+(Ch(Ag_2, PC(Ag_1, Ag_2, t, \phi)) \Rightarrow F^+Jus(Ag_1, PC(Ag_1, Ag_2, t, \phi' \therefore \phi)))$

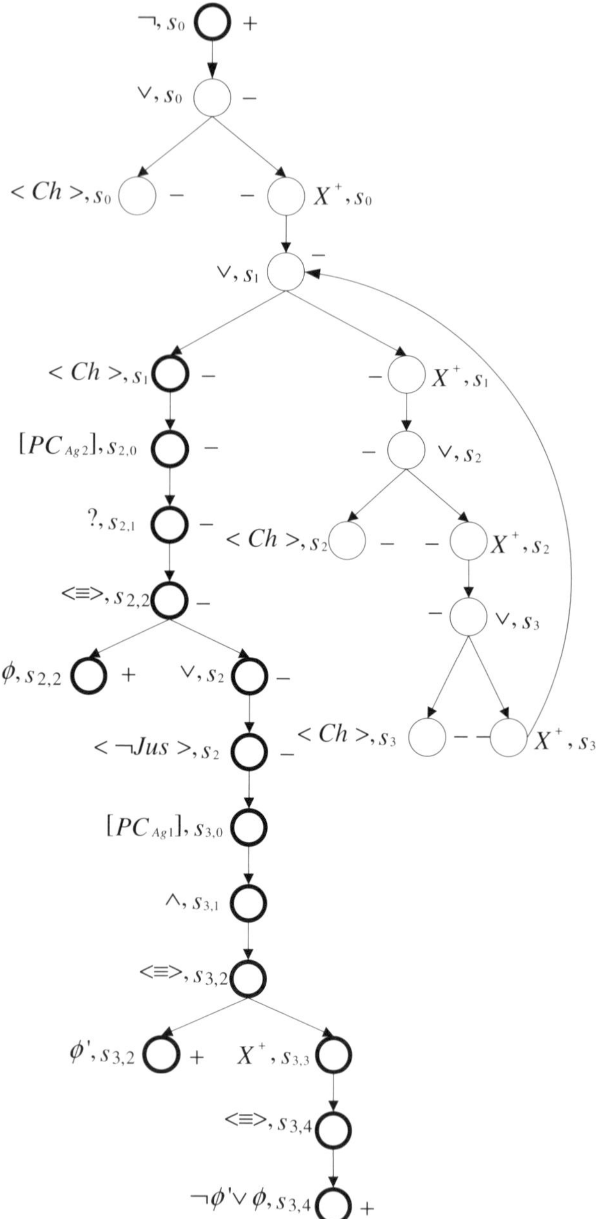

Figure 11. The ABTA product graph

6. Termination and Computational Complexity

In this section, we prove the termination of the translation procedure and we discuss the worst-case time complexity of our model checking[3]. Since the translation procedure is based on tableau rules, we need to prove the finiteness of the tableau. The methodology we follow is inspired by [18,21].

If σ_2 is a CTL*^{CA} formula resulting from the application of a rule to a CTL*^{CA} formula σ_1, then we say that σ_2 is a child of σ_1 in the tableau and σ_1 is the parent of σ_2. The *height* of a tableau [18] is defined as the length of the longest sequence $<\sigma_0, \sigma_1, ...>$, where σ_i is the parent of σ_{i+1}. To prove the finiteness of a tableau, we will establish that each formula has a maximum height tableau.

Intuitively, to show the finiteness of the tableau, we will define a strict ordering relation $\prec$ between CTL*^{CA} formulae and then show that: **1)** if σ_1 is the parent of σ_2, then $\sigma_1 \prec \sigma_2$; **2)** the strict ordering relation $\prec$ has no infinite ascending chains.

The ordering relation $\prec$ should reflect the fact that applying tableau rules results in shorter formulae or recursive formulae. The idea is to prove that the number of nodes of the ABTA is finite. Therefore, the definition of this ordering is based either on the fact that formulae are recursive or on the length of formulae. We notice that in the case of recursive formulae, we obtain cycles which are infinite paths on a finite number of nodes. The length of a formula is defined inductively as follows:

Definition 7 *The length of a formula ψ denoted by $|\psi|$ is the number of variables and operators in ψ i.e.:*

$|\psi| = 1$ if ψ is an atomic formula
$|\neg\psi| = 1 + |\psi|$
$|\psi_1 \wedge \psi_2| = 1 + |\psi_1| + |\psi_2|$
$|\psi_1 \vee \psi_2| = 1 + |\psi_1| + |\psi_2|$
$|?\psi| = 1 + |\psi|$
$|\psi_1 \therefore \psi_2| = 1 + |\psi_1| + |X^+(\neg\psi_1 \vee \psi_2)|$
$|X\psi| = 1 + |\psi|$ where $X \in \{X^+, X^-\}$
$|\psi_1 U \psi_2| = 1 + |\psi_1| + |\psi_2|$ where $(U, X) \in \{(U^+, X^+), (U^-, X^-)\}$
$|PC(Ag_1, Ag_2, t, \psi)| = 1 + |\psi|$
$|C(Ag_1, SC(Ag_1, Ag_2, t, \psi))| = 1 + |PC(Ag_1, Ag_2, t, \psi)|$
$|Withdraw(Ag_1, PC(Ag_1, Ag_2, t, \psi))| = 1 + |\neg PC(Ag_1, Ag_2, t, \psi)|$
$|Satisfy(Ag_1, PC(Ag_1, Ag_2, t, \psi))| = 1 + |\psi|$
$|Violate(Ag_1, PC(Ag_1, Ag_2, t, \psi))| = 1 + |\neg\psi|$
$|Reactivate(Ag_1, PC(Ag_1, Ag_2, t, \psi))| = 1 + |PC(Ag_1, Ag_2, t, \psi)|$
$|Challenge(Ag_2, PC(Ag_1, Ag_2, t, \psi))| = 1 + |PC(Ag_2, Ag_1, t', ?\psi)|$
$|Accept(Ag_2, SC(Ag_1, Ag_2, t, \psi))| = 1 + |PC(Ag_2, Ag_1, t', \psi)|$
$|Refuse(Ag_2, SC(Ag_1, Ag_2, t, \psi))| = 1 + |PC(Ag_2, Ag_1, t', \neg\psi)|$
$|Justify(Ag_1, PC(Ag_1, Ag_2, t, \psi' \therefore \psi))| = 1 + |PC(Ag_1, Ag_2, t', \psi' \therefore \psi)|$
$|Attack(Ag_2, PC(Ag_1, Ag_2, t, \psi' \therefore \psi))| = 1 + |PC(Ag_2, Ag_1, t', \psi' \therefore \neg\psi)|$

---

[3] All the proofs of this section are available at:
http://users.encs.concordia.ca/~bentahar/SoMet2007-Appendix.pdf

$|Defend(Ag_1, PC(Ag_1, Ag_2, t, \psi' \therefore \psi))| = 1 + |PC(Ag_1, Ag_2, t', \psi' \therefore \psi)|$

The ordering relation $\prec$ is defined as follows:

Definition 8 *Let* $\sigma_1 = E(\psi_1)$ *and* $\sigma_2 = E(\psi_2)$ *be two* CTL^{*CA} *formulae. Then,* $\sigma_1 \prec \sigma_2$ *holds if*

    1- $\sigma_1 \leqslant \sigma_2$
    2- $\sigma_1 \not\leqslant \sigma_2$ *and* $|\psi_1| > |\psi_2|$.
    where $\sigma_1 \leqslant \sigma_2$ *iff* $X\psi_1$ *appears in* ψ_2

The first clause is used when we have a recursive formula (this means that an *until* formula). $\prec$ is irreflexive, asymmetric and transitive. The proof is straightforward from the definition since $>$ and $\leqslant$ are strict ordering relations.

In what follows, the notation $\sigma_1 \rightarrow_R \sigma_2$ means that σ_1 is the parent of σ_2 using a tableau rule R. We have the following lemma (see the proof in the appendix[4]):

Lemma 1 *Let* $\sigma_1 = E(\psi_1)$ *and* $\sigma_2 = E(\psi_2)$ *be two* $DCTL^{*}_{CAN}$ *formulae. Then:*

    $\sigma_1 \rightarrow_R \sigma_2 \Rightarrow \sigma_1 \prec \sigma_2$.

To show that the ordering relation has no infinite ascending chains, we use the notion of Fischer-Ladner closure of a formula ψ $(CL(\psi))$ [22]. The idea underlying the definition of this notion is to prove that if a tableau has a root ψ, then all formulae ψ' of this tableau have a formula in $CL(\psi)$ (i.e. $\psi' \in CL(\psi)$). Furthermore, if we prove that $CL(\psi)$ is a finite set, then we conclude that each formula appearing in a given tableau belongs to a finite set. This result will be very helpful to prove that the ordering relation $\prec$ has no infinite ascending chains.

Definition 9 *Let* ψ *be a* CTL^{*CA} *formula. The Fischer-Ladner closure of* ψ, $CL(\psi)$ *is the smallest set such that the following hold:*
    If ψ *is an atomic formula then* $\{\psi\} \subseteq CL(\psi)$
    If $\psi = \neg\psi_1$ *then* $CL(\psi_1) \subseteq CL(\psi)$ *and* $\{\neg\psi_1\} \subseteq CL(\psi)$
    If $\psi = \psi_1 \wedge \psi_2$ *then* $CL(\psi_1) \subseteq CL(\psi)$ *and* $CL(\psi_2) \subseteq CL(\psi)$ *and* $\{\psi_1 \wedge \psi_2\} \subseteq CL(\psi)$
    If $\psi = \psi_1 \vee \psi_2$ *then* $CL(\psi_1) \subseteq CL(\psi)$ *and* $CL(\psi_2) \subseteq CL(\psi)$ *and* $\{\psi_1 \vee \psi_2\} \subseteq CL(\psi)$
    If $\psi = ?\psi_1$ *then* $CL(\psi_1) \subseteq CL(\psi)$ *and* $\{?\psi_1\} \subseteq CL(\psi)$
    If $\psi = \psi_1 \therefore \psi_2$ *then*
        $CL(\psi_1) \subseteq CL(\psi)$ *and* $CL(X^+(\neg\psi_1 \vee \psi_2)) \subseteq CL(\psi)$ *and* $\{\psi_1 \therefore \psi_2\} \subseteq CL(\psi)$
    If $\psi = X\psi_1$ *then* $CL(\psi_1) \subseteq CL(\psi)$ *and* $\{X\psi_1\} \subseteq CL(\psi)$ *where* $X \in \{X^+, X^-\}$
    If $\psi = \psi_1 U\psi_2$ *then*
        $CL(\psi_1) \subseteq CL(\psi)$ *and* $CL(\psi_2) \subseteq CL(\psi)$ *and* $CL(X(\psi_1 U \psi_2)) \subseteq CL(\psi)$
        and $\{\psi_1 U\psi_2\} \subseteq CL(\psi)$ *where* $(U, X) \in \{(U^+, X^+), (U^-, X^-)\}$
    If $\psi = PC(Ag_1, Ag_2, t, \psi_1)$ *then*
        $CL(\psi_1) \subseteq CL(\psi)$ *and* $\{PC(Ag_1, Ag_2, t, \psi_1)\} \subseteq CL(\psi)$

---

[4] http://users.encs.concordia.ca/~bentahar/SoMet2007-Appendix.pdf

If $\psi = C(Ag_1, PC(Ag_1, Ag_2, t, \psi_1))$ then
  $CL(PC(Ag_1, Ag_2, t, \psi_1)) \subseteq CL(\psi)$ and $\{C(Ag_1, PC(Ag_1, Ag_2, t, \psi_1))\} \subseteq CL(\psi)$
If $\psi = Withdraw(Ag_1, PC(Ag_1, Ag_2, t, \psi_1))$ then
  $CL(\neg PC(Ag_1, Ag_2, t, \psi_1)) \subseteq CL(\psi)$ and
  $\{Withdraw(Ag_1, PC(Ag_1, Ag_2, t, \psi_1))\} \subseteq CL(\psi)$
If $\psi = Satisfy(Ag_1, PC(Ag_1, Ag_2, t, \psi_1))$ then
  $CL(\psi_1) \subseteq CL(\psi)$ and $\{Satisfy(Ag_1, PC(Ag_1, Ag_2, t, \psi_1))\} \subseteq CL(\psi)$
If $\psi = Violate(Ag_1, PC(Ag_1, Ag_2, t, \psi_1))$ then
  $CL(\neg \psi_1) \subseteq CL(\psi)$ and $\{Violate(Ag_1, PC(Ag_1, Ag_2, t, \psi_1))\} \subseteq CL(\psi)$
If $\psi = Reactivate(Ag_1, PC(Ag_1, Ag_2, t, \psi_1))$ then
  $CL(PC(Ag_1, Ag_2, t, \psi_1)) \subseteq CL(\psi)$ and
  $\{Reactivate(Ag_1, PC(Ag_1, Ag_2, t, \psi_1))\} \subseteq CL(\psi)$
If $\psi = Challenge(Ag_1, PC(Ag_1, Ag_2, t, \psi_1))$ then
  $CL(PC(Ag_1, Ag_2, t', ?\psi_1)) \subseteq CL(\psi)$
  and $\{Challenge(Ag_1, PC(Ag_1, Ag_2, t, \psi_1))\} \subseteq CL(\psi)$
If $\psi = Accept(Ag_1, PC(Ag_1, Ag_2, t, \psi_1))$ then
  $CL(PC(Ag_1, Ag_2, t', \psi_1)) \subseteq CL(\psi)$
  and $\{Accept(Ag_1, PC(Ag_1, Ag_2, t, \psi_1))\} \subseteq CL(\psi)$
If $\psi = Refuse(Ag_1, PC(Ag_1, Ag_2, t, \psi_1))$ then
  $CL(PC(Ag_1, Ag_2, t', \neg\psi_1)) \subseteq CL(\psi)$
  and $\{Refuse(Ag_1, PC(Ag_1, Ag_2, t, \psi_1))\} \subseteq CL(\psi)$
If $\psi = Justify(Ag_1, PC(Ag_1, Ag_2, t, \psi_2 \therefore \psi_1))$ then
  $CL(PC(Ag_1, Ag_2, t', \psi_2 \therefore \psi_1)) \subseteq CL(\psi)$
  and $\{Justify(Ag_1, PC(Ag_1, Ag_2, t, \psi_2 \therefore \psi_1))\} \subseteq CL(\psi)$
If $\psi = Attack(Ag_2, PC(Ag_1, Ag_2, t, \psi_2 \therefore \neg\psi_1))$ then
  $CL(PC(Ag_2, Ag_1, t', \psi_2 \therefore \neg\psi_1)) \subseteq CL(\psi)$
  and $\{Attack(Ag_2, PC(Ag_1, Ag_2, t, \psi_2 \therefore \neg\psi_1))\} \subseteq CL(\psi)$
If $\psi = Defend(Ag_1, PC(Ag_1, Ag_2, t, \psi_2 \therefore \psi_1))$ then
  $CL(PC(Ag_1, Ag_2, t', \psi_2 \therefore \psi_1)) \subseteq CL(\psi)$
  and $\{Defend(Ag_1, PC(Ag_1, Ag_2, t, \psi_2 \therefore \psi_1))\} \subseteq CL(\psi)$

Lemma 2 *Let ψ be a formula, then $CL(\psi)$ is finite and bounded in size by $2|\psi|$.*

The next lemma establishes the link between tableau rules and Fischer-Ladner closure of formulae.

Lemma 3 *Let $\sigma_1 = E(\Phi, \psi_1)$ and $\sigma_2 = E(\Phi, \psi_2)$ be two $CTL*^{CA}$ formulae. Then:*
  $\sigma_1 \rightarrow_R \sigma_2 \Rightarrow CL(\psi_2) \subseteq CL(\psi_1).$

Intuitively, $\sigma_i \prec \sigma_j$ holds if σ_i is an ancestor of σ_j in some tableau, i.e. if there are rules $Ri, ..., Rj$ such that: $\sigma_i \rightarrow_{Ri} \sigma_{i+1}... \rightarrow_{Rj} \sigma_j$. We have the following lemma:

Lemma 4 *The ordering relation $\prec$ has no infinite ascending chains.*

Now, we can easily prove the finiteness theorem.

Theorem 2 (Termination) *For any $CTL*^{CA}$ formula σ_l, there is a maximum height tableau has σ_l as a root.*

Let us now discuss the worst-case time complexity of our model checking (see the proofs in the appendix[5]).

Lemma 5 *Let ψ be a $CTL*^{CA}$ formula, and let $B_\psi = <Q, l, \rightarrow, q_0, F>$ be the ABTA obtained by the translation procedure. Then $|B_\psi| < 2^{|\psi|}$.*

The complexity of the transition procedure is thus exponential in the size of the formula ($O(2^{|\psi|})$). However, if ψ is a CTL^{CA} formula, $|B_\psi|$ is bounded by $|\psi|$. The complexity is then linear in the size of the formula. This result follows from the fact that in CTL^{CA} we have only state formulae.

Lemma 6 *Let $T = <S, Lab, \wp, L, Act, \rightarrow, s_0>$ be a transition system for a dialogue game, and let $B_\psi = <Q, l, \rightarrow, q_0, F>$ be an ABTA for ψ. The time complexity of the model checking algorithm is bounded by $|T| \times |B_\psi|$ where $|T| = |S| + |\wp| + |\rightarrow|$ and $|\wp|$ is the number of sub-states in all structure transition systems of T.*

The worst-case time complexity of our model checking technique is therefore linear in the size of the model and exponential in the size of the formula to be checked.

7. Conclusion

In this paper, we have addressed the verification problem of communicating agent-based systems, in which knowledge-driven agents communicate by reasoning about dialogue game protocols. We proposed a new model checking technique allowing for the verification of both the correctness of the protocols and the agents' compliance to the structure of the communicative acts. This technique uses a combination of an automata-based and a tableau-driven algorithm to verify temporal and action specification. The formal properties to be verified are expressed in $CTL*^{CA}$ logic and translated to ABTA using tableau rules. We proved that this model checking algorithm working on a product graph is an efficient on-the-fly procedure that always terminates.

Acknowledgments

We would like to thank the Natural Sciences and Engineering Research Council of Canada (NSERC) and le Fond Québécois de la Recherche sur la Nature et les Technologies (NATEQ) for their financial support. We are also grateful to the editors and the four reviewers for their valuable comments which helped us to improve the quality of the paper.

---

[5] http://users.encs.concordia.ca/~bentahar/SoMet2007-Appendix.pdf

References

[1]   Bordini, R.H., Fisher, M., Pardavila, C. and Wooldridge, M. Model checking AgentSpeak. In *Proc. of the 2ⁿᵈ Int. Joint Conf. On Autonomous Agents and Multi Agent Systems*, 2003, pp. 409-416.

[2]   Bordini, R.H., Visser, W., Fisher, M., Pardavila, C., and Wooldridge, M. Model checking multi-agent programs with CASP. In *Computer-Aided Verification*, Hunt, W.A. and Somenzi, F. (eds.), LNCS 2725 Springer, 2003, pp.110-113.

[3]   Giordano, L., Martelli, A., and Schwind, C. Verifying communicating agents by model checking in a temporal action logic. In *Logics in Artificial Intelligence* (JELIA'04), LNAI 3229 Springer, 2004, pp. 57-69.

[4]   Lomuscio, A., Pecheur, C., Raimondi, F. Automatic verification of knowledge and time with NuSMV. In *International Joint Conference on Artificial Intelligence*, pp. 1384-1389, 2007.

[5]   Raimondi, F., and A. Lomuscio. Automatic verification of multi-agent systems by model checking via ordered binary decision diagrams. In *Journal of Applied Logic,* 5(2): 235-251, 2007.

[6]   Kacprzak, M., Lomuscio, A., and Penczek, W. Verification of multiagent systems via unbounded model checking. In *Proc. of the 3ʳᵈ Int. Joint Conf. on Autonomous Agents and Multi Agent Systems*, 2004, pp. 638-645.

[7]   Endriss, U., Maudet, N., Sadri, F., and Toni, F. Protocol conformance for logic-based agents. In *Proc. of the 18ᵗʰ Int. Joint Conf. on Artificial Intelligence*, 2003, pp. 679-684.

[8]   Baldoni, M., Baroglio, C., Martelli, A., Patti, V., and Schifanella, C. Verifying protocol conformance for logic-based communicating agents. In *Proc. of the 5ᵗʰ Int. Workshop on Computational Logic in Multi-Agent Systems*, 2004, pp. 82-97.

[9]   Bentahar, J. A pragmatic and semantic unified framework for agent communication. *Ph.D. Thesis*, Laval University, Canada: 2005.

[10] Bentahar, J., Moulin, B., Meyer, J-J.Ch. and Chaib-draa, B. A computational model for conversation policies for agent communication. In *Computational Logic in Multi-Agent Systems*, vol. 3487 LNAI Springer, pp. 178-195, 2005.

[11] McBurney, P. and Parsons, S. Games that agents play: A formal framework for dialogues between autonomous agents. In *Journal of Logic, Language and Information*, 11(3), 2002, pp. 315-334.

[12] Sadri, F., Toni, F., and Torroni, P., Logic agents, dialogues and negotiation: an abductive approach. In *Proc. of the Sym. on Information Agents for E-Commerce, Artificial Intelligence and the Simulation of Behaviour Conf.*, 2001.

[13] Bentahar, J., Moulin, B., Meyer, J-J.Ch. A tableau method for verifying dialogue game protocols for agent communication. In *Declarative Agent Languages and Technologies*, vol. 3904 LNAI Springer, pp. 223-244, 2006.

[14] Bhat, G., Cleaveland, R., and Groce, A. Efficient model checking via Büchi tableau automata. In *Computer-Aided Verification*, Berry, G., Comon, H. and Finkel, A. (eds.), LNCS 2102 Springer, 2001, pp. 38-52.

[15] Bernholtz, O., Vardi, M.Y., and Wolper, P. An automata-theoretic approach to branching-time model checking. In *Computer Aided Verification*, Dill, D.L. (ed.), LNCS 818 Springer, 1994, pp. 142-155.

[16] Bhat, G. and Cleaveland, R. Efficient model checking via the equational μ calculus. In *the 11ᵗʰ Annual Sym. on Logic in Computer Science*, IEEE Computer Society Press, 1996, pp. 304-312.

[17] Huget, M.-P., Wooldridge, M. Model checking for ACL compliance verification. In *Advances in Agent Communication*, Dignum, F. (ed.), LNAI 2922 Springer, 2004, pp. 75-90.

[18] Cleaveland, R. Tableau-based model checking in the propositional mu-calculus. In *Acta Informatica*, vol. 27(8), 1990, pp.725-747.

[19] Vardi, M. and Wolper, P. An automata-theoretic approach to automatic program verification. In *Sym. on Logic in Computer Science*, 1986, pp. 332-344.

[20] Courcoubetis, C., Vardi, M.Y., Wolper, P. and Yannakakis, M. Memory efficient algorithms for verification of temporal properties. In *Formal Methods in System Design*, vol. 1, 1992, pp. 275-288.

[21] Adi, K., Debbabi, M., and Mejri, M. A new logic for electronic commerce protocols. In *Theoretical Computer Science*, vol. 291, 2003, pp. 223-283.

[22] Emerson, E.A., Jutla, C. and Sistla, A.P. On model-checking for fragments of μ-calculus. In *Computer Aided Verification*, Courcoubetis, C. (ed.), LNCS 697 Springer, 1993, pp. 385-396.

Chapter 6

Program Conversion and Related Software Validation

New Trends in Software Methodologies, Tools and Techniques
H. Fujita and D. Pisanelli (Eds.)
IOS Press, 2007

Constructing higher-level Transformation Languages based on XML

Daniel FOETSCH [a] and Elke PULVERMUELLER [b]

[a] *Department of Computer Science, Christian-Albrechts-Universität zu Kiel, Germany*
[b] *Faculté des Sciences, de la Technologie et de la Communication, Université du Luxembourg, Luxembourg*

Abstract. Based on the experience in the e-commerce domain, we propose a concept for the development of higher-level transformation languages. Transformation is a key factor in this domain as the market requires a fast reaction to frequent changes in the interfaces and exchange data. Moreover, a typical e-commerce system is divided into different services which are offered and hosted by different vendors which results in a complex integration problem.

Our proposed solution is based on the operator hierarchy concept which allows to define transformation operator hierarchies containing different levels of transformation operators. The concrete realization of such a higher-level transformation language construction is demonstrated by an application of the XML operator hierarchy concept to the transformation language XSLT. XSLT serves as an example which is employed to provide the elementary transformation operators. On top of these elementary operators the layered concept allows the definition of new higher-level operators, e. g. domain-independent and domain-specific ones. The construction of the higher-level language XML2DSV is presented, for instance. This is a stand-alone domain-specific transformation language, which creates delimeter-separated values (DSV) files from XML documents, on the base of XSLT.

Keywords. XSLT, e-commerce, higher-level transformation operators, operator hierarchy concept, transformation language

Introduction

In today's competitive and dynamic business environment, the system integration is becoming more and more important. An increasing number of systems are interconnected, both within the system under construction and with systems that are already deployed. However, one of the main problems of integration is, equal to evolution, the adaptation. In the case of integration, the parts have to be adapted to enable communication and exchange (adaptation towards another system unit) while the evolution adapts due to requirements changes (adaptation towards the user).

In this paper, we concentrate on the system integration in the e-commerce domain. Though, not limited to this area, e-commerce is a typical field where the integration and evolution requirements are central. E-commerce systems are constructed from a set of re-usable services. In this, it has several similarities to the telecommunication domain. However, these services are frequently contributed and hosted from different vendors.

The services often change due to technical progress and market competition. Examples for companies, which concentrate on the integration of e-commerce services to customer specific solutions, are Truition Inc. [1] and Intershop Communications AG. Truition Inc., for instance, offers on-demand solutions for specific e-commerce activities (out-sourcing of e-commerce services). Instead of building individual sale and marketing channels, Truition Inc. offers such services in different alternatives (e. g. product data transfer into customer specific online-shops or into market places like eBay). The customers connect their logistic systems, for instance, to the Commerce Management System of Truition and, thus, use the offered sale and marketing channels.

One of the most challenging drawbacks of such an approach is the fact that there does not exist one general standard for the integration of the different interfaces. Either no standard is available at all or there are multiple of them (e. g. BMEcat, EDIFACT or xCBL). Solutions which aim at connecting different e-commerce services have to provide a transformation service for ASCII text, Excel, XML and CSV (Comma Separated Values), for instance. The latter of which, is the most frequently used format (53,7%) in the Truition Inc. business, for instance. Besides the different formats, it is a technical challenge to deal with usually frequently changing APIs (known as agile interfaces). This refers to both, the customers providing the (e. g. logistic) data as well as the sale and marketing platforms. The eBay interfaces, for instance, change approximately all 24 weeks. Examples of such changes are new attributes to classify the products or just new syntactical data structures.

Although the integration and adaptation problem is a key issue in the e-commerce market, the diversity of formats and frequency of individual changes have hindered an efficient automation. In our work, we aim at a contribution to closing this gap. In particular, we address the problem of low-level transformations. Equal to high-level languages for defining and implementing the services or parts, respectively, we aim at suitable higher-level languages to define transformations which are performing the integration and adaptation tasks. As higher-level transformation languages depend on the domain, it is essential to support the definition of appropriate specific transformation languages.

For the realization of higher-level transformation language we rely on XML. XML is often used as an intermediate language (e. g. also in the data transformation approach of Truition Inc.). XML (Extensible Markup Language) [2] is a meta markup-language recommended by W3C in order to create structured documents. Unlike plain text, it contains special tags which decompose the document into logical parts.

One of the most widely used XML transformation languages is XSLT recommended by W3C [3,4]. The origins of XSLT as a language, itself written in XML, lie in the functional paradigm, and in text-based pattern matching languages in the tradition of awk [5]. Accordingly, an XSLT program (called stylesheet) consists of a collection of template rules. Each template rule contains a match condition and a list of operators to construct parts of the target document. In short, if a node in the source document matches the template's rule match condition, the template is instantiated and the operators specified within this template rule are executed. Additionally, a very simple function mechanism using named templates is offered.

Nevertheless, as a low-level transformation language, XSLT has further drawbacks. XSLT does not offer operators to create constructs of a particular class of target documents. The base language supports only the creation of text literals, XML literals, and XML nodes like elements, attributes, comments etc. Even more significantly, XSLT completely ignores target language constraints. An XSLT processor can only ensure that the result XML document is well-formed. It cannot guarantee the validness of a specific XML dialect with respect to the target schema. Other target formats are unsupported at all. This makes XSLT both a powerful and an error-prone low-level transformation language.

The remainder of the paper is organized as follows: The fundamental ideas of the generic XML operator hierarchy concept are presented in section 1. It outlines the principles to the construction of higher-level transformation languages. Based on this introductive background, we propose a concrete operator hierarchy (i. e. a concrete higher-level transformation language) on top of the low-level transformation language XSLT in the following section 2. After identifying several possible domain-independent higher-level operators for XSLT, we describe the definition, usage, and implementation of one example operator. This is followed by an example of a complete domain-specific transformation language. The concrete operators shall only demonstrate the realization of the operator hierarchy and prove the feasibility of the approach. The general concept is independent of the specific technology. Finally, we consider related work and conclude this paper.

1. Fundamentals

In this paper, we support higher-level transformation languages by building new higher-level operators on top of existing ones based on the generic XML operator hierarchy concept. The advantages of higher-level transformation languages are similar to those of general-purpose higher-level programming languages (e. g. Java). Modularizing the code reduces the redundancy and the risk of errors. Since the higher-level operators bear a close resemblance to everyday languages, the readability and maintenance of code is improved. The higher-level operators may increase the programmer productivity. Moreover, domain-specific operators, specified for a concrete XML dialect or another non-XML-based format, allow error messaging and, in general, validation at the domain level. Last but not least, domain-specific operators ensure that the result or at least parts of the result complies/comply with the constraints of target languages.

The operator hierarchy concept picks up existing principles from software engineering. The basic idea is to construct a layered framework that enables the definition of higher-level operators on top of existing ones. This allows a bottom-up stepwise composition and adaptation of operators. A specific closed set of operators on one level forms a transformation language. The higher the level the more domain specific is the language or the operator, respectively. The operator hierarchy and the mapping between the levels bridges the gap between the low-level transformation language (e. g. XSLT) and high-level transformation languages (e. g. even more domain specific).

The starting point of the hierarchy is the lowest level of operators (cf. figure 1). This level comprises the so-called elementary operators offered by the underlying XML transformation technology. For example, these could be the operators provided by the XSLT transformation processor. Elementary operators are used for fundamental operations on the document structure. On top of this elementary level, new levels are introduced in the operator hierarchy. These levels contain more complex operators. Although the figure ends on level 3 further levels may be added depending on the application domain.

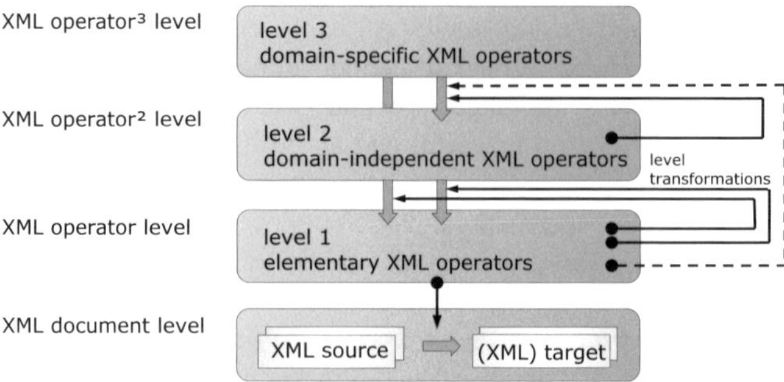

Figure 1. XML operator hierarchy.

We divide the set of new operators (on top of the elementary ones) in domain-independent and domain-specific operators. Domain-independent operators are predominantly defined to encapsulate more than one elementary operator for reuse. For instance, if an XML-based update language does not support the replacement of XML elements, a corresponding domain-unspecific replace operator could be composed from elementary insert and delete operators. Domain-specific operators are composed of elementary as well as domain-independent operators and can be particularly adapted to domain-specific languages and patterns. In contrast to domain-independent operators, these operators are basically intended for reuse in a certain application area. In principle, a more detailed differentiation as well as other kinds of classifications using other criteria is possible. The idea behind this principle to form higher-level transformation languages is similar to higher-level programming languages in general. Programs are compiled to lower-level statements (e. g. C++ is compiled to machine code). With the intermediate representations we have a similar hierarchy.

As shown in figure 1, the layered operator concept is implemented by applying a multi-level transformation process, which transforms operators from higher levels into operators from lower levels. If the transformation language uses itself XML to specify the transformation definitions, the language and the underlying transformation technologies can be reused for this level transformation. Some conceptual details of the operator hierarchy are elaborated in [6]. However, since more than one transformation must be performed in order to resolve higher-level operators, the hierarchical approach may come with some additional costs regarding the performance of transformations. But this additional overhead has no impact on runtime performance. The transformation from higher to lower level operators is performed only once at build-time.

The XML operator hierarchy is a generic concept which can be applied to all XML-based languages which transform or update XML documents. In [7] we present an infrastructure called XTC (XML Transformation Coordinator) that automates the multi-level transformation process for several specific XML-based languages integrating their processors by respective adapters. XTC identifies existing higher-level transformation operators applicable to given level transformation definitions and recursively transforms them into elementary transformation operators. The result is processed by the connected processors (via the adapters).

2. XSLT Operator Hierarchy

As a basic principle, every language has its own operator hierarchy since higher-level operators completely depend on the expressive power of elementary languages or operators, respectively. For instance, an update language such as XUpdate [8] only supports in-place updates. As a consequence, it is impossible to build the same higher-level operators than using XSLT as underlying language. However, if two languages have the same expressive power, higher-level operators and, particularly, the newly built stand-alone domain-specific languages are portable.

In the following, we propose potential domain-independent and domain-specific operators for XSLT. In this case, XSLT is an example for a concrete elementary language providing concrete elementary transformation operators.

2.1. Domain-independent Operators

The level of domain-independent operators offers a well-known set of enhanced functionality to perform common tasks. This large body of reusable code is provided to simplify the XSLT transformation programming. Its usage is not restricted to a specific domain but are, in contrast, cross-cutting to several domains. Various domain-independent operators can be built on top of elementary ones. In the following, we list some possible categories:

> **Math operators** provide facilities for mathematical computation, e. g. computation of the minimum, maximum, average, sum, or multiply of a node set[1]; the highest or lowest node of a node set; absolute, ceiling, or floor value of a number node.
>
> **String operators** provide facilities for string manipulation, e. g. the replacement, splitting, concatenation, or alignment of one or more than one string.
>
> **Date and time operators** provide facilities for date and time formatting and conversion, e. g. returning a date, time, duration, year, month, name of month, days, name of days, minutes, seconds of one date/time string; adding or subtracting a date/time string with another one.
>
> **Set operators** provide facilities for nodes manipulation, e. g. the difference, distinction, intersection, union, equity, exceptions, or counting of two or more nodes.
>
> **Control operators** provide facilities for managing the control flow, e. g. functions, for-loop, for-each-group, while, or repeat operators.

To demonstrate the concept, we concentrate on two simple domain-independent operators. We start with describing the syntax and semantics of these operators followed by a discussion of their usage and implementation. This shows one complete realization and application step from low-level elementary operators to a higher-level domain-independent operator.

2.1.1. The `function` and the corresponding `call-function` Operator

For example, XSLT only offers a restricted function (call) mechanism. To realize a function in XSLT, a named template has to be declared which can be invoked by name. There

---

[1] XSLT 2.0 uses sequences of nodes instead of the node set of XSLT 1.0.

are many restrictions to this concept. For instance, only one template with the same name is allowed. A parameter x, passed to a named template that does not have a parameter for x, is simply ignored without any warning. Particularly, the last restriction is error-prone. Applying the operator hierarchy concept, we can easily build a more flexible and safer function mechanism. By means of these new operators the developer can describe the transformation directly in terms of functions and function calls. The operators ease the transformation work for the developer by eliminating the burden to consider all these error-prone restrictions manually and, in consequence, support to reduce transformation errors. We call the corresponding operators function and call-function operator (the latter is used to call the defined function):

```
<ctrl:function name=qname>
  <ctrl:param name=qname select=expression?>
    <!-- Content: template -->
  </ctrl:param>*
  <!-- Content: template -->
</ctrl:function>

<ctrl:call-function name=qname|varref>
  <ctrl:with-param name=qname select=expression?>
    <!-- Content: template -->
  </ctrl:with-param>*
</ctrl:call-function>
```

The new function and call-function operator has each a required name attribute. The value of this name attribute is a qualified name[2]. The parameters are defined in the same manner as in XSLT 1.0. The with-param is used to specify a parameter passing to a function. The required name attribute sets the respective name. Additionally, either a select attribute, containing an XPath expression [9], or a content can be applied to bind a value to this parameter. Similarly, a parameter can be defined in the function operator. However, in contrast to the named templates of XSLT, a corresponding function operator is identified by the required name attribute and the names of the parameters. Therefore, functions may be defined with the same name and different parameters.

The following simple example shows how to apply the new operators. Assuming, we have a list of orders as source, and we want to convert all time types in an application-specific format. This might be needed to connect two e-commerce services (e. g. the logistic of customer A with the eBay market place [10]). The integration quality depends on a correct data exchange. As before, the stylesheet contains ordinary elementary XSLT operators and the new function operator and the respective call-function operator (cf. listing **1**). Their usage eases the definition of the transformation task and results in a more readable and a more concise representation of the transformation. The operators may be considered as a kind of small reusable transformation patterns or frameworks.

Source
```
<OrderArray>
 <Order>
    <OrderID>2476679</OrderID>
    <OrderStatus>Completed</OrderStatus>
    <AdjustmentAmount currencyID="USD">0.0</AdjustmentAmount>
    <AmountSaved currencyID="USD">0.99</AmountSaved>
```

---

[2]To natively support higher-order functions, the name of the call-function operator may also be a variable reference to a function (name) supplied by a parameter of the surrounded function operator.

```
<CheckoutStatus>
  <eBayPaymentStatus>PayPalPaymentInProcess</eBayPaymentStatus>
  <LastModifiedTime>20070515T08:11:51.000Z</LastModifiedTime>
  <PaymentMethod>PayPal</PaymentMethod>
  <Status>Complete</Status>
</CheckoutStatus>
  ...
</Order>
<Order>
  <OrderID>2698789</OrderID>
  <OrderStatus>Active</OrderStatus>
  <AdjustmentAmount currencyID="USD">0.0</AdjustmentAmount>
  <AmountSaved currencyID="USD">0.0</AmountSaved>
  <CheckoutStatus>
    <eBayPaymentStatus>NoPaymentFailure</eBayPaymentStatus>
    <LastModifiedTime>20070520T18:31:55.000Z</LastModifiedTime>
    <PaymentMethod>None</PaymentMethod>
    <Status>Incomplete</Status>
  </CheckoutStatus>
  ...
</Order>
</OrderArray>
```

Stylesheet

```
<xsl:transform
  xmlns:xsl="http://www.w3.org/1999/XSL/Transform"
  xmlns:ctrl="http://www.informatik.uni-kiel.de/Control">
  <ctrl:function name="convertTime">
    <ctrl:param name="oldTimestamp" />
    <xsl:value-of select="concat(substring($oldTimestamp,'1','4'),'-',
                          substring($oldTimestamp,'5','2'),'-',
                          substring($oldTimestamp,'7','2'))" />
  </ctrl:function>
  ...
  <xsl:template match="//Order/CheckoutStatus">
    <lastChange>
      <ctrl:call-function name="convertTime">
        <ctrl:with-param name="oldTimestamp" select="LastModifiedTime" />
      </ctrl:call-function>
    </lastChange>
  </xsl:template>
</xsl:transform>
```

Target

```
...<lastChange>2007-05-15</lastChange>...<lastChange>2007-05-20</lastChange>...
```

Listing 1. Usage of the function operators.

To generate the desired result, we need a level transformation which translates the domain-independent function operators into elementary XSLT operators (cf. figure 2). This is due to the fact that the underlying processors only understand the elementary operators; similar to a hardware processor which only understands machine code but no higher-level programming language. It is important that the function operators belong to a separate namespace because the corresponding level transformation file is identified by this namespace.

As shown in figure 2, the level transformation file is itself written in XSLT to reuse the XSLT processor. But, if more efficient, other specific XML transformation languages and respective processors may be applied, too. However, the `ctrl.xslt` level transformation file supports and, thus, cross-cuts all domain-independent operators by provid-

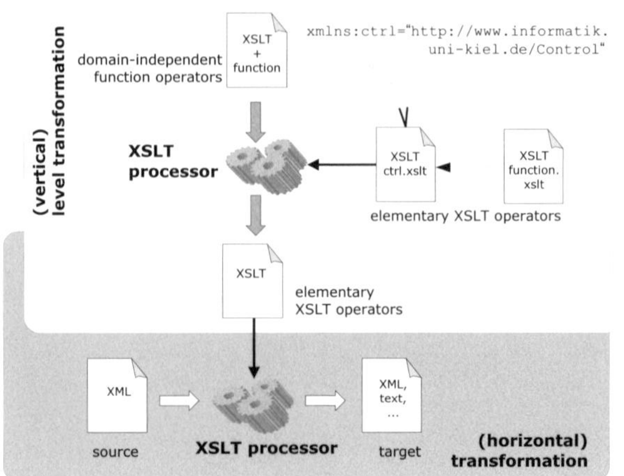

Figure 2. XSLT level transformation (application of figure 1).

ing facilities for managing the control flow of the transformation definitions. Line 2 of listing **2** includes the level transformation definition of the function operators.

```
01 <transform version="1.0" xmlns="http://www.w3.org/1999/XSL/Transform">
02 <include href="function.xslt" />
...
   <!-- ***** starts traversals ***** -->
22 <template match="/">
23    <variable name="errors">
24      <apply-templates mode="validation"/>
25    </variable>
26    <if test="string-length($errors)!=0">
27      <message terminate="yes">
          <value-of select="string-length($errors)"/>
          <text> error(s) detected</text>
        </message>
28    </if>
29    <apply-templates />
30 </template>


   <!-- ***** validation code ***** -->
31 <template match="text()" mode="validation" />


   <!-- ***** copying code ***** -->
32 <template match="@*|node()">
33    <copy>
34      <apply-templates select="@*|node()" />
35    </copy>
36 </template>
37 </transform>
```

Listing 2. Level transformation definition of the `ctrl` stylesheet: `ctrl.xslt`.

The stylesheet of listing **2** starts two traversals: in validation mode (line 24) and in default mode (line 29). The first one checks the syntax of the employed operators. It gathers all thrown error messages. If at least one error occurred in the first traversal, the level transformation is terminated. The second one replaces all domain-independent control operators by appropriate elementary XSLT operators. The other elementary XSLT operators are only copied without further processing (line 32–37).

```
01 <transform version="1.0" xmlns="http://www.w3.org/1999/XSL/Transform"
      xmlns:axsl="http://www.w3.org/1999/XSL/Transform/Alias"
      xmlns:ctrl="http://www.informatik.uni-kiel.de/Control"
      exclude-result-prefixes="ctrl">
02  <namespace-alias stylesheet-prefix="axsl" result-prefix="xsl"/>
03  <variable name="filename" select="'function.xslt'"/>
04  <variable name="id" select="generate-id()"/>

    <!-- ***** validation code ***** -->
05  <template match="ctrl:function" mode="validation">
06    <if test="not(@name!='')">
07      <message>Error reported by <value-of select="$filename"/>: Element
        '<value-of select="name()"/>' must have a 'name' attribute.</message>
08      <text>.</text>
09    </if>
10    <for-each select="@*[not(name()='name' or name()='select')]">
11      <message>Error reported by <value-of select="$filename" />:
        Attribute '<value-of select="name()" />' is not allowed on element
        '<value-of select="name(..)" />'.</message>
12      <text>.</text>
13    </for-each>
      ...
14 </template>

    <!-- ***** level transformation definition ***** -->
15 <template match="ctrl:function">
16    <variable name="create-name">
17      <value-of select="@name" />
18      <for-each select="ctrl:param">
19        <sort select="@name" />
20        <text>-</text><value-of select="@name" />
21      </for-each>
22      <text>-</text><value-of select="$id" />
23    </variable>
24    <axsl:template name="{$create-name}">
25      <for-each select="ctrl:param">
26        <choose>
27          <when test="@select">
28            <axsl:param name="{@name}" select="{@select}"/>
29          </when>
30          <otherwise>
31            <axsl:param name="{@name}">
32              <apply-templates />
33            </axsl:param>
34          </otherwise>
35        </choose>
36      </for-each>
37    </axsl:template>
38    <apply-templates />
39 </template>
```

Listing 3. Validation and level transformation definition of the `call-function` operator: `function.xslt`.

    A possible level transformation definition, implementing a concrete `call-function` operator, consists of two templates (cf. listing **3**; extract of `function.xslt`). The content of the first one (line 6–13) contains exemplary XSLT operators ensuring the correct syntax of the `call-function` operator. Further checks may be specified in the same manner. Examples for further checks might be:

        if a function definition with the same name and parameters exists,
        if the parameters have different names,
        if parameters have either a `select` attribute or a content.

The content of the second one (line 16–37) contains XML literals[3] and XSLT creating operators to transform the `call-function` operator into corresponding elementary XSLT operators. The XML literals use an alias for a namespace in order to avoid namespace conflicts with the XSLT namespace.

Though the new version of XSLT (XSLT 2.0 [4] in conjunction with XPath 2.0 [11]) also allows the declaration of user-defined functions that can be called from any XPath expression. Nevertheless, there are some differences. Our `function` operator is identified by the `name` attribute and the parameter names. This approach differs from the XPath function call in that the values are passed by associating each one with a parameter name, instead of providing an ordered list of values. Therefore, a function may be defined, for instance, with the same name and number of parameters but different named parameters. Furthermore, the structure of our `call-function` operator is reflected in the nesting of XML elements and their attributes. Hence, it can be generated from more higher-level operators easier than the compact textual representation of XPath. Due to the level transformation process, last but not least, our `function` operator natively supports the definition of higher-order functions. It is possible to pass a function (name) as a parameter to another callable function and then invoke it dynamically (cf. in contrast [12]).

However, the `function` operator is only one example for a domain-independent operator. There are many other (more complex) control operators that can be built on top of elementary ones. For instance, the hierarchy concept may be used to create a traditional `for-loop` operator[4] with `start` and `end` attributes as well as an optional `counter` attribute. There is no comparable direct support in XSLT 2.0.

2.2. Domain-specific Operators

Similar to the construction of above, it is also possible to build domain-specific operators which may offer facilities to create parts of a particular class of target documents. With these operators, we overcome the problem of XSLT caused by its universality: XSLT only supports the creation of text literals, XML literals, and XML nodes instead of constructs of a specific language (cf. section introduction).

As outlined for the e-commerce domain this is a severe restriction as a large number of target document categories may be identified. The main distinction is between XML documents and non-XML documents. For XML documents many XML-based vocabularies, languages, and applications exist. This includes, for instance, WSDL, SOAP, ebXML, xCBL, XSD, RDF, OWL, and several more.   Also for non-XML documents several non-XML-based vocabularies, languages, and applications exist. This includes, for instance, EDIFACT, CSV, PDF, LaTeX, DTD, and many more.

Applying the operator hierarchy concept, both categories of documents may be supported. Corresponding domain-specific operators may be defined by extending XSLT. This may even result in a completely new transformation language which consists of a closed set of such domain-specific operators.

---

[3]In point of fact, we apply a bootstrapping process (i. e. applying our own operator hierarchy concept) by using XSLT-specific operators to generate elementary XSLT operators. In contrast to XML literals, this ensures the generation of syntactically correct XSLT operators.

[4]The `for-each` operator of XSLT is not really a loop construct. To solve iterative problems you have to transform them into recursive problems. The resulting code could become easily unreadable.

In the following, we exemplify a small stand-alone domain-specific transformation language which creates delimeter-separated values (DSV) files from XML documents. DSV is a simple data exchange format, supported by many legacy systems and almost all spreadsheet software applications. The DSV format uses specific characters (delimiters) to separate its data items. For example, in CSV files (Comma Separated Values) the data fields and records are delimited using commas and newlines [13].

XML2DSV Transformation Language

An XML2DSV program is represented by a `dsv` element in an XML document. The `dsv` element may contain a separator description and must contain a description for the data fields and records.

The optional separator description, specified with the `separator` element, allows to define the specific delimiters. For instance, the `field-separator` operator states the delimiter, and if the last field may or may not have an ending delimiter. If the separator description is omitted, the default setting corresponds to the values configured in line 3–5 of listing **4**.

```
01 <dsv xmlns="http://www.informatik.uni-kiel.de/DSV">
02   <separators>
03     <field-separator ending-field-break="yes" delimiter="," />
04     <field-escape delimiter='"' />
05     <record-separator ending-record-break="no" delimiter="&#xa;" />
06   </separators>
07   <data escaped-field="yes">
08     <header escaped-field="no">
09       <field>ID</field>
10       <field>STATUS</field>
11       <field>AMOUNT</field>
12       <field>PAYMENT</field>
13     </header>
14     <record match="//Order">
15       <field select="OrderID" />
16       <field select="OrderStatus[text()='Active' or text()='Completed']" />
17       <field select="AmountSaved" />
18       <field select="CheckoutStatus/PaymentMethod" />
19     </record>
20   </data>
21 </dsv>
```

Listing 4. Usage of the XML2DSV transformation language.

The `data` element is used to define the delimited data. The corresponding data selection is specified by adding `record` operators as children of the `data` element. The `record` operator contains a description of data fields. These are instantiated for each node identified by the XPath expression specified by the `match` attribute (line 14). With respect to these context nodes, the concrete data items are selected using the `select` attribute in the `field` operator (line 15–18). If all data fields bind literal data characters (line 9–12) the `match` attribute in the `record` operator may be omitted. There may be an optional header record (`header` operator) appearing as the first record of the DSV with the same format as ordinary records. The `data`, `header` as well as `record`, and `field` operators support an `escaped-field` attribute. It is set if a character, specified in the `field-escape` operator, is used to enclose fields or not; default setting is the latter case. A setting shadows another setting if the setting occurs at a point where the other setting is visible.

```xml
<?xml version="1.0" encoding="UTF-8"?>
<xslt:transform xmlns:xslt="http://www.w3.org/1999/XSL/Transform" version="1.0">
  <xslt:output method="text"/>
  <xslt:template match="text()"/>
  <xslt:template match="/">
    <xslt:variable name="field-separator-delimiter">,</xslt:variable>
    <xslt:variable name="ending-field-break">yes</xslt:variable>
    <xslt:variable name="field-escape-delimiter">"</xslt:variable>
    <xslt:variable name="record-separator-delimiter">
</xslt:variable>
    <xslt:variable name="ending-record-break">no</xslt:variable>
    <xslt:text>ID</xslt:text>
    <xslt:value-of select="$field-separator-delimiter"/>
    <xslt:text>SATUS</xslt:text>
    <xslt:value-of select="$field-separator-delimiter"/>
    <xslt:text>AMOUNT</xslt:text>
    <xslt:value-of select="$field-separator-delimiter"/>
    <xslt:text>PAYMENT</xslt:text>
    <xslt:choose>
       <xslt:when test="$ending-field-break='yes'">
          <xslt:value-of select="$field-separator-delimiter"/>
       </xslt:when>
       <xslt:otherwise/>
    </xslt:choose>
    <xslt:value-of select="$record-separator-delimiter"/>
    <xslt:for-each select="//Order">
      <xslt:value-of select="$field-escape-delimiter"/>
      <xslt:value-of select="OrderID"/>
      <xslt:value-of select="$field-escape-delimiter"/>
      <xslt:value-of select="$field-separator-delimiter"/>
      <xslt:value-of select="$field-escape-delimiter"/>
      <xslt:value-of select="OrderStatus[text()='Active' or text()='Completed']"/>
      <xslt:value-of select="$field-escape-delimiter"/>
      <xslt:value-of select="$field-separator-delimiter"/>
      <xslt:value-of select="$field-escape-delimiter"/>
      <xslt:value-of select="AmountSaved"/>
      <xslt:value-of select="$field-escape-delimiter"/>
      <xslt:value-of select="$field-separator-delimiter"/>
      <xslt:value-of select="$field-escape-delimiter"/>
      <xslt:value-of select="CheckoutStatus/PaymentMethod"/>
      <xslt:value-of select="$field-escape-delimiter"/>
      <xslt:choose>
        <xslt:when test="$ending-field-break='yes'">
          <xslt:value-of select="$field-separator-delimiter"/>
        </xslt:when>
        <xslt:otherwise/>
      </xslt:choose>
      <xslt:choose>
        <xslt:when test="$ending-record-break='yes'">
          <xslt:value-of select="$record-separator-delimiter"/>
        </xslt:when>
        <xslt:otherwise>
          <xslt:if test="not(position()=last())">
            <xslt:value-of select="$record-separator-delimiter"/>
          </xslt:if>
        </xslt:otherwise>
      </xslt:choose>
    </xslt:for-each>
  </xslt:template>
</xslt:transform>
```

We implement two modes for the level transformation: a (default) dynamic and a static mode. The level transformation definition in the dynamic mode generates a respective elementary XSLT transformation definition with delimiter variables and corresponding references (cf. listing above). In the static mode, the specific delimiters are represented by text literals.

The example program in listing **4** creates the following result passing the source of listing **1** as input.

```
ID,STATUS,AMOUNT,PAYMENT,
"2476679","Completed","0.99","PayPal",
"2698789","Active","0.0","None",
```

Due to space limitations, we omit the implementation of the level transformation. Its principle is the same as for level transformations of domain-independent operators.

3. Related Work

The paper presents a concrete realization and application of the operator hierarchy concept to define higher-level transformation languages. The usage of higher-level languages for implementing the system parts (e. g. components, objects) is not sufficient. Facing an increasing integration and evolution pressure, transformations become a major element in the system development. The following outlines related work which is also aiming at providing more convenient (higher-level) languages and tools to express the transformations.

While there exist numerous approaches to modularize low-level transformation operators for the purpose of clarity and reuse (e. g. the `include` and `import` operator in XSLT) extended and XSLT specific reuse mechanisms may be found in the EXSLT community initiative [14]. It proposes a number of modules including named templates to provide extensions to XSLT. These named templates are comparable to our domain-independent operators. The main difference between both concepts is that higher-level operators are like pre-defined language instructions. Therefore, the operators offer an appropriate XML-based notation. Furthermore, the syntax of operators can be validated and corresponding error messages may be thrown. In XSLT, for instance, it is not an error to pass a parameter to a template that does not have a respective parameter definition; the passed parameter is ignored without any warning.

Related work may also be found in further specific extensions and elementary operators (even those already available in XSLT). Closely connected to XSLT is XPath which allows to describe document parts used by both XSLT and XPointer (e. g. to find specific elements or element sets). In addition, often a library of functions is offered. In the case of XPath (in combination with XSLT), these may be considered as a pre-defined set of basic operators. However, such pre-defined sets do not cover all requirements and, moreover, a flexible and extendable hierarchy of highly re-usable operators is not considered.

Some XSLT processors such as Saxon [15] offer extension functions and extension operators for XSLT. For instance, the `saxon:while` operator performs a traditional while loop. The content of the `saxon:while` operator is carried out as long as some conditional expression evaluates to true. But these operators are proprietary extensions of the standard. The respective XSLT programs are not portable. They cannot be processed by other XSLT processors.

Currently, higher-level transformation languages are directly implemented using general-purpose programming languages with APIs such as DOM or its derivates

(JDOM, dom4j, etc.). The XOpT composition concept [16], for instance, follows this approach. There, domain-specific operators are designed to process Java code after a transformation to JavaML [17], an XML representation of Java. Other top-down approaches (e. g. [18,19,20]) develop domain-specific transformation languages and map them on XSLT also using general-purpose programming languages. All these approaches consider only a single level of transformation operators in contrast to the layered hierarchy concept we propose.

The operator hierarchy, however, is not tied to a specific technical implementation. Though presented for the XML-specific transformation language XSLT in this paper, the concept is generic and, therefore, may be also applied to other languages. For instance, program transformation languages (such as ASF+SDF, DMS, Kids, Stratego, Tom, or TXL) may be used as underlying transformation technology, too.

OMG's QVT (Query/View/Transformation) standard [21] and other model transformation languages are on another technological space than our transformation concepts. These existing transformation languages are, therefore, not directly comparable. However, the usage of the operator hierarchy concept may support the realization of higher-level model transformations. They may be realized by means of model-specific transformation operators.

4. Summary and Outlook

In this paper, we propose the development of higher-level transformation languages. To demonstrate the realization of such a higher-level transformation language construction, we apply the XML operator hierarchy concept to the transformation language XSLT. XSLT is only one example which may be employed to provide elementary transformation operators. A specific set of higher-level operators forms the higher-level language. They are defined on top of the elementary operators. The layered concept allows the definition of new higher-level operators without changing the underlying XSLT language and respective processors.

We identified some examples of potential domain-independent and domain-specific operators. Domain-independent operators are basically intended to encapsulate more than one elementary XSLT operator for reuse. In contrast to the domain-specific operators, these operators are applied in several domains. Domain-specific operators, composed of elementary and domain-independent operators, are specialized for a certain target dialect or format. The layer concept may be extended with additional layers depending on the application domain. We demonstrate the definition, usage, and implementation of higher-level operators using corresponding examples.

The experience with an increasing integration and evolution challenge in the e-commerce domain reveals that transformation has been neglected in the past with respect to the language level. Transformation should become a core element in the system development. It should be supported by powerful and suitable language constructs. At the same time, flexibility is required to react on changing or new application domains (and their specific requirements for suitable transformation languages). Modern paradigms and concepts like object-orientation, components, aspect-orientation or patterns for general-purpose programming languages are still missing for transformation languages. The experience in our work has shown that the mapping of such higher-level concepts to transformation languages is not straight-forward. Even more, a pure mapping and knowledge transfer from the general-purpose programming languages may be inappropriate for transformation languages although the investigation is worthwhile.

In general, the proposed composition concept, relying on transformation itself, can be applied to several specific XML-based languages both transformation languages (STX [22], fxt [23], XML Script [24], etc.) and update languages (XUL [25], XUpdate [8], etc.). However, future research has to elaborate the expressive power of the specific XML-based languages and the effects on the expressive power of higher-level transformation definitions.

Further extensions to the work presented may be in the field of design guidelines to support the decision which elementary operators may be encapsulated in domain-independent operators and what measures may be employed to find a well-balanced size of the operators.

References

[1] Truition, Inc. Company profile. http://www.truition.de.

[2] Tim Bray, Jean Paoli, C. M. Sperberg-McQueen, Eve Maler, and Françoir Yergeau, editors. *Extensible Markup Language (XML) Version 1.0 (Third Edition), W3C Recommendation, 04 February 2004.* W3C, 2004.

[3] James Clark, editor. *XSL Transformations (XSLT), Version 1.0, W3C Recommendation 16 November 1999.* W3C, 1999.

[4] Michael Kay, editor. *XSL Transformations (XSLT), Version 2.0, W3C Recommendation 27 January 2007.* W3C, 2007.

[5] Arnold D. Robbins. *GAWK: Effective AWK Programming – A User's Guide for GNU Awk.* Free Software Foundation, Boston, USA, 3 edition, June 2004.

[6] Daniel Fötsch, Andreas Speck, and Peter Hänsgen. The Operator Hierarchy Concept for XML Document Transformation Technologies. Berliner XML Tage 2005 (BXML'05), 12.-14. September 2005 in Berlin. In Rainer Eckstein and Robert Tolksdorf, editors, *Berliner XML Tage 2005*, pages 59–70. XML-Clearinghouse, September 2005.

[7] Daniel Fötsch and Andreas Speck. XTC – The XML Transformation Coordinator for XML Document Transformation Technologies. In *DEXA'06: Proceedings of the 17th International Conference on Database and Expert Systems Applications*, pages 507 511, Washington, DC, USA, 2006 IEEE Computer Society.

[8] Andreas Laux and Lars Martin. *XML Update Language, Working Draft, 14 September 2000*, 2000.

[9] James Clark and Steve DeRosa, editors. *XML Path Language (XPath), Version 1.0, W3C Recommendation 16 November 1999.* W3C, 1999.

[10] ebay Inc. ebay Web Service API Guide, Version 511. http://developer.ebay.com/developercenter/xml/, 2007.

[11] Anders Berglund, Scott Boag, Don Chamberlin, Mary F. Fernàndez, Michael Kay, Jonathan Robie, and Jérôme Siméon, editors. *XML Path Language (XPath) 2.0, W3C Recommendation 23 January 2007.* W3C, 2007.

[12] Dimitre Novatchev. Higher-Order Functional Programming with XSLT 2.0 and FXSL. In *Extreme Markup Languages 2006*, Montréal, Québec, August 2006.

[13] Y. Shafranovich, editor. *RFC 4180 – Common Format and MIME Type for Comma-Separated Values (CSV) Files.* The International Society, October 2005.

[14] EXSLT community initiative. www.exslt.org.

[15] Michael Kay. Saxon XSLT. http://saxon.sourceforge.net.

[16] Elke Pulvermüller and Andreas Speck. XOpT - XML-Based Composition Concept. In Volker Gruhn Hamido Fujita, editor, *Proceedings of the 3rd International Conference on New Software Methodologies, Tools, and Techniques (SoMeT'04)*, volume 111, pages 249 – –262, Leipzig, Germany, September 2004. IOS Press.

[17] Greg J. Badros. JavaML: a Markup Language for Java Source Code. *Computer Networks: The International Journal of Computer and Telecommunications Networking*, 33(1-6):159–177, 2000.

[18] Paula Leinonen. Automating XML document structure transformations. In *DocEng '03: Proceedings of the 2003 ACM symposium on Document engineering*, pages 26–28, New York, NY, USA, 2003. ACM Press.

[19] Mikaël Peltier, Françoir Ziserman, and Jean Bézivin. On levels of model transformation. In *XML Europe 2000*, pages 1–17, Paris, France, 2000.

[20] Tadeusz Pankowski. A High-Level Language for Specifying XML Data Transformations. In *Advances in Databases and Information Systems, 8th East European Conference, ADBIS 2004, Budapest, Hungary, September 22-25, 2004, Proceesing*, volume 3255 of *Lecture Notes in Computer Science*, pages 159–172. Springer, 2004.

[21] Object Management Group. MOF QVT Final Adopted Specification ptc/05-11-01. http://www.omg.org/cgi-bin/apps/doc?ptc/05-11-01.pdf, November 2005.

[22] Oliver Becker. Transforming XML on the Fly – How STX Enables the Processing of Large Documents. In *XML Europe 2003 Conference Proceedings*, May 2003.

[23] Alexandru Berlea and Helmut Seidl. Transforming XML Documents using fxt. *Journal of Computing and Information Technology*, 10(1):19–35, March 2002.

[24] Decisionsoft. XML Script 2.0, X-Trac v2 (XPath) release date 10.10.2002. http://www.xmlscript.org, 2002.

[25] Igor Tatarinov, Zachary G. Ives, Alon Y. Halevy, and Daniel S. Weld. Updating XML. In *SIGMOD '01: Proceedings of the 2001 ACM SIGMOD international conference on Management of data, Santa Barbara, California, United States*, pages 413–424, New York, NY, USA, 2001. ACM Press.

New Trends in Software Methodologies, Tools and Techniques
H. Fujita and D. Pisanelli (Eds.)
IOS Press, 2007

Toward Solving Equations in Kleene Algebras

F. Lajeunesse-Robert and B. Ktari

Computer Science Department,
Laval University, Quebec, Canada.
E-mail: {francois.lajeunesse-robert, ktari}@ift.ulaval.ca

Abstract. This work aims to investigate conditions under which program analysis can be viewed as algebraically solving equations involving terms of subclasses of Kleene algebras and variables. In this paper, we show how to solve a kind of linear equations in which the variables appear only on one side of the equality sign, over an idempotent semiring with identity and zero. Furthermore, we give some ideas showing how to extend the resolution method to other classes of equations and algebraic structures.

Keywords. Program Verification, Program Equivalence, Kleene Algebras, Equation Solving, Resolution

Introduction

Kleene algebras are algebraic structures which are largely used to reason about computer programs. For instance, it could be used to prove equivalence between two programs [1,2] by making various algebraic handling. However, what happens when two programs are not equivalent? Must we stop there or it could be interesting to go further and to ask ourself what does it lacks to one of them so that they become equivalent ? In the context of Kleene algebras, to answer the last question we need to be able to solve equational systems. Another possible application of the resolution of equations in Kleene algebra comes from model checking. For example, given a property and a program, both expressed as terms in Kleene algebra, it could be important to know what is missing in the program so that it satisfies the property. This problem is in fact what motivated us to investigate the resolution of equations in Kleene algebra.

From the beginning, we have decided to restrict ourselves to the resolution of linear equations only. The reason of it is obvious. Higher the degree of equation is, higher is the difficulty to solve it. Also, when we look further to solve this kind of equation, it soon appears that the operator "*" of Kleene algebra is a big challenge. This operator can be seen as an iteration over a program. It surely increases the expressivity of the algebra but it also makes it harder to reason on it, especially when we are trying to solve equations. For this reason we decided to consider equations that do not include the operator "*". Finally, we noticed that there is a significant difference between equations in which variables appear on both side and those in which variables appear on one side of the equal sign. Equations with variables on both side are much more difficult to solve than the others because they are a kind of recursive definition of an expression. For that reason, we mostly considered the equations in which the variable appears on one side of the equal sign.

In universal algebra, the unification theory is commonly used to solve equational systems for the most general case. It consists to find a substitution which will replace the variables of an equation with different terms of the algebra so that the equality hold. For instance, consider this equation:

$$pX + tY = Zq + tp$$

where the set of variables is $\{X, Y, Z\}$ and p, t, q are terms in the algebra. Then, it is easy to find the substitution $[X/q, Y/p, Z/p]$ which allows to unify the equation. The concept of unification is general and theoretically applicable to all classes of algebras. However, if we restrict it to a certain class of algebra it becomes easier to be found and used. From this perspective, work were made on the unification of linear equations in semiring [3], which is significantly closer to the unification in Kleene algebra; algebra which is an idempotent semiring augmented with axioms defining the operator star.

In the literature related to Kleene algebras we have not found much work done on solving linear equations. The only available work [4] tried to use matrices to solve equations of the form

$$X = aX + b$$

where $X = [X_1 \ X_2 \ \ldots \ X_n]^t, b = [b_1 \ b_2 \ \ldots \ b_n]^t$ and a is a matrix of size $n \times n$. Considering the limitation of this approach, we want to find new techniques allowing to solve a larger class of equations.

So we based our approach on finding some laws and hypotheses allowing to solve equations in a similar way we solve them in classical algebra. From there we soon discovered that the comparison of these two algebras for solving equations was very limited. But this gave us a start up and we were able to develop a technique for solving linear equations. This technique is what we present in this paper.

In section 1, we present the definition of Kleene algebra in the sense of Kozen [5] and a variant of it, named Kleene algebra with tests, used to represent *while* programs according to a simple translation function. We will also explain in a more detailed way what we mean by verifying that two programs are equivalent and how solving equations in Kleene algebra can help to create program equivalencies. The actual method developed for solving linear equations in which the variable appears only on one side of the equality sign over an idempotent semiring is given in section 2. To do so, we first introduce some concepts used for solving equations. Then we present the approach itself by showing how to verify that two programs are equivalent and how this could be extended to solve equations. We conclude this section with several examples of resolution. Section 3 is devoted to three possible extensions of the resolution technique to deal with other kind of linear equations that we are currently working on. However, restricting ourselves to idempotent semirings makes it impossible to solve all theses variations of linear equations. Section 4 introduces future works to apply the solving of equations to model checking. Finally, section 5 summarizes the work that we have done and gives some possible applications of solving equations over idempotent semirings.

1. Kleene Algebras

1.1. Idempotent semiring and Kleene algebra

Historically, the concept of Kleene algebra comes from a question raised by Stephen Cole Kleene asking if it is possible to give a sound and complete axiomatization of the equational theory of regular set. Since there, a lot of work were done so that several different axiomatizations of Kleene algebra are available now. Hereafter, we present the axiomatization proposed by Kozen in [5].

Idempotent semiring   An idempotent semiring with identity and neutral element, or idempotent semiring for short, is an algebraic structure $\langle A, +, \cdot, 0, 1 \rangle$ such that :

$$
\begin{aligned}
x + (y + z) &= (x + y) + z & x \cdot 0 &= 0 \\
x + 0 &= x & 0 \cdot x &= 0 \\
x + y &= y + x & x \cdot 1 &= x \\
x + x &= x & 1 \cdot x &= x \\
x \cdot (y + z) &= x \cdot y + x \cdot z & (x + y) \cdot z &= x \cdot z + y \cdot z \\
x \cdot (y \cdot z) &= (x \cdot y) \cdot z
\end{aligned}
$$

Kleene Algebra   A Kleene algebra is an algebraic structure $\langle K, +, \cdot, {}^*, 0, 1 \rangle$ such that $\langle K, +, \cdot, 0, 1 \rangle$ is an idempotent semiring and that the operator "*" satisfies the following axioms :

$$1 + aa^* \le a^* \tag{1}$$

$$1 + a^*a \le a^* \tag{2}$$

$$ax \le x \to a^*x \le x \tag{3}$$

$$xa \le x \to xa^* \le x \tag{4}$$

where $\le$ is the partial order over the elements of K, i.e $x \le y \leftrightarrow x + y = y$. Precedences between operators, from high to low, are "*", "$\cdot$", "+". We use also "xy" instead of "$x \cdot y$" and "x^n" instead of $\underbrace{x \cdot x \cdot \ldots \cdot x}_{n \text{ times}}$. In others words, any idempotent semiring for which one can define an operator "*" satisfying the axioms (1) to (4) is a Kleene algebra. In this paper, we restrict ourselves to idempotent semirings (since Kleene algebras forgetting their "*" operators are idempotent semirings), and let for future works the extension to full Kleene algebras.

We can consider Kleene algebra as being an abstraction of computer programs. It is commonly agreed that "0" indicates the program *halt*, "1" indicates the program *skip*, "+" indicates a non-deterministic choice between two programs, "$\cdot$" indicates the sequencing of programs and "*" indicates the iteration over programs. Therefore, it is easy to define a program in terms of a Kleene algebra expression. However, to put things into perspective, there is an abstraction which is closer to the programs that we use in real life. The following introduces Kleene algebra with tests.

Kleene algebra with tests   A Kleene algebra with tests is an algebraic structure $\langle K, B, +, \cdot, ^*, \overline{}, 0, 1 \rangle$ such that $\langle K, +, \cdot, ^*, 0, 1 \rangle$ is a Kleene algebra, that $B \subseteq K$ and that $\langle B, +, \cdot, \overline{}, 0, 1 \rangle$ is a boolean algebra.

Concretely, it means that instead of having only actions now there are also tests which model conditional structures of control. Let consider the following example of translation of simple programs towards their equivalent in Kleene algebra with tests :

$$p \; ; q = pq$$
$$\textbf{if } b \textbf{ then } p \textbf{ else } q = bp + \bar{b}q$$
$$\textbf{if } b \textbf{ then } p = bp + \bar{b}$$
$$\textbf{while } b \textbf{ do } p = (bp)^*\bar{b}$$

where p and q are atomic programs and b and $\bar{b}$ are tests such that $\bar{b}$ is the complement of b.

With such algebraical representation of programs, we can easily prove the equivalence of two programs. To illustrate that, we take a simple example drawn from the paper of Kozen introducing Kleene algebra with tests [1]. This example is about the equivalence of the program :

$$s; bc + \bar{b}\bar{c};$$
$$\textbf{if } b \textbf{ then begin } p; q \textbf{ end}$$
$$\textbf{else begin } p; r \textbf{ end}$$

where the atomic program p doesn't commute with the test b, that is $bp \neq pb$, and the program :

$$s; bc + \bar{b}\bar{c};$$
$$p; \textbf{ if } c \textbf{ then } q \textbf{ else } r$$

where c is a new test which commutes with p, that is $cp = pc$. By translating theses programs into Kleene algebra with tests (and removing the leading s), the problem of equivalence transforms itself into checking if the equality

$$(bc + \bar{b}\bar{c})(bpq + \bar{b}pr) = (bc + \bar{b}\bar{c})p(cq + \bar{c}r) \tag{5}$$

is valid.

To prove this equation, one way is to simplify the terms on each side of the equation to obtain two identical expressions on each side of the equal sign :

$$(bc + \bar{b}\bar{c})(bpq + \bar{b}pr)$$
$$= \langle \text{ Distributivity of } \cdot \text{ over } + \rangle$$
$$bcbpq + \bar{b}\bar{c}bpq + bc\bar{b}pr + \bar{b}\bar{c}\bar{b}pr$$
$$= \langle \text{ Commutativity of tests } \rangle$$
$$bbcpq + \bar{b}b\bar{c}pq + b\bar{b}cpr + \bar{b}\bar{b}\bar{c}pr$$
$$= \langle \text{ Laws } xx = x \text{ and } x\bar{x} = 0 \rangle$$
$$bcpq + \bar{b}\bar{c}pr$$

$$(bc + \bar{b}\bar{c})p(cq + \bar{c}r)$$
$$= \langle \text{ Distributivity of } \cdot \text{ over } + \rangle$$
$$bcpcq + \bar{b}\bar{c}pcq + bcp\bar{c}q + \bar{b}\bar{c}p\bar{c}r$$
$$= \langle Hypothesis : pc = cp \rangle$$
$$bccpq + \bar{b}\bar{c}cpq + bc\bar{c}pq + \bar{b}\bar{c}\bar{c}pr$$
$$= \langle \text{ Laws } xx = x \text{ and } x\bar{x} = 0 \rangle$$
$$bcpq + \bar{b}\bar{c}pr$$

This example illustrates how Kleene algebras can be useful to reason about programs and in particular about program equivalence. However, once we prove that two programs are equivalent, it remains to know how we can find what is missing in a program in order to make it equivalent to another program. This problem of finding a missing part in a program corresponds in fact to the resolution of an equation where programs are represented as Kleene algebra expressions. An equation in Kleene algebra of the form

$$Xq = pq$$

where X is a variable and p, q are atomic actions means that one wants to know which program must be carried out with the action q so that it is equivalent to the program pq. In that case, the answer is obvious but let us consider the following less coarse example drawn from the example we just presented :

$$X(bpq + \bar{b}pr) = Xp(cq + \bar{c}r)$$

for which we know that a solution is $X = (bc + \bar{b}\bar{c})$ because we prove that the equality (5) is valid. In this case, we can't just simplify each side to obtain the solution. That being said, we will not present a method for solving this kind of equation because it involves tests and developing such a theory would require a new paper.

2. Solving equations

2.1. Setting in context

In the following section, we will show how to solve a kind of linear equations in which the variable appears only on one side of the equal sign, over an idempotent semiring with identity and zero, idempotent semiring for short. Even if we have solely talked about solving equations using Kleene algebras so far, we have decided to restrict the scope of the paper further more to idempotent semirings only. This restriction allows a first step toward solving equations in idempotent semirings equipped with a " * " operator (hence, Kleene algebras).

As we have seen earlier, when reasoning using the Kleene algebra, it's often needed to postulate some hypotheses such as commutativity of "·" for some elements to prove the equivalence of two programs. The method developed for solving equations should be independent of any possible hypotheses in the sense that for any set of initial hypotheses it has to be usable. It's likely that trying to develop such a general technique would not be feasible because the set of all possible hypotheses might not be finite. To avoid this kind of problem, we will only consider idempotent semiring interpreted on the algebra of regular set over an alphabet Σ [6], Reg_{Σ}. Those idempotent semiring can be characterized by the interpretation R_{Σ} defined between the term algebra and the algebra of regular set. This interpretation is defined over the atomic elements as follows :

$$R_{\Sigma}(a) = \begin{cases} \{a\} & \text{if } a \in \Sigma \\ \{\varepsilon\} & \text{if } a = 1 \\ \emptyset & \text{if } a = 0 \end{cases}$$

and extend homomorphically over all elements. Thus we only consider Kleene algebra which have a meaning on the model of regular languages. That been said, there is other models of Kleene algebra such that the relational one [7]. In this model, a Kleene algebra is seen as a set of relation where each element x of Σ is mapped to the relation $\{(x, x)\}$, 1 is mapped to the identity relation, 0 is mapped to the empty relation and extend homomorphically over all elements. Nevertheless there is no natural model of a Kleene algebra that include all the other.

The set Σ corresponds in fact to the minimal generating set of the algebra, denoted by $\mathcal{G}$. Since Σ is of finite size for regular sets, it comes down to say that we restrict the equations to a subclass of Kleene algebra having a finite generating set. Moreover, in order to simplify the reasoning surrounding the idempotent semiring, we define a σ-normal form which is used to standardize the representation of the elements of the universe. In fact, once elements are expressed in this form, it becomes easier to apply various laws which will allow to simplify equations. Before defining the σ-normal form we need to introduce the notion of sequence.

Definition 1 (Sequence). *Let $\mathcal{G}$ be the minimal generating set of an idempotent semiring. A sequence, denoted by σ, is defined in an inductive way as follows :*

- *0 and 1 are sequences.*
- *If σ is a sequence and if $x \in \mathcal{G}$ then $\sigma \cdot x$ is a sequence.*

It is important to note that if the interpretation R_Σ is considered, the sequence σ corresponds to a word generated by the alphabet σ. Moreover, we will designate the set of all the sequences generated from the minimal generating set $\mathcal{G}$ as $\sigma_\mathcal{G}$. It is now possible to define the σ-normal form.

Definition 2 (σ-normal form). *Let $\langle A, +, \cdot, 0, 1 \rangle$ be an idempotent semiring, then the σ-normal form of the element $x \in A$ is defined in an inductive way as follows :*

- *A sequence σ is under σ-normal form.*
- *If x is under the σ-normal form and if σ is a sequence then $x + \sigma$ is under σ-normal form.*

Example 1. *The σ-normal form of the expression "$a(bc + d)(da + bd)f$" is*

$$abcdaf + abcbdf + addaf + adbdf$$

In an intuitive way, an element of the set A in its σ-normal form corresponds to the representation of this element in term of the elements of minimal generating set for which we distributed "$\cdot$" on "$+$" each time it was possible to make it. It appears then obvious that any elements can be represented in a σ-normal form because they all have been generated from a composition of elements of minimal generating set. This enables us to represent any element $a \in A$ of an idempotent semiring by

$$a = \sum_{i \in I} \sigma_i$$

where $\sigma_i \in \sigma_\mathcal{G}$ for all i belonging to a finite set I.

When we consider idempotent semirings under the interpretation R_Σ these are also residual lattices [8]. That is to say, that it is then possible to define operators who play the role of the reverse of "$\cdot$". Nevertheless, independently of the interpretation that we make of Kleene algebra by limiting our scope to residual subclasses of the algebra to solve linear equations facilitate the isolation of a variable by some algebraic manipulations. Having said that, nothing indicates that the resolution becomes simpler because it will be necessary to define more operators. We are therefore going to end this section by introducing residuals structures and what is the exact meaning of an idempotent semiring being a residuated lattice.

The structure $\langle P, \cdot, e, \backslash, /, \leq \rangle$ is named a residual po-monoid [9] if "$\cdot$" is associative, e is the identity element and if it respect the following property :

$$x \cdot y \leq z \Leftrightarrow x \leq z/y \Leftrightarrow y \leq x \backslash z \tag{6}$$

for all x, y, z belonging to P, where "$\leq$" indicates a partial order on the elements of P. It is said that the operators "$\backslash$" and "$/$" are respectively right and left residues. Intuitively, x/y and $y \backslash x$ can be seen as being a generalization of division in classical algebra meaning "x over y" and "y under x". In these two cases x corresponds to the dividend while y corresponds to the divisor. Besides, the existence of the residual operators rises a series of properties which are valid for any residuated po-monoids where the proof are given in [10]. Her some of them that we'll refer to later on.

Proposition 1. *Let P be a residuated po-monoid.*

1. *If $\bigsqcup X$ and $\bigsqcap Y$ exist for any $X, Y \subset P$ then for all $z \in P$, $\bigsqcap_{x \in X} x \backslash z$ and $\bigsqcap_{y \in Y} z \backslash y$ exist and*

$$\left(\bigsqcup X \right) \backslash z = \bigsqcap_{x \in X} x \backslash z \quad \text{and} \quad x \backslash \left(\bigsqcap Y \right) = \bigsqcap_{y \in Y} z \backslash y$$

2. $(xy) \backslash z = y \backslash (x \backslash z)$

It should be noted that the preceding properties have an equivalent mirror form utilizing the operator $/$. To obtain that, we have to read the expressions backward by substituting $x \cdot y$ by $y \cdot x$ and x/y by $y \backslash x$. Therefore each time we will give a result for an expression it will also be true for its mirror form.

The algebraic structure $\langle A, +, \cdot, \backslash, /, 0, 1 \rangle$ is a residual idempotent semiring, or RISR for short, if $\langle A, +, \cdot, 0, 1 \rangle$ is an idempotent semiring and $\langle A, \cdot, 1 \backslash, /, \leq \rangle$ is a residual po-monoid. Note that in these propositions, the operator $+$ is equivalent to join, denoted by $\sqcup$, on behalf of the definition given for $\leq$. Moreover, if A is a lattice [11], then A is called a residual lattice.

A common point in residual structures, that we have just introduced, is that they all have a minimal element and as a consequent of that they also have a maximum element $0 \backslash 0$ which we denote by "∞". The approach for solving equations presented in section 2.2.2 doesn't take into account the existence of such an element. However, latter on in the section 3 we will present the step to be done so that equations using the "∞" element can be handled.

2.2. Approach

Linear equations with one variable are defined over idempotent semiring as well as over Kleene algebra as any equation written in the form

$$\sum_{i \in I} a_i X b_i + c = \sum_{j \in J} d_j X e_j + f \tag{7}$$

where a_i, b_i, c, d_i, e_i, f belong to the universe of the algebra for all i and for all j belonging respectively to finite sets I and J. For its part, X indicates a variable. However, in what follows we shall be interested more particularly in linear equations for which the variable is present only in one side of equality symbol. We will reconsider later, in the section 3, the case where the variable is present on both side. Besides, before talking about the resolution of equations, we need to be able to compare any two elements of the algebra. This is owed to the fact that to solve certain equations we need to prove the equivalence of two programs. Let us take for instance, the equation $pX + q = r$, where $p, q, r \in K$, which can be also written in the equivalent form

$$pX \leq r \wedge q \leq r \wedge r \leq pX + q$$

following the application of the laws

$$x = y \Leftrightarrow x \leq y \wedge y \leq x \qquad y + z \leq x \Leftrightarrow y \leq x \wedge z \leq x \ .$$

It is then obvious that if this equation has a solution it is necessary that q is less than or equal to r.

2.2.1. Equivalence of programs

By expressing the elements of A under the σ-normal form, verifying that two of them are equivalent is like considering the equality

$$\sum_{i \in I} \sigma_i = \sum_{j \in J} \sigma'_j$$

where $\sigma_i, \sigma_j \in \sigma_{\mathcal{G}}$ for all i and for all j belonging respectively to the finite set I and J. From this form it's then easy to apply the following rewriting lemma so that the equivalence of two elements of A becomes a series of equivalences between a sequence and an element of A.

Lemma 1 (Rewriting). *Let $\langle A, +, \cdot, 0, 1 \rangle$ be an idempotent semiring and $x_i, y_j \in A$ for all i and for all j belonging respectively to the finite set I and J. Then*

$$\sum_{i \in I} x_i \leq \sum_{j \in J} y_j \Leftrightarrow \bigwedge_{i \in I} \left(x_i \leq \sum_{j \in J} y_j \right)$$

Example 2. *By applying the rewriting lemma, the equation "$abc + cdd + X = aa + ab + cdadc$" becomes*

$$abc \leq aa + ab + cdadc \wedge cdd \leq aa + ab + cdadc \wedge X \leq aa + ab + cdadc \wedge$$
$$aa \leq abc + cdd + X \wedge ab \leq abc + cdd + X \wedge cdadc \leq abc + cdd + X$$

Then, we only have to be able to prove the validity of expressions having the following form :

$$\sigma \leq \sum_{j \in J} \sigma'_j \tag{8}$$

where $\sigma, \sigma_j \in \sigma_{\mathcal{G}}$ for all j belonging to the finite set J. At this point, we use the hypotheses on which we only consider the idempotent semiring for which the interpretation R_{Σ} can be applied so that it will be possible to verify if the equality (8) is valid or not. By applying R_{Σ} toward inequalities of the form given by (8) we obtain :

$$\{\sigma\} \subseteq \bigcup_{j \in J} \{\sigma'_j\}$$

However, if we refers ourselves to the set theory such an inequality is valid if and only if there is a $j \in J$ such as $\{\sigma\} \subseteq \{\sigma_j\}$. Moreover, we have that $\{\sigma\} \subseteq \{\sigma_j\}$ if and only if $\sigma = \sigma_j$, i.e. the words σ and σ_j are the same one. These properties are translated, in Kleene algebra, by the identities

$$\sigma \leq \sum_{j \in J} \sigma'_j \Leftrightarrow \bigvee_{j \in J} \sigma \leq \sigma_j \tag{9}$$

$$\sigma \leq \sigma' \Leftrightarrow \sigma = \sigma' \tag{10}$$

$$\sigma \cdot x = \sigma' \cdot y \Leftrightarrow \sigma = \sigma' \wedge x = y \tag{11}$$

where $\sigma, \sigma_j, \sigma' \in \sigma_{\mathcal{G}}$ for all j belonging to the finite set J and that $x, y \in \mathcal{G}$, since R_{Σ} is an isomorphism. In fact, such back and forth from an algebra to another tell us that under R_{Σ} interpretation, checking program equivalence of elements of A reduces to check whether they are syntactically equivalent. This result was rather foreseeable due to the fact that R_{Σ} interpretation is considered. Nevertheless, instead of comparing sequences directly between them to know if they correspond, we introduce the residual operators who will be used to make these checks.

We introduce residual operators allowing us to do syntactic comparisons in a purely algebraic way. In fact, residuals will be used to isolate variables in equations. It's well known that residuals are defined by (see [12])

$$X/Y = \{z \in \Sigma^* | (\forall y \in Y) zy \in X\} \qquad Y \backslash X = \{z \in \Sigma^* | (\forall y \in Y) yz \in X\}$$

over the idempotent semiring of the formal languages over an alphabet Σ, i.e. LAN(Σ). Since we are interested in valid equations over R_{Σ} we define residuals according to the above definition.

Theorem 1. *The following laws hold for any idempotent semiring under the R_{Σ} interpretation.*

$$y \backslash x = 1 \qquad \textit{if } x, y \in \mathcal{G} \textit{ and } x = y \tag{12}$$

$$y \backslash x = 0 \qquad \textit{if } x, y \in \mathcal{G} \textit{ and } x \neq y \tag{13}$$

$$1 \backslash x = x \qquad \textit{if } x \in A \tag{14}$$

$$z \backslash (y + x) = z \backslash y + z \backslash x \qquad \textit{if } x, y \in A \textit{ and } z \in \mathcal{G} \tag{15}$$

$$z \backslash (y \cdot x) = (z \backslash y) \cdot x \qquad \textit{if } x \in A \textit{ and } z, y \in \mathcal{G} \tag{16}$$

$$z \backslash (\infty \cdot x) = z \backslash x + \infty \cdot x \qquad \textit{if } x \in A \textit{ and } z \in \mathcal{G} \tag{17}$$

2.2.2. Resolution

Starting from the definition of a linear equation given in (7) and expressing it in term of elements of A under their σ-normal form, the equations where the variable is present only in one side of the equality sign are expressed as

$$\sum_{i \in I} \sigma_i X \sigma_i' + \sum_{j \in J} \sigma_j'' = \sum_{k \in K} \sigma_k''' \tag{18}$$

where $\sigma_i, \sigma_i', \sigma_j'', \sigma_k''' \in \sigma_\mathcal{G}$ for all i, for all j and for all k belonging respectively to the the finite sets I, J, K. To solve this equation, we first apply the rewriting lemma such that we obtain the equivalent equation

$$\bigwedge_{i \in I} \left(\sigma_i X \sigma_i' \leq \sum_{k \in K} \sigma_k''' \right) \wedge \bigwedge_{j \in J} \left(\sigma_j'' \leq \sum_{k \in K} \sigma_k''' \right) \wedge \bigwedge_{k \in K} \left(\sigma_k''' \leq \sum_{i \in I} \sigma_i X \sigma_i' + \sum_{j \in J} \sigma_j'' \right)$$

and then we have to solve simpler equations. Moreover, under this equivalent form, we notice that the equation (18) has a solution if:

$$\sigma_j'' \leq \sum_{k \in K} \sigma_k'''$$

is valid for all $j \in J$. Once theses inequalities are verified we can then further proceed in the solving of the simpler equations.

First of all, we will consider inequalities of the form:

$$\sigma_i X \sigma_i' \leq \sum_{k \in K} \sigma_k''' \tag{19}$$

By applying many times the definition of the residuals given in (6) it is easy to isolate the variable X for all $i \in I$ to obtain inequalities of the form $X \leq p_i$ where $p_i \in A$ for all i belonging to the finite set I. It follows that the elements of A less than p_i, for all i belonging to the finite set I, are solutions. Formally, it means that all elements of the set $\{x \in A | \bigwedge_{i \in I} x \leq p_i\}$ are solutions. And if the meet operator exists, as in the case of the R_Σ interpretation, it's then equivalent to say that every X less than or equals to $\prod_{i \in I} p_i$ is a solution. It follows that:

$$\bigwedge_{i \in I} \left(\sigma_i X \sigma_i' \leq \sum_{k \in K} \sigma_k''' \right) \Leftrightarrow X \leq \prod_{i \in I} \sigma_i \backslash \left(\sum_{k \in K} \sigma_k''' \right) / \sigma_i' \tag{20}$$

This means that to be able to solve (18) under the R_Σ interpretation we have to know how to calculate the meet of any two elements, which is done by using the properties (9)-(11), i.e. doing like we use to do in set theory. Once this solution is obtained, it's easy to verify if (18) has a solution by substituting X by $\bigsqcap_{i\in I}\sigma_i\backslash\left(\sum_{k\in K}\sigma_k'''\right)/\sigma_i'$.

However, if we are interested in knowing the exact solution one has to consider also the inequality of the form

$$\sum_{k\in K}\sigma_k''' \leq \sum_{i\in I}\sigma_i X\sigma_i' + \sum_{j\in J}\sigma_j'' \tag{21}$$

In this case, it is also possible to isolate X for all i belonging to the finite set I by using the fact that the residual defined under the R_Σ interpretation has the monoticity property and that for all $\sigma \in \sigma_G$ we have that $\sigma/\sigma = 1$. Also, it has to be noted that if the equation (21) doesn't have a solution, the equation resulting by dividing each side with the same element may have a solution since the monoticity is obtained from a strict implication. Concretely, this means that once we have a solution to the new inequality we have to validate that it is also a solution of (21), i.e., after substituting X by the solution, the latter inequality must be valid.

Thus if we fix an index i at value l, it is possible to isolate the variable according to

$$\sigma_l\backslash\left(\sum_{k\in K}\sigma_k'''\right)/\sigma_l' \leq X + \sigma_l\backslash\left(\sum_{i\neq l\in I}\sigma_i X\sigma_i'\right)/\sigma_l' + \sigma_l\backslash\left(\sum_{j\in J}\sigma_j''\right)/\sigma_l' \tag{22}$$

Notice that it is possible that we have to calculate $\sigma\backslash X/\sigma'$ for any $\sigma, \sigma' \in \sigma_G$ while trying to evaluate $\sigma_l\backslash\left(\sum_{i\neq l\in I}\sigma_i X\sigma_i'\right)/\sigma_l'$. But as we have not defined residuals over variables, it is impossible to do so. Nevertheless, independently of the result of such a division, it is obvious that any X larger than $\sigma_l\backslash\left(\sum_{k\in K}\sigma_k'''\right)/\sigma_l'$ is a solution of (21) if such a solution exists.

That being said, even if there exists a solution of the inequality it is possible that $\sigma_l\backslash\left(\sum_{k\in K}\sigma_k'''\right)/\sigma_l'$ is not the least one possible for (21) for two reasons. The first one comes from the fact that there might be a constant term on the right side of the inequality sign. To illustrate what is the impact of this on the resolution, let consider the inequality

$$c \leq X + c$$

where $c \in A$. In this cases, by limiting ourselves to the result given in (22) we found that c is a lower limit of X where the true lower limit is "0". This is due to the fact that the meet of the constant terms on each side of the inequality sign is not equal to "0". Intuitively, this is a kind of equivalence found in classic algebra when there is a same element on each side, i.e. $X + a = c + a$. To take into account such cases, we introduce the operator "$-$" as follows :

$$x - y \overset{\Delta}{=} \sum_{z\leq x \wedge z\nleq y} z$$

for all $x, y \in A$, which can be seen as a reverse of the operator "$+$".

From this definition, it follows that:

$$x \leq (x - y) + y \tag{23}$$

$$x - y \leq x \tag{24}$$

for all $x, y, z \in A$. Under the R_Σ interpretation, this operator corresponds, in fact, to the difference between two sets and it is easy to calculate the result of $x - y$ by using the properties (9) to (11). Moreover, it is possible to prove that the residuals operators distribute over "$-$" under the R_Σ interpretation, i.e. :

$$(x - y)/z = x/z - y/z$$

for all $x, y \in A$ and for all $z \in \mathcal{G}$. Thus, if $\sigma_l \backslash \left(\sum_{k \in K} \sigma_k''' \right) / \sigma_l'$ is a solution of (21), then $\sigma_l \backslash \left(\sum_{k \in K} \sigma_k''' - \sum_{j \in J} \sigma_j'' \right) / \sigma_l'$ is also a solution according to the identities (23), (24) and from the distributivity of the residual operators over "$-$", such a solution is less than or equal to the former one.

The second reason which explain why $\sigma_l \backslash \left(\sum_{k \in K} \sigma_k''' \right) / \sigma_l'$ is not necessarily the least solution of (21) comes from the fact that a part of the solution is generated by $\sigma_l \backslash \left(\sum_{i \neq l \in I} \sigma_i X \sigma_i' \right) / \sigma_l'$ when X is replaced by it. As an example, let's consider the inequality

$$adb + aadbb \leq aXb + aaXbb$$

for which we can obtain the solutions $d + adb$ and d whether we decide to isolate X from respectively the sequences aXb and $aaXbb$. In the first case, we realize that this solution is not the least one because when we replace X by $d + adb$ in the term $X + aXb$ the sequence adb is generated by aXb because d is included in the solution. We must then subtract from the solution the sequences generated by the other occurrences of the variable, i.e. the sequences generated by $\sigma_l \backslash \left(\sum_{i \neq l \in I} \sigma_i X \sigma_i' \right) / \sigma_l'$ when X is replaced by $\sigma_l \backslash \left(\sum_{k \in K} \sigma_k''' \right) / \sigma_l'$. This implies that if (21) has a solution it has a least one who is equal to

$$\sigma_l \backslash \left(\left(\left(\sum_{k \in K} \sigma_k''' - \sum_{j \in J} \sigma_j'' \right) - \sum_{i \neq l \in I} \sigma_i \left(\sigma_l \backslash \left(\sum_{k \in K} \sigma_k''' \right) / \sigma_l' \right) \sigma_i' \right) / \sigma_l' \tag{25}$$

for any fixed index l. It's then enough to replace X by this value in (21) and to verify if the inequality is valid so we can be sure that this is really a solution.

2.3. Examples

In this section, we consider several examples of program verification problem and we show how they can be resolved by solving equations involving variables. For the following examples we consider only idempotent semirings under the R_Σ interpretation.

Example 3. *Let's first consider the following program :*

init( );
v := getVal( );
if *(v != null)* **then begin** *f(v);* **end else begin** *g(v);* **end**
exit( );

By stating that $i \stackrel{\Delta}{=} init()$, $a \stackrel{\Delta}{=} v := getVal()$ and $e \stackrel{\Delta}{=} exit()$ are atomic programs, we want to prove that the program starts with i and ends with e, i.e. $ia(f + g)e = iXe$. Rewriting this equation under it's σ-normal form and using the rewriting lemma (1) we have that it's equivalent to $iafe + iage \leq iXe \wedge iXe \leq iafe + iage$.

Thus, let us first consider the inequalities where X appears in the left :

$$iXe \leq iafe + iage$$
$$\Leftrightarrow \langle \text{ Definition of the residuals (6) } \rangle$$
$$Xe \leq i\backslash(iafe + iage)$$
$$\Leftrightarrow \langle \text{ Law (16), (15) } \rangle$$
$$Xe \leq (i\backslash i)afe + (i\backslash i)age$$
$$\Leftrightarrow \langle i\backslash i = 1 \rangle$$
$$Xe \leq afe + age$$
$$\Leftrightarrow \langle \text{ Definition of the residuals (6) } \rangle$$
$$X \leq (afe + age)/e$$
$$\Leftrightarrow \langle \text{ Law (16), (15) }, e/e = 1 \rangle$$
$$X \leq af + ag$$

We could also found this result by directly applying the identity given in (20). Considering that $\sigma_1''' = iafe, \sigma_2''' = iage, K = \{1, 2\}, \sigma_1 = i, \sigma_1' = e$ and $I = \{1\}$, we have to calculate

$$\prod_{i \in \{1\}} \sigma_i \backslash \left(\sum_{k \in \{1,2\}} \sigma_k''' \right) / \sigma_i' = \sigma_1 \backslash (\sigma_1''' + \sigma_2''') / \sigma_1' = i\backslash(iafe + iage)/e$$

then by applying laws (16) (15) and using the properties "$i\backslash i = 1$" and "$e/e = 1$", we find that the previous term is equal to $af + ag$.

Now, let's consider the inequalities where X is at the right side of the inequality symbol:

$$iafe + iage \leq iXe$$
$$\Rightarrow \langle \text{ Monotocity of residuals } \rangle$$
$$(iafe + iage)/e \leq (iXe)/e$$
$$\Leftrightarrow \langle \text{ Law (16), (15) } \rangle$$
$$iaf(e/e) + iag(e/e) \leq iX(e/e)$$
$$\Leftrightarrow \langle e/e = 1 \rangle$$
$$iaf + iag \leq iX$$
$$\Rightarrow \langle \text{ Monotocity of residuals } \rangle$$
$$i\backslash(iaf + iag) \leq i\backslash(iX)$$
$$\Leftrightarrow \langle \text{ Law (16), (15) } \rangle$$
$$(i\backslash i)af + (i\backslash i)ag \leq (i\backslash i)X$$
$$\Leftrightarrow \langle i/i = 1 \rangle$$
$$af + ag \leq X$$

So, we deduce that $af + ag$ is a solution to $ia(f + g)e = iXe$ because the lower limit is equal to the upper limit. As for the upper limit we can apply directly the result given in (25) to calculate the lower limit. Using $\sigma_i, \sigma'_i, \sigma'''_k, I, K$ as previously defined when calculating the upper limit and that $J = \emptyset$, $l = 1$, we have that

$$\sigma_1 \backslash (((\sigma'''_1 + \sigma'''_2) - 0) - 0)/\sigma'_1 = i \backslash (iafe + iage)/e = af + ag$$

Example 4. *Consider the following program :*

> *open(f);*
>   **if** *(f != null)* **then begin** *buff = read(f); write(mem,buff); closeAll( );* **end**
>   **else begin** *buff = read(f); write(mem,buff); close(f);* **end**

By stating that : $o \triangleq$ *open(f)*, $c \triangleq$ *close(f)*, $r \triangleq$ *buff = read(f)*, $c' \triangleq$ *closeAll* and $w \triangleq$ *write(mem,buff)* are atomic programs, we want to prove that $o(rwc' + rwc) = oX(c+c')$, i.e., the program starts with o and ends with either c or c'. Rewriting this equation under it's σ-normal form and using the rewriting lemma (1) we have that it's equivalent to $orwc' + orwc \leq oXc + oXc' \wedge oXc \leq orwc' + orwc \wedge oXc' \leq orwc' + orwc$.

Thus, let us first consider the inequalities where X is at the left of the inequality symbol $\leq$:

<table>
<tr><td>

$oXc \leq orwc' + orwc$
$\Leftrightarrow \langle$ Definition of the residuals (6) $\rangle$
$oX \leq (orwc' + orwc)/c$
$\Leftrightarrow \langle$ Law (16), (15) $\rangle$
$oX \leq orw(c'/c) + orw(c/c)$
$\Leftrightarrow \langle c'/c = 0, c/c = 1 \rangle$
$oX \leq orw$
$\Leftrightarrow \langle$ Definition of the residuals (6) $\rangle$
$X \leq o\backslash(orw)$
$\Leftrightarrow \langle$ Law (16), (15) $, o\backslash o = 1 \rangle$
$X \leq rw$

</td><td>

$oXc' \leq orwc' + orwc$
$\Leftrightarrow \langle$ Definition of the residuals (6) $\rangle$
$oX \leq (orwc' + orwc)/c'$
$\Leftrightarrow \langle$ Law (16), (15) $\rangle$
$oX \leq orw(c'/c') + orw(c/c')$
$\Leftrightarrow \langle c/c' = 0, c'/c' = 1 \rangle$
$oX \leq orw$
$\Leftrightarrow \langle$ Definition of the residuals (6) $\rangle$
$X \leq o\backslash(orw)$
$\Leftrightarrow \langle$ Law (16), (15) $, o\backslash o = 1 \rangle$
$X \leq rw$

</td></tr>
</table>

We know that if $o(rwc' + rwc) = oX(c + c')$ has a solution, then $X = rw$ is one of them. But, if we also want to have the exact solution we need to consider the inequality where the variable is on the right side of the inequality symbol :

$$orwc' + orwc \leq oXc + oXc'$$
$$\Rightarrow \langle \text{ Monotocity of residuals } \rangle$$
$$(orwc' + orwc)/c \leq (oXc + oXc')/c$$
$$\Leftrightarrow \langle \text{ Law (16), (15) } \rangle$$
$$orw(c'/c) + orw(c/c) \leq oX(c/c) + oX(c'/c)$$
$$\Leftrightarrow \langle c'/c = 0, c/c = 1, 0y = 0, y + 0 = y \rangle$$
$$orw \leq oX$$
$$\Rightarrow \langle \text{ Monotocity of residuals } \rangle$$
$$o\backslash(orw) \leq o\backslash(oX)$$
$$\Leftrightarrow \langle \text{ Law (16)}, o\backslash o = 1 \rangle$$
$$rw \leq X$$

So, after replacing X by rw in $orwc' \leq oXc + oXc'$ it is easy to show that the resulting inequality is valid.

All this means that $\quad o(rwc' + rwc) = oX(c + c') \quad$ has a unique solution that is $X = rw$.

Moreover, in the case of the R_Σ interpretation, it can be easily shown that

$$\left(y \cdot \sum_{i \in I} \sigma_i \right) \bigg/ \left(\sum_{i \in I} \sigma_i \right) = y$$

where $y \in A$ and $\sigma_i \in \sigma_\mathcal{G}$ for all i belonging to the finite set I, and that the monoticity of the residuals is also valid for equality. That being said, we can solve $o(rwc' + rwc) = oX(c + c')$ only by calculating $o \backslash (rwc' + rwc)/(c + c')$ and verifying that the result is indeed a solution.

To conclude this section, we want to raise the fact that in the previous examples, it wasn't necessary to verify if inequalities like

$$\sigma_j \leq \sum_{k \in K} \sigma_k'''$$

were valid. Those inequalities only arises from equations in which there is a constant term on the side of the variable. For example, to solve the equation $ab + X = ab + cd$ we must verify that $ab \leq ab + cd$.

3. Further resolution

In the preceding section, we presented a method allowing to solve some kind of linear equations in residual idempotent semirings under the R_Σ interpretation. Although, this method is not complete, for the idempotent semirings, in the sense that not all linear equations, such as we defined them, can be solved. To have a complete method it is necessary to take into account equations containing the element "∞" as well as linear equations where variables appear on both side of the equality sign. We are therefore going to analyze the impacts as well as the limitations to which we are confronted when we consider one of these cases.

But, before doing that, we want to give some comments about linear equations that have multiple variables on one side of the equality sign.

3.1. Multiple variables

Finding if a linear equation with multiples variables on one side of the equality sign have a solution is not different from the case of only one variable. In fact, when we apply the rewriting lemma, the equations where the variables are on the left side of $\leq$ have only one occurrence of a unique variable. For example, let consider the equation

$$Xa + Y = bca + de$$

by applying the rewriting lemma we have that $Xa \leq bca + de$ and that $Y \leq bca + de$. So by isolating X in the first inequality we know that $X = bc$ and $Y = bca + de$ is a solution if $Xa + Y = bca + de$ has one.

On the other side, finding the least values of the variables so that they are solutions of the linear equation is more difficult and it might be possible that in some cases the least solution doesn't even exists. In the above example, such least values are bc and de for X and Y respectively. That been said, we want to investigate on finding this least solution for linear equations with multiple variables on one side of the equality sign.

3.2. The element ∞

We start by considering equations using the element "∞". At first glance, it seems that it is not useful to analyze this type of equations if they are strictly an abstraction of computer programs since these do not have corresponding actions to the element "∞". However, in the context of model checking it makes sense because the element "∞" could be used to specify an arbitrary sequence of actions. According to the resolution procedure developed previously to solve equations, we need to solve three problems.

Firstly, we have to be able to compare elements of the universe using "∞". To make this type of comparisons easy, we begin by modifying the definition of sequences. Instead of having considered sequences as being defined from the elements of the set $\mathcal{G}$, we rather considered the set $\mathcal{G} \cup \infty$. This enables us to represent elements in their σ-normal form so that the comparison of elements turns to check the validity of inequality in the form given by (8). We then proceed in a similar way that we used to do for checking the validity of such inequalities in the absence of the element "∞". That is we simplify progressively the sequence on the left side of the inequality sign by using the definition of the residuals (6) and the laws defined in Theorem 1. However, we can only verify the validity of inequalities where "∞" appears only on the right side of $\leq$ because it is not that obvious how to divide by the element "∞". In fact, we believe that this problem is closely related to solving equations over Kleene algebra under the R_Σ interpretation because in those $R_\Sigma(\infty) = R_\Sigma\left(\left(\sum_{x \in \mathcal{G}} x\right)^*\right)$. That being said, even if we can only verify the validity of inequations where "∞" appears only on the right side of $\leq$ there is still some interesting applications to it.

To illustrate this let us consider an example drawn from model checking. Suppose that we have a property saying that no information can be sent on the network after the reading of file. This property is expressed by the formula

$$\neg eventually(\widehat{r}\, eventually(\widehat{s}\, tt)) \tag{26}$$

in linear μ-calculus, where $r \overset{\Delta}{=} read$ and $s \overset{\Delta}{=} send$. However, instead of verifying directly this property we will rather consider its positive form. In a residual idempotent semiring, this positive form of the formula is translated by "$\infty r \infty s \infty$" and can be seen as the set of all programs in which there is a *read* followed by a *send*. So, any program that satisfies the positive form cannot satisfy (26) and *vice-versa*. We consider also the following program:

```
input(x);
cipherText := read(x);
if (cipherText != null)
```

then
   begin
      output(cipherText);
      plainText := *decrypt*(cipherText);
   end
else
   begin
      plainText := null;
   end
send(plainText);

which means that the user has to give a file name in input and if it could be read successfully, the program prints its content at the screen and send the decryption of this content over the network. Otherwise, it send an empty message (*null*). This program can be translated to $ir(od + n)s = irods + irns$ in an idempotent semiring where $i \overset{\Delta}{=} input(\text{x})$, $r \overset{\Delta}{=} \text{cipherText} := read(\text{x})$, $o \overset{\Delta}{=} output(\text{cipherText})$, $d \overset{\Delta}{=}$ plainText := *decrypt*(cipherText), $n \overset{\Delta}{=}$ plainText := null and $s \overset{\Delta}{=} send(\text{plainText})$. Clearly, this program does not satisfy the property (26) but here is how to prove it in an algebraic way. Since that the property "$\infty r \infty s \infty$" "represents" a set of programs, we just have to verify if the program "$irods + irns$" is included in it (that is, "$irods + irns \leq \infty r \infty s \infty$") to show that the program does not respect (26). In fact, because of the rewriting lemma (1) verifying that $irods + irns \leq \infty r \infty s \infty$ is valid is the same as verifying that the inequalities $irods \leq \infty r \infty s \infty$ and $irns \leq \infty r \infty s \infty$ are valid. However, in this example we shall limit ourselves to give the details for only one. The second could be treated in a similar way.

$$irods \leq \infty r \infty s \infty$$
$\Leftrightarrow \langle$ Definition of the residuals $(6) \rangle$
$$irod \leq (\infty r \infty s \infty)/s$$
$\Leftrightarrow \langle$ Law $(17) \rangle$
$$irod \leq \infty r \infty s \infty + (\infty r \infty s)/s$$
$\Leftrightarrow \langle$ Law (10) and $s/s = 1 \rangle$
$$irod \leq \infty r \infty s \infty + \infty r \infty$$
$\Leftrightarrow \langle \infty r \infty s \infty \leq \infty r \infty,$ Definition of the residuals $(6),$ Laws $(17), (16)$ and $r/d = 0 \rangle$
$$iro \leq \infty r \infty$$
$\Leftrightarrow \langle$ Definition of the residuals $(6),$ Laws $(17), (16)$ and $r/o = 0 \rangle$
$$ir \leq \infty r \infty$$
$\Leftrightarrow \langle$ Definition of the residuals $(6),$ Laws $(17), (16), r/r = 1$ and $\infty r \infty \leq \infty \rangle$
$$i \leq \infty$$
$\Leftrightarrow \langle$ Definition of $\infty \rangle$
true

Secondly, it is necessary to be able to solve inequalities having the form (19). For the inequalities where "∞" appears on the left side of $\leq$ we are stuck because we can't divide by "∞" yet but for the other it is possible to isolate X as we have already did in section 2.2.2 so the solution of (19) is given by (20). It is therefore necessary to be able to calculate the meet of two elements using "∞". Previously, we were calculating $a \sqcap b$ by enumerating all the elements less than "a" and all those less than "b" and doing the sum of the elements that were less than both. This was possible because there was a finite number of elements less than "a" and "b" but as "∞" has an infinite number of elements less than it we no longer can proceed in that way. We thus wondered about different ways of calculating $a \sqcap b$ in the presence of "∞" to come with a technique which seems to be good but for which we do not have a proof yet. This is part of future works.

Thirdly, it is necessary to be able to solve inequalities having the form (21). In addition to the fact that we don't know how to divide by "∞" there is other complications for solving this kind of inequalities. With the element "∞" we can't isolate X as we did before using the monotocity of residuals because $\infty/\infty = \infty$. Also not all equations have a lower limit. For example the equation $r\infty \leq X\infty$ has the solutions $r \leq X$ and $1 \leq X$ but there is no solution to the equation that is under both "r" and 1. Finally, we still have to calculate the difference of two elements using "∞". One quickly realize that it is not possible to do so in general in an idempotent semiring under the R_Σ interpretation. For instance, if we try to calculate "$\infty a\infty$" minus "$\infty a\infty b\infty$", which means the set of all the sequences containing an a from which we removed all the sequences containing an "a" and thereafter a "b", the solution would be similar to "$\infty a(\bar{b})^{*}$", where $\bar{b} = \sum_{x \in \mathcal{G} \backslash b} x$, which means that after the action "a" it is not possible to have "b". But under the R_Σ interpretation there is no such element that have the significance of "$(\bar{b})^{*}$" because the operator "$*$" is not defined yet.

In summary, when we take into account the element "∞", we'll be able to compare any elements between them and to solve inequalities of form (19) after we are able to divide any element by "∞". In general, the inequalities of the form (21) don't have a lower solution.

3.3. Variable on each side

We consider now the case where the variable is present on the two sides of the equality sign in a linear equation. Solving this kind of equations, will possibly enable us to resolve some problem related to the synthesis of controller. It is therefore an interesting case which deserves to be explored. However, unlike the case where variable is present on only one side of the equality sign, these equations do not have, in general, solutions in an idempotent semiring under the R_Σ interpretation.

This is illustrated easily when we consider the equation

$$X = aX + 1$$

for which we know that the solution in a Kleene algebra is "a^{*}" but which does not have a solution in the idempotent semiring under the R_Σ interpretation because there is no element which is equivalent to "a^{*}". However, there are also equations for which the variable appear on the two sides of the equality sign which have solutions in the idempotent semirings. One has that to think of the equation

$$X + 1 = X$$

which is equivalent to the inequality $1 \leq X$ that we can solve. In fact, equations having a solution in the idempotent semirings are all those which can be rewritten as an inequality where the variable appears in one side only.

4. Future work

As a continuity of this work is to extend the linear solution of equations to the entire Kleene algebra. Having this, we will then be able to solve equations using the element "∞" as well as equations in which we find the variable on each sides of the equality sign. Parallel to that and since we want to apply the solution of equations to model checking, it is interesting to develop a translator that transforms formulas of a restricted form of the linear μ-calculus to a term of Kleene algebra. The choice of the linear μ-calculus is not arbitrary but it is based on the fact that it has the same expressivity of the ω-regular languages [13] which can be also expressed in term of the ω-algebra which is an extension of the Kleene algebras [6]. From this perspective, we have started working on the translation of expressions of a simplified version of the linear μ-calculus towards the Kleene algebra. Let's consider the following syntax:

$$\phi ::= \mathsf{tt} \mid \phi_1 \vee \phi_2 \mid \phi_1 \wedge \phi_2 \mid @\,\phi \mid \odot\,\phi \mid \mathit{eventually}(\phi)$$

The translation function is given by :

$$
\begin{aligned}
|tt| &= \infty \\
|@\,\phi| &= a \cdot |\phi| \\
|\odot\,\phi| &= \left(\textstyle\sum_{x \in \mathcal{G}} x\right) \cdot |\phi| \\
|\phi_1 \vee \phi_2| &= |\phi_1| + |\phi_2| \\
|\phi_1 \wedge \phi_2| &= |\phi_1| \sqcap |\phi_2| \\
|eventually(\phi)| &= \infty \cdot |\phi|
\end{aligned}
$$

For instance, the translation of the formula presented in the last section is as following :

$$
\begin{aligned}
|eventually(\textcircled{r}\,eventually(\textcircled{s}\,tt))| &= \infty \cdot |\textcircled{r}\,eventually(\textcircled{s}\,tt)| \\
&= \infty \cdot r \cdot |eventually(\textcircled{s}\,tt)| \\
&= \infty \cdot r \cdot \infty \cdot |\textcircled{s}\,tt| \\
&= \infty \cdot r \cdot \infty \cdot s \cdot |tt| \\
&= \infty \cdot r \cdot \infty \cdot s \cdot \infty \\
&= \infty r \infty s \infty
\end{aligned}
$$

Having said that, it remains to prove that it is sound and complete. Besides, we need to consider a syntax that contains negation which is more complicated to deal with but useful. Also, for other logical formula (e.g. $always(@\,tt) = aaaa\ldots$), we anticipate the use of ω-algebra which is suitable to deal with infinite iteration of an element a (a^{ω}).

Lastly, it would be interesting to develop a method of resolution for other interpretation than R_Σ and syntactic equivalence. This becomes particularly useful when we reason on the equivalence of programs calling upon a first-order logic. To illustrate this, let us take again an example of optimization given by Kozen in [2]. In this one, it was proved by using Kleene algebra with test that the programs $i := \mathbf{expr}; j := \mathbf{expr}$ and $i := \mathbf{expr}; j := i$ are equivalent under the assumption that $\mathbf{expr}$ does not contain any occurrence of i. However, if we limit ourselves to the syntactic comparison of programs those two are not equivalent. Indeed, translated into Kleene algebra those are expressed respectively by the elements pq and pr, where $p \overset{\Delta}{=} i := \mathbf{expr}$, $q \overset{\Delta}{=} j := \mathbf{expr}$ and $r \overset{\Delta}{=} j := i$, which elements are syntactically differents. To all that it is added all the other kinds of equations: with several variables, non-linear, etc.

5. Conclusion

In this paper, we developed a method for solving linear equations in which the variable appears on one side of the equal sign over an idempotent semiring. The choice of this kind of equations and algebraic structure were a consequence of various constrains observed when we asked ourselves whether or not it is possible to solve equations within Kleene algebra. We are now looking for extending this work to be able to solve more equations and to find other applications for them. Model checking was our first motivation behind this work since we wanted to find what a program is missing so that a property become satisfied. However, other possible applications of the resolution of equations are program equivalence and the synthesis of controller.

Acknowledgements

We are grateful to Claude Bolduc and Mohamed Mejri for their many helpful ideas, comments and suggestions.

References

[1]   D. Kozen, Kleene algebra with tests, ACM Transactions on Programming Languages and Systems 19 (3) (1997) 427–443.
URL `citeseer.ist.psu.edu/kozen99kleene.html`

[2]   D. Kozen, M.-C. Patron, Certification of compiler optimizations using Kleene algebra with tests, in: J. Lloyd, V. Dahl, U. Furbach, M. Kerber, K.-K. Lau, C. Palamidessi, L. M. Pereira, Y. Sagiv, P. J. Stuckey (Eds.), Proc. 1st Int. Conf. Computational Logic (CL2000), Vol. 1861 of Lecture Notes in Artificial Intelligence, Springer-Verlag, London, 2000, pp. 568–582.

[3]   W. Nutt, Unification in monoidal theories is solving linear equations over semirings, Tech. Rep. RR-92-01, Deutsches Forschungszentrum für Künstliche Intelligenz GmbH, Erwin-Schrödinger Strasse, Postfach 2080, 67608 Kaiserslautern, Germany (1992).
URL `citeseer.ist.psu.edu/nutt92unification.html`

[4]   D. Suikang, Proseminar kleene algebra und regular expressions (05 2004).
URL   `www-sst.informatik.tu-cottbus.de/~wwwti/Studium/04PSAutomaten/Zusamenfassungen/03DuSuikang.pdf`

[5]   D. Kozen, A completeness theorem for kleene algebras and the algebra of regular events, Information and Computation 110 (1994) 366–390.
URL `http://www.cs.cornell.edu/kozen/papers/ka.ps`

[6]   C. Bolduc, Oméga algèbre: Théorie et application en vérification de programmes, Master's thesis, Université Laval (2006).

[7]   D. Kozen, Kleene algebras with tests and the static analysis of programs, Tech. Rep. 2003-1915, Computer Science Department, Cornell University (November 2003).

[8]   P. Jipsen, From semirings to residuated kleene lattices, Studia Logica 76 (2) (2004) 291–303.
URL `http://www1.chapman.edu/~jipsen/papers.html`

[9]   P. Jipsen, C. Tsinakis, A survey of residuated lattices, in: J. Martinez (Ed.), Ordered Algebraic Structures, Kluwer Academic Publishers, Dordrecht, 2002, pp. 19–56.

[10] B. Müller, Residuals and detachment, Tech. rep., University of Augsburg (2005).

[11] S. Burris, H. Sankappanavar, A Course in Universal Algebra, Springer-Verlag, 1982.
URL `http://www.math.uwaterloo.ca/~snburris/htdocs/ualg.html`

[12] P. Höfner, From sequential algebra to kleene algebra: Interval modalities and duration calculus, Tech. rep., University of Augsburg (2005).

[13] J. Bradfield, C. Stirling, Modal logics and mu-calculi: an introduction (2001).
URL `citeseer.ist.psu.edu/bradfield01modal.html`

New Trends in Software Methodologies, Tools and Techniques
H. Fujita and D. Pisanelli (Eds.)
IOS Press, 2007

Analyzing Software Engineering Processes on Source Code Level

DIRK WILKING [a] and STEFAN KOWALEWSKI [a]

[a] *Embedded Software Laboratory, RWTH Aachen University*

Abstract.

The following paper describes a framework for a software engineering process evaluation based on source code changes. The main aspect is to collect the complete source code during every compile step. A detailed analysis of each change of the source code allows a categorization of the type of change. This can be regarded as atomic actions containing especially the problems that occurred during the development. Initial results collected during a software experiment are analyzed and five hypothesis are discussed.

Keywords. Code Evolution, Agile Methods, Empirical Software Engineering

1. Introduction

Cycle based software engineering approaches recently received attention mainly through the rise of agile methods. A variety of experience reports and case studies [1], [2], [3], or [4] describe the application of short development cycles as a feasible way to control a software project. One aspect of an agile software engineering is the advantage of feedback which is received from a project. By integrating this feedback into the next development cycle, a problem centric development course is chosen. This control loop can be found in almost all of the agile methods as described in detail by Abrahamsson et al. In [5].

A different approach to be mentioned here is code evolution (cf. [6], [7]). The concept of code evolution is to provide a holistic analysis of a software life cycle. By gathering time based data in source code repositories, laws could be formulated and investigated [8]. Code evolution focuses on an analysis over time and measurement is done repeatedly during a project.

These two different concepts can be put together in order to allow insights on software engineering on a very low level and for a small time frame. Measurement can be done early and frequently over the complete course of a project. For this kind of measurement, hypothesis are formulated regarding the nature, the problems and the factors influencing these short development cycles. The agile concept of small development steps and rapid feedback allows a more detailed look on software evolution. The goal is to point out some reasons for why predicting the outcome of a software project is difficult "in the small".

The mechanism and technical realization of the framework are described in section 2 and 3 respectively. After that, results based on a lab course are presented in 4. This chapter also focuses on the hypothesis formulated during the data analysis. Lastly, sections 5 and 6 sketch the future of the framework.

2. Principle of Collecting Data

The collection of source code changes is tied to the compilation of a program. Every time the developer compiles his program, the complete source code is saved to a hidden repository. The reason for this approach is that a compilation is supposed to deliver a first usable part of a program (except when there are syntactical errors). Usable in this case means that new or corrected program behavior may be observed. In addition to a multitude of different versions and states of completeness of a project, especially the changes from one version to another can be observed. These changes over time constitute the main aspect discussed in the following.

One of the advantages of collecting steps in this atomic way is that especially unwanted steps become visible. Problems like missing syntactical knowledge, guessing of configuration values and usage problems with third party modules can be identified. Another aspect is that the complete course of the project is reconstructible to a certain degree. For example the order of completed functionality can be extracted from the course of changes. Design decisions which are implicitly inherent in a project might be revealed, though this was not possible in the initial evaluation. The disadvantages comprise a need for acceptance on the developer side and the question of measurement validity. Acceptance is strongly needed, as reconstructing small development steps might reveal questionable work progress and some longer breaks during the development. Measurement is problematic, as different developers might compile at a different frequency. This behavior might lead to a loss of precision for certain developers.

The approach proposed here is similar to the approach described in [9] which consists of gathering changes directly from an integrated development environment (IDE). Changes that are done with an IDE are on a higher level compared to changes on source code level. These changes mainly consist of refactoring steps modifying the structure of a software project. By collecting these kind of changes, a correct semantical interpretation of the change data can be achieved. Both types of data collection have different advantages and an application of one or the other must be based on the circumstances and aims of a study.

3. System Overview

The framework to collect data mainly consists of a simple tool which copies a specified folder to a hidden source code repository. This collector works like a trojan horse: it changes its name to that of the compiler executable. Every time this executable is called, the copy task is done and after that, the real compiler is called with the same environmental settings.

3.1. Analysis Modules

Currently, the following types of analysis are available for the language C: Lines of code (LOC), cyclomatic complexity, number of files per project, number of functions per project, abstract syntax tree computation (partly), and clusters of functions based on latent semantic indexing (cf. [10]). The folders containing the project files are analyzed based on a visitor pattern. Two interfaces exist for this pattern. The first interface focuses on table based results. Examples of this are LOC, the cyclomatic complexity, the number of functions in a project and so on. Another type of analysis uses tree like data structures. For this type of data, an XML based interface is provided.

4. Initial Results

4.1. Background

The data basis of the entire collection consists of 1.7 gigabytes of source code data so far. They originate from 6 experimental sessions made either during lab courses or software engineering experiments. Due to the duration, an analysis was done so far for only one experiment consisting of ten participants. The task in this lab course was to develop a speed measurement for four input signals, which had to be send over CAN-bus thereafter. The platform for this experiment was an ATMega 16 Microcontroller which was programmed in C. Details of this experiment can be found in [11].

The quality of student participants is a controversial point, but the participants of an experiment are regarded as sufficient for evaluating basic effects [12]. In general, programming expertise highly depends on the aspect being compared (cf. [13] and [14]).

Two basic types of evaluation can be differentiated: syntax and semantics based analysis. Syntax based variables did not show satisfying results. Technically, computing them is simple. But the impact of a changed syntactical part of the program or an added syntactical aspect cannot be rated properly. The reason is that only additional meaning like increased development time or a lower readability of a syntactical change would help in assessing the change. In addition, variables like cyclomatic complexity are only interesting for extreme values, which did not occur during the projects. Thus, results regarding syntactical aspects have been omitted in this evaluation.

4.2. Procedure

In order to analyze the data in detail, a semantic analysis of changes was executed by the authors. On the one hand, this was done because of the failure of syntax based analysis modules. On the other hand, concept based evaluations for program comprehension and for reengineering ([15]) appeared to better suit the kind of data. A simple source code browser has been developed for this task showing the differences between two compile steps. Figure 1 depicts the user interface of the application. For each step, the number of changed lines of code, the duration of the step, and a qualitative description of the change are shown. The description consisted mainly of the software module being developed. The term "module" is a rather subjective description of the topic the participant programmed, which comprised I/O ports to be configured correctly, interrupts for signal detection and precise timing, and CAN-bus amongst others. The reason for this type of classification is the order of the tasks which was to be checked and to compare the length between different groups. A second rating is given for the type of change. These comprise debugging, refactoring, initial coding, make working, and architecture outline.

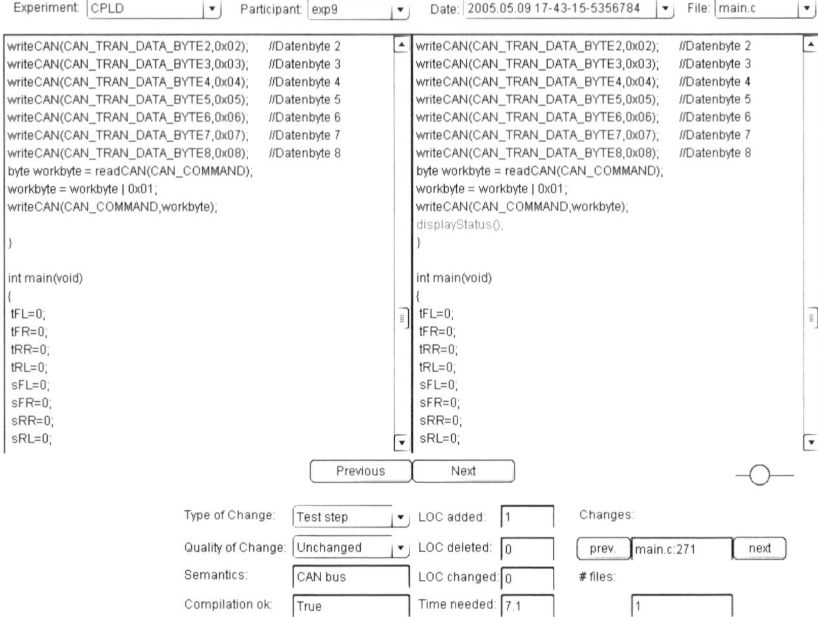

Figure 1. Screenshot of a simple application for browsing changes in the source code.

Refactoring was done rarely with comments as the most important refactoring. Debugging is a step where an additional function was added to make the process of finding a problem faster. Make working is the type of change that describes variation of source code which occurred most often. Initial coding and architecture outline describe the first addition of source code and whether it aims at the software architecture.

Although types of events can be counted, the results must be considered as qualitative in nature due to the subjective review. It must be noted that the review process was done solely by the authors. It is likely that some classifications would be different when done by different reviewers. Nevertheless, the results from this reviewing process lead to novel hypothesis and it is unlikely that a more reliable analysis method would lead to opposite results.

4.3. Resulting Hypothesis

The terminology used in the following used two expressions in particular. In order to describe the phase where a conceptual part of the software was developed, the expression "task" was used. The term "goal" describes the aim of completing a task. An example of this is the correct implementation of the I/O ports, which on the one hand were needed by the interrupts and on the other hand are considered a conceptual part of its own.

4.3.1. Basic Work Cycle

When regarding single steps of changes in a qualitative way, one of the more problematic aspects of software engineering becomes apparent. It is the basic work cycle which consists of varying source code until a certain goal is reached. Goals in embedded software development comprise light emitting diodes (LEDs) being activated, registers pro-

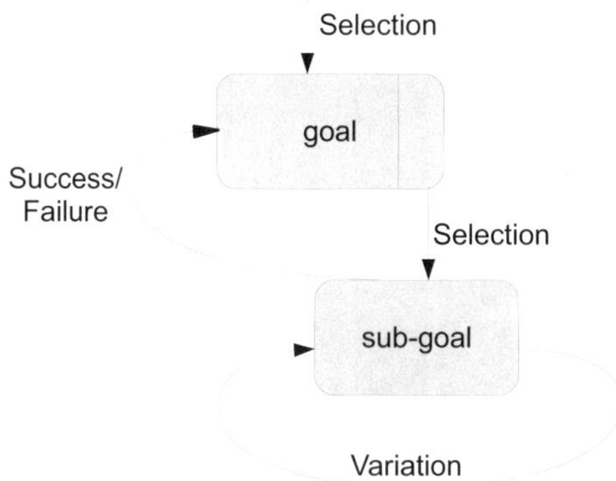

Figure 2. Model for the lowest level of development. Variation consists of code changes until a certain goal is reached and is the main source of randomness.

grammed with a certain value or certain lines of code which must be reached (indicated by LEDs). Variation comprises steps like setting different configurations for a low level hardware device, a different order of programming steps or copying and changing old source code lines.

This approach leads to a cycle which is based on variation, success and a goal as depicted in Figure 2. The arrows indicate a developer's action tied to a certain duration. The boxes indicate goals, which are either obvious and written down (for example in the form of a specification to fulfill) or temporary intentions of the developer. The topmost arrow is meant as a hint to a hierarchical structure of goals. Success is measured by fulfilling a certain goal. Failure exists in the form of reverting to an older version.

Regarding variation of source code, an example based approach appears as a good explanation of this aspect [16]. Creativity and experience may have a strong influence here. Selecting a feasible goal and trying the most promising variation certainly improves over time. This very basic feedback cycle can be plainly described as trial and error development and it is doubtful that a deterministic principle of development exists on this low level of development. In order to make a quantitative prediction at least under laboratory conditions possible, an assessment of the task complexity and the participants' development ability and experience must be measured as additional factors.

Regarding the cycle based nature observed on this level of development, agility with its cycle based planning approach seems to fit to the observation. Although agile planning takes place on a higher level of software development, fast changes to a program resulting in direct feedback appear as an analog approach compared to this hypothesis.

4.3.2. Random Length of Tasks

When regarding goals like a working CAN-bus module or the correct measurement of values, it becomes obvious that the times needed to finish the modules are subject to random length. Figure 3 shows the different tasks of the project for nine participating groups. Because of the different length of tasks, the absolute time to fulfill the requirements is different for each group, too. Apparently, some groups needed around twice the time the fastest group needed. In addition, the times for developing sub-tasks were quite different, too. Some groups managed to fulfill a sub-task right after the initial programming, while others had to correct the syntax or had to add lines for debugging their

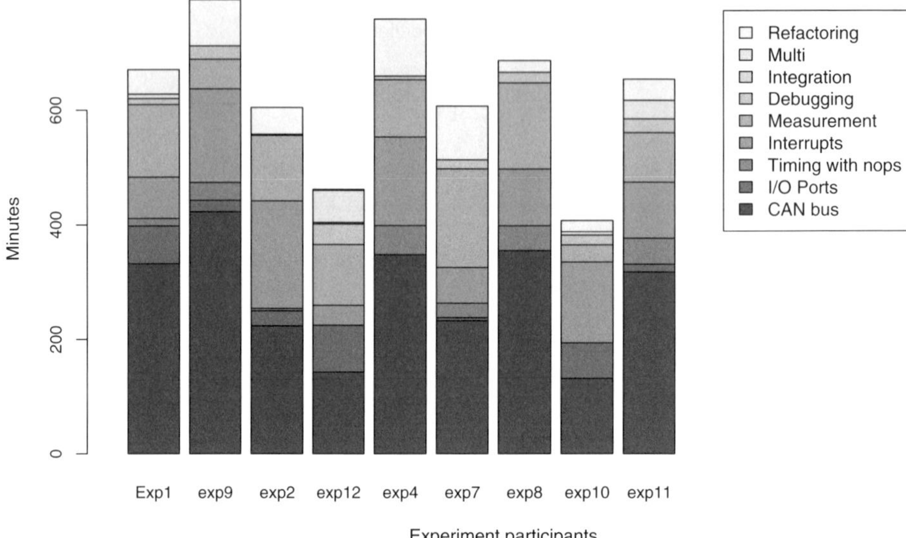

Figure 3. Absolute times for programming sub-tasks.

code. This is a clear reason for the overall randomness of programming: some were lucky enough to create a working solution right at he beginning, others spent for the very same functionality hours of programming.

The problem even for this rather simple task is that a prediction of the course of development is not possible by deterministic models. During experiments, we asked the groups to rate their development knowledge and the number of years they programmed so far. No correlation could be found between development time and knowledge or experience. Due to that, no factor was able to predict the length of the overall development process.

Another observation is that the length of subtasks appears to be as random in length as the length of the complete project. Because of this, a minor hypothesis is that the length of tasks is random on different hierarchical levels, too.

The only aspect which seems to allow some forecasting is the rough length of the tasks. The time needed to program the correct configuration of the I/O ports was different between the participating groups, but overall, this task was rather short. On the other hand the implementation of the CAN-bus was one of the major problems for each group. This rough categorization shows that there is at least some equivalence of the task complexity. In general, these observations are supported by [17], which states that the difference in development performance is a factor around 3.

4.3.3. Non-linearity of Tasks

Project planning consists (amongst other aspects) of creating a time schedule and assigning different development aspects to developers. When assigning tasks, a time for the start and for the end of the task is predefined. The schedule of the length of a programming task is based on experience, as normally the software development is done for the first time. Amongst other assumptions, one implicit assumption is that a task is programmed once and finished in one step.

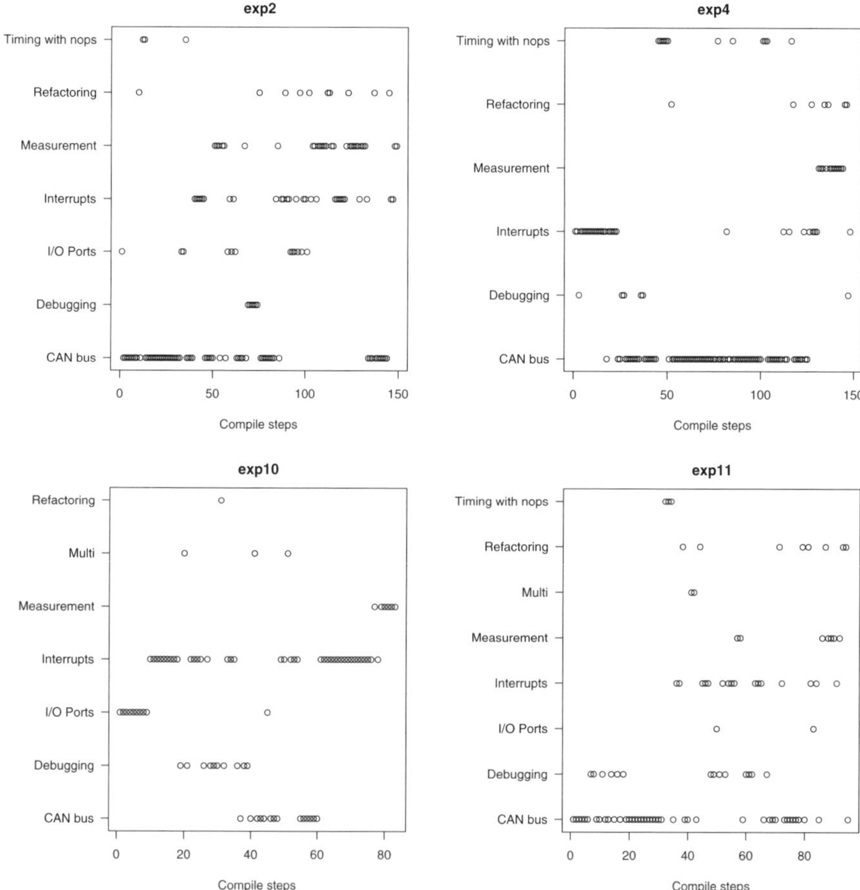

Figure 4. Type of task done in each compile step. Four of the ten groups are shown.

Regarding the data gathered from the first experiment in Figure 4, a trend towards this step-wise development becomes obvious. One reason is that technical constraints exist. Correct configuration of the I/O ports is a precondition to work on the CAN-bus. In addition, the correct measurement of incoming signals is the most high-level task and therefore should be developed last.

Nevertheless, the occurrence of tasks under uncontrolled, natural conditions seems to be not linear. The most random occurrence can be found for experimentation group two (exp2) in Figure 4. Here, tasks are switched frequently and development seems to follow a different concept than the technical approach. Experimentation group eleven (exp11) worked on the integration of interrupts with the CAN-bus part and often switched between both tasks. Group ten faced the same problems with interrupt integration as group 11. The last group shown here had a more linear behavior with only slight interventions. Group four (exp4) stuck to a task longer and only interrupts had to be rechecked during development.

The question arising from this observation is if the switching between tasks would have occurred if the groups planned their development and if they were asked (or forced) to stick to that schedule. There is a trend towards stepwise development of the different tasks visible, but due to this natural switching between tasks, it appears as a problem to maintain a linear development. One of the ultimate problems related to that is the problem of integration. Even when forced to develop in a linear fashion, merging all parts of the software together might again lead to finished modules being touched again. While reviewing the authors got the impression that exactly this happened sometimes. When the developers finished the measurement part and tried to send the measurement results via CAN-bus, this module sometimes had to be changed again. This forced some developers to work on a very basic level where even the correct configuration of the I/O ports had to be checked again.

4.3.4. Inherent Testing of Software Parts

As described above, each sequence of change steps aimed to fulfill a certain sub-goal. When reviewing the added lines of source code, sub-goals were identified. They appeared as certain lines of code to be reached, a calculation which was done with some predefined values, or a configuration which had to be checked externally by looking at some LEDs. These tests normally were short lived, and either were conserved as a comment or were deleted during later development.

Looking at this behavior, collecting these internal tests appears as a sound conclusion. Technically, this leads to the principle of collecting white-box tests as done in Test-Driven Development. Reusing these internal tests to assure a certain behavior during the course of development appears as supporting natural behavior, especially when the possibility exists that a software part has to be touched again.

4.3.5. Anomalies

Totally unexpected changes are best described as anomalies. Anomalies were perceived on different levels of development. One observed problem was a source file which was not added to the makefile for a long time. Another anomaly consisted of removing the current source code and replacing it with an old version. These anomalies appeared rarely and often had a severe effect on a project. A prediction of anomalies has not been tried, as marking them appeared unnecessary due to the rare occurrence and bad prediction variables.

5. Future Analysis

The main aspect of these atomic source changes is the extraction of new variables for the assessment of software engineering processes. One possible addition to verify productive steps is to focus on single lines of code. A "good" line of code could be one that appears unchanged in the final version of the source. The opposite is a change of a line of code which does not even appear in the final version. Hence, the overhead in terms of line numbers and time spent on these lines may be a new variable assessing the software engineering process. In addition, a line may be identified as "parameter" when only a single value was changed frequently within. One technical problem is a missing multiuser support. The integration of changes will be problematic as a merging of code normally is done only when committing to a repository.

One of the main questions for low level measurement is which kind of semantics is important. First of all, concepts appear as a powerful source for assessment. When a classification of the technical aspect a developer is working on becomes a solid variable to classify a change, further hypothesis could be checked. In consequence, techniques to influence this variable might be evaluated. It might be possible to introduce techniques that enforce a more linear approach of development tasks.

One problem encountered during reviewing the changes was to find a taxonomy for the tasks. In addition to the technical concept, it was tried to further classify the change. For example it was tried to differentiate between debugging steps and a full scale test. Debugging was thought as a simple test to check some program behavior and being removed thereafter. A test was considered to be maintained during the whole life cycle. Although this was observed sometimes, the differentiation was not sharp enough.

Apparently, the review process for the semantic evaluation must be executed in a more objective way. To achieve this, different people should execute a review and it must be checked whether their results conform with each other. Another idea is to ask the developer to review his own changes at the end (or beginning) of a day. This could result in a more reliable review as the developer knows best about his intentions.

Eventually, the best way to execute such a low level measurement is an academic environment. Here, control of developers must be seen as part of a study or an experiment. For a non-academic environment, acceptance may be missing and severe dysfunctions might occur (cf. [18] and above). The problematic aspect is that not a record of successful development is done, but negative aspects constitute the most interesting aspect being gathered.

Regarding high level software engineering, low level evaluation may be used to assess the correctness of a project schedule. For example, the level of deviation from a given schedule might be measured in terms of time and order. Additionally, the frequency of anomalies and especially their detection might give feedback for higher level models of software engineering.

6. Conclusions

This papers presented a framework for software process assessment based on source code level observations. The collection mechanism consists of copying the complete source code every time the compiler is executed. The system is described in terms of data analysis modules.

Regarding initial results, hypothesis are formulated based on the review of changes. These reviews provided semantic information of the concepts being changed, which lead to hypothesis concerning low level changes. The first hypothesis describes a basic work cycle consisting of code variation to achieve a certain goal. A probability of failure of a task in this work cycle leads to the hypothesis of random duration of development tasks. The goal of a task represents a minor testing step, which often is not explicitly apparent in the source code. Thus, another hypothesis is the existence of inherent testing during each development step. Another observation revealed that developers tended to change existing, presumably finished modules. Thus, a general non-linearity of development tasks regarding project progression makes up the last hypothesis.

Regarding agile methods, test driven development may be regarded to support the behavior of inherent testing. The addition of the technique of test driven development is regarded as explicitly gathering inherent test steps, which otherwise are dismissed after successful execution. The general idea of rapid changes to the source code as proposed by agile methods appears to be supported by the observed basic work cycle. Especially the probability of failure with the consequence of random length of tasks seems to fit the agile concept.

References

[1] N. Van Schooenderwoert. Embedded agile project by the numbers with newbies. In *Proceedings of AGILE 2006 Conference (AGILE'06)*, 2006.

[2] O. Salo and P. Abrahamsson. Integrating agile software development and software process improvement: a longitudinal case study. In *International Symposium on Empirical Software Engineering, 2005*, 2005.

[3] Pekka Abrahamsson and Juha Koskela. Extreme programming: A survey of empirical data from a controlled case study. In *Proceedings of the 2004 International Symposium on Empirical Software Engineering (ISESE04)*, 2004.

[4] Peter Manhart and Kurt Schneider. Breaking the ice for agile development of embedded software: An industry experience report. *IEEE: Proceeding of the 26th International Conference on Software Engineering (ICSE04)*, pages 6–14, 2004.

[5] Pekka Abrahamsson, Outi Salo, Jussi Ronkainen, and Juhani Warsta. *Agile software development methods. Review and analysis.* VTT Publications, 2002.

[6] Daniel M. German. An empirical study of fine-grained software modifications. In *20th IEEE International Conference on Software Maintenance, 2004*, 2004.

[7] Ahmed E. Hassan and Richard C. Holt. Studying the evolution of software systems using evolutionary code extractors. *Proceedings of IWPSE 2004: International Workshop on Principles of Software Evolution*, 2004.

[8] M.M. Lehman, J.F. Ramil, P.D. Wernick, and D.E. Perry. Metrics and laws of software evolution-the nineties view. In *4th International Software Metrics Symposium (METRICS '97)*, 1997.

[9] Romain Robbes and Michele Lanza. A change-based approach to software evolution. *Electronic Notes in Theoretical Computer Science*, 166:93–109, 2007.

[10] Jonathan I. Maletic and Andrian Marcus. Supporting program comprehension using semantic and structural information. In *ICSE '01: Proceedings of the 23rd International Conference on Software Engineering*, pages 103–112, Washington, DC, USA, 2001. IEEE Computer Society.

[11] Falk Salewski, Dirk Wilking, and Stefan Kowalewski. The effect of diverse hardware platforms on n-version programming in embedded systems - an empirical evaluation. Proceedings of the 3rd International Workshop on Dependable Embedded Sytems 105/2006, Vienna University of Technology, 2006.

[12] Dag I. K. Sjøberg, Bente Anda, Erik Arisholm, Tore Dybå, Magne Jørgensen, Amela Karahasanović, and Marek Vokáč. Challenges and recommendations when increasing the realism of controlled software engineering experiments. *ESERNET 2001-2003, LNCS 2765*, pages 24–38, 2003.

[13] Jean-Marie Burkhardt, Françoise Deétienne, and Susan Wiedenbeck. Object-oriented program comprehension: Effect of expertise, task and phase. *Empirical Software Engineering*, 7:115–156, 2002.

[14] A. Ebrahimi and C. Schweikert. Empirical study of novice programming with plans and objects. In *ITiCSE-WGR '06: Working group reports on ITiCSE on Innovation and technology in computer science education*, pages 52–54, New York, NY, USA, 2006. ACM Press.

[15] V. Rajlich and N. Wilde. The role of concepts in program comprehension. In *Proceeding of the 10th International Workshop on International Workshop on Program Comprehension, IEEE (2002)*, 2002.

[16] Naiyana Sahavechaphan and Kajal Claypool. Xsnippet: mining for sample code. In *OOPSLA '06: Proceedings of the 21st annual ACM SIGPLAN conference on Object-oriented programming systems, languages, and applications*, pages 413–430, New York, NY, USA, 2006. ACM Press.

[17] Lutz Prechelt. The 28:1 grant/sackman legend is misleading, or: How large is interpersonal variation really? Internal Report 18, Universität Karlsruhe, Fakultät für Informatik, 1999.

[18] Dewayne E. Perry, Adam A. Porter, and Lawrence G. Votta. Empirical studies of software engineering: a roadmap. In *ICSE '00: Proceedings of the Conference on The Future of Software Engineering*, pages 345–355, New York, NY, USA, 2000. ACM Press.

New Trends in Software Methodologies, Tools and Techniques
H. Fujita and D. Pisanelli (Eds.)
IOS Press, 2007

Automated Design Improvement by Example

Mark O'KEEFFE [a,1] and Mel Ó CINNÉIDE [a]

[a] *School of Computer Science and Informatics, University College Dublin, Belfield, Dublin 14, Ireland*

Abstract. The high cost of software maintenance could potentially be reduced by automatically improving the design of object-oriented programs without altering their behaviour. We have constructed a software tool capable of refactoring object-oriented programs to conform more closely to design quality models based on a set of metrics, by formulating the task as a search problem in the space of alternative designs. However, no consensus exists on a single quality model for object-oriented design, since the definition of 'quality' can depend on the purpose, pedigree and perception of the maintenance programmer. We therefore demonstrate here the flexibility of our approach by automatically refactoring several Java programs to conform with quality models based on the metric values of example programs. Results show that an object-oriented program can be automatically refactored to reduce its dissimilarity in terms of a set of design metrics to another program having some desirable trait, such as ease of maintenance.

Keywords. Automated Design Improvement, Refactoring, Metrics

1. Introduction

One measure of the quality of an object-oriented design is the level of difficulty encountered in carrying out maintenance programming. This is because the object-oriented approach is geared towards producing designs which are understandable, flexible, and modular. However, it is not uncommon to encounter designs that have become weakened as a side-effect of the repeated addition of functionality during development (a problem referred to as *design erosion* or *software decay* [16]), or have not been properly maintained in the past. Such designs can require significant refactoring in order to increase their maintainability to an acceptable level, thus increasing the cost of carrying out maintenance tasks.

The ideal solution to this problem would be the automation of some portion of the refactoring step by the application of an automated design improvement tool. Such a tool would take the current set of classes as input and output a set with the same external behaviour, but having a design that is more easily comprehended, adapted or extended. In this context, the application of refactorings can be considered movement in the space of alternative designs.

---

[1]Corresponding author; email: mark.okeeffe@ucd.ie

Our novel approach to automated design improvement is the formulation of the refactoring task as a search problem; given a design quality model we apply automated refactorings to a program in order to move through the space of alternative designs and search for those of highest quality. However, no consensus exists on a single model of object-oriented design quality, and none is likely to develop since the perceived quality of a design is highly subjective. In other words, that which makes a design understandable may depend on the skills of the programmer, that which makes a design flexible may depend on his/her purpose, and that which makes a design reusable may depend on the nature of the proposed reuse.

Previous search-based refactoring work by the authors has shown that object-oriented programs can be automatically refactored in order to conform more closely to a given quality model [27]. However, because the priorities of the maintenance programmer can change from day to day and best programming practice can vary between domains, it is unlikely that a single quality model can be defined that will maximise the effectiveness of search-based refactoring across the board. The programmer wishing to take advantage of search-based refactoring is therefore left with the problem of developing a suitable quality model. This paper shows how that complex process can be circumvented by basing a quality model on the characteristics of some other program in the problem domain that is known to exhibit the desired property. Therefore, if any one program is found to have a desirable trait such as high maintainability or reusability other programs can be quickly refactored to more closely resemble the example, using our approach.

2. Related Work

2.1. Search-Based Software Engineering

Search-Based Software Engineering (SBSE) can be defined as the application of search-based approaches in solving optimisation problems in software engineering [17]. Such problems include *module clustering*, where a software system is reorganised into loosely coupled clusters of highly cohesive modules to aid reengineering [14,18,20,23], test data generation [21], automated testing [31] and project management problems such as requirements scheduling [1] and project cost estimation [9,13]. An overview of such work and comprehensive recent references can be found in [12] and [17] respectively. Of particular relevance to this work is [17], in which Harman proposes 'Metrics as Fitness Functions' (MAFF). Harman states that a metric can be used as the evaluation function driving a search-based software optimisation; our approach involves using a combination of a *set* of metric values to guide a search for optimal design.

2.2. Automated Design Improvement

Previous approaches to the fully automated restructuring of software have focussed on improving one particular aspect of design, such as method reuse or code factorisation. However, since object-oriented design involves numerous trade-offs, this narrow focus could result in overall quality loss. Examples of such work include that of Casais [10], who proposed algorithms to restructure class hierarchies in order to maximise abstraction, and Moore [24], who proposed a system where existing classes are discarded and replaced with a new set where methods are optimally factored – meaning code duplication is minimised.

Our approach has two main advantages over previous fully automated refactoring work. Firstly, and most significantly, the use of evaluation functions consisting of combinations of various metric values allows us to employ much richer quality models than the single-goal approaches mentioned above, which do not take into account the numerous trade-offs involved in object-oriented design. Secondly, by careful choice and precise definition of the refactorings employed we can make design-quality affecting changes to an object-oriented program without loss of domain-specific information such as class and member names; a particular disadvantage of [24].

In addition to previous fully-automated approaches to design improvement, semi-automated approaches that require user interaction have been reported. Such semi-automated approaches mainly involve the use of metric-based rules to identify areas in need of improvement, the onus then being on the programmer to make the necessary changes. Such 'bad smell' detection has been proposed by Van Emden [15], and by Tahvildari [30], whose system also recommends 'meta-pattern transformations' that can be applied to ameliorate the defect. Another aspect of semi-automated design improvement is simply the automation of application of refactorings, with the particular refactorings performed determined entirely by the user [28]. The drawback of all semi-automated tools is, of course, that they reduce the level of programmer intervention required somewhat less than fully-automated tools have the potential to do.

Seng et. al. [29] describe a similar approach to ours [25,26,27] but use a genetic algorithm rather than local search or simulated annealing to solve the combinatorial optimisation problem. The evaluation function employed is novel rather than previously validated, but is based on well-known metrics such as *Response For a Class* (RFC) and *Weighted Methods per Class* (WMC) from Chidamber & Kemerer's MOOSE suite [11], among others. The authors report success in automatically repositioning displaced methods in the class structure, not limited to movement within inheritance hierarchies. However, only the Move Method refactoring is considered so the extent of change within the class structure is limited.

3. Experimental Methodology

3.1. CODe-Imp

We have constructed a prototype automated design-improvement tool called CODe-Imp[2] in order to facilitate experimentation with search-based software maintenance. CODe-Imp takes Java 1.4 source code as input and extracts design metric information via a Java Program Model (JPM), calculates quality values according to an evaluation function and applies refactorings to the Abstract Syntax Tree (AST), as required by the search technique employed. Output consists of the refactored input code as well as a design improvement report including quality change and metric information.

---

[2]Combinatorial Optimisation Design-Improvement

3.2. Refactorings

Many refactorings are described in the literature, in particular by Fowler [16]. The precise definition of refactorings is an area of research by itself [28]. Fowler, among others, defines refactorings in natural language, so a degree of interpretation is required in automating these refactorings. In addition, language-specific features such as 'package' visibility in Java must be taken into account.

The refactoring configuration of CODe-Imp for the experiments reported here consisted of the fourteen refactorings described below. We have selected complementary pairs of refactorings so that changes made to the input design during the course of the search could be reversed. This is necessary for some search techniques such as simulated annealing to move freely through the solution space, though not for the hill-climbing approach employed here.

The CODe-Imp refactorings are, in general, based on a Fowler refactoring of the same name. Some reverse refactorings were added, as were some obvious alternative refactorings. Refactorings were selected according to the criteria below:

1. GRANULARITY – only refactorings operating at the level of methods/ attributes and higher were accepted. Lower-level refactorings are generally concerned with rectifying implementation mistakes, and do not have a large impact on the design of a program. An example refactoring that does not meet this criterion is Introduce Assertion ([16], p.267), in which an 'assert' statement is added at the start of a method to ensure some necessary conditions hold.

2. REVERSIBILITY – only refactorings that could be reversed by some other acceptable refactoring were accepted. The preconditions for all accepted refactorings were formulated to ensure this property. An example refactoring that cannot be applied in a reversible fashion, and so fails to meet this criterion, is Remove Parameter ([16], p.277).

3. AUTOMATION – the motivation for some refactorings necessitates programmer input; for example, the refactoring Extract Method ([16], p.110) is useful because the name given to a new method replacing a complex statement tells the programmer what the statement does. An extracted method with a meaningless name would actually make the code harder to understand. For this reason, some refactorings were not selected simply because it does not make sense to automate them.

The refactorings implemented in CODe-Imp are:

1. **Push Down Field** – moves a field from some class to those subclasses that require it. This refactoring is intended to simplify the design by reducing the number of classes that have access to the field ([16], p.329).
2. **Pull Up Field** – moves a field from some class(es) to the immediate superclass. This refactoring is intended to eliminate duplicate field declarations in sibling classes ([16], p.320).
3. **Push Down Method** – moves a method from some class to those subclasses that require it. This refactoring is intended to simplify the design by reducing the size of class interfaces ([16], p.328).

4. **Pull Up Method** – moves a method from some class(es) to their immediate superclass. This refactoring is intended to help eliminate duplicate methods among sibling classes, and hence reduce code duplication in general ([16], p.322).

5. **Extract Hierarchy** – adds a new subclass to a non-leaf class C in an inheritance hierarchy. A subset of the subclasses of C will inherit from the new class. This refactoring is intended to help improve class cohesion and modularity by increasing abstraction in the class hierarchy.

6. **Collapse Hierarchy** – removes a non-leaf class from an inheritance hierarchy. This refactoring is intended to reduce design complexity by removing superfluous classes from the design.

7. **Increase Field Security** – increases the security of a field from public to protected, from protected to package or from package to private. This refactoring increases data encapsulation.

8. **Decrease Field Security** – decreases the security of a field from private to package, from package to protected or from protected to public. This refactoring reduces data encapsulation.

9. **Replace Inheritance with Delegation** – replaces an inheritance relationship between two classes with a delegation relationship; the former subclass will have a field of the type of the former superclass. This refactoring is used to rectify a situation where a subclass does not use enough of a superclass's features to justify the specialisation relationship ([16], p.352).

10. **Replace Delegation with Inheritance** – replaces a delegation relationship between two classes with an inheritance relationship; the delegating class becomes a subclass of the former delegate class. This refactoring can be used in a situation where a delegating class is using enough features of a delegate class that a specialisation relationship would be more appropriate ([16], p.355).

11. **Increase Method Security** – increases the security of a method from public to protected, from protected to package or from package to private. This refactoring can reduce the size of the public interface of a class ([16], p.303).

12. **Decrease Method Security** – decreases the security of a method from private to package, from package to protected or from protected to public. This refactoring can increase the size of the public interface of a class.

13. **Make Superclass Abstract** – declares a constructorless class explicitly abstract. This increases some measures of abstraction, and can facilitate other refactorings.

14. **Make Superclass Concrete** – removes the explicit 'abstract' declaration of an abstract class without abstract methods. This decreases some measures of abstraction.

We have deliberately chosen refactorings that operate at the method/field level of granularity and higher because our focus is on the automatic improvement of the design encapsulated in a program rather than implementation issues such as correct factorisation of methods.

One of the functions of CODe-Imp's Java Program Model (JPM) is to determine where refactorings can legally be applied – in other words, where the corresponding code alterations can be made without altering program behaviour. In order to achieve this we have employed a system of static precondition checking, the details of which are beyond the scope of this paper.

3.3. Dissimilarity Function

The evaluation function employed here is a dissimilarity function based on the eleven object-oriented design metrics of Bansiya's QMOOD[3] hierarchical design quality model [2]. Several metric suites were considered, as described below, but QMOOD was selected in order that the results of this work could be readily compared with the results of previous search-based refactoring approaches [27].

3.3.1. CK

The Metrics Suite for Object-Oriented Design (known as CK) of Chidamber and Kemerer [11] is a seminal work in object-oriented quality measurement and is still frequently cited today. Metrics are defined for properties such as complexity, inheritance, coupling, cohesion and messaging. The CK metrics and subsequent modifications by Li et al. [32] have been independently validated as indicators of such characteristics as fault-proneness [3], but no attempt has been made to combine them in the form of an evaluation function. Several interpretations exist of some CK metrics, such as Lack of Cohesion of Methods (LCOM).

3.3.2. MOOD2

The MOOD (Metrics for Object-Oriented Design) metrics suite [7] was introduced by Fernando Brito e Abreu et al. in 1994 and was subsequently evaluated by the author [6] and others [19]. Because some deficiencies were identified, namely the lack of measures of reuse, polymorphism and external coupling, the MOOD suite was superseded by the MOOD2 metrics suite in 1998 [4]. The MOOD2 metrics are also defined in an English–language paper [5] through extended OCL and the GOODLY design language [8].

The MOOD2 suite is a comprehensive, modern metrics suite including several measures each of coupling, reuse, polymorphism, data-hiding and inheritance. MOOD2 metrics are formally defined, and hence can be directly implemented without resolution of ambiguity. However, nowhere in the literature are evaluation functions defined that combine MOOD2 metric values to give an overall quality index. As a result MOOD2 does not provide a complete quality model suitable for use in search-based refactoring.

3.3.3. QMOOD

The QMOOD (Quality Model for Object-Oriented Design) model of Bansiya [2] was introduced in 2002 and consists of a hierarchy of four levels. The levels in descending order are: Design Quality Attributes such as 'understandability', Object-Oriented Design Properties such as 'encapsulation', Object-Oriented Design Metrics, and Object-Oriented Design Components such as 'class'.

For the purpose of search-based refactoring, the QMOOD model has the advantage that it defines functions from metric values to Quality Attribute Indices (QAIs) for such design attributes as flexibility, reusability and understandability. This provides an excellent foundation for experimentation in automatically refactoring a design to conform

---

[3]Quality Model for Object-Oriented Design

to this quality model. However, while QMOOD provides a detailed model of object-oriented design quality, it is lacking in the area of effective metric definition. Metrics in QMOOD literature [2] are defined in natural language, and are in some cases ambiguous. In order to implement the QMOOD metrics for replicable studies it is necessary to define them more precisely. The QMOOD metrics are as follows:

1. **Design Size in Classes (DSC)**– "A count of the total number of classes in the design."[2] Interpreted as excluding imported library classes. Corresponds to the object-oriented design property of 'design size' in QMOOD.

2. **Number Of Hierarchies (NOH)**– "A count of the number of class hierarchies in the design."[2] Interpreted as excluding hierarchies that consist of a specialised class within the design and a generalised class outside. Corresponds to the object-oriented design property of 'Hierarchies' in QMOOD.

3. **Average Number of Ancestors (ANA)**– "The average number of classes from which each class inherits information."[2] Corresponds to the object-oriented design property of 'Abstraction' in QMOOD.

4. **Number of Polymorphic Methods (NOP)**– "A count of the number of the methods that can exhibit polymorphic behaviour."[2] Interpreted as the sum over all classes, where a method can exhibit polymorphic behaviour if it is overridden by one or more descendent classes. Corresponds to the object-oriented design property of 'Polymorphism' in QMOOD.

5. **Class Interface Size (CIS)**– "A count of the number of public methods in a class."[2] Interpreted as the average over all classes in a design. Corresponds to the object-oriented design property of 'Messaging' in QMOOD.

6. **Number Of Methods (NOM)**– "A count of all the methods defined in a class."[2] Interpreted as the sum over all classes in a design. Corresponds to the object-oriented design property of 'Complexity' in QMOOD.

7. **Data Access Metric (DAM)**– "The ratio of the number of private (protected) attributes to the total number of attributes declared in the class."[2] Interpreted as the average over all design classes *with at least one attribute*, of the ratio of non-public to total attributes in a class. Corresponds to the object-oriented design property of 'Encapsulation' in QMOOD.

8. **Direct Class Coupling (DCC)**– "A count of the number of different classes that a class is directly related to. The metric includes classes that are directly related by attribute declarations and message passing (parameters) in methods."[2] Interpreted as an average over all classes when applied to a design as a whole; a count of the number of distinct user-defined classes a class is coupled to by method parameter or attribute type. We exclude imported library classes from the computation. Corresponds to the object-oriented design property of 'Coupling' in QMOOD.

9. **Cohesion Among Methods of Class (CAM)**– "The relatedness among methods of a class, computed using the summation of the intersection of parameters of a method with the maximum independent set of all parameter types in the class."[2] Interpreted as an average over all classes having at least one method. We have excluded constructors and implicit 'this' parameters from the computation. Corresponds to the object-oriented design property of 'Cohesion' in QMOOD.

10. **Measure Of Aggregation (MOA)**– "A count of the number of data declarations whose types are user-defined classes."[2] Interpreted as the sum of values for all design classes. We define 'user defined classes' as classes defined in the source code of the input program. Corresponds to the object-oriented design property of 'Composition' in QMOOD.

11. **Measure of Functional Abstraction (MFA)**– "The ratio of the number of methods inherited by a class to the number of methods accessible by member methods of the class."[2] Interpreted as the average over all classes in a design (with at least one method available) of the ratio of the number of methods inherited by a class to the total number of methods available to that class, i.e. inherited and defined methods. Corresponds to the object-oriented design property of 'Inheritance' in QMOOD.

The dissimilarity function itself gives the sum of absolute differences between the quotients for subject program metric over example program metric and the identity value of one. More precisely: the dissimilarity value $d\left(P_s P_e\right)$ for a subject program P_s and an example program P_e, where the metric value for metric m on program P is given by $m\left(P\right)$, is defined as

$$d\left(P_s P_e\right) = \sum_{n=1}^{11} \left| \frac{m_n\left(P_s\right)}{m_n\left(P_e\right)} - 1 \right|$$

and is minimised by combinatorial optimisation in a refactored program $P_s{'}$.

3.4. Search Technique

Previous work has shown that a steepest-ascent hill-climbing search is sufficient to produce consistently good results in automated refactoring, though simulated annealing is more effective in some cases [27]. Hill climbing has also been found to be surprisingly effective in solving similar combinatorial optimisation problems such as module clustering [18,22]. For clarity, we have employed steepest ascent hill-climbing alone in this study.

Steepest ascent hill-climbing (HCS) is a local search algorithm where the search examines all neighbouring solutions and moves to the neighbour of highest quality. This is repeated until no neighbour of higher quality can be found, at which point the search terminates. A neighbour of a solution S is defined as a solution that can be generated by one application of one refactoring to S.

Algorithm 1 Steepest Ascent Hill-Climbing

1: currentNode = startNode;
2: madeAscent = TRUE;
3: **while** madeAscent **do**
4:     madeAscent = FALSE;
5:     L = NEIGHBOURS(currentNode);
6:     bestNeighbour = null;
7:     bestNeighbourEval = -INFINITY;
8:     **for** all x in L **do**
9:         **if** (EVAL(x) > bestNeighbourEval **then**
10:             bestNeighbour = x;
11:             bestNeighbourEval = EVAL(bestNeighbour);
12:         **end if**
13:     **end for**
14:     **if** bestNeighbourEval > EVAL(currentNode) **then**
15:         currentNode = bestNeighbour;
16:         madeAscent = TRUE;
17:     **end if**
18: **end while**
19: **return** currentNode;

3.5. Input

Input consisted of two open-source Java 1.4 programs of a maximum size of one hundred classes randomly selected from SourceForge[4] via java-source.net, and a self-contained subset of the *Spec-Benchmarks*[5] standard performance evaluation framework, to which it was known a large number of refactorings could be applied. The programs selected were:

1. **Input A.** *Beaver*, a parser generator

   - 93 classes
   - 4999 SLOC
   - 9 inheritance hierarchies
   - 177 refactorings could initially be applied

2. **Input B:** *SpecCheck*, a benchmarking program

   - 41 classes
   - 4836 SLOC
   - 5 inheritance hierarchies
   - 351 refactorings could initially be applied

---

[4] http://sourceforge.net/
[5] http://www.spec.org/

3. **Input C:** *Mango*, a collections library
   - 51 classes
   - 1131 SLOC
   - 0 inheritance hierarchies
   - 28 refactorings could initially be applied

4. Results

4.1. Overview

The aim of the study described here was to demonstrate that Java programs can be automatically refactored to conform more closely to a quality model extracted from an example program and defined in terms of a set of object-oriented metrics. No assumptions were made as to the quality (or otherwise) of the input programs, nor was the range of dissimilarity values controlled by selection of input programs, which was random. Each of the three input programs was automatically refactored with CODe-Imp, using metric values of the other two programs as alternative quality models.

Experiments were carried out on a 2.2GHz AMD Athlon powered PC with 1GB CL2 RAM. Mean processing time per solution examined was approximately one second, including model building, metric extraction, quality assessment, discovery of legal refactorings, and actual (AST) refactoring. Total run-time varied between less than one minute and 66 minutes, depending on the number of refactorings possible for the input program and the number of refactorings applied. CODe-Imp was designed with robustness rather than speed as a priority and makes no use of concurrent processes, so there is potential to greatly decrease these run-times.

Tables 1– 3 show the total difference function values as defined in section 3.3 for input program and refactored input program, as well as individual metric components given by

	DSC	NOH	ANA	DAM	DCC	CAM	MOA	MFA	NOP	CIS	NOM	$d(P_s P_e)$
					input *Beaver*, example *Spec-Check*							
Beaver	0.268	0.5	1.343	0.296	2.256	0.67	1.952	1	0.401	0.355	0.465	**8.903**
Beaver'	0.268	0	0.952	0.156	2.417	0.059	2.061	0	0.066	0.334	0.422	**6.736**
change	0	-0.5	-0.390	-0.140	0.161	-0.009	0.109	-1	-0.335	-0.021	-0.043	**-2.167**
					input *Beaver*, example *Mango*							
Beaver	0.25	1	1	0.332	1.455	0.248	2.273	1	1	0.266	0.022	**8.846**
Beaver'	0.25	1	1	0.193	1.455	0.216	2.273	0	1	0.258	0.022	**7.667**
change	0	0	0	-0.138	0	-0.0323	0	-1	0	-0.008	0	**-1.178**

Dissimilarity values for input program *Beaver* and refactored program *Beaver'*. Note that dissimilarity quotients rather than actual metric values are shown, so the identity value 1 indicates a perfect match between subject program and example program for that metric. Negative values in the 'change' rows indicate metrics that have been brought closer to the desired value.

Table 1. Results for input program Beaver

	DSC	NOH	ANA	DAM	DCC	CAM	MOA	MFA	NOP	CIS	NOM	$d(P_s P_e)$
				input Spec-Check, example Beaver								
Spec-Check	0.367	0.333	0.573	0.421	0.693	0.063	0.661	1	0.286	0.550	0.869	**5.816**
Spec-Check'	0.467	0.333	0.091	0.000	0.714	0.063	0.684	0.237	0.380	0.400	0.869	**4.238**
change	0.1	0	-0.482	-0.421	0.021	0	0.023	-0.763	0.094	-0.150	0	**-1.578**
				input Spec-Check, example Mango								
Spec-Check	0.025	1	1	0.050	0.246	0.296	0.109	0	1	0.137	0.827	**4.690**
Spec-Check'	0.125	1	1	0.000	0.313	0.295	0.010	0	1	0.005	0.827	**4.575**
change	0.1	0	0	-0.050	0.067	-0.001	-0.099	0	0	-0.133	0	**-0.115**

Dissimilarity values for input program *Spec-Check* and refactored program *Spec-Check'*. Note that dissimilarity quotients rather than actual metric values are shown, so the identity value 1 indicates a perfect match between subject program and example program for that metric. Negative values in the 'change' rows indicate metrics that have been brought closer to the desired value.

Table 2. Results for input program Spec-Check

	DSC	NOH	ANA	DAM	DCC	CAM	MOA	MFA	NOP	CIS	NOM	$d(P_s P_e)$
				input Mango, example Spec-Check								
Mango	0.0244	1	1	0.052	0.326	0.419	0.098	0	1	0.120	0.452	**4.495**
Mango'	0.0244	1	1	0.052	0.326	0.419	0.098	0	1	0.120	0.452	**4.495**
change	0	0	0	0	0	0	0	0	0	0	0	**0.000**
				input Mango, example Beaver								
Mango	0.333	1	1	0.495	0.592	0.330	0.694	1	1	0.362	0.022	**6.833**
Mango'	0.333	1	1	0.495	0.592	0.330	0.694	1	1	0.362	0.022	**6.833**
change	0	0	0	0	0	0	0	0	0	0	0	**0.000**

Dissimilarity values for input program *Mango* and refactored program *Mango'*. Note that dissimilarity quotients rather than actual metric values are shown, so the identity value 1 indicates a perfect match between subject program and example program for that metric. Negative values in the 'change' rows indicate metrics that have been brought closer to the desired value.

Table 3. Results for input program Mango

$$d_{m_n}(P_s P_e) = \left| \frac{m_n(P_s)}{m_n(P_e)} - 1 \right|$$

where $d_{m_n}(P_s P_e)$ is the individual metric difference value of metric m_n for a subject program P_s and an example program P_e. Negative values in the 'change' rows indicate a metric that has been brought closer to the desired value, positive values indicate a metric that has been taken further from the desired value, and zero indicates no metric change.

4.2. Beaver

Results for the input program *Beaver*, a parser generator of 93 classes, are shown in table 1. The dissimilarity value for this program, taking *Spec-Check* as example program, decreased by 24.3%, from 8.903 to 6.736. Eight metrics were brought closer to the example program values, while two moved farther away. These metric changes were effected by one Pull Up Field, two Push Down Method, seven Increase Field Security, one Decrease Method Security and two Replace Inheritance with Delegation refactorings, so very significant changes were made to the class structure.

Taking *Mango* as example program, the dissimilarity value for *Beaver* decreased by 13.3%, from 8.903 to 7.667. Four metrics were brought closer to the example program values, with none moved farther away. These metric changes were effected by two Pull Up Field, one Push Down Method, six Increase Field Security and one Decrease Method Security refactorings, so significant changes were made to the class structure.

4.3. Spec-Check

Results for the input program *Spec-Check*, a benchmarking program of 41 classes, are shown in table 2. The dissimilarity value for this program, taking *Beaver* as example program, decreased by 27.1%, from 5.816 to 4.238. Surprisingly, given the large decrease in dissimilarity value, the same number of metrics were brought closer and moved away from the example program values (4). However, the magnitude of absolute metric quotient change was much greater in the negative/closer changes, with metrics such as ANA and DAM changing from approximately half the desired value to within 1%. These metric changes were effected by one Pull Up Field, three Extract Hierarchy, eleven Decrease Field Security and six Increase Method Security refactorings, so very significant changes were made to the class structure.

Taking *Mango* as example program, the dissimilarity value decreased by only 2.45%, from 4.690 to 4.575, although the input/example dissimilarity value was close to the lowest observed, in this case. Nevertheless, four metrics were brought closer to the example program values while two were taken farther away. These metric changes were effected by one Pull Up Method, four Extract Hierarchy, four Increase Field Security, one Decrease Field Security and six Increase Method Security refactorings, so despite the small change in dissimilarity value very significant changes were made to the class structure.

4.4. Mango

Results for the input program *Mango*, a collections library of 51 classes, are shown in table 3. No decrease in dissimilarity value between the input and refactored program was observed for this input, with either example program. However, only 28 refactorings were possible for this program, compared to 190 for *Beaver* and 351 for *Spec-Check*. This lack of instances where the preconditions for potential refactoring were met in the *Mango* program is the most likely explanation for the failure of CODe-Imp to reduce the dissimilarity value. Inspection of the *Mango* program revealed that its designers had made no use of the inheritance mechanism. Since most of CODe-Imp's refactorings operate on inheritance hierarchies, this explains the small number of possible refactorings for this program.

4.5. Summary

Of three input programs automatically refactored by CODe-Imp, one was made significantly more similar in terms of the metrics suite employed to two example programs, one was made significantly more similar to one example program and slightly more similar to the other, and one was not made any more similar to either example program. Unsurprisingly, the greatest reductions in dissimilarity value were observed where a large number of refactorings were possible for the input program, and there was a relatively high dissimilarity value between input program and example program.

5. Conclusions & Future Work

In this study we have demonstrated that Java programs can be automatically refactored to reduce their dissimilarity to other programs in terms of a set of object-oriented metrics, provided the subject program in question makes use of object-oriented features such as inheritance that make refactoring possible. This work has the potential to contribute to the development of domain-specific object-oriented quality models, which will be of use in both traditional and search-based software maintenance.

Future work will include repeating these experiments with larger input programs, alternative search techniques and other metric suites. The limitations of this work center around the fact that similarity between programs as measured by a metrics suite may not match with the human perception of similarity, particularly in the case of ontological artifacts such as design patterns. We plan to further explore this relationship in the future by supplementing the metrics suite with pattern-detection routines, in order to extract richer quality models from example programs.

References

[1]　Anthony J. Bagnall, Victor J. Rayward-Smith, and I. M. Whittley. The next release problem. *Information & Software Technology*, 43(14):883–890, 2001.

[2]　Jagdish Bansiya and Carl G. Davis. A hierarchical model for object-oriented design quality assessment. *IEEE Trans. Software Eng.*, 28(1):4–17, 2002.

[3]　Victor R. Basili, Lionel C. Briand, and Walcélio L. Melo. A validation of object-oriented design metrics as quality indicators. *IEEE Trans. Software Eng.*, 22(10):751–761, 1996.

[4]　Fernando Brito e Abreu. The MOOD2 metrics set (in portuguese); relatorio r7/98, abril, 1998a. Technical report, Grupo de Engenharia de Software, INESC, 1998.

[5]　Fernando Brito e Abreu. Using OCL to formalize object oriented metrics definitions. Technical report, Grupo de Engenharia de Software, INESC, 2001.

[6]　Fernando Brito e Abreu and Walcélio L. Melo. Evaluating the impact of object-oriented design on software quality. In *IEEE METRICS*, pages 90–99, 1996.

[7]　Fernando Brito e Abreu, Luis Ochoa, and Miguel Goulão. Candidate metrics for object oriented software within a taxonomy framework. *Journal of Systems and Software*, 26(1), July 1994.

[8]　Fernando Brito e Abreu, Luis Ochoa, and Miguel Goulão. The GOODLY design language for MOOD2 metrics collection. In *ECOOP Workshops*, pages 328–329, 1999.

[9]　Colin J. Burgess and Martin Lefley. Can genetic programming improve software effort estimation? A comparative evaluation. *Information & Software Technology*, 43(14):863–873, 2001.

[10]　Eduardo Casais. An incremental class reorganization approach. In O. Lehrmann Madsen, editor, *Proceedings of the European Conference on Object-Oriented Programming*, pages 114–131, Utrecht, June 1992. LNCS.

[11] S. Chidamber and C.F. Kemerer. A metrics suite for object oriented design. *IEEE Transactions on Software Engineering*, 20:476–493, June 1994.

[12] John A. Clark, José J. Dolado, Mark Harman, Robert M. Hierons, B. Jones, M. Lumkin, Brian S. Mitchell, Spiros Mancoridis, K. Rees, Marc Roper, and Martin J. Shepperd. Formulating software engineering as a search problem. *IEE Proceedings - Software*, 150(3):161–175, 2003.

[13] José Javier Dolado. A validation of the component-based method for software size estimation. *IEEE Trans. Software Eng.*, 26(10):1006–1021, 2000.

[14] D. Doval, S. Mancoridis, and B.S. Mitchell. Automatic clustering of software systems using a genetic algorithm. In *International Conference on Software Tools and Engineering Practice (STEP'99)*, 1999.

[15] Eva Van Emden and Leon Moonen. Java quality assurance by detecting code smells. In Arie van Deursen and Elizabeth Burd, editors, *WCRE*, page 97. IEEE Computer Society, 2002.

[16] Martin Fowler. *Refactoring: improving the design of existing code*. Addison-Wesley Longman Publishing Co., Inc., Boston, MA, USA, 1999.

[17] Mark Harman and John A. Clark. Metrics are fitness functions too. In *IEEE METRICS*, pages 58–69. IEEE Computer Society, 2004.

[18] Mark Harman, Robert M. Hierons, and Mark Proctor. A new representation and crossover operator for search-based optimization of software modularization. In William B. Langdon, Erick Cantú-Paz, Keith E. Mathias, Rajkumar Roy, David Davis, Riccardo Poli, Karthik Balakrishnan, Vasant Honavar, Günter Rudolph, Joachim Wegener, Larry Bull, Mitchell A. Potter, Alan C. Schultz, Julian F. Miller, Edmund K. Burke, and Natasa Jonoska, editors, *GECCO*, pages 1351–1358. Morgan Kaufmann, 2002.

[19] R. Harrison, S. Counsell, and R. Nithi. An evaluation of the MOOD set of object-oriented software metrics. *IEEE Transactions on Software Engineering*, 24(6):491–496, 1998.

[20] Spiros Mancoridis, Brian S. Mitchell, Yih-Farn Chen, and Emden R. Gansner. Bunch: A clustering tool for the recovery and maintenance of software system structures. In *ICSM*, pages 50–, 1999.

[21] Christoph C. Michael, Gary McGraw, and Michael Schatz. Generating software test data by evolution. *IEEE Trans. Software Eng.*, 27(12):1085–1110, 2001.

[22] Brian S. Mitchell. *A Heuristic Search Approach to Solving the Software Clustering Problem*. PhD thesis, Drexel University Philadelphia, USA, 2002.

[23] Brian S. Mitchell, Martin Raverso, and Spiros Mancoridis. An architecture for distributing the computation of software clustering algorithms. In *WICSA*, pages 181–190. IEEE Computer Society, 2001.

[24] Ivan Moore. Automatic inheritance hierarchy restructuring and method refactoring. In *OOPSLA*, pages 235–250, 1996.

[25] M. O'Keeffe and M. Ó Cinnéide. A stochastic approach to automated design improvement. In James F. Power and John T. Waldron, editors, *Proceedings of the 2nd International Conference on the Principles and Practice of Programming in Java*, pages 59–62. ACM SIGAPP, Computer Science Press, Trinity College Dublin, Ireland., June 2003.

[26] M. O'Keeffe and M. Ó Cinnéide. Towards automated design improvement through combinatorial optimisation. In *Proceedings of the 4th International Workshop on Directions in Software Engineering Environments (WoDiSEE 2004)*, May 2004.

[27] M. O'Keeffe and M. Ó Cinnéide. Search-based software maintenance. In *Proceedings of the 10th European Conference on Software Maintenance and Reengineering (CSMR 2006)*, pages 249– 260, 2006.

[28] Donald Bradley Roberts. *Practical analysis for refactoring*. PhD thesis, Department of Computer Science, University of Illinois at Urbana-Champaign, 1999. Adviser-Ralph Johnson.

[29] Olaf Seng, Johannes Stammel, and David Burkhart. Search-based determination of refactorings for improving the class structure of object-oriented systems. In *GECCO '06: Proceedings of the 8th annual conference on Genetic and evolutionary computation*, pages 1909–1916, New York, NY, USA, 2006. ACM Press.

[30] Ladan Tahvildari and Kostas Kontogiannis. Improving design quality using meta-pattern transformations: a metric-based approach. *Journal of Software Maintenance*, 16(4-5):331–361, 2004.

[31] Joachim Wegener, André Baresel, and Harmen Sthamer. Evolutionary test environment for automatic structural testing. *Information & Software Technology*, 43(14):841–854, 2001.

[32] Wei Li. Another metric suite for object-oriented programming. *J. Syst. Softw.*, 44(2):155–162, 1998.

New Trends in Software Methodologies, Tools and Techniques
H. Fujita and D. Pisanelli (Eds.)
IOS Press, 2007

Experience of XML-Based Source Code Representation with Parsing Actions

Kazuaki MAEDA [1]

Department of Business Administration and Information Science,
Chubu University, Japan

Abstract. This paper describes PALEX, a new source code representation in XML which contains parsing actions and lexical formatting information. Once a compiler finishes analyzing source code, it can record a list of parsing actions (shift, reduce and reading a token) during a compiling process. PALEX contains the recorded parsing actions and also lexical formatting information, white spaces and comments. It has two features as a source code representation in XML. The first is that it is independent of programming languages. The second is that the original source code can be restored from the PALEX code. For a prototype implementation, the Java compiler GCJ was modified. Syntax rules and lexical definitions are prepared for development of software tools which read the PALEX code and play back the parsing actions. An experiment was designed and the result shows that the size of the generated PALEX code is very large. However, the XML-based source code representation together with parsing actions offsets the cost of the large storage space.

Keywords. XML, source code representation, Java, syntax analysis, parser generator

1. Introduction

A compiler reads source code, analyzes it and builds a tree to represent the hierarchical structure of the source code. The source code is usually kept in the plain text. This is because it is easy to manipulate the plain text using text editors and other software tools. In Unix operating system, for example, we can count lines of the source code using a "wc" command. If we want to get a list of lines including a specified identifier, we usually execute a "grep" command with a regular expression.

The tree which the compiler builds is called abstract syntax tree (AST)[1]. It is widely used in many practical systems which need the syntactic information of the source code. For example, in the early days, Diana was designed as AST for Ada programs[2]. It is suitable for an intermediate representation of the Ada programs in an Ada compiler. AST is not designed for multiple programming languages. In the case of Diana, it is designed only for the Ada programming language.

Several source code representations in XML exist. XML can be used across different platforms (i.e. different computers, different operating systems and different program-

---

[1]Contact information of the author: Department of Business Administration and Information Science, Chubu University, 1200 Matsumoto, Kasugai, Aichi 487–8501, Japan; Email: kaz@acm.org

ming languages). If the source code is analyzed and kept in XML, it is possible to develop software tools using various programming languages and libraries. JavaML[3] and XMLizer[4] are typical XML-based source code representations for AST. XSDML[5] and srcML[6] support the representation of formatting information including white spaces and comments in addition to representing AST. Therefore, the original source code can be restored from the XML document using the formatting information in XSDML or srcML.

This paper describes yet another XML representation of source code called PALEX (PArsing actions and LExical formatting information in Xml). Once a compiler finishes analyzing source code, it can record a list of parsing actions during a compiling process, those are shift, reduce and reading a token. PALEX contains the recorded parsing actions and also lexical formatting information including white spaces and comments. It has two features;

- It is independent of programming languages because there are no language specific elements and attributes in PALEX.
- The original source code can be restored from the PALEX code because it contains enough information for it.

A Java compiler was modified to read Java source code and to produce the PALEX code. Moreover, syntax rules and lexical definitions are prepared for development of software tools which read the PALEX code and play back the parsing actions.

The next section explains a traditional LALR parser and the Java compiler GCJ. Section 3 describes the details of the source code representation in PALEX. Section 4 explains the storage space issue and some experiences about PALEX. Section 5 provides a summary of this paper.

2. Traditional Parsers and the Modification

2.1. LALR Parser

In the 1970s, the parser generator Yacc[7] was developed, which made parser development much easier. Yacc reads user-defined syntax rules with action codes to be invoked when the syntax rules are recognized, and it generates an LALR (lookahead LR) parser written in the C programming language. The LALR parser is a refined version of an LR parser which reads input from left to right and produces rightmost derivations. It uses lookahead sets to make the size of the parsing tables compact.

The LALR parser generated by Yacc uses two tables, *Action* and *Goto*. A procedure for the LALR parser is shown in Figure 1. It is a modified description in a compiler textbook[8]. As you can see in the Figure 1, the parser executes mainly four actions, those are <u>shift</u>, <u>reduce</u>, <u>accept</u> and <u>error</u>.

When we develop a parser using a parser generator Bison[9] which accepts Yacc-compatible syntax rules, we can build it in a debug mode to check the actions during parsing. Let us consider an example of an import statement in Java.

```
import java.*;
```

```
push start state to stack
token = NextToken()
while(true){
  S = top of stack
  if(Action[S,token]==shift Si){
    push token to stack
    push Si to stack
    token = NextToken()
  }else if(Action[S,token]==reduce A -> B){
    pop 2*|B| symbols from stack
    S = top of stack
    push A
    push Goto[S,A]
  }else if(Action[S,token] == accept){
    return
  }else{
    report syntax error
  }
}
```

Figure 1. A procedure for an LALR parser

Figure 2 shows a fragment of syntax rules to analyze the import statement, which is extracted from source code of a Java compiler. The figure also shows lexical definitions to understand token symbols in the syntax rules. When Bison generates a parser and the parser analyzes the import statement in the debug mode, it writes debug information to standard output as shown in Figure 3. In the figure, you can see state transitions using three parsing actions, <u>reading a token</u>, <u>shifting token</u> and <u>reducing stack by rule</u>. The PALEX code described in Section 3 contains the parsing actions.

```
import_declaration: single_type_import_declaration
                  | type_import_on_demand_declaration;
single_type_import_declaration
    : IMPORT_TK name SC_TK;
type_import_on_demand_declaration
    : IMPORT_TK name DOT_TK MULT_TK SC_TK;
name: simple_name | qualified_name;
qualified_name: name DOT_TK identifier;
simple_name   : identifier;
identifier    : ID_TK;
```

Token symbol	Meaning of the symbol
IMPORT_TK	"import"
SC_TK	";"
DOT_TK	"."
MULT_TK	"*"
ID_TK	an identifier

Figure 2. Syntax rules for an import statement in Java

2.2. GCJ and its Modification

GCJ[10] is a Compiler for the Java programming language. It is written in the C programming language. GCJ has been fully integrated and supported as a GCC (GNU Compiler Collection)[11]. One of the advantages is that GCJ can generate both native code and bytecode from Java source code. Programs created by GCJ can dynamically load and interpret class files or native shared libraries resulting in pure, or mixed native/interpreted

```
Starting parse
Entering state 0
Reading a token: Next token is token IMPORT_TK ()
Shifting token IMPORT_TK ()
Entering state 3
Reading a token: Next token is token ID_TK ()
Shifting token ID_TK ()
Entering state 22
Reducing stack by rule 24 (line 702), ID_TK -> identifier
Stack now 0 3
Entering state 26
Reducing stack by rule 22 (line 693), identifier -> simple_name
Stack now 0 3
Entering state 24
Reducing stack by rule 20 (line 688), simple_name -> name
Stack now 0 3
Entering state 23
Reading a token: Next token is token DOT_TK ()
```

Figure 3. Debug information written by an LALR parser

applications. Many commercial applications have already been developed with GCJ. For example, all of the major GNU/Linux distributions use GCJ to support programs like OpenOffice, Eclipse and Tomcat.

The parser for GCJ was developed using a parser generator Bison[9]. In the case of GCJ, Bison reads syntax rules for the Java programming language and generates a parser written in the C programming language to analyze Java source code.

GCJ was modified for a prototype implementation to produce the PALEX code from Java source code. GCJ is a free software so that we can obtain the source code and modify it. The modified version of GCJ is called Mogcj in this paper. Mogcj reads Java source code and produces the PALEX code.

Bison was modified to implement Mogcj and it is called MoBison. MoBison reads syntax rules for the Java programming language and generates a special parser for Mogcj which contains functionality to produce the PALEX code. MoBison is used to embed the functionality in the compiler. Moreover, MoBison generates parsing information for other software tools to analyze the PALEX code written by Mogcj.

3. Source Code Representation and its Creation

3.1. Source Code Representation in PALEX

PALEX is a new XML representation of source code. XML can be used across different platforms. Moreover, many libraries to process XML documents have already been implemented for a majority of programming languages. If source code is analyzed and kept in XML, it is possible to develop software tools using various programming languages and libraries.

The modified Java compiler Mogcj reads Java source code and produces the PALEX code. Once a compiler finishes analyzing source code, the parsing actions (i.e. shift, reduce and reading a token) can be recorded. The PALEX code contains the parsing actions, lexical formatting information, white spaces and comments. To explain the details, let us consider an example of the following source code in Java.

```
import java.*; // simple statement
```

It is a simple import statement with a comment. Mogcs analyzes the source code and produces the PALEX code as shown in Appendix. Table 1 shows the meanings of element names in PALEX and Table 2 shows the meanings of attribute names. Names of some elements and attributes are abbreviated because the size of the XML document should be reduced to save the storage space.

Table 1. Elements in PALEX

Name	Meaning of the element
parseFiles	root document
parse	parsing a file
wsc	white space and comments
lex	reading a token
shi	shift action
red	reduce action
go	action for going to another state
xdc	XML documentation
acc	acceptance

Table 2. Attributes in PALEX

Name	Meaning of the attribute
lang	name of a programming language
pg	name of a parser generator
ver	version number of PALEX
name	name of the source file
st	state number
fr	source state number for shift action
to	destination state number for shift action
tk	kind of a token
va	string image of a token
li	line number
co	column number
ru	syntax rule number

The PALEX code in Appendix contains the parsing actions, which are shi (shift), red (reduce), lex (reading a token), and go (going to another state). The shi element contains a source of a state transition in the fr attribute and a destination of the state transition in the to attribute. The red element contains a state number in the st attribute and a syntax rule number in the ru attribute. The syntax rule has a unique sequential number which is internally assigned to identify each rule. The lex element contains token information. In Appendix, for example, the first lex element indicates that the kind of the token is *IMPORT_TK* shown in the tk attribute, that the string image of the token is *import* shown in the va attribute, and that it starts at the position of line 1 and column 1 shown in the li attribute and the co attribute.

The wsc element contains white space characters and comments. There are two wsc elements in Appendix. The first wsc element contains a space character between *import* and *java* in the import statement. The second wsc element contains a space character, a comment *// simple statement* and a newline character.

3.2. Implementation Methods

The structure of the original compiler GCJ is shown in Figure 4. In GCJ, there are some functions for lexical analysis (scanner), syntax analysis (parser), semantic analysis, optimization and code generation. The parser in the original compiler GCJ is generated by Bison which accepts Yacc-compatible syntax rules.

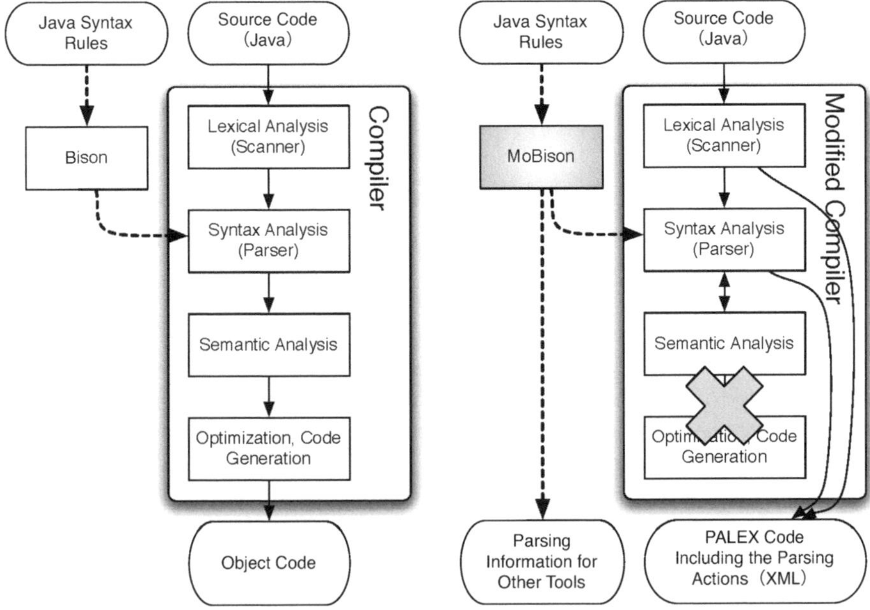

Figure 4. Structure of the original compiler GCJ   **Figure 5.** Structure of the modified compiler Mogcj

GCJ was modified as shown in Figure 5 to implement a translator which reads Java source code and produces the PALEX code. The scanner was modified to provide string image of lexical token and the location information, and to produce wsc elements including white spaces and comments.

Bison was replaced by a modified parser generator called MoBison as shown in Figure 5. MoBison reads syntax rules for the Java programming language and generates a special parser written in C for Mogcj which contains functionality to produce the PALEX code. MoBison is used to embed the functionality in the Java compiler GCJ. Moreover, it generates parsing information for other software tools to analyze the PALEX code produced by Mogcj.

If we want to utilize PALEX features for developing software tools, the first thing we have to do is to develop a program for playing back the parsing actions. The parsing information generated by MoBison contains

- lexical definitions for Java source code and
- syntax rules to analyze the PALEX code.

Generated syntax rules for the import statement are shown in Figure 6. In the figure, MoBison adds, to the end of rules, special symbols REDUCE_20, REDUCE_21, RE-DUCE_22, REDUCE_23 and REDUCE_24 to reduce the corresponding rule. The numbers (e.g. 20, 21, 22, 23 and 24) are unique sequential identifiers assigned to the syntax rules.

The modified Java compiler Mogcj reads Java source code and produces the PALEX code. If Mogcj is used to produce only the PALEX code, it is not necessary to execute the optimization and the code generation in the compiler. At that time, we can specify using an option that Mogcj finishes the execution after producing the PALEX code.

```
name: simple_name REDUCE_20 | qualified_name REDUCE_21;
simple_name    : identifier REDUCE_22;
qualified_name: name DOT_TK identifier REDUCE_23;
identifier     : ID_TK REDUCE_24;
```

Figure 6. An example of grammar rules generated by MoBison

4. Experiment and Tool Development

4.1. Experiment

To examine the storage space of this paper's approach, 535 source files were selected from source code in Groovy[12] version 1.0. Each source file was analyzed using Mogcj and then the size of the generated PALEX code was calculated.

The five largest Java source files are shown to check the size of the generated PALEX code in Table 3. For example, the largest file "GroovyRecognizer.java" is translated to the PALEX code whose size is about 27MB.

Table 3. The five largest Java source files in Groovy

File name	Size of source code (KB)	Lines of source code	Size of the PALEX code (MB)
GroovyRecognizer.java	326.42	12,756	26.61
DefaultGroovyMethods.java	233.76	6,917	9.83
JavaRecognizer.java	189.22	7,686	15.83
AsmClassGenerator.java	132.86	3,280	6.79
GroovyResultSet.java	111.63	2,614	1.23

The size of the PALEX code exceeds the usual XML document. The storage cost, however, is not a serious problem because nowadays the prices of hard disk drives are increasingly getting cheaper year by year.

4.2. Application to Develop a C# Parser

PALEX is independent of programming languages and the platforms. In order to clarify the independence, it was applied to develop a C# parser using the Mono C# compiler[13]. As shown in Figure 7, the conceptual structure of the Mono C# compiler is similar as one of the Java compiler GCJ.

There are some kinds of lexical analysis, syntax analysis, semantic analysis, optimization and code generation which are implemented in the C# programming language. Jay is a parser generator to accept Yacc-compatible syntax rules. In the case of the Mono C# compiler, Jay reads more than 700 syntax rules for C# and generates a parser written in C# to analyze C# source code.

The parser generator Jay used in the Mono C# compiler is replaced by a modified parser generator MoJay. The input specification of MoJay is completely the same as one of Jay. MoJay reads the C# syntax rules and generates the parser written in C#. Moreover, it statically generates lexical information and C# syntax rules to be used for development of software tools effectively using the PALEX code.

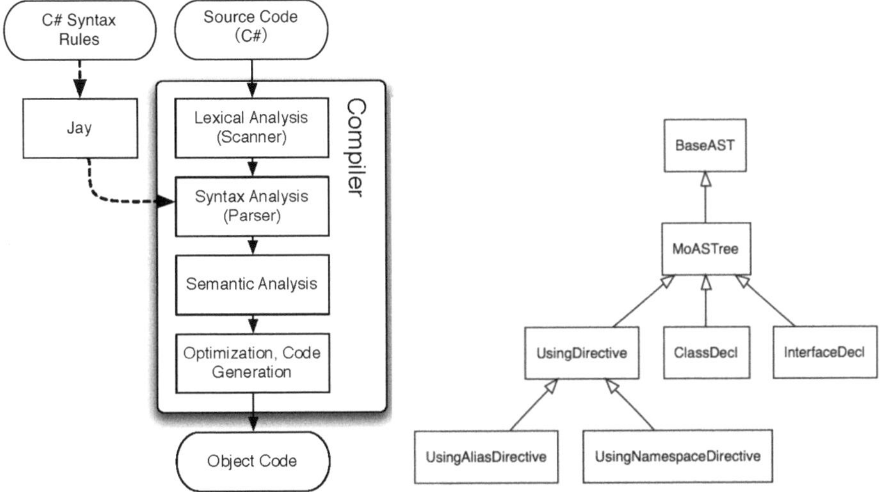

Figure 7. The conceptual structure of Mono C# compiler

Figure 8. An example of the generated class diagram

4.3. Tool Development Using PALEX

If we want to utilize PALEX features and to develop software tools, the first thing we have to do is to develop a program for playing back the parsing actions.

In the author's experiences, it takes only a few hours to implement a simple recognizer which reads the PALEX code and analyzes it. If we develop a reverse engineering tool for C#, we should implement the simple recognizer at first and then build some functions into it to analyze relationship between classes and to generate design documents (e.g. class diagrams, communication diagrams).

The author also developed a program, called UnPalex, to restore the original source code from the PALEX code. Due to the interoperability of XML, we can implement UnPalex in different programming languages. A simple version of UnPalex was developed in C# to debug MoBison and to check correctness of the produced PALEX code.

The author developed a simple reverse engineering tool effectively using PALEX. It reads C# source code and generates the class diagram as shown in Figure 8. The reverse engineering tool consists of 6,750 lines of C# source code and the syntax rules consists of 2,115 lines. Some classes were implemented to build the AST. The tool was developed on Mac OS X using Mono. After completing the development of the production quality version, the source code was transferred to another PC (running on Windows XP), and the author attempted to build the executable file using Cygwin and Visual Studio 2005. This building work was very simple, and it was carried out without any problems. This is because XML and C# function independently of operating systems and computers.

5. Summary

This paper described PALEX which is produced as an XML document containing elements of source code and parsing actions, et. al. The PALEX code contains the recorded parsing actions and also formatting information including white spaces and comments. PALEX has two distinguished features. The first is that it is independent of programming languages because there are no language specific elements and attributes in the XML document. It enables us creation of reverse engineering tools in any programming languages. The second is that the original source code can be restored from the PALEX code because it contains enough information to restore it.

For a prototype implementation, the Java compiler GCJ was modified. Syntax rules and lexical definitions are prepared for development of software tools which read the PALEX code and play back the parsing actions. In the author's experiences, it takes only a few hours to develop a simple recognizer for PALEX using effectively the syntax rules and the lexical definitions.

An experiment was designed and the result shows that the size of the generated XML document is very large. However, the XML-based source code representation together with parsing actions offsets the cost of the large storage space.

Various compilers for some programming languages are now investigated to expand applications of the PALEX code. The development activities and the results will be published in the near future.

References

[1]　Alfred V. Aho, Monica S. Lam, Ravi Sethi, and Jeffrey D. Ullman. *Compilers : principles, techniques, and tools, 2nd Ed.* Pearson Education, 2006.

[2]　G. Goos and Wm. A. Wulf. Diana Reference Manual. Technical report, Carnegie-Mellon University, 1981.

[3]　Greg Badros. JavaML: A Markup Language for Java Source Code. In *9th International World Wide Web Conference.* http://www9.org/w9cdrom/index.html, 2000.

[4]　Gregory McArthur, John Mylopoulos, and Siu Kee Keith Ng. An Extensible Tool for Source Code Representation Using XML. In *9th Working Conference on Reverse Engineering*, 199–209, 2002.

[5]　Katsuhisa Maruyama and Shinichiro Yamamoto. A CASE Tool Platform Using an XML Representation of Java Source Code. In *4th IEEE International Workshop on Source Code Analysis and Manipulation*, 158–167, 2004.

[6]　Jonathan I. Maletic, Michael Collard, and Huzefa Kagdi. Leveraging XML Technologies in Developing Program Analysis Tools. In *4th International Workshop on Adoption-Centric Software Engineering*, 80–85, 2004.

[7]　Steven C. Johnson. Yacc: Yet another compiler compiler. In *UNIX Programmer's Manual*, volume 2, 353–387, 1979.

[8]　Keith D. Cooper and Linda Torczon. *Engineering a Compiler.* Morgan Kaufmann, 2004.

[9]　Bison - GNU parser generator. *http://www.gnu.org/software/bison/bison.html.*

[10]　GCJ: The GNU Compiler for Java - GNU Project - Free Software Foundation (FSF). *http://gcc.gnu.org/java/.*

[11]　GCC, the GNU Compiler Collection - GNU Project - Free Software Foundation (FSF). *http://gcc.gnu.org/.*

[12]　Groovy - Home. *http://groovy.codehaus.org/.*

[13]　Main Page - Mono. *http://www.mono-project.com/.*

Appendix: An Example of Source Code Representation in PALEX

```
<?xml version="1.0" encoding="us-ascii"?>
<parseFiles lang="java" pg="bison" ver="0.5">
<parse name="importExample.java">
<lex st="0" tk="IMPORT_TK" va="import" li="1" co="1"/>
<shi fr="0" to="3"/>
<wsc va=" "/>
<lex st="3" tk="ID_TK" va="java" li="1" co="8"/>
<shi fr="3" to="22"/>
<red st="22" ru="24"/>
<go  fr="3" to="26"/>
<red st="26" ru="22"/>
<go  fr="3" to="24"/>
<red st="24" ru="20"/>
<go  fr="3" to="23"/>
<lex st="23" tk="DOT_TK" va="." li="1" co="8"/>
<shi fr="23" to="43"/>
<lex st="43" tk="MULT_TK" va="*" li="1" co="12"/>
<shi fr="43" to="59"/>
<lex st="59" tk="SC_TK" va=";" li="1" co="13"/>
<shi fr="59" to="80"/>
<red st="80" ru="45"/>
<go  fr="0" to="15"/>
<red st="15" ru="41"/>
<go  fr="0" to="13"/>
<red st="13" ru="33"/>
<go  fr="0" to="10"/>
<wsc va=" // simple statement&#xA;"/>
<lex st="10" tk="$end" va="" li="2" co="0"/>
<red st="10" ru="27"/>
<go  fr="0" to="9"/>
<red st="9" ru="1"/>
<go  fr="0" to="8"/>
</parse>
<accept/>
</parseFiles>
```

Chapter 7

Intelligent Software Design and Maintenance

New Trends in Software Methodologies, Tools and Techniques
H. Fujita and D. Pisanelli (Eds.)
IOS Press, 2007

Normative Systems:
the meeting point between Jurisprudence and Information Technology?
A position paper

Luigi Logrippo
Université du Québec en Outaouais
Gatineau, Québec, Canada
luigi@uqo.ca

Abstract. It is argued that there are many concepts and methods in common between policy systems used in Information Technology and Jurisprudence, i.e. legal theory. These concepts are found in the research area of 'normative systems' which encompasses them and provides a framework for unifying research. It is further argued that advantages can be accrued to both research areas by favoring interchanges of methods and principles in this unifying framework. A distinction is made between norms in rule style and norms in requirements style. Issues of completeness, consistency and conflicts are considered. Concepts that are useful in this research area include defeasible logic and ontologies. Useful tools are theorem provers and model checkers.

1. Background and Motivation

This paper presents the view that legal methodology, Jurisprudence, has many issues and concepts in common with software methodology. There is much that can be learned in both fields by a process of conceptual osmosis, or even convergence. This process will be encouraged by the fact that the behavior of computational agents is increasingly acquiring legal significance. There are several areas in which this is happening: e-business (including e-contracts and security) and IT governance. In these areas, it might even become desirable that laws can be formally translated into computer programs, or that the correspondence of an IT policy with law can be formally audited. For example, a law on privacy may have to be implemented in a set of policies in a language such as XACML [17]. This set of policies may have to be checked for conformance with the law. As the law changes, the XACML policies may have to be changed as well.

A force acting in the converse direction is provided by the fact that computer networks are becoming like social systems, with their own internal norms [19].

At the same time, just as in IT software to help create systems of policies is being developed, in the area of jurisprudence *legislative drafting systems* are being developed [12]. XML is commonly used for syntactic support of both kinds of systems, however for now formal semantics and semantic validation are not primary goals in either field. Surely, developing the necessary formal models is a long-range research task in both areas.

Motivated by these developments, this paper hinges on the view that information systems policies and legal systems have much in common, in fact are special cases of *normative* systems. We identify a *rule* style and a *requirement* style in both areas. Issues of completeness and consistency are discussed in relation to these two styles. Several concepts and tools of common interest are briefly discussed.

It is important to note that we are not claiming to address all aspects of the systems we are discussing. Legal systems are extremely complex and have aspects that are quite difficult to formalize in any logic or any formal theory, since they have their roots in sociology, history, psychology, ethics and politics [9, 15]. Information systems policies are of many different types for many different applications, but they are all formalized because they are executed by machines. In order to identify similarities, we will schematize and simplify. However we claim and we shall show by examples, that there are common concepts for expressing and analyzing some aspects of these systems.

From a Jurisprudence point of view, we are taking a formalistic approach by which laws are seen as having their own self-contained meaning as pure logical statements, outside of consideration of political, sociological, or moral nature. We recognize of course that these considerations exist and open the way to other types of discussion.

2. Normative systems

In 1993, Jones and Sergot wrote: [8]

> "The general position which we here develop and illustrate is that---at the appropriate level of abstraction---law, computer systems, and many other kinds of organisational structure may be viewed as instances of normative systems. We use the term to refer to any set of interacting agents whose behaviour can usefully be regarded as governed by norms. Norms prescribe how the agents ought to behave, and specify how they are permitted to behave and what their rights are. Agents may be human individuals or collections of human individuals, or computer systems or collections of computer systems. Normative systems include systems of law, abstract models of computer systems, and hybrid systems consisting of human and computer agents in interaction."

We subscribe to this view, with two exceptions. First of all, are normative systems sets of interacting agents (legal institutions), or sets of norms? This question has been extensively debated in philosophy of law and therefore it should be avoided if possible. In this paper, we are mostly interested in sets of norms. Second, this view characterizes norms in terms of the deontic concepts of obligation ('ought to') and permission. This is a very common view, endorsed by the best authorities [9]. However in Section 3 we will see that normative systems can exist without deontic concepts.

There are few attempts to define formally norms and normative systems. Most of these attempts take a limitative view, based on specific formalisms. A much-cited book by Alchourron and Bulygin [1], which claims application to social sciences only, loosely defines norms as statements that relate cases to solutions. As in Jones and Sergot, the solutions are expressed in deontic forms.

We shall take the broad view that normative systems are man-made systems of logical statements, the norms, which relate facts to intended consequences. Their intention is to regulate the functioning of sets of interacting agents. Although they may be expressed in deontic terms, the norms can be translated into fact-consequence form. In this sense, normative systems are similar to rule-based systems. We shall see that the systems in this very general class have some common characteristics that are worth comparing and discussing. The similarities thus recognized can lead to the use of common principles and methods across different types of normative systems.

Examples of policy systems encountered in information technology, and to which we will make further reference below, are:

- Firewalls and routers
- Telecommunications features, call control
- Information access control systems (e.g. language XACML)
- Security models (Bell-LaPadula, Chinese Wall, RBAC…)
- Web services orchestration and choreography (e.g. language BPEL)
- E-commerce policies and contracts, service-level agreements

3. Norms that are simple rules

As biologists can learn much by studying elementary life forms, we can learn much by studying elementary normative forms.

The Hammurabi code, written about 3,700 years ago, contains norms such as this:

> "If any one steals cattle or sheep, or an ass, or a pig or a goat, if it belong to a god or to the court, the thief shall pay thirty fold; if they belonged to a freed man of the king he shall pay tenfold; if the thief has nothing with which to pay he shall be put to death."

This can be recognized as written in the well-known ECA: <event, condition, action> format which is widely used in data bases, agent systems, etc. [18]:

Event = any one steals cattle or sheep, or an ass, or a pig or a goat

Condition = if it belong to a god or to the court

Action = the thief shall pay thirty fold

The Hammurabi code is an early example of coherence in legislative style, since it consists of about 300 articles which are almost all written in <event, condition, action> format, another witness of the greatness of the Babylonian culture.

On the IT side, let us consider *firewalls*:

```
DROP     all -- nuisance.com  anywhere
```

This is a rule in a Linux *router* to drop packets having any ("all") protocol that come from node "nuisance.com" and go anywhere. This rule is again in the format <event, condition, action>, although the condition is empty (conditions compare the incoming events with facts that are known in the context, such as the time of occurrence, or the concepts of 'god' or 'court' in the previous example, which presumably are known in an implicit contextual ontology).

These examples show that, in spite of prevalent opinion to the contrary, normative systems can exist without deontic concepts. In fact, we conjecture that all normative systems can be expressed as sets of rules in the ECA format, although this representation may not be finite.

4. Norms in the deontic context

A commonly held view of norms interprets them in a deontic context, for which deontic logic is a frequently used formalization [14]. Deontic logic is a type of modal logic that uses modalities such as *permitted* and *obligatory*, which are mutually related by relationships such as:

> obligatory A = not permitted not A = forbidden not A

In this interpretation, the Hammurabi norm above creates an obligation to pay thirty fold; the firewall norm creates an obligation to drop all nuisance.com packets.

An early example of legal system that is explicitly based on deontic concepts is Moses' law:

> Thou shalt not steal

In other words, *it is forbidden to steal*. In this normative style, we gain abstraction, since the brief statement just given covers a dozen articles of the Hammurabi code, but we lose specificity: what happens if one steals? How is this norm enforced?

In software engineering terminology, one could think of a *compilation* of the Moses Code into Hammurabi terms, or of a *reverse engineering* of the Hammurabi code into Moses terms.

In IT one encounters deontic statements as part of documentation, or in the statement of requirements. For example, a policy in a hospital could be:

> The accounting department shall not have access to the parts of a patient's record that deal with health history

This requirement will be translated in terms of rules, e.g. if an employee of the accounting department attempts to access certain fields in the patient's record, the request will be blocked. High-level languages that allow the direct expression of such requirements are becoming available, but eventually they must be translated into rules.

Obligations can be specified in several policy languages for computing systems (notably access control [17] and business-to-business languages [13]), however in this context they don't seem to have the same meaning. In the computing context, to say that a behavior is forbidden simply means that it will not take place. To say that a behavior is compulsory means that it will take place if the conditions are verified. It could be claimed that such obligations or permissions are in fact rules.

Therefore, there is a difference between the meaning of deontic modalities in law and in IT policies, difference that must be resolved before we can use such concepts interchangeably in the two domains.

It is our view that, although modal logics have been used extensively in both Computing and Jurisprudence, the tendency to make them a ubiquitous paradigm should be resisted, because they add a level of complexity while many types of analysis can be done without them.

5. Rules and requirements

We have therefore identified two normative styles:

- The rule style (of which examples are the Hammurabi and the firewall style)

- The requirements style (of which an example is the Moses style)

This is consistent with the distinction between requirement and implementation in software methodology. The deontic style specifies requirements to be implemented by means of rules, just as software specifications must be implemented by means of programs.

The distinction between 'rules' and 'principles' in legal theory is explored in [24]. This paper makes the point that rules and principles are the extremes of a spectrum, rather than two essentially different normative styles. This is reasonable, however we contend that in a well-structured normative system these two types of norms should be clearly identified and separated.

There are of course many other normative styles, including styles that have a place between the two identified above, and others whose interpretation and classification could be the subject of endless discussion. However as mentioned we shall schematize and reason in terms of these two styles.

6. Common research topics

Within this framework, there are several research topics that are equally relevant in the areas of law and in the area of policy systems in IT. In these topics, common methods can be used. These are the topics of Completeness, Consistency, and Conflicts.

In law, as in software methodology, questions of completeness and consistency can arise:

- Between rules
- Between requirements
- Between rules and requirements

These questions may be difficult to answer because of logical interrelationships among norms. In an access control system, there may be a rule stating that only executives can access budget information, as well as definitions from which it is possible to deduce that receptionists are not executives, so it will be possible to conclude that receptionists cannot access budget information. This derived rule can be inconsistent with respect to others, or can fill an apparent gap.

6.1. Completeness

Are all cases covered in a law, are all cases covered in a software specification or in a program? What are the 'cases'? In law, conceivably they are all possible social situations. In computing, they are all possible inputs to a system, and rigid type systems are used to limit consideration to certain types of inputs; other inputs will simply be ignored, typically resulting in error messages.

In logic, a system is complete if for any statement P, a proof exists for either P or not P. In normative systems and jurisprudence, there are different and more complicated definitions [1,3,4], but one wonders why.

In law, one could at first think that if a situation is not considered, then there is no rule for it, and anything goes. In criminal law, no provision usually means that the situation is tolerated, it is sometimes said that the system contains an implicit *closure norm* to this effect: "nullum crimen sine lege".

To reason more systematically, let us consider the relationships that we have established between rules and requirements.

First of all, consider rules only or requirements only. In programming, we can have a series of tests on a variable of a certain type. If some values of the type are not considered, then the program will go to an explicit or implicit 'otherwise' statement, which plays the role of a closure norm, so incompleteness is impossible.

But normative systems often do not have 'otherwise' clauses, and in the case of law often the data types are not clearly defined. The cases that are not considered remain in some sort of limbo that has generated much literature [1, 3, 4]. The legislator's *intention* comes into consideration, and this can be the result of inductive reasoning. The intention becomes a sort of implicit requirement. Suppose that there is a domain that consists of subdomains some of which are covered by norms, and others that are not, without an explicit norm that covers all subdomains. For example, consider the case where the downtown of a city consists of streets A, B, C, and D. Different rules punish parking on A, B and C with different fines. One can conclude that parking on all downtown streets, except D, is forbidden, or that possibly the system is incomplete.

Other examples are discussed in detail in [1]. Suppose that there are norms for the case where A and B are true, and for the case where *not A* and *not B* are true. What is the norm for the case where only one of A or B is true? The fact that some cases are considered and others are not can point to an implicit requirement that all cases should be considered.

Similar situations of course can arise in the area of software requirements, if these are manually generated and interpreted.

In some domains, it is a requirement that a decision must be always achieved. An example of this situation is provided by firewall systems. A firewall must decide acceptance or rejection for each and every packet. So if there is no rule for a specific packet type, the system must apply some sort of 'default norm' to decide. For example, in Cisco firewalls, if there is no rule for a certain packet, then the packet is refused. In Linux firewalls, the default decision is acceptance. These are the 'closure norms'.

A similar situation exists in inheritance law, where a way must be found to distribute the whole inheritance.

The cases we have discussed make reference to implicit requirements. Of course, incompleteness can also be caused by relating explicit requirements with sets of explicit rules.

For example, the following norm of the Canadian Charter of Rights and Freedoms: 'Everyone has the right to life…' has been used to argue that Canada's law is incomplete because it has no norms to address abortion.

The introduction of new requirements will likely generate incompleteness, which must be filled by the introduction of new rules.

The treatment of incompleteness is very different between legal systems and IT systems. In IT, incompleteness is pathological and the system must be made complete, usually by intervention of the designer.

It is interesting to note that in legal systems filling incompleteness is often considered to be a role of the judiciary. For this reason, it is sometimes said that legal systems cannot be incomplete, because a judge can always find the rule to apply [3,4]. In IT, one could think of providing a system with meta-rules to solve incompleteness, however, unless these rules are very simple (such as the mentioned closure rule), incompleteness or inconsistency can exist at this meta-level.

6.2. Consistency

In classical logic, a system is consistent if there is no statement A for which it is possible to prove both *A* and *not A*. Different rules can cover the same cases with contradictory effects. This situation of course cannot be confused with the similar case in which two rules can be applied, but their results are compatible (e.g. one norm stipulates a repayment, another stipulates a fine). As for incompleteness, we can identify the following cases:

- Inconsistencies between rules
- Inconsistencies between requirements
- Inconsistencies between rules and requirements

In classical logic, in an inconsistent system anything can be derived, because an inconsistency is false and from false anything can be derived. Therefore, any inconsistency has global implications. However this conclusion is insignificant in practice. If an enterprise database contains an inconsistency, users normally still believe the rest, although the more inconsistencies are found, the more confidence will decrease. If an inconsistency is found in rules for a complex game, players will still play the game according to the remaining rules. Therefore the users of an inconsistent system tend more to isolate the inconsistent part, than to say that since the system is inconsistent it can't be used. And in those cases that are not flagrant, users try to iron out inconsistencies by means of interpretation, i.e. by trying to show that different assertions apply to different cases. In other words, it may be possible to interpret the clauses in such a way that the inconsistency disappears. This is a main occupation for judges and lawyers.

In software methodology, inconsistency among requirements is generating a literature [7, 15], and the solutions proposed are complex.

The case of inconsistencies between rules is explicitly considered in several types of IT systems. In most cases (programs, firewalls) the rules are executed top down and this will automatically eliminate inconsistency because one of the mutually inconsistent rules won't be reached. However it remains to be seen whether the result corresponds to the intent of the designer. In other systems there are explicit 'combining algorithms' to solve inconsistencies. For example, in the case of the access control language XACML these are Deny-Overrides, Permit-Overrides, First Applicable, and Only-One Applicable, plus others that can be defined by the user [17].

In Western jurisprudence, some overriding principles have been known for centuries, such as (in their Latin versions): *lex specialis derogat generalis, lex posterior derogat prior, lex superior derogat inferior*, i.e. a law can be modified by a more specific one, or by a later one, or by one of higher hierarchical position.

Still, there is question of whether the application of the chosen algorithm or principle may betray the intention of the author of the norms, who may not fully understand all existing conflicts and their possible solutions.

In IT, much study has been generated by a particular type of inconsistency, called Feature Interaction. This subject attracted the attention of designers of telephony features, when they realized that the combination of several features led in some cases to problems, because one feature could disrupt the intended effect of another. This could occur on one end of the system, or, worse, between ends. The more general case of this problem can be stated in the following way. In a component-based system, some components may have mutually inconsistent requirements. How can this be detected, can they still be combined? A series of workshops and conferences has been dedicated to this topic, they started in 1992 and the most recent has been [17].

An analysis of inconsistency of norms from the legal and deontic point of view is presented in [5].

It appears then that the most practical solution for inconsistency in normative systems is to report the existing inconsistencies to the designer of the system for human resolution.

6.3. Ontologies

Advanced normative systems use extensive sets of definitions to structure the domain on which they act. Family and inheritance laws are typical examples. Companies have organizational structure that is taken into consideration in company policies. For example, employees can be characterized by roles. We are all familiar with call processing systems that forward calls on specific matters to employees with a certain role. The well-known access control method called RBAC (for Role-Based Access Control) [6] uses roles to determine access rights to databases or other resources.

These definitions form ontologies, which are hierarchical data structures containing attributes for the entities in a certain domain, together with their relationships. Some literature [5] refers to ontologies with the name of *world knowledge*, which they contrast with *normative knowledge.*

The conditions that we have mentioned with relation to ECA systems refer to ontologies.

Ontologies and definitions can act as rule generators: e.g. we can have a norm saying that theft is punished in a certain way, then definitions saying that certain behaviors are theft. The combination of these definitions with norms that use them creates new norms. By using RBAC, access control rules are associated to roles rather than to users. Without RBAC, access rules have to be attached to users, so there have to be many more rules, in addition there have to be mechanisms for attaching and detaching rules from users, as the roles of users change. Similarly, in object-oriented languages such as Java, one can define an array of students, and then on this basis one can create a Java class for each student.

Hence, the use of ontologies can substantially simplify and shorten the expression of rules.

Although some normative systems may not contain explicit definitions or ontologies, in reality every such system depends on such information, which may be externally defined or understood in the social context. Firewalls, for example, depend on implicit ontologies such as the structure of the Internet addressing space, the structure of the systems ports, etc.

The study of ontologies for legal systems is arguably the research area in which Jurisprudence seem to be taking the greatest inspiration from Information Technology [2, 22, 23].

6.4. Conflicts between peers

Conflicts can occur between peers when their requests or policies are incompatible, in fact or potentially. In the case where parties are aiming at an agreement, it may be possible to solve conflicts by a negotiation phase, or by concluding that no agreement is possible. In law, this is the material for arbitrators, judges, lawyers. In computing systems, this is material for the operating system, centralized or distributed. The operating system is the government authority in these systems. The difficulty of this subject is visible in many examples. For example, the deadlock problem in operating systems is computationally unsolvable, in the sense that it is impossible to determine that a deadlock is possible or to prevent it.

Although nowadays there is a lot of confidence in peer-to-peer systems and their ability to solve problems by peer-to-peer agreements, issues such as the feature interaction problem and the deadlock problem show that this confidence is unfounded. Authentication also cannot be done on a pure end-to-end basis. It appears that trusted third parties are necessary to solve these problems, as well as others. Trusted third parties are already used in authentication. Hence, distributed systems will acquire some of the architectural characteristics of legal systems, with their legislators, judges and notaries.

7. Normative systems for electronic societies

Societies are ruled by laws and customs. Those who do not abide by them are punished or emarginated. Electronic societies can span the world and these enforcement methods may not be effective, as we all know by our constant fight against spam and viruses. Similarly, we can get into what appears to be a bona fide electronic agreement with a party, and then we are helpless when we see that the party does something we don't believe was agreed.

A model for peer-to-peer agreements and electronic societies may be provided by international law, which is constituted mainly of customs and multilateral conventions.

Collaboration of distributed systems can only be achieved if they all use certain common mechanisms. For example, interprocess communication in a set of distributed Java processes depends on all the processes using synchronized methods. Such tacit agreements constitute customs.

In law and society, many customs exist that are respected by all who want to be considered reliable citizen. For example, if Alice lends a book to Bob, Bob is supposed to check back with Alice if she wants to lend it to Carl. However in telephony Bob can automatically forward to Carl a call from Alice without checking with her. So Alice may find herself talking to Carl, although she may have Carl on her incoming call screening list. This is a well-know example of interaction of telephony features that is possible because of violation of a rule that is well understood in society, but not so in telephony.

Unequal agreements with network entities such as Skype, who dictates terms of operation, may be similar to protectorates. Consortia such as Apache, where participants can collaborate in the evolution of the system, are more similar to alliances. In computing systems we can have multi-faceted situations where a user can be simultaneously in many such agreements, again creating the possibility of inconsistencies. People routinely click the 'Accept all conditions' box, happily no one compares all such clauses that have been accepted.

Network entities will associate with other entities they can trust, and this will establish societies of mutual trust. Concepts and modes of operations will be created in these societies, some of which will slowly gain acceptance, thus enlarging the societies. The concept of Web of Trust is an application of this idea.

8. Useful concepts and tools

8.1. Defeasible logic

We have seen that in some systems there are implicit meta-rules by which some rules take the priority. I.e. in firewalls, the rules that come first take the priority. This is not justifiable in logic terms, because order has no importance in logic. Similarly, in legal system all norms are equally valid unless otherwise said.

Defeasible logic is a logic already well-known in AI and philosophy of law. It is a non-monotonic logic first proposed in [16]. It involves three types of propositions:

- Hard rules: these specify that a fact is always a consequence of another: all packets from spammers.com must be refused.
- Defeasible rules: specify that a fact is *typically* a consequence of another: all packets from nuisance.com must be refused
- Defeaters: specify *exceptions* to defeasible rules: packets from luigi@nuisance.com must be accepted.

Therefore, before applying a defeasible rule, it must be checked for defeaters. Defeasible logic provides a framework for specifying exceptions and priorities. Interestingly, it is difficult to find hard rules in nowadays' legal systems, a fact that creates a lot of work for lawyers and judges...

The closure norm can be seen as a defeasible norm. It exists in the system, but can be defeated by any other norm. It applies only if no other norm applies. If defeasible logic is not used, the closure norm can be constructed as the norm that applies when the conjunction of the negation of the premises of all other norms is true, and this conjunction may be very lengthy indeed.

8.2. Theorem Provers and Model Checkers

The commonality of concepts and issues leads to a commonality of automated tools that can be used in this research area.

Theorem provers and model checkers can be used to prove consistency and completeness, although they face computational complexity constraints and they are difficult to use.

Evidently, the use of such tools is much more difficult in the domain of law, because laws often are not based on precise ontologies. However, this may change in some areas of law, especially those that deal with electronic media.

8.3. Tools for Ontologies

It was mentioned above that there is considerable similarity of methods between Jurisprudence and IT in the use of ontologies. In fact, OWL, the Web Ontology Language for the Semantic Web, together with its tools, is a common reference in both areas [2,10].

9. Conclusions

In the new era of e-commerce and agent societies, IT is encountering some of the problems that have motivated Jurisprudence for thousands of years. Increasingly, the behavior of information systems is gaining legal relevance. On the other hand, IT can contribute to transform these problems by injecting new dimensions, as well as methods and tools for precision and for quick, automatic decisions.

Similarities and relationships can be found in the areas of architecture (the system of legal institutions in Jurisprudence) and norms. In this paper we have concentrated on this second area.

We have argued that there are many principles in common among different types of normative systems, including IT and Jurisprudence. These common principles can be studied in general terms and common methods and tools can be developed. Our classification of normative styles in Section 5 has allowed us to draw several parallels.

Acknowledgment. This research has been funded in part by the Natural Sciences and Engineering Research Council of Canada. I am indebted to Guido Governatori of the University of Queensland for contributing ideas with detailed comments on an earlier version of this paper, and for introducing me to defeasible logic. As well, I am indebted to my PhD student Waël Hassan for many discussions on related topics. I would like to dedicate this paper to the memory of Fritz Paradies, a lawyer and scholar in Frankfurt and Amsterdam, who wrote about normative concepts in programming languages in the 1960s.

References

[1]   Alchourròn, C.E., Bulygin, E.: *Normative Systems*. Springer, 1971.
[2]   Casanovas, P., Biasiotti, M.A., Francesconi, F., Sagri, M.T. (Eds): Proc. of the Workshop on Legal Ontologies and Artificial Intelligence Techniques (LOAIT 2007), June 2007.
[3]   Chiassoni, P.: A tale from two traditions: Civil law, Common law, and legal gaps. Analisi e Diritto, 2006, 51-74.
      http://www.giuri.unige.it/intro/dipist/digita/filo/testi/analisi_2007/ accessed June 2007.
[4]   Conte, A.G. : *Saggio sulla completezza degli ordinamenti giuridici.* Giappichelli, 1962.
[5]   Elhag, A. A. O., Breuker, J. A. P. J., Brouwer, P. W. : On the formal analysis of normative conflicts. Information & Communications Technology Law, 9:3 (2000), 207– 217.

[6]   Ferraiolo, D.F., Kuhn, D.R., Chandramouli, R.: *Role-based Access Control.* Artech House, 2003.

[8]   Gervasi, V., Zowghi, D.: Reasoning about inconsistencies in natural language requirements. ACM Transactions on Software Engineering and Methodology, 14(3):277-330, July 2005.

[9]   Jones, A.J.I., Sergot, M.: On the characterisation of law and computer systems: The normative systems perspective. In: *Deontic Logic in Computer Science: Normative System Specification,* J.-J.C. Meyer and R.J. Wieringa (Eds), Wiley, 1993.

[10] Kelsen, H.: *General Theory of Law and State.* Harvard University Press, 1945.

[11] Lacy, L.W.: *OWL: Representing Information Using The Web Ontology Language.* Trafford, 2005.

[12] Lee, A. J., Boyer, J. P., Olson, L. E., and Gunter, C. A.: Defeasible security policy composition for web services. In Proc. of the Fourth ACM Workshop on Formal Methods in Security (Alexandria, Virginia, USA, November 03 - 03, 2006).

[13] McIver, W.J.: Software support for multilingual legislative drafting. CIRN Conference and Colloquium, Oct. 2004.

[14] Medjahed, B., Benatallah, B., Bouguettaya, A., Ngu, A.H.H., Elmagarmid, A.K.: Business-to-business interactions: issues and enabling technologies. The Very Large Data Base Journal (2003) 12: 59–85.

15] Meyer, J.J.C., Wieringa, R.J. (Eds.): *Deontic Logic in Computer Science: Normative System Specification.* Wiley, 1993.

[16] Nuseibeh, B., Easterbrook, S., Russo, A.: Making Inconsistency Respectable in Software Development, Journal of Systems and Software, 58(2):171-180, 2001.

[17] Nute, D.: Defeasible logic. In *Handbook of logic in artificial intelligence and logic programming, volume 3*: Nonmonotonic reasoning and uncertain reasoning, 353-395. Oxford University Press, 1994.

[18] OASIS, Organization for the Advancement of Structured Information Standards.: XACML, eXtensible Access Control Language. www.oasis-open.org/committees/xacml/ accessed May 2007.

[19] Paton, N.W. (Ed.): *Active Rules in Database Systems.* Springer, 1999.
       Pitt. J. (Ed.): *Open Agent Societies: Normative Specifications in Multi-Agent Systems.* Wiley, 2004.

[20] Reiff-Marganiec, S., Ryan, M.D.: *Feature Interactions in Telecommunications and Software Systems VIII,* IOS Press, 2005.

[21] Sartor, G.: *Legal Reasoning: A Cognitive Approach to the Law.* Springer, 2005.

[22] Valente, A.: Legal knowledge engineering: A modeling approach. IOS Press, 1995.

[23] van Kralingen, R.W., van den Herik, H.J., Prins, J.E.J., Sergot, M., Zeleznikow J. (eds.): Legal Knowledge Based Systems: Foundations of legal knowledge systems. Proc. of Jurix 2006, IOS Press, 2006.

[24] Verheij, B., Hage, J.C., van den Herik, H. J.: An integrated view on rules and principles. Artificial Intelligence and Law, Vol. 6 (1998), No. 1, 3-26

New Trends in Software Methodologies, Tools and Techniques
H. Fujita and D. Pisanelli (Eds.)
IOS Press, 2007

On Implementability of the Formal Specifications[1]

Victor MALYSHKIN
Supercomputer Software Department (SSD),
Institute of Computational Mathematics and Mathematical Geophysics,
Russian Academy of Sciences,
630090, Novosibirsk, RUSSIA
malysh@ssd.sscc.ru, http://ssd.sscc.ru

Abstract. The paper is devoted to the consideration of the problem of formal specifications implementability and program synthesis.

1. Introduction

The idea of the paper is to consider the problem of a formal specification representation, analysis of its implementability and program synthesis. Central point of the consideration is the technological implementability of the formal specification.

This problem came from the investigation of the problem how to automate the construction of parallel programs of large-scale numerical modeling. There are now several well-known and widely used universal numerical methods, like particle-in-cell (PIC) [1,2] or Monte Carlo [3], which are applied to solution of many different problems. Number of experts well experienced in correct application of these methods and correct implementation of the numerical models on this basis is very limited. Therefore, there is the necessity to include numerous details of these numerical models implementation and their parallel implementation into the knowledge base of an intelligent system.

The idea of the paper is to consider the implementable methods of parallel program construction from a formal specification for the large scale numerical modeling.

2. Steps of software construction from the intention.

The following steps of the software construction from an intention can be listed:
`Informal specification` $\to$ `Formal specification` $\to$ `Algorithmation` $\to$ `Program construction/synthesis`. The `Informal specification`, expressed in natural language, is not considered here because there are no now reliable and well implementable methods for understanding of the user's intention and its transformation into the `Formal specification`.

---

[1] The work was supported by the grants: Rosobrazovanie, contract RNP.2.2.1.1.3653; NWO-RFBS, contract 047.016.007; NWO-RFBS, contract 047.016.018.

We say that **Informal specification** is *Not_Implementable*. For the same reason the step of **Formal specification** is divided into two steps: **Formal_specification → Formal_implementable_specification**. The step **Formal specification** is also not considered because not any formal specification is implementable. Only **Formal implementable specification** is considered.

Implementability and Not_implementability of the formal specification. The notion of specification implementability should be now elaborated. For specification implementation the values should be assigned to any variable, to any operation and object of the specification (there exist the proper algorithms). If this is impossible to do, then such a specification is *Not_Implementable*.

Potential implementability of a specification means, that there exists an implementing algorithm, may be unknown for now. *Dynamic implementability* means that a proper algorithm exists and can be chosen/constructed in the course of execution only. For example, the functional specification of the function of matrices multiplication is $c_{ij}=\sum a_{ik}\times b_{kj}$. This functional specification contains the description of all the thinkable algorithms of matrices multiplication, but the choice of the best algorithm to be used in a certain program depends on the properties of the input matrices, on the criteria of the quality of the implementation and go on. The quality of implementation is a substantial part of the notion of implementability. In particular, if the values of matrices entries can be from 10^{-20} to 10^{20}, then a special algorithm of matrices multiplication should be constructed for implementation of the same specification because otherwise the quality of the entry values will be far from the desirable. It is clear, that the correct choice cannot be done statically.

Static implementability provides the choice/construction of an implementing algorithm in the course of compilation (traditional programming languages are mostly statically implementable). The cases of potential implementability and dynamic implementability can be called as *technologically Not_Implementable* specifications, in the latter case because of high complexity of they implementation. In programming this means that high quality of a program cannot be reached in general case. Even low level mathematical specification can be technologically Not_Implementable.

In such a way, we consider only the diagram **Formal_Implementable_specification → Algorithmation → Program_construction/synthesis.** The question is: what formal specifications are suitable, i.e., technologically implementable, and can be used for automation of the human activities. It is well know that not any functional specification is implementable.

Logic derivation of an algorithm. One of the possible implementable treatment of the idea "dream⇒good_program" is given in the paper by Zohar Manna [4], where the dream is represented as functional specification from which an algorithm is derived (problem algorithmation). Unfortunately, this approach did not meet and could not meet good success because it does not provide the derivation of an algorithm and construction of the implementing program of the required quality [5].

Language of mathematics. Another example gives the idea that the best programming language is the language of mathematics. The project for implementation of this idea was formulated in 1963 in the paper by I.B.Zadykhailo [6]. This very attractive idea is also very far from good implementability and should be rejected. Even low level mathematical specification can be technologically Not-Implementable [5].

3. Structural program synthesis

Thus, another idea should be used. Obviously, this is the idea of the program synthesis from some implementable specification. General formulation of the program synthesis problem is. Given:

- class S of input problem specifications,
- class P of resulting programs,
- equivalency relation $\sim$ on P,
- quality relation $>$ on P, that satisfies to the axioms of the partial order.

The algorithm $A{:}S{\rightarrow}P$ should be found that:

- Program $p{=}A(s)$, $p{\in}P$, satisfies to the specification $s{\in}S$,
- p is the best (in the sense $>$) program among $\{p|p{\sim}A(s)\}$

In such a way, the algorithm $A{:}S{\rightarrow}P$ solves a program synthesis problem, that is, for every specification $s{\in}S$, the algorithm A construct an element $p{=}A(s)$, $p{\in}P$, which is the best program among all the programs solving specified problem s.

Generally, the system of program synthesis should contain the following components. First, the description of a knowledge base of an object domain should be prepared. As a rule the knowledge base contains the variables and specification of the actions/operations in order to compute one variable from the others. For example, the knowledge base, that describes numerical computations, should contain the description of the matrices and specification of an operation how to multiply two matrices and to compute their product. Such a specification of an operation can be implementable or no.

The next component can be called as *planner*. If a user says that he knows the values of the variables of a set V and asks, either the variables of a set W can be computed or no, then the planner should construct (derive) the algorithms computing W variables from V variables or explain, that this algorithm can't be constructed and why. Usually this algorithm is represented as a set of functional terms [7, 8, 9] Certainly, all the sets above should be countable sets otherwise the specifications will be initially not implementable.

The third component is the *generator* of a program. It constructs a program implementing derived algorithm, taken into account the peculiarities of the input and output data and the program's executing environment.

Depending on character of object domain formalization several substantially different approaches to program synthesis can be considered. The pure theoretical approach to program synthesis is represented by the method of logical synthesis of programs. The object domain specification here used is a mathematical calculus. This is very attractive approach but, unfortunately, technologically not implementable, because:

- usually for practical object domain there are no chances to develop non-contradictory calculus of proper completeness.

- this approach cannot provide the derivation of an algorithm and construction of implementing program of the required quality

For these reasons we are forced to use in practice the methods with less possibilities for knowledge base description, but more suitable for machine processing. One of such methods is based on imposing a structure on the knowledge base that reflects the associative dependences between the objects of the object domain. In the process of an algorithm derivation the explicit representation of these dependences in computer permits to use the associative search instead of random search in logical programming. This approach to program synthesis is known as the method of structural program synthesis [9]. Rephrased idea of structural program synthesis is:

- there is no any technological sense to develop the universal system for algorithm derivation from functional specification.

- The desirable program should be constructed out of accumulated well developed ready-made modules.

Informally the idea of the method of structural program synthesis method can be demonstrated by the following irresponsible example [10]. Let us imagine themselves the impassable jungle with the dragons, dreadful monsters and animals, etc. (fig. 1a). In order to cross the jungle automatically from point x_0 to point x_3 the careful, in all the thinkable details, description of the jungle should be created (the non-contradictory theory of proper completeness should be developed in logic programming). In practice, such full knowledge base initially does not exist and nobody tries to create it. Therefore, if it is necessary to cross the jungle from point x_0 to point x_3, the pioneers, using currently accumulated knowledge on jungle, beat the path a through the jungle (fig. 1b). Not excluded, that performing this exploit some of them will be eaten by animals, e.g., tigers or lions. But after that the other people will be able to use this path and to cross the jungle even if they have very poor knowledge on jungle. In order to cross the jungle the others should only to go along the path a. Likewise the other paths from y_0 to y_1 and from z_0 to z_2 can be beaten. At the same time it is discovered that the path $x_0x_1z_1z_2$ is also beaten and from x_0 to x_3 two paths $x_0x_1x_2x_3$ and $x_0x_1z_1x_2x_3$ leads (fig. 1c). The latter longer path can be considered as more preferable then the first one in the case a hungry tiger awaits a lone traveler inside the interval x_1x_2.

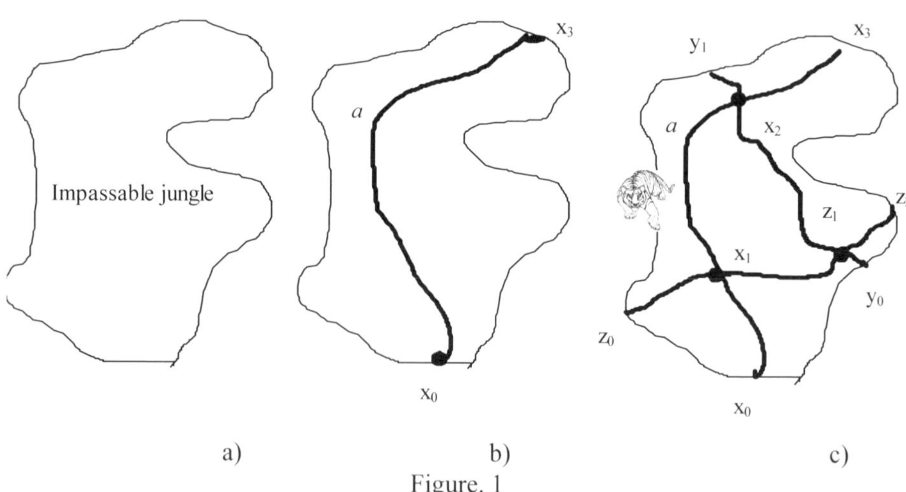

Figure. 1

A path serves here as an image of an algorithm. The sequence of the algorithm's steps/operations a_1, a_2, a_3 corresponds to the path a (fig. 2). The operation a_1 computes the value of the variable x_1 from the value of the variable x_0, etc. An operation can be implemented in a program by a procedure. Thus, the value of the variable x_3 is computed from the value of the variable x_0 by the sequence $x_0 \rightarrow a_1 \rightarrow x_1 \rightarrow a_2 \rightarrow x_2 \rightarrow a_3 \rightarrow x_3$ of the operations.

Likewise the value of the variable z_2 is computed from the value of the variable z_0 (the path $z_0x_1z_1z_2$) by the sequence of the operations $z_0 \rightarrow b_1 \rightarrow x_1 \rightarrow b_2 \rightarrow z_1 \rightarrow b_3 \rightarrow z_2$, the value of the variable y_1 is computed from the value of the variable y_0 (the path $y_0z_1x_2y_1$) by the sequence of the operations $y_0 \rightarrow c_1 \rightarrow z_1 \rightarrow c_2 \rightarrow x_2 \rightarrow c_3 \rightarrow y_1$. Then the variable x_3 can be computed from x_0 by two different algorithms, that correspond to two different paths $x_1x_2x_3$ and $x_0x_1z_1x_2x_3$, that are actually the algorithms $x_0 \rightarrow a_1 \rightarrow x_1 \rightarrow b_2 \rightarrow z_1 \rightarrow c_2 \rightarrow x_2 \rightarrow a_3 \rightarrow x_3$ and $x_0 \rightarrow a_1 \rightarrow x_1 \rightarrow a_2 \rightarrow x_2 \rightarrow a_3 \rightarrow x_3$.

In such a way, in the method of structural program synthesis the knowledge base constitutes the collection of good algorithms (the computational model), well implemented as procedures. The combination (superposition) of the good algorithm also can be good algorithm. It will not be obligatorily the optimal algorithm, but it should not be the worst algorithm. The problem of a good algorithm derivation is now reduced to the restricted controlled search on the graph.

Computational model is used for the knowledge base representation. Program synthesis problem is given in static formulation. Given:
- computational model C (a set of dependences),
- set of input variables V,
- set of output variables W.

A problem s is formulated as: **on C compute W from V**   (1)

An algorithm, solving the specified problem s should be derived and an implementing program P should be constructed. Certainly, this problem formulation can be used in dynamic case too.

Contrary to logic programming functional specification is not given here, the desirable function is defined by the structure of the computational model C. Actually, for problem specification (1) the finite set of algorithms solving a problem is defined by the computational model C. If C contains well implemented dependences (good modules or procedures) then there are good chances that the final program will be of good quality too. From technological viewpoint, the structural synthesis of program [9] is the model that exploits the idea of the module re-use. If there is a set of good programs, then, under proper conditions, new program, assembled out of good modules can be also of good quality.

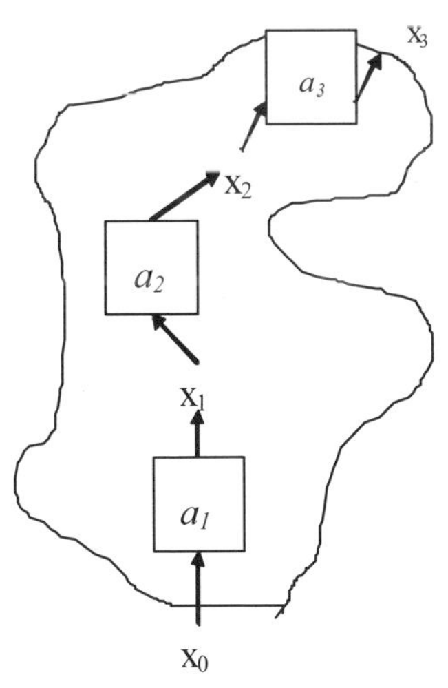

Figure.2

A technologically implementable specification is represented here as very attractive tuple (C,V,W). List of input data V, list of desirable results W are given and implementing software is automatically constructed. But finite model of structural synthesis of program is very restricted model. Obviously, the specified algorithm is well derived on computational model.

4. Conclusion

Suggested structural program synthesis method provides the use of the technologically implementable specification and synthesis of a program with the desirable properties. The specification (C,V,W) is, may be, the best technologically implementable specification for now. It is clear from the consideration above that technologically implementable specification and the method of algorithm derivation from this specification and program construction should be closely coupled.

Accumulating of numerical algorithms, implementing different aspects of the particle-in-cell method application provides the possibility to assemble new application of the PIC out of ready made library modules in the above described manner.

References

[1].	R Hockney R.W., Eastwood J.W. Computer simulation using particles. McGraw-Hill Inc. 1981.

[2].	Yu.N.Grigoryev, V.A.Vshivkov, M.P.Fedoruk Numerical Particle-in-Cell methods. Theory and applications. VSP, Utrecht, Bocton, 2002.

[3].	Jun S. Liu. Monte Carlo Strategies in Scientific Computing. Springer Verlag, Springer Texts in Statistics, 2002

[4].	Z.Manna, R.Waldinger. Synthesis: dreams$\Rightarrow$programs// IEEE Tr. On SE, 1979, Vol. SE-5, pp. 294-398.

[5].	V.Malyshkin. Concepts and Operationalism, Turbulence and Ontology, Specification and Implementation in Software Engineering. – In series New Trends in Software Methodologies, Tools and Techniques, IOS Press, Vol. 111, pp. 49-54. Proceeding of the SoMeT'04 Int. conference, 28-30 September 2004, Leipzig, Germany.

[6].	I.B.Zadykhailo. Sostavlenie tsiklov po parametricheskim zapisyam spetsialnogo vida. Zhurnal vychislitelnoi mathematiki I mathematicheskoi physiki. 1963, Vol.3, No.2, pp. 337-357 (in Russian)

[7].	A.I.Maltsev. Algorithms and recursive functions. - Moscow, Nauka, 1986, in Russian. (Algoritmy i vychislimye funktsii).

[8].	Hartley Rogers. Jr, *Theory of Recursive Functions and Effective Computability,* Mc Graw -Hill, 1967

[9].	A.Valkovskii, V.E.Malyshkin. *Synthesis of Parallel Programs and Systems on the Basis of Computational Models.//* Nauka, Novosibirsk, 1988. (In Russian, Sintez parallel'nykh programm i sistem na vychislitel'nykh modelyakh)

[10].	V.Malyshkin, V.Korneev. Parallel programming of multicomputers. – In series "NSTU Textbooks", Publishing house of the State Technical University of Novosibirsk, 2006, 296 pp. (Parallelnoe programmirovanie multicomputerov).

New Trends in Software Methodologies, Tools and Techniques
H. Fujita and D. Pisanelli (Eds.)
IOS Press, 2007

An Introduction to the Quantitative, Rational and Scientific Process of Software Development (Part 1)

Zenya Koono[a,1], Hui Chen[b] and Hassan Abolhassani[c]

[a] *Creation Project, Kanagawa, Japan*
[b]*Information Science Center, Kokushikan University, Tokyo, Japan*
[c]*Computer Engineering Dept., Sharif University of Technology, Teheran, Iran*

Abstract. Repetitive decomposing of the objective concept hierarchically, developed for design involves a human intentional activity, ranging from management to physical works. This model proved the empirical rules in Industrial Engineering. In addition to these "design" process characteristics, the "test" process is found to be a defect attenuating process with the attenuation rate of its error rate of the second kind. As these are applicable to any software process, they are very useful.

Keywords. Design, Test, Process, Productivity, Man-hours, Defect, Defect intensity, Industrial Engineering

Introduction

After the end of the 19th Century the industrial production of hardware began, and Industrial Engineering (IE)[1] was also born, and overcome many problems and built up the Production Control of hardware. Later at the beginning of the 20th Century, Quality Control made rapid progress. IE achieved the industrialized production.

Japan introduced IE almost 50 years later than advanced countries. Due to this delay, the rapid deployment of IE began. In the middle of the 1960's, the IE's standard time system was introduced in hardware factories and penetrated many industries. In the 1970's to 1980's, Japanese Total Quality Control/Management (TQC/M) grew and it enabled economical production and quality products from Japan poured into the world.

IE's quantitative, rational and scientific technologies achieved these. The purpose of Part 1 is to introduce them to software development. This is the "product" aspect, and Part 2[2] discusses the "process" aspect[3]. Section 1 introduces design by repeated decomposing of the objective concept hierarchically to mean objects; it is common to mental work and to physical work. Section 2 proves the empirical rules of IE. These mean that the basics of IE may be used also in software. Section 3 explains that a test is a defect attenuator, and the decreasing rate is equal to the second kind of error rate of inspection. Various field data are explained to enable a quantitative evaluation of these.

---

¹ Corresponding Author: Representative, Creation Project, Honfujiswa 2-13-5, Fujisawa, Kanagawa, 251-0875, Japan; E-mail:koono@vesta.ocn.ne.jp.

1. Human intentional activity

"Stepwise detailing" by Wilth, N. in 1971 is regarded as the first proposal for a design method in software. Later, it was developed into various structured methods from the 1970's to 1980's. They claim that functions have a hierarchical structure. The hierarchical decomposition is a common structure in various design methodologies. Figure 1[4, 5] shows the authors' design that repeats the hierarchical decomposition of an elementary data flow.

On the left side of Figure 1, data flows show the design record of a Clock program. The specification "clock" is defined by input and output data to form an elementary data flow. It is regarded as a parent and is decomposed to the detailed data flow of the children in the next level. This consists of three *serial* elementary data flows "Obtain time," "Obtain hands" and "Display", following Myers' STS division[6].

As it is a program, an execution sequence of each function is needed. A flowchart starts from a compressed barrel symbol above the first function and goes along the bold line to reach the end mark of a compressed barrel on the last function.

Next, three elementary data flows are decomposed hierarchically. The figure shows that of "Obtain hands." The input and output data of the elementary data flow are hierarchically decomposed, and using the pattern of Jackson's program design[7], the elementary data flow "Obtain hands" is hierarchically decomposed to three *parallel* elementary data flows.

On a lower level a hierarchical decomposition of an elementary data flow "Obtain minute hand" is shown. The detailed result shows that the degree is 6 times sixty minutes, and the next hierarchical decompositions are to convert this from natural language expressions to programming language expressions as the implementation means.

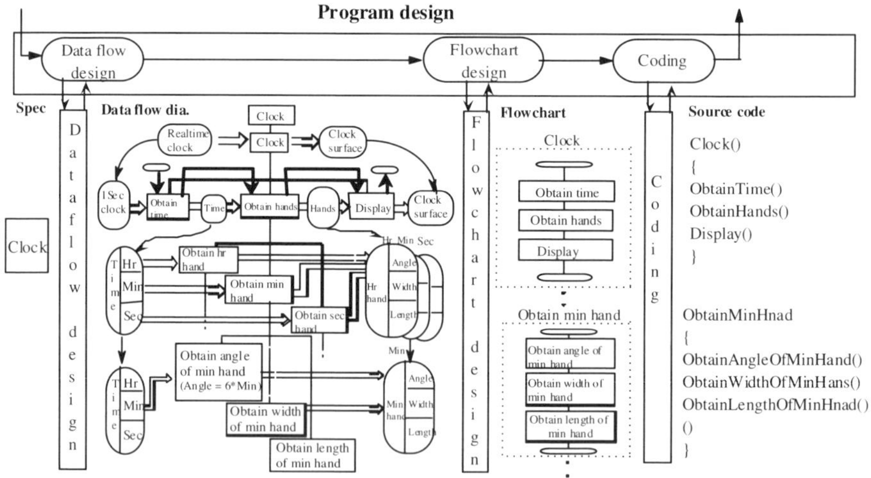

Figure 1. Design records of "Clock Program"

A design is repetitive hierarchical decompositions. As it is repeated, it becomes clearer, more detailed and minute[8]. At the final stage, they are converted to the implementation means (c. f. source code).

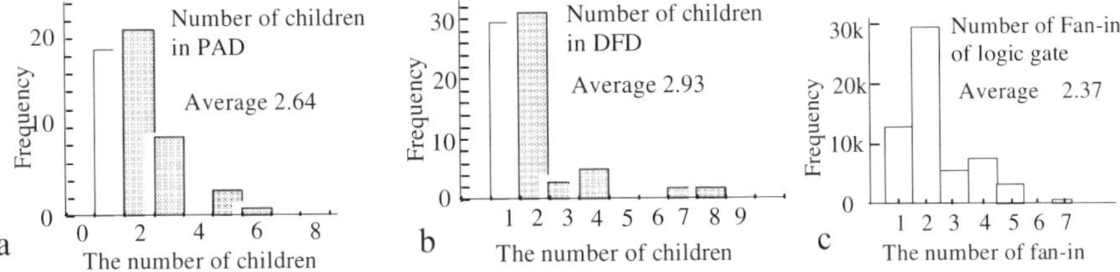

Figure 2. Various expansion rates

As the authors were studying the automatic design learning from human design[20], the aforementioned hierarchical decomposition was standardized. As the experience is accumulated, it was found that it brings about a good design (ease of understanding) and constancy of the expansion rate. Figure 2.a[9] and 2.b[9] are taken from actual designs. Figure 2.c[10] is from a logic circuit design. In logic circuit design, a designer synthesizes a logic circuit using lower level logic signals, which is the same as the hierarchical decomposition. These three show a similar expansion distribution.

The average is a little smaller than 3. It is lower than the usual number of chunks. Surveys in cognitive science found two experiments. The first one is that the expansion rate in a short-term memory is around 2. Another is that larger chunks appear in cases where a long time is allowed for remembering. From these, the average rate seems to appear as a result of a speed neck. A theoretical study shows that e = 2.71828.. is the optimum, but not yet perfect.

Let us examine other cases. Figure 3.a [11] shows the human intention for a physical action, "take a picture." It is hierarchically decomposed to the three implementation means as shown in the figure. Each of these may be further hierarchically decomposed repetitively until they are reduced to nerve signals to drive a muscle as intended.

In military science, "Hierarchy of Object[12]" is an important empirical law in planning a war. It is a repetitive hierarchical decomposition to the details of "occupy island X" as shown in Figure 3.b[11]. This law is explained as follows:

The highest executive of a nation assigns the final objective of the war to the supreme commander. This person decomposes it to several means to attain it, and assigns each to the respective subordinates. Then these people do similar actions. Through repeating thus the plan of the war may be detailed.

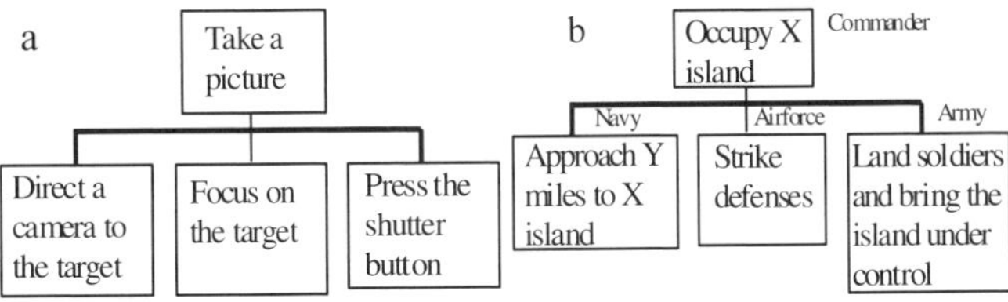

Figure 3. Human intentional activities

Thus continuing, the final objective is broken down to each move of the soldiers involved.

As shown by these three examples of human intentional activity, this repetitive hierarchical decomposition may involve a management objective (at management level), a function (at design level) and then on down to human physical action. All kinds of designs are included in these. The central core of software design is to perform the hierarchical decompositions of concepts in the problem area. The program technique is the implementation means used at the final stage.

2. Constancies of productivity and defect intensity

The axioms in hardware production control and quality control in IE are following simple *empirical rules*. If they are applicable also in software, almost all of the techniques in the IE may be used also in software.

- Linear nature
  Hierarchical decomposition and integration
  (Simple arithmetic operations are possible)
- Productivity
  = (Man-hours)/(number of items)
  = constant
- Defect (build-in) intensity
  = (Number of defects)/(number of items)
  = constant

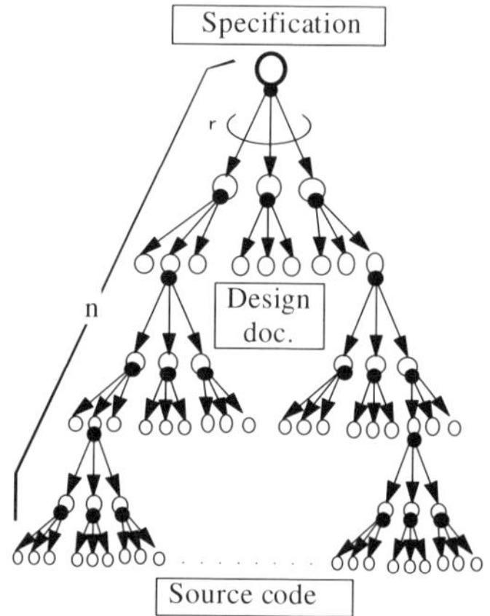

Figure 4. Hierarchically expanding network model

Although more than 100 years had passed since they began to be used, these empirical rules have not yet been theoretically proven. The object of this section is to prove these apply to human intentional activities in general and also in software.

As has been mentioned before, "producing" and "designing" belong to human intentional activity. The central core of the activity is repetitive hierarchical decomposition. Figure 4[13, 5] shows a model of this activity. A white circle is information; a black dot is an elementary processing node. r is the expansion rate, and that is a constant.

In a design, an elementary decomposition node at the top decomposes hierarchically a specification at the top to r intermediate outputs. Next r elementary decomposition nodes operate sequentially. All nodes operate sequentially like the single stroke of a brush, and the final outputs are generated.

Let us assume that a small time t elapses while an elementary decomposition node operates. The man-hours consumed in this network may be evaluated by multiplying them by $t \cdot$(the total number of elementary decomposition nodes). Let us assume that the elementary decomposition nodes err at a small error rate of e, and thus the erred output propagates through to the final output. By $e \cdot$(the total number of elementary decomposition nodes), the total number of errors, namely defects, in the final output may be calculated. Thus through these the total number of outputs, both productivity and defect intensity, may be obtained. If these results proved both constancies, the empirical rules are proved by the aforementioned mechanism, 100 years after they came into use.

When r is constant, the characteristics of the hierarchically expanding network model shown in Figure 4 may be calculated using the formula of a constant-rate increasing series. Let us assume that the network consists of n levels from the top to the bottom. Let N_p be the total number of nodes in the network, and N_o the total number of the output information. These are expressed as follows:

$$N_p = 1 + r^1 + r^2 + r^3 + + r^{n-1} = (r^n-1)/(r-1) \qquad \text{Eq. (1)}$$

$$N_O = r^{n-1} \qquad \text{Eq. (2)}$$

$$N_p/N_O = 1/r = \text{constant, provided that } n>1. \qquad \text{Eq. (3)}$$

Let assume that man-hours for the processing of the network are the sum of small time t consumed at each node for decomposition. The productivity P may be evaluated by (the total number of the output, divided by the man-hours).

$$P = N_O/(t \ \dot{} N_P) = r/t = \text{constant} \qquad \text{Eq. (4)}$$

The following characteristics are obtained:
- The productivity is constant
- The man-hours are proportional to $(\text{size})^1$
- The system is a linear system

These are applicable to both mental work such as design and also physical work in hardware production.

Let assume that each node errs at the small rate of e during the processing of the network and the error propagates to the output. The defect (build-in) intensity E may be evaluated by the total number of the nodes multiplied by e and divided by the total number of the output.

$$E = e \ (N_P/N_O) = e/r = \text{constant} \qquad \text{Eq. (5)}$$

The following characteristics are obtained:
- The defect build-in intensity is constant
- The total number of defects is proportional to $(\text{size})^1$
- The system is a linear system

Empirically used constancies are theoretically proved, and the inner mechanisms are also clarified. The linearity guarantees hierarchical decomposing and integration as well as simple (arithmetic) operations for their characteristics. They are useful for practical use. Also, it is noteworthy that errors during intentional activity arise from human mistakes. The actual field data of software developments verify these relationships.

It is desirable that they are many, not biased, from various applications, ranging from small size to large size and implemented by various languages. The materials chosen are from the 1970's and the 1980's, when the initial difficulties of large software developments were overcome but most developments were new and almost without reuse. Figure 5 is man-hour data and Figure 6 is defect number data, both plotted on both-logarithmic scales, where the horizontal axis is the software size and the vertical axis is man-hours or the number of defects (errors) and the plots show a belt-like distribution.

Figure 5.a[14] is re-plotted from Nelson's RADC (Rome Air Development Center, USA) data, adding two sub-trend lines, being equal distance from the center trend line, one located at 1/3 times (standard deviation) of the center (mean) line and one located at 3 times (standard deviation) of the center (mean) line. Nelson reported that the center trend line equation, gained statistically, is $X^{0.975873}$. (The difference of the exponent of 0.024127/1.0 is not so significant as to deny the linear nature.)

Figure 5.b[15] is re-plotted from Boehm's COCOMO data, and Figure 5.c[16] is re-plotted from Yoshida's Fujitsu data in linear scales. Both plots, as a whole, show a trend of $Y \propto X^1$. They are processed graphically in following way:

- A center trend line of $Y \propto X^1$ is drawn to pass through the center of the plot group. The position of the interceptor of the Y-axis is adjusted as follows:
- Two sub-trend lines are drawn up and down along and equal distance from the center trend line. The distance and the interceptor are adjusted so that a few plots are outside of the belt-like zone. The distance is represented as N, which is the normalized number of the distance by the center (mean) value[2].

These three figures show that, plots in the belt-like zone show a trend of $Y \propto X^1$ or the productivity is constant, or man-hours are productivity multiplied by the software size. Also from these three data the linear nature of the man-hours is verified.

Defect data, Figure 6[17], is re-plotted from Thayers' third project data in linear scales, and the same graphical treatment as above is made. The main trend line shows that $Y \propto X^1$ or defect (built-in) intensity is constant, and the linear nature of the defect intensity is verified.

Thus both constancies of productivity and defect intensity are verified and the linear nature is also verified. As both constancies of productivity and defect intensity share the same body, the node, these are due to the

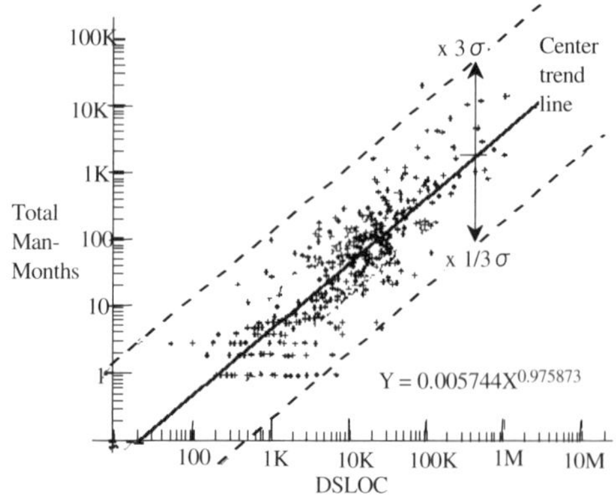

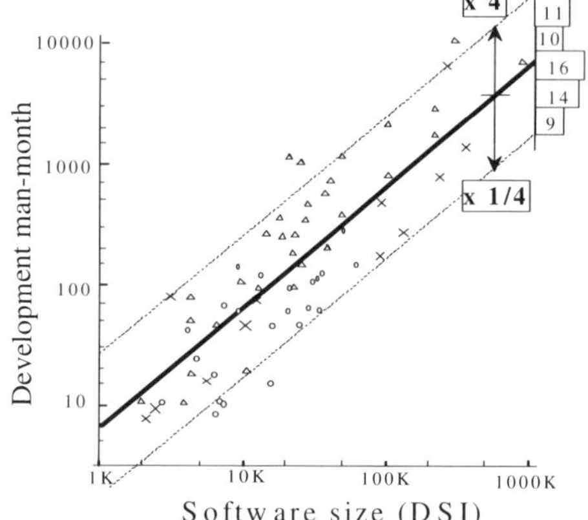

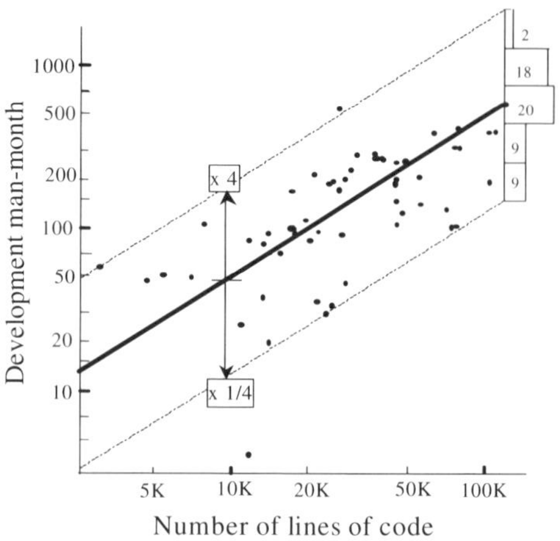

Figure 5. Software size vs. man-month
(Both logarithmic scales)

---

[2] It follows the practice of the Human Reliability Engineering (HRE)[21]. It recommends use of 3 time (N = 3) of the Human Error Probability (average) value for systems evaluation. If it is critical, use N = 5.

conclusion. But, the fact that N = 5 only in this case shows that there must be something particular here. This will be discussed later.

The next problem is to clarify the belt-like zone. In Figure 5.b, 5.c and 6, the belt-like zones, are partitioned to five parallel sub-belts of the same width, and the number of plots in each sub-belt are shown in bar charts at the top right of each figure. They show a bell-like shape, or the facts show a lognormal nature.

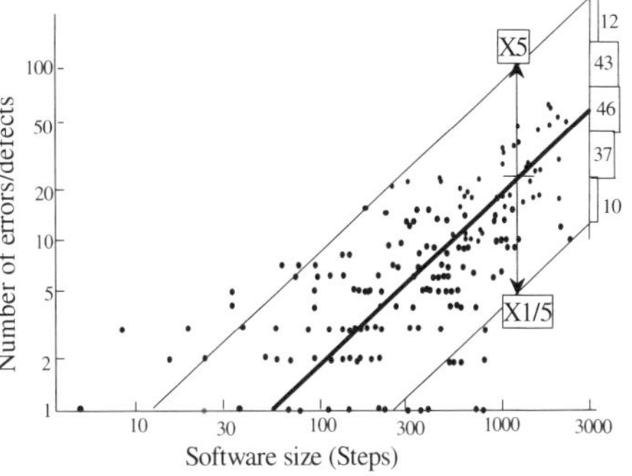

Figure 6. Software size vs. defect (log)

Statistics say lognormal distribution arises as the multiplicative product of many small independent factors. (I.e. epidemiological data and sociological data) In an idealistic lognormal distribution, the plots shown on a log-scale form a normal distribution, and 99.74% of the plots are contained in a range +/- 3·(standard deviation) centered at the average. The standard deviation is proportional to the mean. This is the mechanism that makes the plots show a belt-like zone. Distribution curves in Figure 5 and 6 show their near lognormal distribution nature. Considering the background of lognormal distribution, there are many other similar characteristics.

Figure 7.a[4] shows the growth of "run time." The horizontal axis shows days, and the vertical axis shows the run time in logarithmic scale. It is a "run time" data during an environmental simulation test in the last phase of the system test. A random but heavy load is applied to an online system, and the "run time" is the time from the start to system stoppage by some reasons. When it stops, the cause (usually a software bug) is sought. After it is fixed, the test starts again. The plots show a linear growing trend line, caused by a negative exponential decay of the residual defects. Along the main trend line, two sub-trend lines are drawn, and the normalized number N is written (in the same way as before). From this figure, it is understood that the "run time" shows a lognormal-like distribution multiplied by a negative exponential decay[3], where N is 3.2.

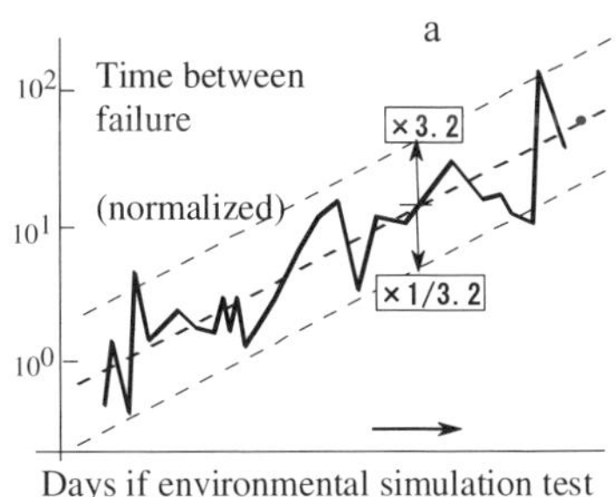

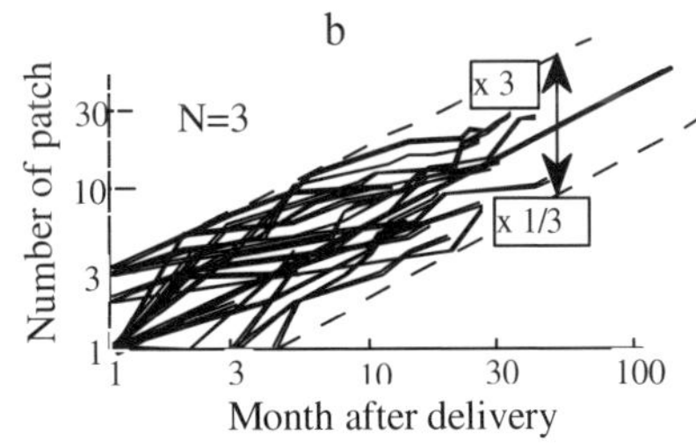

Figure 7. Other lognormal characteristics

---

[3] The central trend line is named the Kudoh line from the name of the finder. Extending trend lines is possible when the system reaches the desired "run time". Brettschneider proposed a way to calculate the number (day) of the residual defects[19].

Figure 7.b[18] shows the growth of the accumulated number of defects of online systems sharing a mother file. The horizontal axis is "days after the system are put into service," and the vertical axis is the accumulated number of the patches, both in log scales. A system operates with a common mother file and the patches. When some trouble is found, it is analyzed and if necessary, the corresponding patch is prepared. Then, the troubled system is stopped, and all yet un-installed patch(es) including the new ones are installed. The Curves are the loci of each system, and they show a belt-like zone. Also this figure shows the similar trend as Figure 7.a, and N is almost 3.

Figure 5.a (N = 3) case seems to be an all in-house development. Also Figure 7.b (N = 3) is the purest case and Figure 7.a (N = 3.2) suffers from the noise (repairing time). In Figure 5.b (N = 4) (COCOMO data case), there are three plot groups. Exponents of each plot group are as follows; 1.05 for in-house small development group and 1.20 for large development by outside people group and N = 1.12 for the intermediate group. Thus, Figure 5.b is estimated to suffer from the noise by (non-hierarchical design). Figure 6, where N = 5, is the worst case. It will be explained later.

The external characteristics of human-related process should show lognormal distribution, caused by many independent factors influencing them as the multiplicative product. When some other causes operate, as the standard deviation increases the distribution becomes broader, resulting in a larger N. Conversely, when some factors in the process are stabilized, the distribution becomes narrow, resulting in a smaller N. Therefore for their intrinsic nature, aforementioned discussion is correct.

3. Quantitative characteristics of defect removal

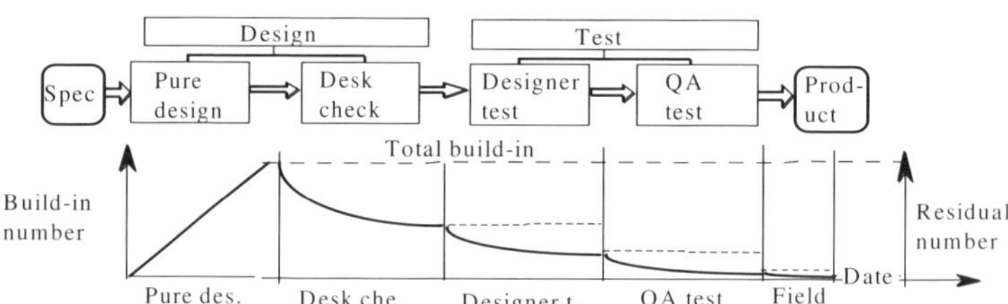

Figure 8. Built-in and decrease of defects

Figure 8[9] in the upper diagram shows a development process. The process flow for design is "pure design" and "desk check," and for the test is "designer's test" and "QA test." (QA is Quality assurance, and some do not have it.) Pure design does not include any checks, and instead desk checks may include any kind of check.

Figure 8 in the lower diagram shows the build-in and removal of defects. In pure design, defects are build-in linearly with time. The total build-in number is E_d and is shown by a broken line. The following desk checks and two cascaded tests are the defect removing process, with negative exponential decay. The number (Ed) is equal to the total number of defects found in following stages, as shown below.

$E_d =$ desk check removed number
　　　+ designer's test removed number
　　　+ QA's test removed number
　　　+ number found after delivery   Eq. (6)

Among the three defects removing processes, the desk check is the most effective.

The defect intensity, namely (the build-in number of defects)/(software size), are the intrinsic external characteristics of a design process. Thus the build-in number of the defects must be measured. This requires that all defects be recorded and removed. Among them those removed during the desk checks are the most important. But many people neglect the importance of the number removed during desk checks. Also Thayers' case neglected these.

Excellent designers remove 80% of built-in defects. However some remove only 10%. In this case, the apparent average defect intensity is decreased from 1 to 0.45, $\{(0.8 + 0.1)/2 = 0.45\}$, of the original. In addition to this, a new variation of the amplitude 0.35, $\{(0.8 - 0.1)/2 = 0.35\}$, is added on the existing one, which is apparently 0.45. This variation amplifying mechanism is the major cause of the larger value of N = 5 in Thayers' case[4]. Thus, the idealistic "design" builds in defects of the logarithmic distribution[5].

In order to count the removed number of defects, a designer declares the closure of a design, and beyond this point every defect found is recorded. Using thus recorded defects; the exact defect intensity may be obtained after a project. A record of desk checks may be simpler than those for the tests. Surely it needs additional man-hours to take all the records, but without this we might loose sight of the quality.

In the bottom level of the diagrams of Figure 8, both the overall decaying curve and the decaying curve for each section may be regarded as a negative exponential decay. When they are plotted on a logarithmic scale chart, the negative exponential decay will appear as a decreasing linear trend line.

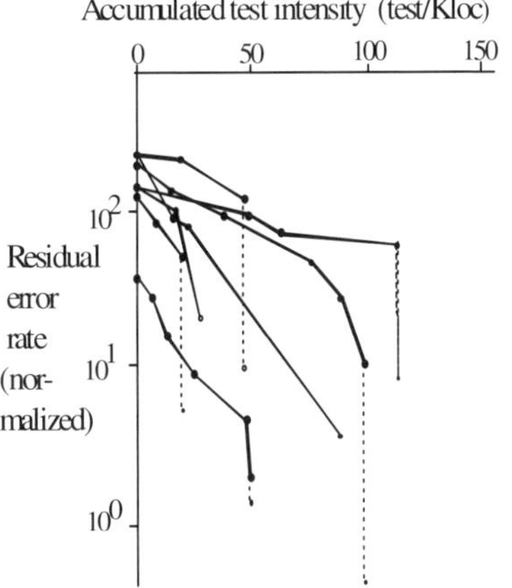

Figure 9. Attenuation by test

Figure 9[4] shows several data that show decreasing trend lines. The gradient of a trend line is named as the "effectiveness of tests" to show the attenuation of defect/test. In the figure, the horizontal axis shows the normalized test intensity (number of test/software size), and the vertical axis shows the normalized residual defect intensity.

The bottom right-most point shows (X = total accumulated test intensity, Y = the residual defect intensity after delivery). The top left most point on the vertical axis is the residual defect intensity after desk checks, or at the start of the test. As the point goes to the left, the number of defects removed is accumulated. As the point goes to the right, the number of tests finished is accumulated[6].

A test is a comparison test of the following two:

---

[4] Thayers' data included other randomness. The data is for routines of one project, and the distribution will have a center axis along the central trend line starting from (X = the total size, Y = the total number of defects) and the shape seems to be like an umbrella without the top part. This explains the spread of the distribution when X is small.

[5] Shiomi in HRE made an elaborate study on 'typing of KB', and proved both the errors and man-hours show a logarithmic distribution by the distribution graph[22].

[6] In Figure 9, vertical dotted lines appear. They are for environmental simulation tests, in the early stage. At that time, various tests of the environmental simulation test were recorded as one test. Later, it was partitioned into many tests.

- program output as the result of so-called design
- expected output derived from a specification.

This test suffers from two kinds of statistical errors. The first kind of error (probability) is to mistake a good item as bad, and the second kind of error (probability) is to mistake a bad item as good. The latter problem is related to the purpose of the tests.

Let us assume the defect intensity of the program is E_D. Then let us assume the second kind of error of the test is E_T. The defect rate after the test/check (the comparison) is $E_D \cdot E_T$. Namely, the initial defect intensity E_D is decreased to $E_D \cdot E_T$. Therefore, a test (desk check) is equal to a small attenuator of defects. It is the reason for the decreasing trend line. But, it should be remembered that these are based on the random nature of defects and tests.

1. If the initial defects are decreased, the curves shift downward.
2. If the number of tests is increased, the trend line is extended to the right by the amount of the increase, and then the final residual defect rate is decreased.
3. If the second kind of error probability is decreased (by making the tests more accurate) the curves go down more sharply, thus the residual defect intensity is decreased.

As these show, following quantitative, rational and scientific treatments are possible in desk check and test.

- Quantitative measurements with quantitative relationships
- Quantitative planning, execution, evaluation and improvement
- Quality control and Total Quality Management

4. Concluding remarks

Part 1 explained the basic structures and the fundamental characteristics of human intentional activity putting emphasis on software, excluding the learning effect. Due to repetitive hierarchical decompositions of human concept, in any human intentional activities, ranging from management (concept level mental operation), design (function level mental operation) and physical works, following fundamental relationships exit.

- Productivity = (The number of output)/(man-hours) = constant
- Man-hours = (The number of output)/productivity
- Time consumed in mental operations causes consumption of resource.
- Defect (built-in) intensity = (The number of defect)/(the number of output)
- (The number of defect) = {Defect (built-in) intensity}•(the number of output)
- Error of a mental operation causes a defect.
- Design is a linear system, where decomposition and integration is possible.
- Defect removing (desk check and test) process is an attenuator of defect, and the attenuation rate is the second kind of the error probability.

These apply in any kind of "process" of all of human intentional activities. This wide applicability based on the scientific foundation is the first salient feature of this system.

Based on aforementioned relationships, Industrial Engineering has brought up various engineering systems, such as production engineering, production control, management engineering, quality control and so on. By them, the present day world has been enjoying prosperity. Software industry has been long staying primitive labor-intensive industry up to now. This system indicates that those engineering systems may also support software industry. Software works may be managed quantitatively, rationally and scientifically. Thus software industry may become industrialization.

Acknowledgements

One of the authors, Koono wishes to express his deep gratitude to superiors, colleagues and forefront people in Totsuka Works, Hitachi, Ltd. for their kind cooperation. This study is the result of their generous help. The authors wish to express their thanks also to those who contributed to the Software Creation Project. They are also very thankful to Mr. Daniel Horgan for his very careful corrections and valuable advice on their English.

References

[1]   G. Salvendi, ed., Industrial Engineering Handbook, 1982, John Wiley &Sons.
[2]   Z. Koono, H. Chen and H. Abolhassani, An Introduction to Quantitative, Rational and Scientific Process of Software Development (Part 2), a companion paper submitted to this conference.
[3]   Z. Koono and H. Chen, Toward Quantitative, Rational and Scientific Software Process, Software Process Workshop 2005, pp. 454-458, May 2005.
[4]   Z. Koono, K. Ashihara and M. Soga, Structural Way of Thinking as Applied to Development, IEEE/IEICE GLOBECOM 1987, pp. 26. 6. 1-6. 6, 1987.
[5]   Z. Koono, H. Chen and B.H. Far B, Expert's Knowledge Structure Explains Software Engineering, Proc. of Joint Conference on Knowledge-Based Software Engineering 1996, pp. 193-197, Sept. 1996.
[6]   G.J. Myers, Reliable software through composite/structured design, John Wiley and Sons, 1979.
[7]   M.A. Jackson, Principles of program design, Academic Press, 1975.
[8]   H. Chen, B.H. Far and Z. Koono, A systematic Construction Method of an Expert System Used for Automatic Software Design, JIJSAI, Vol. 12, No. 4, pp.616-626. 1987.
[9]   A. Kawamata, Electronic circuits of the DEX-1, Development Report of NTT, Vol. 16, N0. 11, pp. 2275-2306, 1967.
[10]   Carl von Clausewitz, Vom Kriege, 1832.
[11]   R. Nelson, Software Data Collection and Analysis at RADC, Rome Air Development Center, Rome, NY, 1978.
[12]   B.W. Boehm, Software Engineering Economics, Prentice Hall, 1981.
[13]   M. Kataoka, S. Hanada, M. Teramoto, S. Yoshida, M. Ohba, and K. Fujino, Panel discussion, State of The Art and Issues in Software Metrics, JIPSJ, Vol. 26, No. 1, pp. 42-52, Jan. 1985.
[14]   Thayers et al., Software Reliability Study, Final Technical Report, RADC-TR-76-238, Rome Air Development Center, 1976.
[15]   R. Brettschneider, Is your software ready for the release?, IEEE Software, Vol. 6, No.4, pp.100,102,108, July/August, 1989.
[16]   Z. Koono, H. Abolhassani and H. Chen, A new way of automatic design of software (Simulating human intentional activity), Proc. Of Software Methodologies, Tools and Techniques 2006, pp.407-420, Oct. 2006.
[17]   A.D. Swain and H.E. Guttman, Handbook of Human Reliability Analysis With The Emphasis on Nuclear Power Plant Application, NUREG/CR-1278, SAND 80-0200 (1983).
[18]   H. Shiomi, On Analysis and Summarization of Human Reliability Data for Simple VDT Operation, BICRMS 92, pp. 372-377, 1992.

New Trends in Software Methodologies, Tools and Techniques
H. Fujita and D. Pisanelli (Eds.)
IOS Press, 2007

An Introduction to the Quantitative, Rational and Scientific Process of Software Development (Part 2)

Zenya Koono[a,1], Hui Chen[b] and Hassan Abolhassani[c]

[a] *Creation Project, Kanagawa, Japan*
[b]*Information Science Center, Kokushikan University, Tokyo, Japan*
[c]*Computer Engineering Dept., Sharif University of Technology, Teheran, Iran*

Abstract. "Product" and "process" are two mutually orthogonal and important aspects of software. As Part 1 discusses "product", Part 2 discusses "process". "Process" is independent of "product" and is used commonly by various "producers". This paper first explains the structure of "process" and then introduces important technique by "divide and conquer". Various important management issues are discussed.
Keywords. Process, Product, Productivity, man-hours, Defect intensity, Industrial Engineering, Learning Effect, Human intelligence

Introduction

In software, there are two aspects, namely "product" and "process". "Product" and "process" are orthogonal concepts. 'The standpoint of both Part 1[1] and 2 is human intentional activity ranging from physical activities to mental operations in design and management. In Part 1, the structure and the quantitative characteristics of a "product" have been shown, which may be applicable in any "process". In Part 2, the main theme is "process[2,3,4]", which is a commonly used technology, for any "product". It is discussed from the viewpoint of knowledge, which is common to all of the physical activities and mental operations in design and management.

Eventually, the "process" in this paper is the same as that in Industrial Engineering (IE) [5]. This means what has been established in IE on an empirical basis agrees with what is concluded here from the aforementioned theoretical viewpoint. Thus, "process" here is the same as that in industry in general. "Process" is the method for achieving manufacture, commonly used by "products," from the viewpoint of management. Thus, it is different from the so-called Software Process or Work Breakdown Structure.

Section 1 explains what is process, and Section 2 discusses how "divide and conquer" is used with "process", or how management uses it. Section 3 explains how the characteristics are used in a process, and Section 4 discusses the various important points for developments, including management.

---

[1] Corresponding Author: Representative, Creation Project, Honfujiswa 2-13-5, Fujisawa, Kanagawa, 251-0875, Japan; E-mail:koono@vesta.ocn.ne.jp.

1. The structure of process

In the early age of software, a software development process used the same names as in hardware. As hardware production had preceded software development by at least half a century, the process had penetrated deeply into society. Furthermore, software design, and not only hardware design but also hardware production work, shared the same structure of human intentional activity, discussed in Part 1. It was only natural for software development to stand upon the process technology developed in hardware, as its basic form.

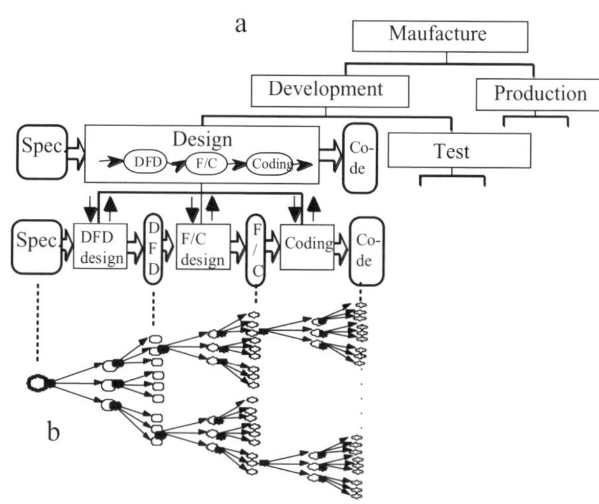

Figure 1. Structure of process

The upper part of Figure 1[3] is the upper part of a "development" process, which is hierarchically structured in the customary manner from IE. "Manufacture" at the top of Figure 1, is decomposed. "Development" is a flow of work to complete design documents[6] (including source code list) for the specification, while *"production" is a repetitive work making identical products*. Further downward, the "design" process is broken down to "data flow design" process, "flowchart design" process and "coding" process, where each interface is chosen to be abstracted and simplified, as in the case of a hierarchically structured software system. *Both interfaces of a process are defined by documents.* A process includes people who are responsible directly for the work.

The hierarchically expanding network at the bottom of Figure 1 shows the design from the specification to the data flow design, flowchart design and coding, correspondingly to the lower process below the "design". (It represents the "product".) The "design" commands "start" at a lower process, and on receiving the "finished" command advances to the next one. By a sequence of clear commands and their responses, the work advances reliably.

The hierarchical processes in Figure 1 constitute a hierarchically expanding network, starting from a final object "manufacture", which agrees with the empirical principle, "Hierarchy of Object[7]" in military science. Similar to a military organization, the usual organization structure for production[2] is a hierarchical one adapted to the process structure. The aforementioned conclusion is supported also by

---

[2] In the early days of IE, there was a dispute about what is the optimum team organization, whether it is hierarchical or not. Actual work was conducted in both ways, and the comparison proved that a hierarchical team is better. From industry to public society, this spread so that the hierarchical organization structure is a basic one now, and the aforementioned high reliability of work, ease of communication and speed of decision making show the superiority of the hierarchical organization structure.

this empirical rule. Thus non-hierarchical organization structures, such as a surgical team system, are special solutions not fitted for general use.

Based on the authors' studies for the automatic design of software[5], "manufacture" in Figure 1 is a human intentional activity. As the decomposition goes on, the work becomes clearer, more solid, more concrete, more detailed and finally it is reduced to the movements of the hands of a worker. The hierarchical decomposition chain starting from the final object "manufacture" is the knowledge of the "manufacture" process. *The hierarchical decomposing network is the knowledge of the "process".* Most of the working knowledge in human beings is a composite of hierarchical knowledge, as pointed out by Minsky in his book, "The Society of Mind". Cognitive science says that around 85% of human knowledge is of a hierarchical-type, and episode-type knowledge is few. Episode-type knowledge in "process" knowledge appears only in the state transition control sequence, as shown in the "design".

The following are keys for the "process" to work together with various "products." IE[3] has established the process concept:

- "Process" is defined at both of its ends (i.e. programming language and documents). It cannot be defined by procedures using natural language.
- "Process" consumes management resources as it progresses. Real time also elapses.
- "Process" does not get into any inside of a 'product'. It understands the inside of a product through measurements of the external characteristics of the process.
- "Process" is a means of control. It is attained through "divide and conquer".

As has already been discussed, "process" in this paper means activities of the people who have rights and responsibility for the work. Thus it is different from the Software Process or Work breakdown Structure, which is a mixture of "product" and "process".

2. Process technology using "divide and conquer"

The conversion from an input to an output belongs to the technology of a "product". The "process" technology is the control technology for better attaining the conversion, and the orthogonal design of the "product". In principle, this control may be applicable not only to physical works in hardware production but also to chemical processes such as in ceramics and biological processes such as brewing. The key point of managing any "process" is said to be "divide and conquer". Figure 2[2, 3, 4] shows the principle involved.

In the right side vibrating string-like figure, the amplitude shows the magnitude of the variation. A design process shown in the second level is constrained at two edges, and the variation becomes greatest at the center. In order to constrain these more severely, two intermediate documents, the data flow diagram and the flowchart, divide it hierarchically into three processes (data flow design, flowchart design and coding). As two intersecting points are added to constrain the vibration, the variation is decreased, as shown in the right side figure. If the variation is not yet sufficient,

---

[3] IE is also called Management Engineering, and systemizes the process technologies applied to the production control of hardware. It started as a cost reduction method in hardware work, and then Quality Control, using statistical methods, started in the early 20th century. It is a compilation of technologies for maximizing the profit of a business. The areas involved are production engineering as the measurement/method/ control/ management/planning of work, quality assurance and various optimization engineering. After 1970's, there was an important progress of Total Quality Control/Management in Japan.

another lower level process is divided into M (in the picture M=3.) processes by intersecting documents, resulting in a reduction to 1/M. If this is not enough, the process is further sub-divided. (It should be remembered that this is effective for internal variations.)

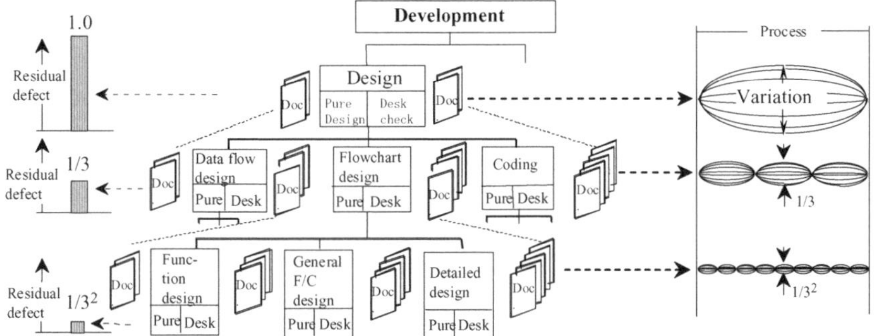

Figure 2. Divide and conquer

Although the principle is simple, it requires an effort to customize it to fit a project. Figure 3[5] shows a record of a first project using both complier language and structured design in the end of the assembler language age. The horizontal axis shows the progress of the processes until coding. The vertical axis shows the accumulated productivity (normalized man-hours/lines of code) of 6 teams as the design progressed. Although the number of processes was increased, the variation was still large. As the contour of curves show, intermediate constraining points do not work.

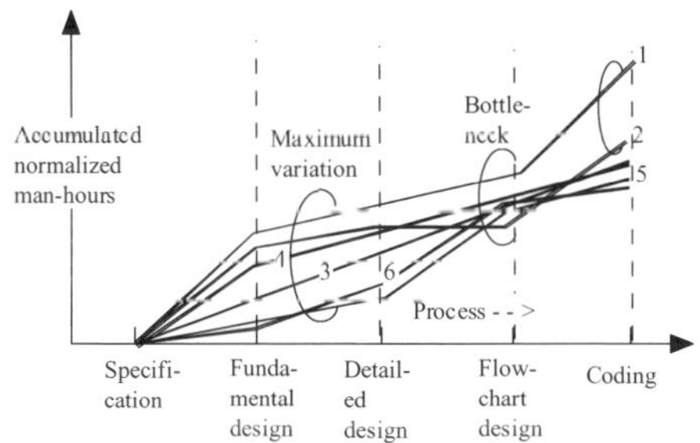

After studies, it was found that the large variation was caused by loose process definitions, which were just indices of each document. The new definitions were not only the indices but also each description standard and sample documents. These regulated everyone's documentation, and the variation was much decreased.

Currently, the best practices are eagerly discussed. It is feared that people might misunderstand that introduction immediately solves problems. If a new practice is introduced, usually it results in some pluses with a certain minus also. More important than the introduction is *the ability to study the problem, use quantitative measures as needed, and localize the cause and then to create some improvements. Namely, what is important is not to imitate, but to apply the principle in own environment.* Otherwise the introduction of this new method does not bring substantial improvements.

Next, regarding the desk checks or quality improvement using "divide and conquer" shown in Figure 2, the manner to remove defects more effectively by desk checks, performed after design, is explained. In Part 1, it was pointed out that any defect removing methods attenuate defects.

In a design on the second level of the figure, after the "pure design", a desk check is made. Let us assume that the defect is random and the defect intensity is D (defects). Let us assume that the probability of the second kind of error is C. The residual defect intensity of the checked program is D·C (defects). In the third level, the program is divided to three of thirds of the entire program size, and each third contains defects of D/3. The errors of each desk check are decreased to 1/3 or the probability is decreased to C/3. Thus three time checks of 1/3 programs are 3 x D/3 x C/3 = D·C/3. If it is divided to M sections, then it is D·C/M. For further decreases, one of the divided processes is further divided to N pair of pure design and desk check. The defects are decreased to D·C/M·N. Bar charts from the second level show this.

The desk checks are effective as the dividing number is large. When thus divided sections are small, or the conversion from the input to the output of the section (or conversion distance) is small, the change is small. In actual desk checks, the check is very easy, and the result is reliable. The following are two examples, each with a different conversion distance.

The first example is that of a telephone switching system. This kind of system is currently called an embedded system. It may be modeled using a Finite State Machine, FSM. A FSM is implemented by memory for remembering states and combinatorial logic for advancing states and for generating necessary signals. When an event driven OS is used including state memory, a state transition route program corresponds to the combinatorial logic. As this system is complex, it is divided into two mutually orthogonal subsystems FSM_A and FSM_B. Both were developed using the same architecture. They were developed by team A and B respectively.

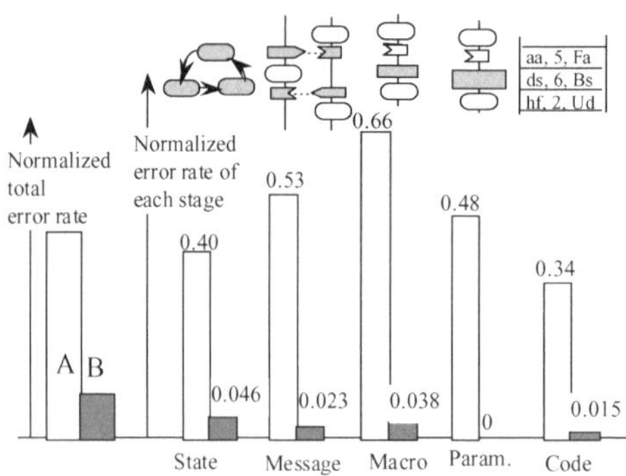

Figure 4. Test detected defects

After the programs were designed, machine tests began. In team A, many defects were found. However, in team B, a few defects were found. But, due to so large a difference, some people worried that the tests would not be done at all. More people were added to team A, and they worked a long time in order to keep to the delivery date. Fortunately, the system was completed, and delivered as scheduled. After all this, team B found a small number of defects.

The bar chart on the left most side of Figure 4[8] shows the overall removed defect intensity found during the test of each switching program. A is around 4 times larger than B. The study focused on the state transition route programs, which is the central core of the switching program. The design process was partitioned into the following five lower level sub-processes, and defects were analyzed from each defect report and they were classified according to each built-in sub- process, thus partitioned. They were in the following order:

1. Partitioning of FSM
2. Message between decomposed FSM's
3. Macro of state transition route programs
4. Parameters of macros and messages
5. Machine code

The right side bar charts show the thus analyzed defect intensity (normalized by defect/state). Very large differences between A and B are clear. During the study, it was revealed that team a desk-checked just a little. On the other hand, in team B as it was their first experience of designing using a state transition diagram, first the leader of B designed and checked by him in a step-by-step manner, and his subordinate checked again in a similar manner. Gradually the leader shifted the workload to the subordinates. If A had done such desk checks in the design, much overtime work and heavy budget overruns could have been avoided.

The next report is of an idealistic desk check performed during the small steps of a design. The program was for pasting a detailed data flow diagram next to the parental elementary data flow diagram for the automatic design system[5], and the size was 147 lines of C code. The design is repetitive hierarchical decompositions of elementary data flows, as shown by the design of the "clock" program in Figure 1 of Part 1.

IPO (Input Process Output) forms are arranged in hierarchical layers to form HIPO (Hierarchical IPO)[9]. The design is recorded on IPO form, and not the IBM way but using data flow diagrams in a sequence of data-function (processing)-data accurately. When the records increase to over one A4 sheet form, the continuing details are recorded in the next page to form HIPO.

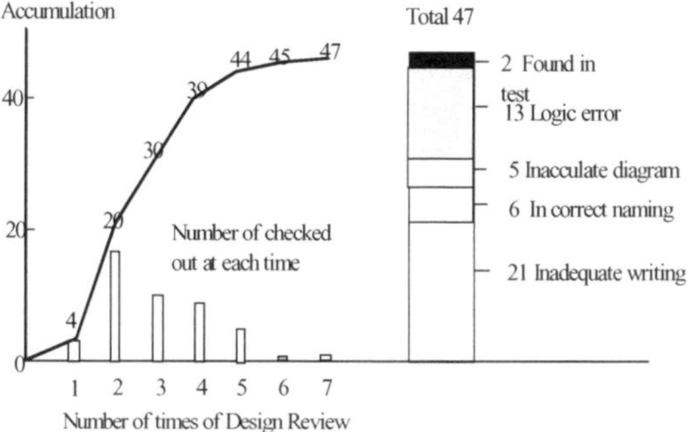

Figure 5. Check in small steps

As the design progresses, review was made at each step of design. A designer explained the design aloud reading data flows on the IPO, and his boss checked the documents while listening to what the designer explained. The left of Figure 5[10] shows the accumulation curve of the number of review times in the horizontal axis and number of check reports in the vertical axis. The right most side of Figure 5 shows a breakdown of the checks.

At first, most checks were mainly related to the drawings not in the design. Next, checks reached natural language expressions as in the diagram. After further progress, checks begin to include processing logics. At the 6th time, all the checks and the checks of amendments were finished, and the review ended. The designer then advanced to the coding, targeting 'no errors'. Actually, two coding errors were found in the test. Among the checked out items, which may relate to program errors, were 13. Adding 2 bugs, the built-in defect density was (13+2)/147 = 102 E/KLOC. (Beginners usually build-in around 100 E/KLOC.) The desk check rate remained 86.7%.

3. Quantitative process characteristics

In Part 1, the quantitative characteristics of human intentional activity in a development process were discussed. The external characteristics are obtained from the actual data. In this section, the "process" is explained using an excellent development taken as the example, with various diagrams and the work records. In an immature team, their process characteristics show a large variation. In an excellent team, however, as the variation is very small, it is thus clear what they are doing.

This is a development of PBX (private branch exchange) software; the development was made in the end of 1980's in GTE (General Telephone and Electronics), which was the largest of the "independent" (non Bell, which had a market share of around 80% of the USA) US telephone companies at that time. Figure 6[3, original data in 11] is reproduced[4] under one of the authors, (Koono)'s responsibility.

These excellent leaders managed this development very well. People eagerly absorbed technical papers, discussed each element, performed trial experiments to gain the data they needed, and thus developed their method for the project. It was impressive to know that there were no disagreements among team members, and their answers were made quantitatively. The situation was like visiting an excellent hardware/components laboratory. During discussion we understood that quantitative measurements and discussion on the results made their opinions agree.

This project adopted various new technologies of that time. They took a compiler language and structured design. The hierarchical products layer was class, sub-program, module and segment. These layers were also used to name the design process. Hierarchical documents in structured design manner were used. They first made a pure design, and then desk checked at each process.

Figure 6 shows the accumulated defect intensity as the development progresses. The vertical axis shows the defect intensity, and the horizontal axis shows the layer name as design process. In "test", it shows the sequence of tests. Below layer names, each desk check method is shown. The final defect built-in intensity was 21.0 defect/kLOC. It was around 1/4 of the previous generation Assembler programs. Desk checks prior to tests removed 82.5% of built-in defects, and the defect intensity removed during tests was only 3.1 defect/kLOC. These are the top-level records at that time. Generally it is difficult for a team to remove more than 80% of defects by desk checks.

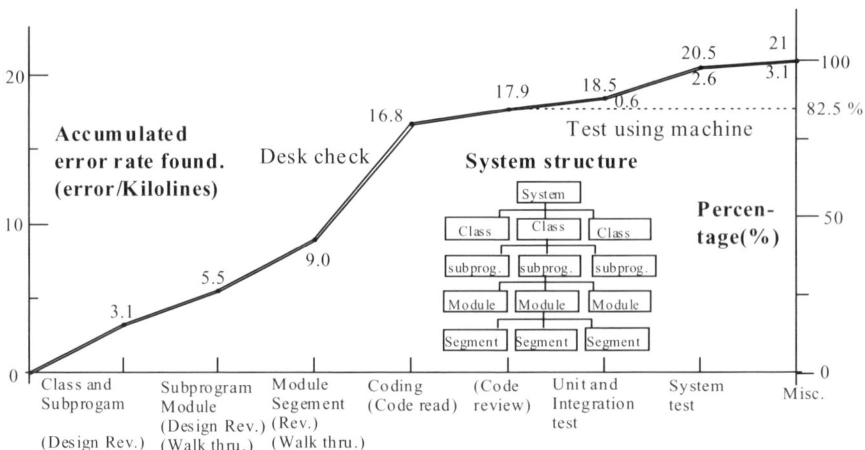

Figure 6. Accumulated defect intensity

---

[4] This excellent development team seemed to be born of GTE's special expectation. The top manager was not only MSEE but also MBA and a member of Tau Beta Pi and so on. The leader was an engineer with a scientific and rational way of thinking based on quantitative measurements, admired by members, and the team members were eager to absorb new techniques.

There were several keys to this result in that project.

(1)   Abundant design documents.

(2)   Emphasis on desk checks prior to tests, encouraged by the quantitative evaluations.

(3)   Desk checks so as to check and correct defects by the preceding pure design.

(4)   Rational man-hours allocated for desk checks.

In the early phase of the checks, Design Review (DR) was done in the originally proposed way[5]. The man-hours consumed by DR were the highest percentage (5.9% of total man-hours) among design checks. But the fact of their very small defect intensity found during tests proved the success of this method.

In the next phase, the weight of DR was decreased but a walkthrough for checking functionalities was added. As their design progressed, the weight of the walkthrough was increased. After coding, they checked the operation of each statement, thus simulating their minds and tracing the entire operation.

Figure 7.a[4] are evaluations after the project, and show the growth of defect intensity in designs. As shown by the upward-pointing arrow, defects are built in during pure design, and as the downward-pointing arrow shows, defects are removed in the following desk check, thus the residual (built-in minus removal) arises. (In this system, the exact built-in intensities of each design process were not known; thus all desk removal ratios are assumed to be equal to 82.5% of built-in defects.)

Figure 7.b[4] shows the decrease of the residual defect intensity as the test progresses. When shown on a logarithmic scale, the total decreasing rate is shown by adding each decreasing rate of a test on a logarithmic scale. (As the defect intensity found after delivery was not available, this is not shown in the figure.)

All defect reports should record each built-in process. (This procedure will be explained 4.2.6.) After a development terminated, and after the growth of defects in the field had been decreased sufficiently, all defect reports are summarized, and the accurate defect build-in intensities of each pure design process and defect removal rates of each desk check process are known.

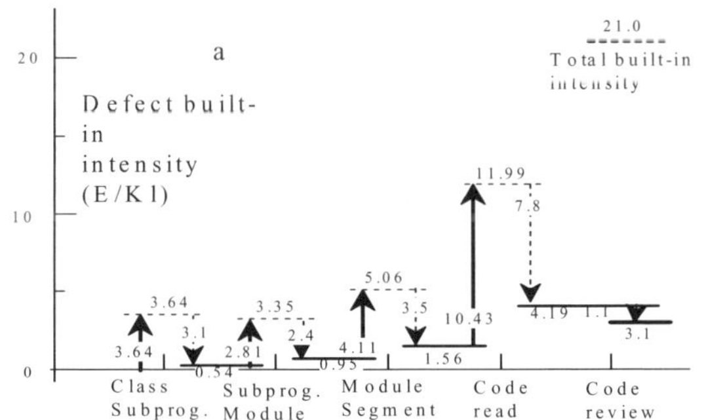

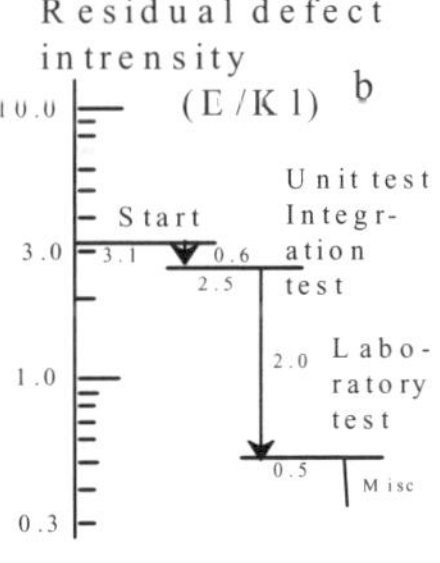

Figure 7. Defect intensity level diagrams

---

[5] Experts were chosen from the fields of planning, installation, operation, service and maintenance. They examined external specifications and performances, with which most designers were not familiar, through documents prepared by designers. Most designers do not touch such aspects, and defects are built-in. A designer knows, through the review item list, what are the problems, and learns a lot about the technology and the system performances, through preparing the description documents. Thus the designer's workload is very heavy. Nominated experts have to read and check thick volumes of documents, prepare each comment, and explain them at the DR meeting. In such cases, GTE telephone company's co-operation was obtained.

Figure 8 shows man-hour statistics. Figure 8.a shows the accumulated man-hours, where the horizontal axis shows the progress of development, using the name of the layer in the design, and the vertical axis shows the accumulated normalized man-hours. Figure 8.b shows the productivities of each process (normalized man-hours)/(source code lines), where source code lines are normalized to 1.

- The hatched parts in the bar chart show the defects attenuating or removing man-hours. The percentage ratio of (man-hours of de check)/(man-hours of pure design) shows the intensity of the desk checks. They were as follows: Class and sub prog. process: 59%, Module and segment process: 35.1%, Coding process: 33.1%

As these show, in order to encourage people to do their best desk checks, the corresponding man-hours for them must be allowed in the budget. Based on past data, this estimation is possible as shown in model diagrams in Figure 9[12]. The upper one shows the time of the pure design and desk checks when the number of people is constant; it shows also man-hours. In the bottom figure, the horizontal axis shows time, normalized by the pure design. The vertical axis shows the residual defect intensity, which grows linearly during pure design (namely until time = 1), and decreases negative exponentially, after desk checks start.

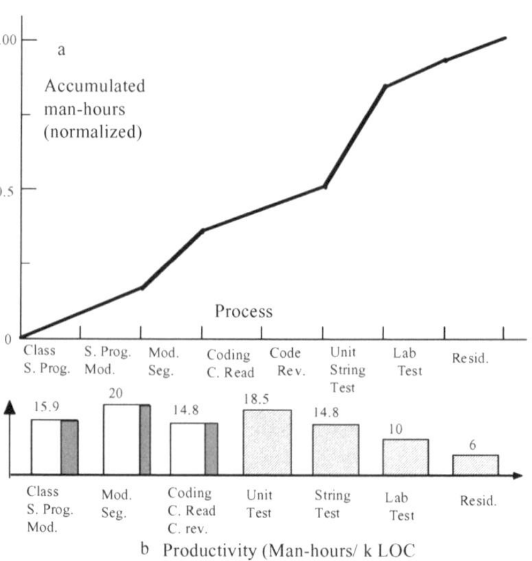

Figure 8. Man-hour data

The residual defect intensity is shown by e^{-aC}, where C is normalized time beginning at the start of desk checks and desk check removal rate $D = (1 - e^{-aC})$.

Let us denote the past data as normalized time C0 and desk removal rate D0, and the new targeting desk removal rate is D1 and the normalized time is C1. From two equations $(1 - e^{-aC0}) = D0$ and $(1 - e^{-aC1}) = D1$, C1 is given by $C1 = C0 \cdot Ln (1 - D1)/Ln(1 - D0)$.

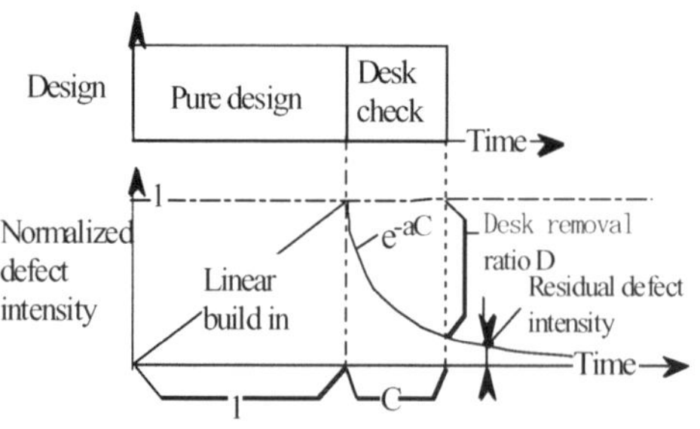

Figure 9. Desk check man-hours

In accordance with increasing allotted man-hours to C1, the method of the desk checks must be improved as to reach the targeted removal rate.

Another example is to allocate reasonable man-hours for tests. Man-hours of test process include works of:
1. test design,
2. pure test operation (with no defects),
3. defect fixing and amending (repair).

Pure test consumes (number of test) x (man-hours for a test), and fixing and amending consumes (number of defect) x (man-hours for a repair).
Each characteristic may be measured or estimated through calculations[5].

If quantitative measurements are made in various cases, the standard model becomes clear. If measurements of each component are made, and each contribution as well as various losses becomes apparent. By correcting the cause of each loss, the productivity is increased and the quality is also increased. Present state without monitoring quantitatively, the situation is like a blind person drives on a highway. When people reached this level, they are approaching hardware production processes.

4 Progresses

4.1 Learning Effects

When a person learns a new sport (physical work) or a new game (mental work), the person shows rapid progress at first. Then the growth rate decreases gradually, but it continues to grow. This is called a Learning Effect. As hardware production work is an N-time repetitive work, the Learning Effect has been known from early times, and since 1936 it (Logarithmic learning efect) has been included in industrial planning.

Figure 10.a[13] was published by one of Hitachi's software factories. The horizontal axis shows the number of designs, the vertical axis shows productivity (man-hours/kLOC) and the two curves are the data for each year. The curves show a rapid decrease at first and the improvement gradually decreases, as mentioned earlier. These are the Learning Effects.

Figure 10.b [3] is re-plotted in both-logarithmic scales from Figure 11.a. It is assumed on the author's responsibility that each software size is constant and their average value. Linear trend lines appear. This type of Learning is known as a Logarithmic Learning Effcct[5]. In logarithmic Learning Effect, the work time for Xth is expressed by the following equation:

$$Y = K \cdot X^{-A}$$

Where X is the number of repetitions, K is the first work time, and A is a characteristic index of Learning Effects.

The gradient of the trend line is proportional to the improvement efforts, and it grows linearly as long as the same efforts are made.

The Learning Effect is supposed to be caused by the accumulation of the memory of the experience. The authors found that as experiences are repeated, the new

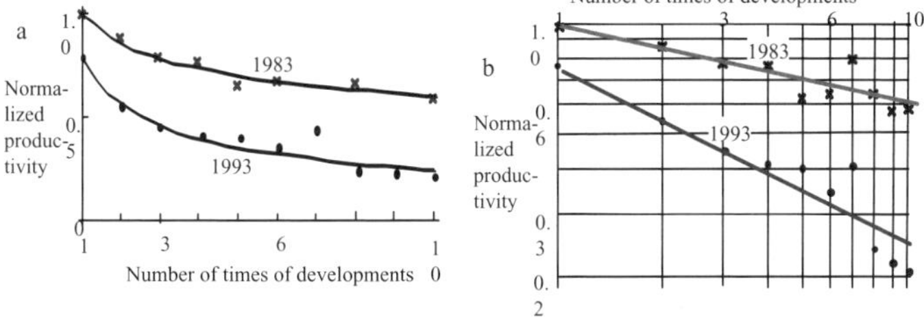

Figure 10. Logarithmic learning curve

knowledge (a pair of a parent and children) grows in logarithmic way[5]. The increase brings the increase/decrease of the characteristic figures. This means that *an improvement is a reflection of the knowledge accumulated.*

Most external characteristics of human related processes (as well as the product) show a Logarithmic Learning Effect. As the future value may be easily predicted, it is used for planning of the productivity of future projects, evaluation of the effectiveness of tools and future trend estimations such as the cost of new devises, etc.

Figure 11.a[14] shows the learning curves of productivity of several categories of software for pure new designs. The horizontal axis shows the accumulated normalized software size. Figure 11.b[15] shows the learning curves of defect build-in intensity for hardware production work and software design. These two graphs were the world's first reports of the Learning Effect of productivity and quality of software by Koono.

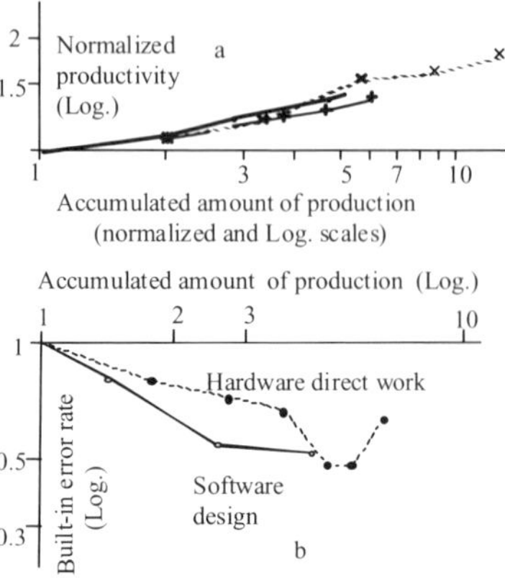

Figure 11. Learning curves

4.2. Business improvements

4.2.1 Independent quality organization

The top manager must be at the head of the improvement movement and has to lead by creating an improvement strategy that cannot be attained by other people. The following is a proposal to provide a quality organization responsible for all quality problems in a company, but independent of the line of design and production.

The Inspection or Quality Assurance department is under the top person in an organization and directly reports to that person and follows their instructions. They direct the whole organization on quality problems, educate people about quality, and, based on the tested results, have a right even to stop the delivery of products, and thus reflect top management's quality policy on all the products and services involved. Formerly, they applied a sampling test based on a statistical quality control, but as the overall quality of products has been improved, they changed to applying tests to all products. Besides such direct work, such quality controllers contact users as representatives of the company. Top management allocates excellent people to such work, and invests in quality related devices and systems. The number of these can reach from several to more then ten percent of the total number of people in a company.

In software, the Quality Assurance (QA) test is applied after the designers' test. After the designers' test has proved to show better results so then at the specified level, QA testing begins. But if the quality level is below the QA's specification, QA turns the system around to the designers. The improvements are shown in Figure 12. The top Figure 12.a[16] and 12.b[16], are from the first study. In Figure 12.a, the horizontal axis shows the number of defects found during the designers' tests and the vertical axis shows those found during QA test, both on a logarithmic scale. Figure 12.b shows similar data of QA in numbers vs. number of defects found after delivery for some

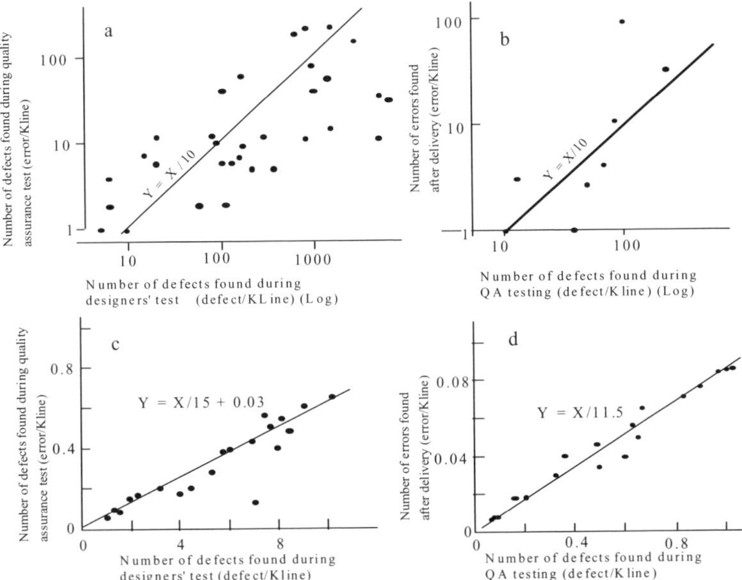

Figure 12. Correlations between the first test and the second test

period until the appearance of the defects decreased sufficiently. The two graphs show the period until the appearance of the defects decreased sufficiently. The two graphs show a correlation of roughly 1:10, namely a series of test defects decreasing to 1/10.

Based on this result, an elaborate study was made. The results[17] are shown in Figure 12.c and 12.d (both shown in linear scales) on the lower level. The variation is much smaller and the correlation is very clear. The attenuation is around 1/10. Although the data used in Figure 12.a and 12.b were gathered from all the past data in a factory, Figure 12.c and 12.d were taken from a group of products. Constraining the process strongly decreases the variation.

The QA's test is black box test, while the designers' test is white box test, and numbers of both tests are equal. QA's tests are designed to check the weak points of the designers' group, the specialties of the market and customers as well as the respective weak points of inexperienced designers. In short, QA people are on the same level as designers and in some fields they are superior to designers. These are the secret keys for an organization that improves the quality level 10 times.

4.2.2 Common problems of both 'product' and 'process'

In software, quantitative measurements and their use reveal many problems. The first theme is the development cost. Figure 13 shows examples of software size. Figure 13.a[18] is from DeMarco's paper, for showing the distribution of program size. After a lesson on software design, he gave the participants the specification and they designed and coded (not tested). He was impressed by the fact that the ratio of the largest/smallest is 8, and thought it is a Rayleigh distribution. As the distribution has a fast rise and slow decay, it may be regarded as a lognormal distribution.

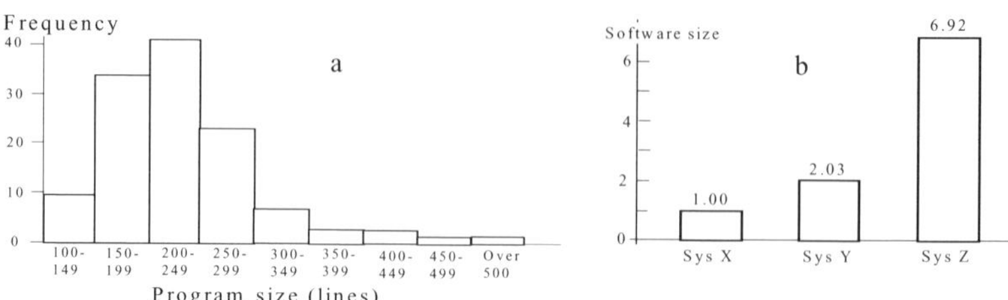

Figure 13. Software size

Figure 13.b[19] shows the size of switching system software of roughly the same specification. If the central system Y is taken with a normalized size of 1, the size range is from {1/2 - 1 - 3.4}. It is near to the {1/3 - 1 - 3} range and of lognormal distribution, which is supposed to be in accord with the statistics. These two examples mean that the software size ranges from the least, 1/3 times to the largest, 3 times of the average, and the ratio of largest to smallest reaches $3^2 = 9$. As these two samples show, not only the characteristic of a human related "process", but that of a human created "product" also shows lognormal distribution.

The development cost of a system is expressed by the software size multiplied by the productivity. The productivity shows lognormal distribution as shown in Figure 5 of Part 1. Using the power sum law ($3^2 + 3^2 = 4.26^2$), the largest /the smallest ratio for development cost (measured by the software size) is 18. If the development cost varies to such an extent, is the management of a software development project possible?

The software size problem affects other aspects. Most software, after its initial development, increases the total size approx. 10%/year[6]. The software size relates not only to the initial development cost but also to annual upgrading (so-called maintenance) cost. In addition to these, the software size relates to the real-time characteristics (i.e. processing power and response time) and the reliability.

In any other engineering, the product's cost is regarded to be shown by (number of items) multiplied by (cost/item). In software, the former is software size and the latter is the productivity. In these 10 years, process improvement has been discussed. But, not only the "process" but also the "product" should be managed. Therefore, it is important to measure both "process" and "product".

4.2.3 PDCA management cycle

PDCA are abbreviations of the Plan, Do, Check and Action (cycle) of management. This system was developed originally by Shewhart, W. A., and further developed later by Deming, W. E, and both pioneers in the quality field. The cycles are as follows:

Plan: establish a work plan.

Do: execute the plan.

Check: monitor to ensure all is going as planned.

---

[6] The trend was found in a telephone switching software in the 1970's[20], and it had been confirmed by various embedded systems at that time. The telephone switching software continued to grow at this trend; most systems' size had reached mega line in the 1990's.

Action: take corrective actions to correct the discrepancies from the initial plan.

When one cycle ends, the people involved must have advanced through PDCA. *The next plan must aim at a better target than before*, as people will have advanced. Through thus repeating these cycles the people involved continue to advance. It is like a spiral progress. In other words, the progress shows a logarithmic Learning effect.

This management system is used in the following manner.

PLAN: Before planning, the manager, who is responsible, gives the strategy to the head of the team responsible for it, and shows how the work should be done. This person decomposes the given strategy to several means to attain it. It is important to establish a tactic for the strategy. Then the person discusses the way to attain it with his/her subordinates, and by leading and encouraging the subordinates details it to the plan for implementation. There will be various difficulties in the implementation of the plan. The countermeasures for these are listed, and some margins to allow individual initiatives are included in the plan. (IE inhibits plans without reasonable margins.) Thus all the members commit it themselves to it.

DO: The weekly performance is gathered and displayed on a screen by two curves of the target (budget) and the reality. The leader monitors the curves.

CHECK: When a discrepancy is detected, the leader calls the members to help them understand and clarify what is the problem.

ACTION: Then they discuss how to resolve the discrepancy, and the countermeasures are determined. Hereafter, people must work coordinating the original plan with the countermeasures. If the recovery is not made or might not be made, the leader must immediately report to the manager. The manager gives advice to the people involved. If this is still ineffective, the manager has to report to the director of the company. The director does the same.

A human person has two sides, one is lazy and another is industrious. In order not to be lazy, it is forbidden not to aim at the target, and this enables people to see the reality quantitatively in contrast to the work target. In order to improve themselves of their own accord, let people join in the meeting, encourage them to speak, propose, and challenge them to be successful. Thus feeling the joy of achievement, people improve.

By acting thus, most troubles are solved in the stipulated period, as people have improved their work during that time. In the next planning session, the manager orders leaders under him/her to analyze the major causes of the discrepancies, establish the countermeasure not to repeat them and encourages leaders and others to establish a plan aiming at a higher target. By thus *repeating quantitatively, people advanced, and the achievements in business are improved. Due to the accumulation of knowledge, the learning curve also grows linearly.*

4.2.4 Approach for Improvements

The following is some advice for applying these improvements efficiently.

1. Eliminate "waste", "strain" and "imbalances" first, in order not to undermine the improvement efforts.
   - Top management and managers are expected to eliminate "waste", "strain" and "imbalances" prior to people's efforts at improvements. Their causes may include some beyond the human level, where the forefront people have rights and responsibilities. If top-level people challenge others to improve on these and they succeed in this, that fact will not only encourage people but also stimulate them.

2. Variations on various phases of a development must be decreased enough prior to other improvements. Tightening up by dividing the process improves the variations caused by internal reasons, and these contribute to decreasing other problems.

3. Concentrate improvement efforts on a few targets at a time and overcome them early. Pareto analysis is a good tool for the selection of these.

4. An improvement is to correct some part of a person. As every person makes his/her best effort already, the person may not be changed easily. It is important to help people to identify the seeds of growth so they can improve by themselves.

5. At the beginning of the improvement efforts, do not require too precise/accurate data. But as improvements go on, measurements may be made for precision and accuracy, to learn what is more effective and what is not.

6. Provide an opportunity for people to think by themselves, be creative in using their own knowledge, implement things in front of others, make presentations before people, etc. so that they may thus make others know about their work and enjoy a sense of satisfaction. It is important to stimulate people's minds also.

4.2.5. Quality control

The fundamental cause of defects is human error, which is common also to production works. Quality control has been developed for hardware production, and the techniques can be applied also to software works. The Pareto[7] analysis, for screening problems, is the most popular technique in software. Figure 14[3] is a model Pareto chart. The horizontal axis shows the items concerned sorted in descending order, and the vertical axis shows the amount of loss. The bar charts show the amount of loss for each item, and the Pareto curve is an accumulated graph of loss.

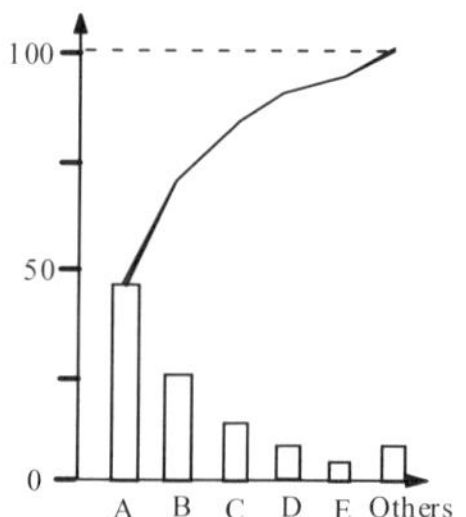

Figure 14. Pareto chart

Juran, J. M. (one of the pioneers in the quality control field) pointed out that *a few vital* elements constitute the majority of the losses. (The rule is also known as the 20%/80% law.) It means that improvements of a few (20%) parts decrease the majority of losses (80%). Therefore, this is used in selecting improvement themes for solving quality problems. If the vital 20% constituting loss of 80% are not found, repeat to change the viewpoint and re-calculate the curve until the a *few vital* is found.

4.2.6 How not to repeat the same errors

A defect arises as a result of a human error. In order to decrease defects, there are two ways, namely to attenuate defects and not to build-in defects. Here, the latter way is discussed. It is impossible not to err in every respect. The only thing possible is to provide some countermeasures **through feedback** to **prevent people repeating errors**. Rather than read the 100 best practices, it is better not to repeat the same error/mistake again. This was found in Total Quality Control/Management (TQC or TQM), and has

---

[7] This law was originally found by Pareto, V., (an Italian economist), where the reality was that a few rich people possessed the majority of the wealth.

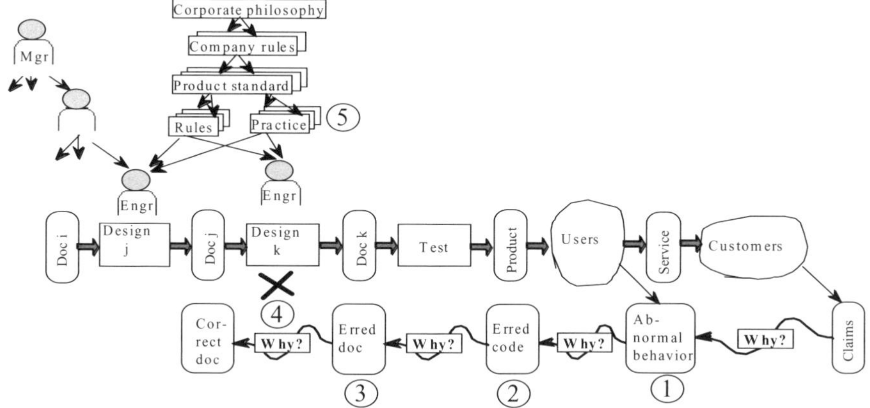

Figure 15. Cause and effect network

resulted in substantial improvements.

Figure 15[3,20] shows a method from the viewpoint of "process." (Originally, it was said to repeat "why and why". But, outside people cannot understand this.) The middle level shows the process flow of a development. After finishing design then tests, a product is delivered to a user and then served to a customer on the right. The customer had trouble and made a claim at the maintenance center.

(1) Responding to a claim on the right side, a service person asks the customer "what happened, when, how, where and what were you doing?" For the records, the problematic behavior is noted.

(2) Based on the record, the faulty mechanism is analyzed, and the mistaken code is identified. For repairs, the correct code is designed, tested and after the QA's approval, the product is repaired. But, the search continues.

(3) Trace upward from the erred code to where the error is built-in. Trace backward from the result to the cause: code -> flowchart -> data flow and so on.

(4) The erred process is where the output documents include error related information but the input document does not include any error related information. In the figure, it is "design k process".

If a person understands the flow of the process, that person can identify the build-in process easily. (It should be noted that the process is divided into many finer processes and enables the identification of the detail of the erred process.)

Each hierarchical decomposing has another side. Any cross-section of a design consists of the following processes:

"Cognition" – "decision" – "conversion".

"Decision" is the selection of the manner of the conversion (algorithm).

"Conversion" is to convert the input information to the output information. Prior to these, there is 'cognition', such as of procedural errors like misreading or mistyping, misunderstanding of the problem, etc. Referring to the input document and the erred document, estimate the erred process from the above three.

An error is the result of a cause at an earlier phase. Trace-back upward to find the cause. During the process, a vital cause X is found that invited the error. In continuing the tracing further, there is a process Y, where if there were no Y there would be no X. Thus the countermeasure to avoid repeating the same error again is to change Y to Y'.

Let us assume that the problem belongs to "cognition" and that a designer in design process k misread the input document. Further upward cause analysis revealed that this is a special case where more additional detailed requirements must be written prior to the design. Then in the earlier phase of standard design practice, an addition is made "in case ⋯, use design rule ⋯," and in that part of the work "yyyyyy" is added.

Based on these updates of the standard design practice, special notice is sent to all design teams and people read about the updates as well as about the cause of the trouble and the problem fact sheet. After all the people involved changed their work methods and use this new way, the countermeasure becomes effective in preventing the same error again.

This prevention method is rational and scientific. Moreover, as it is an improvement method for the process, it may be used not only in hardware production work but also in any human intentional activities where design is involved as well as management. TQC/M was developed originally in hardware production. But as it penetrated into industry it attained various improvements. "Improvement by feedback" is one of them. As it may be applicable to a "process" irrespective of component, hardware or software, the application achieved remarkable progress from the 1970's to 1990's.

5. Discussion

Figure 16[21] shows a very long-term learning curve (in bold line) with the distribution graph of a characteristic. The horizontal axis shows years, and the vertical axis shows the characteristic value. Each small distribution curve of the characteristic (rotated 90 degrees in counter clockwise direction) is pasted on several points of the horizontal axis. The left most side edge of the learning curve shows an initial phase large average value with large variations. After the end of the 19th Century, hardware people had accumulated much experience, acquired various empirical rules, and new engineering bloomed. Based on such efforts up to the present, they are now near the right most ends, where Y is near 0. The enormous accumulation of the knowledge achieves these.

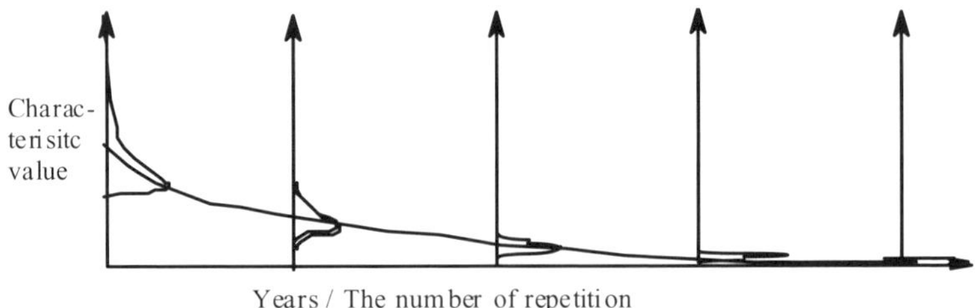

Figure 16. Very long-term learning curve

Where is the software industry located now? In a software development project, after the initial planning and the fundamental design, the number of software people increases rapidly. After the peak has passed, the number decreases, and finally just a few people are left. In some cases, the people come from the outside. As soon as that part of the person's work ends, the person leaves the project and goes away. In the worst case, the person's "product" contribution stays in the software, but what the person achieved in the project (process aspects) is not passed on, or the knowledge is not accumulated.

In such cases, every project starts from the left most side edge of the learning curve and the project ends at the second line with still large characteristic value with still large variations, and thus the characteristics of the project show a large variation.

- Due to the too large variations of process characteristics, the forefront people miss the information to measure and collect the projects' data.
- Likewise, researchers also might lose confidence that the "scientific approach reveals the secret".

Thus, all quantitative, rational and scientific approaches are discarded. That is the worst-case scenario and the best method is to concentrate on a particular field and to accumulate all the knowledge involved.

In hardware, most companies specialize in a narrow area, and put emphasis on accumulating knowledge. In the early age of PC, it was difficult to co-exist with the "Gulliver". The situation has been much improved and the market of software has widened much. It is important for most software venders to specialize in some area.

Ford's conveyor system is the "key of a factory;" it enables various simple level workers to participate in production. In this case, "the conveyor" is the main body of knowledge. Japan's "software factories[19]" have not disclosed their secrets, but education, work practices and production systems together with reusable components would constitute the "conveyor".

Anyway, it is important for a software company to consider "what is your business model"; in reference to the knowledge they have accumulated.

6. Conclusion

Part 1 discussed the "product". It explained the basic structures and the fundamental characteristics of human intentional activity putting emphasis on software. What was discussed in this may be applied to any human intentional activity, from management to design and physical work. Part 2 discussed the "process". The "process" is for the control of the various "products", thus it is orthogonal to the "product". The basic structures and the fundamental characteristics, including the Learning Effect have also been discussed. These explain the theoretical basis of empirically evolved Industrial Engineering practices and their use in various fields, including software.

As "process" is for control on the aforementioned basis, there are huge quantitative measurements, planning and control techniques involved. Thus, major techniques for management are discussed in the last half of Part 2. Most of them are similar to what has already been done in industry.

Both the first part and the last part show the principles involved. As has been reported in Section 2 (referring to Figure 3), it requires additional efforts to make a "best practice" work as intended. Through the process, one acquires one's own knowledge. Through repeating thus, the amount of knowledge accumulated increases.

Various relationships, methods, rules and principles reported here become valuable when people use them, make efforts to master them and finally achieve success, based upon the structures described earlier. The key that enabled the Japanese hardware industry to grow was the fact that all the people involved, including forefront people, learned introductory IE's and all the people worked on the same basis targeting the same objectives.

What the authors hope is that what they have studied will be used and found effective by many others. Various discussed quantitative, rational and scientific engineering undoubtedly increase peoples' productivity and quality.

Acknowledgements

The author wishes to express his sincere thanks to his superiors, colleagues and forefront software people in the Hitachi, Ltd. Totsuka Works, This study is the result of their kind cooperation. The authors also wish to express their gratitude to those who joined the Software Creation Project in Saitama University. They are also very thankful to Mr. Daniel Horgan for his corrections and valuable advice on their English.

References

[1]	Z. Koono, H. Chen and H. Abolhassani, An Introduction to Quantitative, Rational and Scientific Process in Software Development (Part 1), companions paper this conference, 2007.
[2]	Z. Koono, H. Chen and B.H. Far: Expert's Knowledge Structure Explains Software Engineering, Joint Conference on Knowledge-Based Software Engineering (1996), 193-197.
[3]	Z. Koono and H. Chen: Toward Quantitative, Rational and Scientific Software Process, Proc of Software Process Workshop 2005 (2005), 454-458.
[4]	Editor G. Salvendi: Handbook of Industrial Engineering, John Wiley & Sons, Hoboken, 1982.
[5]	Z. Koono, H. Abolhassani and H. Chen, A new way of Automatic design of software (Simulating human intentional activity), SOMET 06, pp. 407-420, 2006.
[6]	Carl von Clausewitz: Vom Kriege, Dummlers Verlag, Bonn, 1832.
[7]	Z. Koono, K. Ashihara and M. Soga: Structural Way of Thinking as Applied to Development, IEEE/IEICE Global Telecommunications Conf. (1987), 26. 6. 1-6.
[8]	IBM, HIPO-Design aids and documentation technique, IBM publication GC20-1851-1, 1975.
[9]	E. B. Daly and D.A. Mnichowicz, The management of large software development for stored program controlled switching systems, International Switching Symposium 979, pp. 1287-1291, 1979.
[10]	Z. Koono and H. Chen, Empirical quantitative model enables quantitative planning of a development, International Symposium on Empirical Software Engineering 2003, Vol. 2, pp13-14, 2003.
[11]	Y. Morioka, F. Nagano, O. Ohno, On learning effect of program development works in Eagle/P (CANDO) environment, National Conference of IPSJ 1991 later half, 5-385, 1991.
[12]	Z. Koono, H. Tsuji and M. Soga: Structural Way of Thinking as Applied to Productivity, IEEE International Conf. on Communications (1990), 204. 2. 1-7.
[13]	Z. Koono, K. Igawa and M. Soga: Structural Way of Thinking as Applied to Improvement Process, IEEE Global Telecommunications Conference, (1988), 40. 1. 1-6.
[14]	Z. Koono and T. Ohotsubo, Evaluation of build-in and check-out of software errors, Research report of IPSJ, Software Engineering 95-5, pp. 31-38, 1993.
[15]	J. Watanabe, H. Ogata and E. Kobayashi, Prediction methods of software quality and software productivity, 2nd Symposium of Software Production Control, A-2, pp.7-14, 1982.
[16]	T. DeMarco and T. Leister, Software development; State of the art vs. state of the practice, 11th International Conference on Software Engineering, pp. 271-275, 1989.
[17]	Z, Koono, Kondo, T., Igari, M. and Soga, M., Structural way of thinking as applied to good design (Part 1. Software size), IEEE COMSOC Global Telecommunications Conference 1991, pp.24.3.1-8, 1991.
[18]	Z. Koono, M. Toiya, T. Matsuida and M. Soga, In-Service quality improvement activities, IEEE Journal on Selected Areas in Communications, Vol. 6, No. 8, pp. 1299-1304, 1988.
[19]	M. A. Cusumano: Japan's Software Factories; A challenge to U.S. Management, Oxford press, 1991.
[20]	Koono, Z., Processor systems in High integration age, Joint Conference of Four Electrical institutes 1979, No. 27-3, 1979.

New Trends in Software Methodologies, Tools and Techniques
H. Fujita and D. Pisanelli (Eds.)
IOS Press, 2007

Measurement Analysis and Fault Proneness Indication in Product Line Applications (PLA)

Zeeshan Ahmed
Mechanical Engineering Informatics and Virtual Product Development Division,
Vienna University of Technology,
Getreidemarkt 9/307 1060 Vienna Austria
zeeshan.ahmed@tuwien.ac.at

Abstract. In this paper we propose an approach to handle the additional level complexity and indicate the rate of increase or decrease of fault proneness in software product line applications. The proposed approach is based on measurement analysis and consisting of three main components .i.e., Analysis, Measurement and Visualisation to dynamically analyse the internal preprocessed source code characteristics, calculate metrics and visualise results in two dimensional diagrams .i.e., graphs, bar chart and tree maps. To evaluate the effectiveness of proposed approach we first implemented it in a real time software application and then performed experimentation using some real time data sets. Narrowing the scope of our research, we only focus on analysing software product line applications developed in C++ programming language.

Keywords— Fault proneness, Measurement analysis, Product line, Variability

Introduction

The software industry is growing with high speed along with the high customer's expectations for high quality products with in short time and low budget, yet the problem of maintaining high success rate is still alive. In the beginning of software product development products were developed using single line product engineering concepts. Each time for a new product new design was implemented because there was no as such concept of reusability. With the passage of time products started becoming larger and more complex. This increase in size and complexity made negative impact on software development productivity, effort and schedule. To cope with these challenges and improve the quality and productivity of software products researchers started considering the Product line engineering concept, already known from the manufacturing industry. Product line is a family of products, based on two key properties Commonality and Variability, designed to take the advantage of their common aspects and predicted variabilities [3].

For the time being product line approach was considered as a good solution to adopt in producing the high quality product with in low cost and short time. But with the passage of time additional level of complexity, feature interaction and composition problems were identified [16], which may increase the fault proneness and reduce the potential productivity gains. To improve the quality of product line applications it was mandatory to identify and reduce the rate of fault proneness by resolving feature interaction and composition problems.

The root cause of identified and shortly discussed problems is the increase of variabilities in product line architectures. To resolve the additional level complexity problem by maintaining the rate of increase in variabilities a comprehensive quantitative project management approach is required because a successful quantitative project management is in turn the base for meeting aforementioned market demands [8]. In order to quantitatively manage the variabilities of product line applications it is mandatory to identify and trace the areas where the rate of variabilities is increasing which itself a complex task. Then calculate some required source code metrics which identifies the rate of fault proneness in product line applications. A number of measurement analysis based solutions have already been proposed and developed including Polymorphism Measure [1], Assessing Reusability of C++ Code [5], Evaluation of Object Oriented Metrics [7], Relation-based Approach [6] and Columbus [14] but still the problems are not completely solved.

In this paper, focusing on the targeted problems, we propose a solution based on measurement analysis; consisting of three components .i.e., Analysis, Measurement and Visualization to dynamically analyse preprocessed source code of product line applications to trace variabilities, calculate metrics and visualise results in two dimensional diagrams.

1. Measurement Analysis Using ZAC

Measurement analysis of internal software source code characteristics can be helpful in indicating the potential reliability and maintainability problems [11]. In order to provide a comprehensive solution to the software practitioners in identifying the additional software level complexity introduced by product line architectures, we present an approach called *Zeeshan Ahmed C-Preprocessed source code analyser (ZAC)*. ZAC is designed to dynamically analyse the internal preprocessed source code characteristics of product line applications, calculate some source code metrics to identify the rate of fault proneness and visualise results in two dimensional diagrams. To full fill the desired jobs and obtain required result ZAC is divided in to three main components .i.e., ZAC-Analyser, ZAC-Measurer and ZAC-Visualizer as shown in Figure 1 and explained in Section 1.1.

1.1 Work Flow Description of ZAC

As the first step, product line application is given to the ZAC as an input. The whole application is divided into possible number of components based on the number of artifacts and then filtration is performed with respect to the types of the artifacts because only the source code artifacts are treated by the system. Process to analyse the preprocessed code is initiated in the first component ZAC-Analyser. During the analysis part preprocessed source code is dynamically analysed to identify the internal source code characteristics .i.e., headers, decisions, macros, directives, expressions, methods, classes and namespaces; these characteristics can contribute in increasing the complexity and decreasing the quality of the software products. To full fill the jobs ZAC-Analyser is further divided into two sub components .i.e., ZAC-Lexer and ZAC-Parser. ZAC-Lexer is designed to generate lexical tokens from each input source code artifact where as ZAC-Parser perfom parsing using generated lexical tokens to understand and validate the semantic of the input source code with respect to the parser rules based on grammar of language used in the development of application. The resultant output of ZAC-Analyser consisting of the information about the total number of artifacts, classes, components, control flows, decisions, defines, directives, parameters, exceptions, expressions, features, headers, macro expressions and namespaces is stored and maintained in designed repository called ZAC-Database. This stored information is further used by the other two components .i.e., ZAC-Measurer and ZAC-Visualiter to take advantage in producing more informative results.

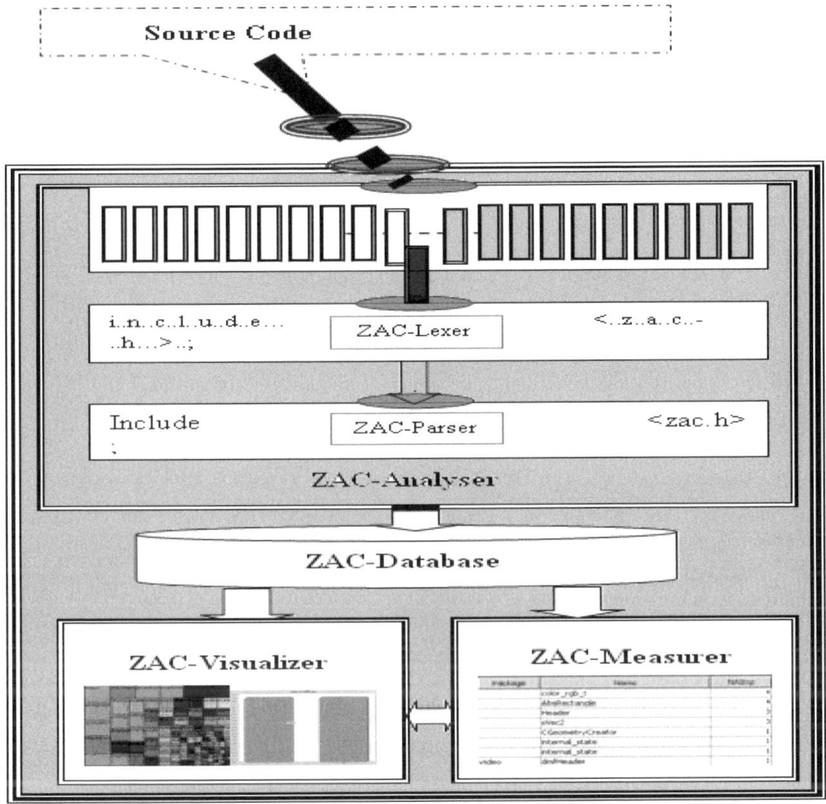

Figure 1. ZAC

ZAC-Measurer using Goal Question Metrics (GQM) [4] approach is desinged to calculate the following metrics .i.e., Class leaf depth (CLD) [12], Number of Children (NOC) [2], Depth of inheritance (DIT) [2], Namespace Inheritance Tree (NIT), Number of Artifacts (NOA) and Class Inheritance Relationship (CIR) from already analysed preprocessed internal source code characteristics by ZAC-Analyser. The reason to select and calculate these six metrics is the indication of fault proneness, the increase in number of these metrics indicates the increase in fault proneness of a product line architecture based applications.

ZAC-Visualizer is designed to have better understanding of the results obtained from ZAC-Analyser and ZAC-Measurer by producing several visual two dimensional diagrams including graphs, line charts, bar charts and tree map.

1.2 ZAC Implementation

To evaluate the effectiveness of proposed approach using open source and freely available development language Java[17], APIs Graphviz[19], DBGen [20], ANTLR C++ Grammar[21] and relational database management systems MySQL [18] ZAC is implemented in a real time software application called ZAC-Tool. The scope of our current implementation is limited because we are only considering the product line applications developed in C++ language for measurement analysis and visualization.

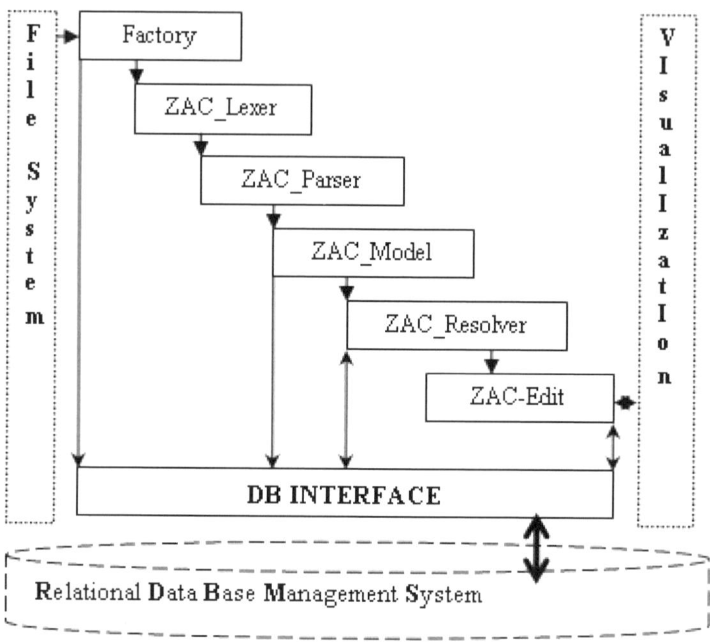

Figure 2. ZAC-System Architecture

Designed and implemented system architecture of ZAC-Tool as shown in Figure 2 is composed of nine components .i.e., File System, Factory, ZAC_Lexer, ZAC_Parser, ZAC_Model, ZAC_Resolver, ZAC-Edit, DB Interface and Visualization. Each component has to play an important role in achiving the final goal. These nine components all togeather works in a way that the product line architecture based application is inputed from File System and only the preprocessed C++ source code files from input application are extracted using Factory. Then ZAC-Lexer treats all extracted preprocessed source code files one by one and generate lexical tokens which are then used by ZAC-Parser to evaluate and validate the semantic of source code with respect to the C++ grammar rules. Based on the resultant information of ZAC-Parser a code model is created by ZAC-Model as shown in Figure 3 which is then stored in database using DB Interface. Code model is concerned with maintenance of results by building the over all code model according to the structure of relational databas. ZAC-Model is comprised of over all twelve distict main and sub elements .i.e., system, namespace, artifact, component, macros, enum, include, struct, union, class, template, feature, flow and expressions. The designed code model is based on the grammatical structure C++ programming language. Constructed code model is then used by ZAC-Resolver to resolve the existing relationships between source code elements .i.e., headers, declared macros, classes and namespaces. These resolved relationships are also stored and maintained in repository using in DB Interface.

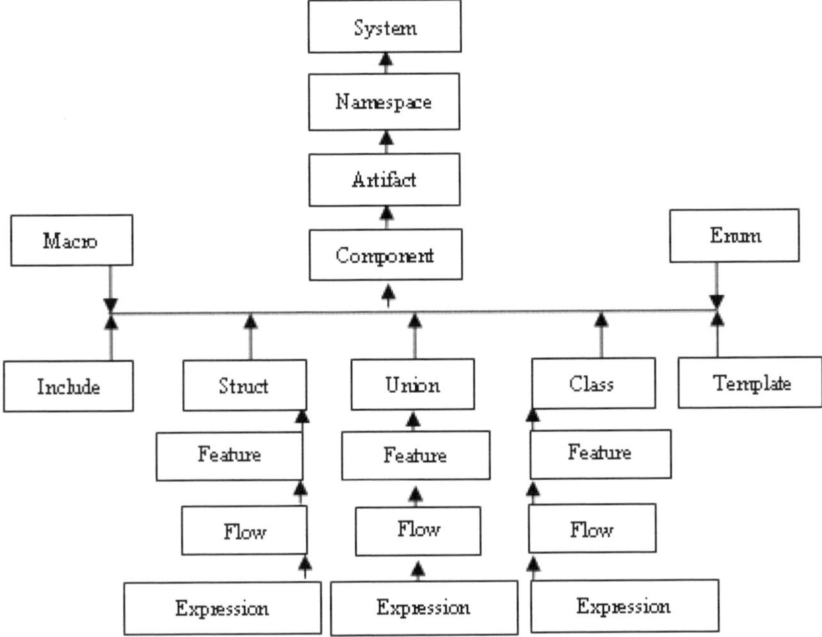

Figure 3. ZAC-Code Model

We have desgined an editor ZAC-Edit to write, import, export and run queris (scripts) to extract and utilise the obtained results to take advantage in making analytical decisions by making statisticcal calculations and measrements. Further more using Visualisation most of the results can be visualised in two dimensional diagrams including graphs, bar charts and tree maps.

1.3 ZAC-Tool

The implemented system architecture of ZAC in the form of ZAC-Tool as shown in Figure 4 is capable of performing the following tasks

1. Take complete software product line applications as an input.
2. Identify, read, analyze and generate lexical tokens of each C++ source code file.
3. Parse the generated lexical tokens to understand the semantics of input source code with respect to parser rules based on C++ language grammar.
4. Identify and resolve variabilities from preprocessed C++ source code.
5. Store the results in a database.
6. Provide options (query editor and generator) to manipulate stored results in database

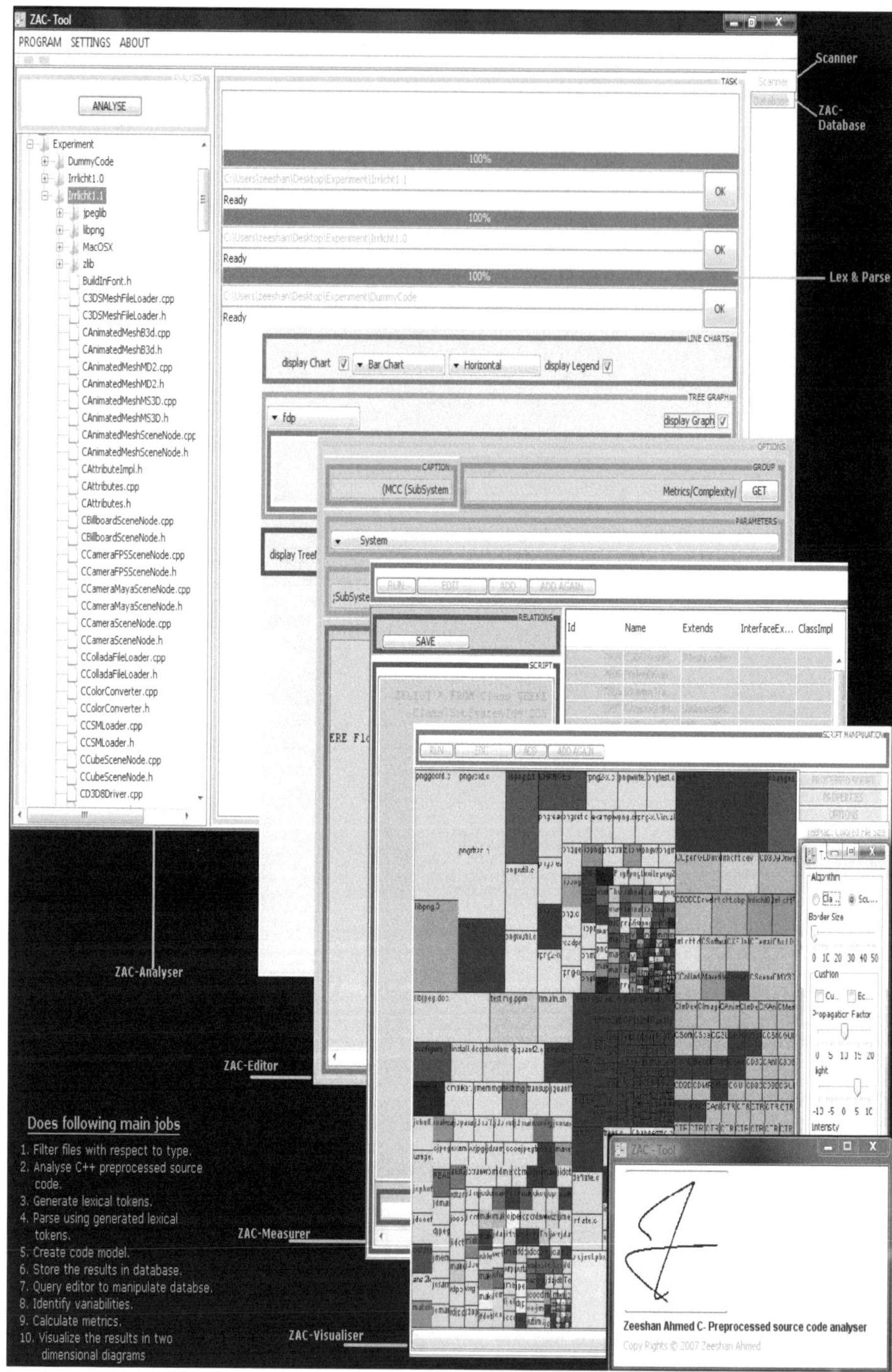

Figure 4. ZAC-TOOL

7. Calculate size measures .i.e., number of artifacts, components, macros, classes, includes and parameters.
8. Calculate complex measures .i.e., number of control paths (MCC) and number of internal level class complexities based on number of methods and statements.
9. Calculate inheritance measures .i.e., Class to leaf depth (CLD -), Depth of Inheritance (DIT), Class inheritance relationship (CIR), Namespace inheritance tree (NIT).
10. Calculate coupling measure to evaluate performance .i.e., Coupling between caught exceptions of classes, attributes of classes and methods in classes
11. Visualise results in Graphs, Tree Maps and Charts.

1.4 Experimentation using ZAC-Tool

We present an experimentation to evaluate the effectiveness of ZAC. We have used Irrlicht (1.0 & 1.1) [9] as the context for experiment. Irrlicht is an open source freely available 3D engine for game programming based on product line architecture and developed in C++ programming language. In our evaluation using ZAC-Tool we first performed the preprocessed C++ source code analysis of the Irrlicht 1.0 & 1.1 and the resultant information about source code characteristics .i.e., artifices, namespaces, components, decisions, define macros, pragma directives, macro expressions, classes and includes is stored in database. Next, using already analysed and stored results in database calculated the metrics .i.e., CLD, NOC, DIT, NIT, NOA and CIR to evaluate the rate of increase / decrease in fault proneness of Irrlicht 1.1 as compared to Irrlicht 1.0, and as the last step pf experiment produced visualisation of results using ZAC-Tool.

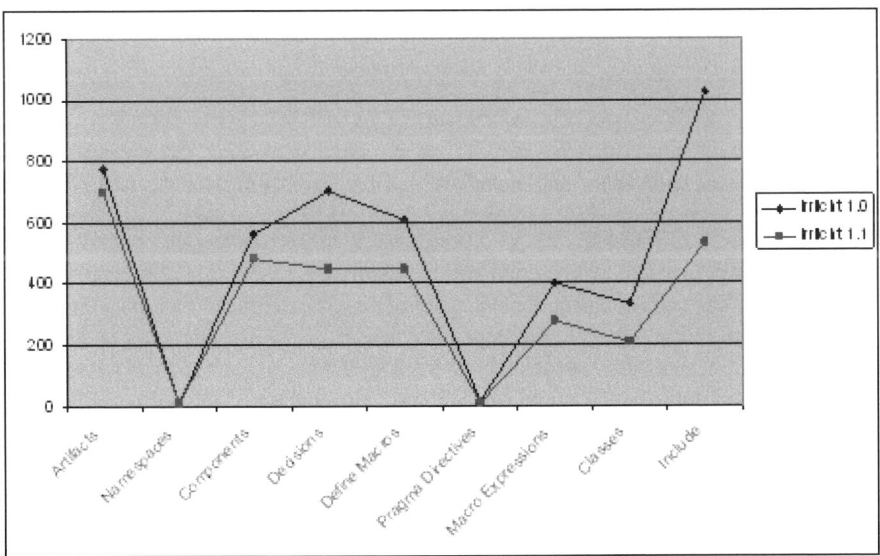

Figure 5. Source Code Analysis

Results of preprocessed source code analysis and calculated metrics are presented in Figure 5 and Figure 6 in line chart. Figure 5 reveals that the number of preprocessed source code characteristics is decreased in Irrlicht 1.1 as compared to Irrlicht 1.0. Figure 6 that reveals the number of calculated metrics based on analysed preprocessed source code characteristics of both Irrlicht 1.0 and 1.1 is decreased in Irrlicht 1.1 as compared to Irrlicht 1.0 as shown in Figure 3. As we have already discussed in section 1.1 that the reason to calculate these selected six metrics is the indication of fault proneness, the increase in number of these metrics indicates the increase in fault proneness, so on the basis of this we can say that the Irrlicht 1.1 is less fault prone than Irrlicht 1.0.

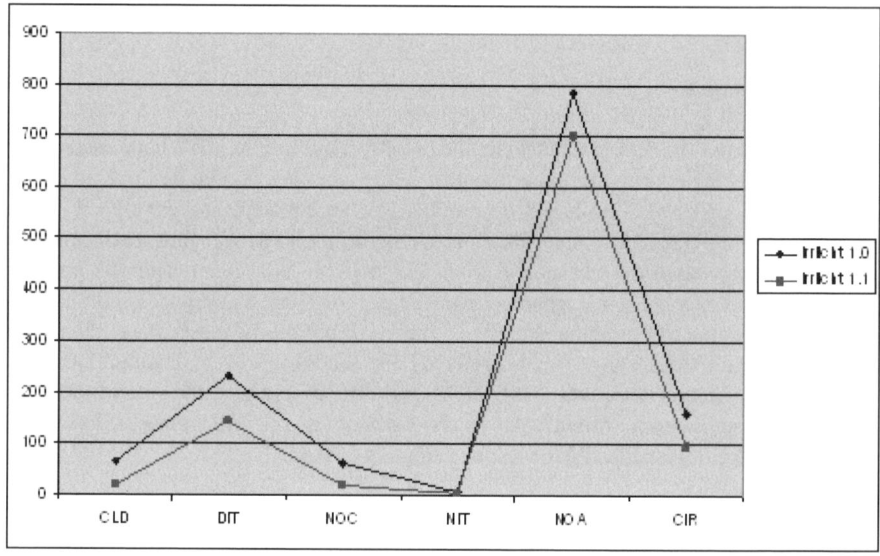

Figure 6. Fault Proneness

Furthermore, in the end using ZAC-Tool we have generated and presented some visual diagrams .i.e., namespace and include graph, file size bar chart and artifact tree map of Irrlicht 1.0 as shown in as shown in Figure 7 (a)(b)(c)(d) and Irrlicht 1.1 as shown in as shown in Figure 7 (e)(f)(g)(h). These diagrams are based on traced variabilities and artifacts of product line applications and can help software practitioners in understanding the over all product line based product's architecture e.g. namespace graph helps in getting information about the number of created namespaces in a product and their relationships with each other, file size bar chart helps in comparing the size of source code files, include graph provides the information about created and used include (headers) in source code and their relationships with each other, moreover coloured tree map gives the information about total number of artifacts, their current location and relationships with each other.

These diagrams are based on traced variabilities and artifacts of product line applications and can help software practitioners in understanding the over all product line based product's architecture e.g. namespace graph helps in getting information about the number of created namespaces in a product and their relationships with each other, file size bar chart helps in comparing the size of source code files, include graph provides the information about created and used include (headers) in source code and their relationships with each other, moreover coloured tree map gives the information about total number of artifacts, their current location and relationships with each other.

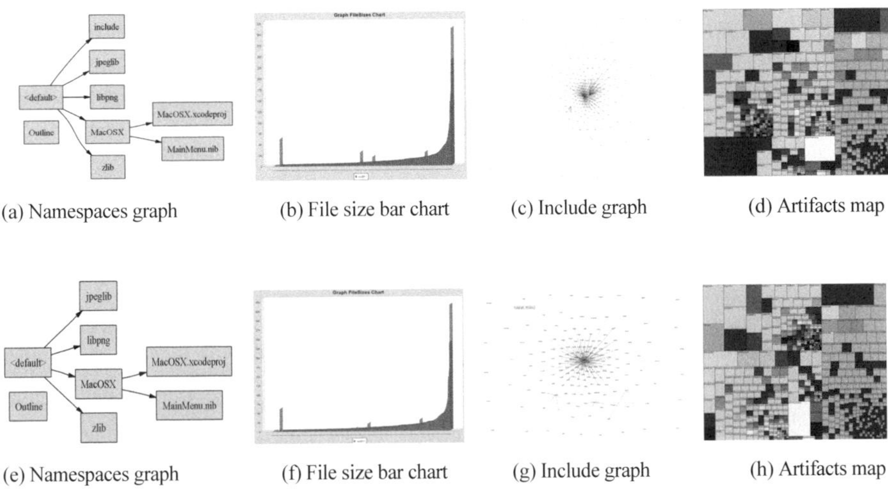

(a) Namespaces graph   (b) File size bar chart   (c) Include graph   (d) Artifacts map

(e) Namespaces graph   (f) File size bar chart   (g) Include graph   (h) Artifacts map

Figure 7. Visual Results

1.5 Current Limitations with ZAC-Tool

As we have already discussed in section 1.2 that this currently implementated version of ZAC can only analyse product line applications developed in C++. Further more during the preprocessed source code analysis of Irrlicht 1.0 & 1.1 some experimental units .i.e., enumerators and templates are not considered in evaluation because the current ZAC-Tool was not able to resolve them. These units neither analysed nor stored in to the database by ZAC-Tool. During the development phase of product life cycle development we have developed the features to analyse these missing components and tested as well using some raw datasets but unfortunately we could not able to find and fix these issues (happened during the experimentation) properly but as the future work of our research and development we are taking care of these issues.

2. Conclusion

We proposed a solution ZAC, to the problem of additional software level complexity introduced by product line architectures. ZAC can be very helpful in creating a new understanding towards quantitative measurement analysis by analysing, measuring and visualising preprocessed C++ source code to indicate the rate of fault proneness in product line application. We implemented our proposed solution in a software tool and tested its effectiveness in an experiment; Resultant information can be helpful to the software practitioners in quickly analysing the internal source code characteristics of product line application as well as measuring rate of fault proneness to identify the current quality level of product and how much improvement is still required. Furthermore it also helped in managing variabilities by tracing and visualizing areas having high variability rate.

Due to the dynamic nature of the field there will always be room for the improvements, therefore, it is very important that the software product line community is to be continuously reviewed itself. As the future work, we will be improving our C++ source analyser, increasing the capability of calculating more size and complex measures to evaluate the effectiveness of products, improving two dimensional visualization to three dimension and working on writing new preprocessed source code analyser called Zeeshan Ahmed Java-Preprocessed source code analyser (ZAJ) to analyse product line architecture based products developed in Java [17] language.

References

[1]   Benlarbi S. Melo W., "Polymorphism Measure for Early Risk Prediction", *In Proceeding of 21st international conference on software engineering, ICSE 99*, Los Angeles USA. 1999

[2]   V. R. Basili, L. C. Briand, and W. L. Melo, "A Validation of Object-Oriented Design Metrics as Quality Indicators", In IEEE Transactions on Software Engineering, volume 22, pages 751–761, Oct. 1996.

[3]   D.M Weiss & C.T.R Lai, Software Product-Line Engineering: A Family-based Software Development process. MA: Addison Wesley: Reading MA, 1999

[4]   Victor R. Basili, Gianluigi Caldieram, H. Dieter Rombach, "THE GOAL QUESTION METRIC APPROACH". Encyclopedia of Software Engineering, pp. 528-532, John Wiley & Sons, Inc., 1994

[5]   Fatma Dandashi, David C. Rine, "A Method for Assessing the Reusability of Object- Oriented Code Using a Validated Set of Automated Measurements", *In proceedings of the 2002 ACM symposium on Applied computing*, Pages: 997 – 1003,ISBN:1-58113-445-2, 2002

[6]   Giancarlo Succi, Eric Liu. "A Relations-Based Approach for Simplifying Metrics Extraction". In Department of Electrical and Computer Engineering, University of Calgary. 2500 University Drive NW, Calgary, AB T2N 1N4. 1999

[7]   Giovanni Denaro, Mauro Pezz`e, Luigi Lavazza. "An Empirical Evaluation of Object Oriented Metrics in Industrial Setting", *In the proceedings of 5th Caber Net Plenary Workshop*, Porto Santo, Portugal 2003

[8]   The Standish group report, August 2005, <http://www.standishgroup.com/quarterly_reports/index>

[9]   Irrlicht, June 2006, <http://irrlicht.sourceforge.net>

[10] J. Viega, J.T. Bloch, Y. Kohno, G. McGraw, "ITS4: A static vulnerability scanner for C and C++ code", *In proceedings of 16th Annual Computer Security Applications Conference (ACSAC'00)*, p. 257, New Orleans, Louisiana, USA, 2000

[11] L.   Briand, J. Wüst, "The Impact of Design Properties on Development Cost in Object-Oriented System", IEEE Transactions on Software Engineering, vol. 27, no. 11, November 2001

[12] L. Briand, J. Wuest, H. Lounis, "Replicated Case Studies for Investigating Quality Factors in Object-Oriented Designs", Empirical Software Engineering: An International Journal, 2001

[13] S. Chidamber and C. Kemerer.s A metrics suite for object oriented design. IEEE Transactions on Software Engineering, 20(6):476–493, June 1994

[14] Rudolf Ferenc, ´ Arp´ad Besz´edes and Tibor Gyim´othy. "Extracting Facts with Columbus from C++ Code". In Tools for Software Maintenance and Reengineering. Published by Franco Angeli Milano, pages 16-31, 2004.

[15] Rudolf Ferenc, Juha Gustafssony, L´aszl´o M¨ullerz, and Jukka Paakkix. Recognizing Design Patterns in C++ Programs with the Integration of Columbus and Maisa, Acta Cybern, 15(4): 669-682, 2002

[16] Silva Robak, Bogdan Franczyk, "Feature interaction product lines", *In Proceedings of Feature Interaction in Composed Systems*, Budapest, Hungary, 2001

[17] Sun   Microsystems's   production,   Java   Development   Kit,   June   2006, <http://java.com/en/download/index.jsp>

[18] MySql Relational Database Management System, June 2006, <http:// www.mysql.com>

[19] Graphviz: Graph Visualization Software, June 2006 <http:// www.graphviz.org>

[20] DBGen June 2006, <http:// dbgen.sourceforge.net>

[21] ANTLR, June 2006, <http://www.antlr.org>

Chapter 8

User Requirement Engineering and Development

Clayworks: Toward User-Oriented Software for Collaborative Modeling and Simulation

Sergei GORLATCH [a] Jens MÜLLER [a] Martin ALT [a] Jan DÜNNWEBER [a]
Hamido FUJITA [b] Yutaka FUNYU [b]
[a] *University of Muenster, Germany*
[b] *Prefectural University of Iwate, Japan*

Abstract. We deal with the problem of developing a software system which integrates collaborative real-time modeling and distributed computing. The main challenge is user-orientation: we need a collaborative workspace for geographically dispersed users with a seamless access of every user to high-performance servers. We describe a particular system, Clayworks, that allows modeling of virtual clay objects and running computation-intensive deformation simulations for objects crashing into each other. To integrate heterogeneous computational resources, we adopted modern Grid middleware and provided the users with an intuitive graphical interface. We parallelized the computation of simulations using a Higher-Order Component (HOC) which abstracts over the Globus Web service resource framework (WSRF) used to interconnect our worksuite to the computation server. Clayworks is a representative of a large class of demanding systems which combine collaborative, user-oriented modeling with performance-critical computations, e.g., crash-tests or simulations for biological population evolution.

Keywords. user-oriented software development, collaboratvie environments, real-time modeling, high-performance simulation

Introduction

Distributed computing over the Internet has become a broadly used approach in a variety of applications for business, science, engineering and entertainment. Two important aspects in this area are: a) *Computer-Supported Collaborative Work (CSCW)* which allows specialists to work together on a single project from different locations, and b) *High-Performance Computing* (HPC). We present a novel user-oriented approach to develop a software infrastructure which combines both aspects, such that usual desktop PCs are interconnected in a CSCW environment and resource-intensive operations are outsourced to specifically configured, high-performance remote machines.

Our work is motivated by a large class of demanding applications that require distributed worksuites which combine features from both CSCW and HPC areas. While contemporary synchronous CSCW systems provide responsive, soft real-time user interactions and can rely on event- and distributed-objects-based middleware like *Java RMI* or *CORBA*, they do not provide adequate mechanisms for running high-performance simulations. In contrast, typical frameworks for distributed HPC and Grid computing [5] like the *Globus Toolkit* [7] or *Unicore* [15] provide transparent access to remote computing resources, but do not provide the means necessary to let several users collaborate and interact in a synchronous way.

We implemented Clayworks as a distributed worksuite allowing the users to collaboratively model clay objects and execute deformation experiments with them. In the modeling mode, several users concurrently model objects in a shared design workspace using virtual clay. Changes to objects are immediately shown at all user clients, which requires soft real-time communication and computation. In the simulation mode, clay objects are deformed when they crash into each other, which is simulated using a remotely located high-performance server. This way, Clayworks facilitates an integrated and seamless workflow for collaborative modeling and simulation; it exemplifies the main features of a large class of demanding scientific and engineering applications, e.g., CAD, biological evolution, or geophysical simulations.

Section 1 presents Clayworks and its distributed three-tier architecture. Section 2 describes the distributed CSCW part for modeling clay objects. The deformation algorithm and its parallel implementation on top of the Globus middleware are presented in Section 3. Finally, we discuss related work and conclusions from the development of Clayworks in Section 4.

1. Clayworks

This section gives an overview of our target application and the design of Clayworks. We discuss the three-tier architecture (Client, CSCW-server, parallel computation) designed for the Clayworks implementation. We briefly explain the main operations which can be performed by the users and discuss the integrated workflow of cooperatively modeling and simulating in Clayworks.

1.1. Clayworks: Integrating CSCW & HPC

Clayworks is a result of combining techniques from two active research areas: Collaborative environments and HPC. Distributed collaborative applications allow experts from different locations to work together on a single project, while HPC deals with accessing remote computational resources like processing power or storage space in a transparent way. For a large group of applications, the integration of both these concepts into a single worksuite is very promising: CAD engineering, biological simulations or virtual physical experiments require a) an interactive construction part to model the objects of interest and to define and set up the simulation, and b) a resource-intensive simulation part.

However, the use of nowadays' HPC is still complicated for application developers, because it requires a lot of specific know-how about how to write jobs and configuration files and how to remotely start computations. Furthermore, current problem solving environments built on top of Grids expose a lot of technical details to the end users, who, besides their own area of interest, have to become experts in the area of Grid computing. Our vision, therefore, is to provide the "invisible Grid". Clayworks is a case study for such an integrated "HPC-powered CSCW" application, which allows non-experts to make full use of a remote high-performance server without caring about details of the underlying network infrastructure.

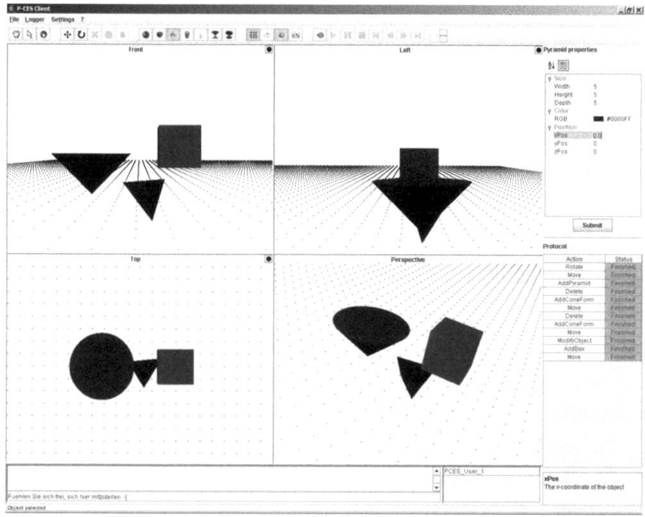

Figure 1. Screenshot of the Clayworks User Client

In the CSCW part of Clayworks, several users, each connected via a graphical client to a shared workspace (Fig. 1), model objects made of virtual clay:

- Users can create, delete, merge or modify the shape of objects, which will be immediately visualized at all connected clients.
- Objects can be grouped or locked for exclusive access, such that users can easily split up the work on complex objects among themselves and collaboratively create large scenarios involving a lot of objects.
- Objects can be saved to a database and reloaded later, even in other workspaces and projects, which allows the user to build a library of reusable objects.

In the simulation part, the computation of the objects' deformations is started on a multiprocessor remote server:

- Users assign a velocity and a direction vector to each object and define other simulation parameters.
- For each object, it can be defined whether the object is solid or should be deformable.
- Users view the result of the simulation as a movie and freely move the camera to scale and rotate the scene.

This architecture can execute deformation simulations among the moving objects, for which we used the deformation algorithm described in [3] as a basis. However, since the computation requires a lot of memory and processing time for larger scenarios, we parallelized the algorithm and embedded it into a software component, which we deployed to a Globus WSRF Grid-container. This setup enables the use of a server with a multiprocessor architecture for running the computations efficiently (see Section 3 for details).

Following the 2x2 classification of CSCW systems described by Ellis et al. [4], the interactions of users in a particular CSCW system can be classified to be local/distributed and asynchronous/synchronous. Although Clayworks allows to work asynchronously as well, it mainly aims at providing a synchronous distributed workspace, as we discuss in Section 1.2 in detail. In order to enable synchronous collaborative work, modeling actions of users have to be visualized immediately at other connected clients. These actions do not only have to be carried out with the maximal possible performance, but they are subject to strong real-time constraints [9]. In fact, Clayworks is not used for controlling any physical machinery, like a hard real-time system where deadline violations lead to serious damage, but any timeout is fatal, as, thereafter, the system state can no longer be maintained correctly. Thus, Clayworks belongs to the most demanding class of applications regarding processing power and computation bandwidth of a distributed CSCW system.

Several other applications like distributed and collaborative CAD/CAE (Computer Aided Design/Engineering) are similar to the virtual clay modeling offered by Clayworks. The simulation part is very relevant to industrial scenarios as well, where, for example, the time-intensive computation of the aerodynamic resistance for a collaboratively modeled car using a similar HPC infrastructure would increase the efficiency of the car's development.

1.2. Three-tier Architecture of Clayworks

The main challenge in the development of Clayworks was the integration of the CSCW and HPC part, which in some sense have contradictory requirements: The CSCW part is a soft real-time system which requires timely communication and computation for a high responsiveness of the application. However, the computations for the modeling are not very expensive and can be executed on a standard, modern desktop PC. In contrast, the simulation algorithm, which iteratively moves and deforms the clay objects, needs a computer with a very high computational power, but has no real-time requirements for the communication.

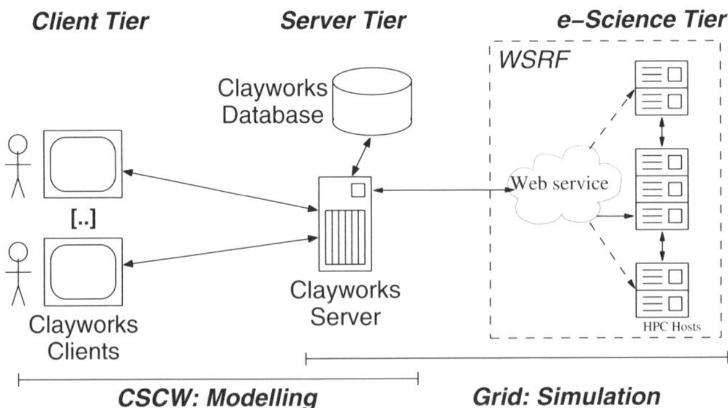

Figure 2. Three-tier Clayworks' Architecture

In order to integrate these different requirements of the CSCW modeling and HPC in Clayworks, we developed a three-tier architecture shown in Fig. 2. The server tier is in the middle, consisting of the Clayworks server and a database put in between the user clients and the HPC tier, thus decoupling the clients from the HPC host. The use of a Web service for interconnecting the Clayworks server and the HPC host enables us to flexibly exchange the HPC host according to the application requirements without affecting the client, as indicated by the dashed lines in the figure.

The clients together with the server form the modeling part which is optimized for immediate communication, while the server together with the HPC host(s) constitutes the high-performance computing facility of Clayworks for the deformation simulations. In the following, the three tiers and their respective functionality are briefly discussed.

Client Tier:　The clients run at the users' desktop computers and provide an access to all functionality: Users can connect to a shared workspace on a Clayworks server, model objects and observe and discuss the work of other users in real-time, and they can start and view simulations.

Server Tier:　In this additional middle tier, we realized functionality which is not feasible to be run on the HPC host(s). In particular, current Web services-based middleware provides no possibility to implement real-time interactions of users; therefore, all real-time communication of the collaborative modeling is handled by the Clayworks server. The database, residing at the Clayworks server, allows the system to reuse objects and to recover a workspace in case of a server failure. For simulations on the HPC host, the server prepares datasets for the remote computation; it starts and monitors the progress of the computations performed by the remote HPC host and finally returns the result to the clients.

HPC Tier:　The HPC tier of Clayworks runs a parallel implementation of the clay deformation algorithm [3] used for the simulation. The implementation is realized as a HOC (Higher-Order Component) in Java. Higher-order components, introduced in [10], abstract over the middleware used to connect to the HPC host performing parallel computations, i.e., in our application, the simulated clay deformation. As discussed in Sect. 3.2, HOCs allow the developer to concentrate on implementing a particular algorithm, while the middleware support, required to exchange data in portable formats, is pre-packaged with the HOC and thereby hidden from the developer.

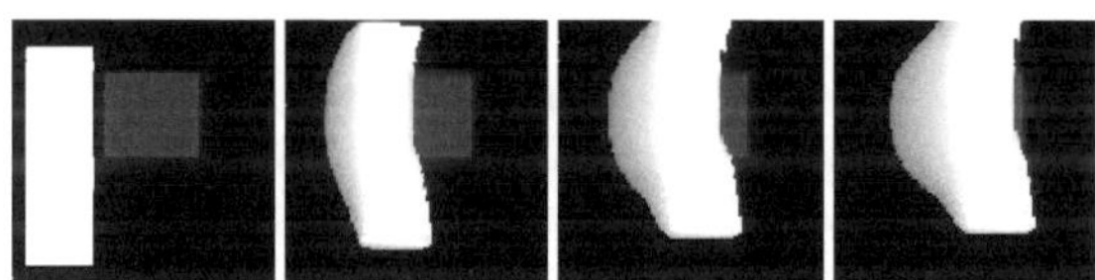

Figure 3. Screenshots of a Simulation Sequence

The HOC used in Clayworks is built on top of the Globus WSRF, so that a Web service is used to outsource computations. To start a simulation, the server sends all objects in the workspace and additional simulation information, like the objects' velocities and movement direction vectors, to this Web service. The deformation algorithm then iteratively moves and deforms the objects, resulting in a sequence of single simulation "screens", see Fig. 3. Upon completion of the simulation, i.e., when all objects have spent their kinetic energy for movement and deformation, the server downloads the simulation results from the Web service and sends them to the clients. To reduce the size of the transferred data, the ZLIB-compression utilities from the `java.util.zip` package are employed. Due to the low number of differences between subsequent pictures in an animation, the size of the result files, which must be transferred over the network, can be compressed to less than a hundredth of their original size.

1.3. Collaboration in Clayworks

The Clayworks clients allow the users to form, resize, reposition, rotate, split up, merge or logically group objects. Objects can be built either by using built-in primitives to create base objects for further refinement or by drawing and spinning 2D shapes to directly sculpt complex objects. Clayworks allows its users to collaboratively work synchronously as well as asynchronously.

Synchronous collaboration connects several users to a single workspace at the same time. The users can immediately see the changes to objects made by other users, which allows them to collaborate in a tightly-coupled manner. In practice, users often split up the work on a complex object among them, each user working on different parts of the object. Clayworks immediately shows the updated object if a user changes the shape of a specific part of the object. Other users can immediately react and adapt the shape of their own parts to the changes or discuss the change with the initiator of the update using the built-in chat functionality. Additionally, Clayworks allows to lock objects, such that no other user can interfere if a specific user wants to execute a complex series of modifications to a specific object.

Asynchronous collaboration does not require the users to be connected simultaneously; moreover, they can work on the same workspace or on the same objects one after the other. Clayworks allows this type of collaboration by providing two technical mechanisms: a) arbitrary leaving and joining a session, and b) persistent workspaces and objects in the Clayworks database:

- The arbitrary joining allows users to connect to an already existing workspace. The objects are version-controlled at the server, such that a later joining client can download the latest version data, even if other users proceed with the modeling during that download.
- The Clayworks database allows asynchronous collaboration due to the possibility to save a complete workspace and load it later on. It is possible to shut down a server and restart the session from the last state some time later. Furthermore, we use the database for a recovery mechanism, based on the frequent storing of backups.

2. CSCW: Distributed Real-time Modeling

In this section, we present the technical realization of the collaborative real-time modeling in Clayworks, in particular the data structures used for representing clay objects and the distributed execution of user actions.

2.1. The Clayworks Client

The Clayworks client makes use of OpenGL via the Java 3D API for the visualization of the workspace. All the different functionalities, like user communication via chat, managing the workspace by locking or saving objects and the modeling of objects, are seamlessly integrated into a single graphical application. Additionally, the parameters for simulation runs, like the velocity and direction of the objects' movement, can be set up.

Completed simulations can be viewed in a special window allowing to freely rotate and move the observer position (see Fig. 3 for an example view).

2.2. Asynchronous Command Processing

The Clayworks server process maintains one or several independent collaborative workspaces. All modeling actions of users are implemented as remote methods residing on the server, which serializes these actions and guarantees consistency of the shared workspace. The server methods remotely called by clients insert a specific command-object (which can, for example, represent a translation, rotation or reshaping of a particular clay object) into a queue and then immediately return. This mechanism makes the originally synchronous Java Remote Method Invocation become asynchronous: The client does not have to wait until the remote computation is finished, but can continue to process user inputs immediately after issuing a command.

At the server, several worker threads execute the commands from the queue in parallel as long as the commands affect different objects. This allows to speed up the command execution for independent commands on multi-processor or multi-core CPU servers, thus increasing the responsiveness of the client, while the correct order of commands affecting the same objects is still guaranteed.

2.3. Command Communication

When the server executes a modeling command from the queue, it transmits that command to all clients, which in turn execute the command locally. This way, instead of a huge polygonal mesh, only a small command has to be transferred to the clients. Conflicts between commands, e. g., a concurrent movement of a single object into multiple directions, are avoided using the locking mechanism, already mentioned in Section 1.3: a locked object can be manipulated exclusively by one user at a time. With this mechanism, actions never need to be reset and we avoid the bouncing of objects and other unnatural movements due to command synchronization. Transitions between subsequent actions are always performed smoothly, since the placement of the command queue on the Clayworks server prevents effects of jitter or network latencies. Due to the fact that each client executes all modeling operations of all users, clients should be run on well-performing desktop systems with a 3D-accelerated graphics card for the Java 3D display. The clients perform well on standard Intel P4 2.6 GHz desktop computers with GeForce 4 graphics cards, so that the hardware requirements of the client can be considered reasonable.

2.4. Two Optimized Representations for Clay Objects

Besides communicating user commands between clients, the server has to hold the central copy of all objects, which have two different representations: *polygonal* or *voxel-based* in a three-dimensional grid. Fig. 4 shows a sphere-shaped object in two different formats: the polygonal version is shown left and the coarser version on the right illustrates the voxel-based version. In the cut-away view of the voxel-based version, it can be seen that only the visible external part of the object is covered by voxels while its inside is unfilled, thus reducing the data size of this format.

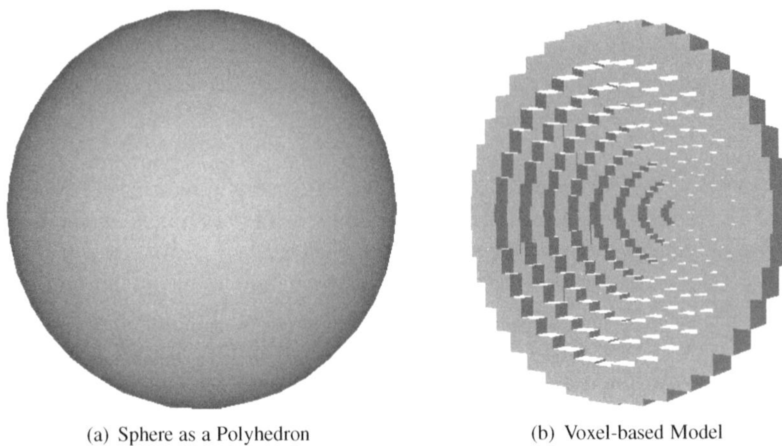

<table>
<tr><td>(a) Sphere as a Polyhedron</td><td>(b) Voxel-based Model</td></tr>
</table>

Figure 4. Two representations of a clay object

The polygonal representation is used in the modeling part and allows the user to build the objects in an intuitive way by defining vertices and faces. The voxel-based representation is required by our parallel simulation algorithm.

Upon the start of the simulation, the server converts the polygonal objects into the discrete voxel-based representation using the algorithm described in [11]. This initialization step forms only a very small fraction of the simulation computation. It is therefore performed directly on the Clayworks server. This way, only a single representation of the object data is required on the remote HPC host which performs the largest part of the computations in parallel. Upon completion of the parallel computations, the server runs the *Marching Cubes* algorithm [12] for re-polygonalizing the objects on each scene of the simulation sequence.

Our solution of transforming data representations at an intermediate application server is feasible for many other distributed applications: This allows clients to operate on a data structure which is most suitable for visualization and editing, while the simulation operates on a data structure optimized for high performance or a specific algorithm.

3. Simulating Clay Deformations in Parallel

This section presents the concept and implementation of the HPC server tier of Clayworks. We briefly describe the basic algorithm used for the simulation and discuss how multiprocessor servers can be used to speed up the required computation. For the implementation, we developed a new Higher-Order Component [10] (HOC), called *Deformation-HOC*. HOCs are software components, pre-packaged with a reusable implementation of an algorithm plus middleware support. The algorithm provided by the *Deformation-HOC* computes a simulation of a material deformation and is an adaptation of the algorithm from [3].

By packaging the component code together with all necessary configuration files, these files, which are typically coded in multiple XML-based formats, become invisible to HOC programmers. The programmer does not need to instruct the middleware on how to handle the communication among heterogeneous resources, but he only writes Java code and is freed from dealing with any XML at all.

3.1. The Multilayer Deformation Process

Once the collaborative construction of the clay objects is finished, the users can specify a direction and a velocity for each object. When a user starts the computation of a simulation, the scene description containing the object coordinates plus the movement information is sent to any available HPC host which runs the simulation algorithm. The simulation algorithm used to compute such scenes is implemented as a multithreaded Java program and, therefore, SMP-servers that map Java threads to different processors are the most appropriate choice of architecture for computing simulations. While multiple simulations can be computed by multiple servers simultaneously, the single simulations are always computed independently, using one dedicated server. All our experiments were conducted using a SunFire 880 computer with 8 UltraSparc-III processors, each running at 1200 Mhz.

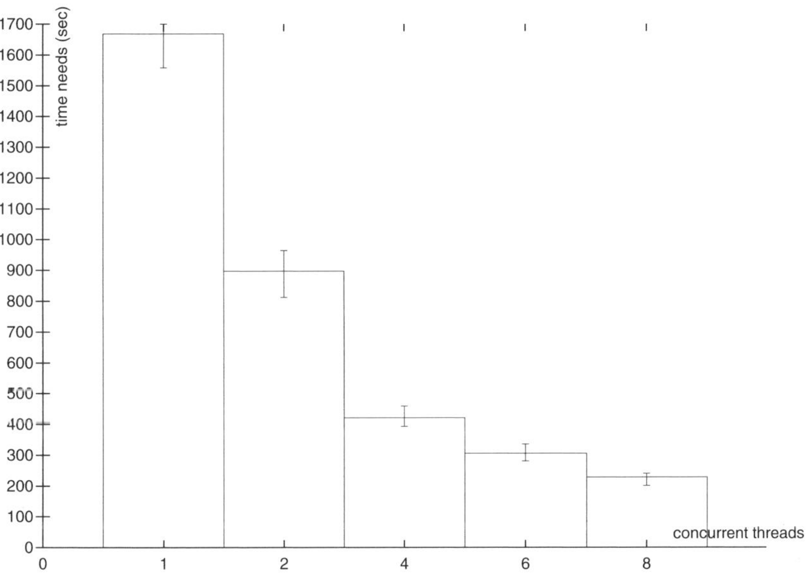

Figure 5. Experimental Results

Fig. 5 shows the average runtime for computing a deformation of two clay cubes (see Fig. 3). There is a good speedup when the number of threads is increased. For 8 threads, e. g., we measured a speedup of 7.2, for a scene where the moving clay objects were evenly distributed.

Inside the simulation algorithm, the voxel-based representation of the objects is held in a 3-dimensional array, the *cubic voxel universe*. Each element of this array is an instance of the Voxel-class, holding the two attributes density and velocity. For each voxel, the density attribute stores the density of the clay at the voxel. All voxels have the same constant volume, which depends on the grain of the cubic voxel universe, which must be specified before the simulation starts. Before the start and after the completion of the algorithm, the clay density of all voxels ranges between 0 and 1, but during the computation, values above 1 are possible. Voxels with a density value above 1 are called *congested*. The impact of congested cells on the computation is discussed below. The second attribute of the `Voxel`-class, `velocity`, is a vector describing the movements taking place in the universe. These movements are always linear shifts, triggered by the Clayworks users.

Basically, we run the sequential algorithm from [3] in parallel on multiple partitions of the cubic voxel universe. In contrast to [3], our implementation does not require the presence of a solid tool object, i. e., all objects in the virtual universe can be built of clay. We also extended the algorithm by introducing energy reduction, which terminates the deformation process in a natural way without requiring the user to stop it. As suggested in [3], our implementation performs a 3-layer traversal, but additional layers can be added using particular parameters.

In each single traversal, all voxels are visited once and new density values are computed for them. During the first layer traversal, the shifting of voxels is computed. As long as the position of a voxel after a shift does not collide with the position of another voxel, there is no clash and the direction of the velocity vector belonging to this voxel is preserved. The magnitude of the vector is altered by multiplying it with an energy reduction factor α in each traversal. To find a good assignment for the energy reduction α, we experimented with multiple different factors, including simple linear ones. Empirically, we verified that the reduction of energy during a shift is simulated very realistically when the exponential function is used to compute the energy reduction factor α, as follows:

$$\alpha = exp\left(\frac{-1.0 * \rho_1}{\rho_2}\right) \tag{1}$$

where ρ_1 and ρ_2 are the density values of the clashing voxels. When voxels clash into each other, a new velocity vector is computed using the formula

$$\delta = \frac{1-\alpha}{2}\delta_1 + \frac{1+\alpha}{2}\delta_2 \tag{2}$$

where δ_1 and δ_2 are the original velocity vectors of the clashing voxels. α adheres to definition (1) reflecting the intensity of the clash, which is reduced proportionally to the reduction of energy.

The computations in this layer are performed quickly, but density congestion in the resulting voxels is allowed (see Fig. 6(a), where a shift between two voxels results in a density congestion). The purpose of the successive layers is to adapt the results of the first layer, such that congested voxels distribute their density overplus among their neighbors.

Each layer of the deformation algorithm is parallel in nature, as the cubic voxel universe can be partitioned into sub-cuboids (slices) as shown in Fig. 6(b), and each layer can be applied in parallel to the slices, while only the ordering of the layers must be preserved. The partitioning depends on the distribution of the clay objects specified by the user. Synchronization and communication is required whenever an operation inside one slice affects voxels in another slice. The irregularity of this partitioning is due to the load-balancing: smaller slices (slices 2 and 3 in the figure) contain more congested voxels, such that the number of dependencies between slices is approximately balanced.

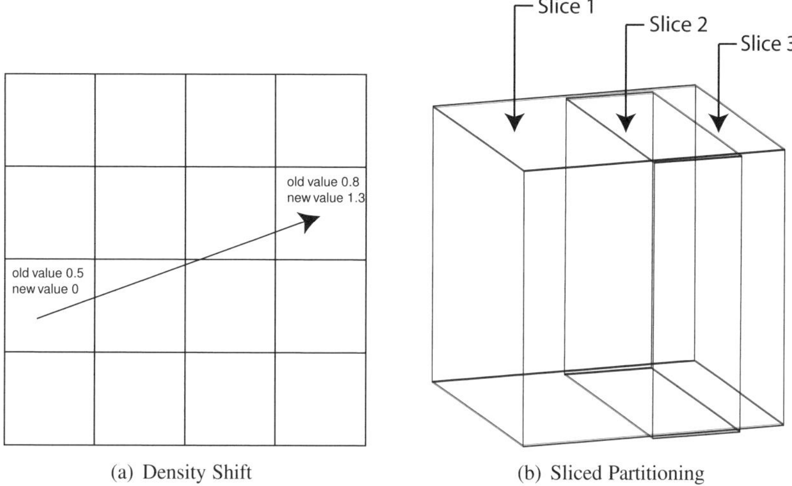

(a) Density Shift   (b) Sliced Partitioning

Figure 6. Density Shift and Sliced Partitioning

3.2. HOCs: Parallel HPC Components

The simulation algorithm described in Section 3.1 can be used for the parallel implementation of a broad class of spacial simulations. It is suitable to compute a realistic presentation of any scene where an arbitrary material is deformed, e. g., the diffusion of gases or the freezing of fluids. It is a recurring program structure and therefore a candidate for a reusable implementation as a Higher-Order Component (HOC)[10].

Our *Deformation-HOC* provides the simulation algorithm via a customizable Web service. The setup, which enables, e. g., asynchronous communication between the Clayworks server and the *Deformation-HOC*, is included in the HOC. The application-specific parts are sent to the HOC using Web service parameters. In the case of the *Deformation-HOC*, only the procedures during density shifts in the first layer and the procedures to correct overfull voxels in the remaining layers are application-specific. Therefore, the *Deformation-HOC* takes one customizing parameter which carries a serialized Java class. This class must be accessible using the following interface:

```
public interface DeformationParameter {
    public boolean isSolid(int objectID);
    public double getMaxDensity( );
    public double powTrans(double nrg);
    public double densTrans(int layerNr, double dens);
}
```

The methods in this interface are as follows:

isSolid returns, for a given `objectID`, whether the respective object is built of a solid material and therefore not affected by the deformation process.

getMaxDensity determines when a voxel is overfull. When a value above 1 is specified, less corrections must be performed, speeding up the higher-layer computations, but the accuracy of the simulation is reduced this way.

powTrans converts kinetic energy into deformation energy, as it happens during the deformation process.

densTrans is used to distribute density among neighboring voxels in a layer > 1, i. e., within a correction.

Users can customize the *Deformation-HOC* by submitting to it their own implementations of the `DeformationParameter`. If no such parameter is specified, the HOC uses the `DefaultDeformation` class, wherein the above methods are implemented according to the mathematical definitions (1) and (2) in Section 3.1; i. e., as long as no different `DeformationParameter` is specified, the *Deformation-HOC* computes the deformation of clay objects. Writing a specific `DeformationParameter` for a different application requires some knowledge about the physical properties of the material which is simulated. When, e. g., a steel brick is simulated, the required `DeformationParameter` is derived from the `DefaultDeformation`-parameter and the methods `isSolid` and `powTrans` are overridden, such that `isSolid` returns `true` and `powTrans` returns a constant, depending on the weight of the brick.

Our *Deformation-HOC* facilitates code reuse and customization. Its full implementation comprises approximately 600 Lines of Java code plus 300 Lines of XML code for the WSRF support. When a new `DeformationParameter` is derived from the `DefaultDeformation`-parameter for different simulations, a programmer using the *Deformation-HOC* has to write no more than 20–30 lines of Java code.

4. Related Work and Conclusion

The main contribution of the Clayworks worksuite is that it tightly integrates collaborative modeling with a HPC infrastructure, allowing end users to collaborate and easily access high-performance servers in a transparent way. Clay deformation is an example application for a large class of problems in industry and science like crash tests, physical simulations or virtual biological experiments.

the opment using osely coupled the

When compared to other distributed problem solving environments like CU-MULVS [6] or NetSolve/GridSolve [14], Clayworks' novel feature is the support for tightly-coupled, synchronous collaboration with soft real-time deadlines. The three-tier architecture of Clayworks satisfies the different requirements of collaborative modeling and HPC. The real-time requirements are combined with the HPC infrastructure in a transparent way for the end users. Furthermore, the transformation of the clay objects from polygonal to voxel-based representation and vice versa allows to use the representation most suitable for visualization and computation, respectively.

The contribution of Clayworks in the area of parallel and distributed programming is the development and use of the *Deformation-HOC*. For the parallel implementation of the deformation simulation, the Deformation-HOC proved to be a very suitable way of programming a Globus WSRF-based service without dealing with the details of middleware technologies. Clayworks confirms the advantages of a Grid middleware and a component-based approach to Grid programming, exemplified by systems like GAT [1], ASSIST [13] and Fractal [2]. Changing the underlying technology of our parallel implementation in a way that multiple servers (which can also operate/communicate using non-Java methods, e. g., MPI) process parts of our cubic voxel universe simultaneously, will not affect the CSCW part of our system, due to the loose coupling between the clayworks server and the HPC host(s) via a Web service. Our experimental results were conducted on a single high-performance server. Our future work will deal with Grid systems comprising several, geagraphically distributed servers.

The concept of seamless integration of remote HPC servers into application software can be expanded into novel areas beyond traditional industry and science: Video editing software could outsource transcoding processes, or online computer game players could start new game sessions on a remote server from the game client. In order to make e-Science suitable for the mass market and non-experts in the area of computing, the access to HPC resources has to be made as transparent as possible. Clayworks is a step in this direction, providing an easy-to-operate application suite.

5. Acknowledgments

We thank the following students for their work on implementing the Clayworks system: P. Bennour, S. Dabek, M. Hiersche, R. Kappus, T. Lohe, P.-L. Lott, P. Lüdeking, M. Rapp, P. Rhiem, C. Sassenberg, and K. Walenta.

We are grateful to the anonymous referees for their helpful comments on the preliminary version of this paper.

References

[1]   G. Allen, et al. The Grid Application Toolkit: Towards Generic and Easy Application Programming Interfaces for the Grid. In *Proceedings of the IEEE, vol. 93, no. 3*, 2005.

[2]   F. Baude, D. Caromel, and M. Morel. From distributed objects to hierarchical Grid components. In *International Symposium on Distributed Objects and Applications (DOA)*. Springer LNCS, Catania, Sicily, 2003.

[3]   G. Dewaele and M.-P. Cani. Interactive global and local deformations for virtual clay. *Graphical Models*, 66(6), 2004.

[4]   C. Ellis, S. Gibbs, and G. Rein. Groupware: Some issues and experiences. *Communications of the ACM*, 3(1), 1991.

[5]   I. Foster and C. Kesselmann, eds. *The Grid: Blueprint for a New Computing Infrastructure*. Morgan Kaufmann, 1998.

[6]   G. A. Geist, J. A. Kohl, and P. M. Papadopoulos. Cumulvs: Providing fault-tolerance, visualization and steering of parallel applications. *International Journal of High Performance Computing Applications*, 11(3):224–236, 1997.

[7]   Globus Alliance. http://www.globus.org.

[8]   e-Science Definition http://www.e-science.clrc.ac.uk.

[9]   A. Burns and A. Wellings. Real-Time Systems, A&W 2001.

[10]   S. Gorlatch and J. Dünnweber. From Grid Middleware to Grid Applications: Bridging the Gap with HOCs. In *Future Generation Grids*. Springer Verlag, 2005.

[11]   J. Huang, R. Yagel, V. Filippov, and Y. Kurzion. An accurate method for voxelizing polygon meshes. In *VVS*, 1998.

[12]   W. E. Lorensen and H. E. Cline. Marching cubes: A high resolution 3d surface construction algorithm. *Computer Graphics*, 21(4):163–169, 1987.

[13]   M. Aldinucci, et al. The implementation of ASSIST, an environment for parallel and distributed programming. In H. Kosch, L. Böszörményi, and H. Hellwagner, eds., *Euro-Par 2003*, number 2790 in lncs, Springer, 2003.

[14]   K. Seymour, et al. Netsolve: Grid enabling scientific computing environments. In *Grid Computing and New Frontiers of High Performance Processing*, 2005.

[15]   Unicore UNICORE-Grid, http://www.unicore.org.

New Trends in Software Methodologies, Tools and Techniques
H. Fujita and D. Pisanelli (Eds.)
IOS Press, 2007

A Unique Trial of Developing Software for the Actual Application by an Engineer with Non-Software Background

Shogo Hayashida, Noriko Taniguchi and Rikio Maruta
SANGIKYO CORPORATION
Yokohama, 224-0053 Japan

Abstract - An attempt to develop a full-fledged software system by an engineer who has no software experiences is described. It is shown that use of the LYEE methodology made the attempt possible and practical with a little assistance and guidance by an experienced engineer. It is confirmed that the method developed through this attempt is useful for nurturing system architects, thereby enabling to realize our ultimate goal that is to transform a non software company to a software company.

Keywords: Software development methodology, System architect, Lyee, LyeeAll3, System development process, Java Server Pages (JSP), Screen transition diagram

1. Introduction

In our previous paper [1], we presented our attempts for transforming a non-software company to a software company utilizing the LYEE methodology [2]. For the successful transformation, two issues needed to be resolved; one was if the LYEE methodology can be implanted in the company who had no base for utilizing such an unpopular methodology with almost none of available literatures for evaluating its applicability, and the other was if necessary system architects can be developed from company's thin engineering resources where those who have software background are very limited.

As already reported in the above paper, the first issue was successfully resolved through receiving LyeeAll2 training provided by Catena Corporation and developing two own actual software systems by an engineer who had ample expertise in software system development. For the second issue, it became apparent that qualification criteria are very important. Through experiments by putting five engineers with various backgrounds into training, necessary qualification was determined to be the logical analyses and synthesis capabilities.

Thus, in addition to the above engineer who developed two actual LYEE-based systems, another engineer who had not ever worked on software development but had shown strength in logical handling of problems through his prior research work on antenna technology, was selected as an additional candidate for the system architect to be fostered. After writing the previous paper, the latter engineer was put into the development of a full-fledged actual application system as the primary developer in order to evaluate how he can be adapted to the software system development work.

In this paper, we will demonstrate that the above mentioned second issue can also be resolved, by showing the primary developer's experiences in understanding the required essential processes for software development, incorporating user requirements into design specifications, conducting LYEE-based programming and performing system debugging. In addition, what could be achieved through own logical approaches by the primary developer with non-software background and what portions required assistances by the well-experienced engineer will be described.

2. Making a Non-Experienced Engineer Develop a Full-Fledged Actual Application System

2.1. System Overview

A human resource management system (HRMS) as shown in Figure 1 was chosen as the target system. The system was actually in need for an employment agency business in the authors' company.

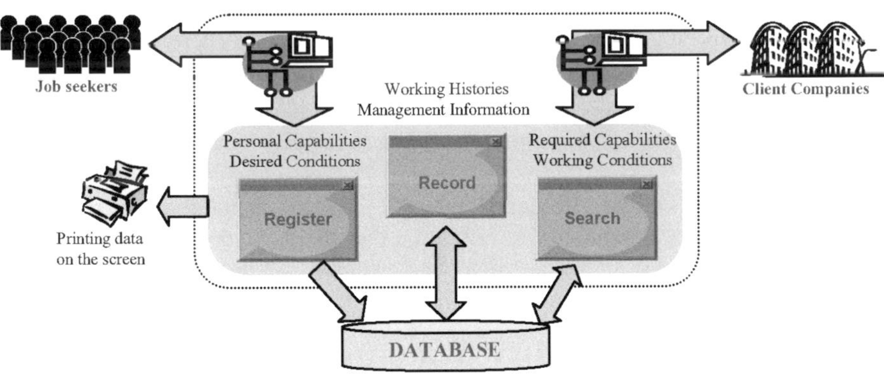

Figure 1: Targeted human resource management system

In order to satisfy user requirements, the system becomes fairly, complex. The major functions to be realized by the system are:

1) To register information of job seekers into the database
2) To search the database to sort out a job seeker who matches the conditions required by clients
3) To update the information of registered workers according to the new employment status and/or additional inputs from the workers
4) To print out the necessary information
5) To maintain the system by the system administrator.

2.2. *System development process*

As the first step, the primary developer (the first author of this paper) who had no software system development experience was advised to strictly follow the software system development process (Figure 2) defined by the well experienced engineer who is the second author of this paper and had developed two software systems using LyeeAll2 and LyeeAll3 as introduced in our previous paper [1].

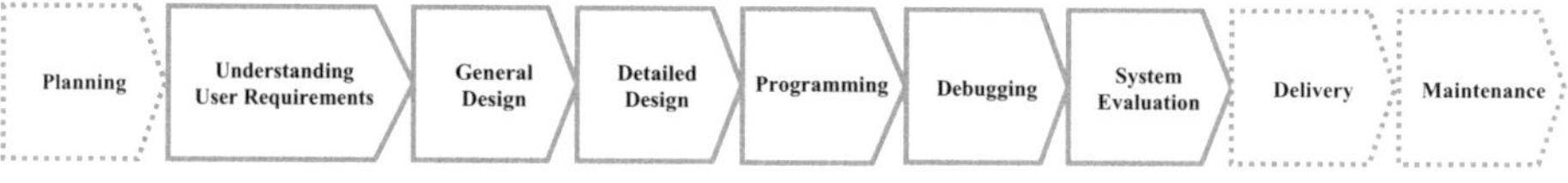

Figure 2: Employed system development process

Definitions of each step in the process are given below:

1) Understanding User Requirements – to extract essence of user requirements from often ambiguous and obscure expressions of users, and to transform them into a system requirements specification.

2) General Design – to determine the required system configuration, system's operating environment (OS, PC specs, database management system), and user interface (user commands, system responses, screen layout and screen transitions among subsystems)

3) Detailed Design – to define names for screens, input/output variables on the screen, database files, tables and their fields, to distinguish data types, and to write state transition diagrams for sub-processes and the total process flow diagram.

4) Programming – to fill out LyeeAll3 templates by the above defined names, data types and the necessary conditions defined by the state transition diagrams for generating executable files, and manually to program Java Server Pages (JSP) for user interface.

5) Debugging – to check if the system operates as desired and to identify and to correct bugs in the program.

6)   System Evaluation – to evaluate if the system works properly responding to user's commands under various actual environments.

2.3. Actual development experiences

2.3.1. The initial attempt

The primary developer was first involved in this development in August 2006. Although the existing another assignment prohibited his concentration on the new job, by the end of August, the general design was able to be completed by understanding user requirements through several meetings with users. The required capability in this phase was to sort out users' wishes and desires in logical ways. The primary developer could be adapted to this work relatively easily, but converting them into a user requirements document, the expertise of the second author was inevitable.

Then roughly by the end of September, detailed design was completed. Since the primary developer had learned how to use LyeeAll3 already by this time, the second author's demonstration of a design example and occasional advices could lead to completing the remaining jobs by him smoothly.

The programming phase took a relatively long period (one and a half months) despite of using the LYEE methodology. This is because of the system's complexity and that screen design capabilities are insufficient in LyeeAll3 [3]. Therefore, rather than relying on LyeeAll3, the screen design was done by using JSP. Since the primary developer did not have the capability of using JSP, he wrote the programs for this portion by modifying sample programs provided by the second author.

Debugging and system evaluation required another half month, and at mid December, the beta version of the system was able to be released to the user. As expected from using the LYEE methodology, the system was free from bugs relating to coding errors, but there were bugs caused by coding errors in the JSP portion and also by data incompatibilities between definitions in LyeeAll3 and in the database.

Table 1 shows the resulting system's complexity measure. As the first attempt to develop a software system by a non-experienced engineer, the system was complex enough.

Table 1: Complexity measure of the developed system

Item	Number
Number of screens	16
Number of DB handling	83
Number of registration	70
Number of search condition	12
Number of personal record	14

Table 2 summarizes time directly consumed by the first author for developing the application system. The time was counted from his actual work time sheet. In addition to this, the second author also needed to allot her time for training the first author, which will be discussed in a latter section.

Table 2: The development time for the beta version of the target application system

Process	Used time in hours
General Design	29
Detailed Design	76
Programming/Testing	203
Total	308

2.3.2. *Incorporating user feedbacks*

The developed system described above was released to the user organization as the beta version in mid December. Then the user organization came up with the detailed lists of required improvements as shown in Table 3.

Required modifications and additions were significant, but thanks to such a nature of LYEE that additions of new subprograms and/or modifications of existing subprograms do not interfere with the remaining programs due to its excellent nature of program sequence independency, finalization of the software system was done more easily than expected. The total time required for this upgrading was 103 hours as can be known from Table 3.

The resulting system complexity became a little larger than the beta version. Table 4 shows how much system complexity increased. The overall system behavior of the developed system can be understood by the screen transition diagram shown in Figure 3. The shaded boxes in the figure indicate the added portions in responding to the user feedback.

Table 3: Improvement requests by user feedback and their implementation time

	Improvement requests	Corresponding screen	G*	D**	P***
1	Modifying screen design	Main			6
2	Providing a special print form for personnel data registration	Register			
3	Maintaining previous versions of registration form with associated revision numbers	Register			
4	Adding a free description column to a list of selectable items with check box	Register			20
5	Providing more precise check items for the skill for using office application software	Register			
6	Providing a separate check box for the driver license	Register			
7	Providing more precise check items for driving skill	Register			
8	Modifying sorting out conditions so as to include the revision number	Register	11	22	
9	Modifying the data updating process so that unauthorized personnel cannot access	Register			15
10	Modifying the form of registration database	Register			
11	Deleting media information for application	Register			0.5
12	Providing a special print form for personnel working history	Record			
13	Providing more precise search conditions for the skill for using office application software	Search			
14	Displaying the sorted out staff information	Search			29
15	Providing printing function with dedicated screen	Print			
16	Displaying all personnel names with the associated ID number	Staff list			
	Total time required in hours		11	22	70

   *   Column G indicates time required in hours for general design.
   **   Column D indicates time required in hours for detailed design
   *** Column P indicates time required in hours for programming and testing

Table 4: Complexity measure of the upgraded version

Item	Number	Additional
Number of screens	19	+3
Number of DB handling	89	+6
Number of registration	83	+13
Number of search condition	15	+3
Number of personal record	14	0

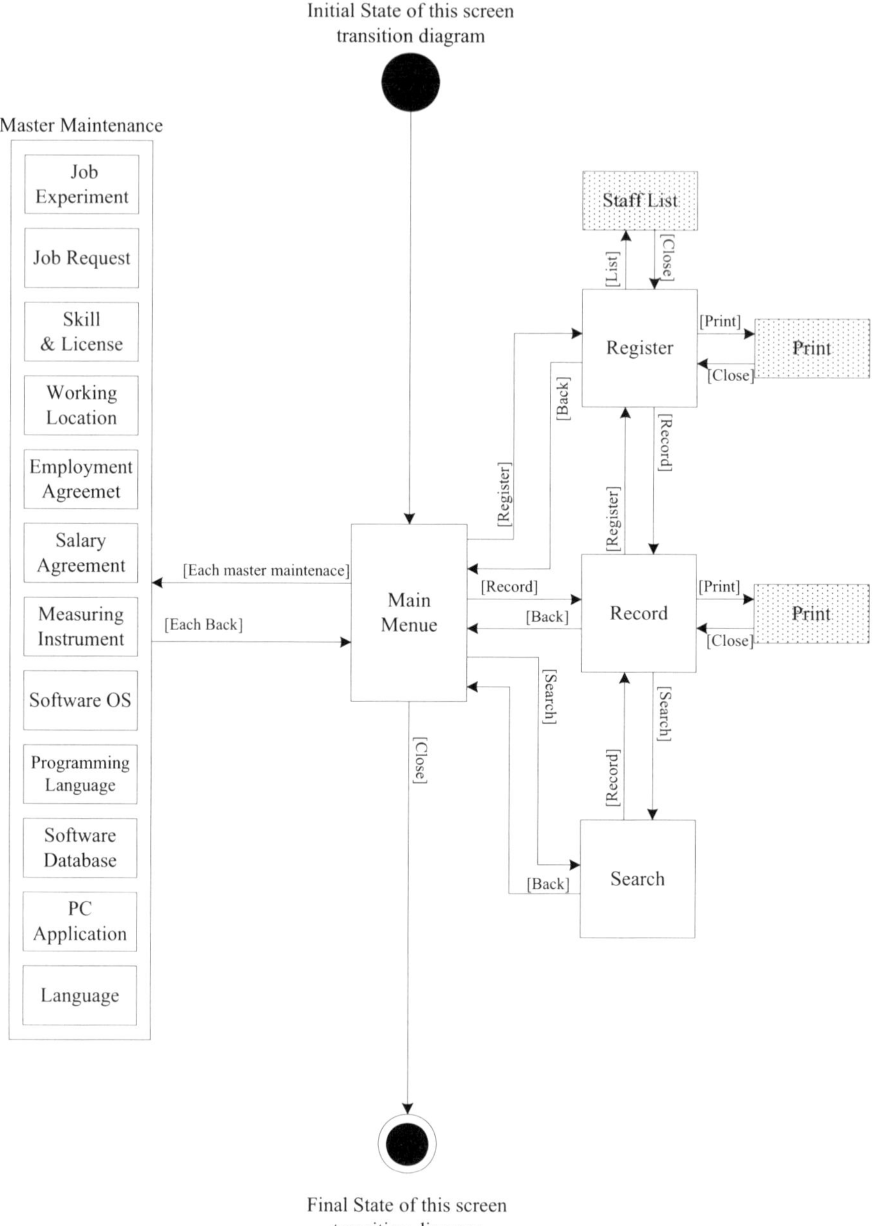

Figure 3: Screen transition diagram in the target application system

3. Assessing the Effectiveness of the LYEE Methodology for Fostering System Architects

As described above, even without prior software knowledge, the first author could develop a fairly complex software system in a relatively short time frame by exploiting the LYEE methodology. Through repeating a couple of additional system developments, it is expected that the first author would be able to conduct any assigned development work on his own as the system architect. Hereafter, we will assess if the achievement by the first author can be similarly gained by other candidate engineers so that our corporate objective to transform a non-software company to a software company can be met.

3.1. *What needed to learn to complete development – trainee's review*

Before being assigned to the project, the primary developer received a Catena's 9-hour LyeeAll3 training course customized to our request. The course was focused on only how to use the tool without any explanation of the so-called LYEE theory. Other software knowledge was quite general one from lectures received in his college age.

Therefore, all other knowledge needed for developing the above explained system was learned in the current project:

1) First, upon the assignment, he carefully read the manual prepared by the second author and understood the required system development process.

2) In the first three phases, i.e., understanding user requirements, general design and detailed design, following the second author's work, set as an example, he tried to complete the remaining portion by himself. For about initial 15% of the process he needed blindly follow the example given by the second author. In about next 35% of the process he wrote the specification documents only with occasional helps by the second author. For the remaining 50% of the process he wrote the specification by himself with the second author's final check.

3) Specifications for testing could be written by just referring to the documents for the second author's previous projects.

4) Preparations of the development environment, including LyeeAll3, Java development software JDK, web application server Tomcat, My SQL driver as DBMS API, open database connectivity ODBC and Java database connectivity JDBC made no sense to him at the beginning, and the thorough on-the-job training by the second author was needed.

5) In the programming phase, there were occasions where the learned knowledge on LyeeAll3 was not enough to complete the design, having required consulting with the second author.

6)	In the programming phase, the database design portion required the training from scratch. Following the second author's work the primary developer tried to complete the remaining portion by himself.

7)	As described before, it was decided that the screen design was done by using JSP. The primary developer wrote the programs for this portion by modifying sample programs provided by the second author.

8)	Trouble shootings require the most expertise from broad knowledge and experiences. Therefore a full involvement of the second author was inevitable at least in the beginning. Through on-the-job training the primary developer could learn how to locate causes of bugs by analyzing logs and could be able to conduct trouble shootings mostly by himself.

3.2. *How to let a novice complete the development – trainer's review*

The second author tried to be the trainer rather than to be a co-developer. Therefore, the basic stance was to let the first author do the development work under the involvement of the second author with a necessary and sufficient condition at each phase of the process. Since writing the system specifications properly incorporating user requirements is the most important portion of the system development and the key portion for the system architect, the second author's involvement was heightened to thinking together rather than instructing. For the programming and testing phase, her involvement was kept minimal so as to assist only when the primary developer was facing to some problems.

The points that the second author checked in laborious detail are the following:

1)	If the true intensions or desires of users are understood through analyses?

2)	If the graphical user interface and database are defined so that the system specification can be written without ambiguity?

3)	If the transitions among all defined screens are specified completely?

4)	If the trainee is confirming the system operation at the testing phase so that the system meet the defined performance?

5)	If the trainee is locating the real cause when the system does not work as defined?

6)	If the trainee is able to find the optimum resolution when encountered a problem?

Time consumed by the second author as the trainer for the primary developer during the system development process is summarized as shown in Table 5. It can be understood from comparisons between two columns, i.e., beta version phase and upgrading phase, that time required by the second author has decreased, meaning that the first author became possible to conduct the development work on his own.

Table 5: Time to train the primary developer by the second author

Process	Beta version phase	Upgrading phase
1) Basic programming training	0	0
2) General design	23	1
3) Detailed design	56	2
4) Programming for screen design (JSP)	62	0
5) Programming (LyeeAll3 template filling)	0	0
6) System testing	22	0
7) Trouble shooting	29	1
Total	192	4

3.3. *System architect training program*

From the above explained actual system development and experiences by a trainee and a trainer, a corporate training program for nurturing system architects has been established, and currently in the trial operation in the authors' company. The program consists of ten steps as described below:

Step 1 To select the candidate with a strong logical mind

Step 2 To assign a specific and effective development target

Step 3 To let the trainee study the system development process shown in figure 2 for the complete understanding

Step 4 To make the trainee prepare the necessary development environment (LyeeAll3 software package, Java development software JDK, Web application server Tomcat, My SQL driver as DBMS API, Open database connectivity ODBC and Java database connectivity JDBC) according to the manual established in the current project

Step 5 To make the trainee acquire how to use LyeeAll3 using the prepared examples

Step 6 To let the trainee lead the meetings with users, let extract essence of user requirements from often ambiguous and obscure expressions of users, and let transform them into a system requirements specification under the coaching by the trainer

Step 7 To let the trainee make specifications by defining required items (required system configuration, system's operating environment, user interface, names for screens, input/output variables on the screen, database files, tables and fields in the database table, data types, state transition diagrams for sub-process, total process flow diagram) under the trainer's assistance on demand

Step 8   To make the trainee modify the Java Server Pages (JSP) for user interface prepared by the trainer, and make fill out LyeeAll3 templates by the above defined names, data types and the necessary conditions defined by the state transition diagrams for generating executable files under the trainer's assistance on demand

Step 9   To let the trainee check if the system operates as desired and to identify and to correct bugs in the program under the trainer's assistance on demand

Step 10   To let the trainee evaluate if the system works properly responding to user's commands under various actual environments under the trainer's assistance on demand

4. Conclusion

In our previous work [1], we showed that the LYEE methodology can be implanted into a third party company as an effective software development tool that could be used by engineers even without software background. Our motivation behind this was to establish a fast and efficient approach to develop system architects from our thin engineering resources in order to transform a non-software company to a software company.

We evaluated in this paper, if even an engineer with non-software background can develop a full-fledged software system as the primary developer, what became essential roadblocks in each part of the development process, and what must be taught by an experienced engineer. As the conclusion of the evaluation, even a novice can develop a fairly complex software system if appropriate guidance and assistance are given by an experienced engineer. Based upon analyses of this experiment we developed our own system architect training program for realizing our corporative objective.

It is believed that the work reported here will be helpful to those who have interests in LYEE but have not been able to step out towards its adoption or in establishing software development capabilities for their own.

References

[1]   R. Maruta and N. Taniguchi, "Transforming a Non-Software Company to a Software Company by Exploiting the LYEE Methodology", Proceeding of the 5th SoMeT_06, pp. 133-145, 2006.
[2]   F. Negoro, "Principle of Lyee Software", Proceedings of 2000 International Conference on Information Society in the 21st Century (IS2000), pp. 441- 446, 2000.
[3]   K. Nakamura and T. Orii, "An Introduction to Lyee Program", Document provided in Catena Corporation's LyeeForum to be found in https://lyee.catena.co.jp/forum-e/servlet

Algorithm Library based on Algorithmic CyberFilms

Yutaka WATANOBE [a,1], Nikolay MIRENKOV [a] and Rentaro YOSHIOKA [a]

[a] *Graduate Department of Information Systems,*
University of Aizu, Aizu-Wakamatsu, 965-8580, Japan

Abstract. A library of algorithms developed as algorithmic cyberFilms is presented. The algorithmic cyberFilms are a new type of software components for presentation, specification/programming, and automatic code generation of computational algorithms. The algorithmic cyberFilm format is implemented as a set of multimedia frames (and scenes), and each library component is demonstrated by frames of algorithmic skeletons representing dynamical features of an algorithm, by frames of integrated view providing static features of the algorithm in a compact format, and by corresponding program templates supporting the code generation. We developed the library which is a collection of typical algorithms taught in university courses, including computation on grids, trees, and graphs. In this paper, we show basic constructs of visual languages which are used for representing cyberFilms as well as for demonstrating the library components. We also show a general overview of the library and its features. In addition, we discuss results of an experiment which was conducted to verify the usability of the library components and their usefulness in education.

Keywords. Visual Programming, Algorithmic CyberFilm, Algorithm Library

Introduction

The use of library components is one of the most effective ways to facilitate the development of software and to ensure its high performance and reliability. Knowledge about advanced algorithms and numerical calculus is vital for solving complex problems and is widely used in existing systems, simulations, and applications. However, although traditional libraries and corresponding tools generally provide better computational performance, functionality, reliability, accuracy, etc., they do not pay enough attention to human performance. Many programming language systems provide algorithms as libraries (e.g. a set of codes) of "black boxes," which reduce the understandability of internal features of algorithms. The user can use the libraries as rather convenient tools, but if he/she wants knowledge embedded in the library components, or wants to customize algorithms, in many cases, he/she has no chance to do such things without laborious efforts. For the pedagogical use, such libraries also reduce motivation for learning algorithmic solutions.

---

[1]Corresponding Author: Tel.: +81-242-37-2541; fax: +81-242-37-2553
E-mail: yutaka@u-aizu.ac.jp (Yutaka Watanobe)

One of the sources of difficulties in current library components is a great gap between a text-based program code and its computational meaning. Conventional programs consist of a list of instructions in a text format based on too abstract concepts and constructs, as well as on too implicit forms of manipulations with these constructs. Complex views of program codes, where dynamical features and static features of algorithms are involved in the same construct, are also the sources of difficulties. That is why, it is very difficult to reuse the library components as "white-boxes [1]." One of ways to solve such problems is related to, so called, visual languages [2]. However, current versions of these languages have very limited supportive features and do not provide serious hopes for breakthrough in the programming production.

To solve the above mentioned problems, we have introduced a new user-oriented (visual, multimedia) programming environment based on algorithmic cyberFilms (self-explanatory software components) [3,4,5]. The algorithmic cyberFilm is a set of multimedia frames (cyberFrame). In the programming process, the user creates or selects some structures of 1D, 2D, or 3D types to define a model of a space. Then, he/she introduces flow of activity in this space by selecting traversal schemes on the structures. After that, he/she defines structure parameters, variables assigned to the structure, and operations performed on the nodes within the traversal schemes. So, the cyberFrames are mainly arranged into special groups in multiple views related to: (1) algorithmic skeletons representing structures and flows of activity on the structures, (2) variables assigned to the structures and the operations performed during the flows, (3) input/output operations defining inter-component communications, and (4) an integrated view presenting a compact form of groups (1)-(3). In the environment, cyberFrames of these groups are developed and analyzed rather independently through focusing on different aspects of algorithmic features. Each group is represented/specified by a corresponding visual programming/modeling language. A set of algorithmic skeleton frames is supported by template programs to generate executable codes in C++. In fact, the user rarely create a cyberFilm from scratch, but he/she can use existing components and their fragments from the library. In the previous research, we have already presented a number of algorithmic cyberFilms related to sequential and parallel matrix multiplications [6], solving algebraic and partial differential equations [7,4], solving matrix equations [8], cellular automation-like algorithms [9], and inter-component communications [10]. Within these case studies, that are good examples of usability of the approach as a whole, a great compactness of our icon language [4,8] in comparison with C language, as well as measurements of understandability and usability of its symbols [9,11] have been demonstrated. Recently, we have also enhanced the cyberFilm format and the corresponding visual notations and constructs for some graph algorithms [5]. However, further consideration of new algorithms in our format is still very important to verify whether the format has the expressive power for representing various types of algorithms, and to make generalization of our results. It is also important to establish a systematic approach for developing an idea of open sets of visual notations [3]. The main contribution of this paper is an open library of algorithms currently including 34 items (they are available from web-site [12]). Each item is presented as a multiple view component: in an icon language, an animation/tile language, and in C++. The novelty of results is in developing the library of a new type, in comprehensive covering the advanced algorithms courses of the university level, as well as in providing statistical features of the library and its usability tests.

In this paper, we show basic constructs of visual languages which are used for representing cyberFilms as well as for demonstrating the library components, and a general overview of the library contents, examples of components, some component characteristics, and example usage of the library. In addition, we discuss the results of an experiment which is conducted to verify that library components are easy to understand and are useful for educational materials as well as for programming.

The rest of this paper is organized as follows. In Section 2, related works are considered. In Section 3 and Section 4, the algorithmic cyberFilm concept and the library are presented. In Section 5, the usability experiment and its results are discussed.

1. Related Works

There are a lot of existing general purpose libraries which include algorithmic solutions, such as Standard Template Library (STL) [13], boost C++ Library [14], NAG C Library [15], and GNU Scientific Library [16]. For advanced algorithms, Graph Template Library (GTL) [17], Combinatorica [18], Knuth's GraphBase project [19], and Boost Graph Library [20] have been developed. These libraries and tools provide a significant amount of potentially comprehensive algorithms and data structures which are rather powerful and reliable. However, they typically do not provide essential support for improving usability and understandability of algorithmic components.

On the other hand, to increase the understandability, some works are related to visualization tools or libraries for algorithm explanations. Especially, there are many tools for graph algorithms such as LEDA [21], LEONARDO [22], LINK [23] and others. LEDA is one of representative library based tools which has been commercially successful and is used by many companies and universities. LEONARDO is an integrated environment for developing and animating C programs based on a declarative language for specifying visualizations. However, even if they employ the visualization techniques, programming in conventional languages is still a major part of activity to use these libraries and tools. As a rule, the user has to embed special codes to visualize intermediate data results. They support visualization of the data in a very appealing way, but the algorithm specification itself is based on conventional text in languages like C/C++ or other text based declarative languages. So, library components are essentially black-boxes. Specifying (programming) algorithms without primary orientation to structure sizes and displaying intermediate step results, as well as without developing large-scale codes in conventional languages, is an attractive direction to be considered.

In the field of algorithm visualization, most existing techniques are of low quality, and the content coverage is skewed heavily toward easier topics [28]. For example, many of sorting visualizations are variations of the classic "sorting out sorting" video [29,30], where important algorithmic features and corresponding topics are poorly covered or difficult to recognize and use. It is also worth to mention that most algorithm visualizations are based on displaying intermediate data of computation (e.g. they are represented by just showing bars being swapped) rather than on displaying operations of corresponding algorithms. There are no essential collections of algorithm visualization where each item is described as multiple view components, and it is difficult to discover other types of well organized collections. In fact, in a huge bibliography [2], there are no papers on visual algorithm libraries.

In the field of visual programming languages, we should mention Spreadsheet programming and Forms/3 as one of general-purpose visual programming languages in a spreadsheet-like approach [24]. Forms/3 includes a set of forms (frames) and a graphical syntax for defining formulas in the form cells, and it also provides animation functionalities for supporting program/algorithm understanding. The main difference between Forms/3 and the algorithmic cyberFilm language is related to when and how a program shows different views. An important aspect of the Spreadsheet programming approach is built-in mechanisms for error checking and testing [25].

Real reusability of components acquired is an important aspect of any library. So, we are also interested in approaches employed in "conventional" (non visual) libraries. From this point of view, Generic Graph Component Library (GGCL) [26] is a collection of generic algorithms and data structures which allows basic algorithm patterns to be applied in different ways for building up more complicated algorithms, resulting in significant code reuse. This library based on the paradigm of generic programming [27] is an attractive example, though still algorithm implementations are described in C++ language.

2. Algorithmic CyberFilm Concepts

This section presents a brief overview of the algorithmic cyberFilm concept. First of all, fundamentals of the multiple views are presented. Then, the algorithmic skeleton view and the integrated view which represent important algorithmic features, and the corresponding program templates, are briefly explained. A programming environment, where algorithmic cyberFilm specifications are prepared, is also considered. Further explanations of the language constructs and symbols as well as additional details of the algorithmic cyberFilm formats can be found in our previous papers [31,3,4,5].

2.1. Multiple Views

The algorithmic cyberFilm represents a software component as a set of multimedia frames (cyberFrames). CyberFrames are arranged into special groups to organize multiple views of component features. The multiple views mainly include:

1. **Algorithmic skeleton view.** Data structures and computational schemes (flows) on these structures.
2. **Variables and Formulas view.** Variables attached to the structures and activity expressions used in space-time points of the algorithmic skeletons.
3. **Internal Input and Output operations view.** Links of sub-components and their input and output operations, i.e. inter components communications.
4. **Integrated view.** A combined view simultaneously displaying the features of items (1)-(3) in a compact form.

Each feature (view) is represented and specified by the most suitable way in a visual modeling/programming language, so called algorithmic cyberFilm language [31], which consists of sub-languages oriented to the corresponding features.

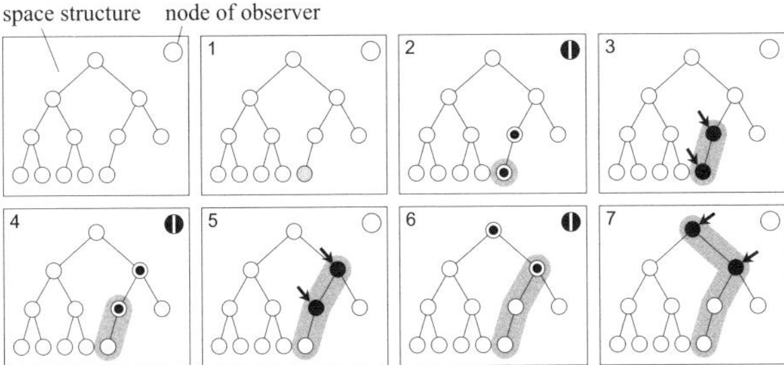

Figure 1. Algorithmic skeleton frames for the computation on a tree

2.2. Algorithmic Skeleton View

The algorithmic skeleton view shows algorithmic steps and thus dynamical features of algorithms. Figure 1 depicts algorithmic skeleton frames oriented to the computation on a tree space. Algorithmic skeleton frames represent the space and the computational schemes in the space. A cyberFrame represents a computational step, and a series of cyberFrames represents a scheme. The space includes 1D, 2D, or 3D structures that consist of a set of nodes connected by edges. Very often an independent node is added to the space. We call it "the node of observer." This node is related to common data of scalar or indivisible types representing sequential (centralized) process of computation. Operations of the node of observer include the access to activity attributes of any nodes in the space structures and controlling them. The schemes are shown by rendering the movement of the node flashing, meaning that some operations are performed on the flashing nodes. Nodes are flashed in different patterns/shapes and colors. The patterns/shapes depend on types of operations and the colors differentiate formulas/procedures that should be executed on the corresponding nodes. For example, cyberFrame 1 of Figure 1 shows that the computational scheme is started on a gray highlighted node of the leaf layer. CyberFrame 2 shows that some decision on place and type of the next step activity is performed on the node of observer. The decision is based on data taking from two nodes highlighted on the tree structure. After that, cyberFrame 3 shows results of the decision (the place of activity - by arrows and a type of activity - by black highlighted nodes). The decision can also include the break of computation. This means, if some conditions are not satisfied, the computation will be terminated here as a result of the decision. Exact activities on the nodes are not defined in the skeleton view, but they are specified in the other views. To clarify the computational flows as well as to give additional aspects to the flashing nodes, special foreground and background objects can be applied as annotations to the cyberFrames. Such objects also decrease or control the level of abstractness of the cyberFrames. In this example, we do not consider output operations, which should be in the real computation. One algorithmic skeleton can be used for programming of a lot of algorithms by attaching different structure parameters, variables, and activity expressions.

2.3. Integrated View

The integrated view shows not only space-time features of computational schemes, but also parameters of space structures, variables declared on the structures, and activity

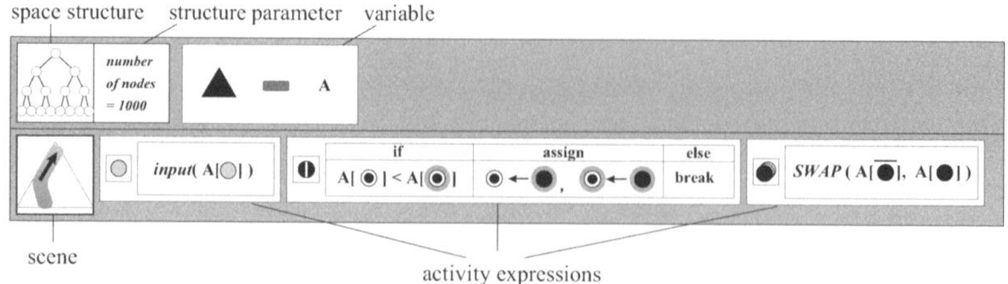

Figure 2. An integrated view of the Up-Heap operation

expressions (including input/output operations) related to different flashing nodes. For representing all these things, a special icon language is used.

Figure 2 depicts an integrated view of the Up-Heap operation obtained by attaching the necessary structure parameter, variables, and activity expressions to the algorithmic skeletons of Figure 1. In Figure 2, there are two horizontal stripes of boxes, which respectively represent a header and a body of the integrated view. The header defines structures and variables. The first and the second boxes with white background in the header define the structure, and the third box defines the variables. In this example, a binary tree structure with 1000 nodes and variable A of the integer type for tree nodes are declared. It means that one element of A is attached to each node of the tree structure. The body of the integrated view defines activities expressions (formulas) related to operations, including possible input/output, on flashing nodes of algorithmic skeletons. In this example, the left side of the body has an icon representing all cyberFrames of Figure 1 in a compact form. In this way, the algorithmic skeleton is represented by an icon in the integrated view. The right side includes three boxes representing activity expressions behind three types of flashing nodes: an input operation for a gray node of cyberFrame 1, a decision operation for the observer node at cyberFrames 2, 4, and 6, and finally, a swap operation for a set of two highlighted nodes at cyberFrames 3, 5, and 7.

2.4. Program Template

The algorithmic cyberFilm is used for the specification and explanation of corresponding algorithms, as well as for the generation of executable codes. Each algorithmic cyberFilm or its cyberScenes are supported by program templates, that consist of a set of template codes and template control data. The template code corresponds to the algorithmic skeleton, and the template control data corresponds to the integrated view. Figure 3 shows how an algorithmic cyberFilm is interpreted to an executable code. It depicts a program template (in this case, with only one template code) which supports the integrated view of Figure 2 and the algorithmic skeleton frames of Figure 1. The template code represents a repetitive construct with predefined formal "keywords" (in Figure 3, the keywords have gray background). The formal keywords are related to the structure parameters, the variables, and the activity expressions. In the template control data, these keywords are gathered and accompanied by real data, that will replace the keywords in the code generation process. For example, the real structure parameters and variables specified in the header as well as activity expressions specified in the body of integrated view are transformed into the template control data as C++ language expressions. Template programs are usually developed by users of the system programmer level and acquired as special

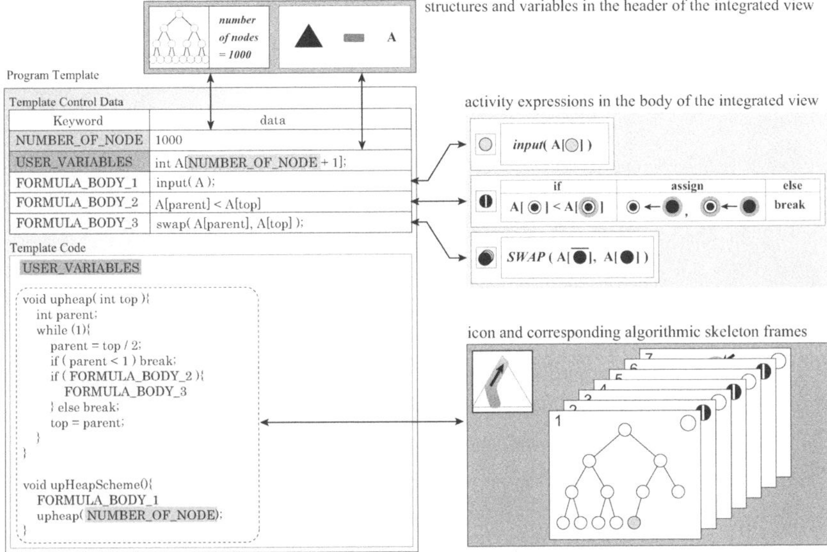

Figure 3. A program template for the algorithm presented in Figure 1 and Figure 2

knowledge of computational scheme implementation. Under some conditions (we do not discuss these here), template programs are automatically generated.

2.5. Programming Environment

A multimedia programming environment based on the algorithmic cyberFilms where the user can present, specify/program, and execute computational algorithms by manipulating the algorithmic features, has been developing. The environment employs the algorithmic cyberFilm language [31] supported by icon languages for representing contents of cyberFrames. So, the end-users can program algorithms without laboriously encoding the source code using the traditional textual format. The multiple views and the corresponding visual languages enable these users to directly manipulate visual symbols to specify/program algorithms.

An important advantage of the approach is that the users, in many cases, should not create cyberFilms from scratch. They can present and program algorithms by retrieving cyberFilms as pieces of "active" knowledge from a cyberFilm library, and use them as they are or after editing them. Within the framework of this environment, an activity for programming of algorithms/applications is centered on searching, browsing, editing, composing, and executing of the cyberFilm components.

3. Library of Algorithmic CyberFilms

The development of the library of algorithmic cyberFilms is important to expand our programming environment both quantitatively and qualitatively. It is also very important to continue brushing up the algorithmic cyberFilm language by verifying its expressive power on various algorithms. In addition, we also promote a systematic approach for

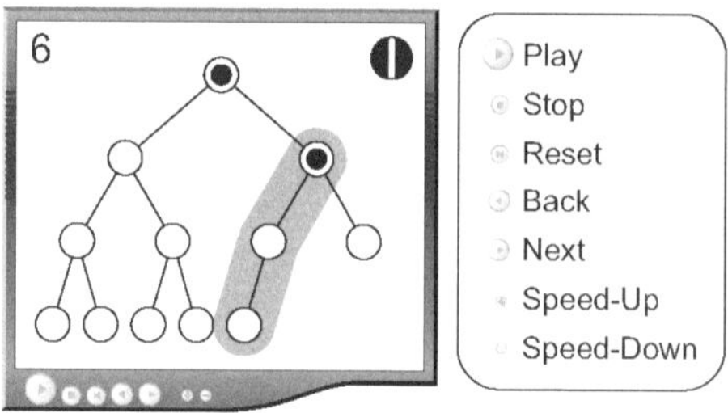

Figure 4. The animation mode

developing an idea of open sets of visual notations [3]. One more goal of the library development is its application as an educational material.

In this section, library contents with some illustrative examples, library component characteristics, and example usage of the library are considered.

3.1. Contents and component browsing

We have developed algorithmic cyberFilms oriented to basic and advanced algorithms of university courses related to computer science and engineering departments. Currently our library includes 34 items presented in Table 1. All library items are available from web-site [12]. Each item has been developed as a multiple view component including an algorithmic skeleton view in the animation/tile language, an integrated view in the icon language, and a program template in C++ language.

The algorithmic skeleton view is observable in an animation mode or as a set of tile cyberFrames. The animation mode is supported by a special browser shown in Figure 4, and the tile view is available as a static picture like Figure 1. When the user watches cyberFrames in the animation view, he/she can use "Non-stop" or "Step-by-step" modes. The "Non-stop" mode is ideal for watching a sequence of cyberFrames smoothly from the first cyberFrame to the last cyberFrame. The user can start the animation by clicking "Play" button and can also adjust the speed of animation. Even if the user employs the "Non-stop" mode, he/she can stop the animation any time by clicking "Stop" button to analyze what he/she has just seen. The user can also continue the animation after stopping. The "Step-by-step" mode is ideal for watching the cyberFrames in frame-by-frame manner through clicking "Next" and "Back" buttons. When the user watches the cyberFrames in the tile view, he/she can scan them by eyes in any special manner. Such a scanning can be attractive even without the animation of flashing nodes.

The integrated view is provided as cyberFrames of Figure 2 type. Each cyberFrame is a static picture and "Step-by-step" mode is used to watch all cyberFrames.

The program template is provided as two part text including the template control data and the template program codes. The text can be divided into conventional pages if it is necessary.

3.2. Illustrative examples

To provide some additional details and hints about the library contents, we show some illustrative examples of the library items. Our first example is related to the Down-Heap

Table 1. A list of developed algorithms

Categories	Algorithms/Problems
Sorting	· Bubble Sort · Selection Sort · Merge Sort
Operations on Heaps	· Up-Heap · Top-Down Construction · Down-Heap · Bottom-Up Construction · Heap Sort
Tree traversals	· Pre-order Traversal · In-order Traversal · Level-order Traversal · Post-order Traversal
Depth First Search (DFS)	· Depth First Search Tree · Articulation Points/Bridges Detection
Breadth First Search (BFS)	· Breadth First Search Tree · Shortest Path Problem
Minimum Spanning Tree (MST)	· Prim's Algorithm · Kruskal's Algorithm
Shingle Source Shortest Path (SSSP)	· Bellman-Ford Algorithm · Dijkstra's Algorithm · Priority First Search
Network Flow	· Edmonds-Karp Algorithm
Dynamic Programming	· Fibonacci Number · Matrix Chain Multiplication · Longest Increasing Subsequence · Longest Common Subsequence · Knapsack Problem
Compression	· Huffman Encoding
Search	· Binary Search
Numerical Analysis	· Gauss Elimination Method · Gauss Jordan Method · LU Decomposition
String Matching	· Brute Force Algorithm · Knuth-Morris-Plat Algorithm

operation. Figure 5 depicts algorithmic skeleton cyberFames oriented to the computation on a tree. The scheme is to move the element on the tree root toward leafs with some possible operations. The same scheme is represented (explained) by two different sets of cyberFrames. This means the algorithmic skeleton view can consist of several variations of the scheme to explain it. Semantics of the node flashing in these cyberFrames is the same as in the cyberFrames of Figure 1. One exception is related to a new half-highlighted node in cyberFrames 2, 5, and 8. Its meaning is similar to the meaning of the observer node flashing in cyberFrames 3, 6, and 9, but without assuming the computation break. Figure 6 depicts an integrated view of the Down-Heap operation obtained by attaching necessary parameters, variables, and expressions to the scheme of Figure 5.

Our second example is related to algorithms based on systematic traversals of all graph edges. Figure 7 depicts algorithmic skeleton frames for such a traversal. Cyber-Frames 1 and 2 are related to the start node selection and variable initialization, respectively. The main cyberScene of cyberFrames 3-14 starts with scanning of an edge indicated by two different highlighted nodes, and each directed edge is scanned exactly one-time in this cyberScene. Figure 8 depicts an integrated view of the Bellman-Ford algo-

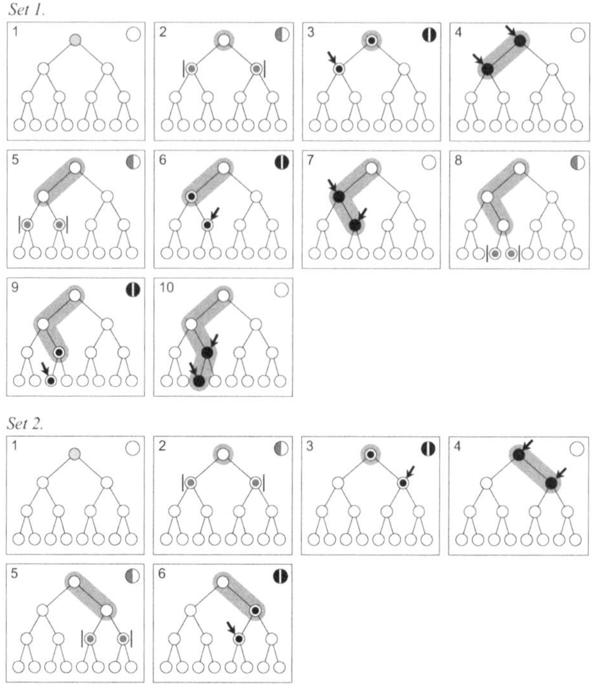

Figure 5. The algorithmic skeletons to represent the same computation scheme

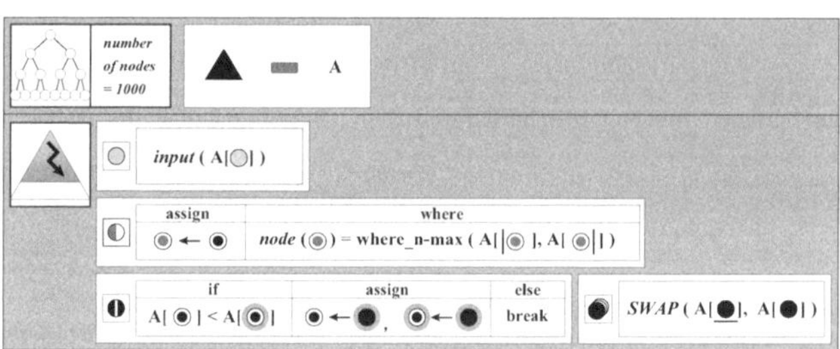

Figure 6. An integrated view of the Down-Heap operation

rithm for solving the single source shortest path problem based on the scheme of Figure 7. The header declares a graph structure with 1000 nodes and edges constructed from file "A." Then, the header declares two variables D and GR of the integer type for graph nodes and edges respectively. It means that one element of D is attached to one node, and one element of GR is attached to one edge. The bottommost part of the integrated view includes an icon of "for-loop" iteration. The expression represented by this icon means that operations (cyberScene) described next to the icon is performed **n** times. In this example, **n** equals **N**, i.e. the number of nodes.

Our third example is related to network flow problems. Figure 9 depicts algorithmic skeleton frames oriented to such problems. The computational scheme is to make a path from the source to the sink, and then to perform some possible operations on the path. Figure 10 depicts an integrated view of the Edmonds-Karp algorithm for computing the maximum flow on the network based on the scheme of Figure 9. The body is represented

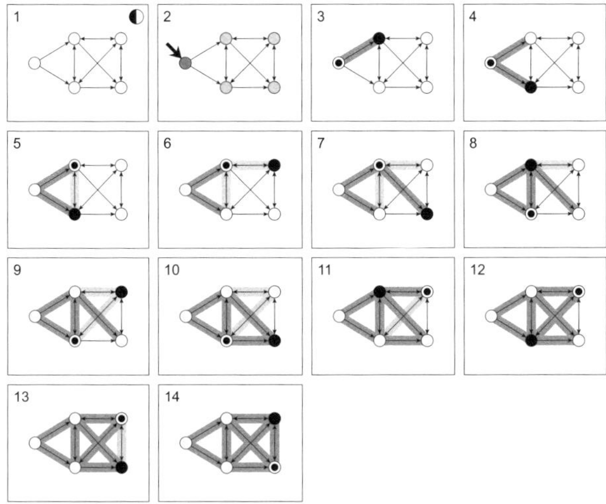

Figure 7. Algorithmic skeleton frames for the All-edges traversal

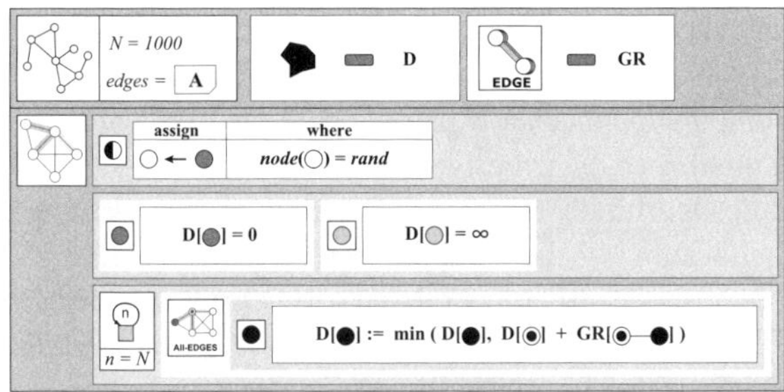

Figure 8. An integrated view of the Bellman-Ford algorithm

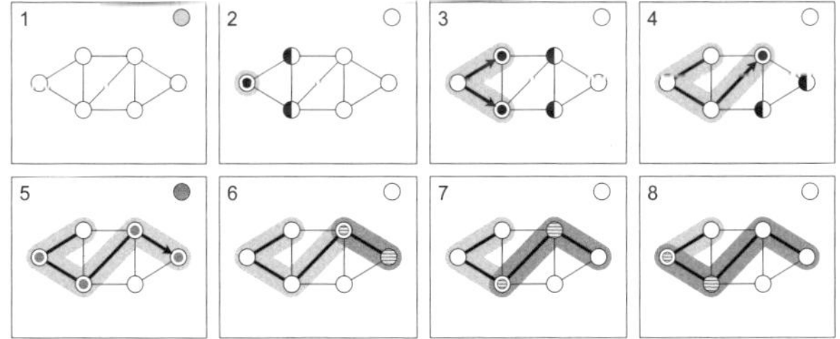

Figure 9. Algorithmic skeleton frames for the generalized graph search on a network

by an icon of "while-loop" iteration. The icon is followed by two sections related to the main cyberScene and a section where the condition is defined.

3.3. Library Components Characteristics

We have comprehensively analyzed the library components characteristics. In the development stage, all the library items have been developed by system programmers. When they develop cyberFilms, there are no restrictions related to the number of structure nodes

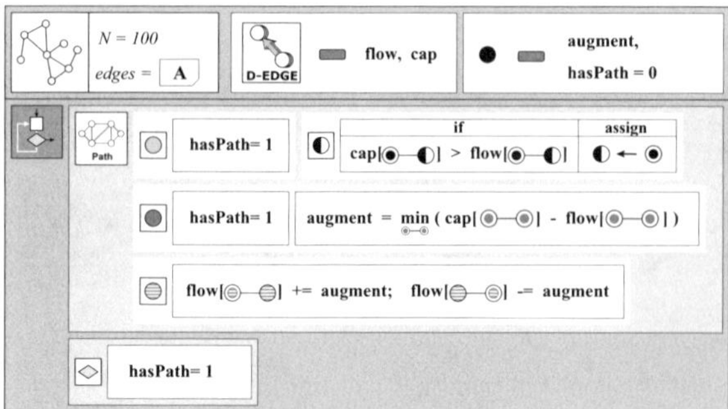

Figure 10. An integrated view of the Edmonds-Karp algorithm

and cyberFrames. However, they should try to minimized the sizes without sacrificing the understandability of the corresponding schemes.

The number of the algorithmic skeleton frames is very small, and they are watchable as short movies. Table 2 shows average numbers of cyberFrames in the algorithmic skeletons related to 1D grids, 2D grids, trees, and graphs, respectively. For example, a graph algorithm is presented by only 14.3 cyberFrames of the algorithmic skeletons in average. The compactness of the cyberFilm is an advantage. The average numbers show that a rather complex computational scheme can be presented by a small number of frames. The overall small number of the cyberFrames is due to the sizes of space structures used in the corresponding algorithmic skeletons. The sizes of the structures, which are necessary to explain the meaning of the computational schemes, are very small. Table 3 denotes average sizes of space structures related to 1D grids, 2D grids, trees, and graphs, respectively, and shows their example views. The table denotes that the average number of nodes in a skeleton frame for algorithms on 1D grids is 7.3, the average number of row or column in a skeleton frame for algorithms in 2-D grids is 4.6, the average height of the trees in a skeleton frame for algorithms on trees is 3, and the average number of nodes in a skeleton frame for graph algorithm is 7.4. The example views show that the explanations and specifications of the computational schemes are performed in very small structures. The overall small size of the structures can be accomplished since the cyberFrames are not directly related to the real data used for the computation.

In this library, each algorithm is presented by only one cyberFrame of the integrated view. CyberFrames of the integrated view are essentially compact. The integrated view frames use at most a half-page of an A4 sheet. The essential compactness is due to the simplified nested loops, the simplified index expressions and activity (formula) expressions, as well as to the reduced number of variables and statements. The compactness makes the components more reliable and secure, because such programs can keep making errors and mistakes at a minimum. The reasons for the significance of this compactness are also described in [4].

3.4. Library Usage

In conventional programming, the users write their code fragments and employ existing functions/components from the libraries. To find the components, and confirm their functionalities, they should do special efforts. In many cases, searching operations are per-

Table 2. The Number of cyberFrames in a skeleton

	1D Grids	2D Grids	Trees	Graphs
average	18.9	24.8	16.2	14.3

Table 3. Size of space structures

	1D Grids	2D Grids	Trees	Graphs
average	7.3 (nodes)	4.6 (rows/cols.)	3.0 (height)	7.4 (nodes)
views				

formed by names or keywords, or by exploring hierarchical structures. As for confirming the functionalities, the users need to read some documents or analyze program codes.

In our programming environment, the users also need to find and understand components, but there is a good basis for that. For example, algorithmic features related to structures, the skeleton schemes, etc. which are represented by visual symbols, can be used both for searching and confirming of the components [32]. In fact, we are developing a special multimedia language and corresponding sub-systems for describing algorithmic semantics, which can be used for the searching and confirming [33]. This basis can support the development of software components in the algorithmic cyberFilm formats, which can be more reusable and adaptable.

Our approach is oriented to two levels of users: 1) end-users and 2) system developers. The end-users just should use library items, and if necessary, they can edit the items with help of special editors. In the programming process, the end-users can understand and directly manipulate programs with visual symbols to accomplish their tasks without referencing to conventional codes in the template programs. Any library item including the algorithmic cyberFilm as a whole and its cyberScenes can easily be imported/exported from/into any user's application cyberFilm. The goal of this library is to avoid or at least essentially decrease coding in conventional ways by introducing all basic algorithmic cyberFilms which can enable the end-users to express their ideas. However, when the necessity arises, then new items (of the cyberFilm or cyberScene levels) should be developed. Any user, capable to do it, is allowed to develop new items, but we consider that this activity should be performed by system developers. When the users (developers) introduce new components, they have to create corresponding template programs as well as the algorithmic cyberFilms (or at least skeleton views) and pass through a refereeing process.

A special feature of the library items is that they can be useful to educate the end-users as students. The algorithmic cyberFilm components are very suitable for explaining algorithms as well as for programming. Beside, the library covers a rather comprehensive set of basic and advanced algorithms of university course levels. The template programs are useful to generate executable codes, but they are also very attractive as educational materials for leaning algorithms and programming. Students can read algorithms in the template programs written in C++, and they can also check how they look like in corresponding animation frames. The students can also see cyberFrames to imagine the algorithms, and then check their specifications in the template programs, to obtain knowledge of the technical implementation in C++ language.

4. Usability Experiment and Discussion

The introduction of new visual constructs and the application them for presenting contents of algorithmic cyberFrames are challenging issues. So, we are permanently performing various experiments to test their usability and understandability by considering new algorithms and by inviting new students to participate in the evaluation of the cyberFilm formats. Some results related to measurements of understandability and usability of visual symbols have been presented in [9,11]. Here we describe a usability experiment related to the student evaluation of the library items.

4.1. Subject

Eighteen undergraduate students enrolled in Advanced Algorithms course (intended for juniors) at University of Aizu have been involved in the experiment as volunteers. Algorithmic cyberFilms related to operations on heaps have been selected for this experiment. These cyberFilms include important aspects to be tested: the use of different types of flashing nodes, data/formula dependent schemes with the half flashing nodes, the use of the node of observer, and special background/foreground images.

Most of participants have already been familiar with coding in conventional programming languages (e.g. C/C++ and Java), but none of them have used the algorithmic cyberFilm language before the experiment. So, first of all, participants were asked to read a tutorial of the algorithmic cyberFilm language. This tutorial provides descriptions of concepts, visual symbols and constructs, the minimum needed for this experiment (we have not forced them to learn the full language specification). We confirmed that the majority of the participants reasonably understand the language as well as the concept of the heap.

4.2. Materials

The library includes the algorithmic cyberFilms for the different types of operations on heaps including Up-Heap, Top-Down Heap Construction, Down-Heap, and Bottom-Up Heap Construction. The four algorithms were described as shown in Table 4. The participants were requested to observe cyberFrames of algorithmic skeletons and integrated views for these four algorithms.

4.3. Procedure

Each participant has got an access to a "questionnaire form" provided through the Java Servlet application. The form consists of: the introduction of the experiment, a link to the tutorial, a question about comprehension of the algorithmic cyberFilm language, a question about programming skills, a link to the support materials for explanation of the heap concept, and a set of questions used to evaluate four library items in the experiment.

For each item, first, the participants were requested to read the description of the algorithm presented in Table 4. Then, the participants were requested to observe algo-

Table 4. Descriptions of the four algorithms

Up-Heap.

The Up-Heap is an operation which moves up an element of a node, whose value is now changed, while the heap condition is violated, toward the root. This operation is mainly performed when a new element is inserted to the end of the heap. The movements of the elements are performed by comparing and swapping elements of parent-child nodes.

Top-Down Heap Construction.

A maximum (minimum) heap of size n can be constructed by inserting n elements into an empty heap. Each element is inserted to the end of the heap, and an Up-Heap operation is performed starting at the end element.

Down-Heap.

The Down-Heap is an operation which moves down an element of a node, whose value is changed, while the heap condition is violated, toward leaves. This operation is mainly performed when the element of the root is changed. The movements of the elements are performed by comparing and swapping elements of parent-child nodes. Before the comparison, an operation which selects the corresponding child is performed.

Bottom-Up Heap Construction.

A maximum (minimum) heap of size n can be constructed by the down-heap operations. First, all elements of the heap are inserted (the heap does not satisfy the maximum or minimum heap condition). Then, nodes become the *source* of the down-heap operations from the node which has at least one child and has the maximal index ($n/2$ where n is the size of the heap) to the root.

---

rithmic skeleton frames (i.e. computational schemes) by watching the cyberFrames in the animation view or analyzing the cyberFrames in the tile view. The participants could choose the animation mode or the tile mode according to their preferences during the observation. The participants were allowed to observe each scheme as many times as they liked, but they should take a note how many times and in which mode did they observe a scheme before its understanding.

After that, the participants were requested to observe the corresponding integrated view and answer a question about the comprehension of the given algorithm.

After observing all the four algorithmic cyberFilms, the participants were requested to answer some additional questions of a "general observation" type. An opportunity to provide comments or suggestions for improvement, has also been available for them.

4.4. Results and Discussion

The experiment has been focused on the understandability of the library components in the algorithmic cyberFilms. So, a part of the experiment related to the algorithmic skeleton views aimed getting fewer number of the observations. We think the lesser number of observations leads to the higher understandability. However, we recommended the participants to observe each scheme at least a few times in either the animation view or the tile view. On the other hand, a part of the experiment related to the integrated views

Table 5. The number of observations respondents tried before understanding schemes

| | Up-Heap | | | | | | | | | Top-Down Const. | | |
| | scheme 1 | | | scheme 2 | | | scheme 3 | | | scheme 1 | | |
R	A	T	$A+T$	A	T	$A+T$	A	T	$A+T$	A	T	$A+T$
r1	0	1	1	0	1	1	0	1	1	1	0	1
r2	2	0	2	2	0	2	2	0	2	2	0	2
r3	1	1	2	1	1	2	1	2	3	1	0	1
r4	1	2	3	1	1	2	1	1	2	1	1	2
r5	1	0	1	1	0	1	1	0	1	1	0	1
.	.	.	.	.	.	.	.	.	.	.	.	.
.	.	.	.	.	.	.	.	.	.	.	.	.
.	.	.	.	.	.	.	.	.	.	.	.	.
r18	2	1	3	2	2	4	2	1	3	2	2	4
average	1.28	1.17	2.77	1.00	1.00	2.33	0.94	1.00	2.27	1.17	1.06	2.55

| | Down-Heap | | | | | | | | | Bottom-Up Const. | | |
| | scheme 1 | | | scheme 2 | | | scheme 3 | | | scheme 1 | | |
R	A	T	$A+T$	A	T	$A+T$	A	T	$A+T$	A	T	$A+T$
r1	2	0	2	0	0	0	0	0	0	1	0	1
r2	2	0	2	2	0	2	2	0	2	2	0	2
r3	1	0	1	1	0	1	1	0	1	1	2	3
r4	1	1	2	2	2	4	1	2	3	2	3	5
r5	1	0	1	1	0	1	1	0	1	1	0	1
.	.	.	.	.	.	.	.	.	.	.	.	.
.	.	.	.	.	.	.	.	.	.	.	.	.
.	.	.	.	.	.	.	.	.	.	.	.	.
r18	1	2	3	1	2	3	1	2	3	1	2	3
average	1.17	1.06	2.55	0.94	0.67	1.94	0.89	0.83	2.05	1.28	1.39	3.00

Table 6. The number of respondents on the number of observations

| | UH | | | TDC | DH | | | BUC |
N	s1	s2	s3	s1	s1	s2	s3	s1
1	4	6	6	6	4	7	6	5
2	6	8	6	6	8	6	6	5
3	5	2	3	2	4	2	3	3
4	2	2	2	4	2	1	1	2
5	1	0	0	0	0	0	0	2
6	0	0	0	0	0	0	0	1
0	0	0	1	-	0	2	2	-
Total	18	18	18	18	18	18	18	18

UH: Up-Heap   TDC: Top-Down Construction
DH: Down-Heap   BUC: Bottom-Up Construction

aimed getting the higher average scores, which rate the higher understandability of visual symbols and constructs.

Table 5 shows a part of the raw scores of the experiment related to the algorithmic skeletons view. This table denotes the number of observations that each respondent tried before understanding a given scheme in the animation mode (A) and the tile mode (T), and shows the total number of A plus T ($A + T$). This table also shows average scores of the number of observations. Table 6 also shows the raw scores which denotes the number of respondents on the corresponding number of observations (N) for each scheme in the animation and tile views. Figure 11 depicts the corresponding histograms of Table 6. Table 5 shows that the respondents observed each scheme less than or equal to three times in average. It is interesting to note that there are no an essential difference between

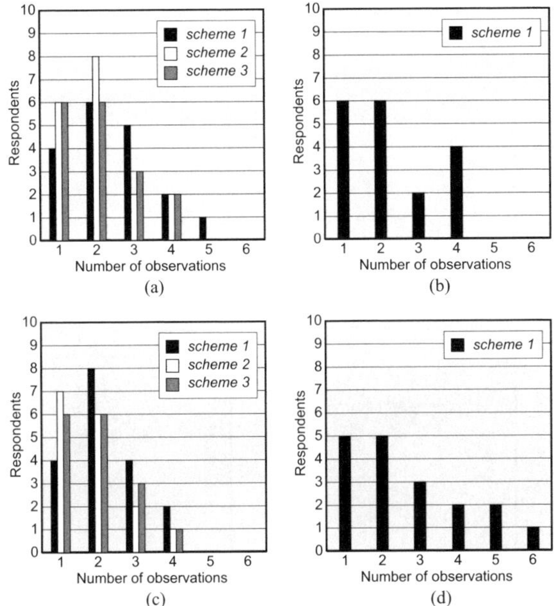

Figure 11. The corresponding histograms of Table 6. (a)Up-Heap, (b)Top-Down Construction, (c)Down-Heap, and (d)Bottom-Up Construction

Table 7. Average scores on the understandability of the integrated views

	UH	TDC	DH	BUC
average	3.11	3.11	3.11	3.05

average scores related to the animation modes and the corresponding tile mode. This result means that both the animation mode and the tile mode are useful. On the other hand, Table 6 and Figure 11 show that the majority of the respondents could understand each scheme by observing it one or two times. Another positive result is that nobody observed each scheme more than six times before he/she understood it.

Table 7 shows average scores related to the understandability of the integrated views of the four algorithms respectively, and Figure 12 depicts how the participants rated their comprehension. The question was rated on a scale of $4 - 1$: 4 = understood well, 3 = understood, 2 = could not understand, and 1 = could not understand at all. These table and histograms show that the majority of the participants could understand the algorithms through the corresponding integrated views. On the other hand, it is still arguable that a few participants could completely understand the algorithms.

As mentioned above, the respondents were also asked about their general observation on the approach used in the library components. Table 8 shows the questions and the corresponding average scores.

The results affirm that incorporating the library of the algorithmic cyberFilms into programming environments could help improve programmers' productivity. The results also show that the library items can be useful as educational materials. They are promising because the experiment was conducted without special promotion efforts and within a very limited period of time. The participants were just requested to read the simple

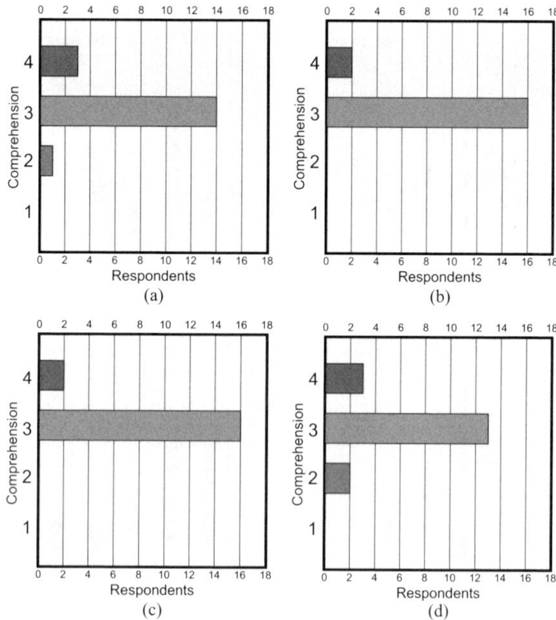

Figure 12. The corresponding histograms of Table 7: (a)Up-Heap, (b)Top-Down Construction, (c)Down-Heap, and (d)Bottom-Up Construction

Table 8. General questions and the corresponding average scores

questions	scores
Were algorithmic skeletons helpful to understand corresponding algorithms?	3.27
Were background and foreground images helpful to understand flow of computation?	3.27
Were integrated view helpful to understand corresponding algorithms?	3.11

tutorial which can be readable for approximately 10-15 minutes, and the majority of the participants finished answering all the questions for approximately 20-40 minutes.

Table 9 shows free comments from the participants. They made fruitful comments of both positive and negative types. Here, we would like to give our answers to some negative comments.

In this experiment, the integrated view has been provided as just a picture, but in the actual environment, the components are more easy to understand. For example, if the user wants to know the semantics of a scheme icon in the integrated view, he/she can click and open the unfamiliar scheme to watch it either in the animation view or in the tile view (if the user already familiar with the scheme, he/she does not need to watch the scheme). The activity expressions and functions can also be explained by the other view related to the variable and activity expressions. In this manner, certain constructs of the language represent semantic features of other constructs. The user generally does not need an external help like online help or printed reference manuals. Semantics of symbols such as structure, scheme, nodes, and all the other visual symbols, will be provided through

Table 9. Free comments from the respondents

pros

- The algorithmic skeletons views are easy to understand because I could see them as "pictures."
- The animation mode is better than the tile mode, but tile mode is useful when I could not follow the speed of the animation. So, it is nice that we can select either the animation mode and the tile mode as well as the step-by-step mode.
- The token movements on the foreground in the algorithmic skeleton frames were useful to understand. "Movement" of data (even without concrete values) are attractive.
- At first, I was not motivated to understand the algorithmic cyberFilm language because I am familiar with programming in text based languages. However, now I'm sure that I will be able to understand this multimedia language in time shorter than that required for mastering the conventional programming languages I currently use.
- The contents of the web-page is useful for understanding algorithms, because it shows animations.
- Degree of my understanding of the heap was increased.

cons

- I think it is difficult or requires time for beginners of your language to understand meaning of structures, nodes, schemes, etc.
- Though the integrated view employs icons, I was not motivated to read it (I think it varies with individuals), because I felt the sense of reading mathematical formulas and requiring time to understand.
- If you provide something that helps people to understand, you should make it more accessible (motivate people), otherwise we need another "help" to understand your "helps."
- I think it is useless for people who want to understand "what is the heap" (I mean it is useful to confirm algorithmic movements, but not useful for understanding theoretical issue).

the environment when he/she click a corresponding object on the screen. Thus in general, there is no need for an external help. In addition, the environment is also responsible for links to materials where theoretical and other features of algorithms are provided.

5. Conclusion

A library of algorithms developed as algorithmic cyberFilms has been presented. The algorithmic cyberFilm represents an algorithm as a set of multimedia frames displaying dynamical and static features of the algorithms. An important aspect of the approach is that the frames, especially related to dynamical features, can be used for programming of many other algorithms by defining configurations of actual structures, variables, and activity expressions. Other important aspects of the approach are related to the high compactness of the integrated view and space structures, and composing program templates for executable code generation without direct referencing to conventional program codes.

The library has been described through the library contents, examples of components, some component characteristics, and example usage of the library. Currently, this library includes 34 components and can be used for developing new algorithmic cyber-Films and for educational purposes. To illustrate the library contents and the idea of the filmification of methods, original solutions for cyberFrames related to multiple views of Bellman-Ford, Edmonds-Karp, and heap-based algorithms have been provided. To show understandability and usability of the library components, a special experiment, its details and results, have been presented. The majority of the experiment participants could understand an algorithmic skeleton by observing it only a few times, and the most of them could also understand algorithms through the corresponding integrated views. These facts are promising for the use of the library in new programming environments and in new educational processes.

Acknowledgements

We would like to thank the anonymous referees for their constructive suggestions and comments that helped to improve this paper. This work was supported by JSPS Research Fellowships for Young Scientists for Yutaka Watanobe.

References

[1] T. Ravichandran and M.A. Rothenberger, Software Reuse Strategies and Component Markets, *Communications of the ACM*, Vol. 46, No. 8, pp.109–114 (2003).

[2] http://web.engr.oregonstate.edu/burnett/vpl.html.

[3] N. Mirenkov, A. Vazhenin, R. Yoshioka, T. Ebihara, T. Hirotomi, and T. Mirenkova, Self-explanatory components: a new programming paradigm, *International Journal of Software Engineering and Knowledge Engineering*, Vol. 11, No. 1, pp.5–36 (2001).

[4] R. Yoshioka and N. Mirenkov, Visual computing within environment of self-explanatory components, *Soft Computing Journal*, Vol. 7, No. 1, pp.20–32 (2002).

[5] Y. Watanobe, N. Mirenkov, R. Yoshioka, and O. Monakhov, Filmification of methods: A visual language for graph algorithms, *Journal of Visual Languages and Computing*, Elsevier. (Accepted to be published)

[6] R. Yoshioka and N. Mirenkov, A multimedia system to render and edit self-explanatory components, *The Journal of Internet Technologies*, Vol. 3, No. 1, pp.1–10 (2002).

[7] A. Vazhenin, N. Mirenkov, and D. Vazhenin, Multimedia representation of matrix computations and data, *International Journal of Information Sciences*, Vol. 141, No. 1, pp.97–122 (2002).

[8] T. Ebihara, N. Mirenkov, M, Nemoto, and R. Monoto, Filmification of Methods and an Example of Its Applications, *International Journal of Software Engineering and Knowledge Engineering*, Vol. 15, No. 1, pp.87–115 (2005).

[9] M.A. Saber and N. Mirenkov, A visual representation of cellular automata-like systems, *Journal of Visual Languages and Computing*, Vol. 15, pp.407–438 (2004).

[10] R.R. Roxas and N.N. Mirenkov, A visual environment for specifying global reduction operations, *International Journal of High Performance Computing and Networking*, Vol. 1, No. 1/2/3, pp.100–116 (2004).

[11] R. Roxas and N. Mirenkov, A Visual Approach that Facilitates Program Comprehension, *International Journal of Software Engineering and Knowledge Engineering*, Vol. 15, No. 6, pp.941–975 (2005).

[12] http://borealis.u-aizu.ac.jp/aks/film/.

[13] M.M. Josuttis, *The C++ Standard Library: A Tutorial and Reference*, Addison-Wesley (2001).

[14] http://www.boost.org/.

[15] http://www.nag.co.uk/.

[16] M. Galassi, J. Davies, J. Theiler, B, Gough, G. Jungman, M. Booth, and F. Rossi, *GNU Scientific Library Reference Manual*, 2nd Edition (2005).

[17] http://infosun.fmi.uni-passau.de/GTL.

[18] S. Pemmaraju and S. Skiena, *Computational Discrete Mathematics*, Cambridge University Press (2003).

[19] D.E. Knuth, *The Stanford GraphBase*, Addison-Wesley (1993).

[20] J.G. Siek, L.Q. Lee, and A. Lumsdaine, *Boost Graph Library, The: User Guide and Reference Manual*, Addison Wesley Professional (2002).

[21] http://www.algorithmic-solutions.com/.

[22] P. Crescenzi, C. Demetrescu, I. Finocchi, and R. Petreschi, Reversible Execution and Visualization of Programs with LEONARDO, *Journal of Visual Languages and Computing*, Vol. 11, No. 2, pp.125–150 (2000).

[23] J.W. Berry, N. Dean, M.K. Goldberg, G.E. Shannon, and S. Skiena, LINK: A system for graph computation, *Software: Practice and Experience*, Vol. 30, No. 11, pp.1285–1302 (2000).

[24] M. Burnett, J. Atwood, R.W. Djang, H. Gottfried, J. Reichwein, and S. Yang, Forms/3: A First-Order Visual Language to Explore the Boundaries of the Spreadsheet Paradigm, *Journal of Functional Programming*, Vol. 11, No. 2, pp.155–206 (2001).

[25] D. Brown, M. Burnett, G. Rothermel, H. Fujita, and F. Negoro, Generalizing WYSIWYT Visual Testing to Screen Transition Languages, in *Proceedings of IEEE Symposium on Human-Centric Computing Languages and Environments, Auckland, New Zealand, pp.203–210 (2003).*

[26] L. Lee, J.G. Siek, and A. Lumsdaine, The generic graph component library, in *Proceedings of the 14th ACM SIGPLAN conference on Object-oriented programming, systems, languages, and applications*, pp.399–414 (1999).

[27] M.H. Austern, *Generic Programming and the STL*, Addison Wesley Longman, Inc (1998).

[28] C.A. Shaffer, M. Cooper, and S.H. Edwards, Algorithm Visualization: A Report on the State of the Field, in *Proceedings of SIGCSE '07*, Covington, Kentucky, pp.150–154 (2007).

[29] R. Baecker, Sorting out sorting: A case study of software visualization for teaching computer science, in *Software Visualization: Programming as a Multimedia Experience*, J. Stasko, J. Domingue, M. Brown, and B. Price (eds.), The MIT Press (1998).

[30] M.H. Brown, *Algorithm Animation*, The MIT Press, Cambridge, MA (1998).

[31] Y. Watanobe, N.N Mirenkov, and R. Yoshioka, Algorithmic CyberFilm Language, in *Proceedings of IEEE Japan-China Joint Workshop on Frontier of Computer Science and Technology*, Aizu-Wakamatsu, Japan, pp.178–185 (2006).

[32] Y. Watanobe, R. Yoshioka, and N.N. Mirenkov, A Searching Method Based on Problem Description and Algorithmic Features, *International Journal of Computational Science and Engineering*, Inderscience Publishers, Vol. 2, No. 5/6 (2007).

[33] Y. Watanobe, N.N. Mirenkov, and R. Yoshioka, A visual language for the description of algorithmic semantics, in *Proceedings of IASTED International Conference on Software Engineering*, Innsbruck, Austria, pp.91–96 (2006).

New Trends in Software Methodologies, Tools and Techniques
H. Fujita and D. Pisanelli (Eds.)
IOS Press, 2007

A Novel Intuitive GUI Method
for User-Friendly Operation

Kohei Sugawara and Rikio Maruta
SANGIKYO CORPORATION
Yokohama, 224-0053 Japan

Abstract. A novel Push-Pin icon is introduced as an intuitive graphical user interface (GUI) in associations from free layouts of printed paper sheets on a pin-up board. It is shown that necessary commands for GUI implementation can be represented by Push-Pin states. Detailed state transition diagrams for actual GUI implementation based on this icon are given. Superiority of the new GUI method to the conventional one was demonstrated in a typical application. It is firmly believed that use of the proposed method will significantly improve work efficiency of computer users.

Keywords: GUI (Graphical User Interface), Icon, Pointing device, Cursor pointer, Windows operating system, Intuitive operations, Drag and drop, Resizing, Display control, User command, Work efficiency, State transition diagram,

1. Introduction

This paper deals with an innovative end-user display control approach that enables users to customize displayed information with freedom. In business applications, users often need to display multiple data on the screen for comparing them at a glance. In order to achieve this with the conventional software, multiple operations such as, cursor pointing, drag-and-dropping, and resizing, must be repeated for each display object. However, this approach is not as convenient as manual handling of printed paper sheets. If data representation on the screen can be done with freedom as manual handling of printed sheets, users may augment their analytical power and creativity significantly, thereby improving work efficiency.

Authors' idea is to assign a Push-Pin as an icon for a display object and to control the Push-Pin for changing the object display location, modifying the object size, and selecting the item to be displayed. When there are plural numbers of objects to be displayed on a screen, there will be the same number of Push-Pins on the screen. All user's commands are given to the Push-Pins by the pointing device (mouse) of the computer. Users therefore do not need fuss around with the mouse on the screen, simply controlling the selected Push-Pin according to intuition.

2. GUI as a Means to Assist User's Thinking Process

The advent of GUI, or Graphical User Interface, helped the widespread use of computer systems among ordinary people [1]. From stand-alone applications of personal computers with Apple's Macintosh or Microsoft Windows operating systems through recent internet browsing, GUI has become an indispensable component of any electronic devices to which human-beings interact. Essence of GUI is intuitive operation. The initial GUIs were intuitive. However, as the functional complexity of applications increased, it became difficult that all of operations consist of intuitive ones. Moreover, frequent cursor operations by the user became necessary in order to give appropriate commands to the system.

As a typical example of GUI operations, let's look at Microsoft Windows [2]. In Microsoft Windows, multiple application/document windows can be displayed on a screen. A window is a rectangular visual area, containing user interface, allowing user inputs, displaying the output from the application system. The user interface includes such functions as to minimize, to restore, to change size, to move, to maximize, and to close. Minimized windows disappear from the screen and can be restored by clicking their title-bar button. Maximizing windows causes them to take up the whole screen space, except the area taken by the title-bar. Windows are closed by clicking the "X" button at top-right, resized by dragging their border, and moved by dragging their title bar.

Among the above explained operations, resizing by dragging window's border is intuitive, but other operations are not necessarily intuitive. For example when a window needs to be moved, the portion to be dragged may be different for application by application. It requires pre-learning if the window can be moved by dragging the title bar. Since places to be grabbed and buttons to be controlled are spread over the corners of the target window, users must fuss around with the cursor pointer on the screen. When users want to compare multiple data at a glance, all these procedures must be repeated for window by window or target application by target application, sometimes losing their concentrations on issues to be analyzed or resolved because of cumbersome operations.

Here let's imagine an office scene where business people are brain-storming their business strategy. In such a scene, various data and/or graphs may be displayed in front of them by using a pin-up board as in Figure 1. In order to stimulate their imagination and enhance their creativity, the display arrangement may be changed according to the progress of discussions.

Authors of this paper thought if this pin-up board approach is incorporated into the computer system, office worker's efficiency would be significantly enhanced, and came to an idea of using Push-Pin images as an icon through which all necessary user commands are given to the application system. Each object window or target application is represented by a Push-Pin icon. Moving an object window or target application can be realized by moving the representing Push-Pin icon. This is an associated implementation of the actual pin-up board operation. In order to resize the target object or the target window, Push-Pin is rotated. This action is from an association to a speaker volume control button. Also on/off switch of the target objects is realized by the push/pull of the Push-Pin icon from an association with the volume control button.

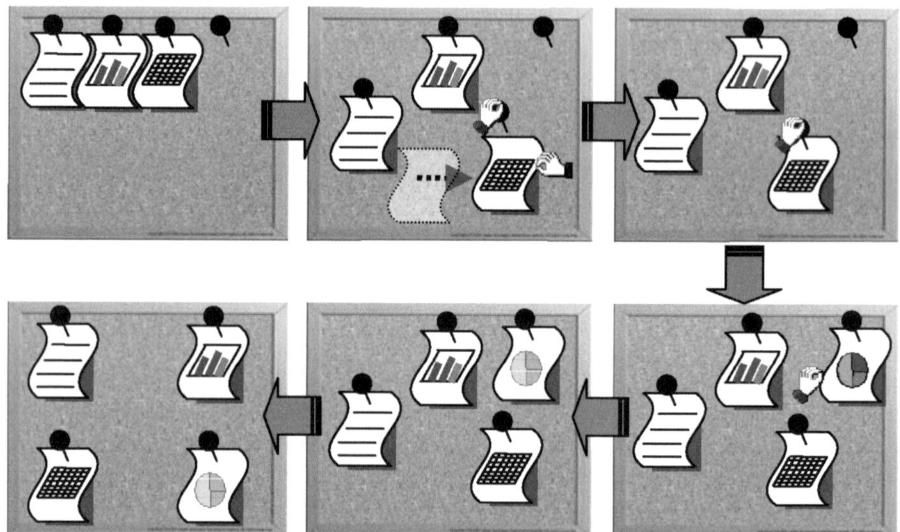

**Figure 1: Displaying and rearranging of multiple data
in business analysis on a pin-up board**

As described above, all user commands for a target window or object can be given to the system through a Push-Pin. This concentration of points of control can significantly reduce the moving distance of the cursor pointer, leading to work efficiency improvement.

3. Intuitive GUI Commands realized by Push-Pin Icon

3.1. Defining a new icon with Push-Pin image

Figure 2 shows definition of the proposed new icon which represents an associated target object. The new icon consists of a push-pin and its shadow. A push-pin is composed of head and nail. The associated target object is nailed down by the push-pin icon. The target object may appear or disappear depending on user's command.

The push-pin icon defined above can express basically three states, i.e. "floating (not being stuck)", "being stuck intermediately", and "being stuck firmly". In addition to these three intuitive states, two extended states, rotating push-pin and concealed buttons in push-pin's shadow, are added as shown in Table 1 to enhance realizable functionalities.

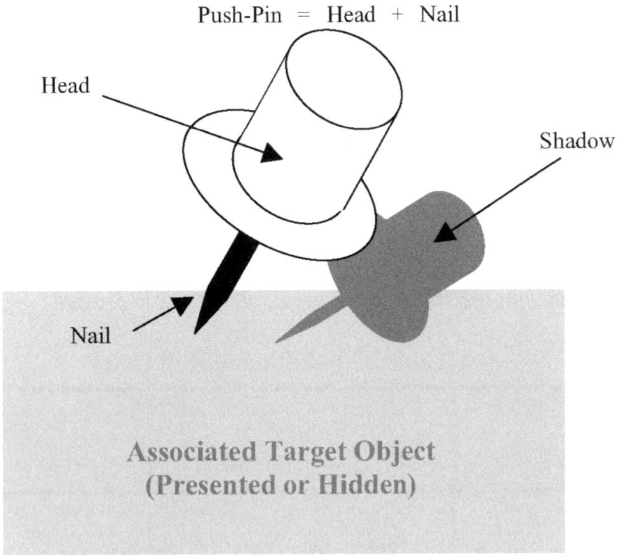

Figure 2: Definition of "Push-Pin" icon

Table 1: States represented by a Push-Pin and its shadow

	State		Image	
			Intuitive	Extended
Main body of Push-Pin	Floating		●	—
	Being stuck intermediately		●	—
	Rotating	Clockwise	—	●
		Counterclockwise	—	●
	Being stuck firmly		●	—
Shadow of Push-Pin	Floating		●	—
	Being stuck intermediately		●	—
	Being stuck firmly		●	—
	Showing concealed buttons		—	●

Table 2 shows six states that can be represented by combinations of main body of push-pin and its shadow. "Icon state **A**" represents that push-pin is floating, thus being ready for moving. "Icon state **B**" indicates that target object is put on the location where the push-pin is located. "Icon state **C**" and "Icon state **D**" show that the target object is under resizing. "Icon state **C**" is for enlarging and "Icon state **D**" is for shrinking. "Icon state **E**" is used for representing the status that push-pin is pressed to switch on the target object. Lastly, the sixth icon state ("Icon state **F**") is introduced for extended functions, showing concealed buttons that can execute some additional functions in the application of the target object.

In order to distinguish the condition of the associated target object (shown or hidden), the above defined states **A** through **F** are given two representations. States **A** through **F** are defined to represent the states when the target object is hidden and states **A̲** through **F̲** represent the states when the target object is present.

Table 2: Definition of icon states

			Shadow's state			
			Floating	Being stuck intermediately	Being stuck firmly	Showing concealed buttons
Pin's state		Floating	Icon State **A** or **A̲**	—	—	—
	Being stuck intermediately	Still	—	Icon State **B** or **B̲**	—	Icon State **F** or **F̲**
		Rotate clockwise	—	Icon State **C** or **C̲**	—	—
		Rotate counter-clockwise	—	Icon State **D** or **D̲**	—	—
	Being stuck firmly		—	—	Icon State **E** or **E̲**	—

Note: States **A** through **F** represent the states when the target object is hidden and states **A̲** through **F̲** represent the states when the target object is present.

3.2. *Functional execution by the Push-Pin icon*

In order to control the target object as desired, the user needs to give an appropriate command to the icon defined in Table 2 by a pointing device. User's meaningful actions with the pointing device are defined to be the following;

User Action **a**: This action is to point the head of the selected push-pin and to push the execution button of the pointing device in order for rotating the push-pin when the target object is shown or making the push-pin stuck firmly when the target object is hidden.

User Action **b**: This action is to point the nail of the selected push-pin and to push the execution button of the pointing device for making the push-pin float.

User Action **c**: This action is to release the execution button of the pointing device for making the push-pin intermediately stuck and still.

User Action **d**: This action is to move the cursor of the pointing device for making the push-pin to move together with the target object.

User Action **e**: This action is to point the shadow of the selected push-pin and to push the execution button of the pointing device for showing or hiding the additional buttons in the shadow.

User Action **f**: This action is to click the appropriate button in the shadow of the selected push-pin for executing the additional functions.

Table 3 depicts all possible commands specified by the user actions defined above. For User Action **a**, only rows **B**, **B̲**, **C̲** and **D̲** are meaningful. Likewise, for User Action **b** rows **B** and **B̲**, for User Action **c** rows **A**, **A̲**, **C̲**, **D̲** and **E**, for User Action **d** rows **A** and **A̲**, for User Action **e** rows **B̲** and **F̲**, and for User Action **f** row **F̲** are only meaningful.

Here, let's assume such a situation that a push-pin icon is stuck intermediately at a place on the screen and the target object is hidden. In Table 3 this situation is corresponding to the row represented as state **B**. Possible user actions in this situation are User Action **a** or **b**. If the user points the head of the push-pin and push the execution button of the pointing device (User Action **a**), the push-pin is stuck firmly (moves to state **E**), and when the execution button of the pointing device is released, the associated target object appears and the current state moves to the row represented as state **B̲**. At the current state **B̲**, User Actions **a**, **b** or **e** can be accepted, thereby enabling resizing (to enlarge or to shrink), moving or showing up concealed buttons for additional functions.

		User Action					
		a	**b**	**C**	**d**	**e**	**F**
Current Icon State when target object is hidden	**A**	—	—	The current icon state moves to Icon State **B**.	Icon location is moved following the cursor pointer.	—	—
	B	The current icon state moves to Icon State **E**.	The current icon state moves to Icon State **A**.	—	—	—	—
	C	—	—	—	—	—	—
	D	—	—	—	—	—	—
	E	—	—	Target object appears and the current icon state moves to Icon State **B**.	—	—	—
	F	—	—	—	—	—	—
Current Icon State when target object is present	**A**	—	—	The current icon state moves to Icon State **B**.	Icon location and target object are moved following the cursor pointer.	—	—
	B	If the previous direction was enlarging, moves to Icon State **C**. If it was shrinking, moves to Icon State **D**.	The current icon state moves to Icon State **A**.	—	—	The current icon state moves to Icon State **F**.	—
	C	Target object is enlarged.	—	Resizing direction is changed to shrinking and the current icon state moves to Icon State **B**	—	—	—
	D	Target object is shrunk. If the size is shrunk to a predetermined level, display of the target object ceases and the current icon state moves to Icon State **B**.	—	Resizing direction is changed to enlarging and the current icon state moves to Icon State **B**	—	—	—
	E	—	—	—	—	—	—
	F	—	—	—	—	The current icon state moves to Icon State **B**.	The assigned function is executed

4. Software Implementation

For intuitive operations, icon's appropriate reactions to user commands are very important. This means icon image needs to be dynamically changed according to the user command. In order to realize the proposed Push-Pin icon, image components shown in Figure 3 are used. The resulting icon image is realized by a superposition of five image groups (3.1 through 3.5) in Figure 3 in layers. For superposition, the image component in a higher image group number is placed on the surface side of the screen.

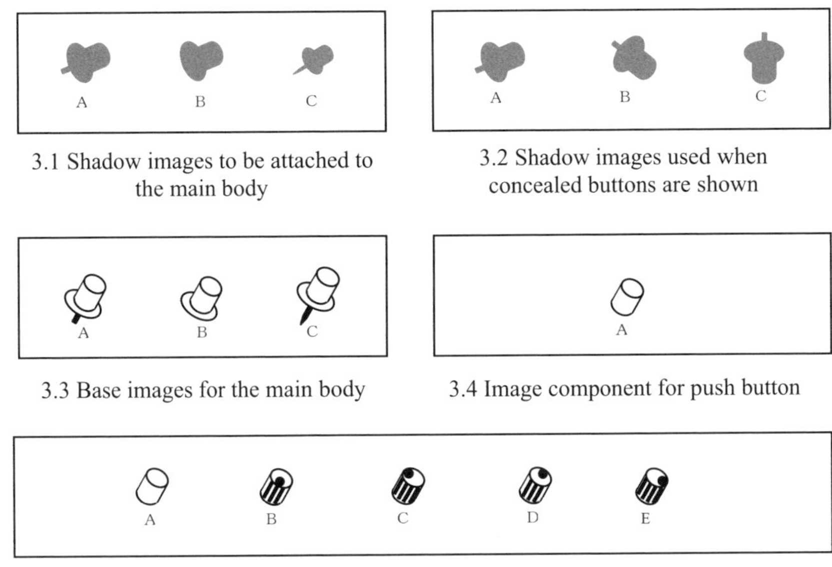

3.1 Shadow images to be attached to the main body

3.2 Shadow images used when concealed buttons are shown

3.3 Base images for the main body

3.4 Image component for push button

3.5 Image components for rotating Push-Pin

Figure 3: Image components for Push-Pin icon

Actual software development can be done according to state transition diagrams shown in Figure 4 through Figure 7. In the state transition diagrams, state transitions occur by user actions. User Actions **a** through **f** in the figures are the same as the user actions defined in Section 3.2.

Figure 4 shows initial settings and the state transition from Icon State **B** to Icon State **A**, or to Icon State **B** via Icon State **E**.

By initial settings, the icon image for Icon State **B** is formed so that the push-pin is located on the screen but the target object is hidden. At Icon State **B**, according to Table 3, either User Action **a** or User Action **b** will occur. User Action **b** is to make the push-pin icon floated for moving. Therefore, the icon image for Icon State **A** is generated and the state is made ready (through jumping to #4) for User Action **d** in Figure 7.

When User Action **a** occurs, according to Table 3, the state should move to Icon State **E**. Therefore, the icon image for Icon State **E** is formed. Since Icon State **E** is a transitional state to be existed only during the execution button is pressed, as soon as the execution button is released, the state moves to Icon State **B̲**. Therefore, the icon image for Icon State **B̲** is formed, and operations in Figure 5 will follow.

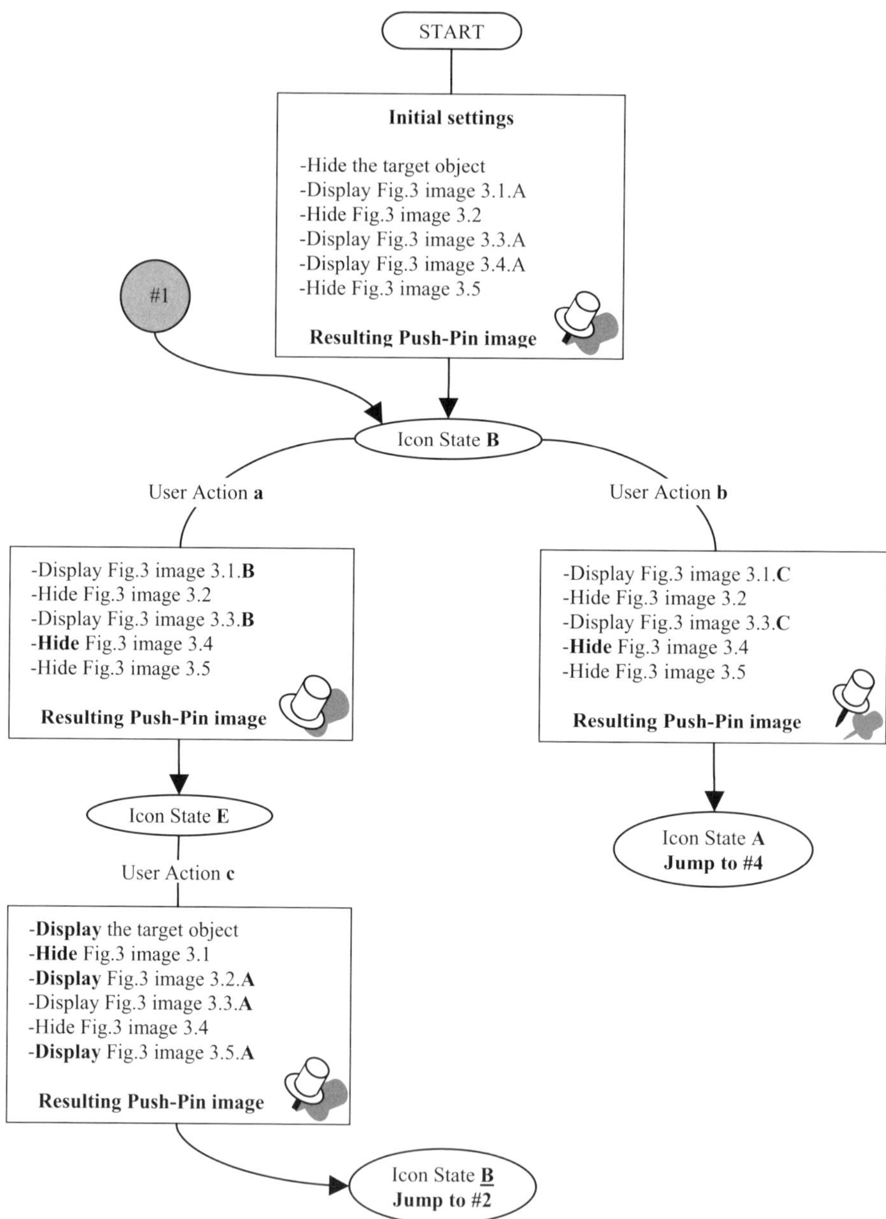

Figure 4: State transitions from Icon State B

Figure 5 is the state transition diagram for the transition from Icon State **B** to either; Icon State **A**, Icon State **F**, Icon State **B** via Icon State **D**, or returning to own state via Icon State **C** or Icon State **D**.

When User Action **b** occurs at Icon State **B**, the icon image for Icon State **A** is generated and the state is made ready (through jumping to #5) for User Action **d** in Figure 7. If User Action **e** occurs at Icon State **B**, the icon image for Icon State **F** is generated and the state is made ready (through jumping to #3 in Figure 6) for selecting any one of concealed buttons in the shadow of the push-pin.

User Action **a** at Icon State **B** is to resize the target object. Resizing includes enlarging or shrinking. If the size of the target object becomes less than a predetermined level, the target object is hidden. Although there are other implementation approaches (such as using right click and left click), a toggling approach is used in the present application for determining the resizing direction (to enlarge or to shrink).

Therefore, when User Action **a** (pointing head of push-pin and pushing the execution button of the pointing device) occurs at Icon State **B**, previous direction of resizing is first determined if in enlarging or shrinking. When the previous direction was in enlarging, Icon State **C** is exhibited and clockwise rotation begins with continued User Action **a**, resulting in the continued expansion of the target object. If User Action **c** occurs, or the execution button is released, at Icon State **C**, resizing direction is reversed to the shrinking mode. When the previous direction was in shrinking, Icon State **D** is exhibited and counter-clockwise rotation begins with continued User Action **a**, resulting in the continued shrinking of the target object as long as the size of the target object is above the predetermined size. If the size of the target object becomes smaller than the predetermined level, push-pin rotation stops and the target object disappears, returning to Icon State **B**. If User Action **c** occurs, or the execution button is released, at Icon State **D**, resizing direction is reversed to the enlarging mode.

Figure 6 is the state transition diagram for the transition from Icon State **F** to Icon State **B**. In this state, the desired command allotted to a concealed button can be ordered by the user action.

Figure 7 is the state transition diagram for the transition from Icon State **A** or **A** to Icon State **B** or **B**. In this state, icon location and target object can be moved following the cursor pointer by the user action.

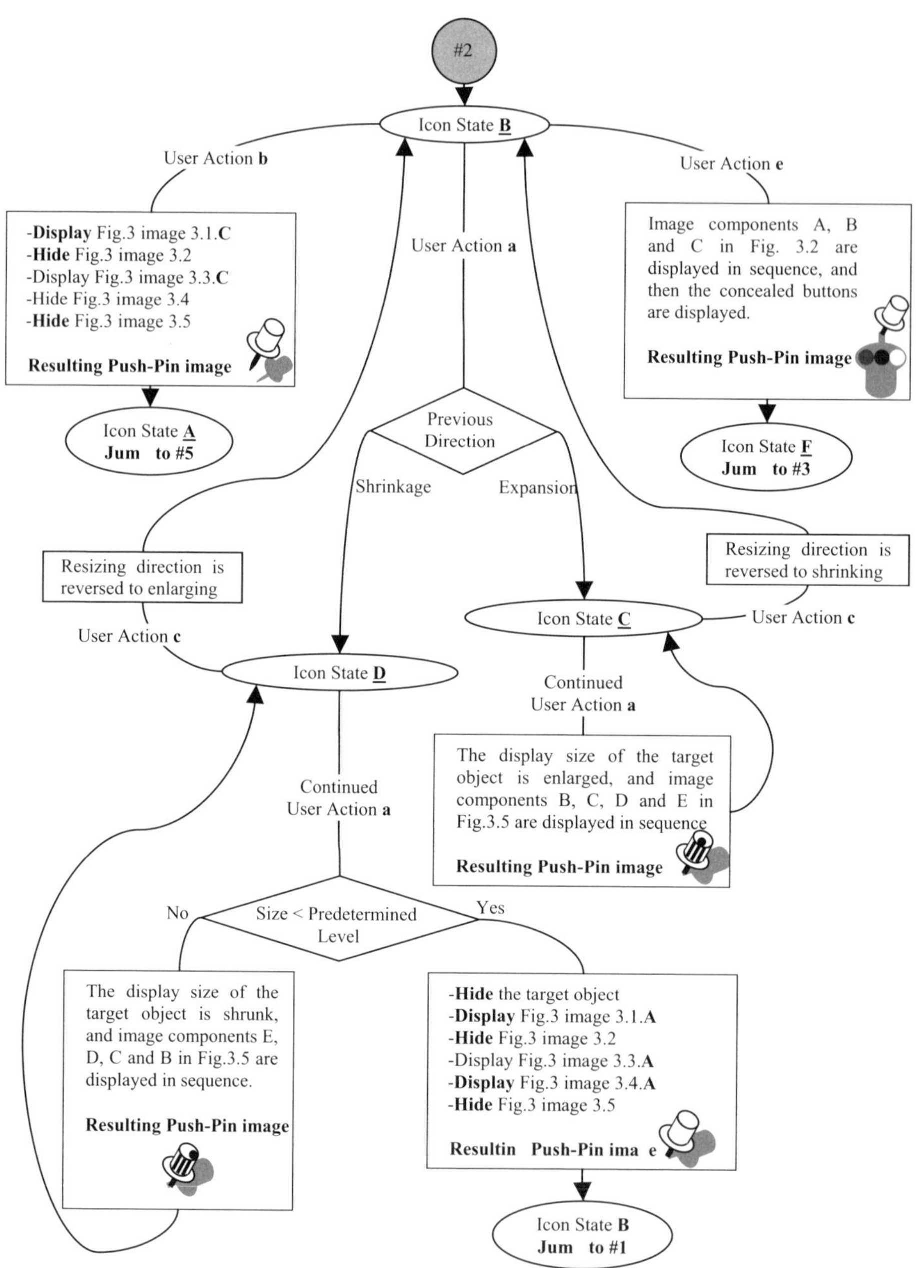

Figure 5: State transitions from Icon State B

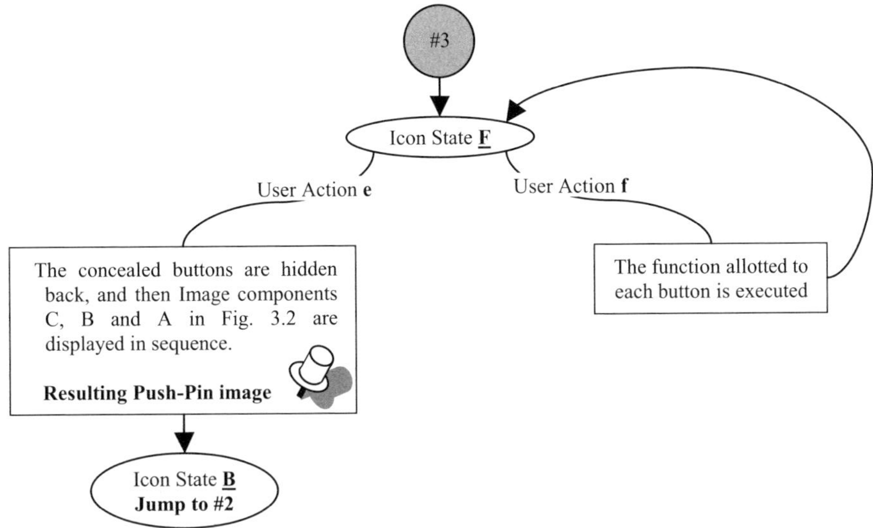

Figure 6: State transitions from Icon State F

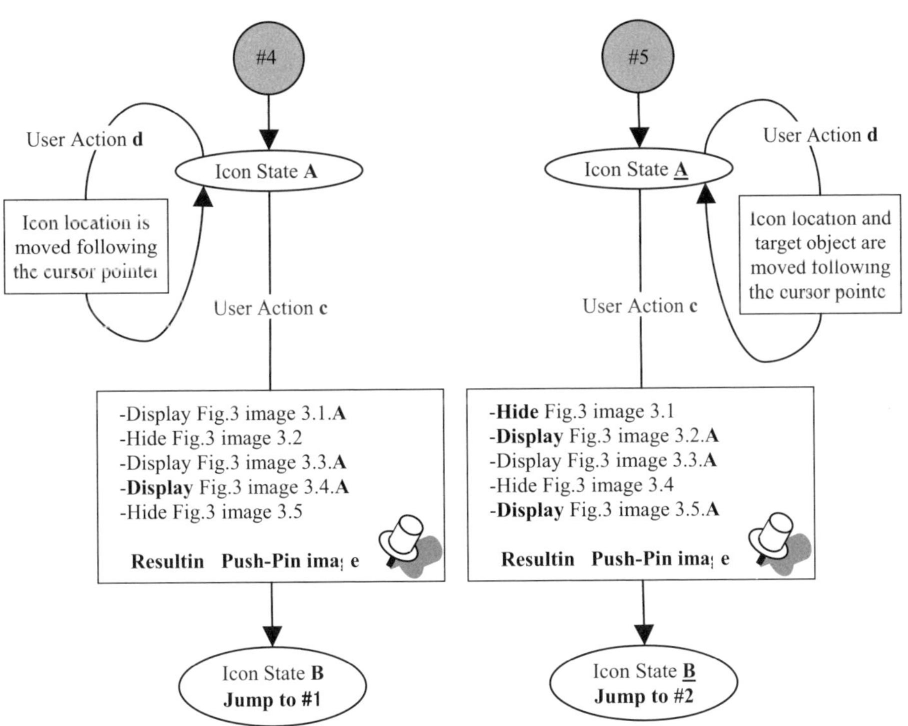

Figure 7: State transitions from Icon State A or A

5. Effectiveness of the Proposed Approach

In order to see the effectiveness of the proposed approach, let's look at a situation where a business person is observing data, e.g., order receipt forecast, sales forecast, and estimated gross profit, in an application using Microsoft Excel as shown in Figure 8.

When the user wants to display a target object, he or she will select the corresponding button. If the user wants to display another target object, another button will be selected. For changing the graph size, the user will drag the border of the graph. To move the graph location on the screen, the user will grab the specified part of the graph and drug it to the desired location on the screen and drop there. If the user wants to look at one specific graph only, other graphs will be put into the non-display mode by pushing dedicated buttons.

By using the new GUI method, the same application can be realized as shown in Figure 9. Three push-pins are assigned to order receipt, sales, and gross profit. As described in the previous sections in detail, just by handling an appropriate Push-Pin icon, changing the object display location, modifying the object size, and selecting the item to be displayed can be easily done. To be noted here is that the total distance of cursor movements is much smaller and constraints in graph layouts on the screen are far less in the new method as compared to the conventional approach, where the layout design is basically fixed by the system design.

Figure 10 illustrates comparisons between the two methods in necessary number of user actions for conducting consecutive four basic operations, namely "to display a target object", "to resize the target object", "to move the display location of the target object", and "to hide the target object". The proposed approach requires only four actions while the conventional approach requires eight actions. Therefore, the proposed approach's superiority is apparent in quantitative comparison, too.

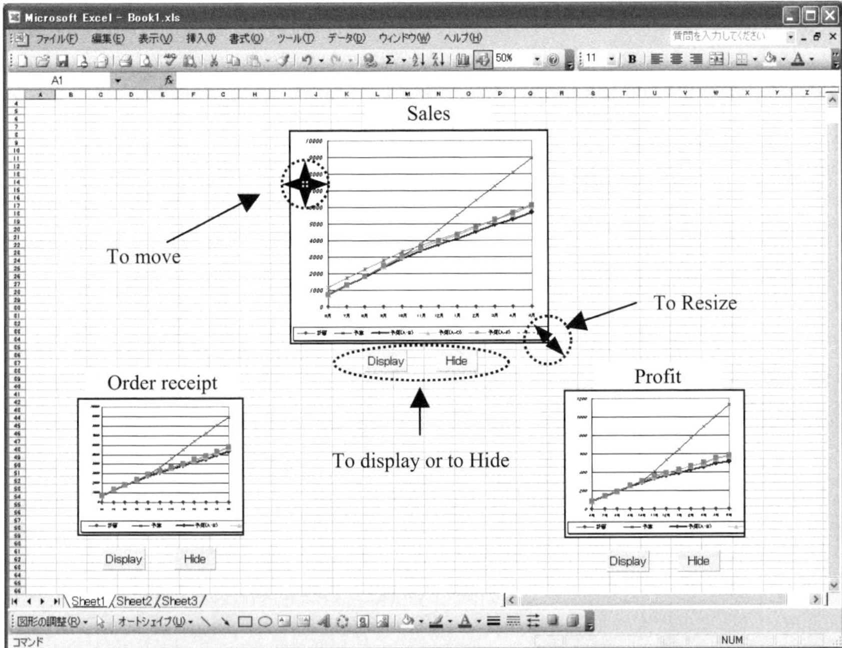

Figure 8: Observing graphs in business analysis using a conventional GUI

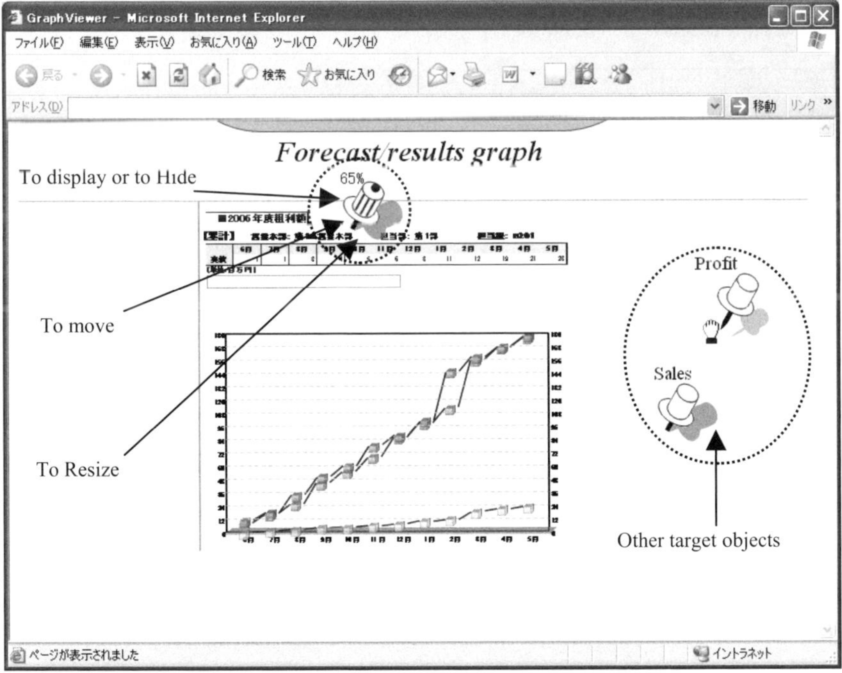

Figure 9 Observing graphs in business analysis using the proposed GUI

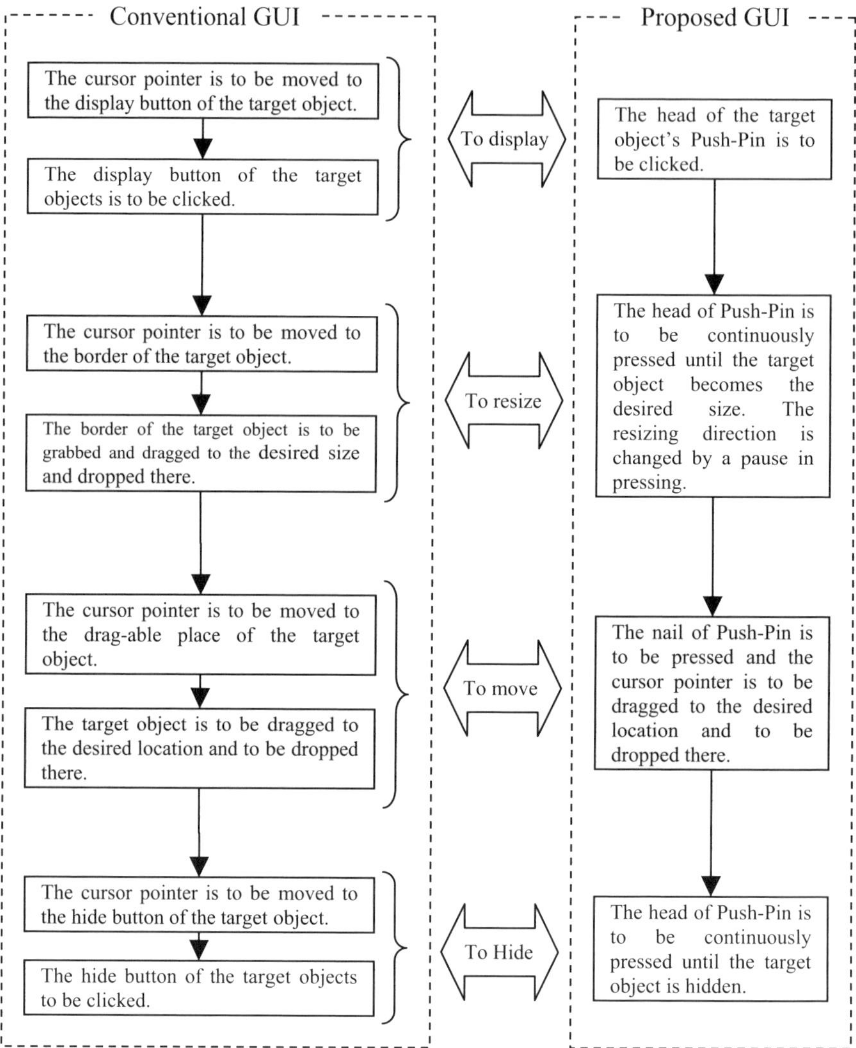

Note: The shaded boxes are actions that require cursor movement beyond an icon area.

Figure 10: Comparison of required actions between the conventional and proposed GUIs

6. Conclusion

A novel intuitive GUI method derived from an association with the use of the pin-up board for brain-storming was proposed and its implementation was fully described. Its effectiveness as compared with the conventional GUI was demonstrated.

In addition to the merits for users, the use of the proposed GUI will bring another merit to system designers. Because the system designer does not need to think about GUI designs, e.g., location, order, size, and etc. of display objects, he or she can fully concentrate on the main functions of the target application.

Although the push-pin icons were used only for application programs in the above explanations, the proposed push-pin icon can also be used to represent folders or short cut icons in Microsoft Windows OS or Apple's Mac OS. In such applications, use of different colors may be useful to distinguish the kind of application windows.

The proposed GUI may also be useful for cell phones, or PDAs, because the number of cursor pointer operations can be reduced.

Acknowledgment

The first hint of the proposed push-pin icon was born when the first author of this paper received a training course provided by HOWS corporation in Tokyo, where Mr. W. Shoji, vice president of the company and the lecturer of the course, emphasized the importance of thinking what users expect tangibly or intangibly for the application system in the process of system design. The authors want to express their appreciation to him for his insightful hints during the course. The authors also appreciate their team members, Ms. N. Taniguchi and Dr. S. Hayashida of Sangikyo Corporation for their useful comments and advices in the development of this work.

References

[1] Jeremy Reimer, "A History of the GUI", Ars File: Paedia from Ars Technica, LLC (http://arstechnica.com/articles/paedia/gui.ars), May 05, 2005 - 01:40AM CT
[2] Microsoft Corporation, "Windows Help and How-to", Microsoft Windows Homepage (http://www.microsoft.com/Windows/default.mspx), © 2007 Microsoft Corporation

Chapter 9

Service Oriented Systems

New Trends in Software Methodologies, Tools and Techniques
H. Fujita and D. Pisanelli (Eds.)
IOS Press, 2007

Determinants of Service Reusability

George Feuerlicht and Amalka Wijayaweera
Faculty of Information Technology,
University of Technology, Sydney,
PO Box 123 Broadway Sydney NSW 2007 Australia
jiri@it.uts.edu.au

Abstract. Software reuse is regarded is as a key software development objective leading to reduction of costs associated with software development and maintenance. However, there is mounting evidence that software reuse is difficult to achieve in practice, and that software development approaches such as component-based development, and more recently service-oriented computing have failed to achieve anticipated levels of reuse. In this paper we identify the determinants of service reusability and argue that the design of services plays an important role in achieving high levels of reuse. We examine the relationship between service granularity and reuse and note that extensive use of coarse grained, document-centric services by SOA practitioners makes achieving reuse particularly challenging.

Keywords. SOA, Web Services, service reuse, service granularity

1. Introduction

Software reuse is important as it reduces the costs associated with design, development, testing and maintenance of software [1]. Many experts believe that reuse is inherent to Service Oriented Architecture (SOA) and studies show that organizations regard reuse as the top driver for SOA adoption [2]. However, in practice, reuse is difficult to achieve and involves design-time effort to identify and design reusable services. Once services are externalized, it becomes very difficult to improve the level of service reuse by runtime intervention, or by modifying the service interfaces. It can be argued that the perception of improved reuse for SOA can be mainly attributed to the ability to derive business value from legacy applications by externalizing existing functionality as Web Services, and is not a direct consequence of SOA adoption [3]. Others have noted that the relatively low levels of service reuse can be attributed to poor design [4]. Reuse in the context of SOA is particularly challenging as the design of services frequently involves domain-wide considerations and relies on domain standardizations of message formats. Furthermore, the emphasis on coarse-grained, document-centric services by SOA practitioners reduces the potential for reuse (see discussion in section 3).

In this paper we first discuss the determinants of software reuse in the context of services identifying the mechanism of service reuse noting the close relationship between service reuse and composability. We then review research efforts to improve reusability of software components and discuss the applicability of such approaches to SOA (section 2). In section 3 we focus on service granularity and discuss the relationship between service granularity and reuse, exploring techniques for optimizing service granularity, and describing industry efforts to specify a standard component model for services (Service Component Architecture). The main contribution of this paper is a clear analysis of the determinants of software reuse leading to the identification of key software design principles and their adaptation to the design of reusable services. We conclude by noting that further research is needed to develop a comprehensive methodological framework for making design decisions about service granularity so that reuse can be maximized (section 4).

2. Software Reuse in the Context of Services

The promise of software reuse was the main driver for the introduction of the object-oriented approach to software construction [5].However, there is evidence that this promise has not been fully realized [4], [6], [7]. More recently, component-based development was seen as a solution to poor levels of software reuse, but the lack of standards for component interoperability prevented significant improvements in software reuse [8], [9], [10]. The service oriented paradigm is the latest approach that is widely regarded as having the potential to significantly improve software reuse and avoid duplication of application functionality [4], [11], [12].

Services share the basic characteristics of components such as modularization, abstraction and information hiding. Design strategies used in earlier software development approaches can be adapted to service design leading to improved service reusability. However, there are significant challenges to overcome as services are typically implemented at a higher level of abstraction than components [13], and reuse potential is limited by the extensive use of coarse-grained, document-centric services [14]. Granularity (i.e. the scope of functionality) of services is a key determinant of reuse, with increased granularity of services diminishing the potential for reuse. It has been argued that the design of service oriented applications should be governed by the same principles as the design of other types of distributed systems, and that maximizing service cohesion and minimizing service coupling by appropriate design of service interfaces can result in improving service reuse [15], [16].

Table 1. Supporting software reuse and evolution in various software development approaches

	Procedural Programming	Object-Oriented Programming	Distributed Components	Service Oriented Computing
Mechanism for Reuse	procedure containment aggregation	class inheritance containment aggregation	component aggregation	service aggregation (assembly and composition)
Mechanism for Evolution	code modification	code modification	component replacement and versioning	service versioning

For the purposes of this analysis it is important to understand the mechanism for service reuse and how it differs from supporting reuse in earlier approaches to software development (Table 1). Service reuse relies entirely on service aggregation, i.e. the ability of a service to participate in multiple service assemblies/compositions can be regarded as a measure of the reusability [3]. We explore the relationship between reuse and composability of services further in the next section.

2.1. Service Composability and Reuse

Services can be used to implement single (atomic) functions such as credit card verification. However, in most cases it is necessary to use the functionality of several services (i.e. service composition) to implement a business requirement. Service composition allows the construction of complex pieces or application functionality by means of recursively composing services [17]. For example a composite service could implement a hotel reservation, airline booking and a car rental to form a travel agency service. In order to allow composition, the individual services need to have characteristics which make them suitable for reuse in composing services [4]. Service compositions are implemented using languages such as the Business Process Execution Language for Web Services (BPEL) to form complete business processes [18]. BPEL implements the composition of the Web Services by specifying the Web Service interfaces (i.e. operations and the input and output messages) and using procedural programming constructs to implement business logic based on existing Web Services [19], [20].

In order to achieve high levels of service reuse and composability, detailed consideration needs to be given to service properties at design-time. More specifically, services should be self-contained and have clearly defined boundaries and endpoints. These requirements are related to the concepts of cohesion and coupling, and it has been argued that both factors determine the level of service composability [21].

2.2. Service coupling

Coupling refers to the degree of interdependence between services, and has been used in traditional software design (e.g. structured programming) as an indicator of software quality. Minimization of coupling leads to loosely coupled software components and is regarded as a key characteristic of high quality software [22], resulting in increased adaptability and reusability in distributed systems [23], and at the same time reducing duplication and redundancy. Coupling in the context of software design has been extensively explored and a number of different types of coupling identified as of relevance to service design [15]. We discuss the various types of coupling in the context of service design in the following sections.

2.2.1. Data coupling

Data coupling refers to the exchange of data parameters between software modules, e.g. passing a data parameter to a service operation. Data coupling can be minimized by only exchanging data which is necessary for the service operation to perform its task [24]. Therefore analysis needs to be carried out to ensure that parameters exchange data that is necessary to implement the service operation. As the service interface constitutes a contract, careful attention needs to be paid to the minimization of data coupling at design time, avoiding unnecessary externalization of interface parameters [23], [22]. It was shown that data normalization techniques are applicable to the design of service interfaces and that normalized service interfaces lead to minimization of data coupling [14].

2.2.2. Stamp coupling

Stamp coupling refers to a situation where data is exchanged between services in the form of composite parameters as is the case in document-centric services that use complex XML message payloads. Since the data is passed as a part of a composite message structure, the service operations are typically *hidden* (implicit) within the data structure, making reuse difficult to achieve. Furthermore, services tend to use only a part of the composite data structure to perform a given business function (e.g. flight booking), resulting in unnecessary coupling via externalized (optional) data structures [22]. Care should be taken to avoid data structures that use optional data elements (i.e. elements not consistently used by the service), as changes to the data structure will affect all services that use the data structure [24]. In general, stamp coupling is an undesirable type of coupling and should be avoided. It may be acceptable in some cases where grouping of data elements significantly reduces interface complexity and the externalized data structure is not likely to change.

2.2.3. Control coupling

Control coupling refers to a situation where a service parameter controls the execution logic of the service. This results in a lack of design clarity (as control logic is split across several services), difficult maintenance, and reduction in service cohesion. Control logic should be implemented directly within the service (or using BPEL for service compositions), not via control parameters as this increases coupling between services and can lead to unpredictable side effects. Control coupling is regarded as highly undesirable with significant negative impact on service reusability [22].

In summary, to maximize reuse service design should aim to minimize data coupling, avoid stamp coupling whenever possible, and avoid control coupling altogether. Reducing coupling increases reusability by creating simpler service interfaces with fewer data parameters. Minimization of data coupling can be achieved by analysis of functional dependencies between interface parameters resulting in well-defined service interfaces and reduction of undesirable side effects [25].

2.3. Service cohesion

Cohesion refers to the strength of the relationship between elements within a software module [26]. Maximizing service cohesion results in low coupling and minimization of the impact of changes on related services improving the stability of the service-oriented applications [15] and increasing the potential for reuse [3]. We discuss the relevance of different types of cohesion to service design in the following sections.

2.3.1. Functional cohesion.

Functional cohesion refers to a situation where all the service operations are highly interrelated and contribute to the execution of a single clearly defined task [15]. The relationship between functional cohesion and software reusability has been noted in the literature [26], [27], [28]. The following heuristics have been proposed to assist software designers in achieving high levels of functional cohesion [26]:

- The function of the service can be described in one simple sentence (if the function must be described as a compound sentence using conjunctions like "and", the service is probably not functionally bound).
- The description of the function should not contain time related words, such as "then", "after", "when". (Presence of time related words indicate the service has sequential or temporal cohesion but not functional cohesion).
- The description of the function should not contain words such as "initialize" and "clean up" which would indicate temporal binding

2.3.2. Informational cohesion

Informational cohesion refers to a situation where all service operations use the same data and is closely related to functional cohesion. In general, the relationships between the service operations are not as strong as in functional, thus making informational cohesion less desirable type of cohesion form the viewpoint of reusability [3].

Other types of cohesions have been defined in the literature, including procedural, temporal, and coincidental cohesion. Procedural cohesion refers to a situation where a number of unrelated operations are grouped together into a service, often in an attempt to reduce coupling. This type of cohesion has a negative impact on service reuse and should be avoided. Similarly, temporal cohesion that groups the execution of otherwise unrelated operations in a time sequence has negative impact on service reuse. Finally, coincidental cohesion refers to the situation where service operations defined for a given service are largely unrelated and should also be avoided [22].

3. Service Granularity Considerations

The importance of coupling and cohesion lies largely in that these service characteristics determine service granularity, i.e. the scope of the functionality implemented by a given service [29], and granularity in terms impacts on service ruse. The design choice is between fine grained services that typically implement a single atomic operation and exchange limited amounts of data, and coarse grained services that implement high-level business functions. It follows that fine grained services are highly reusable as they encapsulate simple functions that are readily reused [15]. However service designers must also consider the impact of using services over the Internet and deal with the design constraints that this environment imposes. Such considerations include network latency and reliability and lead to a preference for coarse grained services that minimize the number of interactions needed to implement a given business function, reducing the complexity of the message interchange dialogue [16]. However, this leads to complex message structures, often including not only data, but also instructions for processing the message, in effect introducing control coupling into the message interchange dialogue. Coarse grained, message-oriented design of services is used extensively in industry-wide, e-business applications, for example, in the Open Travel Alliance (OTA) specification. The use of complex data structures as messages payloads results in stamp coupling, increasing the interdependencies between services and violating a fundamental principle of design of distributed applications. The use of fine grained services, on the other hand, results in complex interaction dialogues and potential issues related to failure recovery [18], [21]. Studies have confirmed that fine grained services produce loosely coupled service-oriented applications with good maintenance properties [18]. It is evident that a methodological framework is needed to support making decisions about the optimal level of service granularity for a given implementation scenario [16].

3.1. Optimizing Service Granularity

In the absence of a comprehensive design methodology decisions about the level of service granularity are typically made using various heuristics. For example, Schmelzer [29] suggests that granularity can be determined by studying the extent to which a service can be reused and proposes a design process for services which combines top down and bottom up approaches. The top down design involves decomposing business processes until the lowest level of processes is identified, producing candidate services. Schmelzer [29] points out that the candidate services identified using this (top down) approach may not be reusable and recommends using bottom up approach to identify reusable business logic in existing code and exposing this business logic as reusable fine grained services. Keen et. al. [30] suggest that a façade design pattern can be used to construct coarse grained services from fine grained services in order to minimize the number of message interchanges. According to Larman [31] this design pattern has been widely used in distributed systems to reduce network traffic. Other alternatives include using BPEL compositions to externalize aggregate services built from low granularity service operations. Another emerging idea involves the use of service components to aggregate fine grained services into a higher-level, coarse grained service, preserving the benefit of reuse inherent in low granularity services and at the same time taking advantage of coarse granularity, aggregated services to simplify the interaction dialogue.

3.2. Service Components

A composite Web Service implemented using a composition language such as BPEL has limited reuse. Yang [19] suggests that adopting concepts from component-based development can facilitate reuse. A composite Web Service can be used to implement complete business processes that consist of activities, flow control, data flows and process definitions. Processes are composed of activities and implement a complete business process such as travel booking. Data flows represent the data that flows between these activities, and control flows specify the order of execution of the activities. Each service component represents a module with high level business functionality (i.e. similar to components in component-based development), and has an interface consisting of service operations and input and output messages. Service components are specified as a class and generated from a WSDL specification or BPEL process specification. The service component class can then be reused, extended or specialized using object-oriented techniques, i.e. by extending or overriding class definitions. Additional service components can be constructed as a combination of existing components to form new applications.

The Service Component Architecture (SCA) is an industry effort by BEA, IBM and Oracle to provide an open, technology neutral model for implementing service components [32]. The SCA aims to provide a model for the assembly of service components from a collection of services. An important aspect of the SCA approach is that it supports the building of coarse grained service components as assemblies of fine grained services, and provides a mechanism for implementing business logic at a higher level of abstraction. SCA components provide and consume services through service interfaces also known as service references. The SCA components can be assembled into business applications by connecting the components via service references. The SCA approach reduces the need to invoke low level APIs to directly access (service) methods combining the advantages of fine grained services (i.e. reuse) with the advantages of coarse granularity services.

4. Conclusions

With the transition to SOA it is essential that the challenge of service reuse is effectively addressed. As noted in the introduction, existing approaches to software development had only limited success in achieving high levels of reusability. While SOA has the potential to greatly increase software reuse, there are indications that this potential is not being fully exploited, and that little research is being carried out in this area [33], [34].

We have argued in this paper that service reusability and composability is determined to a large extent by service granularity. Service reuse, granularity, cohesion and coupling are closely interrelated and need to be considered in the context of a methodological framework to balance out the tradeoffs between performance and reusability for a given application scenario. Earlier approaches to software development, including structured programming, object-oriented approach, and component-based development all use minimization of coupling and maximization of cohesion to optimize reusability. These principles are clearly relevant to SOA, however the situation is complicated by the extensive use of coarse granularity, document-centric services that do not conform to traditional software design principles. Service reusability requires further investigation so that comprehensive service design methodologies based on software engineering principles can be applied in practice.

5. References

[1]　Erl. T. 2005, Service-oriented architecture : concepts, technology, and design. Prentice Hall , London.

[2]　Hurwitz. J. Bloor. R. and Baroudi. C. 2005, Thinking from Reuse-SOA for Renewable Business, viewed 20th May 2007: http://www.hurwitz.com/PDFs/IBMThinkingfromReuse.pdf

[3]　Feuerlicht, G. and Lozina, J. 2007, 'Understanding Service Reusability', accepted for publication in the Proceedings of the 15th International Conference Systems Integration, Prague, Czech Republic

[4]　Sillitti, A., Vernazza, T. & Succi, G. 2002, 'Service Oriented Programming: A New Paradigm of Software Reuse' in Gacek, C.(ed.), Proceedings of the 7th International Conference on Software Reuse: Methods, Techniques, and Tools, Austin , pp. 268-280.

[5]　Capretz, L.F. 2003, 'A brief history of the object-oriented approach', ACM SIGSOFT Software Engineering Notes, vol. 28, issue 2, pp. 1 – 10.

[6]　Blake, B.A. & Jalics, P. 1996, 'An Assessment of Object-oriented Methods and C++', Journal of Object-Oriented Programming, vol.9, no. 1, pp. 42-48.

[7]　Harrison, R., Samaraweera, L.G., Fobie, M.R. & Lewis, P.H. 1996,'Comparing programming paradigms: an evaluation of functional and object oriented programs', Software Engineering Journal, vol. 11, issue 4, pp. 247-254.

[8]　Fingar, P. 2000, 'Component based frameworks for E-commerce', Communication of the ACM, pp. 61-85.

[9]　Vitharana, P. 2003,'Risks and challenges of component based software development, Communications of the ACM, vol. 46, no. 8, pp. 67-72.

[10] Pour, G. 1998,'Moving toward component-based software development approach', Proceedings of the conference on Technology of Object-Oriented Languages, pp.296 – 300

[11] Natis, Y. 2003, 'Service-Oriented Architecture Scenario', Gartner, Stamford, viewed 5 May 2007, <http://www.gartner.com/DisplayDocument?id=391595>.

[12] Herr,M., Bath,U. & Koschel,A. 2004, 'Implementation of a Service Oriented Architecture at Deutsche Post MAIL', Lecture Notes in Computer Science, vol. 3250 , pp. 227 - 238 .

[13] Zimmerman. O. Krogdahl.P. Gee. C. 2004. Elements of Service Oriented Analysis and Design. Viewed 10th May, http://www.ibm.com/developerworks/library/ws-soad1/

[14] Feuerlicht, G. 2005, Design of Service Interfaces for e-Business Applications using Data Normalization Techniques, Journal of Information Systems and e-Business Management, Springer-Verlag GmbH, pages 1-14, ISS:1617-98

[15] Papazoglou M.P. and Yang. J. 2002, Design Methodology for Web Services and Business Processes. In Proceedings of the 3rd VLDB-TES Workshop, pp. 54-64, Hong Kong, Springer.

[16] Feuerlicht, G. 2006, 'Service granularity considerations based on data properties of interface parameters ', International Journal of Computer Systems science & Engineering, Vol. 21, no. 4, pp 315-327.

[17] Dustdar,S. & Schreiner, W. 2005, ' A survey on web services composition', International Journal of Web and Grid Services, vol. 1, no.1 pp. 1 – 30

[18] Perepletchikov, M., Ryan, C. & Frampton, K. 2005, 'Comparing the Impact of Service-Oriented and Object-Oriented Paradigms on the Structural Properties of Software', in R.Meersman (ed.), On the Move to Meaningful Internet Systems 2005: OTM Workshops, Springer-Verlag, Berlin, pp. 431-441.

[19] Yang, J. 2003, 'Service-oriented computing: Web service componentization ', Communications of the ACM, vol. 46, issue 10, pp. 35-40.

[20] Milanovic, N., Stantchev,V. , Richling,J. & Malek, M. 2003, Towards Adaptive and Composable Services, Proceedings of IPSI2003, Montenegro, viewed 21st march 2007, <http://www2.informatik.hu-berlin.de/~milanovi/services.pdf>.

[21] Papazoglou, M.P. & Heuvel, W.V.D. 2006, 'Service-oriented design and development methodology', International Journal of Web Engineering and Technology , vol. 2, no. 4, pp. 412 – 442.

[22] Vinoski, S. 2005, 'Old measures for new services', IEEE Internet Computing, vol. 9, issue 6, pp. 72 – 74

[23] Kaye, D. 2003, Loosely Coupled: The Missing Pieces of Web Services, RDS Press, California.

[24] Page-Jones, M. 1988, The Practical Guide to Structured Systems Design, 2nd edn., Prentice Hall, New Jersey.

[25] Feuerlicht , G. & Meesathit, S. 2004, 'Service requirements and design methodology: Design framework for interoperable service interfaces', Proceedings of the 2nd international conference on Service oriented computing, New York, pp. 299- 307.

[26] Stevens, W., Myers, G,. & Constantine, L. 1999, 'Structured Design' , IBM Systems Journal, vol. 38, no. 2-3, pp. 231-256.

[27] Booch, G. 1993, Object-Oriented Analysis and Design with Applications, Benjamin Cummings Publishing Company, California.

[28] Rumbaugh , J., Blaha, M., Premerlani, W., Eddy, F.,& Lorensen, W. 1991, Object-oriented modeling and design, Prentice Hall, New Jersey.

[29] Schmelzer, R. 2006, 'Solving the service granularity challenge', The SOA Magazine, viewed 21st April 2007, http://searchwebservices.techtarget.com/tip/1,289483,sid26_gci1172330,00.html

[30] Keen, M., Bishop, S., Hopkins, A., Milinski, S., Nott, C., Robinson, R., Adams, J., Verschueren, P., Acharya. A. 2004, Patterns: Implementing an SOA using an ESB, IBM Redbook

[31] Larman, C. 2004, Applying UML and Patterns: An Introduction to Object-Oriented Analysis and Design and Iterative Development, Third Edition. Prentice Hall PTR;

[32] BEA, IBM, and Oracle, 2005, Service Component Architecture: Building Systems using Service Oriented Architecture, A Joint Whitepaper by BEA, IBM, and Oracle, Available online: http://xml.coverpages.org/ni2005-12-07-a.html

[33] Carminati, B., Ferrari E. & Hung, P.C.K. 2005, "Exploring privacy issues in Web services discovery/agencies," IEEE Security & Privacy Magazine, vol. 3, issue 5, pp. 14-21.

[34] Kearney, P., Chapman, J., Edwards, N., Gifford, M. & He, L. 2004, 'An Overview of Web Services Security,' BT Technology Journal, vol. 22, no. 1, pp. 27 - 42

New Trends in Software Methodologies, Tools and Techniques
H. Fujita and D. Pisanelli (Eds.)
IOS Press, 2007

Development of a Maintenance Environment that Enabling Users to Revise Existing Web Applications

Hidaka YANO [a], Sota HONDA [a], Jun SASAKI [a], Michiru TANAKA [a], Keizo YAMADA [a] and Yutaka FUNYU [a]

[a] Iwate Prefectural University, JAPAN

Abstract. Recently, the number of Business to Consumer (B2C) web applications has increased yearly. In particular, the increase in participation in the B2C market by small companies has been noticeable. This paper focuses on the use of B2C web applications by small companies. These businesses, typically, have little money to maintain web applications and also lack the skills to do so. In this paper, we present a self-maintenance model for the implementation of web applications in small business environments. We have surveyed current technologies in this area and have developed an actual maintenance environment for a B2C web application. This paper describes three experimental results for the environment. Finally, issues for future work and a new architecture are proposed to realize an ideal maintenance environment.

Keywords: Software maintenance, End user development, Adjustable software, Web application

1. Introduction

Recently, the number of Business to Consumer (B2C) web applications has increased yearly. The web application has become an accessible business tool not only for big companies, but also for mid-sized and smaller companies. We focus on the small companies' B2C web applications and their users, because we expect the market of small companies to grow rapidly in the near future.

The term "user" has many meanings in B2C web applications; a "user" may be, for example, a consumer, owner or even a shop assistant. It is therefore, necessary to define the term "user" clearly in this paper:

Definition: "User" in this paper indicates a person who provides information services in a small B2C company by using a web application.

In this paper, we assume that the user can understand and use HTML. Web applications enable users to provide their customers with new facilities on their web sites: searching for items, shopping carts, electronic settlement, etc. However the web applications are more complex than conventional web sites. As the "presentation", i.e. the view of a web application, has many relationships to business logic, users can no longer revise these themselves. The presentation is a fundamental component of B2C web application marketing [1][2]. Typically, users have only a small budget to maintain their web applications and lack the skills to change the logic. Consequently, we have developed a web application maintenance environment to enable users to revise and improve their own web sites. In this paper, we propose the self-maintenance model of maintaining the "presentation", that is, web design, appearance and user interface of web applications, without affecting the logic.

This paper is structured as follows. In Section 2, we explain our approach to enable the user to revise the web application's presentation. We touch on the motivations for, and difficulties of, web application maintenance. In Section 3, we consider related work. In Section 4, we describe the development of the web application maintenance environment, which features easy operation using a web browser. In Section 5, we report on some experimental results obtained from using the environment to maintain a real B2C web application.

2. Self-Maintenance Model: Motivation and Approach

2.1 Self-Maintenance Model

We define the term "self-maintenance model" as follows.

> **Definition:** A "self-maintenance model" is a model of software maintenance for the "user", as defined previously, to revise the "presentation" of a web application without affecting its logic.

Here, the meaning of "self-maintenance" is different to that in autonomic computing.

The motivation for our research on the self-maintenance model originates from our experience in the development of a B2C web application [3]. After completing the system development, we spent many man-hours revising the system, due to the numerous and frequent requests of the users. As a result, we investigated a fundamental solution to solve the problem and generated the concept of the self-maintenance model as shown in Figure1.

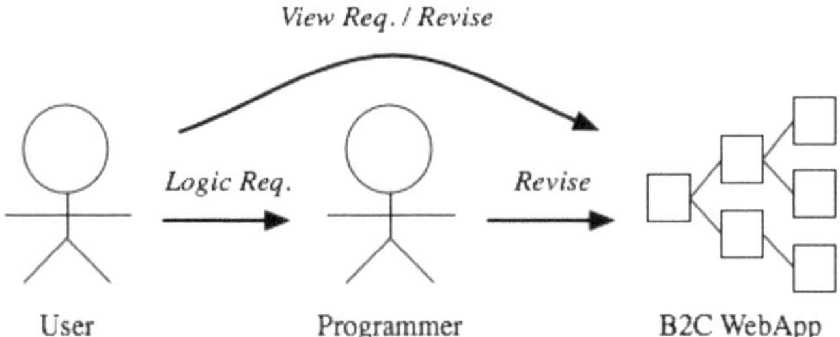

Figure 1.   Self-maintenance model

The basic idea of the self-maintenance model originates from the idea of self-support, that is, doing it oneself. In the model, the user has an obligation to maintain the presentation layer, and can revise it whenever he chooses. This is a reasonable approach with the aim of minimizing maintenance costs.

A self-maintenance model has a difficult issue to resolve. Normal web applications complicate matters by mixing the presentation layer with business logic. General users are not skilled to maintain these advanced web applications. We therefore, decided to develop a new environment that enables a user to revise only the presentation part of a web application.

2.2 Software Structure for User Maintenance

In a normal web application, if a user could revise the presentation part of the application, there would be a gap between the specification and the actual system. This would result in the risk of the system crashing. We, therefore, propose the idea of a software structure for user maintenance, called the "Dress structure" (Figure 2).

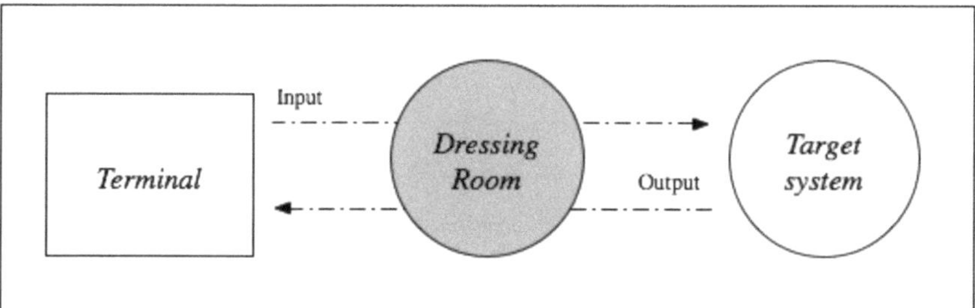

Figure 2.　Dress structure

The structure has a segment which can be revised by a user. This segment is an independent element from the basic specification. We call the revised segment a "Dress", and the Dress storage the "Dressing room". If a user revises the presentation of a web application, the output information is stored in the Dressing room as a new Dress. Then, this Dress is applied automatically to the same kind of output in the Dressing room. Furthermore, a user can prepare and select many kinds of Dresses to apply to the presentation of the target web application system.

2.3 Our approach

Our road map for this study, which aims to realize true user maintenance, is as follows.

a) We implement the environment based on the self-maintenance model and evaluate the effect thereof. This step is important to get positive feedback of user maintenance.
b) We redesign and expand the environment based on dress structure. In this step, we evaluate the effect of *maintainability,* which is essential in realizing user maintenance.
c) We expand the range of applicable users and the software field.

By using the road map given above, we aim to realize user maintenance. This study is the first step and we discuss the development of the maintenance environment in this paper.

3. Present Approaches and Technologies for Maintaining Web Applications

There are many conventional studies that deal with maintaining web applications, such as [13][14][15][16]. However, studies focusing on the user are rare. In this section, we introduce previous work that makes it possible for the user to revise the view (presentation) of web applications.

3.1 Model-View-Controller (MVC) Model and Template Technology

The *MVC Model* is a *Design-pattern* model that has its roots in the *Smalltalk* community at *Xerox*. This model separates the presentation from the business logic (Figure 3) [4][5].

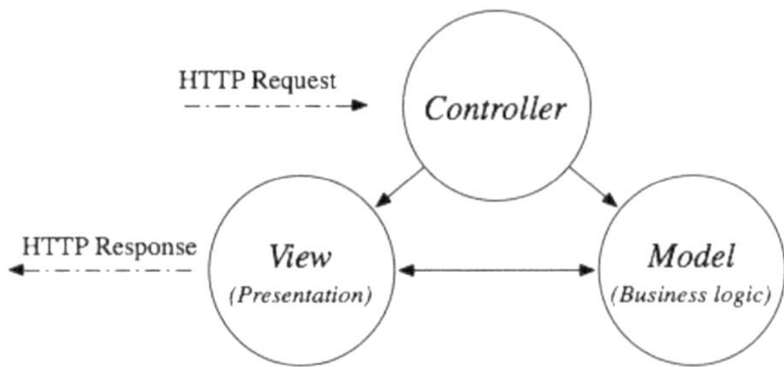

Figure 3.   Model-View-Controller model

Because of the separation between the different aspects of the application, a programmer and a designer can work simultaneously without interfering with each other. Nowadays, various frameworks based on this model are used by vendors and personal programmers. It provides the backbone for most web application development projects. *Struts* is, perhaps, the most well-known of these frameworks [6].

This model brings order and elegance to web application projects, where previously there was chaos. Speaking with our purpose in mind, the user is not the designer. The user has no sense of color, no theory of layout, and moreover, lacks the skills to maintain the web application. Specifically, the user cannot understand the architecture of the web application. He may ask, "Where is the presentation file we are looking at now?".

Template Technology is commonly used for view control in implementations of the MVC model [7]. It creates a view as plain html, which is a useful technology for a web designer. *JSP, WebMacro, XMLC* and *Smarty* are well-known template technologies. Additionally, *StringTemplate* is the most maintainable approach.

This technology increases the possibility of the user maintaining a web application, however, there still remains the need for a clear understanding of the architecture of the program.

3.2 Authoring Tools

There are currently many useful *Authoring Tools* for designers, but none for users. These generally belong to the suite of visual programming tools that generate source code from "look and feel" operations (Figure 4).

Figure 4.   Screen shot of Dreamweaver

In the commercial world, *Dreamweaver* is the biggest name, whereas in the academic world, *Web Flexible Editing (WFE)* stands out in Japan [8][9].

These tools are useful not only for designers, but also for users to revise presentations. However, the tools do not consider web applications that include business logic. Combining *Template Technology* and *Authoring Tools* may solve the problem for the designer. However, this combination is not enough for users, because they are not specialists in web structure. This environment should, however, lessen the gap between the maintenance skills of designers and those of users.

4. Development of a Maintenance Environment for Users

4.1. Design Concept and Development Conditions

We have developed a prototype of the web application maintenance environment to realize the self-maintenance model in an actual field. The reason why the target is web applications, is that many users are using these in the B2C world. In order to construct the user self-maintenance environment on an existing target web application, the environment should not depend on the internal state. We have thus developed a new system, called "phpClip", which is a web application that enables us to construct the internal state independently of the environment by setting a limiting condition. The condition is as follows. Table 1 gives the environment for "phpClip" development.

Condition; Target web application is build using PHP and the template engine "Smarty", which is a well-known tool in PHP programming.

Table 1.   Environment for "phpClip" development

OS	MacOS 10.4
Program language	PHP4
Database	None
Web server	Apache

4.2. Installation of "phpClip"

The method for installing "phpClip" is as follows.

a) The programmer uploads "phpClip" to the target web application. Generally, *FTP Client Software* is used for this phase.
b) The programmer installs and sets up "phpClip" with a web browser. This set up phase constructs the internal state of the target web application. Parameters in the construction include the web server URL and path information for "phpClip".
c) After "phpClip" has been installed, the user can revise the View of the target web application by making use of user access and uses "phpClip" with the web browser.

If an existing web application satisfies the limiting condition that was mentioned in Section 4.2, "phpClip" can be installed to any web applications. We call this "portability", because users can revise the View of the target web application from anywhere.

4.3. Features of phpClip

PhpClip can easily be operated from within a web browser, which enables the user to find and revise the presentation file. Figure 5 illustrates this feature and the use of the environment.

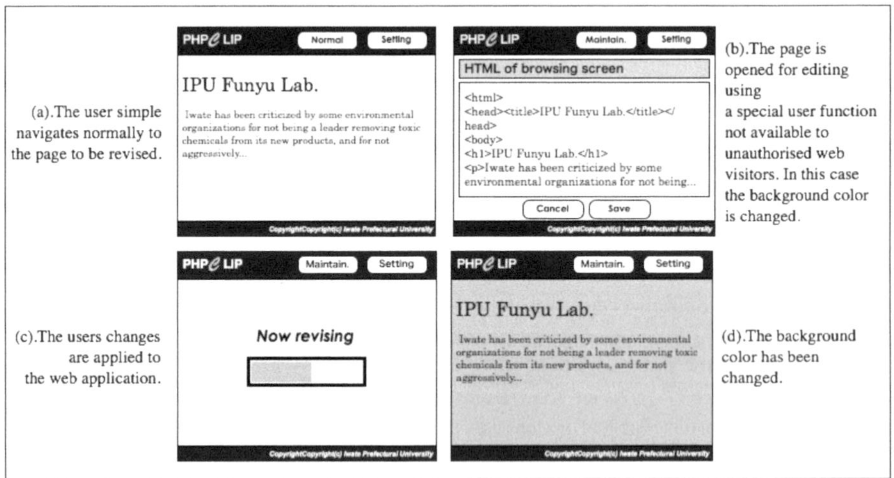

Figure 5. Procedural steps in the maintenance environment

(a) The user finds the target page to revise by standard use of a web browser that does not need knowledge of the web structure. (b) The user revises the HTML as in a *Wiki*. In the process an *Authoring Tool* may be used to assist the user who has little skill and experience with editing HTML. (c) Upon completion by the user, phpClip saves the revision to the existing web application. (d) PhpClip displays the altered page.

Let us look at the relationship between phpClip and the target web application in the revision process (Figure 6).

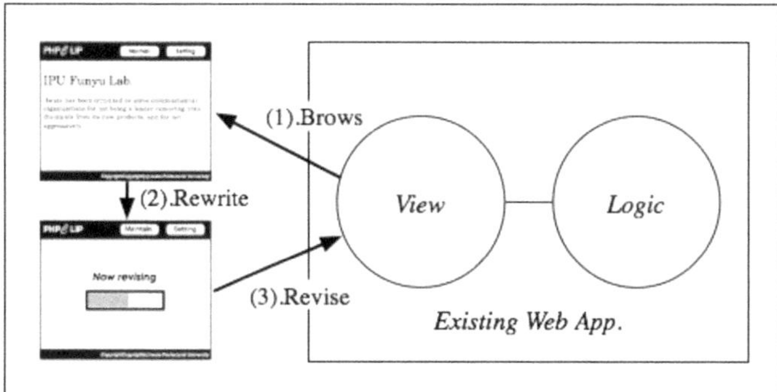

Figure 6. Relationship between the environment and the target web application

(1) After phpClip sends an HTTP request to the target web application, a presentation of the target is returned to phpClip. The target web application then processes a great deal of business logic. PhpClip does not, however, depend on the internal state, since it only considers the presentation ("View"). (2) and (3) The user revises the presentation flow by altering the HTML code, and thus does not depend on the target web application. We are of the opinion that general users have a basic HTML knowledge. If they do not, they can still do the revision using a commercialized HTML authoring tool.

5. Experiments

The experiments performed were evaluated using the following three criteria: ease with which a user can revise the system, portability and the performance record of operations on a real B2C web application. This record revealed a new concept for user self-maintenance.

5.1. Experiment 1: Ease of User Revision

5.1.1. Purpose

This paper has repeatedly made mention of the gap between designers' and users' maintenance skill levels. Experiment 1 aims to demonstrate the feasibility of user revision of web applications using the environment.

5.1.2. Method

We assembled twelve persons as test subjects. Nine of these had experience writing HTML, while three did not. Although our target user should have experience writing HTML, we used some inexperienced users in this experiment. The subjects were asked to make a simple update to a web application using one of two methods. The first method is an established one, FTP access, which requires seeking the relevant HTML file and rewriting it using a text editor. The other is our proposed method. We compared the established method to the proposed method with respect to the time required to make the revision.

5.1.3. Results

The results in Figure 7 clearly show the advantage of using the maintenance environment.

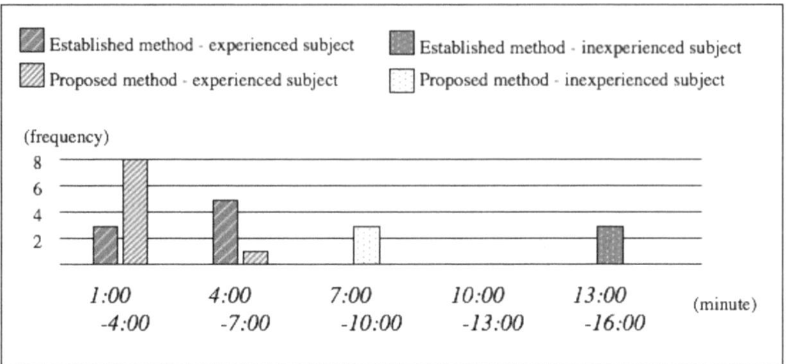

Figure 7.   Results comparing the established and proposed methods

Specifically, the results for inexperienced subjects demonstrate the speed advantage provided by the environment. Results for experienced subjects show a similar tendency. In our opinion, the experienced subjects' maintenance skills are higher than those of inexperienced subjects. That is, the lower the user's skill level, the more beneficial is the environment. On the whole, the results confirm that the proposed model is much easier to use than the established method; thus, the proposed model is a success in this respect.

5.2. Experiment 2: Portability

5.2.1. Purpose

Portability is important for web application environments that are constructed on existing web applications. This experiment aims to show the ease of adopting the maintenance environment.

5.2.2. Method

We assembled three programmers and five web applications for testing. The subjects were asked to add the maintenance environment to the web applications with the help of the installation manual. We measured the time taken to install the environment.

5.2.3. Results

Overall, the time required to implement the system was short (Figure 8).

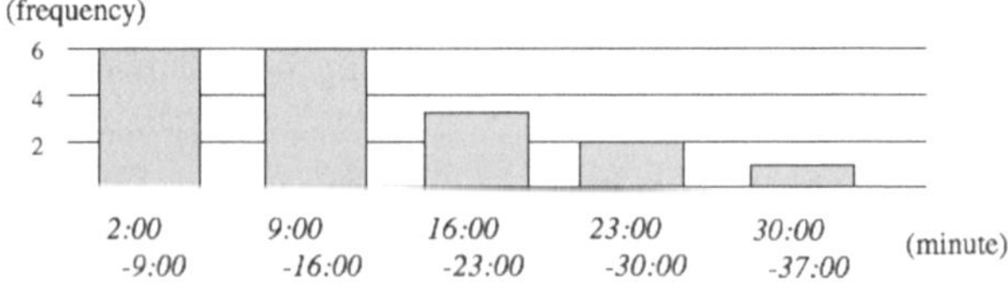

Figure 8.   Results showing ease of adopting the maintenance environment

The results confirm that the maintenance environment is highly portable. This comment from one of the programmers illustrates the result clearly.

"At first, I was flustered. However, adding my experience solved the problem."

As with any system, experience is an important factor in the use or installation thereof. This experiment confirms that the environment has the necessary foundation for it.

5.3. Experiment 3: Record of Operation on an actual B2C Web Application

5.3.1. Purpose

Theoretical study is indispensable for academic pursuits. However, empirical study is also of great benefit, in this case, in testing if the environment is of practical use in the operation of real B2C web applications.

5.3.2. Method

A web shop owner entered into an experimental collaboration with us. The owner maintained his web application using the environment. We asked the owner to record maintenance details including: date, lines of code, etc..

5.3.3. Results

These results confirm that our study has a practical use (Table 2).

Table 2.   The results of a real operation

Consultation period	11/2004-1/2005 (three months)
Revisions	6
Revision: lines of code	105
The Owner's impression	*Following*
I used to feel like revising web shop But the environment motivates me!	
Freeness of maintenance is very good.	

The owner told us he wants to use the environment for many years to come. However, unexpectedly, during continued operation, the owner informed us of a new maintenance problem.

6. Conclusion

We introduced our study by stating that the number of Business to Consumer (B2C) web applications have been increasing from year to year. The users or owners of these applications have limited resources and skills to maintain their web applications. This led us to propose the user self-maintenance model. We first surveyed current technologies available for web application maintenance, and then developed an actual maintenance environment for a B2C web application. This paper describes three experimental results using this environment.

As our study is still in the first step of the self-maintenance model research, we have developed a prototype environment and evaluated it. Applicable users for the maintenance environment are still restricted (users need to have HTML skills). We are aiming to expand the range of applicable users as we would like to realize a true user maintenance environment. Our research approach adopts a bottom-up approach, because we construct a user development and maintenance environment from a possible part.

On the other hand, there is a top-down approach where fundamentally new software should be developed to realize a true user development and maintenance environment. For example, Lyee may be considered a top-down approach, because it is aimed at user oriented software by reconstructing the software structure fundamentally [11][12]. As a top-down approach requires a long time to become established, we are going to continue with our bottom-up approach. We would like to accumulate more experimental results for the user oriented software development and maintenance.

References

[1] N.Dholakia, A.Pandya, "Conceptualizing B2C Businesses as Services", Journal of Electronic Commerce in Organizations, Volume 3, no.1, pp1-12, 2002.

[2] H.Kiely, AMR Research Staff, "Sell-Side Content Management-Your Web Production System", 2000.

[3] J.Sasaki, T.Yoneda, Y.Funyu, "A Reliable and Useful Information Distribution System: the "Kuchicomi Network"", Proc. Of the 15th European-Japanese Conference, Information Modeling and Knowledge Bases XVII, pp.180-190, 2006

[4] G.Krasner, S.Pope, "A description of the model-view-controller user interface paradigm in the smalltalk-80 system", Journal of Object Oriented Programming, issue3, Volume 1, 1988.

[5] E.Gamma et al., "Design Patterns: Abstraction and Reuse of Object-Oriented Design", In Proceedings, ECOOP '93, pp 406-421, 1993.

[6] http://struts.apache.org/

[7] T.Parr, "Enforcing strict model-view separation in template engines", Proceedings of the 13th conference on World Wide Web, 2004.

[8] http://www.adobe.com/jp/products/dreamweaver/

[9] K.Nishi T.Shintani, T.Matsuo, N.Tashiro, T.Ito, "Implementing an Online Writable Web Page System and Its Applications", IEEJ Trans. EIS, Vol.125, pp 660-665, 2005.

[10] S.Gorlatch, T.Kameda, I.H.Fujita, M.Tanaka, Y.Funyu, O.Arai, "Towards Developing Adjustable Software: A Case Study with the Lyee Approach", New Trends in Software Methodologies, Tools and Techniques 2006, pp 423-438, 2006.

[11] F.Negoro, "Lyee's Hypothetical World", New Trends in Software Methodologies, Tools and Techniques 2002, pp 3-22, 2002.

[12] H.Suzuki, T.Yamane, T.Yoneda, J.Sasaki, Y.Funyu, "A Framework for User Accessible Boundary Software", New Trends in Software Methodologies, Tools and Techniques 2003, pp 157-166, 2003.

[13] P.Atzeni, G.Mecca, P.Merialdo, "Design and Maintenance of Data-Intensive Web Sites", Proceedings of the 6th International Conference on Extending Database Technology: Advances in Database Technology, pp 436-450, 1998.

[14] S.Ceri, P.Fraternali, S.Paraboschi, "Design Principles for Data-Intensive Web Sites", ACM SIGMOD Record, Volume28, pp 84-89, 1999.

[15] M.Fernandez, D.Florescu, J.Kang, A.Levy, D.Suciu, "Catching the Boat with Strudel: Experiences with a Web-Site Management System", ACM SIGMOD Record, pp 414-425, 1998.

[16] P.Fraternali, "Tools and Approaches for Developing Data-Intensive Web Applications: A Survey", ACM Computing Surveys, Volume 31, pp 227-263, 1999.

ROME: a Reference Ontology in Medicine

Domenico M. PISANELLI[a], Massimo BATTAGLIA[b], Claudio DE LAZZARI[c]
[a] *National Research Council, Inst. of Cognitive Science and Technology, Rome, Italy*
[b] *National Research Council, Inst. of Neurobiology and Molecular Med., Rome, Italy*
[c] *National Research Council, Inst. of Clinical Physiology,Section of Rome, Italy*

Abstract. Many people today acknowledge that ontologies may help building better and more interoperable information systems, also in medicine. On the other hand, many others are skeptical about the real impact that ontologies - apart from the academic world - may have on the design and maintenance of working information systems. In order to ensure semantic consistency to the heterogeneous information systems that may be applied to the health-care domain, we defined a Reference Ontology in MEdicine (ROME). It consists of about 200 general entities and it is designed to act as a bridge between more specific systems.

Keywords. Ontology, Medicine, Semantic Interoperability

1. Introduction

Medicine is a very complex domain from the point of view of modeling and representing intended meaning. In such a discipline we find different activity domains (e.g. clinical vs. administrative knowledge), different scientific granularities (e.g. molecular vs. organic detail), different user requirements for the same service (e.g. physician-oriented vs. patient-oriented views), ambiguous terminology (polysemy).

Many people today acknowledge that ontologies may help building better and more interoperable information systems, also in medicine. On the other hand, many others are skeptical about the real impact that ontologies - apart from the academic world - may have on the design and maintenance of working information systems.

If "no man is an island", "no system is an island" anymore: data and knowledge integration (may we say "globalization"?) are no longer an optional, but a clear necessity. In fact, the overwhelming amount of information stored in various data repositories - including those available over the web - emphasizes the relevance of knowledge integration methodologies and techniques to facilitate data sharing. The need for such integration has been already perceived for several years, but telecommunications and networking are quickly and dramatically changing the scenario.

However, the ever-increasing demand of data sharing has to rely on a solid conceptual foundation in order to give a precise semantics to the terabytes available in different databases and eventually traveling over the networks. The actual demand is not for a unique conceptualization, but for an unambiguous communication of complex and detailed concepts (possibly expressed in different languages), leaving each user free to make explicit his/her conceptualization.

2. Which ontologies for medicine?

Ontologies are the talk of the day in the medical informatics community. Their relevant role in the design and implementation of information systems in health care is now widely acknowledged. Ontologies are nowadays considered as the basic infrastructure for achieving semantic interoperability. This hinges on the possibility to use shared vocabularies for describing resource content and capabilities, whose semantics is described in an unambiguous and machine-processable form. Describing this semantics, i.e. what is sometimes called the intended meaning of vocabulary terms, is exactly the job that ontologies do for enabling semantic interoperability.

But what kinds of ontologies do we need? This is still an open issue. In most practical applications, ontologies appear as simple taxonomic structures of primitive or composite terms together with associated definitions. These are the so-called lightweight ontologies, used to represent semantic relationships among terms in order to facilitate content-based access to data produced by a given community. In this case, the intended meaning of primitive terms is more or less known in advance by the members of such community. Hence, in this case, the role of ontologies is more that of supporting terminological services (inferences based on relationships among terms – usually just taxonomic relationships) rather than explaining or defining their intended meaning.

On the other hand, however, the need to establishing precise agreements as to the meaning of terms becomes crucial as soon as a community of users evolves, or multi-cultural and multilingual communities need to exchange data and services.

To capture the precise meaning of a term and removing ambiguities, we need an explicit representation of the so-called ontological commitments related to these terms. A rigorous logical axiomatisation seems to be unavoidable in this case, as it accounts not only for the relationships between terms, but – most importantly – for the formal structure of the domain to be represented. This allows one to use axiomatic ontologies not only to facilitate meaning negotiation among agents, but also to clarify and model the negotiation process itself, and in general the structure of interaction.

We should immediately note that building axiomatic ontologies for these purposes may be extremely hard, both conceptually and computationally. However, this job only needs to be undertaken once, before the interaction process starts.

Axiomatic ontologies come in different forms and can have different levels of generality, but a special relevance is enjoyed by the so-called foundational ontologies, which address very general domains.

Foundational ontologies are ultimately devoted to facilitate mutual understanding and inter-operability among people and machines. This includes understanding the reasons for non-interoperability, which may in some cases be much more important than implementing an integrated (but unpredictable and conceptually imperfect) system relying on a generic shared "semantics".

The role and nature of foundational ontologies (and axiomatic ontologies in general) is complementary to that of lightweight ontologies: the latter can be built semi-automatically, e.g. by exploiting machine learning techniques; the former require more painful human labour, which can gain immense benefit from the results and methodologies of disciplines such as philosophy, linguistics, and cognitive science.

An alternative, and orthogonal, point of view is that of classifying ontologies according to their scope, i.e. according to the nature of what they represent. Domain-independent ontologies, or top-level ontologies, accounts for general concepts, like "object", "process", "time", common to different domains. Domain ontologies, on the other hand, are focused on a specific context (e.g. an ontology of surgery, of cars, of food and so on).

The tri-dimensional (3D) top-level ontologies are based on a fundamental distinction between enduring and perduring entities, i.e. between what philosophers usually call continuants and occurrents, a distinction still strongly debated both in the philosophical literature [1] and within ontology standardization initiatives.

Classically, the difference between enduring and perduring entities (which we shall also call endurants and perdurants) is related to their behavior in time. Endurants are wholly present (i.e., all their proper parts are present) at any time they are present. Perdurants, on the other hand, just extend in time by accumulating different temporal parts, so that, at any time they are present, they are only partially present, in the sense that some of their proper temporal parts (e.g., their previous or future phases) may be not present. E.g., the piece of paper you are reading now is wholly present, while some temporal parts of your reading are not present any more. Philosophers say that endurants are entities that are in time, while lacking however temporal parts (so to speak, all their parts flow with them in time). Perdurants, on the other hand, are entities that happen in time, and can have temporal parts (all their parts are fixed in time).

Reference ontologies, like that presented in this paper, constitute an intermediate layer between top-level and domain ontologies. Technically they are domain ontologies, since they refer to a well-defined context, like law, agriculture or medicine. Neverthless they can be seen as "top-level" with respect to the domain they address.

3. The Reference Ontology

In order to ensure semantic consistency to the heterogeneous information systems that may be applied to the health-care domain, we defined a Reference Ontology in MEdicine (ROME). It consists of about 200 general entities and it is designed to act as a bridge between more specific systems (e.g. a clinical guideline manager and an epidemiology database).

ROME is based upon the DOLCE top-level ontology [2]. From DOLCE it inherits the basic distinction between "endurants" and "perdurants".

Classically, endurants (also called continuants) are characterized as entities that are 'in time', they are 'wholly' present (all their proper parts are present) at any time of their existence.

On the other hand, perdurants (also called occurrents) are entities that 'happen in time', they extend in time by accumulating different 'temporal parts', so that, at any time t at which they exist, only their temporal parts at t are present. For example, the book you are holding now can be considered an endurant because (now) it is wholly present, while "your reading of this book" is a perdurant because, your "reading" of the previous section is not present now.

In the clinical context, we may say that a medical device is an endurant, whereas a specialty-care visit a perdurant.

The main sources for building the ROME ontology – which is written in OWL and can be browsed by tools such as Protégé – have been the UMLS Semantic Network (UMLS-SN) [3] and the topmost terms of the Foundational Model of Anatomy (FMA) [4].

In the next paragraph we will see how anatomical basic concepts are represented in ROME.

As far as the UMLS-SN is concerned, we certainly took profit from the precious work of synthesis that has been done by its authors. Many of the most general concepts managed in the health-care context have been singled out in such a semantic network. Nevertheless, we find that not all the "semantic types" – as they call them – are adequately defined and they sometimes lack of semantic precision. As an example we may cite: "Body Space or Junction", "Body Part, Organ, or Organ Component" and "Body Location or Region". Strange relationships between types are defined too, like "conceptual_part_of", for instance.

Figure 1 reports the top entities of the ROME ontology: "endurant", "perdurant" and "quality". The main kind of endurants are "physical endurants" – which can be biologic (e.g. anatomical entities) or non-biologic (e.g. devices) – and "non-physical endurants" (see next paragraph).

"Functions" – both biologic and non-biologic – are other kinds of endurant.

Similarly, also perdurants are divided into biologic processes (e.g. pathologic processes) and non-biologic processes (e.g. diagnostic investigation).

"Quality" (fig.2) is another feature by DOLCE. It refers to the abstract quality of an endurant. "Congenital anatomical structure abnormality", for example, does not represent the anatomical entity itself, but it is the abstract quality attached to it.

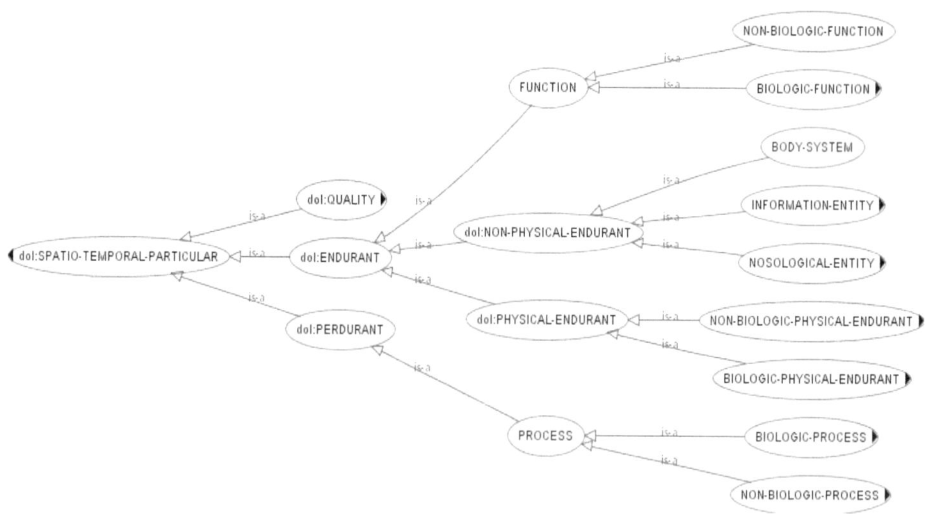

Figure 1.
Top entities in the ROME ontology.

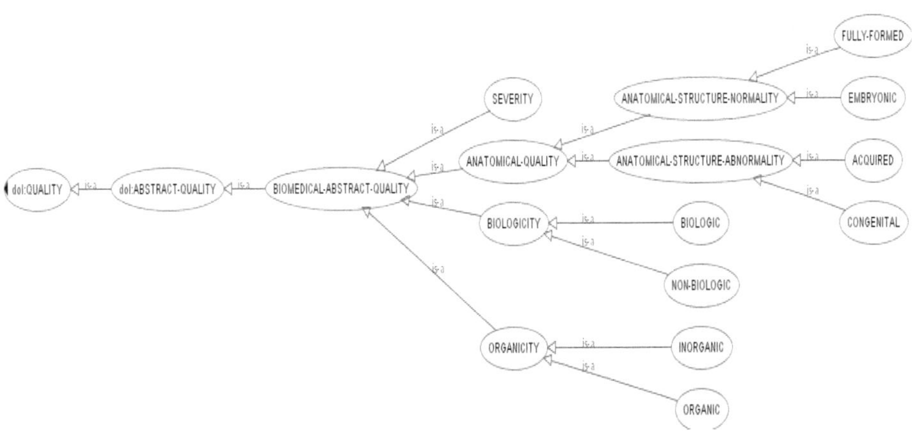

Figure 2.
Hierarchy of qualities.

4. Non- physical and non-material entities

It is natural for a realist based ontology of particulars to take into account physical and tangible objects, but other immaterial and non tangible entities must be considered too.

Non-physical endurants are represented in ROME, such as messages and patient folders (regardless of their physical realization). Another relevant non-physical entity which has a peculiar representation is "diagnosis". On the "Webster Dictionary of Medicine" [5] we read the following definition:

1.a   the art or act of identifying a disease from its signs and symptoms
1.b   the decision reached by a diagnosis
2   a concise technical description of a taxon

Some instances of the three sense singled out in the dictionary could be:

1.a   "the investigation process carried out by dr.Dobbs"
1.b   "my presenile dementia as diagnosed by dr.Dobbs on July 8th 2005 ...."
2   "presenile dementia" (code 290.1 in the ICD-9-CM)

The examples make clear that the first definition (1.a) refers to a process (perdurant), whereas the other two are endurants: 1.b is the result of a diagnostic process made by some physician (two physicians, two diagnoses) and 2 is the abstract piece of knowledge as represented in some classification. This is how we represent the different senses of diagnosis in our ontology:

1.a   "diagnostic investigation" --> "non-biologic process" --> "perdurant"
1.b   "diagnosis" --> "information entity" --> "non-physical endurant"
2   "disease" --> "nosological entity" --> "non-physical endurant"

Anatomy is obviously a key feature of the ROME reference ontology. Basically the top-level of the Foundational Model of Anatomy was adopted in our ontology, including the basilar distinction between material and non-material entities (see fig. 3).

The former may be divided into anatomical structures (e.g. body-parts, organs), body substances and body topographic entities. We defined this new category in order to account for similar entities such as compartments, body regions and surfaces.

Non-material anatomical entities are body junctions and spaces, they certainly have anatomical relevance, but not a material counterpart. From the philosophical literature we mutuated the distinction between bona-fide and fiat junctions [6].

Junctions are boundaries between different anatomical structures (e.g. abdominopelvic junction), borders delimit anatomical structures (e.g. inferior border of tympanic plate). Inner boundaries involving spatial discontinuity (holes, fissures, slits) or qualitative heterogeneity (of material constitution) are called bona fide junctions (e.g. neurocentral junction of lumbar vertebra). They are classified under: confluences, junctions between cavities, junctions between anatomical structures, commissures and borders. On the other hand, fiat junctions are conventional anatomical surfaces or lines (e.g. Reid's base line). As far as body spaces are concerned, they are divided into lumina, cavities and orifices (see table 1). The table reports example of leaf entities in italic. It should be pointed out that leaves are classes without sub-classes, not to be mistaken with instances)

This feature of our ontology is an extension and refinement of the UMLS-SN semantic type "Body Space or Junction" which collapses in a single category a bunch of heterogeneous entities, both material (e.g. joints) and non-material (e.g. cavities).

Table 1.

Classification of body spaces.

<table>
<tr><td>

Body space
  Lumen
        Lumen of aorta
        Lumen of urinary bladder
        Lumen of oesophagus
  Cavity
      Cavity inside organ
          Cavity of left atrium
          Cavity of incisor tooth
      Cavity inside joint
          Carpal tunnel
          Synovial cavity of hip joint
  Orifice
        Pyloric orifice
        Orifice of parotid duct
        Orifice of prostatic duct
        Tympanic orifice of right auditory tube

</td></tr>
</table>

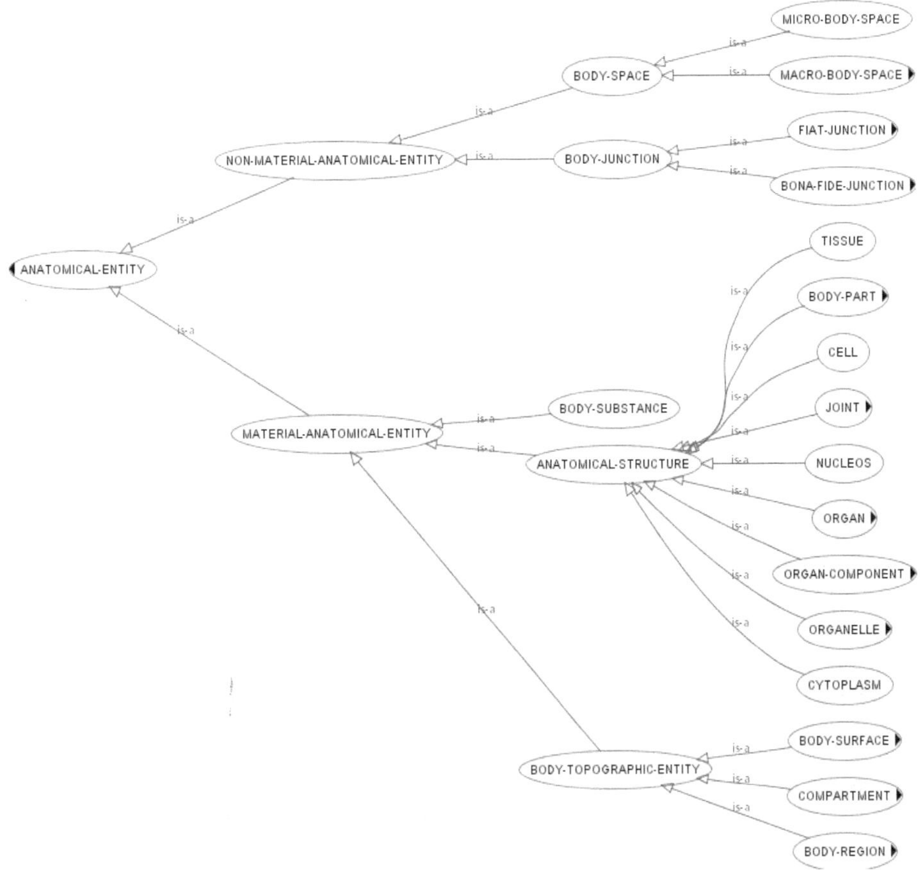

Figure 3.

Top anatomical entities.

5. The application of the reference ontology

We designed several domain-specific ontologies that are mapped to the reference ontology (ROME) and may be regarded as a specialized plug-ins covering different domains.

As an example, we report here the ontology of Mechanical Circulatory Support Systems (MCSS), a particular kind of devices mapped into ROME as non-biologic physical endurants [7].

About 30 different types of MCSS (e.g. Abiomed BVS 5000, HeartMate 1000, Novacor N100) have been represented in the domain ontology. They have been classified according to their features (e.g. pulsatile or continuous flow, synchronized or not with ECG, right, left or bi-ventricular assistance). Such features are classified under qualities in ROME.

The ontology is linked to a tool which is able to perform two types of queries, i.e. both to find a model of machine given a set of features (qualities), and to retrieve actual machines installed in a given ward or department.

Therefore the very same system can be used both as a knowledge base representing performances and characteristics of the different MCSS models and as a database of MCSS installed in a given health-care structure.

Such an asset is a peculiar result of the ontological approach, being the tool able to perform knowledge management at an "abstract" level (retrieving classes of machines according to desired features) and at a "concrete" level (retrieving actual machines according to desired features and availability).

In this way, the ontology can be used to give suggestions to a cardiac surgeon who is looking for the optimal device to implant in a patient. For example, if the patient's heart must be helped to recover, by browsing the ontology it will be possible to analyze the different features of intra-aortic baloon pumps.

Another field of application that we experimented is that of ontologies supporting continuity of care [8]. In consideration of the growing incidence of cardiovascular diseases, also due to the increase of the proportion of older population (a phenomenon now commonly observed worldwide), in May 2002 the Province of Trento launched a three-year research project called e-Heart Failure. The aims of this project include the design and development of a computer-based cooperative work environment based on an electronic patient record (EPR). In fact, in the case of heart failure patients, critical issues are the continuity of care, the shared care, the education of the patient and the active participation of his/her family. Such an EPR has to allow all health care professionals involved in the heart failure patients' care process to provide a shared and continuous care.

Current limitations in the information management of these patients are caused mainly by a poor communication among the different actor involved in the shared process of care, since continuity of care must rely on information systems providing no misunderstanding.

In consideration of the complexity of the clinical domain knowledge regarding the management of a chronic disease, an approach based on ontologies is proved to be useful. In such a way patients' clinical information can be managed with flexibility and effectiveness, preserving its semantic consistency.

As an example of the work done, we will show how the information elements of a particular patient-record view are mapped into the ROME reference ontology.

The view chosen for this example is reported in [8]. It refers to the "Chronology of contacts" (in Italian "Cronologia contatti precedenti"). The field "Comorbilità" (comorbility) refers to "Comorbidity-element", which is part of our reference ontology. "Esami e visite specialistiche" (exams and specialty care visits) correspond respectively to "Diagnostic-investigation" and "Speciality-care visits".

Another relevant application of this reference ontology is in the field of drug representation.

What is a drug? How do we identify it univocally?

It is not possible to give acorrect answer to this question unless we adopt a rigorous ontological approach, since a drug can be identified either by its commercial name and its physical realization.

A commercial name is an abstract thing and is classified in ROME under "information entity" which is a "non-physical endurant". On the other hand, the actual drug, the pill we ingest for example, is clearlya "physical endurant".

This is a significant distinction which found a relevant application in the context of a European funded research project whose aim is to deliver personamized health care services [9]. In fact, in the context of the prototypes implemented for this project, it is essential to distinguish between the identity of drug as a name and drug as a concrete thing, the former being used in monitoring a patient's behaviour, the latter for useful advices.

6. Conclusions

The interconnection of information processing systems, in order to make optimal use of medical and administrative data, will be the basis for improved care and higher efficiency in future health-care information systems.

Without an ontological grounding, like that we provide, the same information may shift its sense according to the context in which it is placed and according to the tacit knowledge of the human agent who specifies its meaning. For example, how do we know if "blood pressure" is a value or a measurement in a given record? Humans understand the context and have no problems, but computers need ontologies.

References

[1]   Hawley K, "How Things Persist", Clarendon Press, Oxford, 2001.

[2]   C Masolo, S Borgo, A Gangemi, N Guarino, A Oltramari, L Schneider. "The WonderWeb Library of Foundational Ontologies." WonderWeb Deliverable 18, http://wonderweb.semanticweb.org, 2003.

[3]   http://www.nlm.nih.gov/pubs/factsheets/
       umlssemn.html

[4]   C Rosse, JLV Mejino Jr. "A reference ontology for biomedical informatics: the Foundational Model of Anatomy". J Biomed Inform 36 (6), 478-500, 2003.

[5]   Webster Medical Dictionary; online at: www.intelihealth.com

[6]   Smith B., Varzi A. C., `Fiat and Bona Fide Boundaries', in Proc. COSIT-97, Springer--Verlag 1997, 103--119

[7]   C De Lazzari, E Guerrieri, DM Pisanelli, "A domain ontology for Mechanical Circulatory Support Systems". Proceeding of the IEEE 30th Annual Conference of Computers in Cardiology, pp. 417-419, 2003.

[8]   C Eccher, B Purin, DM Pisanelli, M Battaglia, I Apolloni, S Forti. "Ontologies supporting continuity of care: the case of heart failure". Comp. in Biology and Medicine, Spec. Issue on Ontologies in Medicine, 2006.

[9]   PIPS Portal: www.pips.eu.org

New Trends in Software Methodologies, Tools and Techniques
H. Fujita and D. Pisanelli (Eds.)
IOS Press, 2007

A Collaborative Environment for User-initiated Development of Web Applications

Sota HONDA [a] , Hidaka YANO [a] , Michiru TANAKA [a] , Keizo YAMADA [a] ,
Jun SASAKI [a] and Yutaka FUNYU [a]

[a] *Iwate Prefectural University, Japan*

Abstract. Many projects that develop information systems fail because system developers do not understand the user's requirements completely. The term "user" here means the customers that requests the software development to system developers. The reasons for failure include incomplete specifications of the user's requirements and the frequent changes thereof. We propose a new development method for a collaborative development model between users and system developers in developing Web application. In our method, users first create a part of the screen images and screen transition images in HTML. Next, the Web-app-skeleton generation tool we have developed, automatically generates a skeleton of the Web application from the HTML files. The system developers then add logical function to it. The Web-app-skeleton generation tool works to generate an optimal skeleton, after analyzing the structure of the HTML file, evaluating any similarity to other HTML files and clustering the pages. This paper describes the new user initiative collborative development environment. In addition, the prototype Web-app-skeleton generation tool is discussed and experimental results obtained from using the tool are reported.

Keywords. Web application, User initiative, Skeleton auto-generation, Collaborative development environment, Information system

1. Introduction

In the last few years, companies and research institutes have used many different development methods and technologies to develop high-quality information systems rapidly. However, many projects for developing information systems have resulted in failure because developers do not understand the user's requirements completely [1][2]. The reasons for failure include incomplete specifications of the user's requirements and the frequent changes thereof [3]. These are assumed to be as a result of defective requirements definitions or design phases, both of which are early processes in information systems development.

On the other hand, empowering users to develop information systems has become attractive as a new development methodology [4]. Users might succeed in developing information systems, which meet their requirements, rapidly if they were to develop the systems themselves.

The benefits of having users develop information systems by are the following:

- Users working in a field can easily define the requirements for their own information systems because they have the relevant work-related knowledge.
- Users can operate and maintein the system themselves.
- Users can respond flexibly to changes in the requirements of the system.

Under the present circumstances, however, it is difficult for users to develop information systems by themselves as they do not have sufficient knowledge of the development process or of the software environments in which they can develop the systems.

It is important for the development or reliable, ideal software that user's requirements are reflected completely and flexibly. This is known as the "Flexible and User Oriented Software Development Approach". In this approach, it is desirable for users to participate directly in the design phase. Therefore, we aim to develop a practical collaborative development environment for users and system developers as a first step in the flexible and user oriented software development approach [5]. In this study, we select a particular web applications as the target information systems. Web applications have been used extensively of late and have progressed rapidly. In addition, the intended users are those who understand HTML or can use authoring tools, for example Microsoft Frontpage, Macromedia Dreamweaver etc., and constantly use web applications.

In this paper, we present the collaborative development environment and a method of generating Web-app-skeletons as the key technology. In later sections, we describe a prototype system and discuss the results of an experiment to confirm the effectiveness of the proposed method.

2. Previous Work

"Himekami" is a collaborative development environment for users and system developers, and was proposed and developed by Mitsui et al. [6]. The proposed web application architecture allows users easily to join in the development of information systems. Mitsui has also developed a web application development tool.

"Himekami" makes it possible for users to participate in system development by completely separating the work of users from that of the system developers. The users first define the "screen contents" and "screen transitions" in natural language. Next, system developers code these with reference to the definition. However, this does not decrease the workload system developer's workload of the system developers. Moreover, communication between users and system developers is not supported in "Himekami", although this is fundamental. In addition, it is difficult to obtain a perspective of the whole system because screen contents and screen transitions are defined independently.

3. Collaborative Development Environment

In this work, we adopt the "Himekami" concept, but add a new function to derive the user requirements flexibly using the "screen contents" and "screen transitions" expressed by the users. For this purpose, the appearance of the web applications (screen contents and screen transitions) are described as HTML files. "Web-app-skeleton" files are then generated from these HTML files. The term "Web-app-skeleton" here means templates and transitional conditions between the templates in a web application, and resembles the frame structure of the web application.

The tasks in the collaborative development between users and system developers in a web application development are summarized below.

(1) Users create screen contents and screen transitions of a web application in HTML.
(2) The Web-app-skeleton files are generated from the HTML files created by users.
(3) System developers add program code to the Web-app-skeleton where required.
(4) Users edit screen contents and add new pages as required.
(5) Users and system developers add, change and confirm their requirements by communicating with each other.

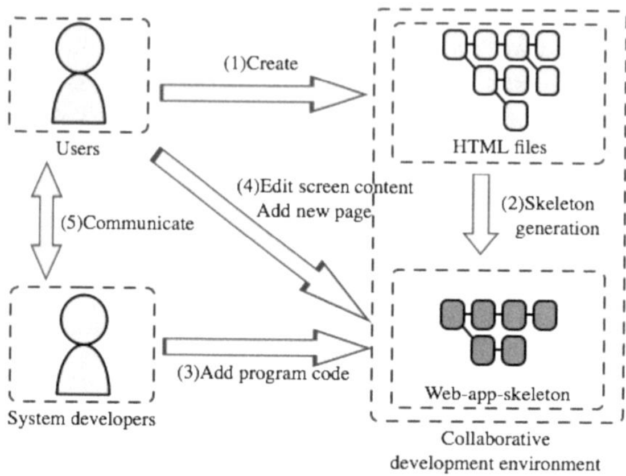

Figure 1. Model of collaborative development

The following functions are necessary in a web application development environment based on the proposed model:

- **Skeleton generation:** Web-app-skeletons are auto-generated from the HTML files created by users.
- **Skeleton editing:** Users and system developers edit the generated Web-app-skeleton.
- **New page addtion:** Users and system developers can add new pages using the generated templates.
- **Communication:** Users and system developers communicate with each other.

Figure 2 shows a screen image of this collaborative development.

The skeleton generation function is dealt with in detail in the next section.

For the skeleton editing function, users and system developers edit the templates, add and edit the program code in the Web-app-skeleton that was actually generated. Users can edit the HTML files and can use the comments as a tool for communicating with the system developers. System developers can use part of the program operation in that they can edit the program code concerning screen transitions and functions in addition to the two function that users can use.

System developers only add program code cardinally because the templates and transition conditions are configured automatically in the Web-app-skeleton that forms the base of the editing. This increases the amount of participation by the users in the system development and reduces the system developer's load.

In the process of adding new pages, users can add pages that have a similar structure (e.g. details of some items), without understanding whether the page has been auto-generated or not.

The function of communication is vital to ensure that the requirements of both users and system developers is communicated to the other party effectively.

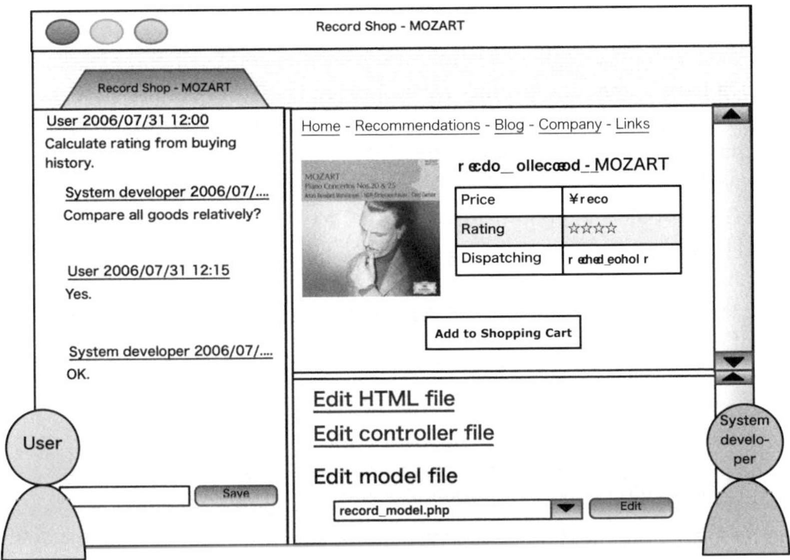

Figure 2. Screen image in collaborative development

4. Skeleton Generation

The tasks for the Web-app-skeleton generation are as follows:

(1) Structural analysis of pages: The HTML files created by the users are analyzed and relationships between the parent page and child pages are extracted.

(2) Calculation of the degree of similarity: Degree of similarity between child pages that have a common parent are calculated for all combinations.

(3) Page clustering: Similar pages are clustered together.

(4) Template selection: Templates are selected for every page cluster.

4.1. Structural analysis of pages

The structure of pages are analyzed to extract parent-child relationships between the pages. Hyperlinks are extracted using regular expressions and page data and relationship data are obtained recursively in a depth-first manner.

4.2. Calculation of degree of similarity

Most pages are generated and output dynamically in web applications. Pages using a common template are often similar because dynamic pages are generated by adding arbitrary data to the template. Conversely, similar pages have a high probability of being generated from a common template. The term "degree of similarity" here means the degree of similarity of structure, not of contents of the page. We argue that child pages which have a common parent page and that are similar can be tied together in a common template. Therefore, the degree of similarity is calculated for all combinations of child pages which have a common parent. We employed tf-idf weighting and a vector space model [7] for calculating the degree of similarity between the pages. Tf-idf weighting is often used in information retrieval and text mining, etc. In a vector space model, it used together with cosine similarity to determine the similarity between two documents. Shimizu et, al. [8] have applied tf-idf weighting to calculating the degree of similarity between HTML documents.

We extract each tag using regular expressions and calculate the degree of importance. We then calculate the degree of similarity between pages from the degree of importance of each tag.

4.3. Page clustering

To find the set of pages which use the same template, we apply an original clustering method. Clustering is a general technique aimed at partitioning of a data set into subsets, so that the data in each subset share some common trait and often used in machine learning and search result categorization [9], etc. In the literature there exist several different clustering algorithms [10], with different properties. We have adapted the agglomerative hierarchical clustering algorithm (hereinafter referred to as AHC).

We improve the AHC in order to reduce the number of calculation on making clustered page groups.

We first ignore low-level related pages with under a threshold of the similarity. We next skip the recalculation process of the similarity in AHC and we stop making clustered pages if there is no high-level related pages with over the threshold.

We explain the detail process of our clustering method.

Step 1) The page, which has the highest average degree of similarity with other pages, becomes a starting cluster in all clusters.

Step 2) The page, which has the highest degree of similarity with the starting cluster, is added to the current cluster.

Step 3) If there is a page, which has a degree of similarity with all pages in the current cluster, it is added to the current cluster. Otherwise, the current cluster are eliminated and we return to Step 1. Once all pages have been clustered, the process halts.

Figure 3 gives an example of page clustering.

There are five pages, A - E, in the example in Fig. 3. The numbers in the upper right hand corners represent the average degree of similarity with other pages and the lines between pages are drawn only when the degree of similarity between these pages is high. That is, if a page is not connected with a line to another page, there is no significant similarity between these pages. The numbers on the line represent the degrees of similarity.

In this example, page E becomes a parent node because its degree of similarity is the highest of all the pages (Step 1). Page E and page A are clustered together, because page A's degree of similarity with page E is the highest of all connected pages (Step 2). If we search for pages, which have a high degree of similarity with both page A and page E, we find page C, which is added to the cluster. The procedure returns to Step 1 because there are no further pages, which have a high degree of similarity with page E, A and C (Step 3).

Next (Step 1 repeated), page D becomes a parent node because its degree of similarity is the highest of all remaining pages. Page D and page B are clustered because page D's degree of similarity with page B is the highest of all pages. The process then terminates as all pages have been clustered.

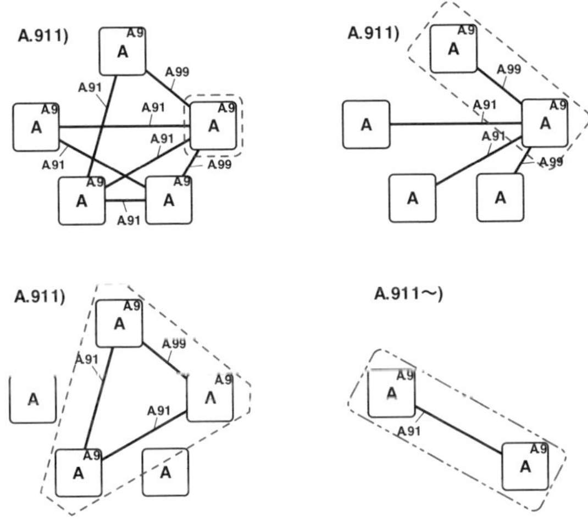

Figure 3. Example of page clustering

4.4. Template selection

At present a template is selected for every page cluster. One of the pages in each cluster is used as the template. The adopted page is the one that has the highest average degree of similarity of all pages in that cluster. The other pages are saved as data.

In the future, we are going to extract the template as the longest common subsequence of the pages in each cluster.

5. Prototype System

5.1. Implementation details

We have impremented four functions presented in section 3. The details of the implementation are shown in Table 1.

Table 1. implementation details

OS	MacOS 10.4
System configuration	Web application
Program language	PHP4
Library	Smarty
DBMS	MySQL
Web server	Apache

we especially describe the two functions with screen shot of each function.

5.2. Skeleton generation

First, users create images of the web application as HTML files in a predetermined folder. Next, they access the prototype system and input a directory name and click on the button for analysis. Finally, the Web-app-skeleton is generated by clicking on the buttons for each process. Since the result of each process is displayed step by step, if there are any inadequacies, we can identify them and modify the original HTML files. With this approach, we expect to reduce the workload and user errors during the process.

Figure 4 shows a screen dump of the results of the structural analysis of the HTML files as an example of a stage in the Web-app-skeleton generation in the prototype system.

The structure of the HTML files, obtained from extracting parent-child relationships, is displayed in a tree format by linking the parent-child and the sibling relationships to rules. This ensures that if the structure of HTML files is flawed, it will be quite obvious and the user can immediately correct the HTML files.

5.3. Skeleton editing

This function allows editing of visual effects and adding business logic to the Web-app-skeleton that was generated by the Web-app-skeleton generation function.

Both users and system developers can edit the web-app-skeleten. Users can use the HTML file editing function that is tied to view effects and the comment function, which serves as a communication tool with the system developers. In addition to these two functions, system developers can use the function for model file editing that is tied to the business logic and the function for controller file editing that is tied to screen transitions and function calls.

In this editing process, each user or system developer can specify a page which he wants to edit immediately. This allows the program code, tied to the page, to be edited easily.

Figure 5 shows a screen shot taken during the editing phase as part of the Web-app-skeleton editing function in the prototype system.

The Upper right hand portion displays the web application based on an auto-generated Web-app-skeleton. The lower right hand portion displays and links, which are connected to each page in the edited file that corresponds to the page currently displayed. Users and system developers can edit the corresponding file by clicking on the link. The portion on the left is used by the commenting function, to enter comments on the displayed page.

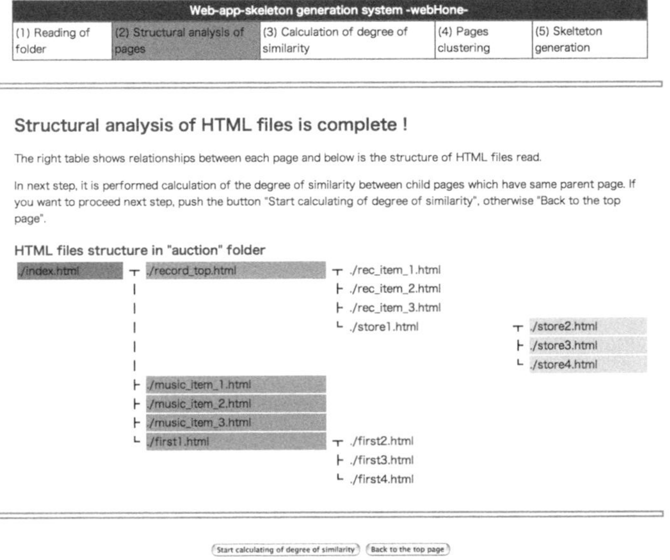

Figure 4. Screen shot of structural analysis of HTML files

Figure 5. Screen shot of Web-app-skeleton editing

6. Experiment

6.1. Purposes

We evaluate the following using the Web-app-skeleton generation of the prototype system: (1) whether or not the prototype system runs according to our expectations, and (2) whether or not the method of Web-app-skeleton generation in the prototype system performs according to our proposal.

6.2. Procedures

The experimental procedure is described as follows:

1. Rebuild the view effect of an existing web application as HTML files.
2. Input the latter to the prototype system and transform them to Web-app-skeleton.
3. Evaluate whether or not the structural analysis of the HTML files, the calculation of the degree of page similarity and the page clustering are carried out appropriately, and whether or not the Web-app-skeleton is generated correctly by comparing it to the expected Web-app-skeleton.

6.3. Targets

The web applications that have been adopted as the experimental targets are given below. The default threshold used in the calculation of the degree of similarity is 0.8. Figure 6 illustrates the construction of the HTML files which are built from the view effect of each web application.

Target1 a personal-produced music CD management system
      - number of pages : 15, number of tags : 213, number of tag varieties : 19
Target2 an auction system for a major web site such as *Yahoo!*
      - number of pages : 16, number of tags : 710, number of tag varieties : 152

For Target1, we expect that nine pages from *cd1.html* to *cd9.html* will be clustered and that the total number of clusters will be seven. For Target2, we expect that three pages from *music1.html* to *music3.html*, three pages from *record2.html* to *record4.html*, and three pages from *store2.html* to *store4.html* will be clustered separately and the total number of clusters will be ten.

7. Results

All functions of the prototype system operated according to our expectations in the experiment.

For Target1, the pages from *cd1.html* to *cd9.html*, which are music CD detailed pages, are similar to each other and were clustered correctly. In addition, *blog.html* and *link.html*, which include blog contents and related links respectively, were also clustered correctly. However, *company.html*, which shows a corporate profile, was clustered incorrectly with the CD detail pages. Moreover, *recommend.html* and *policy.html*, which has recommended CD and site policy information respectively, were clustered together although the degree of similarity of the page contents is low. The percentage of HTML files that were clustered correctly is 78.6%.

For Target2, the expected results were obtained. Most of the pages were clustered correctly. However, although the degree of similarity of page contents was low, the pages from *music1.html* to *music4.html* and the pages from *first1.html* to *first3.html*, which include details of music goods and contents intended for beginners respectively, were clustered together. The percentage of HTML files that were clustered correctly was 80.0%.

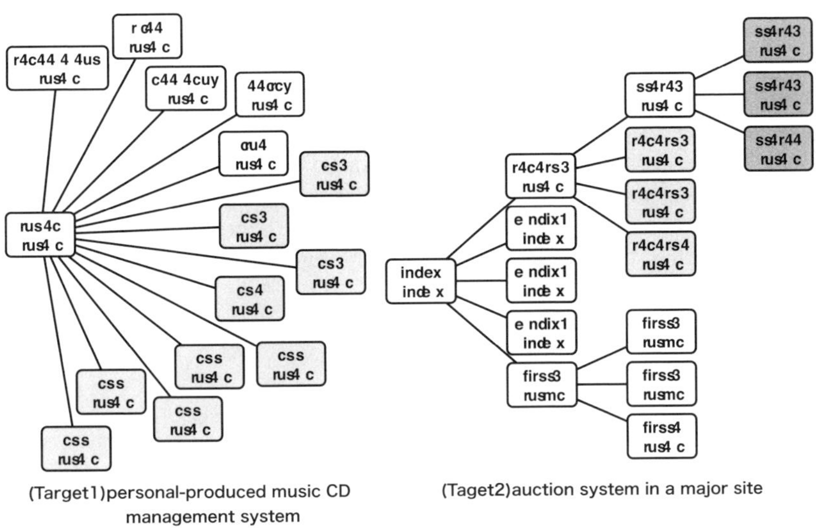

Figure 6. Construction of HTML files which are experimental targets

8. Discussion

We now discuss the appropriateness of the threshold and the cause of the resulting of page clustering based on the results of the evaluation experiment.

All of the pages that we expected to be clustered were in fact clustered. However excrescent pages and pages we did not anticipate being clustered sometimes added to the clusters. One of the reasons for this may be that the degree of similarity was calculated more highly than was expected. Consequently, we generated the Web-app-skeleton again after changing the threshold. As a result, the percentage of correct clustering in Target1 rose to 85.7% with the threshold set at 0.92. It is thus possible to adjust the results of page clustering by changing the threshold. The applicable threshold is different for Target1 and Target2 because it seems to be dependent on the scale of the web application (i.e. number of tags, number of tag varieties etc.) which differs for the two targets.

The structure of tags is not considered because the degree of similarity is calculated only from the frequency of appearance of tags in tf-idf weighting. There is currently a problem in that the degree of similarity is calculated to be high in pages where the frequency of appearance of tags is similar, but where the structure of tags is not.

We could verify the effectiveness of the prototype system, but the calculation of the degree of similarity of pages first needs to be improved in many aspects.

9. Conclusions and Future Work

In our work, we have proposed a collaborative environment for user initiative in developing web applications to enable users to participate actively in web application development. In particular, we have proposed an algorithm for auto-generating Web-app-skeleton from the view effects which users have created and a development approach based on the Web-app-skeleton. We have implemented a prototype system and have evaluated its effectiveness.

In the future, we aim to construct a mechanism of auto-calculating an applicable threshold for the calculation of the degree of similarity based on the scale of HTML files. In addition, we will consider a method of calculating the degree of similarity which can take into account the structure and frequency of appearance of tags.

References

[1]   The Standish Group, "2004 CHAOS Demographics and Project Resolution", http://www.standishgroup.com/, 2004.
[2]   Kensuke Nakamura, Ryutaro Yaguchi, "The success rate of projects is 26.7% survey of informatization in 2003", Nikkei Computer, Nov 17, 2003.
[3]   The Standish Group, "The CHAOS Report", http://www.standishgroup.com/, 2000.
[4]   Takeshi Chusho, Katsuya Fujiwara, Hisashi Ishigure and Kei Shimada, A Form-based Approach for Web Services by Enduser-Initiative Application Development, SAINT2002 Workshop (Web Service Engineering), IEEE Computer Society, pp.196-203, 2002.
[5]   Sota Honda, Tae Yoneda, Jun Sasaki, Yutaka Funyu, A Proposal of a Method of Web-app-skeleton Generation on user Initiative Collaborative Development Environment, In Proc. of the 68th Information Processing Society of Japan national conference, 2006.
[6]   Kohei Mitsui, Tae Yoneda, Jun Sasaki, Yutaka Funyu, A Web Application Architecture for Collaborative Development between users and SEs, Faculty of Software and Information Science, Iwate Prefectural University, 2005.
[7]   Gerard Salton, Michael J. McGill, "Introduction to Modern Information Retrieval", McGraw-Hill, 1983.
[8]   Chikara Shimizu, Hitoshi Aida, Information Extraction from the WWW by Mining Frequent Graph Patterns in HTML Structures, IPSJ SIG Technical Report, Vol.2004, No.36, pp.71-78, 2004.
[9]   Hiroyuki Toda, Ryoji Kataoka, Search Result Clustering Method at NTCIR-5 WEB Query Term Expansion Subtask, In Proc. of NTCIR-5 Workshop Meeting, 2005.
[10] Charles Romesburg, Cluster Analysis For Researchers, Lulu.Com, 2004.

New Trends in Software Methodologies, Tools and Techniques
H. Fujita and D. Pisanelli (Eds.)
IOS Press, 2007

505

Author Index

Abolhassani, H.	361, 372	Kurematu, M.	145
Adi, K.	185	Lajeunesse-Robert, F.	285
Ahmed, Z.	391	Langar, M.	200
Alt, M.	403	Logrippo. L.	343
Arai, O.	225	Maeda, K.	330
Battaglia, M.	485	Malyshkin, V.	355
Ben Sta, H.	93	Mao, M.	73
Bentahar, J.	239	Maruta, R.	416, 448
Bilda, Z.	166	Mechri, T.	200
Borovikova, O.	105	Mejri, M.	200
Chai, X.	73	Meyer, J.-J.	239
Chen, H.	361, 372	Mirenkov, N.	427
Danylak, R.	166	Müller, J.	403
De Lazzari, C.	485	Ó Cinnéide, M.	315
Di Sciullo, A.M.	126	O'Keeffe, M.	315
Dünnweber, J.	403	Pisanelli, D.M.	485
Edmonds, E.	119, 166	Pulvermueller, E.	269
Feuerlicht, G.	467	Qumer, A.	83
Foetsch, D.	269	Sacha, K.	36
Fujita, H.	145, 200, 225, 403	Sasaki, J.	475 ,494
Funyu, Y.	200, 403, 475, 494	Solms, F.	52
Ghedira, K.	93	Sugawara, K.	448
Gorlatch, S.	403	Tanaka, M.	475, 494
Hakura, J.	145	Taniguchi, N.	416
Hamza, L.	185	Watanobe, Y.	427
Hayashida, S.	416	Wijayaweera, A.	467
Henderson-Sellers, B.	3, 83	Wilking, D.	305
Honda, S.	475, 494	Yamada, K.	475, 494
Jiang, Y.	73	Yano, H.	475, 494
Koono, Z.	361, 372	Yoshioka, R.	427
Kowalewski, S.	305	Zagorulko, Y.	105
Ktari, B.	285